THINK
MARRIAGES & FAMILIES
CENSUS UPDATE

JENIFER KUNZ

West Texas A&M University

PEARSON

Boston   Columbus   Indianapolis   New York   San Francisco   Upper Saddle River
Amsterdam   Cape Town   Dubai   London   Madrid   Milan   Munich   Paris   Montreal   Toronto
Delhi   Mexico City   Sao Paolo   Sydney   Hong Kong   Seoul   Singapore   Taipei   Tokyo

Editorial Director: Craig Campanella
Editor-in-Chief: Dickson Musslewhite
Publisher: Karen Hanson
Editorial Project Manager: Maggie Barbieri
Editorial Assistant: Christine Dore
Director of Marketing: Brandy Dawson
Executive Marketing Manager: Kelly May
Marketing Assistant: Janeli Bitor
Full-Service Project Management: PreMedia Global

Senior Production Project Manager: Roberta Sherman
Manufacturing Buyer: Megan Cochran
Manager of Design Development: John Christiana
Manager, Visual Research: Beth Brenzel
Image Interior Permission Coordinator: Richard Rodrigues
Image Cover Permission Coordinator: Tara Gardner
Front Cover Image: Ariel Skelley/Blend Images/Getty Images
Back Cover Image: Skip O'Donnell/iStockPhoto
Composition: PreMedia Global

> This book is dedicated to my goodly parents, Phillip and Joyce, my four siblings, their spouses, and my twenty-one nieces and nephews. **I love you all.**

This book was set in 8.5/12 Helvetica Neue Light.

Credits and acknowledgments borrowed from other sources and reproduced, with permission, in this textbook appear on appropriate page within text (or on pages 296–315).

Cataloging-in-Publication data unavailable at press time

10 9 8 7 6 5 4 3 2 1   CRK   15 14 13 12 11

www.pearsonhighered.com

ISBN-13: 978-0-205-16760-9
ISBN-10: 0-205-16760-8

BRIEF CONTENTS

CONTENTS

01

INTRODUCTION TO MARRIAGE AND FAMILY

02

HOW TO STUDY MARRIAGE AND THE FAMILY

03

COMMUNICATION, POWER, AND CONFLICT

04

THE ROLE OF GENDER

07

CHOOSING A PARTNER

08

PREPARING FOR CHILDREN AND PARENTING

11

THE EFFECTS OF WORK AND THE ECONOMY

12

FAMILY AND SOCIAL INSTITUTIONS: EDUCATION, RELIGION, POLITICS, AND THE LEGAL SYSTEM

13

STRESS, VIOLENCE, AND ABUSE IN MARRIAGES AND FAMILIES

14

SEPARATION AND DIVORCE

xi

CONTENTS

This book began when I was young and my parents taught my siblings Jay, Jody, Johnathan, Jana, and me that family is important. I would like to thank them for that. They instilled in me a desire and motivation to know my family and to help preserve my heritage. I also thank my grand-parents, who have long since passed on, who shared with me stories from their youth and left a record for those still alive. I also express gratitude to Matt, Rachel, Kristina, Mallory, Heidi, Logan, Kate, Parker, Coulson, Paul, Jane, Parley, Brigham, Clayton, Truman, Adam, Jameson, Alice, Adelaide, Lucy, and Ella for loving your aunt and sharing your lives.

There are many people who have made this book possible and have contributed to the project in their own way. I would like to thank them for their assistance and support. I owe a debt of grati-tude to Maggie Barbieri, Karen Hanson, Nancy Roberts, Claudine Bellanton, and Dickson Musslewhite. I also have had the opportunity to work with the following staff members at *Words & Numbers:* Melissa Amen, Peter Traskey, Salimah Perkins, Adam Noll, and Russ Hall, and I thank them for their expertise in the editorial and production processes.

I appreciate the reviewers who extensively reviewed each chapter of this book and the members of my editorial review board who worked hard to make sure that the information in the book is accurate and timely. I especially thank:

Rebecca Adams, Ball State University
Jeremy Boyle, Kansas State University
Victor Harris, Utah State University
Nicole Loftus, Saddleback College
Timothy Loving, The University of Texas
Romana Pires, San Bernardino Valley College
Margaret Preble, Thomas Nelson Community College

2010 Census Update Edition—Features fully updated data throughout the text—including all charts and graphs—to reflect the results of the 2010 Census.

A Short Introduction to the U.S. Census—A brief seven-chapter overview of the Census, including important information about the Constitutional mandate, research methods, who is affected by the Census, and how data is used. Additionally, the primer explores key contemporary topics such as race and ethnicity, the family, and poverty. The primer can be packaged at no additional cost.

A Short Introduction to the U.S. Census Instructor's Manual with Test Bank—Includes explanations of what has been updated, in-class activities, homework activities, discussion questions for the primer, and test questions related to the primer.

JENIFER KUNZ's interest in studying the family grew out of the experiences she had growing up in her own family. She reflects, "We worked hard, played hard, and had fun together. I came to learn and understand that the family is the most important and most influential social institution in the world."

Her travels around the globe have expanded her understanding of marriages and families. Living abroad for 18 months in Uruguay gave her the deeper understanding that people are more similar than different. "These experiences have affected my professional and private life in profound ways. It affects how I teach, what I research, and my interactions with others."

Jenifer Kunz received her Ph.D. from Brigham Young University in 1994 and began teaching at West Texas A&M University in 1993. She is a Professor of Sociology and currently serves as the Department Head.

Jenifer has made several scholarly presentations about the family on the national and international level, and her articles and publications have appeared in many academic journals and books. She has received numerous awards for teaching and has been an international visiting professor several times at the University of Calgary in Alberta, Canada. She has also served as a consultant and a facilitator for various government and independent agencies. She is actively involved in the community and mentoring. Jenifer's area of specialization is marriage and the family. She has a special interest in the effects of divorce on children. She is a member of many professional associations and academic organizations that focus on the family.

Jenifer lives in Texas. In her free time she enjoys mountain biking, snorkeling, traveling, playing the piano, speaking Spanish, and spending time with family and friends.

Jenifer Kunz welcomes your comments and suggestions about this *THINK Marriages & Families* text at: jkunz@wtamu.edu.

THINK

MARRIAGES & FAMILIES
CENSUS UPDATE

Harvard

graduate Ellen Gulden, the central character in the film *One True Thing*, is on the brink of an exciting new writing career at *New York* magazine. Set to cause a stir with an investigative article about a politician tainted by scandal, Ellen's future as a reporter looks promising. However, when she returns to her hometown for the weekend to celebrate her father's birthday, Ellen receives some bad news. Her mother, Kate, is about to undergo surgery for cancer. The surgery will be grueling, and Kate will need a lot of help during her recovery. Ellen's father, George, makes it clear that he expects Ellen to move back home to look after her mother. Horrified at the thought of jeopardizing her career, Ellen argues that the family should hire a housekeeper or that George should take a sabbatical from his job as an English professor and look after Kate himself. After a heated discussion, Ellen reluctantly agrees to come home.

Back in her childhood home, Ellen begins helping her mother with the domestic chores, while her father carries on with his life as usual. Ellen starts to realize that, growing up, she idealized her father and dismissed her mother's lifestyle as frivolous. Kate is very involved with community activities, enjoys making curtains and taking care of the house, and comforts friends when they are in need. Looking at her parents through an adult's eyes, Ellen begins to see them differently. She realizes that her mother is the glue holding the family together and that her father is a philanderer who does very little to help out around the house. When he invites two work colleagues to a private family Thanksgiving dinner—likely the last Thanksgiving the family will spend together—Ellen loses all patience with him. After a bitter confrontation, her father tells her to go back to her life in New York. However, before the situation is resolved, Kate takes a turn for the worse, and the family discovers that her cancer is terminal.

Anxious to resolve the situation between her husband and daughter, Kate calls Ellen into a room to talk. She explains that marriage is full of highs and lows, that she knows everything about her husband, and that removing him from her life would only have left a huge hole. She emphasizes the importance of family and tries to help Ellen see the situation from her point of view. Ellen eventually comes to realize that her parents love each other in their own way and that her father is suffering from her mother's impending death just as much as the rest of the family.

At the end of the film, Kate gets increasingly weaker and begs Ellen to help her end her life. Ellen cannot and when her mother eventually dies of a morphine overdose, Ellen suspects that her father was responsible. She goes to plant flowers on her mother's grave and runs into her father, who denies that he had anything to do with her mother's death. They realize that Kate took the overdose by herself. George reiterates how much he loved his wife, his "one true thing," and Ellen begins to forgive him for his fallibility.

INTRODUCTION TO MARRIAGE AND FAMILY

CHAPTER 01

What does *One True Thing* teach us about family relationships? **The film explores the** complex bonds **that** exist between husband and wife **and** between parent and child, **and how these bonds change and develop over time.**

communication between individuals in a family and between different generations in particular. The film also considers how **stressors** such as illness can put added pressure on strained family relationships, as well as emphasizing the difficulty of balancing work life and home life—relatable issues for the majority of families in today's society.

One day, when I was four years old, while I was riding my bicycle down a hill, the chain came off my bike. I couldn't stop the bike or steer it to safety, and I crashed into a 1966 red Ford Mustang convertible that was being lovingly washed by its owner. The car was a wreck, the owner was furious, and I ended up in the hospital with several stitches in my elbow.

We can compare the bicycle to the family in society. When all the interrelated parts of the bicycle are working well together, the bike operates in an orderly way. Similarly, when all the different parts of society perform their designated functions, society is balanced and in harmony.

Throughout this chapter, we will examine the various definitions of marriage and family, look at historical and current trends in American families, and consider the role of families in society. We will also take a look at different theoretical perspectives of family and finally ask ourselves, "What is the meaning of family?"

STRESSOR is a situation or event causing stress.

At the beginning of the film, Ellen is in danger of becoming just like her father—cold and career-driven—but she gradually comes to see the important role that Kate plays in keeping the family together. It takes an honest and frank discussion with her mother for Ellen to truly understand her parents' relationship, suggesting the importance of

∧
∧ Sometimes, family relation-
∧ ships are more complex **than they initially appear.** What defines a **"normal" family?**

Introduction to Marriage and Family

marriage – a legally recognized union between a man and a woman

and

family – a group of two or more people related by birth, marriage, or adoption that live together

vary across cultures and throughout history

economic security – financial security and stability
social prestige and status – a sense of place and belonging
education and socialization – raising and educating children according to cultural norms and values

protection – physical protection of all family members
religious tradition – providing family members with a religious identity
recreation – family members entertain each other
affection – family members provide intimacy and comfort

however, functions of the family remain unchanged and include

get the topic: WHAT DEFINES A FAMILY, AND WHAT ARE THE HISTORICAL AND CURRENT TRENDS IN MARRIAGES AND FAMILIES?

Defining Marriage and Family

"Family: A social unit where the father is concerned with parking space, the children with outer space, and the mother with closet space." — Evan Esar (1899–1995)

Take a moment to consider the definition of a family. What images spring to mind? If you are picturing a husband, wife, and two smiling children, you are envisioning a traditional or nuclear family—a family unit consisting of two parents and their children. A nuclear family does not include extended family members such as aunts, uncles, and grandparents. But only about 25 percent of families in the United States today fit this model. Many students reading this book likely come from single-parent families, same-sex families, or families that include stepparents and stepsiblings. Some may have been raised by their grandparents or by other relatives, and a quick poll would probably confirm that readers come from a variety of cultural and ethnic backgrounds. An accurate definition of marriages and families must take all of these different forms of marriages and families into account.

WHAT IS MARRIAGE?

In 1866, Britain's House of Lords stated that marriage is the "voluntary union for life of one man and one woman to the exclusion of all others."[1] This definition has survived in legal doctrine, and **marriage** in the United States is typically defined as a legally recognized union between a man and a woman who are at or above a specified age and who are not legally married to someone else. The union is assumed to be permanent, although the joined parties can legally separate or have the union dissolved through divorce. Although widely accepted by many people, this definition of marriage is extremely narrow, excluding cohabiting couples in committed heterosexual or homosexual relationships that function in the same way as legal marriages, but without the same legal rights and protections. A broader definition of marriage might take these relationships

> **MARRIAGE** is a legally recognized union between a man and a woman.
> **MONOGAMOUS MARRIAGE** is a type of marriage in which one person is married to another person of the opposite sex.
> **POLYGAMOUS MARRIAGE** is a type of marriage in which one person is married to multiple husbands or wives.
> **ARRANGED MARRIAGE** is a type of marriage in which the families of the bride and groom negotiate an arrangement before the two parties enter into a relationship.

into account and describe marriage as a union between two people in a committed relationship, in which they are united sexually, cooperate economically, and may give birth to, adopt, or rear children. However, even this description is culturally specific and does not accurately depict many marriages in non-Western cultures.

Types of Marriage

Marriages around the world are either monogamous or polygamous. In Western cultures, marriages are assumed to be **monogamous**—one person is married to another person and the relationship remains exclusive. In some parts of the world, **polygamous** marriages are the accepted form, in which one person is married to multiple husbands or wives. Polygamy is legally practiced in many parts of the world, including the Middle East, South America, Asia, and some parts of Africa. As we will see in Chapter 9, polygamy is illegal in the United States, although it is still practiced in some states.

Among non-Western cultures, rules about marriage vary greatly from those in Western society. In some parts of India, Africa, and Asia, children as young as six years old may marry other children (and sometimes adults), although they may not live together until they are older. Many cultures organize **arranged marriages**, in which the families of the bride and groom negotiate an arrangement before the two parties enter into a

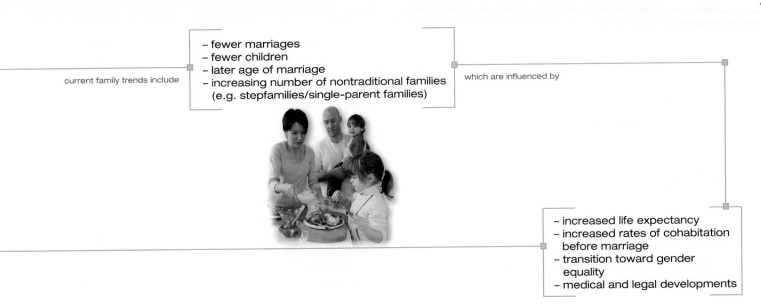

current family trends include

- fewer marriages
- fewer children
- later age of marriage
- increasing number of nontraditional families (e.g. stepfamilies/single-parent families)

which are influenced by

- increased life expectancy
- increased rates of cohabitation before marriage
- transition toward gender equality
- medical and legal developments

Family Groups 2010

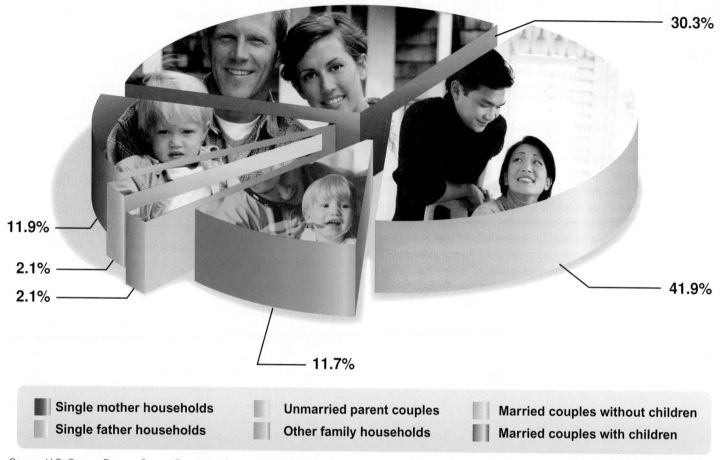

30.3%

41.9%

11.7%

11.9%

2.1%

2.1%

| ■ Single mother households | ■ Unmarried parent couples | ■ Married couples without children |
| ■ Single father households | ■ Other family households | ■ Married couples with children |

Source: U.S. Census Bureau, Current Population Survey, 2010 Annual Social and Economic Supplement.

> Although traditional families still make up **the largest percentage of family groups in the United States,** many families today consist of unmarried couples **or single-parent households.**

relationship. Arranged marriages are common in some parts of Asia, Africa, and the Middle East. However, changing attitudes toward gender roles and the influence of Western culture may be affecting traditional ideas about marriage in these countries. A recent report indicated that divorce rates in India are soaring among the middle classes as working women of independent means refuse to submit to arranged marriages.[2]

Although there are many cultural variations of marriage, family historian Stephanie Coontz notes that all arrangements defined as marriages share three common characteristics: They establish rights and obligations related to gender, sexuality, extended family relationships, and legitimacy of children; they establish specific roles within the wider community; and they allow the organized transfer of wealth and property from one generation to the next.[3]

WHAT IS FAMILY?

Walk around a busy shopping mall, and you will likely see many types of families—single-parent families, married couples, stepfamilies, same-sex

families, and multigenerational families, to name just a few. With all this diversity, how can we limit the definition of family to a sentence or two?

According to the United States Census Bureau, a **family** consists of "a group of two people or more related by birth, marriage, or adoption and residing together," and a **household** is made up of "all people who occupy a housing unit" regardless of a relationship.[4] In other words, according to the federal government, a married couple and their children constitute a family, whereas an unmarried, cohabiting couple makes up a household. This definition of family is used for a variety of official purposes, including statistical analysis of family change, measuring poverty, and determining eligibility for many social programs. For example, under Social Security laws, only a worker's spouse, dependent parents, and children are eligible to claim benefits based on that worker's contributions. Nontraditional families such as same-sex partners and cohabiting partners do not qualify as family members under the federal government's definition of family (although several states now legally recognize same-sex marriage and domestic partnerships).

Although useful for analytical purposes, limiting the definition of family to include only relatives within the same household makes it difficult for sociologists to fully examine the patterns of support and caregiving that take place across households.[5] Many people have close ties with relatives who live nearby, or close ties with **affiliated kin**—nonrelated individuals who are accepted as part of the family. Among Latino and African American communities in particular, ties with affiliated kin are often stronger and more lasting than the ties established by blood or marriage.[6] For the purposes of this book, we will use the term *family* to refer to a social institution common to all societies that organizes and unifies people into cooperative groups to care for one another.

History of the American Family

Popular 1970s television shows such as *The Waltons* and *Little House on the Prairie* idealized the "good old days" of the American family, in which people were poor but happy, and strong family ties were the norm rather than the exception. But did this golden age ever actually exist? A look at the history of the American family may debunk some of the persistent myths surrounding family life.

∧
∧
∧ **Women developed increasingly liberal attitudes** toward divorce in the 1960s **and were less likely to remain** in unhappy marriages.

FAMILY is a group of two people or more related by birth, marriage, or adoption and residing together.
HOUSEHOLD refers to all people who occupy a housing unit regardless of relationship.
AFFILIATED KIN are nonrelated individuals who are accepted as part of a family.

U.S. COLONIAL PERIOD TO 1899

When the first settlers arrived in North America in the 17th century, they joined more than a million Native Americans. By the end of the century, immigrants were arriving from all over Europe, and Africans were being forcibly shipped into the colonies to be sold as slaves, which disrupted their family ties. From the very beginning, families in the United States were culturally, ethnically, and religiously diverse.

Early colonial families were primarily nuclear families, made up of husband, wife, and children.[7] However, unrelated individuals such as children from other families, apprentices, and hired laborers often joined colonial households to live and work. Fathers were regarded as the head of the family and exercised control over wives and children, often using physical force to discipline their young. The chances of a colonial child surviving to adulthood were far lower than they are today, with an infant mortality rate of one in every three children in some communities.[8] Those children who did survive did not enjoy the lengthy childhood that an American youngster might expect today—by the age of six or seven, girls were put to work sewing or spinning, and boys were sent into the fields to help their fathers. By the age of 14, most colonial children were sent to live with other families to learn a trade.[9]

Marital roles in colonial households were divided by gender, with husbands responsible for planting, harvesting, bookkeeping, and supervisory tasks, and wives in charge of cooking, sewing, milking, cleaning, and gardening. Colonial families were primarily a unit of production—they worked hard and were often beset by accidents, illness, and disease.

UNITED STATES: 1900 TO PRE-WWII

By the late 19th century, economic and political changes were altering traditional gender roles in American families. Women began campaigning for the right to vote and increasingly took on roles outside the home, attending universities and pursuing careers. Technological advances led to the mass production of goods, lessening the need for child labor, and schools assumed more responsibility for socializing and educating children. Medical advances also assisted the changing family structure, with decreasing infant mortality rates lessening the need for couples to have large families to ensure that some of their children survived.

During this time, public concern over family violence, child neglect, declining middle-class birth rates, divorce, and infant mortality was increasing, resulting in more government intervention in family life. Reformers helped pass compulsory school attendance laws and child labor restrictions. Organizations offering advice about child-rearing, parenting, and social policy were formed, leading to a shift in the way people viewed the family. Rather than a functional unit of production, the new family ideal was the companionate model, based on mutual affection, sexual fulfillment, and the sharing of domestic tasks and child rearing.[10] From the large 19th-century family units developed smaller, more private family groups that focused on the emotional well-being of their members. Interpersonal relationships between spouses became the linchpin of family life.

Although these changes promoted positive, caring relationships, they also led to an increase in divorce rates. Once spouses expected marriage to go hand in hand with emotional fulfillment, they became more willing to terminate unhappy relationships.

U.S. MODERN ERA (WORLD WAR II TO PRESENT)

Many people look back to the 1950s as the golden age of the traditional family, but was it really? Teenage pregnancy rates were higher in the 1950s than they are today, although a higher proportion of teenage mothers were married (primarily due to "shotgun weddings," a colloquialism that developed from the idea that many fathers of pregnant girls had to force, possibly with a weapon, a man to marry his daughter once she became pregnant). Many families were unable to survive the traumas of war and its aftermath, and the divorce rate rose from one in six in 1940 to one in four marriages in 1946.[11] Although many families prospered in the years following World War II, many others suffered from economic hardship. In 1948, *Newsweek* reported that most of the 27 million schoolchildren in the United States were badly in need of medical or dental care, while more than 900 thousand children were malnourished.[12]

The "golden age" of the 1950s was also a contributing factor to rising divorce rates in the 1960s and 1970s. When soldiers returned from the war, many women were forced to give up their factory jobs to make way for the returning veterans and encouraged to stay at home and assume domestic roles. As a result, birth rates increased and the average age at first marriage decreased. However, women began to feel increasingly trapped in their limited roles, and this tension eventually boiled over, resulting in the formation of the women's liberation movement in the 1960s. The typical family structure began to shift from father as breadwinner to dual-income families, in which both husband and wife worked outside the home. Since the 1960s, families have also grown smaller—in 2004, only 10 percent of women produced four or more children, compared to 36 percent of women in 1976— and more diverse.[13] We will examine contemporary types of family variation in Chapter 9.

Current Trends in Families

By the end of *One True Thing*, Ellen begins to see the importance of the domestic role her mother played in the family. Supporters of traditional families argue that society functions best when families are made up of a breadwinner husband and a supportive wife who takes care of the domestic responsibilities at home. What implications might this have for

Marital Status of U.S. Population (over Age 15) 2010

Percentage

70 65 60 55 50 45 40 35 30 25 20 15 10 5 0

White   Black   Asian   Hispanic

Married   Never Married   Divorced   Widowed

Source: U.S. Census Bureau, Current Population Survey, 2010 Annual Social and Economic Supplement.

contemporary families? Current trends include fewer marriages, fewer children, later age of marriage, and an increasing number of single-parent families and stepfamilies.[14] Let's take a look at some recent U.S. statistics:

- Of 66.9 million opposite-sex couples living together in 2008, 60.1 million were married, and 6.8 million were not.[15]

- The percentage of women aged 40 to 44 who were childless increased from 10 percent in 1976 to 18 percent in 2008.[16] Families typically have fewer children today compared to earlier generations, with the birth rate over the last 20 years averaging around two births per woman (compared to four births per woman in the early 1900s).

- In 2009, the United States had an estimated 5.3 million "stay-at-home" parents: 5.1 million mothers and 158,000 fathers.[17]

- In 2010, about 10 percent of all children (7.5 million) lived in a household that included a grandparent. Fifty-four percent of children living with a grandparent had no parent present.[18]

- American families are overworked: In families without children, husbands and wives worked a combined average of 68 hours of paid work a week in 2000, compared to 58 hours a week in 1968. In families with children, parents worked an average of 64 hours of paid work a week in 2000, compared to 53 hours a week in 1968.[19]

FACTORS AFFECTING CURRENT TRENDS

Demographic Factors

Sociologist John Weeks believes there are several reasons for the changing composition of modern households.[20] People are living longer, increasing the likelihood that they will eventually be widowed or divorced—now that "till death do us part" might involve 60 or 70 years of living with the same person, people may be less inclined to follow through with their wedding day promises. Increased life expectancy also reduces the pressure to marry and have children early, resulting in a trend toward delayed marriage and the tendency to leave the parental nest at a much later age than previous generations. Between 1970 and 2000, the proportion of women who had never been married increased from 36 percent to 73 percent among women aged 20 to 24, and from 6 percent to 22 percent among 30- to 34-year-olds. Similar results were found for men.[21] As we will see in Chapter 9, these statistics may be partially explained by the increasing rates of cohabitation before marriage. The longer cohabiting couples delay tying the knot, the less likely they are to eventually marry.

Lifestyle Factors

Over the past 40 years, a transition toward gender equality and the empowerment of women has also contributed to changing family structures. A combination of longer life and lower fertility means that women have more opportunities to pursue other goals and achieve economic and social independence. Prior to the 1970s, women typically worked only until they got married or became pregnant, which was reflected in the number of women in the labor force. In 1950, there were 29 female year-round full-time workers for every 100 males; by 2000 this figure had increased to 70 females working full-time per 100 male workers.[22] Today, it is socially acceptable for women to juggle higher education and a career with raising a family, or to choose not to have a family at all—as we noted earlier, one in five women of childbearing age in the United States was childless (involuntarily without children) or "child-free" (voluntarily without children) in 2006. Despite the transition toward gender equality, however, it appears that we are not quite there yet. In 2001, the average female full-time worker earned just 75 percent of the income earned by males.[23] And although Hillary Clinton came close in the 2008 presidential campaign, no female leader has yet served as President of the United States.

In addition to changing attitudes in the workplace, medical and legal developments have enabled women to have more choices when it comes to marriage and children. The advent of the contraceptive pill in the 1960s, combined with the legalization of abortion in 1973, gave women more reproductive options. Previously, women had little control over if or when they would have a family, but the pill allowed women the ability to plan when they were going to have a pregnancy as well as the number of children they had (if any). This allowed women to have relationships without being married and not worry about becoming pregnant. The reduced stigma of having a child out of wedlock also meant that women no longer felt the social pressure to marry or even remain in a relationship in the event of a pregnancy. In 2004, 1.2 million children in the United States were born out of wedlock.[24]

Women are not the only demographic to benefit from a shift in attitudes concerning the family. Several states have legalized same-sex marriage in the past decade, with more likely to follow suit in the near future. Since Massachusetts became the first state to pass legislation in 2004, more than 10,000 gay and lesbian couples have exchanged vows there.[25] Many same-sex couples are raising biological or adopted children. In 2005, an estimated 65,000 adopted children in the United States were living with a gay or lesbian parent.[26]

IS MARRIAGE IN TRANSITION OR DECLINE?

Some social commentators view the high divorce statistics and increasing numbers of nontraditional families as symptoms of the weakening of the family and as an indication of its imminent demise. However, these doom-and-gloom predictions are nothing new. In 1927, psychologist John B. Watson believed that family values had broken down to such an extent

<<< **Hillary Clinton** hoped to become the first female American president **but lost the Democratic party nomination** in the presidential primaries **to Barack Obama in 2008.**

Major Trends Affecting Families: South America in Perspective

Between 1950 and 2000, major structural changes took place in the countries of South America. Rapid urbanization shifted the majority of the population from rural areas to cities, and the number of women in the labor force rose from 20 percent to 40 percent.[29] Urban poverty levels increased, affecting more than half the population in some countries. Most countries also experienced major political changes, with dictatorships giving way to democracies in the 1980s. With the new democratic governments came changes in legal and policy issues related to the family. So, how have these structural changes affected family dynamics in South America?

Changes in Family Structure

Although nuclear households are the most widespread form of residence in South America, the number of single-person households is on the increase. In Argentina, a country with a large number of older persons, the number of single-person homes rose from 11.3 percent in 1986 to 15.5 percent in 1999.[30] Researchers attribute this partly to an aging population, but also to the growing number of young adults living by themselves before they marry and to the increasing number of divorcés who live alone.[31] High rates of poverty and unemployment in urban areas have resulted in an increasing number of extended family households, in which family members move in together to pool their resources. In Brazil and Argentina, legislation has been proposed to legitimize same-sex unions for homosexual couples, and there has been a slow increase in the number of same-sex families.

As in the United States, statistics indicate lower marriage rates and higher cohabitation rates in the majority of the region.[32] Greater freedom of choice and the reduction of social stigma have also resulted in higher divorce rates—a trend also attributed to the increasing financial independence of women, allowing them to escape violent or unhappy marriages. An increase in educational opportunities for women has also lowered birth rates, as women delay marriage and childhood to pursue professional opportunities. However, recognition of reproductive rights is a slow legal process in South American countries, with strong opposition from institutions such as the Catholic Church. Many women surveyed did not want an additional child when they became pregnant, and there is a clear gap between ideal family size and actual number of children.[33]

Emerging Issues

Several countries in South America have increasingly aging populations, resulting in progressively greater need for financial aid and care. Traditionally, families lived in extended networks with children taking care of their elderly parents, but a growth in state welfare services has taken some financial responsibility away from family members. As a result of increasing unemployment and poverty, the care process may be reversed in some cases, with elderly family members using their pensions or homes to help younger generations who are struggling.

Despite many social and legal advances, some family issues in South America have yet to be resolved. Living with HIV or AIDS carries great social stigma, yet the availability of preventive health services for sexual and reproductive services is scarce (with a lack of government action attributed to the strength of the Catholic Church).[34] Although the problem of domestic violence has started to gain social visibility and legal attention, there is a tendency toward silence because victims feel shame and guilt. One study found that 80 percent of women in Mendoza, Argentina, reported that they had been victims of physical or emotional violence in their lives. Family violence is a pattern of learned behavior, and many South Americans are raised in patriarchal families in which violence toward women or violence as a means of socializing children is the norm.[35]

∧
∧
∧ **Factors such as** urbanization and new political regimes **are changing family dynamics** in South America.

that marriage was in danger of extinction, stating, "In 50 years, unless there is some change, the tribal custom of marriage will no longer exist."[27] Other professionals look at marriage and family as being in a state of transition rather than decline.[28] They view changes in family structures as evidence of the flexibility of marriage and family and the ability of each institution to adapt to modern life. In your opinion, is the American family in transition or decline?

FUNCTIONS OF THE FAMILY

Although families differ widely in structure, they all perform similar functions. In the 1930s, sociologist William Ogburn identified seven roles that families fulfill: economic security, social prestige and status, education and socialization of children, protection, religious tradition, recreation, and affection. More than 60 years later, contemporary sociologists have produced very similar lists, suggesting that although the structures of today's families might have changed, the expectations for the roles of the family in society have remained relatively consistent.

FAMILY OF ORIGIN describes the family in which an individual is raised.

Economic Security

One of the most important roles of a family unit is to provide financial security and stability for its members. This includes all the material resources needed for the family's physical survival, such as food, shelter, and clothing. Due to the recent economic downturn and the collapse of large companies such as GM and Chrysler, many families are finding it increasingly difficult to provide financial security for their loved ones. A survey of 25 cities between October 2007 and September 2008 reported an 18 percent increase in the demand for food assistance, as well as an increase in homelessness of up to 30 percent in some cities.[36]

Social Prestige and Status

Being part of a family provides us with a sense of place and belonging in society. The family in which we grow up is known as our **family of origin**, and it has many influences on our experiences in later life (see diagram).

The Importance of Family of Origin

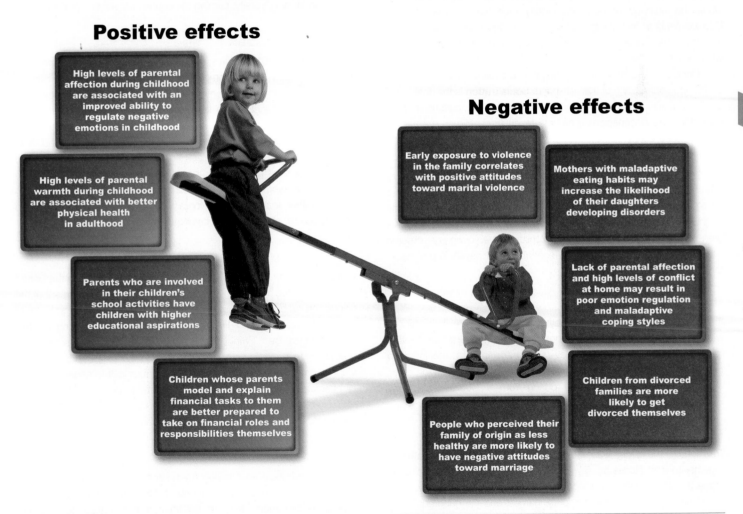

Positive effects

High levels of parental affection during childhood are associated with an improved ability to regulate negative emotions in childhood

High levels of parental warmth during childhood are associated with better physical health in adulthood

Parents who are involved in their children's school activities have children with higher educational aspirations

Children whose parents model and explain financial tasks to them are better prepared to take on financial roles and responsibilities themselves

Negative effects

Early exposure to violence in the family correlates with positive attitudes toward marital violence

Mothers with maladaptive eating habits may increase the likelihood of their daughters developing disorders

Lack of parental affection and high levels of conflict at home may result in poor emotion regulation and maladaptive coping styles

People who perceived their family of origin as less healthy are more likely to have negative attitudes toward marriage

Children from divorced families are more likely to get divorced themselves

∧
∧ **Being born or adopted into a loving family is arbitrary,** but the effects of childhood family experiences are far-reaching.

SOCIALIZATION is the shaping of an individual's behavior to conform to social or cultural norms.

FAMILY DIVERSITY refers to the variation in family structures, experiences, and circumstances between families.

RACE is a group of people who are classified according to their phenotype.

PHENOTYPE refers to the anatomical and physical characteristics that distinguish one race from another.

ETHNIC GROUP is a group of people characterized by cultural factors, such as language, religion, and shared customs, that are passed from one generation to the next.

Our families place us in a particular socioeconomic class, such as working class, middle class, or upper class. As you will learn in Chapter 11, social class affects many aspects of family life, including when people marry, how many children they have, and how they raise their children.[37]

Education and Socialization

Although an increasing number of married couples are choosing to remain child-free, many plan to have a family. Procreation is an essential function in society—without the production or adoption of children, there would be no way of replacing elderly members as they die off. Developments in technology such as artificial insemination and in vitro fertilization have enabled many couples to reproduce who might otherwise remain childless.

Once a couple becomes parents, they are responsible for the education and socialization of their offspring. Socialization is the shaping of an individual's behavior to conform to social or cultural norms. Consciously or unconsciously, parents teach their children the values, attitudes, and beliefs of their culture.

Protection

Whom did you run to as a child when you fell off your bike and cut your knee? The family provides physical as well as economic protection for its members. This is a reciprocal relationship between parents and children—while parents take care of their children at a young age, children later return the favor by providing economic and psychological assistance in their parents' old age.

Religious Tradition

If parents belong to a religion, they will usually provide their children with a religious identity by performing traditions particular to that religion. A Christian family may say grace before meals, read passages from the Bible together, and celebrate Christmas and Easter, while a Jewish family may fast during Yom Kippur and celebrate Hanukkah together.

Recreation

Traditionally, the family was a source of recreation. Families gathered together to read stories or play musical instruments. Some sociologists argue that this function is being replaced by outside agencies such as Little League sports teams, computer games, and the hundreds of TV channels now available in the average American home.[38]

Affection

Studies consistently show that married couples and adults who live with others are happier and healthier than people who live alone.[39] Intimacy and affection are basic human needs, and families provide each other with a source of companionship.

DIVERSITY IN FAMILIES

No two families are the same—families differ in socioeconomic status, structure, race, ethnicity, sexuality, and lifestyle choice. There are many interpretations of family diversity, although we generally use it to mean variation in family structures, experiences, and circumstances between families. Let's take a look at one aspect of family diversity in depth: race and ethnicity.

DIVERSITY IN RACE AND ETHNICITY

Race and ethnicity are frequently confused, but they are not synonymous. A race is a group of people who are classified according to their phenotype—anatomical and physical characteristics of individuals, such as skin color. An ethnic group is a group of people characterized by cultural factors, such as language, religion, and shared customs, that are passed from one generation to the next. As we noted earlier, the United States was home to hundreds of diverse groups of people before the colonists even arrived. Since then, immigration has further increased racial and ethnic diversity, earning the country its "melting pot" moniker.

African American Families

According to the 2010 Census, more than 38.9 million African Americans live in the United States, comprising 12.6 percent of the total population.[40] Although they are no more likely to be divorced or widowed, a greater percentage of blacks than whites have never been married (46 percent compared with 28 percent). African Americans have higher divorce rates and unmarried birth rates than the general population, and more than 30 percent of black households are headed by women with no husbands present, compared to 12 percent in the population overall.[41] However, many of these characteristics are associated with poverty rather than race; if divorce rates are adjusted according to socioeconomic status, racial differences are minimal.

Hispanic Families

Hispanics are the largest and fastest growing ethnic group in the United States; projected figures indicate that by 2050, at least 25 percent of the population will be of Hispanic origin. The combination of immigration and higher birthrates among Hispanics are the primary reasons for this projected increase.[42] Within the Hispanic community, there is considerable diversity in ethnic heritage (for example, Mexican, Puerto Rican, or Cuban), and socioeconomic status, making it difficult to generalize familial characteristics. For example, the percentage of unmarried Hispanic mothers ranges from 27 percent among Cubans, to 41 percent among Mexicans, to 60 percent among Puerto Ricans.[43]

Asian American Families

In 2010, there were 14.7 million Asian Americans in the United States, comprising just under five percent of the total population.[44] Asian Americans are more likely to be married than whites (61 percent compared with 55 percent), but only half as likely to be divorced (5 percent compared with 11 percent). They typically have fewer children than other groups and tend to have their children later and within marriage. Only six percent of Asian American births occur to teenage mothers, compared to 23 percent of African American births and 18 percent of

Socioeconomic Status of U.S. Population: 2009

	All Races	White	African American	Hispanic	Asian
Median Family Income	$62,363	$69,530	$40,698	$42,445	$78,330
Percentage of Families Below Poverty Level	14.3	9.4	25.8	25.3	12.5
Percentage of Unemployed Adults over 16	7.2	6.1	13.3	8.7	5.8

Source: Social Explorer Tables: ACS 2005 to 2009 (5-Year Estimates) (SE), ACS 2005–2009 (5-Year Estimates), Social Explorer; U.S. Census Bureau; Carmen DeNavas-Walt, Bernadette D. Proctor, and Jessica C. Smith, "Income, Poverty, and Health Insurance Coverage in the United States: 2009," *Current Population Reports*, U.S. Census Bureau.

Hispanic births.[45] Although there is diversity within Asian American groups, most are very family-oriented, and place a high value on educational achievement, cultural values, and independence.[46] Family structure and values may vary depending on how recently the family immigrated to the United States, with more recent immigrants likely to retain more of the traditional cultural characteristics of their home countries. Studies have shown considerable differences in the attitudes of first-, second-, and third-generation Japanese family members.[47]

American Indian Families

Nearly 2,932,248 million Americans identify themselves as American Indians or Alaska Natives, comprising around 0.9% percent of the total population in 2010.[48] Although some identify with a particular tribe, such as Navajo, Cherokee, or Sioux, most of those in cities tend to call themselves Native Americans or Indians. Since World War II, many Native Americans have migrated from reservations to urban areas, as a result of poverty or pressure to assimilate in the modern world. As with Hispanic and Asian American groups, there is much variation between different tribal groups, although several generalizations can be made: Native Americans often live in extended families that revolve around clan membership rather than birth, marriage, or adoption; Native Americans are increasingly marrying non-Indians; and as with African Americans, conclusions about family characteristics are affected by Native Americans' low economic status.[49]

From Classroom to Community } Diversity in Homeless Families

Every other weekend, Tyler visits his local homeless shelter to help prepare meals for families and individuals in need. He has been volunteering at the shelter for more than two years.

"Before I started helping out at Doorways, I had an image of the stereotypical homeless person in my head—an elderly war veteran with an alcohol abuse problem.

"I've seen maybe a few people at the shelter that fit the type, but they are definitely in the minority.

"Most of the people we provide with transitional housing—probably about 70 percent—are families with children.

"This was completely shocking to me because I grew up in a very middle-class neighborhood and had the attitude that homelessness was caused by mental illness or drug abuse.

"Meeting families similar to mine that had fallen on hard times was a shock.

"We have a lot of them at the moment because of the economic downturn—people who lost their jobs and couldn't pay the rent or mortgage.

"Most of the families we take in, though, are young-single mothers and their children.

"Sadly, they're usually escaping from violent husbands or partners. Since I've been helping at the shelter, the regular staff have managed to get many families into permanent affordable housing, which is a very satisfying feeling."

THEORIES OF THE FAMILY

Social scientists use experiments, surveys, observation, and secondary data analysis to test hypothesis and form theories—or proposed explanations that have not been proven as fact—about family dynamics. Qualitative research attempts to provide a full picture of family issues through case studies, ethnographies, and focus groups. Sociologists have many opposing theories about the structure, composition, and behavior of families and family members. In this chapter, we will examine nine different viewpoints.

Structural-Functional Theory

Remember the story about the bike at the beginning of the chapter? The explanation about all the different parts of society functioning in an interrelated way is an example of structural-functional theory (commonly known as functional theory). Functional theorists examine the family from a macro level, looking at society from a broad, global approach. Imagine looking out of an airplane window from 30,000 feet up. You can't see the finer details, but you are able to see the Earth's surface right out to the horizon.

One of the most influential functionalists was Talcott Parsons, who developed his theories in the 1950s and 1960s. Parsons believed that human behavior is driven by people's efforts to conform to the moral codes of society and that these moral codes constrain human behavior to promote the common good. For society to survive, its subsystems (families and other organizations) must function in a way that promotes the maintenance of society as a whole. There are two central assumptions in functional theory: The main function of families is to procreate and socialize children, and the family, as a system, needs to maintain its basic structure.

For Parsons, the ideal structure was illustrated by the Gulden family in One True Thing—a post-World War II isolated nuclear family style, consisting of husband, wife, and children. Parsons argued that the husband's role was breadwinner of the family and the wife's role was to maintain family relations; these were the dominant social values and norms. When men and women conform to the norms of society, they raise healthy children, but failure to conform throws society into disequilibrium, resulting in dysfunctional outcomes such as divorce and juvenile delinquency.

Structural functional theory ground to a halt in the 1960s and 1970s, with the huge increase in same-sex couples, single-parent families, and blended families. Having no way of accounting for these family variations except to label them as "deviant," the weakness of structural functionalist theory was exposed—it was unable to account for social change. However, elements of functionalism still survive today. Members of the marriage movement promote traditional marriage and protest legal policies that would legalize same-sex marriage. Researchers study the effects of divorce on children and question whether working mothers negatively affect their children's well-being. And the nuclear or traditional family is still used as the benchmark against which all alternative or "deviant" lifestyles are measured.

Conflict Theory

Conflict theory stems from Karl Marx's idea that those who control the resources have all the power. Whereas functionalists believe that conflict plays a minor role in family life and that the ultimate goal is for a balanced and peaceful household, conflict theorists believe that conflict is inevitable and necessary. Individual family members are motivated to pursue their own needs, values, and goals, which often conflict with the needs, values, and goals of other family members, resulting in a struggle for power. For example, at the beginning of One True Thing, Ellen wants to stay in New York to pursue her career, while her father wants her to return home to take care of her mother. According to conflict theorists, sources of power within a family include legitimacy, money, physical coercion, and love. In the film, George uses both his position as Ellen's father and her love for her mother to persuade her to return home.

Conflict theorists believe that conflict within families is necessary because it results in change and adaptation. People who have power want to maintain the status quo, while people without power want to change the system to make it fairer. Current examples include the campaign for same-sex marriage legislation, demands to close the salary gap between men and women, and affirmative action policies that support equal opportunities for racial and ethnic minorities. Conflict theorists examine how these inequalities may be passed down through different generations, for example, via the socialization of children and traditional male/female division of household labor.

Feminist Theory

Compare the portrayal of women in family sitcoms before 1950 and after 1980 and you will likely see a marked difference in gender roles. For example, June Cleaver from Leave It to Beaver is often seen in the kitchen fixing meals for her family or entertaining the ladies of the neighborhood as part of her social club. On the other hand, Clair Huxtable from The Cosby Show works outside the home as a lawyer and is often seen as the disciplinarian of the family. These changes reflect a cultural shift during the 1960s and 1970s, known as the modern feminist movement or the second wave of feminism (the first wave occurred during the late 19th and early 20th centuries, when women campaigned for the right to vote). During the second wave of feminism, leaders such as Betty Friedan, Gloria Steinem, and the National Organization for Women (NOW) campaigned on issues such as equal pay and job training for women, reproductive choice, maternity leave, child care, and an end to sex discrimination.[50] Today, feminists support equality for men and women in all contexts of public and private life.

From the feminist movement grew feminist theory, in which scholars base their work on several assumptions. They view women's experiences as central to an understanding of the family as a whole, focusing on women's perspectives and feelings. They believe that gender is socially constructed and that the roles of husbands and wives are defined by society rather than biology. Contrary to the functionalist viewpoint, feminist theorists believe that the nuclear family is an inadequate description of families in modern society and that limiting families to the nuclear description restricts women's roles to subordinate positions. Rather than the maintenance of social order, feminist theorists place emphasis on social change and challenging the status quo. Finally, feminist theorists believe that there is no neutral observation of humans—rather than treating the family as a whole, feminist theorists explore the individual experiences of each family member.[51]

Symbolic Interaction Theory

Symbolic interactionists figuratively put families under a microscope on a daily basis, by examining the family on a micro level. Interactionists believe that individuals develop a sense of self through their interactions with others. We develop a sense of self based on the reactions of the people we care about and by our perception of these reactions. The way in which we interpret people's opinions of us then becomes a dominant aspect of our own identities—a concept that sociologist Charles H. Cooley referred to as the "**looking-glass self**."[52] In other words, some of our actions and behaviors may be the result of self-fulfilling prophecies. For example, a teenaged boy might interpret his father's coldness toward him as an indication that he is not good enough for his father. Feeling that he is unable to gain his father's approval, the teenager begins to cut

LOOKING-GLASS SELF is a concept of self in which interpretations of other people's opinions become a dominant aspect of identity.

SELF is the concept of identity that develops through interactions with others.

SOCIETY refers to the process of socialization in which we interpret meanings of symbols and learn about our roles.

ROLE is the part we are expected to play in society, learned through interactions with others.

classes in school and eventually flunks out. His father is disappointed in him, fulfilling the son's expectations that he will never be good enough in his father's eyes.

Symbolic interactionism involves three main concepts: the **self** (a concept that develops through interactions with others), **society** (the process of socialization in which we interpret meanings of symbols and learn about our roles), and **role** (the part we are expected to play in society, learned through interactions with others). Contemporary family research from a symbolic interactionist perspective deals with

∧
∧ **Conflict theorists view** the current dispute over same-sex marriage **as a power**
∧ **struggle,** with the people in power fighting to maintain the status quo. **Is change**
inevitable as society evolves?

MICROSYSTEM is a child's immediate environment, including any immediate relationships or organizations that the child interacts with.

MESOSYSTEM is the description of how different parts of the child's microsystem interact.

EXOSYSTEM refers to the outside influences that a child may not interact with personally, but that have a large impact on the child.

MACROSYSTEM is the culture in which an individual lives.

CHRONOSYSTEM is the research model that examines the impact of normative and nonnormative life transitions on family processes and child development over time.

REWARDS are the pleasures or satisfactions we enjoy from participating in a relationship.

COSTS are the negative outcomes, energy invested, or rewards foregone as a result of choosing one behavior over another.

COMPARISON LEVEL OF ALTERNATIVES is the evaluation by individuals of their relationships in the light of available alternatives.

BOUNDARIES are emotional barriers that define a system and separate the system from its environment and other systems.

RULES OF TRANSFORMATION are the means by which a system governs the way in which inputs from the environment are changed to outputs.

SUBSYSTEM is part of a system that can be analyzed separately in relation to its exchanges with the system and with other subsystems.

VARIETY is the extent to which a system is able to adapt to changes in the environment.

the roles that individuals play within families, for example, how the roles of husband and wife are defined during different stages of family life, and how factors such as gender role conceptions may affect spousal interactions.

Ecological Theory

Developmental psychologist Urie Bronfenbrenner argued that in order to study a child's development, it is necessary to look beyond the child's immediate environment and consider the interaction between the child's biological makeup and wider external factors.[53] Bronfenbrenner identified five environmental systems that influence the family: microsystems, mesosystems, exosystems, macrosystems, and chronosystems.

The **microsystem** is the child's immediate environment, including any immediate relationships or organizations that the child interacts with, such as family members or teachers at school. The **mesosystem** describes how different parts of the child's microsystem interact. For example, children whose parents play an active role in their education often do better in school than children with poorer home-school linkages.[54] The **exosystem** includes outside influences that the child may not interact with personally, but that have a large impact on the child, such as parents' workplaces or members of the extended family. If a parent receives a promotion and spends many more hours at work, the relationship with his or her child may be affected. Many studies consider the impact of mothers working full-time, the effects of parental unemployment on families, and the amount of time parents spend with their children.

On a wider level, the **macrosystem** describes the culture in which an individual lives, including the relative freedoms permitted by the national government, cultural values, and the economy—all of which may affect a child positively or negatively. Finally, Bronfenbrenner considers **chronosystems**, research models that examine the impact of normative and nonnormative life transitions on family processes and child development over time. Normative transitions might include puberty, changing schools, marriage, and retirement, whereas nonnormative transitions might include unexpected events within a family, such as death or divorce.

Social Exchange Theory

Why might you choose to live with your parents instead of moving into an apartment by yourself? Or opt to get married rather than remain single? According to social exchange theorists, human behaviors and interactions are based on a series of rewards and costs. **Rewards** are the pleasures or satisfactions we enjoy from participating in a relationship—the comfort we gain from having someone to confide in or the trust that is earned over a long period of time, and **costs** are the negative outcomes, energy invested, or rewards foregone as a result of choosing one behavior over another—the inability to flirt with members of the opposite sex at a bar after marriage, or the petty arguments that result from living in close confinement with another person. As long as the rewards of a relationship outweigh the costs, the relationship will likely continue.

Social exchange theorists also consider the **comparison level of alternatives**, in which individuals evaluate their relationships in the light of available alternatives. This may vary greatly between relationships. For example, one person may believe that he can easily find a more caring and generous partner, increasing the likelihood that he will end his current relationship. Another person may believe that his current partner is the best he can hope for, and that there are few alternative options. This may help explain why some people stay in violent or unhappy relationships.[55]

Family Systems Theory

According to family systems theorists, individuals cannot be understood in isolation because they are part of an interconnected and interdependent system—a family. Family systems theory originated in Ludwig von Bertalanffy's work on general systems theory in the 1940s, which posited that organisms are complex, organized, and interactive. Family systems theory includes several key concepts:

1 Systems have **boundaries**. Every system has emotional barriers that define the system and separate the system from its environment and other systems. No family is a completely open or closed system, although some families may be more willing than others to allow outsiders into the household.

2 Systems have internal **rules of transformation** that govern the way in which inputs from the environment are changed to outputs. For example, family inputs might include goods and services, and outputs might include the behaviors of family members and socialization of children.

3 Systems have **subsystems** that can be analyzed separately in relation to their exchanges with the system and with other subsystems. In family units, these subsystems might include parent-child subsystems, sibling subsystems, and marital subsystems.[56]

4 Systems have different degrees of **variety**—the extent to which the system is able to adapt to changes in the environment. Systems that are unable to adapt to change may malfunction (or develop family rifts). For example, a family with strict Catholic views about sex before marriage may be unable to adapt to a teenage pregnancy within the family, causing a rupture in the family system.

Family Life Course/Development Theory

How do relationships between husbands and wives change with the birth of their first child? Does the relationship shift when that child goes to school or leaves the family home? Family development theorists attempt to answer questions such as these by studying transitions within marriage and family over time. Early development theorists viewed family development as proceeding through life cycle stages, with each stage marked by a different set of norms or expectations. Typical stages included early marriage, living with young children, children leaving home, and the empty nest.[57]

However, the concept of stages is problematic, partly because there are many different ways of categorizing the stages of family development, and partly because the traditional stages (marriage, children, retirement) do not include relevant categories for single-parent families, childless families, remarried families, and many other family forms. Early researchers developed the misleading view that if certain conditions were met in a stage, then the family could successfully move onto the next stage of development, implying both a causal effect and suggesting that there was a "normal" process of family development. Furthermore, some stages may not be mutually exclusive. For example, Duvall and Hill included "families with schoolchildren" and "families with adolescents" as two separate categories, yet many families have children of both ages.[58]

To address some of these criticisms, Joan Aldous suggested modifying the idea of a family life cycle, instead focusing on a "family career."[59] This allowed for the possibility that different families had different "career" paths, which might include divorce, remarriage, cohabitation, and remaining single.

> **NEPOTISM** is favoritism shown to one's kin.
> **RECIPROCITY** is the exchange of favors.
> **COERCION** is being forced to act against one's interests.

Despite the criticisms, family development theory has been applied in many areas of academic research, including turning points in blended families and sexual orientation in family development.[60]

Biosocial Theory

Biosocial theorists view human behavior in the family setting as an intricate interaction of genes and the environment. Developed from Darwin's theory of evolution, anthropologist P.L. van de Berghe argued that the human family was the earliest social institution and could be reduced to three principles: **nepotism** (favoritism shown to one's kin), **reciprocity** (the exchange of favors), and **coercion** (being forced to act against one's interests).[61] Of these, the concept of nepotism, or kin selection, is the most important. Individuals attempt to maximize the transmission of their genes to the next generation. Because we share genes with our siblings, their reproductive success is related to ours. In other words, we are genetically predisposed to favor our siblings to ensure that they reproduce and carry on the family genes. Van de Berghe argues that parents also maximize their chances of reproductive success by either having few children and investing a lot of care and attention in them or by having many children to ensure the survival of some. The chosen method depends on the environment—higher fertility is preferable in a hostile, unstable environment (for example, where there is a high likelihood of disease, war, or famine), whereas lower fertility is suited to a stable environment (for example, in Western cultures with good health care, food, and educational resources.)[62]

Although biosocial theory has been criticized for its overstatement of biological influences, much research has focused on the interaction between biological and societal influences, including odor communication between mothers and infants, kin recognition and attachment, and violence and abuse within families.

Bronfenbrenner's Environmental Systems

Chronosystem
Macrosystem
Exosystem
Microsystem and Mesosystem

Child

Normative events (e.g., puberty, marriage, retirement)
(e.g., family, school)
(e.g., extended family, parents' workplace)
(e.g., government, cultural values, economy)
Nonnormative events (e.g., death, divroce)

WRAP YOUR MIND AROUND THE THEORY

Functionalists believe that social deviance results from failure to conform to the dominant set of values and norms in Western societies. Do you agree that children from nontraditional homes are disadvantaged by their backgrounds?

FUNCTIONALISM

According to functionalists, an individual is given the best possible chance of success if he or she is raised in a traditional nuclear family. When a family consists of a breadwinner husband, a wife who maintains strong family relations, and their biological children, it conforms to the dominant set of values and norms in Western societies. As a result, the family performs its intended function within society and the children grow up to be happy, healthy, and well-adjusted individuals. Conversely, children who grow up in nontraditional households (for example divorced or single-parent homes) are more likely to participate in deviant behavior. Although functionalism died out in the 1960s and 1970s, many Americans still consider the nuclear family the ideal family type and use it as a benchmark against which to measure nontraditional families.[63] When researchers consider the impact of divorce on children, the educational attainment of children from single-parent families, or the behavior of adopted children in same-sex families, they also use children from nuclear families as a benchmark for comparison.

CONFLICT THEORY

Conflict theorists believe that individuals within a family are motivated to act in their own interests. Because these interests often differ from the interests of other family members, conflict becomes inevitable. Siblings fight over the TV remote control, husbands and wives compete for time with the children, and parents argue with their children about completing homework on time. Families are divided into hierarchies, with parents exerting power over children and men traditionally exerting power over their wives. These family hierarchies reflect wider inequalities in society in relation to race, class, and gender. Conflict theorists view conflict as an instrument for social change, in which people who have power struggle to maintain the status quo, whereas people without power fight to change the system to make it fairer. If we look at the family as a microcosm of society in general, we can see how families teach children the principles of conflict and negotiation from an early age.

HOW DO FAMILIES INFLUENCE INDIVIDUALS?

SYMBOLIC INTERACTIONISM

From a symbolic interactionist perspective, individuals are shaped through their interactions with others. Through these interactions (and our interpretation of them), we develop a sense of self. Since we spend a large proportion of our time with immediate family members, the family plays an important role in developing our identities, or self-concepts. According to symbolic interactionists, we learn to see ourselves as other people do—their reactions to us serve as a type of mirror reflecting our image so that we can see it (the "looking-glass self" concept).[64] One study that supported this concept examined the behavior of three groups of schoolchildren. The children in the first group were repeatedly told that they *were* tidy. The children in the second group were told that they *should be* tidy, while the third group was not told anything unusual. After observing the amount of litter each group dropped, researchers noted that the children in the first group were the tidiest—being labeled as tidy caused them to develop a new self-concept and behave accordingly.[65]

Conflict theorists view conflict as a means of social change and adaptation. How might a struggle for power lead to a change in social structure?

According to symbolic interaction theory, we develop a sense of self through our interactions with others. Can people's reactions to us influence our own personalities?

discover marriages and families in action:

Perspectives of the Family

What is a family? As we have already observed, there are many different opinions about what constitutes a family, making it difficult to formulate a single definition. Let's look at the family from three different angles: the perspective of society, the perspective of small groups, and the perspective of the individual.

SOCIETAL PERSPECTIVE

In many countries, *family* has a very narrow legal definition, meaning either a nuclear family of married parents and their biological children under the age of 18, or blood relatives. Other groups of people who might consider themselves a family, for example same-sex couples or cohabiting couples, do not qualify for Social Security benefits or other types of governmental aid. Stepparents have no legal rights over their partners' biological children unless they legally adopt them. Organizations from multinational companies to small businesses may also assume this narrow definition of family, limiting employees' rights to a leave of absence after the death of a relative or after the birth of a child.

SMALL-GROUP PERSPECTIVE

Examining the concept of family from a small-group perspective, we may classify particular groups of people as families or not. Do a single parent and child make up a family? What about a cohabiting couple with a child? Or a married couple without children? A family may be seen to include large numbers of people related by blood or marriage. This same group may also be classified as extended family, or a kin group. In some non-Western cultures, obligations toward extended families may be stronger than obligations toward more immediate family members. For example, in one form of Cantonese marriage, women do not live with their husbands until at least three years after their marriage, because their primary duties are to their own extended families.[66]

INDIVIDUAL PERSPECTIVE

On the most personal level, we can look at the family from the perspective of the individual. Some people consider their pets to be members of their family, while others might only include their parents, children, or siblings. Being biologically related might not even be sufficient to be counted as a family member. One researcher found that 19 percent of the children living with biological siblings did not identify their brothers or sisters as family members, while stepparents, stepsiblings, stepchildren, and absent or divorced parents were also frequently omitted from the list.[67]

> **ACTIVITY**
>
> Write down a list of everyone you consider to be a member of your family. Compare your list with your family and friends.

MAKE CONNECTIONS

Marriage and Family

As you have learned in this chapter, there is no standardized definition of the family. Personal experiences and individual living situations cause family to mean something different to everyone. In Chapter 4, we will look at how gender affects marriage and family and examine traditional and nontraditional gender roles within families.

Although some argue that functionalist theory may be outdated, its notion of family as the most important unit within society still holds true. As the feminist slogan says, "The personal is the political." In other words, things that happen in society can and do affect the family, and vice versa. In Chapter 12, we will examine how the family relates to other social institutions, including education, politics, religion, and the legal system.

>>> ACTIVITIES

1. Ask three of your friends to write a definition of what family means to them.

Compare their answers with your own. Are there similarities and differences? Why or why not?

2. Locate a scholarly social science database at your university library. You may be able to access this via the Internet. Perform a search using the key word family. What type of articles do you locate about the family? Browse through the search results. Are there similar themes or different topics?

CHAPTER

01

Theory

FUNCTIONALISM   14

- an individual is given the best possible chance of success if he or she is raised in a traditional nuclear family
- the nuclear family is a benchmark against which to measure nontraditional families

SYMBOLIC INTERACTIONISM   15

- individuals are shaped through their interactions with others
- the family plays an important role in developing self-concept

CONFLICT THEORY   14

- individuals within a family are motivated to act in their own interests
- families are divided into hierarchies, which reflect the hierarchies in society

Key Terms

stressor is a situation or event causing stress   4

marriage is a legally recognized union between a man and a woman   5

monogamous marriage is a type of marriage in which one person is married to another person of the opposite sex   5

polygamous marriage is a type of marriage in which one person is married to multiple husbands or wives   5

arranged marriage is a type of marriage in which the families of the bride and groom negotiate an arrangement before the two parties enter into a relationship   5

family is a group of two people or more related by birth, marriage, or adoption and residing together   6

household refers to all people who occupy a housing unit regardless of relationship   6

affiliated kin are nonrelated individuals who are accepted as part of a family   7

family of origin describes the family in which an individual is raised   11

socialization is the shaping of an individual's behavior to conform to social or cultural norms   12

family diversity refers to the variation in family structures, experiences, and circumstances between families   12

race is a group of people who are classified according to their phenotype   12

phenotype refers to the anatomical and physical characteristics that distinguish one race from another   12

ethnic group is a group of people characterized by cultural factors, such as language, religion, and shared customs, that are passed from one generation to the next   12

looking-glass self is a concept of self in which interpretations of other people's opinions become a dominant aspect of identity   15

self is the concept of identity that develops through interactions with others   15

(continued)

society refers to the process of socialization in which we interpret meanings of symbols and learn about our roles   *15*

role is the part we are expected to play in society, learned through interactions with others   *15*

microsystem is a child's immediate environment, including any immediate relationships or organizations that the child interacts with   *16*

mesosystem is the description of how different parts of the child's microsystem interact   *16*

exosystem refers to the outside influences that a child may not interact with personally, but that have a large impact on the child   *16*

macrosystem is the culture in which an individual lives   *16*

chronosystem is the research model that examines the impact of normative and nonnormative life transitions on family processes and child development over time   *16*

rewards are the pleasures or satisfactions we enjoy from participating in a relationship   *16*

costs are the negative outcomes, energy invested, or rewards foregone as a result of choosing one behavior over another   *16*

comparison level of alternatives is the evaluation by individuals of their relationships in the light of available alternatives   *16*

boundaries are emotional barriers that define a system and separate the system from its environment and other systems   *16*

rules of transformation are the means by which a system governs the way in which inputs from the environment are changed to outputs   *16*

subsystem is part of a system that can be analyzed separately in relation to its exchanges with the system and with other subsystems   *16*

variety is the extent to which a system is able to adapt to changes in the environment   *16*

nepotism is favoritism shown to one's kin   *17*

reciprocity is the exchange of favors   *17*

coercion is being forced to act against one's interests   *17*

Sample Test Questions

MULTIPLE CHOICE

These multiple-choice questions are similar to those found in the test bank that accompanies this textbook.

1. Which of these statements is TRUE of marriages in all cultures?
   a. Marriage is a legal union between one man and one woman.
   b. Marriage is a voluntary union between two parties.
   c. Marriage establishes rights and obligations related to gender.
   d. Marriage is only legally recognized if individuals are over the age of 16.
2. Which of these is NOT a current trend in modern households?
   a. fewer marriages
   b. fewer children
   c. delayed marriage
   d. more nuclear families
3. Which of the following theorists examine the family on a micro level?
   a. Functional theorists
   b. Conflict theorists
   c. Feminist theorists
   d. Social interactionist theorists
4. One effect of increased life expectancy is:
   a. a trend toward delayed marriage.
   b. a trend toward lower divorce rates.
   c. a trend toward higher birth rates.
   d. a trend toward early marriage.
5. Which of these statements would MOST LIKELY be voiced by a functionalist?
   a. Variety in family structures shows that marriage and family are in transition.
   b. Conflict within families is a necessary instrument for social change.
   c. Family members develop a sense of self through their interactions with others.
   d. The traditional nuclear family is the only form that promotes stability within society.

ESSAY

1. Discuss the current trends in marriage and family in the United States.
2. What factors should you keep in mind when reading and interpreting statistics about racial diversity?
3. Discuss whether the "golden age" of the traditional nuclear family ever really existed.
4. Choose three theories of marriage and family, and discuss the advantages and disadvantages of each.
5. Discuss how definitions of family may vary according to perspective.

WHERE TO START YOUR RESEARCH PAPER

For more data on current marriage statistics, go to
http://www.cdc.gov/nchs/nvss.htm

For more data on current trends in household compositions, go to
http://www.census.gov/population/www/socdemo/hh-fam.html

For more information about marriage laws in the United States, go to
http://www.usmarriagelaws.com/search/united_states/index.shtml

To find out more about changing trends in the working family, go to
http://www.pbs.org/livelyhood/workingfamily/familytrends.html

To learn more about legal trends in marriage, including information about the campaign to legalize same-sex marriage, go to
http://www.hrc.org/issues/marriage.asp

For more information about Hispanic households in the United States, go to http://www.lasculturas.com/aa/spec/blcensus2000b.htm

To find out more about the history of the family, go to
http://encarta.msn.com/encyclopedia_761558266/family.html

For global statistics on marriage and family, including birth rates and size of households, go to http://www.nationmaster.com/index.php

ANSWERS: 1. c; 2. d; 3. d; 4. a; 5. d

Remember to check www.thethinkspot.com for additional information, downloadable flashcards, and other helpful resources.

In the

movie *It Runs in the Family*, the Grombergs, who appear to be a highly successful American family, are preparing to celebrate Passover. The family's patriarch, Mitchell, has been retired for many years after founding a successful New York law firm. He has survived a recent stroke, but he is physically frail and his speech is impaired, although his mind remains sharp. Throughout Mitchell's life, his wife Evelyn has given him counsel on emotional and family matters, but now she is undergoing kidney dialysis.

Alex, their son, and Rebecca have been married for 22 years. Alex is a partner in his father's law firm; Rebecca is a psychologist. They have two children: Asher is in his fifth year of college, and E.J. is 11, just coming into the turmoil of adolescence.

In some ways, the Grombergs seem to have it all. But you can't base the true strength of a family on its economic and social status alone. As the movie reveals, the Grombergs are a unique, intricate, and flawed family.

Mitchell's skill in the courtroom never translated to the touchy business of raising Alex. Mitchell's tongue has always been sharp, and Alex feels that Mitchell is disappointed in him. Alex reacts to one of Mitchell's frequent barbs by noting that his father is still as harsh as ever, but the stroke has made it "more difficult to enunciate his insults."

Alex became a lawyer in his father's firm largely because it was what his father expected. Now he is immersed in the same type of work his father did, although it's the last thing he would have wished. He is much more interested in offering free legal help to the poor and volunteers at a soup kitchen. In midlife, he and his wife have grown apart, and their children reflect some of the gaps in their parenting. Asher barely maintains his grades and is more interested in life as a party deejay and a marijuana supplier than in more respectable careers. E.J. is so serious that his adolescent relationships with girls are painfully awkward, and he communicates his need for an allowance increase through a computer spreadsheet illustrating his income and expenses.

Over the course of the movie, Mitchell senses his coming death and tries to repair his relationship with his son. Mitchell's brother, a decorated veteran, dies after a long and painful period in a wheelchair, during which he loses the ability to communicate. Alex's dissatisfaction with his work and marriage leads to a near-affair with a co-worker at the soup kitchen, interrupted only by chance. Asher gets himself and a new girlfriend arrested for growing marijuana on the eve of an important college presentation. E.J. searches for trustworthy guidance as he comes of age, but finds little.

There's no single happy ending for a complex family like the Grombergs. There are still stressful events to come, and it isn't obvious how each family member will react. But it is clear that, behind the social façade presented by even the most successful or "normal" American families, lies a complicated and unique web of relationships, bound together by biological and social ties that go deeper than stereotypes and simplistic definitions.

HOW TO STUDY MARRIAGE AND THE FAMILY

CHAPTER 02

Although *It Runs in the Family* is generally classified as a comedy, **there are enough painful moments in the film** to make many viewers stop and think about their own families.

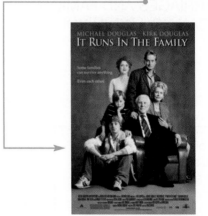

Over the years, the Gromberg family has changed markedly. Mitchell's stroke has made him vulnerable, and Evelyn's treatments require time and emotional energy previously reserved for the family. There was little communication between Mitchell and Alex as he grew up, but now Mitchell awkwardly tries to repair the damaged relationship.

Furthermore, the Grombergs live in a world where drug use is common, and technology makes it easy to avoid face-to-face communication. But for all these challenges, the Grombergs show a resiliency and a deep connection that help them face another day.

I was in my early twenties when I met the family I will call the McKinneys. Ken and Marsha McKinney were married when he was 24 and she was 23, and they had six children.

Their third child, Mike, was born with Down

∧
∧ Families undergo changes
∧ for many reasons, **including health issues.**

syndrome. Ken and Marsha worked hard to provide the extra care Mike needed and watched him struggle to learn basic tasks and relate to others. In the end, Mike progressed enough to support himself.

The couple retired, sold their home in Minnesota, and moved to Arizona. They made friends and volunteered with several service organizations.

At 82, Ken had a serious stroke and died. Marsha and Ken had been nearly inseparable for 57 years, and his death was very hard for Marsha to accept. However, she is still in good health and continues to volunteer.

The changes the McKinney family experienced illustrate some important concepts in family development. Social scientists see the family development as a series of stages. There is some disagreement over the best ways to study families or apply these stages to individual families, but it's clear that all families change considerably over their life cycle.

How to Study Marriage and the Family

Family development theory – suggested families go through similar stages

social scientists produced 3 models

Quantitative research – uses numbers to describe families and their actions
Experiments
Surveys
Observation
Secondary data analysis

Quantitative research – uses words to describe families and their actions
Case studies
Ethnographies
Focus groups

get the topic: WHAT MODELS AND METHODS DO SOCIAL SCIENTISTS USE IN ASSESSING THE DEVELOPMENT OF FAMILIES?

Family Development Theory

People have thought about families and the ways they change and grow for hundreds of years. **Family development theory**, or the idea that families move through common stages, can be traced back to the late 1700s. During the period after World War II, theorists began to identify and name critical stages in family development, using the term **family life cycle** to indicate the eight stages of growth that begin after marriage.[1] Since then, there has been considerable debate about the best ways to assess family development. Some have criticized family development theory for placing too much emphasis on family structure as opposed to interactions among family members and for a lack of empirical studies that back up the theory of common stages of development.[2] In this chapter, we'll look at three basic ideas in applying family development theory.

FAMILY LIFE CYCLE

The graphic on the following page displays the eight distinct stages in family development identified by the family life cycle approach. Note that they are identified by the presence of children, their ages, or the ages of the couple.[3,4]

Soon after the family life cycle stages were identified in the late 1950s, some researchers found them extremely helpful in doing statistical studies on a family's economic status or other demographic information. They felt that, in most studies, a person's age was less important in influencing their behavior than their status in the family life cycle, suggesting that "the critical dates in the life of an individual may not be his birthdays so much as the days a change occurs in his family status, for example, when he marries or his first child is born."[5]

The usefulness of the family life cycle approach in research today has been reduced because fewer families go through all of the identified stages, or the order of the stages has been changed because of divorce, remarriage, stepfamilies, adoptions, couples who choose not to have

FAMILY DEVELOPMENT THEORY proposes that families proceed through common, identifiable stages.

FAMILY LIFE CYCLE is a theory that identifies eight specific stages for families beginning after marriage.

STRATIFICATION is a division into similar layers or groups.

FAMILY LIFE COURSE is a model that focuses on how families integrate changes over time and the meanings that individual family members give to those changes.

children, and same-sex couples.[6] A 1979 study also stated that using the stage of family life cycle as a means of **stratification**, or division into similar layers or groups, was no more useful than using dates of marriage or ages in predicting behavior or status, and suggested the need to develop other stratification schemes.[7] Some believe that the family life cycle model could still be an important tool if the identification of stages is modified to address the length of marriage and the presence of children.[8]

FAMILY LIFE COURSE

In the early 1990s, some social scientists proposed a new perspective on family development, called family life course. Instead of dividing family life into standard stages according to the age of the couple and children, **family life course** focuses on how families integrate changes over time and the meanings that individual family members give to those changes. For example, it focuses on how unique individuals respond to a particular event, such as the death of a spouse, because of their background, personality, age when the death occurs, or length of time living together. What are the differences if the spouse was deeply involved in family life or was relatively remote and removed? What about the differences in reactions to the death of a spouse who is the sole breadwinner and one who was part of an economically equal couple? How do individuals react if the death followed a long illness or was the result of a sudden accident or health problem?

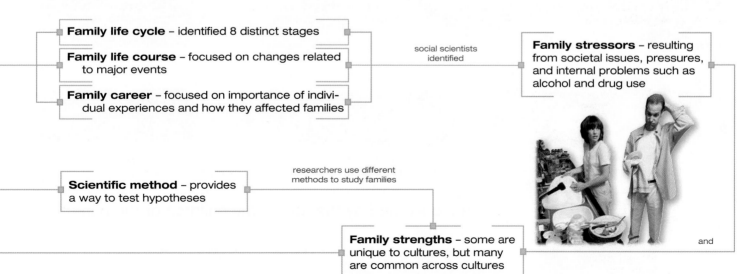

Family life cycle – identified 8 distinct stages

Family life course – focused on changes related to major events

Family career – focused on importance of individual experiences and how they affected families

social scientists identified

Family stressors – resulting from societal issues, pressures, and internal problems such as alcohol and drug use

Scientific method – provides a way to test hypotheses

researchers use different methods to study families

Family strengths – some are unique to cultures, but many are common across cultures

and

Family Life-Cycle Stages

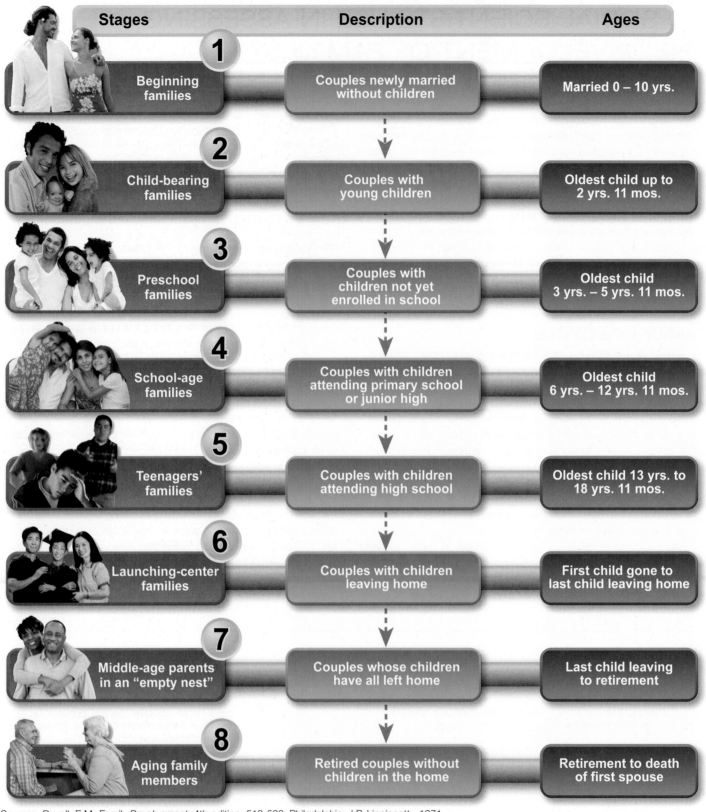

Stages	Description	Ages
1 Beginning families	Couples newly married without children	Married 0 – 10 yrs.
2 Child-bearing families	Couples with young children	Oldest child up to 2 yrs. 11 mos.
3 Preschool families	Couples with children not yet enrolled in school	Oldest child 3 yrs. – 5 yrs. 11 mos.
4 School-age families	Couples with children attending primary school or junior high	Oldest child 6 yrs. – 12 yrs. 11 mos.
5 Teenagers' families	Couples with children attending high school	Oldest child 13 yrs. to 18 yrs. 11 mos.
6 Launching-center families	Couples with children leaving home	First child gone to last child leaving home
7 Middle-age parents in an "empty nest"	Couples whose children have all left home	Last child leaving to retirement
8 Aging family members	Retired couples without children in the home	Retirement to death of first spouse

Sources: Duvall, E.M. *Family Development*, 4th edition, 519-532. Philadelphia: J.P. Lippincott., 1971.
Kunz, J. 1989. *Marital Satisfaction Over the Family Life-Cycle.* Thesis for Brigham Young University, Sociology Department.

∧ Most family life cycle stages **are governed by the age of the children or the parents.**
∧ What stage is your family currently in?

This approach avoided the more rigid categories established by the family life cycle and allowed for unique, individual responses to transitions in the family caused by internal or external events. However, this perspective still addresses traditional, two-parent families, without allowing for the increase in nontraditional families such as single-parent families, stepfamilies, and same-sex couples. [9]

FAMILY CAREER

Most of us think of a career as a job classification that may extend over an adult's working life. But a family career is different. The **family career** perspective on family development focuses on families and individuals and how their experiences affect family development throughout the life of the family. These experiences are further divided into four **subcareers**, or specific aspects of family life experienced by individuals, which affect the family. One person may experience conflicting or complementary effects from several subcareers at the same time or be involved in none at a given time.

The family career perspective views the intersections or transitions between these subcareers as crisis points—times when family relationships are changed. For example, when a child is born to a married couple, a parent-child subcareer is added to a marital subcareer. Another example of a crisis point occurs when a divorce ends a marital subcareer (and possibly a parent-child subcareer), but a sexual subcareer continues, possibly with another partner.

The sexual experience subcareer generally occurs between people of about the same age. Their sexual experiences, good and bad, affect how the individual relates to the family, whereas the family structure affects the individual's sexual experience at the same time. Some years ago, the common expectation was that most people's sexual experiences would begin with marriage. Today, that is not the case because sexual experimentation and premarital sex are much more common and occur at younger ages. Another subcareer is the marital career, also experienced primarily between people of similar ages. One study by sociologist Harold Feldman found that married

∧
∧ Married couples are generally
∧ more satisfied **with their marriages**
in early and later years. Why do you
think **this might be true?**

people without children are most satisfied with their marriages in the early and later years, with people in the middle years of marriage showing less satisfaction.[10]

The parent-child subcareer involves a parent and a child and an unequal power relationship. Often, this subcareer can extend well beyond the point when a child leaves the home and can affect family members long after the child becomes an adult. The fourth subcareer is

> **FAMILY CAREER** is the family experience of an individual over a lifetime.
> **SUBCAREER** is one of four distinct roles that a person may experience at any time and that affect the individual and the family.

the relationship between two adults as marital partners, which ends with the death of one spouse. In some cases, the end of this subcareer entails giving economic or social control of the family to a younger member so that the older adult can retire and relax in his or her old age.[11]

Regardless of the perspective used—family cycle, family life course, or family career—observing families over a long period of time can offer insights into how families grow and change over the years. Observing the Grombergs or the McKinneys as they moved from marriage to parenthood and working careers and later to an empty nest, retirement, death, and involvement with a third generation provides vivid examples of how a family grows and changes.

FAMILY STRESSORS

Before we take a closer look at how sociologists study families, let's build a foundation for understanding the family by talking about the basic ups and downs of family life: the stresses and successes our families encounter on a regular basis. There's no doubt that creating a loving family has been a challenge since the dawn of time. Consider the stories of rival biblical brothers Cain and Abel, Henry VIII and his wives who lost their heads, and the sadistic Lizzie Borden who gave her parents 40 whacks with an ax. It's obvious that many families have been filled with conflict. Over the years, social scientists have identified a variety of family stressors, or conditions that cause stress.

A 2007 study by John DeFrain and Sylvia Asay listed 12 different areas in which families in the United States experience stress. The list began with the fast pace of life and the competitive and materialistic nature of our society. Change is always a source of stress (even though it may have a positive outcome) and the pace of economic, social, and technological change has quickened in recent years. People in the United States feel driven to be the best and to be compared favorably to others. This includes competition through material possessions; whoever has the newest and most expensive watch, car, phone, computer, clothes, etc., is a winner. Those who don't have such possessions feel the stress of being a Loser with a capital L. Spending on a credit card to keep up with the fast crowd only adds stress when there's no plan for paying it back.[12] This culture of

∧
∧ In the board game called *Life*, **players make career and economic choices as they**
∧ **drive through the years.** In the end, **"The player with the highest dollar amount wins!"**
How important is acquiring money and goods for individuals and families?

excessive consumption contributed to the economic recession that start-ed in the United States in 2007 and spanned the globe a year later, adding even more stress to people's lives in the form of unaffordable mortgage payments, plummeting stock portfolios, and widespread job loss.

The need for many people to work long hours and keep up with social and community commitments results in a lack of personal and family time. Healthy people need time alone to decompress from busi-ness and social interactions. They also need time with their families to simply enjoy each other's company. In many families today, both parents work outside the home full- or part-time. The percentage of children liv-ing with a working mother has increased from 10 percent in 1940 to 60 percent in 1990. This shift means that families increasingly turn to peo-ple outside the family for help with child care.[13] Studies show that many parents feel stress about the hours their young children spend under the care of others.[14]

Changes in our society place added stress on families. DeFrain and Asay suggest that the repeated instances of extramarital affairs and mar-ital conflict shown on TV and in movies contribute to a "culture of divorce" in the United States. They also suggest that America has an obsession with sex exhibited in ads, movies, TV, and the Internet and indicated by large numbers of teen pregnancies and extramarital affairs for both men

and women. The fear of rising rates of violent crime both within the fam-ily (domestic violence and child abuse) and on the streets adds stress to family life, especially for women and children.[15]

Family stress is also increased by overcrowding in cities and preoc-cupation with the differences in ethnic and cultural groups when people see dangers and threats rather than common ground. Ever since the attacks of 9/11 and the ensuing wars in Iraq and Afghanistan, terrorism and armed conflict have added another stressor for families. And with the American and global economy at a low point—who imagined that huge banks would fail and GM could go bankrupt?—economic worries are even more common.[16]

More stressors come from within the family. More than half of all American adults come from a family background that included alcoholism or problem drinking, and more than 9 million children current-ly live with people who abuse alcohol or other drugs.[18] One legal drug, alcohol, contributes to the deaths of about 85,000 people each year. Another legal drug, tobacco, is even more deadly, contributing to 433,000 deaths in 2000, while illegal drugs contributed to 17,000 deaths in the same year.[19]

Over time, family roles have changed as well. Within families, there has been a need to renegotiate and restructure gender and parenting roles.

Work Stress Increases around the World

In industrialized countries such as the United States and countries in Europe, work outside the home has been a stressor for families for many years. As societies changed from a rural, agrarian economy to an urban, capitalistic, manufacturing economy, families experienced stress due to long work hours and the associated problems related to child care, lack of family time together, and household management.

Today, the global economy is bringing many of these stresses to families in under-developed countries that are undergoing similar economic changes. The World Health Organization of the United Nations issued a report in 2007, which noted many negative health effects from work stresses, including high blood pressure and cardiovascular disease, which in turn create family stress

>>> Families in countries which are **becoming more industrialized** are experiencing stresses related to **health problems, child care, and family time together.**

because of poor health, poor economic conditions, and early deaths.

The report suggested steps to assess the level of stress for workers and address the identified issues, and several case studies showed that these steps could be implemented successfully. In Vietnam, Mexico, and the Netherlands, small companies and government agencies were initially resistant to changes that promoted safer working conditions and healthy lifestyle activities for work-

ers. However, when it was shown that less stress for workers resulted in greater productivity, fewer sick days, and reduced payments for health claims, the companies embraced the programs wholeheartedly.[17]

Stressors on Modern American Families

Cultural and ethnic tensions
Violence and crime rates
Alcohol, tobacco, other drugs
Lack of personal time
Obsession with sex
Poor economy
Culture of divorce
Use of day care
Competitive lifestyle
Terrorism and war
New gender roles
Overcrowded cities

The increase in the number of women working outside the home and their success in many types of careers make the traditional role of "housewife" less appropriate and less applicable to millions of American women. At the same time, men are challenged to engage in roles that have not traditionally been assigned to American men. In many cases, they need to participate in different family activities such as child care, housework, cooking, driving the kids to school, and so on. Although these changes often have positive outcomes, the transition to a new family role can be a source of stress as well.[20]

By now, you're probably aware that even stable and supportive families face a lot of significant challenges. How do families survive—and even thrive—without falling apart? Remember the Grombergs? Even though they suffered many of the types of stress listed above—including a competitive lifestyle, little personal or family time, child care outside the home, drug use, and new gender roles – they managed to stay together and provide essential support to family members when needed. In the next few pages, you'll learn about a few different ways in which families like the Grombergs build strengths and neutralize stressors.

<<< American families **are subjected to stress from our society and culture** as well as from family members' actions. **Which sources of stress were you aware of growing up?**

FAMILY NARRATIVE is made up of family stories that are told and retold to help define family history and character.
MICRO-SOCIAL PERSPECTIVE focuses on individuals and single family groups.
MACRO-SOCIAL PERSPECTIVE focuses on groups of families at the community or cultural level.

FAMILY STRENGTHS

One way in which a family can build strength is through a **family narrative**. A family narrative consists of stories that are told and retold to help define the family's history and character. Whether or not these stories are, strictly speaking, factually accurate, they can persuade family members that their family is special and different from other families in important ways. Such stories can help explain a family's methods of managing both success and failure and help each individual in the family gain a stronger sense of identity.

For example, a grandfather might tell a story about looking for work for months during hard times and finally getting a job over 30 other applicants because he had carefully shined his worn-out shoes. The employer said that his efforts showed he was someone who would take pride in his work. The message for children and grandchildren is that their family is special because of their persistence, that continuing to look for work in the face of many rejections is the way the family copes with a tough economic situation, and that each individual has a connection with the pride and persistence of the grandfather.[21]

Low-income families experience high degrees of stress because of a lack of resources such as housing, food, clothing, a safe neighborhood, educational resources, and more. But researchers have also identified some ways in which families address these issues and remain strong. Members of strong families with low incomes usually communicate well with other family members, assist each other in solving problems, agree on basic family values, and participate in many family activities together. They also have a network of friends in the community and don't hesitate to ask for their help.[22]

Families with two parents who work full-time may feel stress over child care, changing gender roles, and decreased personal time, but they can build family strengths in several ways. One important way is to focus on managing household tasks efficiently. This may involve new roles for both parents and children. A father may cook supper on some nights as a child does the laundry. Involvement in making the house run smoothly builds family strength and a feeling that everyone is working together.[23]

Social scientists have also studied strengths in families with specific racial, ethnic, and cultural backgrounds. Each group of families has developed unique ways to address the stressors that commonly arise in their cultures. For example, Native American families consistently face adverse economic challenges. But the successful families in these communities show respect between family members, generosity within the family and toward other community members, and a unified belief in spiritual constructs.[24]

Research Your Family History

Irene is 20 and just finishing her sophomore year.

"We had an assignment in high school to create a family tree. My grandmother is still alive, but I didn't know much about my great-grandmother's background.

"I spent time at her house when I was little, before she died, and I knew she didn't speak English well, but that was about all I remembered. My grandmother said she didn't talk much about her early years, just that she had come from Latvia and their family was very poor.

"Last summer I spent some time looking through immigration records for Ellis Island on the Web.

"At first I couldn't find anything, but then I used a different spelling for her last name and there she was! I've read about what it was like for immigrants when my great-grandmother came over in the early 1900s, and I'm amazed at what they survived. They were incredibly brave to come here with just a few clothes and very little money, but the war and poverty they were leaving behind was even worse. I'm proud to come from such a strong immigrant family.

"I'm thinking of changing my name back to its original spelling."

∧ ∧ ∧ **Many family narratives in the United States** include stories of hardships related to immigration.

African American families in the United States are also likely to face economic challenges and social and economic discrimination. Just as successful families in other racial and ethnic groups in the United States do, strong African American families show a powerful bond among family members, an emphasis on the value of work, the ability to adapt and change with shifting economic conditions, an emphasis on academic and social achievement, and strong religious beliefs.[25]

Common Factors in Strong Families across Cultures

Recently, several researchers worked together to identify common factors within strong families that crossed national and cultural boundaries. As a result of this work, the researchers developed the International Family Strength Model, widely used today, using studies involving thousands of family members in the United States and 28 other countries. It identifies six major qualities of strong couples and families:

International Family Strength Model: Common qualities of strong families	
Appreciation and affection	Members care for each other deeply and regularly communicate these feelings.
Commitment	Couples and family members are dedicated to each other and do not let work or other activities take too much time and energy away from the family.
Positive communication	Members talk to each other and listen carefully, both to solve problems and to learn more about each other.
Spending enjoyable time together	Members enjoy spending time together at celebrations and in everyday activities.
Spirituality or religion	Strong families show a common spiritual sense through organized religion or their own constructs of hope and optimism.
Managing stress and crisis effectively	Strong families are good at avoiding crises and at managing minor, daily crises and larger, life-changing ones.[26]

This model provides a **micro-social perspective**, one that focuses, like a microscope, on individuals and small groups. But researchers also feel that families are heavily influenced, positively and negatively, by the communities they live in and their cultures. This is a **macro-social perspective**, where society is seen as if from an airplane, and entire communities and cultures are viewed as a whole.[27]

>>> Strong Native American families **show a common belief in spirituality** and have extensive ties to their community. **Does your family share these characteristics?**

They have identified five important community factors that influence the strength of families:

Ways that some communities support strong families	
A supportive environment	Family and friends are willing and able to provide support when families need it
An effective educational system	A community-sponsored system provides effective academic, social, and cultural education
Support for families practicing religion	Families have opportunities to practice their chosen religion
Services for families needing assistance	Services sponsored by the community or government provide necessary economic and social assistance to families
A safe, secure, and healthful environment	Families are protected from violence and environmental hazards[28]

You can probably provide a positive and negative example for each of the ways communities can influence families. For example, an effective educational system allows parents to entrust their children to educational experts who will help educate and social- ize their children

to be positive community members; an ineffective one leaves educational burdens on the family and may draw children into negative social behaviors rather than positive ones.

Using a macro-social perspective, researchers also identified five important ways that cultures affect families:

Ways that some cultures support strong families	
A rich cultural heritage	Cultures can provide families with meaning, direction, and inspiration.
Shared cultural meanings	Families understand words and phrases unique to their culture, which helps them understand their history and circumstances.
Political stability	Families do not have to worry about whether the current government will survive and what might replace it.
A stable economy	Families are able to plan an economic future and gain access to food, shelter, and clothing.
An understanding of global culture and society	Families can gain knowledge from other cultures, including social, economic, and technological advances.[29]

Again, examples of positive and negative cultural effects on families come to mind easily. A stable economy can allow families to provide for their children the essentials and extras that enhance their growth; economic instability leaves many families uncertain and unable to provide for their basic needs, let alone extras.

DeFrain and Asay, the same researchers who listed areas of challenge for American families, provided two visual models that illustrate relationships between family, community, and cultural strengths. This graphic illustrates their belief that the strongest families are created when the greatest number of family, community, and cultural strengths intersect. But they also believed that if one or

>>> Researchers have identified **16 different factors that may affect formation of a strong family.** Do you think any single factor can create a strong family if many others are absent? **Do you think any single factor can prevent a strong family if many others are present?**

more of the three areas are weak or lacking, families can adapt to create a strong family.[30]

THE SCIENTIFIC METHOD

Now that you've read about family stressors and family strengths, maybe you'd like to learn more about the topic by studying real-life families yourself. You know that some families have successful techniques for overcoming challenges, and you'd like to learn more about those techniques. But where do you start? How have the researchers we've discussed in this chapter obtained data and drawn conclusions about the information they've collected? Before we go much farther into our discussion of families, let's take a few steps back and talk about that cornerstone of the social sciences, the scientific method.

Suppose you're talking to a friend over lunch. The two of you are discussing your mutual friends' romantic relationships, and you say, "People who are in long-term relationships are happier than people who go in and out of lots of short relationships." Your friend isn't so sure he agrees with you. "Are you sure?" he asks. "Can you prove it?" Well, can you?

You can certainly try. For several centuries, people have relied on the scientific method to try to prove what they believe. Your statement about long-term relationships and happiness is called a **hypothesis**, a proposed explanation of behavior that is not proven but can be tested. The **scientific method** is a systematic approach to observing phenomena, drawing conclusions, and testing hypotheses. It requires that a hypothesis be verified through tests and that the results of those tests can be repeated.[31]

Factors Identified Internationally as Important in Strong Families

FAMILY STRENGTHS
- Appreciation and affection
- Commitment
- Positive communication
- Spending enjoyable time together
- Spirituality or religion
- Managing stress and crises effectively

The strongest families are created when the most factors intersect.

COMMUNITY STRENGTHS
- Supportive environment
- Effective educational system
- Support for families practicing religion
- Support for families needing assistance
- Safe, secure, and healthful environment

CULTURAL STRENGTHS
- Rich cultural heritage
- Shared cultural meanings
- Political stability
- Economic stability
- Understanding of global culture and society

Source: Defrain, John, and S. Asay. Epilogue. *Marriage & Family Review* 41 (3) 2007: 447-466 http://dx.doi.org/10.1300/J002v41n03_10 MARRIAGE & FAMILY REVIEW by Defrain, John and S. Asay. Copyright 2007 by Taylor & Francis Informa UK Ltd - Journals. Reproduced with permission of Taylor & Francis Informa UK Ltd - Journals in the format Textbook via Copyright Clearance Center.

The scientific method consists of six steps, which must be completed in order:

Step	Example for your relationship hypothesis
1. Ask a question about a specific topic.	Are people in long-term relationships happier than people in short-term relationships?
2. Do background research on the topic.	Talk to friends and family members, and read books and journal articles about happy relationships.
3. Formulate a hypothesis.	People in long-term relationships are happier than people in short-term relationships.
4. Test your hypothesis by conducting research and gathering data.	Perform interviews or conduct a survey of many different people in both short-term and long-term relationships.
5. Analyze your data and decide on a conclusion.	Study the results of your interview or survey to determine the accuracy of your hypothesis.
6. Write up the results.	Write a report to describe your hypothesis, tests, and results.

There are several important points to remember about the scientific method. First, a hypothesis has to be something that can be tested and measured objectively. For example, hypotheses concerning a car's speed or its braking distance can be tested and measured, but a hypothesis concerning which brand of jeans looks the best cannot because it is a subjective judgment. A hypothesis can always be stated as an "if-then" statement, such as "If sports cars with different width tires are driven from a standing start, then the one with the widest tires will reach 60 miles per hour first."

The tests for the hypothesis also must be fair. It wouldn't be fair to ask each of your interview subjects different questions or hand out different surveys, since the different questions will yield results that you can't compare to each other. Nor would it be fair to have several different people conducting interviews for you, because some interviewers might be more intimidating than others. And it wouldn't be fair to compare long-term daters in their 30s with short-term daters in their teens, since the age difference between the two groups would complicate your results.

Using the scientific method for family research involves testing human beings rather than inanimate objects. Devising accurate tests or comparisons so that all conditions are the same except for one variable is a great challenge for social scientists. For example, you might compare the academic achievements of children raised by same-sex couples to those of children in traditional, two-parent families. But because some children in same-sex families were originally born into traditional families, they might be more likely to have experienced a parental divorce or death. A more accurate comparison might involve children raised by same-sex couples and children in other families who have experienced the divorce or death of a parent.

One of the earliest sociological thinkers, Max Weber, proposed in the early 20th century that social research should be as objective as possible. Researchers should be neutral and "value-free" and should not let

HYPOTHESIS is a proposed explanation of behavior that is not proven but can be tested.
SCIENTIFIC METHOD is a systematic approach to observing phenomena, drawing conclusions, and testing hypotheses.
QUANTITATIVE RESEARCH uses the scientific method to test a specifically defined hypothesis; uses numbers to describe and explain the issues being studied.
QUALITATIVE RESEARCH examines and interprets an issue to discover underlying meanings or patterns of relationships; uses words, pictures, or objects to describe the issues being studied.

personal values affect the gathering of data or their interpretation. This is the ideal of the scientific method, but the reality of social research may be different for two reasons. First, every experiment or study requires the researcher to interpret the data that involve personal judgment and personal values. Second, every research project is a political issue for someone. Research related to families who benefit from public assistance programs or those involved in organized religion could be used to promote or eliminate public assistance or encourage or discourage religious involvement. These possible effects necessarily influence those designing the tests and interpreting the data and may influence the subjects of the tests as well. In the end, Weber believed that researchers could never be totally value-free, but instead should be clear about the values brought to the research in the first place.[32]

RESEARCH METHODS

Once you've settled on a topic to study, you'll need to gather information through research. **Quantitative research** uses the scientific method to test a specifically defined hypothesis, using numbers to describe and explain the issues being studied. These numbers are gathered through instruments such as questionnaires, in which a person can give a number value to a question, answer yes or no, or select one of multiple choices. Interpreting the data involves adding up the numbers of identical or similar answers. Quantitative research may also involve interpretation of statistical data gathered previously.

However, the research question you want to answer may not lend itself to quantitative research. For example, you may want to study a young child living in a single-parent household over a period of several years, recording how the child grows and changes emotionally. **Qualitative research** examines and interprets an issue to discover underlying meanings or patterns of relationships. Qualitative methods such as case studies gather information about a particular issue, including the reasons people give for a particular behavior or what factors they believe influenced a decision. Researchers may choose to investigate a particular issue with only a question in mind, rather than a hypothesis as required by the scientific method.[33]

Quantitative Research Methods

One way quantitative family researchers gather data is through experiments. Thinking of scientists' conducting experiments on families may conjure up images of rats in a maze or Dr. Frankenstein creating his monster. Instead, most experiments on marriage and families simply select particular groups of families and then try to control the conditions so that their "if-then" statement can be tested. One experiment in the 1970s selected 5,000 low-income families, divided them into four groups, and provided them with different levels of financial assistance, including no assistance. One hypothesis was that financial assistance would make single mothers more attractive as potential spouses and their marriage

INDEPENDENT VARIABLE is the factor that is manipulated by the researcher during an experiment.

DEPENDENT VARIABLE is the factor that is affected by the independent variable during an experiment.

CONTROL VARIABLES are factors that remain constant across experimental subjects and throughout experimental trials.

RANDOM SAMPLING is a procedure through which participants in an experimental study are chosen at random.

rate would increase, and another was that assistance would prevent couples from divorcing. Both were proven to be false.[34]

In an experiment, a researcher will usually have an **independent variable**, a **dependent variable**, and several **control variables**. The independent variable is the factor that the researcher manipulates, and the dependent variable is the factor that changes based on the manipulations of the independent variable. The control variables are factors that remain constant across all experimental trials and conditions. For example, in the experiment described above, the level of financial assistance was the independent variable, and the marriage rate was the dependent variable. The experimenters most likely had to control such variables as the mothers' age, income, education, psychological history, and other factors that could ultimately affect the women's marriage rate if not taken into account.

In many cases, experimenters want to be able to take the results they glean from a small group of subjects and generalize those results to an entire population. In order to make these generalizations in an academically rigorous way, experimenters choose their subjects through a process called **random sampling**. As an experimenter, you

can ensure that your subjects are representative of a larger population by choosing them at random *from* that population. If you are selecting a group of 5,000 low-income single mothers, for example, not all of the mothers should be from one racial or ethnic group, not all of them should be in the same age bracket, and not all of them should come from a certain religious background. Your sample of low-income single mothers should resemble the entire population of low-income mothers across the country.

Experiments have several advantages over other types of research studies. For example, if experiments are performed well, they are replicable, which means that they can be performed by other people under similar conditions with similar results. Each new set of similar results lends strength to a researcher's hypothesis. However, experiments have their disadvantages, too. Although researchers attempt to control the conditions of the experiment, outside forces may intervene. For example, during the experiment on family assistance and marriage, a state could change its laws related to family assistance for married couples, which would probably affect the marriage rate. Societal changes may also make an experiment hard to repeat.[35]

Quantitative researchers may use surveys to collect information for statistical analysis. Surveys require a large number of people to respond to the survey, and they usually involve closed questions, which means that people have a limited number of ways to respond, similar to a multiple choice test. Surveys can be conducted over the phone, in person, by mail, or on the Internet, and the answers are numerically coded and analyzed using computer programs.[36] Surveys have several advantages: They are relatively inexpensive, they can be administered from remote locations, and they can involve a large sample that makes the results more reliable. Because

Source: Neill, J. Qualitative vs. Quantitative Research. Outdoor Education and Research Center. University of New Hampshire 2007. http://wilderdom.com/research/QualitativeVersusQuantitativeResearch.html

∧ **The graphic** illustrates **some ways to distinguish between** quantitative **and** qualitative
∧ research. **What advantages do you think one type of research has over another?**

responses are limited to a few choices, measurements are relatively easy and standard. However, survey questions and answers may not address significant areas of concern or provide an answer that truly describes a person's thoughts or feelings. The people who choose to respond to a survey may not represent a true picture of a group, since a significant percentage may not reply.[37]

Researchers can also observe specific types of situations and record what is seen. Valid scientific observations must meet five criteria: the observation must serve a specific research purpose; the observation must be planned systematically; the observation must be recorded systematically; the observation must be related to general principles rather than specific examples; and the observation must be checked for reliability and validity. In one example of an observational study, a researcher observed families with children younger than five years old in three different settings and found that the primary caretaker was more likely to be male if the child or one of the older children was male, and the setting was recreational as opposed to a restaurant or a commercial setting.[38]

Observation is especially useful for very young children who are not good candidates for a written or oral survey. It may also provide an "insider" perspective when the subjects know the researcher and know they are being observed. Observational studies are also commonly performed over long periods of time (a **longitudinal study**) or in several different cultures (a **cross-cultural study**). However, observation is sometimes done without the subjects' knowledge, which some researchers feel is an unethical invasion of privacy. Observation is also time-consuming and hard to duplicate, and there may be large variations in the ways different observers catalogue and interpret actions.[39]

The final way to perform quantitative research on marriage and families is through **secondary data analysis**. Researchers take studies that have already been completed, such as those by the U.S. Census Bureau and other government and private organizations, and analyze the findings in new ways. For example, a researcher could analyze U.S. Census data to show a correlation between a family's economic status and the number of children in the family, or a correlation between a family's ethnic background and the probability of owning their home.

Secondary data analysis is sometimes called "inobtrusive" since no contact with the subjects is required, and there is no influence by the researchers on the subjects. There are many sources of statistical information on families sponsored by the government and private institutions. This approach is relatively cheap since no new information needs to be gathered, and it provides a very large sample size, which is sta-

∧
∧ **Secondary data analysis** can draw on huge
∧ **statistical databases** to draw correlations.
Researchers never see **the subjects who are being** analyzed.

LONGITUDINAL STUDY is a research study in which subjects are observed over a long period of time.
CROSS-CULTURAL STUDY is a research study in which subjects from two or more cultures are observed.
SECONDARY DATA ANALYSIS is quantitative research that uses studies that have already been completed and analyzes the data in ways not originally planned.
CASE STUDY is an intensive study of a single case or a small number of cases that share common characteristics.

tistically appealing. Because the data are all gathered using a standard set of questions, the data are very reliable. But in certain cases, data applicable to a proposed hypothesis may not be available because the appropriate questions weren't asked. For example, one survey only asked questions about child care to parents of young children. Analyzing data on child care for older children is not possible because the data simply don't exist.[40]

Qualitative Research Methods

Researchers who are looking for an understanding of marriage and family matters beyond what statistics can tell them engage in qualitative research. They interpret information provided by a single source or several sources to provide a full picture of a family, its members, or a particular issue. They use three primary techniques: case studies, ethnographies, and focus groups.

A **case study** is an intensive study of a single case or a small number of cases that share common characteristics. For example, a case study might describe a single Asian American immigrant family in the United States to illustrate how Asian values affect the family within U.S. culture. Or a case study could focus on families in which the head of the household is employed by a large corporation to understand how company policies on maternity or parental leave affect families. Cases or families are selected because they are presumed to present an "average" experience that will help describe other similar cases. Most case studies involve in-depth interviews with individuals or families, but also may involve observation.[41]

Case studies allow in-depth reporting and provide the full context for a situation and complete details. They may be designed as exploratory, explanatory, or descriptive case studies. Exploratory cases allow researchers to investigate an issue before forming a hypothesis; explanatory cases may begin with an "if-then" hypothesis and attempt to prove or disprove a theory; and descriptive cases begin with an assumed pattern and compare the case to that pattern. However, like all qualitative research, case studies are criticized because the findings are based on a single case or a few cases that may not be applicable to a broad population. Many researchers use case studies in combination with quantitative methods to provide background for a statistical analysis.[42]

Ethnography attempts to understand a group from the point of view of its members—to describe it from "the inside." Researchers essentially participate in the lives of the group they are studying over an extended period, using observation, interviews, and other methods to understand the events that happen as well as the meanings people give to them. An ethnography may require several years to complete and may begin with only a general question to guide the research. The researcher must be trusted by the group being studied or they won't divulge meanings unknown to outsiders.[43] The researcher runs the risk of actually changing the lives of the people because of the researcher's involvement. Although the ethnography provides a rich and detailed picture of a particular family or group of families, the results can't automatically be generalized to other families or groups because the study involves such a small sample.[44]

A **focus group** is a small group, usually consisting of about seven to ten people who are brought together to discuss a subject of interest to the researcher. Focus groups are commonly used today in business and politics; that flashy slogan you heard for a political campaign or a new toothpaste was almost certainly tested in a focus group to gauge people's reactions. Social researchers may use a focus group to help design questions or instruments for quantitative research or to study the interactions among group members on a particular subject. In most cases, researchers ask predetermined questions, but the discussion is unstructured. Focus groups are a relatively cheap method of research and can be completed quickly. They also allow for the flexible discussions and answers that are desirable in qualitative research. However, they definitely require a skilled leader to avoid leading participants in a predetermined direction, to establish an atmosphere in which all participants feel comfortable speaking, and to allow discussion of uncomfortable or challenging topics. It is also possible for two different researchers to analyze the discussion in different ways.[45]

∧ **Focus groups** are used to test reactions to a wide variety **of consumer products**
∧ **and political ideas.** How do you think members of a focus group are chosen?

think marriages and families:

The three theoretical perspectives discussed in Chapter 1—functionalism, symbolic interactionism, and conflict theory—see marriage and families in different ways and ask different questions to help describe and understand them. Researchers supporting each perspective may choose a variety of research methods. For example, a functionalist, symbolic interactionist, and a conflict theorist might all use a case study to illustrate family relationships or devise a survey to judge family attitudes and behaviors. At the same time, their answers to a specific question would vary widely.

Functionalism

Functionalists see the family as a group within the social system that affects individuals and the larger social and cultural systems, as well as being affected by those systems. Marriage and families help create a stable society by fulfilling two important, interrelated functions. The family socializes children so that they understand social expectations and can become positive members of society. The family also places adults in the role of parent, which encourages them to act responsibly in relation to their children and the larger society.

This emphasis on the relationship between families and society points researchers to areas where society and families intersect and affect each other. They may study family structures and compare different structures such as nuclear families with nontraditional families such as single-parent families and stepfamilies. They may look into the family functions discussed in Chapter 1: socialization, regulation of sexual behavior, social placement, and material and emotional security. They may search for universal factors within families across cultures and consider how different cultures define families. Functionalists may also look

at changing family roles, such as women working outside the home, and how these changes affect society as a whole.[46]

Conflict Theory

Conflict theory states that people act primarily out of self-interest and that this causes inevitable conflicts between individuals and groups over power and material resources. Families reflect these same conflicts. Researchers are interested in the conflicts created by inequalities and power relationships within families and the ways these conflicts are resolved. They may study formal and informal power struggles between parents, parents and children, and siblings. The struggle for control of economic resources between spouses and among family members is also a subject of interest for conflict theorists. Physical conflicts such as spousal and child abuse or family violence also reflect conflict theory. Another area of research concerns social policies that either address inequalities or promote them, such as welfare programs and the struggle for legal rights for same-sex couples.[47]

Symbolic Interactionism

Symbolic interactionists believe that the family is the product of the day-to-day interactions of family members and the meanings they give to these interactions. Families are socially constructed by their members and vary in their reactions to significant events. Researchers might focus on changes in a family and marriage because of the birth or death of a family member. They might study the ways family interactions change over the entire family life cycle or marital career, when a member begins a job or loses a job, or when children grow into adolescence. Researchers may even study the way families celebrate certain holidays to see the meanings that the family members give them.[48]

discover marriages and families in action:

A Family Worksheet

All families have strengths as well as weaknesses. If you and your family were asked to describe them, you would probably give long, rambling accounts of personal experiences but have a hard time classifying them into categories. In 2002, the School of Family Life at Brigham Young University created a worksheet (available on the Internet) designed to make a family's job easier. They separated family interactions into nine distinct categories and provided a rating system for them (see the Family Strengths Chart on p. 39).

Family members over the age of eight complete the chart, and then they can compare areas of agreement or disagreement about family strengths. These differences should be the basis for positive family discussion. But the aim of this chart is also to direct the family to a Goal-Setting Worksheet, using the same categories to set goals for improvement, activities, and dates for completion of the goals.[49]

ACTIVITIES

1. Fill out the worksheet to identify the strengths in your family. Have the members of your family also fill out the worksheet. Compare your answers.
2. Imagine that you moved to a different country or culture and the family structure that you enjoy today was banned. How might you feel? What would you do to adapt?
3. Find two people from other racial or ethnic groups. Ask them if they think there are particular family strengths that accompany their racial or ethnic group. Compare and contrast their answers with your own. What are the similarities and differences?

WRAP YOUR MIND AROUND THE THEORY

Early functionalists **identified economic roles according to gender.** What economic roles existed in your family?

FUNCTIONALISM

Early functional theory, published in the 1950s, saw families as reflecting clear roles identified by gender. Men worked outside the home, provided the economic resources for the family, and made most of the decisions related to the external world, including economic decisions. Women controlled a different world—the home—and guided family decisions related to internal family relationships and management of the household. Women's work at home was not considered an economic contribution to the family even though it took many hours and significant skills. Functional theory has not fully addressed the changes in families in recent decades. They might point to the traditional roles of 50 years ago and suggest that the husband in a family should be the sole breadwinner and make most economic decisions. This view doesn't address the millions of nontraditional families today or the economic changes that often require both parents to work outside the home.

CONFLICT THEORY

Conflict theorists believe that families reflect the conflicts in society: Conflicts are automatically created by groups or individuals who are acting in their own self-interest to gain control of scarce resources. In previous years, family conflict theorists could point to the unequal pay for work—males were paid for their labor outside the home while female home-makers received no economic rewards for their work at home—as a clear example of a certain class (male breadwinners) retaining power and control over a group that was treated unfairly. Today, families still experience many conflicts over economic contributions and control. Women often work outside the home, but may feel compelled to continue all of their domestic duties as well. Some women work a full day at an office, then rush home to make dinner and do the laundry. Conflict theorists would propose new roles to allow for more equitable division of economic contributions and division of labor.

WHO CONTRIBUTES TO AND CONTROLS FAMILY FINANCES?

SYMBOLIC INTERACTIONISM

Symbolic interactionists believe that each family defines its own roles and meanings through interactions among family members. For example, one family may have negotiated or created a role for a single male wage-earner, another for a single female wage-earner, and another for both parents to work full- or part-time outside the home. Families may create unique structures for handling economic decisions as well. In certain cases, one spouse may "bring home the bacon," while the other spouse may decide how to cook the bacon and distribute it. In some cases, children may both contribute to the family economic resources and participate in economic decisions.

Conflict theorists argue **believe that families inevitably have conflicts over** the importance of different types of work **and control of economic resources.** What does your own experience reveal about this?

Families were forced to change economic roles during World War II. **How many of those changes have continued in today's world?**

Strength Area	Very Strong	Some Growth Needed	Much Growth Needed
Caring and Appreciation			
Time Together			
Encouragement			
Commitment			
Communication			
Adaptive Ability			
Spirituality			
Community and Family Ties			
Clear Responsibilities			

MAKE CONNECTIONS

Family Changes and Common Factors

Both the movie *It Runs in the Family* and the story of the McKinneys illustrate concepts discussed in this chapter. In these two family stories—one fictional and one real—we can see many of the stressors families face as well as the strengths they develop. If we studied either of these families over time, we might have used the family life cycle, family life course, or the family career perspective to frame some of their changes. We might have use qualitative techniques to address their unique characteristics or they might have been part of a large sample that yielded quantitative results.

In Chapter 1, we reviewed the diversity in current families which connects to unique family strengths. In Chapter 8, we will see how one event, the birth of a child, can change families in important ways. In Chapter 16, we will review in depth some of the characteristics of strong families that apply across racial and ethnic groups.

From Classroom to Community } Coping with Alcoholism and Domestic Violence

One day a week, Marlena volunteers at a domestic violence shelter where women stay with their children for a short time to escape a dangerous situation at home. Most of the time she plays with the younger children there, trying to make them comfortable in a frightening situation.

"I know what it's like to be afraid when your father comes home. My father was a good man most of the time, but if he started drinking, he wouldn't come home until late at night and then there would always be fights.

"Most of the time it was only yelling, but sometimes my parents would hit each other, and I was afraid one of them would get killed.

"A teacher at school got me hooked up with Alateen, and it really helped. That's one of the reasons I help at the shelter now.

"I can't believe how many of the kids here are affected by their parents' use of alcohol. Lots of them say that things are pretty good when their parents are sober, but they never know when that will be or how long it will last.

"They're nervous all the time, and they never really relax. I feel sorry for them. It takes away so much of their energy and enjoyment of the world."

<<< **Millions of children in the United States** fear domestic violence related to alcoholism **or drug abuse.**[50]

Family development theory suggests that families move through distinct stages. The family life cycle theory of the 1950s identified eight stages that are related to the presence of children, their ages, or the ages of the couple. The family life course model looks at how families change in relation to significant events. The family career model identifies four subcareers and looks at ways an individual and the family are affected by the intersection of these experiences. Families face stressors related to rapid societal change, but they also develop strengths. Social scientists use the scientific method to test hypotheses with both quantitative and qualitative research.

Researchers can study marriage and the family from the perspectives of functionalism, conflict theory, or symbolic interactionism.

You can conduct research in your own family to work out strengths and weaknesses that might be there. This gives an opportunity to build on the strengths and improve on the weaknesses.

Theory

FUNCTIONALISM   37

- the family socializes children to become members of society and socializes adults through the role of parent
- looks at family structure and family functions

SYMBOLIC INTERACTIONISM   37

- people construct families through their interactions and the meanings they give the interactions

- looks at how families react to changes such as a birth or a death, loss of a job, growth of children, etc.

CONFLICT THEORY   37

- people act out of self-interest and conflicts over resources are inevitable
- looks at power struggles and power relationships between parents, parents and children, and siblings

Key Terms

family development theory proposes that families proceed through common, identifiable stages   25

family life cycle is a theory that identifies eight specific stages for families beginning after marriage   25

stratification is a division into similar layers or groups   25

family life course is a model that focuses on how families integrate changes over time and the meanings that individual family members give to those changes   25

family career is the family experience of an individual over a lifetime   27

subcareer is one of four distinct roles that a person may experience at any time and that affect the individual and the family   27

family narrative is made up of family stories that are told and retold that help define family history and character   30

micro-social perspective focuses on individuals and single family groups   31

macro-social perspective focuses on groups of families at the community or cultural level   31

hypothesis is a proposed explanation of behavior that is not proven but can be tested   32

scientific method is a systematic approach to observing phenomena, drawing conclusions, and testing hypotheses   32

quantitative research uses the scientific method to test a specifically defined hypothesis; uses numbers to describe and explain the issues being studied   33

qualitative research examines and interprets an issue to discover underlying meanings or patterns of relationships; uses words, pictures, or objects to describe the issues being studied   33

(continued)

independent variable is the factor that is manipulated by the researcher during an experiment *34*

dependent variable is the factor that is affected by the independent variable during an experiment *34*

control variables are factors that remain constant across experimental subjects and throughout experimental trials *34*

random sampling is a procedure through which participants in an experimental study are chosen at random *34*

longitudinal study is a research study in which subjects are observed over a long period of time *35*

cross-cultural study is a research study in which subjects from two or more cultures are observed *35*

secondary data analysis is quantitative research that uses studies that have already been completed and analyzes the data in ways not originally planned *35*

case study is an intensive study of a single case or a small number of cases that share common characteristics *35*

ethnography is a study that attempts to understand a group from the point of view of its members *36*

focus group is a small group brought together by a researcher to discuss a particular subject *36*

Sample Test Questions

MULTIPLE CHOICE

These multiple-choice questions are similar to those found in the test bank that accompanies this textbook.

1. The family life cycle model is less important today because:
   a. quantitative research has disproved it.
   b. it doesn't apply to families in other cultures.
   c. fewer families go through all the stages or experience stages in the same order.
   d. more parents are taking on nontraditional roles.

2. The sexual subcareer for people today has changed because:
   a. premarital sex is more common and sexual experimentation begins younger.
   b. people have access to more sexual information.
   c. sexually transmitted diseases have reduced sexual contacts.
   d. more teens remain abstinent than ever before.

3. The International Family Strength Model suggests that:
   a. each culture has a unique family structure and unique family strengths.
   b. the later people marry, the more likely they are to remain married.
   c. international groups need to be more involved in family issues.
   d. strong families share similar traits across cultures.

4. Which of the following is NOT a criticism of qualitative research?
   a. It is hard to generalize to a large group.
   b. It doesn't explain the context for many issues.
   c. It is hard to duplicate.
   d. A researcher may be biased in a certain direction.

5. Secondary data analysis:
   a. is rare because there aren't enough data sources.
   b. provides valuable information for case studies.
   c. usually involves only a small sample size.
   d. is unobtrusive because no further contact with the subjects is required.

ESSAY

1. How important is the scientific method in studying families?
2. What stressors do you think have the greatest effect on modern families?
3. Which do you think is the most important in building strong families: individual family strengths, community support, or cultural support?
4. Discuss the strengths and weaknesses of quantitative research.
5. Compare a case study to an ethnography.

WHERE TO START YOUR RESEARCH PAPER

For basic information on family development theory, family life cycle, family life course, and family career, go to
http://family.jrank.org/pages/519/Family-Development-Theory.html

For an analysis of family life cycle, go to
http://www.jstor.org/stable/351728

For information on family stressors and family strengths, go to
http://dx.doi.org/10.1300/J002v41n03_04

For information on community and cultural effects on families, go to http://dx.doi.org/10.1300/J002v41n03_10

For information on the scientific method, go to http://www.science buddies.org/science-fair-projects/project_scientific_method.shtml

To find out more about the differences in quantitative and qualitative research methods, go to
http://wilderdom.com/research/QualitativeVersusQuantitative Research.html

For more information on quantitative research design, go to
http://www.sportsci.org/jour/0001/wghdesign.html

For more information on surveys, go to http://www.socialresearch methods.net/kb/survey.php

For more information on qualitative research, go to http://www.social researchmethods.net/kb/qual.php

ANSWERS: 1. c; 2. a; 3. d; 4. b; 5. d

Remember to check www.thethinkspot.com **for additional information, downloadable flashcards, and other helpful resources.**

Caleb

Holt is a young firefighter in Albany, Georgia. In the opening scene, he reminds a rookie of the firefighters' most important rule: "Never leave your partner behind." Caleb is married to Catherine, a public relations officer at the local hospital.

Caleb and Catherine have been married for seven years, and their relationship is suffering. The two are growing quickly apart, and Catherine realizes that she cannot be married to Caleb anymore.

When Caleb's father hears about the impending divorce, he challenges Caleb to a "love dare," explained in detail in a book he had handwritten while going through a similar crisis with Caleb's mother.

The book contains instructions for Caleb to follow for 40 days, each complemented with a relevant quotation from the Bible. Caleb agrees to follow the instructions just to please his father, or to prove him wrong. For the first several days, Caleb avoids conflict with Catherine, sends her flowers and chocolates, calls her at work, and even prepares a romantic candlelit dinner. Catherine, however, is unmoved by these gestures.

Caleb is now sick of trying to save his marriage. Caleb's father points out that God loves all people even when they turn away from Him. Caleb understands that he needs to redefine love as a lifelong commitment, and he revisits the love dare with renewed energy and belief.

Catherine is still determined to obtain a divorce, until one day she finds out about Caleb's love dare. Catherine acknowledges that Caleb has changed over the past few weeks, but she is not yet ready to make a decision.

The following day, Catherine finds out that Caleb had used his savings to buy her sick mother a new expensive wheelchair. She runs to the fire station where Caleb works and tells him that she loves him and that she is ready to commit to him again. The movie ends with Caleb and Catherine renewing their vows in a religious ceremony and promising to live together for the rest of their lives.

COMMUNICATION, POWER, AND CONFLICT

CHAPTER 03

What lessons can we learn **from *Fireproof*? Despite its** strong religious message, *Fireproof* **has something to say**—even to people of different cultures and beliefs—**about managing family conflict.**

It stresses the importance of commitment in conflict resolution and shows how conflict can arise when people stop communicating effectively with each other. People face different challenges at different times of their lives, and it is important that family members understand the kind of pressures that the other members face. The firefighters' adage, "Never leave your partner behind," is central to the story. It implies that commitment means working together through hardship and cultivating closeness even when individual and outside factors seem determined to move people apart.

A few days before I began the second grade, I went to buy school supplies with my parents at a local department store. As I was browsing through notebooks and pencils, I suddenly heard someone screaming at the end of the aisle. "What's wrong with you? You are such a dumb, stupid, idiot boy!" I turned around, startled, and dropped the notebook that I was holding. A little boy had dropped a glass bottle of rubber cement, and his father was screaming at him. As the boy sulked and began to cry, his father only intensified his verbal attacks and even swore a few times. That event made a huge impression on me. Perhaps because the boy did not drop the rubber cement on purpose—it had been an accident. Perhaps I was shocked that a father could talk like that to his son. Whenever I think about that day, I realize how lucky I am to have parents who have never treated me like that. It also makes me wonder about how the things we say affect other people, especially those in our families.

In this chapter, we will examine the dynamics of communication, power, and conflict in family life and the theories behind them. We will also observe how family therapy deals with issues of communication, power, and conflict.

>>> **Communication involves the use of words, signs, and gestures that can be sometimes be misinterpreted and generate conflict.**
During the 2008 presidential campaign, Barack and Michelle Obama exchanged a gesture of complicity that was surprisingly interpreted by a media pundit as a "terrorist fist jab."

Family Communication

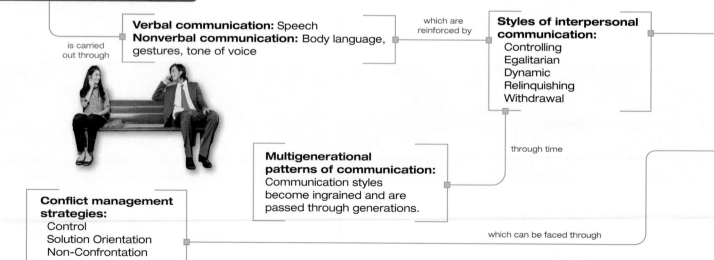

is carried out through

Verbal communication: Speech
Nonverbal communication: Body language, gestures, tone of voice

which are reinforced by

Styles of interpersonal communication:
Controlling
Egalitarian
Dynamic
Relinquishing
Withdrawal

through time

Multigenerational patterns of communication: Communication styles become ingrained and are passed through generations.

Conflict management strategies:
Control
Solution Orientation
Non-Confrontation

which can be faced through

get the topic: HOW DO PATTERNS OF COMMUNICATION, POWER, AND CONFLICT AFFECT FAMILY LIFE?

Communication

People are constantly communicating with each other, whether they realize it or not. In fact, **communication** happens not only when we talk to each other. Generally, we communicate every time we use speech, signals, and writing to exchange ideas and information. We can say that there are three main types of communication. When we talk to each other, we use **verbal communication**. When we read or otherwise interpret visual cues such as typographical signs, illustrations, and images, we use **visual communication**. When we interpret each other's body language, gestures, and facial expressions, we use **nonverbal communication**. Whenever we communicate, we use a mix of verbal and nonverbal communication. Sometimes, the verbal and nonverbal elements reinforce each other, but they express very different feelings at other times. Just think about a little girl, prompted by her father to apologize to her little sister. The girl might say, "I'm sorry" (i.e., her verbal communication) to indicate apology, but her angry expression, lowered eyes, impatient stance, and low voice (i.e., her nonverbal communication) may convey something very different.

COMPONENTS OF FAMILY COMMUNICATION

The mother of a six-year-old boy gives him permission to watch his favorite movie. He has watched that movie many times, but knows he could watch it a million more times. He asks his mother to sit down and watch the movie with him. His mom agrees and tells her son to start the movie as she finishes emptying the dishwasher. She misses the opening scenes and, throughout the movie, she continues to do other small chores, talk on the phone, and flip through a magazine. Whenever her son calls her attention to a scene in the movie, she looks up smiling but never looks engaged. The boy feels hurt and pouts.

COMMUNICATION is the act of conveying verbal and nonverbal information to another person.
VERBAL COMMUNICATION is the information conveyed through spoken language.
VISUAL COMMUNICATION is the information conveyed through visual cues such as typographical signs, illustrations, and images.
NONVERBAL COMMUNICATION is the information conveyed through body language, gestures, and facial expressions.
COGNITION is the process of logical thought.

Situations like this can help us understand the components of family communication. The interaction described above shows both verbal and nonverbal communication. However, what is most important to examine is the way mother and son interpret each other's behavior and words. As explained by researchers Yerby, Buerkel-Rothfuss, and Bochner in *Understanding Family Communication*, family communication is influenced by the interaction of individual perceptions, emotions, and the result of their reasoning, or **cognition**.[1] How do these components work? When family members interact, they receive information through their senses. Then, they react to the information, and last, they interpret the information. Interpretation can either be done rationally, or it may be influenced by the person's emotions. For example, during a family argument, a person may be overly angry and need to take time away from the interaction before being able to rationally interpret what the family member is saying.

To link this to the situation above, we can say that the boy saw the mother walk away from the movie (individual perception), felt dismissed (emotion), and probably reasoned that his mother did not care about him (cognition). Sometimes, verbal and nonverbal communication may contradict each other. For example, in the situation described above, the mother says she enjoys the movie, but cannot hold her attention for more than a few minutes. On the one hand, she is trying to be supportive; on the other hand, she is communicating impatience and a lack of interest. This kind of

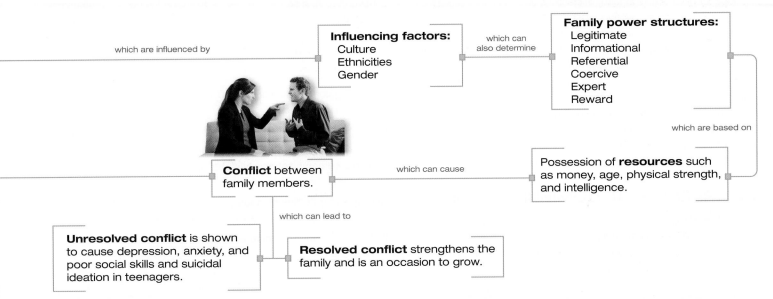

which are influenced by

Influencing factors:
Culture
Ethnicities
Gender

which can also determine

Family power structures:
Legitimate
Informational
Referential
Coercive
Expert
Reward

which are based on

Conflict between family members.

which can cause

Possession of **resources** such as money, age, physical strength, and intelligence.

which can lead to

Unresolved conflict is shown to cause depression, anxiety, and poor social skills and suicidal ideation in teenagers.

Resolved conflict strengthens the family and is an occasion to grow.

Personality Types and Communication

	Analytical	Driver	Amiable	Expressive
Characteristics	logical and meticulous	self-reliant and resolute	considerate and trustworthy	sociable and enthusiastic
Favorite Question	How?	What?	Why?	Who?
Communication Style	• Provides accurate facts • Wants information to be presented logically	• Talks fast and to the point • Likes to solve problems	• Likes listening to others • Avoids conflicts	• Uses exaggerations • Expresses ideas in an enthusiastic manner

∧∧∧ **The Merrill-Reid model is still a popular categorization of personalities according to their communication styles. Based on the information in the table,** what personalities do you think are more likely to experience conflict communication?

discrepancy often occurs in family interactions and can cause problems. Incidentally, research shows that, when faced with such contradictions, people tend to rely on nonverbal cues to interpret other people's behavior.[2]

Another fundamental component of family communication is the context in which the communication takes place. The context includes not only the physical space in which communication occurs, but also the cultural background that affects the interaction. For example, a couple's public display of affection varies according to the location—think about kissing your partner on a tropical beach as opposed to in the accountant's office—and the acceptability of such nonverbal communication in the context of the culture.

INTERPERSONAL COMMUNICATION STYLES

The term **interpersonal communication** refers to the verbal and nonverbal messages that two or more people exchange. In any interpersonal communication, a **sender** conveys a message through a **communication channel** (e.g., speech, gestures, writing) and a **receiver** interprets that message. One of the biggest challenges of family life is to adapt and correctly interpret different styles of interpersonal communication. What are some of the different styles?[3]

Controlling communication style The sender does not allow the receiver to express his or her ideas.

Egalitarian communication style The sender encourages feedback from the receiver.

Dynamic communication style The sender uses motivational phrases to encourage the receiver.

Relinquishing communication style The receiver is invited to participate in the communication as much as the sender.

Withdrawal communication style Either participant shows no interest in the exchange.

These styles are mostly applied to define interpersonal communication in the workplace. Yet, it is apparent that these modes of communication can occur in a family. Think about a family in which a parent assumes a clear authoritarian role. He or she might adopt a controlling style of interpersonal communication by establishing strict rules that the children are not allowed to discuss.[4]

WIDENING OF THE FAMILY CIRCLE

When talking about family communication, what kind of family do scholars refer to? The conventional image of a family is a **nuclear family** constituted by married parents of opposite sex with dependent children. However, members of the **extended family**, such as grandparents, often have a significant influence on the dynamics of family communication. Besides, what about families with divorced parents or families in which children are now adults? After all, the communication behavior between two siblings changes dramatically from when they are toddlers and fight over toys to when they are adults and need to take care of their elderly parents.

In recent years, a new trend in the study of family communication has emerged to examine communication for a more diverse family representation. New studies have included the relationships between parents and their adult children, adult siblings, stepfamilies, families after divorce, and so on.[5]

CONCLUSIONS ABOUT FAMILY COMMUNICATION

What are the challenges of studying family communication? As discussed above, modern studies of family communication need to take into account the kaleidoscopic variety of family structures today. Factors such as race, ethnicity, **sexual orientation** (or the sex one is attracted to), and demographics have an enormous influence of patterns of communication within a family. Some cultures, for example, do not value open communication that much. And for cultures that do, open communication is not always positive.

Communication within the family also affects the way communication and personal interactions occur in society, especially in cultures that regard family as the foundation of society. The United States is one such culture, and it is estimated that more than 90 percent of Americans marry at some point in their lives.[6] This must certainly be related to values and beliefs that are taught in the family.

Last, it must be understood that external social and economical factors affect family communication. The use of the Internet has already reshaped the rituals of courtship with the availability of online dating Web sites. Medical advancements enable couples to have children more easily through practices such as artificial insemination, in vitro fertilization, and **surrogacy**, the process through which a woman agrees to carry and give birth to a baby for another couple.

The concept of family is a shifting one, and so are the patterns of family communication. Only the acknowledgement of the intrinsic diversity and changeability of family structures can lead to a successful analysis of family communication.

> >>> Parents communicate with their children through different styles of interpersonal communication.
> **Choose one of the styles explained above. What kind of verbal and nonverbal communication do you think characterizes that style?**

INTERPERSONAL COMMUNICATION is the verbal and nonverbal messages exchanged by two people.

SENDER is the person who conveys a verbal or nonverbal message.

COMMUNICATION CHANNEL is the method through which information is conveyed, such as speech, gestures, and writing.

RECEIVER is the person to whom a verbal or nonverbal message is addressed.

CONTROLLING COMMUNICATION STYLE is one in which the sender does not allow the receiver to express his or her ideas.

EGALITARIAN COMMUNICATION STYLE is one in which the sender encourages feedback from the receiver.

DYNAMIC COMMUNICATION STYLE is one in which the sender uses motivational phrases to encourage the receiver.

RELINQUISHING COMMUNICATION STYLE is one in which the receiver is invited to participate in the communication as much as the sender.

WITHDRAWAL COMMUNICATION STYLE is one in which either participant shows no interest in the exchange.

NUCLEAR FAMILY is a group constituted by the parents and their own or adopted children.

EXTENDED FAMILY is a group constituted by a nuclear family and their relatives.

SEXUAL ORIENTATION is the sex a person is attracted to.

SURROGACY is the process through which a woman agrees to carry and deliver a baby for another couple.

Communication Patterns

GENDER DIFFERENCES IN CONVERSATIONAL STYLES

"Talk to every woman as if you loved her, and to every man as if he bored you, and at the end of your first season you will have the reputation of possessing the most perfect social tact."

A Woman of No Importance, Oscar Wilde
Anglo-Irish author and playwright (1854–1900)

Until the achievements of the feminist movement in the past century, the debate over the differences in the **communication patterns** of men and women was mostly characterized by the stereotypical image of men as aggressive and dominant and women as passive and nurturing. Communication patterns are the recurring characteristics of verbal and nonverbal exchange between two or more people. Even today, the discussion over gender-based differences in conversational style can turn into a quagmire of stereotypes and generalizations. Researchers argue that society and the media tend to stress the differences rather than the similarities between men and women, and this emphasis alters people's perception of gender styles. For example, consider the popular image of the inarticulate, childish husband in many commercials and sitcoms, which is aptly parodied in satirical TV shows such as *The Simpsons* and *Family Guy*.

What researchers agree on is that the differences in communication styles between genders rely more on the genders' interpersonal orientation. Men tend to talk to provide information and to solve problems. They provide facts and focus on things rather than people. Women instead are more likely to ask for information and talk to connect with others. For these reasons, women are more prone to smile or establish eye and physical contact.[7] Where do these differences come from? As opposed to what some people would think, these differences are not genetic but rather the product of the gender expectations and **gender roles**—those sets of expected behaviors associated with males and females—communicated by society and the family. These differences are also the result of socialization, or the world and culture we live in influencing our behavior. In this sense, the inequality of power between genders that has been transmitted throughout history still affects gender roles today.[8] Researchers also point out that, from a young age, women are more likely to be taught to be polite and diplomatic, whereas men are encouraged to be assertive and unemotional.[9] Of course, the process of equalization in the past decades has reshaped these conversational styles, and women in society and in the family are more assertive than their stereotypical images may convey. [10]

MULTIGENERATIONAL TRANSMISSION OF COMMUNICATION PATTERNS

A 14-year-old girl begs her dad to let her stay at a friend's the night before an important exam at school. The father resists her pleas. Finally, in frustra-

Gender and Communication

Women are more likely to...	Men are more likely to...
understand nonverbal cues	interrupt others and change topic
talk about problems and weaknesses	lecture the listener
ask for help	express clear demands
communicate to establish connections	communicate to establish status

Sources: Yorburg, B. Family Realities: A Global View, 147–157. Prentice Hall: Saddle River, NJ. 2002. http://www9.georgetown.edu/faculty/bassr/githens/tannen.htm

<<< **In her book** *You Just Don't Understand: Women and Men in Conversation* (1990), **sociolinguist Deborah Tannen argued that** men and women have different conversational styles. **Do you think younger generations today display the same differences?**

tion he turns to her and barks, "You want to know why you're not going? Because I said so!" Suddenly, a horrifying thought strikes him as he realizes he has shouted at his daughter: "Did I just turn into my father?"

It is fairly general knowledge that people inherit traits and behaviors from their parents. How does this happen? As mentioned earlier in the chapter, families inform the behavior of their children and the way they communicate with others. When parents communicate with each other, verbally and nonverbally, they often resort to communication patterns of which they are unaware (for example, the re-enactment of prescribed gender roles). Over time, these communication patterns become increasingly engrained and may turn into a **script**, or a sequence of automatic behaviors that people enact without even realizing it. When a communication pattern becomes ingrained, it is easily transferable to the children, a concept known as **multigenerational patterns of communication**. The transfer of communication patterns not only affects the way the children communicate and react to the outside world, but will also affect the way the children behave once they have a family of their own. In multicultural families, the communication patterns that are inherited by the family of origin can even lead to misunderstandings and conflict.[11]

RESEARCH FINDINGS ABOUT COMMUNICATION PATTERNS

What trends in family communication has research brought to the surface? Scholars from different theoretical perspectives agree that patterns of family communication influence relationships outside the family. They also associate parents' communication behavior with the social well-being of their children.[12] In particular, it has emerged that families with a higher degree of **conversation orientation**—the degree to which families encourage open exchange of ideas on a variety of subjects—help their children develop social skills that will allow them to interact more positively with the outside world. A 2009 study published by the International Communication Association reveals that adolescents from families with a high level of conversation orientation have more face-to-face interactions with their same-gender friends, which leads to friendship closeness.[13]

The positive effects of conversation orientation have been identified even across different cultures. A 2008 study by the School of

> **SCRIPT** is a sequence of automatic behaviors.
>
> **MULTIGENERATIONAL PATTERNS OF COMMUNICATION** are the transfer of communication patterns from one generation to the next.
>
> **CONVERSATION ORIENTATION** is the degree to which families encourage open exchange of ideas on a variety of subjects.
>
> **AFFECTIONATE COMMUNICATION** is the way affection in expressed.

Communication at East Carolina University analyzed the communication patterns in American and Japanese families. Although American and Japanese families belong to different types—the former encourage discussion and promote the family's values, whereas the second allow children to develop their own ideas with almost no interference from the parents—it emerged that conversation orientation leads to greater communication satisfaction for both the American and Japanese participants.[14]

Research has not only focused on the effects of family communication, but also on the way family communication takes place. For example, researchers have revealed that adolescent girls are more likely to interrupt their mothers than mothers are to interrupt their daughters in a conversation.[15] The interruptions, though, seem to be a sign not of dominance, but of involvement. Interestingly, mothers kept a slower, turn-taking style, most likely because they were used to talking more slowly and clearly when their children were growing up and learning to speak.[16]

Family Affection Patterns

Affection is obviously a form of communication, and family affection patterns were found to be important in children. How is affection displayed? **Affectionate communication**, or the way affection is expressed, can be nonverbal, verbal, and supportive. Nonverbal affection is made by physical demonstration of affection such as hugging, kissing, and holding hands. Verbal affection refers to expressions such as "I love you." Supportive affection refers to the support provided to a family member in times of crisis. In a study of Asian American children whose parents still displayed strong cultural bonds with their country of origin, it was evident that parental verbal affection and affective responsiveness were beneficial in overcoming the cultural gap because they improved the relationship between parents and children, especially for father–son and mother–daughter relationships.[17]

∧∧∧ **Research has shown that verbal and physical displays of affection can positively affect the cultural gap between generations of immigrant families.** Why do you think affection can minimize a cultural gap in immigrant families?

Breakdowns in the Family: Solutions

PROBLEM

SOLUTION

Fathers and Daughters
Father finds it hard to talk about the daughter's problems. Daughter is uncomfortable opening up to him.

The father should make an effort to build trust by talking to the daughter when she is young.

Mothers and Sons
Mother is overprotective. Son keeps his activities from her so that she does not worry too much.

The mother should talk to her son when he is young and show more trust.

Fathers and Sons
Father has come back into the son's life after a long period of time, or the two are complete opposites.

Father and son should find a common ground and make an effort to like each other.

Mothers and Daughters
Mother wants the daughter to behave in a certain way. Daughter feels pressured and stops talking to her mother.

The mother should learn to show more acceptance and engage less in arguments.

Mothers and Fathers
Mother and father have stopped communicating with each other for a number of reasons.

Mother and father should make an effort to talk to each other openly about their feelings.

Sources: http://www.helium.com/items/461845-dealing-with-communication-breakdowns-in-your-family

∧
∧ **There are** many negative patterns of communication that can affect family members.
∧ **What do you think are the characteristics of good communication?**

Problems and Solutions in Family Communication

A daughter shows her mother her latest purchase, a T-shirt of her favorite band. The mother fakes a smile, looks away, and comments, "The important thing is that you like it." Then she leaves the room, as her daughter darts angry looks into her back.

This example represents, as you might imagine, poor communication on the mother's part. What causes poor communication? Criticism—even the kind presented as a compliment, as in this case—can be negative not only because it hurts the receiver of the message, but also because it can be used to hide the sender's own shortcomings. The mother in our example is subtly saying that her daughter is not capable of choosing an appropriate shirt. Defensiveness and the refusal to continue with a discussion are

barriers to open communication. Imagine if the daughter in the above situation had responded to her mother by saying "You never liked the way I dressed," or the mother refused to hear why her daughter's feelings were hurt. Instead of the issue being resolved, an argument might have escalated. Certain people present themselves as the only ones who care about the other or pretend they can read the hidden reasons behind the other's supposed faults. Again, let's return to the example of the T-shirt. The mother may get upset that the daughter is making certain assumptions about her comment. This is an example of poor listening skills. Have you ever had an argument with your partner that started with an insignificant disagreement that led to the disapproval of all of each other's past actions and attitudes? This is the case when communicators stray from the issues at hand and fail to address the real problem. In sum, poor communicators are those who use discussion to compete and blame the other or find scapegoats to avoid addressing their own responsibilities. In such scenarios, protecting their egos becomes more important than growing the relationship.

What can families do to improve their communication style? According to Rick Peterson and Stephen Green from Virginia Tech, families should attempt to communicate frequently, even when work and school take much of their time. Communication then should be clear, honest, direct, and, most importantly, matched by a willingness to listen without prejudice. To achieve successful communication, being an active listener is key, which means listening carefully and asking questions to make sure one person understands the other's point of view. Nonverbal messages should also be observed carefully and interpreted. Last, families should try to focus on expressing positive communication such as complimenting, encouraging, and supporting other family members.[18]

The responsibility to establish good communication patterns lies first with the parents, who need to teach their children to be effective communicators. When dealing with small children, it is important that parents teach by example, communicating clearly and listening actively. In doing so, parents will communicate that their children's messages are important to them, thus encouraging the children to express their ideas freely. Second, parents should teach their children to be active and respectful listeners. Patricia Tannen Nelson, from the Department of Individual and Family Studies at University of Delaware, suggests that family conversations take place without interruptions or distractions, and that parents encourage children to repeat in their own words what they have heard from them.[19]

Family Power

Family communication is also affected by the dynamics of power within a family. Scholars define power in terms of which family members make important decisions or manage resources such as money, time, and values. In the model of the **patriarchal family**, for example, the father is completely responsible for the wife and children but also has complete authority over them. It is important to remember that, more often than not, different members of the family share power at different stages of the family cycle. Researchers have outlined six types of power bases within families[20]:

Legitimate power comes from the belief that power should be delegated to a specific member of the family. Legitimate power occurs, for example, when a family believes that the mother should take care of the family budget, or only the parents have the right to educate their children. Legitimate power might also be shown by a wife having the power to ask her husband to clean up after she has prepared a meal.

Informational power is based on one family member having access to information that is denied to the other members of the family. For example, a mother may have access to more information than her husband about the children's private lives and use it to claim responsibility for decisions about the children.

Referential power is based on affection and the creation of bonds between members of the family. For example, a husband might help in the garden and learn about the plants his wife is growing because she enjoys gardening.

Coercive power implies that a family member uses, or threatens to use, physical or psychological force to impose his or her will on others. Coercive power can be characterized by aggression, abuse, and competition. An example could be a partner withholding sexual intimacy if the other partner does not comply with a request. A parent might also use this tactic to force a child to get ready for school in the morning.

Expert power is based on the specific expertise of a member of the family that leads him or her to make decisions in that area. For example, a parent who works for an insurance company might make the decisions about insurance for the entire family.

Reward power implies offering physical and psychological rewards to family members who comply with certain requests. A classic example is when parents promise to buy ice cream for their young children if they behave at the grocery store.

THE RESOURCE THEORY OF POWER

Although almost 50 years have passed since Blood and Wolfe developed their **resource theory** of power, their assumptions are still considered valid today. The resource theory states that the family member who controls the

>>> **The Mosuo people of southwestern China are one of the few examples of matriarchal societies.** Mosuo women are in charge of the household and are free to choose, marry, and leave their spouses when they want. **How are Mosuo families an example of legitimate power?**

EGALITARIAN RELATIONSHIPS are unions in which power is shared equally between partners.

AFFECTIVE behavior is that in which people tend to rely a lot on nonverbal communication.

CONTROL is the conflict-management style that is carried out through the use of blame, personal attacks, and mean jokes.

SOLUTION ORIENTATION is the conflict-management style that involves logical reasoning, compromise, and a focus on mutual agreement.

NON-CONFRONTATION is the conflict-management style that involves withdrawal and avoidance.

most resources is the one who has the most power.[21] To formulate their theory, Blood and Wolfe interviewed almost 500 wives about their husbands' income, social prestige, and educational achievements. It emerged that the higher the husbands scored in each category, the more entitled they felt to make decisions for the family.[22] The theory helped highlight the shift in power balance in families in which women had good jobs and a higher education level compared with women in the past.

What do we really mean when we talk about resources? Resources can be economic, such as income or property ownership. They can also be educational, meaning the level of education of a family member. Physical resources include health, size, and even strength—imagine a family working in the fields for their sustenance. Psychological resources such as self-confidence, self-esteem, and intelligence can also play an important role in determining who has the most power in a family.

Success and Criticism of the Resource Theory

The resource theory formulated by Blood and Wolfe has been very influential in the discussion of family power. It shows that individuals hold power because of their access to specific resources rather than for biological reasons. It also implies that granting women more access to economic and educational resources could lead to more **egalitarian relationships**. International studies also seem to support the theory. For example, a study of 113 non-industrialized countries showed that women's power inside the marriage corresponded to their contribution to food production.[23] Blood and Wolfe's theory has also attracted criticism. The idea that the spouse with more resources holds more power in the family is contradicted by the fact that there doesn't seem to be any shift in power when women earn more money than their husbands.[24] In fact, many family scientists believe that the dominance of the father in the traditional family structure comes from gender distinctions that have been transmitted through the centuries.[25]

WAYS TO INCREASE YOUR POWER IN THE FAMILY

By now, you must probably be thinking about the way power is distributed in your family. If you are ambitious, you might ask yourself, "How can I have more power?" Increasing your own power has its benefits, but you do not have to limit someone else's power when you increase your own.

Researchers have outlined a few ways to increase one's power in the family. One way is to broaden one's horizons by taking courses to improve one's education and obtain better professional opportunities. Another way is to minimize the rewards received by others. For example, a couple who receives constant economic help from their in-laws may implicitly allow the in-laws to exert control over their economical decisions. People can also learn to minimize the negativity received from others or exaggerate the hurt they receive in order to diminish the likeliness of being hurt again. Children often respond to punishment by pretending they don't care or by reacting with heartbreaking cries. People can also try to draw attention to their good behavior by telling others of compliments and rewards received at work or school. Last, people can gain power by ingratiating themselves with another member of the family; for example, when a teenager prepares an elaborate dinner for her parents to make amends for the massive dent she left in the back of the family car, she can gain power by showing her better side to her parents.

Decision Making in Marriages and Families

A couple wins a big sum of money at the state lottery. As they celebrate at a fancy restaurant, they wonder, "Should we start a college fund for the kids, or should we just run away to a tropical island and leave the kids to their destiny?" The couple could discuss the matter, argue for hours, or even toss a coin to determine what course they should take. Whatever their conclusion, they will follow a specific decision-making process.

How do families approach decision making? Researchers identified five different approaches to decision making in marriage and families. First, families can appeal to authority and status, thus giving the decision-making power to the family member or members who are perceived to have the highest authority. Another approach involves following established rules. One rule can be that no decision can be made until all family members agree with each other. Families can also rely on their values. If the couple in this scenario is very religious, they could decide to devote all their money to their church or to a religious charity. Decisions can be taken through discussion and consensus, which means all members of the family are invited to share their opinions on a decision. Decision can also be made by default if a family is not engaged in a decision-making process, such as when families postpone decisions. For example, the couple that won the lottery may postpone the decision about how to spend their money, and then find themselves giving it all away to hordes of relatives and friends in need of a loan.[26]

Of course, the process of making decisions is never straightforward. According to researchers, there are many factors that can affect decision

<<< During a pregnancy, couples are faced with many important decisions concerning health care, time management, expenses, education, etc. **Can you give at least three examples of how religion or culture of origin can influence the decision-making process of an expecting couple?**

World's Most Emotional Countries

What we might see as an "effective" communication style within families in the United States could be perceived as the exact opposite in other countries. A questionnaire by the Center for International Business Studies in the Netherlands identified different styles of communication among different countries.[26] Countries such as Mexico, Switzerland, China, Brazil, and Italy have been defined as **affective**, which means that people tend to rely a lot on nonverbal communication (such as hand gestures and physical contact) and openly expressed emotions.

In these countries, people are more likely to greet people with enthusiasm and talk more loudly when excited. In affective communication, the receiver must work harder to be able to decode these nonverbal signals.

Countries such as Japan, the United Kingdom, Indonesia, Argentina, and the United States emerged as "neutral" countries, meaning that people in these countries tend to keep their emotions in check and not express them publicly. Voice intonation, timing, and facial expressions all help communicate messages. Because of differences in cultures, there are variations among countries. The Japanese prefer a more indi-

rect style of communication, whereas Americans communicate directly to convey a specific objective.[27]

Families in affective countries are more likely to have loud arguments and affectionate reconciliations than families in neutral countries. Because families in affective countries express their emotions, communication is not always effective. Receivers still need to pay attention to the real significance of nonverbal clues. Although America is considered a neutral country, it is also more personal; people are more likely to use first names in business, for example. This can carry over to how people interact inside the home.

---

making in marriages and families, such as the presence of children, gender roles, and individual interest in the outcome of the decision.[29] Families are also influenced by outside factors. If a student is burdened with tons of weekend homework, his or her family will find it difficult to plan a getaway during that time. The government's decision to promote or reject subsidies for low-income families can also be a relevant factor in the decision-making process of many families.

Different family types will also show different decision-making approaches. Studies reveal that gay couples strive for equality of power between the spouses, thus actively rejecting traditional gender roles of heterosexual couples.[30] Studies on stepfamilies show how parents often take the decision to join two families without involving their children.[31] Families also make decisions on the basis of their culture and ethnicity. A study revealed that Vietnamese women are mostly responsible for administering the family's economic resources to such a degree that they are referred to as "chiefs of domestic affairs."[32]

Conflict and Managing Conflict

WHAT IS CONFLICT?

Think about your relationship with your parents, your friends, or even your teachers. Despite the love, friendship, and/or respect you might feel for them, it is highly likely that at some point you've experienced some kind of conflict in these relationships. Conflict is an inescapable component of human relationships. Even those who are terrified of conflict and try avoiding it at all costs are still not immune to it. But how can we define *conflict*? Conflict happens when people differ in their feelings, thoughts, or behaviors. Conflict can be beneficial if it forces people to confront problems. However, when conflict is not resolved and does not enable personal growth, it can become harmful and may even lead to violence and abuse.

REACTIONS TO FAMILY CONFLICT

How do you react to conflict? Do you voice every single thought that crosses your mind, no matter how hurtful? Do you try to keep calm and focus on the issue, not your ego? Do you avoid any kind of confrontation, staring into the distance with a frozen smile and murmuring to yourself that everything is great?

Conflict Styles

	Control	Solution Orientation	Non-Confrontation
Tactic	Uses blame and accusations.	Uses reasoning and compromise.	Uses withdrawal and avoidance.
More likely to say...	"You are always thinking about yourself!"	"This makes me feel unappreciated. Can we talk about it?"	"I just remembered I need to go out and buy some groceries."

<<< **The family in the hit TV series *The Sopranos* employed all conflict styles when dealing with the father's involvement in organized crime.** How do you think power structures within the family can influence conflict style within a family?

Sources: Turner, L.H., R. West. Perspectives of Family Communication, 165. McGraw Hill: New York, 2006.

TACTICS are the behaviors that people adopt to carry out their conflict-management styles.

CONFLICT RESOLUTION is the process of attenuating or eliminating a source of conflict.

SUICIDAL IDEATION refers to thoughts about committing suicide.

CONFLICT MANAGEMENT is the process of dealing with conflict.

There are many ways in which individuals in families can react to conflict. Often, an individual's response to conflict affects the outcome of the conflict. In the previous paragraph, we described the three different styles of dealing with conflict. These styles are referred to as **control**, **solution orientation**, and **non-confrontation**. According to Turner and West, authors of *Perspectives on Family Communication* (2006), each of these styles is characterized by the use of **tactics**, or behaviors that individuals adopt to carry out their styles.[33] The control style is the most aggressive and makes use of blame, personal attacks, and mean jokes. The control style often brings to the surface important issues and may even represent a sign of commitment. The solution-orientation approach involves logical reasoning, compromise, and a focus on mutual agreement. Not surprisingly, this approach is identified as the most positive approach to **conflict resolution**. The non-confrontation approach, which involves withdrawal and avoidance, is adopted for fear of strong negative reactions from one or more family members.

CONSEQUENCES OF FAMILY CONFLICT

Family conflict can lead to positive outcomes if managed effectively. A family that manages to resolve a conflict displays more motivation to face and solve problems. Effective conflict management encourages positive interactions between family members, together with understanding and mutual acceptance. Once feelings are out in the open, families learn to express themselves more effectively and change their behaviors to promote family happiness. A 1989 study published by the American Psychological Association showed that couples that had conflict and managed to work through it have higher levels of marital adjustment over time.[34] A more recent study, from 2004, looked at couples during the first two years of their marriage. Couples who expressed unhappiness in their marriage were more likely to exhibit negative communication behaviors such as withdrawing.[35]

When conflict is not resolved in a functional way, it can have serious negative effects. Research has documented links between conflict

∧
∧ **According to family scientists,** conflict can be an
∧ occasion to strengthen a relationship. **Based on this assumption, what kind of verbal and nonverbal communication should a couple try to keep during an argument?**

in the marriage and feelings of depression and anxiety.[36] Regarding children, a 2006 study of 170 boys with a median age of eight years concluded that children from conflicted families have fewer friends compared with children from families with less conflict.[37] A survey of over 450 adolescents, published by the National Council on Family Relations associated family conflict with adolescents' self-derogatory feelings and even with adolescent **suicidal ideation**, or suicidal thoughts.[38] Unresolved family conflict has also been associated with drug abuse and homelessness for young adult children[39] and the likelihood of occurrence of domestic violence.[40]

MANAGING CONFLICT

In *Fireproof,* Caleb manages his conflict by continually demonstrating his commitment to his wife, even though she is no longer receptive to his love. Just as in the movie, we need to learn how to manage the conflict that exists in our families and relationships.

Addressing and resolving conflict is called **conflict management**, and family researchers have been studying conflict resolution and conflict management for several decades. The strategies adopted for conflict management vary from person to person and depend on the ultimate goal that an individual pursues—even if the individual is not aware of pursuing it. In a marriage, for example, a fairly common goal for the spouses is to preserve intimacy. When intimacy is threatened, spouses may decide on different strategies, such as talking and compromising or even avoiding the conflict. Anderson and Sabatelli, in their book *Family Interaction: A Multigenerational Developmental Perspective* (1995), explain that research has revealed general trends in the conflict management styles of men and women. It seems that women are more apt to talk problems through, whereas men tend more often to avoid confrontation.[41]

No matter what conflict management strategies are adopted, though, the conflict styles of happily married couples share a few common characteristics. In particular, spouses in effective marriages maintain an open dialogue in which they listen attentively to each other and emphasize positive over negative interactions. Professor John Gottman even suggests that couples should maintain a five-to-one ratio of positive and negative interaction to maintain marital happiness.[42] In addition, studies have shown that couples with similar conflict-management styles are more likely to be satisfied with their union because similar conflict-management styles are less likely to cause misinterpretation. For example, if one spouse insists on discussing problems, while the other tries to avoid confrontation, there is a high risk of frustration for both spouses.[43]

think marriages and families: WHAT ARE THE
THEORIES BEHIND FAMILY INTERACTION?

Adjusting to Divorce: Theoretical Perspectives

How do family scientists view the role of communication in the family? Here are three perspectives:

FUNCTIONAL THEORY

Can good communication skills in the family translate to good communication skills in society? The functions of the family in society, already discussed in Chapter 1, belong to the scope of **functional theory**. According to functional theory, the family performs an important function in the preservation of social order. One of the functions identified by a functionalist is the socialization of its members. Through socialization, parents teach their children to become well-adjusted and valuable members of society.

How does this relate to communication? Communication is functional to socialization, because effective communication helps people make good decisions and solve problems. In a way, functional theory is concerned with the outcome of family interactions and how these interactions affect social order. From a functionalist point of view, communication needs to be carried out through logical thinking, a preoccupation with the family's best interest, and the establishment of criteria and values to guide the family. For example, when a family decides to go on a vacation, members might discuss how much money they are willing to spend, who is going to organize the trip, what chores will be performed by each member, and how much time the family will allot to joint or individual activities. Good communication will improve the chances to experience a smooth and fun vacation for everybody that also strengthens family unity.

CONFLICT THEORY

Often toddlers go through a period in which they say "no" to everything. Experts suggest that this is the child's first attempt at independence.[44] Parents often get frustrated, and conflict is born.

The **conflict theory** analyzes the patterns of conflict resulting from competition over resources. It is easy to see how conflict theory relates to

> **FUNCTIONAL THEORY** asserts that the family performs an important function in the preservation of social order.
>
> **CONFLICT THEORY** is the theory that analyzes patterns of conflict resulting from competition over resources.
>
> **SYMBOLIC INTERACTION THEORY** is the theory that people attach symbolic meaning to elements in the world around them.
>
> **SYMBOLS** are objects, events, or ideas that have acquired cultural significance beyond their literal meaning.

communication: Individuals often use verbal and nonverbal communication to coerce someone to go along with their own interests and thus maintain control of the relationship. Communication is especially relevant in conflict management. When family members argue, they need to communicate effectively to come to an understanding and a possible compromise. Conflict can even aid communication, because it makes people address problems more directly and learn more about the other's feelings and motivations. When a child says "no" all the time, it is actually a great opportunity for parents to establish rules and teach about acceptable compromises.

SYMBOLIC INTERACTION THEORY

The main assumption of the **symbolic interaction theory** is that people attach symbolic meaning to elements in the world around them. **Symbols** are very important in all types of communication. Symbols create meaning in communication through gestures, words, nonverbal signs, objects, and body language. The meanings assigned vary not just across cultures, but also from family to family. If a father grounds his son for ditching classes, the son may decide to give his father the silent treatment, which may communicate that the son is angry because his father punished him. When two siblings are involved in a heated confrontation in which they say a lot of mean things that they may not really believe, they may solve the problem by discussing it, or by simply giving each other a high five to show that everything is all right and the argument is over. They could also use a special phrase or joke that they share to reinstate complicity and closeness.

MAKE CONNECTIONS

Effective and Ineffective Communication

As you have learned in this chapter, all families deal with communication issues, power issues, and conflict. In Chapter 14, you will see how poor communication results in conflicts within the family, and you will examine the consequences of not managing conflict constructively.

Earlier in the chapter, you read about different communication styles and learned how ineffective communication, power

imbalance, and poor conflict-management skills can negatively affect the family. Alternatively, effective communication, combined with balance of power and effective conflict management, can improve and strengthen family relationships. To promote family unity, family members need to learn to communicate their thoughts and feelings clearly and honestly. They also need to learn to listen to the others' point of view without judgment and interpret correctly nonverbal messages. You will learn more about the characteristics of success-

ful marriages and effective families in Chapter 16.

>>> ACTIVITIES

1. Write a handwritten letter to one of your relatives, explaining what you admire about him or her.
2. Prepare a homemade meal for your family and then sit down to eat and talk with them.
3. Plan a day out with your family to visit a landmark in your neighborhood, town, or state.

55

Communication, Power, and Conflict

WRAP YOUR MIND AROUND THE THEORY

Functionalists **believe that communication is functional to socialization. What do you think might be the** effect of a family's poor communication skills on the social lives of their children?

FUNCTIONALISM

Functional theory states that families perform a fundamental role in the preservation of an orderly society. In particular, functionalists focus on the role of the nuclear family as the primary group[45] that teaches individuals to become valuable members of society. Functional theory is concerned with the outcome of communication in relationship to the role of the family in society. Families should promote effective communication by committing themselves to make the best decisions for the family and for individuals, by establishing values and criteria to make decisions and solve problems, and by developing and evaluating alternative solutions. This approach is related to the function of socialization, with which families teach their children values and skills that will help them contribute positively to society.

CONFLICT THEORY

Conflict theorists believe that society is composed of groups that are competing over resources. This approach also applies to families, in which balance is affected by resources such as money, age, physical strength, intelligence, and education. Conflict can originate internally from family interactions, and externally from events such as work problems, economic crises, and health issues. Communication is vital in conflict management, as families need to negotiate and compromise to overcome the conflict. In this sense, conflict can be an occasion for growth and learning. Teenagers' desire for independence initiates one classic family conflict. Parents need to relax their rules and trust their children more, but that implies a redefinition of their power over their children. Through negotiation and understanding of each other's points of view, the relationship between parents and teenage children can become stronger and more meaningful.

? WHY IS THE GOAL OF COMMUNICATION IN THE FAMILY?

SYMBOLIC INTERACTIONISM

Symbolic interactionists examine the meanings that people give to their behavior and to the behavior of others. Theorists also believe that families are defined by their verbal and nonverbal communication, not just by their genetic makeup. The symbols that affect family interactions are determined by the families but also derive from their families of origin, their religious beliefs and cultures, and the society they live in. During a family life cycle, members need to learn and adjust to common and individual interpretations of those interactions. For example, an adult son might think that calling his mother once a week means showing her his affection, whereas the mother might think that affection can only be shown through frequent visits. The relationship between mother and son will improve only if they are willing to learn about and understand each other's interpretation of affection.

Conflict theorists consider conflict **an occasion for growth in the family.** How can poor communication skills reverse this process?

According to symbolic interaction theory, culture and religion can affect the way people interpret and experience family interaction. **How do you think this can affect multicultural families and families of different religious beliefs?**

discover marriages and families in action:
HOW DOES FAMILY THERAPY ADDRESS ISSUES OF COMMUNICATION, POWER, AND CONFLICT?

Marriage and Family Therapy

In this chapter, we analyzed patterns of communication, power, and conflict in marriages and families. Successful marriages and effective families are able to enjoy open communication and honesty, to maintain a functional balance in their responsibilities and roles, and to manage conflict so that it becomes an occasion for the relationship to grow.

But what happens when couples and families fail in one or more of these tasks? That is when marriage and family therapy can come in handy. As opposed to more traditional individual therapy, marriage and family therapy tends to be short term and focused on solutions. Marriage and family therapists may treat one spouse or member of the family, or couples and families together. Among the problems addressed by marriage and family therapy are marital and family conflict, mental and emotional disorders, drug abuse and alcoholism, marital distress, depression, and obesity.[46] According to the American Association for Marriage and Family Therapy, there are more than 50,000 marriage and family therapists operating in the United States today.[47] In some cases, family therapy is mandated by law. For example, troubled adolescents and abusive parents are sometimes required to meet with a family therapist instead of serving jail time.[48] All this shows that good communication and effective conflict-management skills are fundamental to the emotional well-being of individuals and families alike.

ACTIVITIES

1. Use online or print resources to locate a marriage and family therapist or family counselor in your neighborhood. Set up an interview with him or her about communication patterns and skill, power balance in the marriage and in the family, and conflict management.
2. Research stories of couples and families who have resolved issues of communication, power, and conflict in their relationships. Can you identify common patterns or factors that have helped them resolve their issues of communication, power, and conflict?

From Classroom to Community } Helping Families Communicate

Once a week, Chris volunteers as an English language tutor for immigrant families. Chris teaches them basic grammar and useful expressions, but he also gives families information about U.S. culture and traditions.

"I have been teaching English for two years now, and it has been a very interesting experience.

"Most of the adults that I teach know only basic English and want to learn to communicate better to improve their working conditions and deal with everyday problems. Many also want to become more 'American,' learning about idioms and culture.

"I often use role playing to get my students to learn English. That way my students get to practice vocabulary and expressions, as well as the tone of voice, the gestures, and the level of politeness or directness that Americans use every day.

"Before I became a tutor, I didn't realize that our language is so nuanced. I never realized how body language and tone of voice change from culture to culture. Verbal language is really only part of the process. Nonverbal communication is also important in the way we present ourselves to strangers and to our bosses.

"Some of my students have children who were born here in the United States. The parents sometimes tell me that their children speak perfect English and behave in a more 'Americanized' way.

"By learning to speak English, a few parents say they feel closer to their children. They feel they have more control and influence over them. I found this fascinating."

CHAPTER

03

Family interactions are based on patterns of verbal and nonverbal communication that are often based on the balance of power within the family. Families experience conflict, which can originate with poor communication and other internal or external issues. When managing conflict, it is important that families use communication effectively to solve problems and improve their relationships.

Functional theory sees effective communication as a necessary element for socialization, which helps children become valuable members of society. Symbol interactionists analyze the symbols we attach to verbal and nonverbal communication, and how contrasting interpretations of language can create conflict. Conflict theorists believe family conflict is originated in one's desire to promote his or her own interests despite the other's.

Marriage and family therapists teach couples and families to communicate openly and honestly, to maintain a functional balance in their responsibilities and roles, and to manage conflict so that it becomes an occasion to grow.

Theory

FUNCTIONALISM 55

- socialization is an important function of the family
- socialization is promoted through effective communication that involves exchange of ideas and establishment of common values

SYMBOLIC INTERACTIONISM 55

- people give meanings to words, signs, and body language
- family interactions can be positively and negatively affected by people's perceptions

CONFLICT THEORY 55

- spouses and family members compete over resources
- effective conflict management can strengthen the family

Key Terms

communication is the act of conveying verbal and nonverbal information to another person 45

verbal communication is the information conveyed through spoken language 45

visual communication is the information conveyed through visual cues such as typographical signs, illustrations, and images 45

nonverbal communication is the information conveyed through body language, gestures, and facial expressions 45

cognition is the process of logical thought 45

interpersonal communication is the verbal and nonverbal messages exchanged by two people 46

sender is the person who conveys a verbal or nonverbal message 46

communication channel is the method through which information is conveyed, such as speech, gestures, and writing 46

receiver is the person to whom a verbal or nonverbal message is addressed 46

controlling communication style is one in which the sender does not allow the receiver to express his or her ideas 46

egalitarian communication style is one in which the sender encourages feedback from the receiver 46

dynamic communication style is one in which the sender uses motivational phrases to encourage the receiver 46

relinquishing communication style is one in which the receiver is invited to participate in the communication as much as the sender 46

withdrawal communication style is one in which either participant shows no interest in the exchange 46

nuclear family is a group constituted by the parents and their own or adopted children 47

extended family is a group constituted by a nuclear family and their relatives 47

sexual orientation is the sex a person is attracted to 47

surrogacy is the process through which a woman agrees to carry and deliver a baby for another couple 47

communication patterns are the recurring characteristics of verbal and nonverbal exchange between two or more people 48

gender roles are sets of expected behaviors associated with males and females 48

script is a sequence of automatic behaviors 49

multigenerational patterns of communication are the transfer of communication patterns from one generation to the next 49

conversation orientation is the degree to which families encourage open exchange of ideas on a variety of subjects 49

affectionate communication is the way affection in expressed *49*

patriarchal family is a family structure in which the eldest male has the most authority *51*

legitimate power is based on the belief that power should be delegated to a specific member of the family *51*

informational power is based on one family member having access to information that is denied to the other members of the family *51*

referential power is based on affection and the creation of bonds between members of the family. Feelings like affection, friendship, and attraction can help create alliances within the family. *51*

coercive power is based on a family member using physical or psychological force to impose his or her will on others, often with a threat of fear or loss of privilege *51*

expert power is based on the specific expertise of a member of the family that leads him or her to make decisions in that area *51*

reward power offers physical and psychological rewards to family members who comply with certain requests *51*

resource theory is the idea that power originates from the control of resources *51*

egalitarian relationships are unions in which power is shared equally between partners *52*

affective behavior is that in which people tend to rely a lot on nonverbal communication *53*

control is the conflict-management style that is carried out through the use of blame, personal attacks, and mean jokes *53*

solution orientation is the conflict-management style that involves logical reasoning, compromise, and a focus on mutual agreement *53*

non-confrontation is the conflict-management style that involves withdrawal and avoidance *53*

tactics are the behaviors that people adopt to carry out their conflict-management styles *54*

conflict resolution is the process of attenuating or eliminating a source of conflict *54*

suicidal ideation refers to thoughts about committing suicide *54*

conflict management is the process of dealing with conflict *54*

functional theory asserts that the family performs an important function in the preservation of social order *55*

conflict theory is the theory that analyzes patterns of conflict resulting from competition over resources *55*

symbolic interaction theory is the theory that people attach symbolic meaning to elements in the world around them *55*

symbols are objects, events, or ideas that have acquired cultural significance beyond their literal meaning *55*

Sample Test Questions

MULTIPLE CHOICE

These multiple-choice questions are similar to those found in the test bank that accompanies this textbook.

1. Based on research, how do men differ from women in their conversational styles?
   a. Women are more assertive.
   b. Women express clear demands.
   c. Women talk to give information.
   d. Women understand verbal cues more.

2. How is control better than non-confrontation as a conflict-management strategy?
   a. Family members pause to listen to each other.
   b. Family members are forced to deal with a problem.
   c. Family members learn to keep their emotions in check.
   d. Family members become aware of their own shortcomings.

3. What is one effect of conversation orientation in the family?
   a. social adjustment of the children
   b. ingrained communication patterns
   c. egalitarian relationships between parents
   d. open display of affection among individuals

4. Which of the following types of power originate in the belief that power should be delegated to a specific member of the family?
   a. reward power
   b. coercive power
   c. legitimate power
   d. informational power

5. How can increasing one's options as far as work and education also increase one's power in the family?
   a. It minimizes other people's accomplishments.
   b. It helps manage with external source of conflict.
   c. It helps gain the affection of other family members.
   d. It grants more economical and educational resources.

ANSWERS: 1. d; 2. b; 3. a; 4. c; 5. d

ESSAY

1. Discuss the gender-based differences in conversational style according to research.

2. What are the resources that determine how power is distributed in a family?

3. What type of communication can positively affect conflict management?

4. How do sociologists from the three sociological paradigms view family communication?

5. Discuss the three different strategies of dealing with conflict: control, solution orientation, and non-confrontation. What communication style do you think belongs to each strategy?

WHERE TO START YOUR RESEARCH PAPER

For more information about family communication, go to: http://www.familycommunication.org/

For more information on gender-based difference in conversational styles, go to http://www.my-counseling-site.com/gender_differences.html

For information about gender differences and feminism, go to http://feminism.eserver.org/gender-differences.txt

To find out more conflict management styles, go to http://disputeresolution.ohio.gov/schools/contentpages/styles.htm

For more information about conflict resolution for parents, go to http://school.familyeducation.com/page/57476.html

To find out more about functional theory applied to the family, go to roxbury.net/images/pdfs/eftchap1.pdf

To find out more about conflict theory applied to the family, go to www.public.iastate.edu/~hd_fs.511/lecture/Sourcebook15.ppt

To find out more about symbolic interaction theory applied to the family, go to http://chass.utoronto.ca/~salaff/SYMBOLIC%20INTERACTIONISM%20THEORY.pdf

Remember to check **www.thethinkspot.com** for additional information, downloadable flashcards, and other helpful resources.

Teena

Brandon is an unhappy young woman living in Lincoln, Nebraska. Not yet 21, she has broken away from her family and is living in a small trailer with her cousin Lonnie, who is gay. She has had several brushes with the law and has an important court date coming up. But the true source of her unhappiness goes even deeper. She was born with the biological makeup of a woman, but she has always felt, inside, that she was a man.

Teena cuts her hair short and dresses in flannel shirts, blue jeans, and boots, the common wardrobe of the men her age in Lincoln. She perfects the art of "strappin' and packin'"—flattening her breasts by wrapping a gauze bandage around her chest and stuffing a sock down her pants to simulate male sexual organs. She switches her name to Brandon Teena and proves very successful at picking up young women in bars for short-term romances, so good in fact that some young men become resentful and attack Lonnie's trailer. Lonnie tries to warn Teena that her actions might provoke violent reactions—people in small towns "kill fags," he says—and in frustration shouts out, "You're not a boy." But Teena just grins and responds, "Then how come they say I'm the best boyfriend they've ever had?"

An encounter at another bar brings Candace and Brandon together. "He" throws himself into a fight with a much bigger man to defend her. Candace and her friends, John and Tom, are impressed and invite Brandon to come "hang out" in the small town of Falls City, about 75 miles away. Brandon takes them up on the offer and soon is the talk of Falls City—making fast friends with the ex-cons John and Tom and the rough crowd they run with, becoming a temporary boyfriend to lonely girls starved for any bit of sensitive attention, and living with Candace and her appealing sister, Lana. Soon, Brandon and Lana are acting like lovers, even though John still feels possessive of Lana because she wrote him letters when she was a young teenager and he was in prison.

But things unravel quickly. John and Tom rapidly become more violent and unstable. After Brandon is arrested on a traffic charge, he is put in the woman's section of the jail. When Lana visits, Brandon lies to her and says that he was born with both male and female sexual organs, and she professes her continuing love. But the rest of the town isn't so gullible or forgiving, especially John and Tom. They kidnap Brandon, ripping his clothes off in front of Lana to reveal the truth about his sexual identity. Lana still doesn't turn against him, but John and Tom brutally rape Brandon. When Brandon/Teena files charges, the local sheriff treats her like the criminal and does nothing to help her. In the end, John and Tom react again, because of Brandon's accusations to the police and because of John's overwhelming jealousy of Brandon and Lana. In a drunken rage, they kill Brandon and Candace with Lana looking on.

It is a sad and brutal movie. But the saddest part may be that it is based on the true story of Teena Brandon, murdered in Falls City, Nebraska, in 1993.

THE ROLE OF GENDER

CHAPTER 04

The murders associated with **the tragic story of** Teena Brandon/Brandon Teena **occurred in** 1993 **and generated nationwide headlines.**

The movie is set in Nebraska, but everyday experience suggests that the same types of people and communities exist throughout the United States and probably worldwide. Why are some people uncomfortable even acknowledging sexual issues that vary from the heterosexual norm? And why would some people in our society feel it necessary to kill others because of their sexuality?

Just a little research reveals violence against homosexuals throughout history, in the United States and other countries. As they pursued the policy of genocide, Adolf Hitler's Third Reich arrested homosexuals along with Jews, Gypsies, and political opponents for extermination in the death camps. Police raids on gay bars in New York City in 1969 resulted in the Stonewall riots, a series of confrontations that promoted the revolutionary idea that people couldn't be arrested simply because of their sexual orientation.

When I was 10 years old, I had a friend I will call Marilyn. She was what everyone called a tomboy. One summer, when we often wore shorts, she began carrying a big leather wallet in her back pocket. It was obviously a man's wallet, unlike any of the handbags or coin purses we saw our mothers carrying. She carried two one-dollar bills in it and loved to show them off.

We were playing jump rope one day when her father came out and told her to give him the wallet. Marilyn took it out of her back pocket sadly and started to give it to him, but she couldn't resist asking why. Her father acted as if the answer was obvious and he was surprised that we didn't know the answer. "Because girls don't carry wallets," he said. "A girl carrying a wallet in her back pocket is like a man wearing a woman's bra."

He was absolutely certain of what he said, and I've never forgotten that day. His view of gender and sex roles was simple and involved cultural expectations unconnected to any innate, biological differences. I was forced to think about the ways that an individual can be affected by family and cultural expectations. Marilyn enjoyed her wallet, and it seemed a harmless bit of fun. But the conflict with her father's stereotypes was too great for him to allow her to continue.

The Role of Gender

usually begins with

Biological facts:
sex – determined by chromosomes, organs, etc.
sex roles – determined by biology; include giving birth, natural strength

affect

are affected by

Cultural influences:
gender – cultural definitions of masculine and feminine
gender roles – attitudes and activities culturally acceptable for males and females
Mead's research showed culture more important than biology in gender roles
socialization – family, school, peer groups, and mass media teach gender roles to children and adults
gender norms – expectations for behavior for males and females

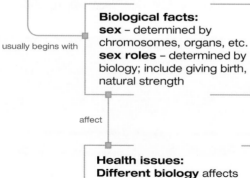

Health issues:
Different biology affects certain diseases and conditions.
Other differences may account for different rates of disease, response to treatments.

affect

get the topic: WHAT ARE THE DIFFERENCES BETWEEN SEX AND GENDER?

Sex vs. Gender

"As far as I'm concerned, being any gender is a drag." — Patti Smith (1946–)[1]

Many people in our society use terms related to sexual identities interchangeably. For example, most people would consider the two following questions to be the same: What sex is that person? What gender is that person? This reflects the common social view that there is a single, acceptable sexual identity for people—either male or female—and that each identity will act in predictable and similar ways.

However, as the Teena Brandon story illustrates, not everyone fits into a single mold. Social scientists have distinguished terms that apply to different areas of sexual identity. **Sex** refers to the biological differences that differentiate men and women, including internal and external sexual organs, hormonal profiles, and chromosomes. **Gender** describes the social practices that a culture defines as masculine and feminine. **Sexuality** consists of social practices related to erotic desire, pleasure, and reproduction.[2, 3]

Examples from *Boys Don't Cry* and my childhood experience with Marilyn can help make these distinctions clear. Teena's sex was female because her internal and external sexual organs were female. However, in most of her public life, her gender was male because she met the cultural expectations for males—she hung out with the guys, dressed like them, fought willingly, and generally fit in with the male crowd. She also showed romantic interest in the women in the story, which is consistent with the male gender. Her sexuality made her erotically attracted to women and gave her pleasure, although reproduction wasn't an option. For young Marilyn, her sex was female, and her father forced her to comply more closely with the cultural expectations of the female gender by giving up her man's wallet.

SEX ROLES VS. GENDER ROLES

Another area of confusion involves the roles people play in society. Roles are the behaviors expected by people of a certain category or status. A **sex role** consists of the attitudes and behavioral expectations that go along with the biological aspects of being male or female. These sex roles are determined biologically and don't change because of societal attitudes. For example, females are capable of giving birth, and males are most often physically stronger than females. On the other hand, gender roles are attitudes and activities a culture determines as acceptable for males and females. These vary from culture to culture and change over the years. For example, 50 years ago, a woman working on a construction site was a rare occurrence and outside accepted gender roles. Today, women in hard hats are much more commonly seen and accepted.[4]

Most of us have a conception of what traits align with masculine and feminine gender roles. Most males realize that they have a few traits that would be considered feminine, and females know they have some traits traditionally associated with men. For example, a woman may have a deep voice, something more typical in males, or a man may have smaller hands, a typically feminine characteristic. But the term **androgynous** refers to a person who has a balance of both male and female characteristics so that neither predominates.[5]

Over the years, social scientists have done a great deal of research on defining culture and its influences on individuals, families, and other groups within it. In 1957, one social scientist suggested

---

SEX refers to the biological differences that differentiate men and women, including internal and external sexual organs, hormonal profiles, and chromosomes.

GENDER is made up of the social practices that a culture defines as masculine and feminine.

SEXUALITY is made up of social practices related to erotic desire, pleasure, and reproduction.

SEX ROLES are attitudes and behavioral expectations that go along with the biological aspects of being male or female.

ANDROGYNOUS describes a person who has a balance of both male and female characteristics so that neither predominates.

---

have resulted in

patriarchy – societal system of male domination over females

sexism – belief that one sex is superior to the other; used to keep women in inferior jobs and social positions

"his and her" experiences of marriage where marriage is a much greater benefit for men than for women

a **"second shift"** of household work for women after a job outside the home

emotional differences in what men and women feel and express

affect

sexuality – social practices related to erotic desire, pleasure, and reproduction

sexual orientation – the sex to which a person is sexually, romantically, and emotionally attracted

that culture consisted of "whatever it is one has to know or believe in order to operate in a manner acceptable to its members"[6] A current dictionary defines culture as "the totality of socially transmitted behavior patterns, arts, beliefs, institutions, and all other products of human work and thought."[7] Regardless of the exact definition, it is clear that culture exerts a powerful force on nearly every aspect of individuals' lives. This is true in the area of sex and gender as well.

A simple example illustrates how culture can affect our gender roles. Every culture has **norms**—expectations for appropriate behavior—that include different expectations for males and females. Travelers from the United States to India, Southeast Asia, and much of Africa are often shocked to see men who are friends walking down the street holding hands. This practice simply indicates friendship with no intimation of a homosexual relationship. It is a simple gesture, accepted by those cultures as well within gender norms. However, in the United States, men do not hold hands as a sign of friendship. If they do hold hands, this act is considered to be outside the male gender norms for our society and is usually deemed an indication of a homosexual relationship. Most men from the United States would cringe or shy away from a heterosexual friend's attempting to hold hands, while men from Asian and African cultures might seek out this contact. The difference in these reactions is attributable to gender roles and norms created by different cultures rather than by a person's sex, which is determined by biology.

One of the earliest researchers who documented the primacy of culture over biology in gender roles was Margaret Mead. In *Sex and Temperament in Three Primitive Societies*, published in 1935, she argued that if male and female behavior is based on biology, then male and female roles would be essentially the same in all societies. On the other hand, if culture influenced male and female roles, then behavior would vary in different cultures. Her studies of three distinct cultures in New Guinea showed a wide variety of roles for males and females. In a mountainous area, she found a culture in which males and females generally worked together cooperatively, assisting in a wide variety of tasks in a manner that is often classified as "feminine." Neither males nor females were expected to act competitively or aggressively, and any that did were considered abnormal.

Further to the south, she found males and females both acting aggressively "masculine" in a culture that promoted competition and

∧
∧ Modern entertainers often exhibit a mix of male
∧ and female characteristics. **Do you think this androgynous quality helps their popularity or hurts it?**

conflict. Mothers, daughters, and wives often competed violently for the attention of a single male, and both sexes were anxious to show off their wealth and social status. Males and females were expected to enjoy fighting and to be sexually aggressive, and those that didn't were, again, considered abnormal.

A third culture showed more distinct sexual roles, but they were reversed from what Western cultures might expect. The women of the tribe managed the economic affairs and fulfilled the role of providers. They controlled most of the property and were thought to have the stronger sex drive. The men, on the other hand, were considered weak, emotional, and inefficient and were expected to nurture children as they grew. Again, males and females who didn't fit these roles were considered abnormal.[8] Mead concluded, "[T]he evidence is overwhelming for the strength of social conditioning" in the formation of gender roles in comparison to any biological influence.[9]

In many modern industrial cultures, gender roles have long been generalized to expect men to be more aggressive and competitive, while women are expected to be more nurturing and cooperative. In *Boys Don't Cry*, for example, Brandon defends Candace in a bar fight, and Lana comforts Brandon when he's in jail. As more women have entered the workforce and business world in recent years, researchers have wondered whether there would be a change in those types of personality traits. Would women become more competitive and aggressive because of their work experiences? Would men become more nurturing and cooperative because they experienced new roles at home and shared the workplace with women? Data from 40,000 people on six continents actually indicate that the opposite is true! Men and women in industrialized countries, where there are often two wage earners in the family, are strongly aligned with these traditional competitive/cooperative expectations. In rural agrarian societies, the differences between men and women are less marked.[10]

Patriarchy and Sexism

Throughout history, many societies have been **patriarchies**—a system of male control over females. Male control ranges from making the laws and controlling religion to owning the goods and directing education. A patriarchal culture provides very limited gender roles for women, none of which involves power over men. For example, many early religions only allowed men to be priests and practice religion. In many countries, women could not own property until the 20th century. Divorce laws often allowed men to easily cast out a wife but prevented women from initiating separation. In some patriarchies, men were free to beat their wives, and sexual assault or rape did not exist if the husband was the perpetrator and the victim was his wife. Women only gained the right to vote in the United States in the 20th century, and some view the current abortion rights debate as an instance of a patriarchal society denying women control over their own bodies. The control over women by patriarchal societies extended into every corner of life.[11] Ira Reiss points out a patriarchal double standard among teenagers. He says that some teen males feel they are ready for sex, but also believe the girl they are going steady with is not. This leads to the males seeking a more permissive girl to have sex with while they date only virgins.[12]

In contrast, there are few known instances in which a **matriarchy**—female control over males—existed in society. Beyond Margaret Mead's tribe in New Guinea, there are some cultures in Indonesia, Africa, and elsewhere that are matrilineal—meaning that material possessions and family heritage are passed down on the female side—but women in these societies don't repress and control men in the same ways that a patriarchy does women. In most of them, power is shared between men and women rather than being dominated by one group.[13]

One of the common characteristics of patriarchal societies is **sexism**, the belief that one sex is superior to the other. In many societies, especially those that are or were patriarchies, males believe they are superior to females in many different ways: in physical strength, mental capabilities, business acumen, political ability, economic management, leadership qualities, and nearly every other area not related to child-rearing and household tasks. In the United States today, some men even believe that they are naturally better drivers than women and better at cooking hamburgers on the grill!

NORMS are societal expectations for appropriate behavior, including those for gender.
PATRIARCHY is a social system in which men dominate women.
MATRIARCHY is a social system in which women dominate men.
SEXISM is the belief that one sex is superior to the other.

Sexism can be expressed at two levels—in the relationships of individuals with this attitude to other males and females, and by institutions such as businesses, churches, and governments whose policies favor men over women. Sexism and some culturally created gender roles are used as a way to exploit women and benefit men. On a personal level, sexism may allow a husband the freedom to seek enjoyment on some nights "out with the boys," while a wife may be relegated to duties at home. Institutions practice sexism if they don't consider women for jobs with strenuous physical or mental requirements or those requiring leadership of teams. The benefit for men? They don't have to compete with qualified women to gain those favored positions. Institutional sexism has also created a work environment in which women are consistently paid less than men for doing the same work.[14,15]

Although sexual discrimination in employment is illegal under U.S. employment law, there are thousands of cases alleging sexual discrimination filed each year with the Equal Employment Opportunity Commission (EEOC).[16] Persistent discrimination in a wide variety of institutions has created a "glass ceiling" for many women—an unofficial barrier that prevents them from rising above a certain level of employment because men control the hiring and promotion process. This is evident in many different corporations and other institutions, including colleges and universities. A few years ago, a female professor at one of the top academic research laboratories in the world showed that women were paid lower salaries than men, provided less in research funding, and given inferior lab space and facilities. In some cases, women's responsibilities for child care have interfered with their ability to advance in a career.[17]

One type of sex discrimination at work is sexual harassment, defined by EEOC as "unwelcome sexual advances, requests for sexual favors, and other verbal or physical conduct of

∨
∨
∨ Different cultures have different norms for male and female gender roles. **Do you find any of these images offensive or disturbing because of your cultural norms?**

Gender Norms in Different Cultures

<<< Women had to fight hard to gain the right to vote in the United States and other countries.

How was this a sign of a patriarchal society?

a sexual nature," that affects a person's work. Sexual harassment will be covered in more detail in Chapter 12.[18]

The Process of Socialization

The example of U.S. men's reactions to hand-holding with other men illustrates how deeply embedded gender roles and norms can be in our personalities. But if gender roles vary in different cultures, and it is cultures that define acceptable gender roles, how are these roles taught to young people? We are taught about gender roles through socialization. Socialization is the process by which culture is passed from one generation to the next. Note that socialization is not a single event or a process that ends at a certain age, such as entry into adolescence or adulthood. Socialization continues throughout our lives as we learn from others about values, attitudes, behaviors, and beliefs that are considered appropriate by society's standards. Socialization can be natural and unconscious as well as planned and intentional. Many people debate whether certain characteristics are with us at birth (nature) or learned through others (nurture).

∨ Men and women are subjected to powerful messages about gender roles.
∨
∨ **Which do you think have been the most powerful in your life?**

Socialization in Gender Roles

What aspects of how we view gender come from socialization, and what is innate?

We all learn about our gender roles from many different sources. Our first influences, and often the most lasting, come from our families.

FAMILIES

According to a popular saying, "You can choose your friends, but you can't choose your family." Our parents and siblings influence us from the moment we are born, and the messages we receive concerning gender roles are vivid. One study showed that parents may have different expectations for boys and girls as soon as 24 hours after they are born![19] Boys and girls are treated differently throughout early childhood, often being dressed in specific colors according to gender—girls in pink and boys in blue—and receiving toys that adults assume they will like—boys like balls and trucks, while girls like dolls.[20] Later, children are rewarded for participation in activities that fit within their gender roles—girls receive positive feedback for playing with dolls and housekeeping activities, while boys get a pat on the back for playing with trucks and participating in sports.[21] Even household tasks are often assigned according to gender roles, with boys mowing the lawn and girls cooking and doing the laundry. This type of differentiation encourages children to identify certain types of work with different genders.[22] Both mothers and fathers contribute to this type of socialization, but men have been found to be more likely to reinforce stereotypes.[23]

Parents continue influencing gender roles as children grow into and beyond adolescence. Differing messages are often relayed to male and female adolescents related to sexual experiences. For example, a recent survey indicated that in Latino families teenage boys are either overtly or covertly encouraged to have sex as a way to "become a man," while girls are watched closely, sometimes even prohibited from dating, to try to prevent sexual experiences before marriage.[24] Parental gender expectations can also play a role in how children view their own abilities. When parents of junior high students expected girls to struggle with math, the girls reflected this view, finding fault with their achievement even if it was equal to that of boys.[25]

Siblings can also play a large role in socializing younger children. Little brothers and sisters look up to their older siblings and often model what they see. They may be influenced by the ways an older brother or sister accepts and adapts to gender roles. It's a common sight to see a younger brother dressing like an older brother or a younger sister trying on an older sister's jewelry or playing with her makeup. Several studies indicate that younger girls in particular are influenced by older sisters' sexual choices, including their age at first sexual intercourse, how consistently they use contraception, and rates of pregnancy and childbearing.[26]

SCHOOL

Messages in schools reflect other areas in society, so it's no surprise that schools reinforce some gender roles for children. Boys participate in more physical activities at school, while girls are more likely to help teachers with housekeeping activities. Boys are generally louder and more aggressive in school, while girls are usually quieter and show fewer behavior problems. However, teachers can also provide strong role models that combat gender role stereotypes. A gifted woman math or science teacher can inspire girls to consider greater involvement in an area in which they have often been previously discouraged.[27]

PEER GROUPS

Peer groups can exert a strong influence on young people as they mature. They can influence everything from the way a person walks,

talks, and dresses to political thoughts and personal dreams for the future. Gender roles are no exception. If teenagers hang with a crowd that thinks boys shouldn't study hard for school or that girls shouldn't be involved in sports, an individual's opinions may follow the crowd. Choices related to sexuality are especially susceptible to peer pressure. If "everyone's doing it" (or they think everyone's doing it), boys and girls are more likely to engage in sexual experimentation and activity. Other gender roles can be affected as well, including participation in sports or clubs, inclinations toward certain training or careers, and leisure activities. Gender roles may encourage the girls to go shopping, while the boys form a rock band or toss a football with the guys.[28,29]

and chattering away about how beautiful the moon is. How do you think you would react? The stereotypical reactions expected for the man might be annoyance or anger with no hesitation about asking the person to go elsewhere. The woman might be expected to be frightened at first, or else to attempt to help the person find the address and be sure the person was calm and coherent before leaving.

Some research shows that, from an early age, boys and girls are encouraged to feel and express certain emotions and not others. Mothers are more apt to ignore boys' crying and expressions of pain, which may desensitize them to feelings of distress. Fathers often teach boys to ignore or deny fear and label it as excitement instead. Boys are also allowed to be more negative and aggressive, showing

MASS MEDIA

Television, movies, and the Internet are so integrated into our lives today that people often forget what a strong influence they can be. Children spend an average of three to four hours *every day* watching television and spend more time each year in front of the tube than in the classroom or in activities with their parents.[30,31] What do children learn about gender roles when they watch *Survivor*, *American Idol*, or *The Sopranos* on TV or music videos on their iPod? What about movies like *Ice Age* or *Wall-E*? Even billboards and signs on buses broadcast messages about the acceptable gender roles in our society.

It's clear that children (and adults) are exposed to a wide variety of messages concerning gender roles. Religious groups, job experiences, and particular racial or ethnic groups may have a strong effect on individuals as well. With such a wide range of influences—from the highly sexualized dancing of women in popular music videos to the sober intelligence of our Secretary of State, Hillary Clinton, from the hard-bitten profile of military men fighting for survival to the gentle healing of a beloved family doctor—it's no wonder that people often feel confusion over their own best expression of gender.

GENDER ROLES AND EMOTIONS

One aspect of gender roles involves the emotions we feel and those we express. For example, a man and woman may react to the same event in very different ways. Imagine that you were one person in a heterosexual couple enjoying a quiet moment at night on an isolated park bench when a disoriented and distracted person appears before you, asking for directions to an obscure address

∧
∧ **Generally it is more permissible for men** to show
∧ emotional anger than it is for women. **What emotions do you think** are more permitted for women to show?

Tips on Being a Good Housewife in the 1950s

them that anger is an appropriate emotion for them, while the opposite is true for girls.[32] In *Boys Don't Cry*, Brandon is accepted as a man because of his aggression. The title itself presents the gender stereotype that men should not show certain emotions.

Gender Roles and Marriage: Is It Better for Men than for Women?

In 1972, the researcher Jesse Bernard published a study that compared the institution of marriage for men and women. Her conclusion? Marriage is generally two different experiences: one for her and one for him, termed the "his and hers" marriage. For men, marriage meant better mental and physical health, better job and economic prospects, and less involvement in crime than for unmarried men. The same was found to be true when comparing married and unmarried women. So, in general, marriage was a positive step for both men and women.

However, comparing the health of married men and married women showed that marriage provided much greater physical and mental health benefits to men than to women, because unmarried men had much higher rates of physical and mental illness and criminal involvement than unmarried women did. Bernard concluded that marriage was good for both men and women, but it was much better for men. Her explanation was that the common role of "housewife" at the time was unstructured and isolating; it cut women off from the social contacts enjoyed in work outside the home and involved constant, tedious demands.[33]

Since publication, Bernard's research has been challenged for a variety of reasons. Currently, social conditions have changed considerably from the time of her study. One simple example indicates significant changes: In the 1970s, only about 40 percent of married women were employed, while that

Housekeeping Monthly 13 May 1955

The good wife's guide

1. Have dinner ready: Plan ahead, even the night before, to have a delicious meal — on time. This is a way of letting him know that you have been thinking about him, and are concerned about his needs. Most men are hungry when they come home and the prospects of a good meal are part of the warm welcome needed.

2. Prepare yourself: Take 15 minutes to rest so you will be refreshed when he arrives. Touch up your makeup, put a ribbon in your hair and be fresh looking. He has just been with a lot of work-weary people. Be a little gay and a little more interesting. His boring day may need a lift.

3. Clear away the clutter. Make one last trip through the main part of the house just before your husband arrives, gathering up school books, toys, paper, etc. Then run a dust cloth over the tables. Your husband will feel he has reached a haven of rest and order, and it will give you a lift, too.

4. Prepare the children: Take a few minutes to wash the children's hands and faces if they are small, comb their hair, and if necessary, change their clothes. They are little treasures and he would like to see them playing the part.

5. Minimize the noise: At the time of his arrival, eliminate all noise of washer, dryer, dishwasher or vacuum ... to encourage the ch... to b...

Source: Housekeeping Monthly May 13, 1955.
http://www.snopes.com/language/document/goodwife.asp

∧ Messages like these **probably**
∧ **contributed to the "his and her" marriage experiences** of the 1950s and beyond. What basic male and female gender **roles are expressed here?**

number had risen to 60 percent by 2001.[34] This certainly means that fewer women can be defined as "housewives." However, it's not clear if this change has erased the "his and hers" experience of marriage. For example, men are still more likely to work full-time than women, get paid more, and have jobs with a higher status. Women still do a much larger share of household and child care work, even if they are also working outside the home, and they say they have less choice than men about these responsibilities. Men have increased their proportion of housework and child care in recent years, but the responsibilities for these tasks still fall overwhelmingly on women.[35]

The title of the book by Arlie Hochschild refers to the household responsibilities of working women as *The Second Shift*, published in 1997. After studying 50 households in which both spouses worked, she found that many women work one job and then come home to a second shift of preparing dinner, cleaning, doing laundry, and other household work. Later, she found that women work an average of 15 hours longer each week than men when both paid and household jobs are included! When gender roles expanded to allow (or force) women to work outside the home, the corresponding gender roles at home did not contract enough to allow a similar experience of marriage for women as men. "Her" experience now allows greater self-esteem and self-satisfaction through work than offered by the traditional role of housewife, but it has also added the stress of needing to succeed in two complex arenas: the workplace and the home.

The inequality of responsibilities at home is a significant source of stress for many couples. Hochschild suggests that the stresses on women from the second shift can be mitigated in two ways: Husband and wife can discuss and negotiate equitable responsibility for household tasks, and employers can offer work policies that allow more leeway for working mothers and fathers.[36]

HETEROSEXUAL describes those who are attracted to the opposite sex.
HOMOSEXUAL describes those who are attracted to members of the same sex.
BISEXUAL describes those who are attracted to members of both sexes.
ASEXUAL describes those who are attracted to neither sex.
PANSEXUAL describes those who display a broad range of sexual attractions, including attraction to those who do not fall into the simple gender categories of males and female.

Sexuality and Sexual Orientation

As stated earlier, sexuality consists of social practices related to erotic desire, pleasure, and reproduction. Sexuality provides the means for our continuation as a species and encompasses a wide variety of feelings and behaviors. What attracts or stimulates one person sexually may repel another. For example, one woman may find that her feet are an extremely sensitive, erogenous zone, while another may feel uncomfortable when a partner offers a foot massage. The range of erotic stimuli runs from what you or another person is wearing—high heels or sneakers? a tuxedo or a leather jacket? —to words and phrases, scents, and every type of touch from gentle to rough.

In many cases, sexuality is only part of the reason one person is attracted to another. Our society's gender roles have often made people feel uncomfortable about one or more parts of their sexuality. Men may feel that one erotic desire or dream isn't manly, and women often struggle with the conflicting messages sent by our society about the pleasures and importance of sex.[37]

Sexual orientation refers to the sex of the person someone is sexually, romantically, and emotionally attracted to. Most social scientists use four basic classifications for sexual orientation: **Heterosexuals** are attracted to the opposite sex; **homosexuals** are attracted to members of their own sex; **bisexuals** are attracted to members of both sexes; and **asexuals** are attracted to neither sex.[38] A new term—**pansexual**—is being used to describe a person who displays a broad range of sexual attractions, including attraction to those who do not fall into the simple gender categories of males and female.[39] By applying these definitions, Teena Brandon would be classified as a homosexual, because she was attracted to females and her biology made her female, even though she felt she was male.

Over the years, homosexuals have often been the target of violence, abuse, and ridicule. The dominant forces in many societies have portrayed homosexuality as a sickness, leaving people to explore and understand their sexuality alone while hiding it from others. Some religious and other groups have claimed that homosexuality can be "cured" through certain types of therapy. However, medical research consistently shows this to be false. The American Psychological Association removed homosexuality from its list of mental disorders in 1973 and has reaffirmed that position several times, as recently as 2000.[40] Research has also shown that homosexuals are no more likely to suffer from other mental disorders than heterosexuals and are just as likely as heterosexuals to be capable parents.[41]

A Difficult Truth

Jeff will graduate from college next year. He "came out of the closet" more than a year ago by telling his parents that he was gay.

"I went through a lot in high school, trying to figure out whether I was gay or not. It wasn't something I could talk to my parents about, and there wasn't anyone else I could go to in our small town without everyone knowing about it.

"But in my heart I knew I was gay and eventually I came to accept it. There's a great support group here at school, and we talk for hours about how confusing things can be.

"Anyway, I decided that I needed to tell my parents because I love them. I wanted them to understand who I really am so we could have a true relationship.

"I worked on a letter to them for over a month, just in case I couldn't manage to get the words out. But in the end, I did, and I gave them the letter later. They knew something big was coming because of the way I was acting. And right away, my mom started to cry. It made me feel terrible until she said she was crying for me, that she thought I'd already felt a lot of pain because of it and I'd probably feel a lot more.

"My dad didn't say much right away, but he never does. He was pretty shocked, but a couple of weeks later at dinner, he said, 'We love you son, no matter what your feelings are.'

"They still struggle with it sometimes, trying to figure out what to tell their friends and the rest of the family, who aren't very understanding, but I feel so much better when I'm home. It's not like I tell them much about boyfriends and my lifestyle, but at least I can look them in the eye and not feel like I'm deceiving them."

<<< "Coming out of the closet" can be a frightening and painful experience, depending on a family's reaction.

A recent study indicates an interesting difference in the sexuality of men and women. Researchers showed groups of men and women erotic images and then measured their biological responses to the images. Heterosexual and homosexual men responded as expected; heterosexuals responded to female images and homosexuals to male images. However, heterosexual and homosexual women showed biological stimulation to images of both men and women. This indicates that women's sexual orientation is more than a matter of sexual stimulation; they are capable of feeling sexually aroused by other women, but the overwhelming majority chooses solely heterosexual relationships.[42]

The Effect of Sex on Health

"Every cell has a sex." — "Exploring the Biological Contributions to Human Health: Does Sex Matter?" Institute of Medicine of the National Academy of Sciences, 2001[43]

<<< Differences between males and females at the cellular level **may affect susceptibility to disease or response to a treatment.**

For years, medical researchers have recognized that males and females have differing rates of disease, death, and injury, as well as differing responses to medical treatments. However, in many studies, the importance of these differences has been minimized, with many studies not identifying differences according to sex. Often, research done on human cells has not even recorded whether the tissue being tested had two XX chromosomes (originating from a female) or an X and a Y (originating from a male). Another issue that could change cellular response to different diseases and treatments is the differing levels of particular hormones in males and females. The National Academy of Sciences Report quoted above stresses that future studies should note these differences at the cellular level so that research can more accurately address the differing biology of men and women and their different responses to a variety of health issues.[44]

Of course, some health issues are clearly linked to one sex, such as conditions of the reproductive organs like ovarian and testicular cancer, or practices such as female genital mutilation as performed in Africa and other cultures. But many other

Prevalence of Female Genital Mutilation (FGM) in Africa and Yemen (Women, Ages 15–49)

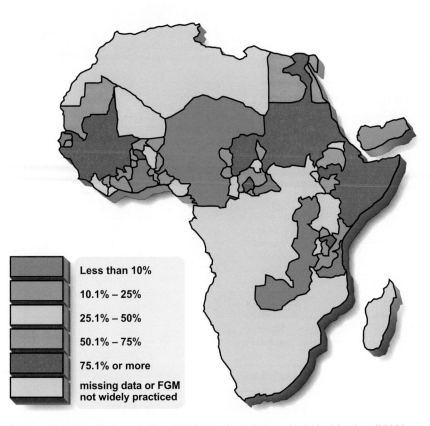

Less than 10%

10.1% – 25%

25.1% – 50%

50.1% – 75%

75.1% or more

missing data or FGM not widely practiced

Source: World Health Organization, 2007. http://whqlibdoc.who.int/publications/2008/9789241596442_eng.pdf

<<< Female genital mutilation (FGM) includes, among other things, **removal of the clitoris and/or restricting the vaginal passage** by sewing the labia together. **Although there is some debate within cultures about its meaning and importance,** the World Health Organization of the United Nations has concluded that **FGM is a significant health hazard for women and is working to eliminate the practice.**[50]

▶▶▶ GO GL🌐BAL

Women in Belarus

Belarus became an independent country in 1991 after the breakup of the Soviet Union. Although many of its gender roles are very traditional—women are the only ones, for example, who are expected to set the table for dinner[55]—its new constitution made women equal to men under the law. They are provided equal rights to property acquired during marriage, as well as the rights to inherit and own property and gain bank loans. Women enjoy freedom of movement and dress and equal civil liberties to men. The minimum age for marriage is set at 18 for both men and women, and laws protect women from physical attack and abuse.

Although there are numerous ways used to assess the status of women in different countries, the international group Organization for Economic Co-operation and Development (OECD), based in France, developed a new measurement in 2009 that measures women's formal legal status and other data that show a bias against women. This index, called the Social Institutions and Gender Index, addresses what the OECD considers the "root causes" of gender inequalities around the world. It is used to rank 102 countries around the world according to the level of discrimination against women. (Countries in North America and most of Europe are not ranked.) In this ranking, Belarus is placed at number 19 of 102, showing a low level of institutional and cultural dis-crimination. The list below shows the 10 countries rated as having the least discrimination against women and the 10 showing the most discrimination.

>>> New constitutions in some countries have **established equal rights for women.** How do you think **the United States would compare in women's rights?**

Degrees of Discrimination Against Women[56]

Rank of countries with least discrimination		Rank of countries with greatest discrimination	
1	Paraguay	93	Iraq
2	Croatia	94	Pakistan
3	Kazakhstan	95	Iran
4	Argentina	96	India
5	Costa Rica	97	Chad
6	Russian Federation	98	Yemen
7	Philippines	99	Mali
8	El Salvador	100	Sierra Leone
9	Ecuador	101	Afghanistan
10	Ukraine	102	Sudan

Source: 2009 Social Institutions and Gender Index, Organization for Economic Co-operation and Development (OECD), http://genderindex.org/ranking

diseases and conditions that don't have a clear sexual link show a marked difference in their rates for men and women. For example, women show lower rates of coronary heart disease and stroke, but are more likely to die from a stroke.[45, 46] Men are shown to lose weight more easily because it is easier to metabolize fat stored in abdominal areas, the common location in men, compared to fat in the hips and thighs, which is more common in women.[47] Mental illnesses such as depression and narcissism show huge differences in rates for men and women: Women suffer depression at twice the rate of men, while three-fourths of people suffering from narcissism are men.[48, 49]

The choices men and women make related to health also show clear differences. Men show much higher rates of alcohol abuse and drug use, including marijuana.[51] Overall life expectancy is much greater for women—about 80 years for women in the United States in 2005 compared to about 75 years for men[52]—even though women experience more illnesses than men.[53]

Researchers have not yet clearly identified reasons for these differences, although scientists have suggested many possibilities. Because of cultural conditioning and the experiences of pregnancy and childbirth, women may be more cognizant of pain and other physical symptoms and may be more willing to seek medical help. Women's common role as primary caretaker for children may expose them to more communicable illnesses from their children, but protect them from illnesses in the workplace. Men are more likely to be involved in outdoor work or recreational activities that increase general health, but also expose them to more injuries and illnesses. In summary, men and women do have clear differences in many aspects of health issues, but we don't currently know definitive reasons for these differences.[54]

think marriages and families:
WHAT INFLUENCES A PERSON'S GENDER ROLE?

FUNCTIONALISM

Functionalists see society as a large, integrated system that requires people to act in particular ways to ensure that the system survives. The great functional thinker Talcott Parsons believed that society required and supported distinct male and female roles so that society would remain stable and continue to function. Male and female roles helped families procreate, which ensured human survival. Parsons also saw male and female gender roles as natural, establishing a division of labor within the family and producing family and cultural stability. The male performed the "instrumental" role as primary breadwinner, partially because of a natural advantage in physical strength. He directed the family's relationship to the outside world by making economic, social, and educational decisions. The female filled the "expressive" role that governed internal family relationships, nurtured the children, and managed the household. Each role helped build a stable family and a stable society and at the same time provided individuals with clear guidelines with which to measure their behavior. The culture socializes each member as both a child and an adult so that these members can accept an appropriate gender role and function properly in society.[57,58]

CONFLICT THEORY

Karl Marx and Friedrich Engels established the basis for conflict theory in 1846 with the publication of the *Communist Manifesto*. This theory suggests that people suffer from inevitable conflicts between individuals and groups over power and material resources. In general, individuals and groups strive to attain a disproportionate amount of power and material goods and actively work to repress other groups and individuals to maintain their advantage. From this perspective, relationships between males and females reflect males' struggles to maintain power and control. Engels argued that capitalism as an economic system increased and extended male control over females. Because males participated in the economy as workers or at the higher levels of capitalism as business owners and managers, and women were either relegated to the home as housewives or the lowest level of jobs and wages in factories, women were more dependent than ever on men for economic survival. They suggested that middle-class men—called the "bourgeoisie"—viewed wives and women as an economic benefit that supported their economic and social status rather than as partners chosen for love or affection.[59,60]

SYMBOLIC INTERACTIONISM

Symbolic interactionists believe that families define their roles through interactions among family members. These roles are not necessarily "natural" as suggested by functionalists, but require people to take on the role of an actor by understanding the expectations of the family. Mead suggested that the self mirrors society, or that the smaller scale family mirrors larger organizations such as neighborhoods and schools. Social ideas such as the role of age, gender, and class are shown in these large-scale structures and shape family interactions.[61] These expectations are crucial because if expectations are unclear, then an individual can't meet them and the rest of the family can't judge the person's behavior.

The variability among family's expectations is crucial to the symbolic interactionists' views. For example, in one household the male might handle the checkbook, while in another it might be the female. In some families, the male might do all of the gardening, and in another the female might be tending to the flowers and weeds. Cooking might be a male, female, or shared responsibility and skill. These expectations may change suddenly or gradually over time. Other considerations may influence these gender roles as well. Parents may assign household chores to a boy when he is young out of necessity and the same chores to a girl years later for the same reason.[62]

WRAP YOUR MIND AROUND THE THEORY

Functionalists believe **gender roles are natural and provide a clear division of labor.** How are/were household responsibilities divided in your family?

FUNCTIONALISM

Functional theory would suggest that the natural gender roles that cultures teach and support through socialization are positive forces for all levels of society: individuals, families, and society as a whole. Individuals are provided with clear expectations about their behavior as males and females. Families are separated into natural and obvious roles that produce a stable family and simple division of labor. Societies benefit from stable families and procreation through a predictable transition from one generation to the next. However, functional theory has not addressed the reality of social change in recent years. For many men and women, traditional gender roles—men as sole breadwinners and women as housewives—just don't fit changing individual and societal expectations and needs. Nontraditional families also don't fit neatly into the functionalist framework. The stable, functional societal system seen by Parsons about 70 years ago doesn't address the changing gender roles of today's society.

CONFLICT THEORY

Conflict theorists suggest that gender roles in society are used to support male domination over women and allow men to maintain power and control over economic and social resources. Male sexism relegates women to lower levels of employment and social power in government or other institutions. Conflict theorists originally criticized capitalism as an economic system because it relegated most men to low-paying jobs in factories while limiting women to work in the home at no pay. Today, the economy has changed considerably, but the same struggles for power and control are seen. Sex discrimination, the "glass ceiling," and research that continually shows women are paid less than men for the same jobs support the view that gender roles support male domination at work and in society.

HOW DO GENDER ROLES AFFECT INDIVIDUALS, FAMILIES, AND SOCIETIES?

SYMBOLIC INTERACTIONISM

For symbolic interactionists, gender roles are negotiated within each family. Economic need may play a big part in these roles – many families today need two wage earners to make ends meet. This fact may necessitate unique roles for family members: Males may need to participate equally or even predominantly in areas such as household management and child care, while females may add responsibilities for work outside the family *in addition* to those for household and child care. The role expectations within a unique family are crucial for each member to be able meet those expectations. These may change quickly or gradually over time. For example, a family member who changes from a day job to a night shift may need to assume new roles in the morning—helping children get to school, for example—while giving up previous roles involved with family time at supper or in the evenings.

Conflict theorists believe **that sexism helps men restrict women's economic and social power.** Have you observed instances in which sexism **restricted women's opportunities?**

Families may **negotiate gender roles to meet different needs.** Did you have specific family roles growing up that were **influenced by gender or other issues?**

discover marriages and families in action:
WHAT EFFECT DO GENDER AND SEXUAL ORIENTATION HAVE ON INDIVIDUALS?

Violating a Norm

As discussed previously, men holding hands as a sign of friendship in some cultures but not in others is an example of a gender norm—an expectation about what is appropriate behavior for males and females. These norms have strong effects on our reactions and behaviors. They can affect how we walk and talk, the emotions we express, the jobs we choose, the recreation we enjoy, the people we are attracted to as lovers and spouses, and so on. Even such things as hairstyles and clothing can be involved in norms for your gender. For example, in the 1960s male "hippies" violated a norm by wearing their hair very long, a style expected of females, until the norm changed and it became acceptable for males to have long hair.

Some entertainers, such as Elton John and the late Michael Jackson, have gained fame and notoriety as "gender benders"—their look, clothing, and mannerisms fell outside the norms for a particular gender. Debate over gender norms also dominates employment issues. Should women work as firefighters, police officers, or combat soldiers? Should male nurses be banned from assisting in labor and birth? Should men work in day care centers and women on construction sites?

ACTIVITIES

To judge your own and other people's reactions to norms associated with gender roles, plan to violate a gender norm and observe your own feelings and the reactions of other people.

1. Decide on which norm you will violate, without violating your moral code. Make a list of norms associated with your gender. These can be in the area of appearance and dress, manners, expression of emotions, attitudes, recreation, etc. Then select one and plan how you will challenge it.
2. Carry out your norm violation. Make sure that you don't engage in illegal or dangerous activities.
3. Afterward, write down how violating the norm made you feel and how other people reacted.[63]

MAKE CONNECTIONS

Make Connections

Families vary considerably in the ways they instruct their children on gender roles and influence them through behavior. Your family of origin, as covered in Chapter 1, has had a strong influence on your life. The effects of socialization can affect your sexuality and sexual orientation, your health, and the gender roles you choose and accept in an intimate relationship. In Chapter 6, we will investigate how the socialization process can affect your sexual behavior. Chapter 7 explores how your socialization can affect your patterns of dating and who you choose as a long-term partner.

>>> ACTIVITIES

For one week, pay attention to all of the stereotypical comments you hear in conversation, in reading, and in the media. Record the comments in a notebook.

From Classroom to Community } "Boys Will Be Boys"

Nick helps run a park program in the summer that attracts kids from about 5 to 15 years of age.

"I'm amazed at the energy the young boys have. They'll chase after a soccer ball all morning.

"The girls start out playing too, but because the boys are faster and stronger, the girls usually lose interest. But a girl counselor gets them to play jump rope for hours.

"One thing that surprised me was how much a lot of the boys like art projects, like gluing together craft sticks or doing papier mache.

"It seems like the girls like drawing and coloring more. But for the older kids—once they're teenagers or almost teenagers—the boys and girls stay as separate as possible unless we make them play a game together.

"The boys are always wrestling and chasing each other and the girls might do one of the hand crafts and just talk quietly to each other.

"Every once in a while there's an exception. Last year Samantha—everyone called her Sam—wouldn't leave the boys alone, and she beat them at most of the rough games they played. She was just having fun, and the boys accepted her as one of the gang."

Theory

FUNCTIONALISM 73
- society needs predictable gender roles to ensure procreation and create a stable society
- people are socialized into natural gender roles that provide a division of labor between men and women
- men are responsible for the "instrumental" role governing economic and social functions outside the family, and women govern "expressive" functions including family relationships and household management

CONFLICT THEORY 73
- the *Communist Manifesto* suggests that capitalism supports gender roles that allow men to exploit women and maintain power and economic dominance
- even though many economic conditions have changed, men continue to use sexism to keep women in jobs and positions with lower pay and less power and responsibility

SYMBOLIC INTERACTIONISM 73
- people negotiate gender roles within families according to prior experiences and current needs
- gender roles within families may change quickly or gradually and may depend on exterior circumstances such as economic challenges

Key Terms

sex refers to the biological differences that differentiate men and women, including internal and external sexual organs, hormonal profiles, and chromosomes 63

gender is made up of the social practices that a culture defines as masculine and feminine 63

sexuality is made up of social practices related to erotic desire, pleasure, and reproduction 63

sex roles are attitudes and behavioral expectations that go along with the biological aspects of being male or female 63

androgynous describes a person who has a balance of both male and female characteristics so that neither predominates 63

norms are societal expectations for appropriate behavior, including those for gender 64

patriarchy is a social system in which men dominate women 64

matriarchy is a social system in which women dominate men 65

sexism is the belief that one sex is superior to the other 65

heterosexual describes those who are attracted to the opposite sex 70

homosexual describes those who are attracted to members of the same sex 70

bisexual describes those who are attracted to members of both sexes 70

asexual describes those who are attracted to neither sex 70

pansexual describes those who display a broad range of sexual attractions, including attraction to those who do not fall into the simple gender categories of males and female 70

Sample Test Questions

MULTIPLE CHOICE

These multiple-choice questions are similar to those found in the test bank that accompanies this textbook.

1. Margaret Mead's research in New Guinea proposed the idea that:
   a. men created patriarchies in many different geographical areas and types of culture.
   b. sex roles were more important than gender roles for individuals.
   c. a matriarchal society could be just as exploitive as a patriarchal society.
   d. gender roles were more dependent on cultural expectations than on biology.

2. As more women have become involved in work outside the home, the differences in personality traits for men and women have:
   a. been shown to rely heavily on economic circumstances.
   b. become even more pronounced than previously documented.
   c. shown that biology is the most important factor in socialization.
   d. allowed men and women to share more of the emotional responsibilities at home.

3. The socialization process:
   a. begins at birth and ends in adolescence.
   b. extends throughout a person's entire life.
   c. involves only internal family relationships.
   d. has little effect on most people's gender roles.

4. A "his and hers" marriage experience involves:
   a. men and women both experiencing equal positive effects from marriage.
   b. men and women negotiating equal responsibilities for household management.
   c. more positive effects from marriage for men than women.
   d. dividing household responsibilities along traditional gender roles.

5. Recent medical research has often:
   a. neglected to take into account differences between men's and women's susceptibility to certain diseases.
   b. divided men and women into separate groups that cannot be compared.
   c. disproved previous research that shows differences for sexes in response to certain treatments.
   d. shown that hormonal differences in men and women have no effect on health.

ESSAY

1. Compare the importance of sex roles with the importance of gender roles for individuals.

2. What influences do you think were most important in the development of your own gender role?

3. Describe the division of labor among adults and children in your own family. Do you think most two-parent families in the United States experience "his and her" marriages?

4. Do you think sexual orientation is more a result of a biological predisposition or of family and cultural socialization? Why?

5. Speculate on some reasons you think there are such significant differences for men and women in their respective rates for health issues.

WHERE TO START YOUR RESEARCH PAPER

For basic information on sex and gender roles, go to
http://www.gender.org.uk/about/index.htm

For more information on gender roles, go to
http://www.faqs.org/health/topics/8/Gender-roles.html

For more information on Margaret Mead and her research in New Guinea, go to http://www.loc.gov/exhibits/mead/field-sepik.html

For information on sexism and sexual harassment, go to
http://www.understandingprejudice.org/links/sexism.htm

To find out more about gender role socialization in children, go to
http://gozips.uakron.edu/~susan8/parinf.htm

For more information on Hochschild's "second shift," go to
http://familystressencyclopedia.blogspot.com/2007/08/second-shift-for-employed-mothers.html

For basic information on sexual orientation, go to
http://www.apa.org/topics/sorientation.html

For more information on how sex may impact health, go to
http://www.nytimes.com/2001/04/25/us/sex-differences-called-key-in-medical-studies.html

Answers: 1. d; 2. b; 3. b; 4. c; 5. a

Remember to check www.thethinkspot.com for additional information, downloadable flashcards, and other helpful resources.

HOW DO FRIENDSHIP, AFFECTION, LOVE, AND INTIMACY AFFECT MARRIAGES AND FAMILIES?

WHAT ARE THE THEORIES BEHIND LOVE IN MARRIAGES AND FAMILIES?

HOW CAN COUPLES ADDRESS INTIMACY PROBLEMS?

Sally

Albright is perky, driven, optimistic, and fussy about details. Harry Burns is dark, pessimistic, lazy, and sarcastic. They meet in the summer of 1977, when newly graduated Sally agrees to drive from Chicago to New York with Harry, who is her best friend's boyfriend. During the trip, Sally and Harry get to know each other and clash on almost every issue they discuss. In particular, the two argue about the possibility of friendship between women and men. Sally asserts that it is completely possible; Harry counters that sex is bound to get in the way, especially because men tend to be sexually attracted to every woman they come in contact with. When the pair arrives in New York, they exchange awkward good-byes.

Five years later, Sally and Harry find themselves on the same plane. Sally is in a new relationship, and Harry is about to get married. They start arguing again about friendship between men and women, each of them holding the same views as five years before. When the plane lands, Harry and Sally again part awkwardly.

Five years later, Sally and Harry meet once more, this time at a bookshop. Sally has broken up with her boyfriend after realizing that she wants a family and her boyfriend does not. Harry is divorcing from his wife, who has fallen in love with someone else. The two decide to go to dinner together and talk about the end of their relationships. This time, their conversation is easy and pleasant, so much that Harry and Sally decide to become friends. From that day on, Harry and Sally become inseparable: talking on the phone until late, exchanging stories about their dates, and even trying to set each other up with their friends.

Then one night, Sally calls Harry in tears. She has received a call from her old boyfriend, who has announced that he is about to get married. Sally feels like a failure because she believes her boyfriend never proposed to her because he considered their relationship temporary. Harry tries to console her. While he is holding her in his arms, the two kiss for the first time and end up spending the night together. The morning after, Harry is obviously uncomfortable with the new intimacy and leaves Sally's apartment in a hurry. Sally is offended and confronts Harry. When Harry says that he had sex with her only out of pity, their friendship ends.

Feeling guilty for what he said to Sally, in the following weeks Harry does all he can to be forgiven, with no success. On New Year's Eve, Harry walks alone in the streets of New York and realizes he is in love with Sally. He hurries to the party she is attending and declares his love to her. Sally realizes she is in love with him, too, and the two finally make up and kiss. The movie ends with a scene in which Harry and Sally are talking to an interviewer, sharing their stories about how they met and about their wedding.

FRIENDSHIP, AFFECTION, LOVE, AND INTIMACY

CHAPTER 05

The movie *When Harry Met Sally. . .* is based on the question, "Can men and women be friends, or does the possibility of sex prevent this?"

The movie also makes us reflect on the relationship between love, friendship, and intimacy. When the protagonists end up in bed together, they are forced to deal with changes in their relationship. Many people agree that it is important for people in a relationship to be friends as well as lovers. Love at first sight, friendship, passion, intimacy. . . How do people navigate through these different experiences and feelings?

When I was in my early 20s, I became engaged to Jeff (not his real name) after dating for a few months. We were studying at the same university and spent a lot of time together. He was kind, loyal, smart, funny, and a great kisser, too. After we became engaged, though, I started having second thoughts. I was not so sure that he was the "right one" and that I should marry him. I realized that I was not feeling the passionate, romantic love that I expected to feel for my fiancé. It turned out that it was more than simply pre-wedding jitters; I actually broke off my engagement with Jeff. It was painful for both of us at first, but I had come to the conclusion that Jeff and I were actually just friends. Years have passed, and I don't regret that decision. Getting married without being truly in love would have been a mistake. From that experience, I learned that the boundaries between friendship, affection, love, and intimacy in relationships can sometimes become blurry. In this chapter, we will examine the differences between friendship, affection, love, and intimacy in marriage and family, and we will learn the theoretical perspectives behind those emotions. We will also learn about what happens when couples lose intimacy.

∧
∧ **Research shows that** good friendships
∧ are linked to positive psychological effects on the individual. **What characteristics of friendship contribute to a person's emotional well-being?**

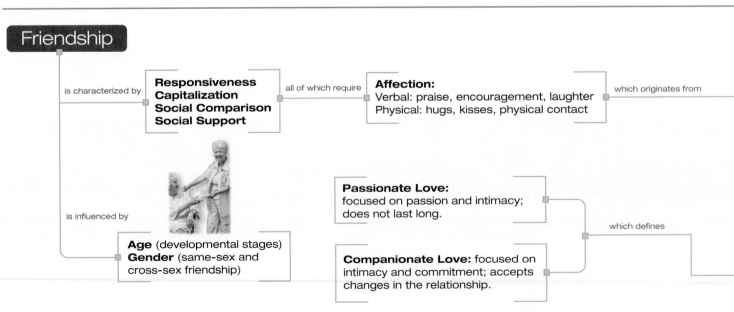

Friendship

is characterized by → **Responsiveness Capitalization Social Comparison Social Support**

all of which require → **Affection:** Verbal: praise, encouragement, laughter Physical: hugs, kisses, physical contact

which originates from

is influenced by → **Age** (developmental stages) **Gender** (same-sex and cross-sex friendship)

Passionate Love: focused on passion and intimacy; does not last long.

Companionate Love: focused on intimacy and commitment; accepts changes in the relationship.

which defines

get the topic: HOW DO FRIENDSHIP, AFFECTION, LOVE, AND INTIMACY AFFECT MARRIAGES AND FAMILIES?

What Is Friendship?

"Friendship is the only thing in this world concerning the usefulness of which all mankind are agreed." — Marcus Tullius Cicero (106–43 B.C.), Roman philosopher

What should a true friend do? Call you often, give you advice, make you laugh, support your decisions, tell you that your new jeans make you look great? The concept of friendship varies across cultures, age groups, eras, and individuals. After all, friends' relationships are not regulated or codified like those between spouses, co-workers, or even neighbors. The difficulty of defining friendship is confirmed by an interview conducted with about 120 adults between the ages of 55 and 87 in 2000, who came up with 17 different criteria to describe friendship, ranging from self-disclosure to day-to-day assistance.[1]

So, how can we define friendship? On a general level, it can be stated that friendship is a **dyadic relationship**, or a relationship between two people, that involves some kind of closeness and mutual affection. Often, friendship is defined as a set of behaviors, like self-discourse and shared activities. Other times, friendship is described as a relationship characterized by trust, empathy, loyalty, and compatibility of interests. Good friends see and talk to each other often and share their most private thoughts and feelings. Good friends are also happy about each other's success and do everything they can to help the friend in need. But is this all there is to say about friendship?

CHARACTERISTICS OF FRIENDSHIP

To better define friendship, we can compare it to another feeling, love. If viewers were allowed to sneak a peek at the lives of the protagonists of *When Harry Met Sally. . .* after their wedding, they would likely see that the relationship has changed quite a bit. We all know that friendship is different from love, but how? First, friendship is not usually exclusive and

DYADIC RELATIONSHIP is a relationship between two people, that involves some kind of closeness and mutual affection.

RESPONSIVENESS is the affectionate and supportive understanding of another's needs, values, and desires.

CAPITALIZATION is being sincerely happy about a friend's well-being and success.

SOCIAL COMPARISON refers to the habit of evaluating one's skills and qualities by comparing them to others.

SOCIAL SUPPORT is the emotional, verbal, and material help received by others.

does not involve the same amount of verbal and physical affection that lovers usually give each other. Second, friends are allowed to pursue their personal interests on their own or with other people, and are not expected to spend most of their free time together.

Researchers have also come up with a few general characteristics that can be attributed to a meaningful friendship. According to Rowland Miller and Daniel Perlman, authors of *Intimate Relationships,* true friendships are characterized by six factors.[2] At the base of all deep friendships lie respect and trust. Then there is **responsiveness**, or the affectionate and supportive understanding of each other's needs, values, and desires. When friends are sincerely happy about each other's successes, they interact in a pattern call **capitalization**. Good friends also compare each other's beliefs and skills to know themselves better in a process called **social comparison**. Because male friendships tend to be more competitive than female friendships, social comparison for men can sometimes be more problematic. Finally, good friends give each other **social support**, or help to one another in times of need. Social support can be provided in the form of emotional support (reassurance and affection), advice support (opinions and guidance), and material support (money and goods).[3]

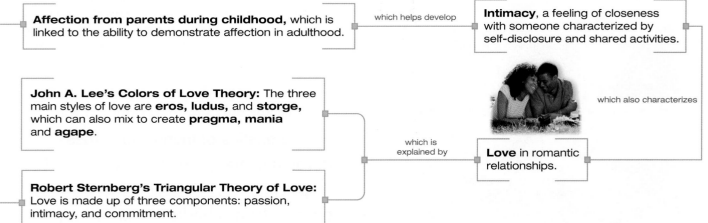

Affection from parents during childhood, which is linked to the ability to demonstrate affection in adulthood.

which helps develop

Intimacy, a feeling of closeness with someone characterized by self-disclosure and shared activities.

John A. Lee's Colors of Love Theory: The three main styles of love are **eros, ludus,** and **storge,** which can also mix to create **pragma, mania** and **agape**.

which is explained by

which also characterizes

Love in romantic relationships.

Robert Sternberg's Triangular Theory of Love: Love is made up of three components: passion, intimacy, and commitment.

Friendship across the Life Cycle

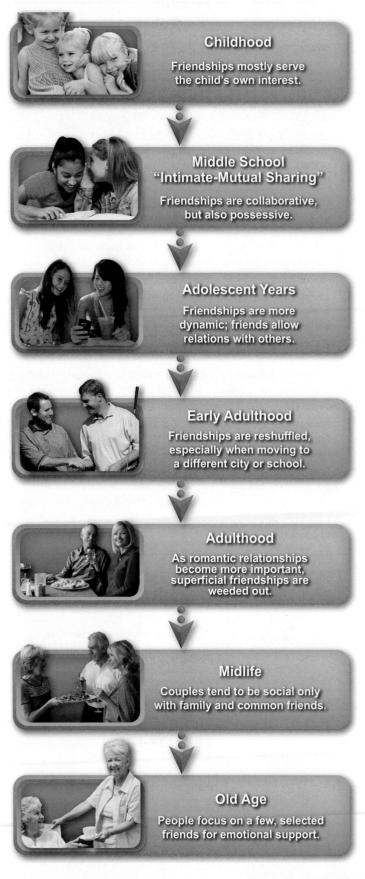

Childhood
Friendships mostly serve the child's own interest.

Middle School "Intimate-Mutual Sharing"
Friendships are collaborative, but also possessive.

Adolescent Years
Friendships are more dynamic; friends allow relations with others.

Early Adulthood
Friendships are reshuffled, especially when moving to a different city or school.

Adulthood
As romantic relationships become more important, superficial friendships are weeded out.

Midlife
Couples tend to be social only with family and common friends.

Old Age
People focus on a few, selected friends for emotional support.

FRIENDSHIP THROUGH LIFE

Miller and Perlman also discuss how friendships change throughout our lives. Two middle-school girls might consider themselves best friends because they share each other's secrets about their crushes. As they grow up, they might show support by babysitting each other's children. Friendships also change in the emotional requirements and expectations of the individuals.

How does friendship change during one's life? Children are mostly interested in having someone to play with, and their friendships are more centered on personal needs.[4] In middle school, friendships become more exclusive and based on mutual interests. Adolescents acknowledge that one friendship cannot fulfill all of their emotional needs, and they start creating independent relationships based on mutual respect and shared sensibilities.[5] College students often have to find new friendships if they leave town to attend school. A 2009 study of 489 first-year psychology students shows that students tend to develop more intense friendships, even at early stages of acquaintance, with people they perceive as having similar interests.[6] After graduation, young adults tend to focus on few meaningful friendships and "weed out" more superficial acquaintances. This tendency becomes more pronounced as people enter important romantic relationships, in a pattern referred to as **dyadic withdrawal**. By midlife, friendship with members of the opposite sex diminishes considerably, as couples tend to spend more time with common friends and family. In old age, research shows that people tend to focus more and more on a few, selected friends rather than acquaintances. In a 2000 study of elderly women, the interviewees explained that mutual support is extremely valued, especially when it provides validation and advice on the challenges of growing old.[7]

ONLINE AND OFFLINE FRIENDSHIPS

In the past few years, social networking sites such as MySpace, Facebook, and Twitter have become hugely popular across all ages. We seem to have developed a veritable obsession with our online personas, so much so that someone mocked the virtual world of *Second Life,* a computer game that allows subscribers to create their own world and interact as avatars, with the invitation to "get a first life."

Despite the opinions of some that young people are in danger of turning into crouching androids glued to their computers, research shows that the majority of friendships are still maintained offline.[8] Offline friendships are characterized by more interdependence, depth, understanding, and commitment, but online friendships can gain some of these qualities with time.[9] Most online friends tend to be rather cautious about disclosing personal information. However, this does not apply to people with a negative view of themselves and others; they instead seem to share more information, possibly in an attempt to become more self-confident in their interactions.[10] Interestingly, even in online friendships people seem to gain more satisfaction when befriending people of a similar age and place of residence.[11]

<<< **Miller and Perlman outlined the characteristics of friendship across developmental years.** How do you think responsiveness between friends may change from childhood to old age?

SAME-SEX AND CROSS-SEX FRIENDSHIPS

In *When Harry Met Sally. . .* there is a scene in which Harry is talking to his male friend Jess about his new friendship with Sally. Harry explains how refreshing it feels having a platonic relationship with a woman: He can get her perspective about dating and sex, and he can finally stop lying about himself because he is not constantly thinking about having sex with her. Do you have a platonic friendship with a member of the opposite sex?

In the past, studies indicated that most people tend to be friends with people of their own sex.[12] However, recent studies show that cross-sex friendships are more common today. Still, sociologists have observed that men and women display different attitudes toward friendships. Women tend to talk more on the phone with their friends and disclose more personal information. Men's friendships instead tend to be more focused on group activities, such as playing sports, rather than on sharing emotions.[13]

Going back to the basic question in *When Harry Met Sally. . .*—"Can men and women truly be friends?"—researchers agree that they absolutely can. Besides, cross-sex friendships have many benefits. Befriending a person of the opposite sex can give one a unique perspective on the other sex, and gender roles become mitigated. Cross-sex friendships are even associated with higher self-esteem and self-confidence.[14] However, cross-sex relationships diminish considerably when people enter into long-term relationships, as these friendships may lead the uninvolved partner to feel threatened in his or her role as a third wheel.[15]

Hooking Up

One day, dating might be considered an old-fashion quirk of almost Victorian taste and prudery, as quaint as a woman dropping an embroidered handkerchief to encourage a man to approach her. On that day, "hooking up" will be the norm. This postmodern view of romance may just be one of the latest fashions of the sometimes alarmist media. Before losing all hope, we should ask ourselves, "What does 'hooking up' really mean?"

"**Hooking up**" is a term used to describe casual sexual activity with no strings attached between heterosexual college students who are strangers or brief acquaintances. When did people start to hook up? Although the term became common in the 1990s, its use with its modern meaning has been documented as early as the mid-1980.[16] Studies from

<<< Online networking sites make it easier for people to meet friends through the Internet. **How do you think online friendships handle responsiveness, capitalization, social comparison, and social support compared with offline friendships?**

the early 2000s show that hooking up was already a fairly common practice on U.S. campuses, practiced by as much as 40 percent of female college students.[17] More recent studies have shed some light on the demographic and psychological correlatives of hooking up. In a 2007 study involving 832 college students, it emerged that hooking up is practiced less by African-American than Caucasian students.[18] Hooking up is also associated with the use of alcohol and, interestingly, with higher parental income.[19] Increased financial resources may give teens and young adults more opportunities to socialize and hook up. As far as personality traits, hookups seem to be more common for people displaying extroversion, although it is also common in neuroticism. **Neuroticism** is a personality trait characterized by negative emotions such as depression, anxiety, anger, embarrassment, vulnerability, and impulsiveness. Impulsiveness combined with emotional instability may lead neurotics to hook up as a way to cope with fears and anxieties.[20] The emotions stirred by hookups are varied, and women seem to be more likely than men to experience regret after a hookup, especially when sexual intercourse is involved.[21]

Not surprisingly, hooking up has received much criticism. Psychologists blame the hookup culture for young people's fear of commitment, saying that focusing only on sex does not teach people to respond to the emotional and romantic needs of the partner. In this sense, hookups are described as the worst possible preparation for long-term relationships and marriage.[22] Other critics argue that the hookup culture has its risks, too, especially when it's strongly characterized by alcohol consumption. A 2007 study of 178 college students concluded that 23 percent of women and 7 percent of men had ex-

>>> A 2003 study of the phenomenon of "hooking up" among college students revealed that people thought their peers were more comfortable with hookups than they were. **Based on these results and on personal experience, how do you think peer pressure affects sexual behavior in teenagers and young adults?**

perienced unwanted sexual intercourse, including regretful or harmful sexual behavior such as assault and rape (although assault and rape were reported only by a small minority of interviewees).[23] More significantly, 78 percent of unwanted sexual intercourse experienced by the interviewees took place during a hookup. Of course, unwanted sexual intercourse is not characteristic of hookups only, and dating is not exempt from it.

HOOKUPS AND DATES

How does "hooking up" differ from dating? According to author Kathleen A. Bogle, the most significant difference lies in the timing of sex, where the term "sex" refers to any sexual activity from kissing to sexual intercourse.[24] In dating, sex usually is postponed until the couple has gone on a few dates, whereas in a hookup, sex frequently happens on the first encounter. Second, when dating, two people get to know each other and possibly start a romantic relationship, which is not required in hooking up. Alcohol consumed in large quantities is also more characteristic of hookups than dating, since casual sex is more likely when inhibitions are lowered. Hooking up also differs from dating in terms of privacy: Dates tend to have a public nature (they take place in restaurants, movie theaters, etc.), whereas hookups are more spontaneous and often private. The private nature of the hookup culture has also been facilitated by technology advancements in the last decades, such as mobile phones and the Internet.[25] This new technology makes it much easier to get in touch with acquaintances through private channels.

In a time of economic crisis, it might be tempting to hook up just to save money. Unlike dates, hookups do not require spending any money on nice dinners and flowers. It is also important to realize that hooking up is most common among college students, and that it is not necessarily representative of the entire single population. College years are often viewed as the last chance to have fun before settling down, so hookups may represent a chance to experiment sexually—something that dating does not provide.

Hookups also show more gender equality in the initiation of the script, or sequence of automatic behaviors, although research shows that men still maintain more power in deciding whether the hookup will be a one-night stand or lead to something more. In this regard, sexual exploitation is still very common both in the hookup and dating cultures, meaning that men are often capable of keeping a partner just for sexual enjoyment, regardless of the woman's true desires. This seems to stem from the fear that women have of being rejected if they don't perform to a man's standard. There is still a stigma attached to women with a more intense sexual life or those who have had many sexual partners. As liberating as the hookup script might seem, the **sexual double standard** that condemns women and praises men for the same level of sexual experience is still present today.

What Is Affection?

Affection is an important factor in any healthy relationship. Friends, couples, and families express both **physical affection** and **verbal affection**. Even though the type of desired affection varies, some researchers believe that the need for affection is innate. In this respect, Kory Floyd, a professor of human communication, postulated the **affection exchange theory**, according to which affectionate communication is an adaptive behavior that is instrumental in human survival and procreation.[26] Another study added that affection is essential for humans. It is given and received, especially during difficult times, and requires effort on the part of all involved in the exchange.[27]

PHYSICAL AFFECTION

Anthropologists agree that physical affection has physiological and emotional benefits for babies. Hugging, kissing, and caressing help calm a crying baby, and, according to teacher trainer Gigi Newton, these activities create the fundamental bond between parent and child.[28] Studies have also demonstrated that children need physical affection from their parents to develop self-esteem, and when they don't receive it, they have a hard time expressing affection as adults.[29]

Physical affection is also positively associated with higher relationship and partner satisfaction.[30] In a survey conducted on over 100,000 women, 72 percent of respondents stated that they would prefer nonsexual physical affection to having sex with an unaffectionate partner.[31] Of course, individuals have their own preference in physical affection. Some people consider holding hands an expression of love, whereas the partner might prefer a long hug. Partners who are able to identify and interpret the other's needs for physical affection have a better shot at a rewarding relationship.

The perception and modality of physical affection are also influenced by the social context a couple lives in. For example, a 2005 survey on public displays of physical affection among adolescents concluded that interra-

Hooking Up versus Commitment

Kara is a sophomore in college. She hooked up a lot during her first year of school, but is now ready for a deeper relationship.

"When I first got to college, I was ready to have fun. Leaving home for the first time gave me a sense of adventure that carried over into my idea of relationships. I didn't want anything serious, but I wanted to see what was out there. During the first months of school I hooked up with a lot of guys, mostly people I met at parties. I loved not having the pressure of a relationship on top of school.

"Then I hooked up with Bill, a guy from my biology class. Since he wasn't a stranger, this encounter was slightly more intimate than what I'd been used to. I'd never thought about Bill romantically, but after we made out, I started to think that way.

"Bill and I didn't become a couple, but our relationship made me realize that hooking up can be fun for a while, but ultimately I'd like to have someone to get close to. I want a guy who doesn't leave first thing in the morning and who calls me for something other than one passionate night."

cial couples are less likely to express affection in public than intra-racial couples, because of the still-present stigma against interracial relationships.[32]

VERBAL AFFECTION

Verbal affection can be provided through affectionate expression such as "I love you," but also through laughter, approval, praise, affectionate notes, and other expressions of appreciation. Different families display different degrees of verbal affection, and a 2007 study of African American infants showed that children from a higher socioeconomic status received more verbal affection than infants from working-class families.[33] Researchers have also examined verbal affection in association with gender. In particular, it emerged that when fathers communicate with their sons, they tend to express affection through shared activities rather than direct verbal statements.[34] This tendency is linked in stereotypical gender roles, but also in **homophobia** (overtly affectionate men are often viewed as effeminate). This is confirmed by the fact that fathers tend to be more affectionate toward their heterosexual sons than to their homosexual or bisexual sons.[35]

What Is Intimacy?
AUTONOMY AND INTIMACY

Intimacy usually describes a feeling of closeness that characterizes meaningful relationships. Intimacy, then, refers to the sharing of personal experiences, thoughts, and emotions with people we love, such as family members, love partners, and close friends. The purpose of intimacy is to establish trust: When we share our secrets with someone, we make ourselves vulnerable. If the other person honors that openness, then the relationship grows. So, when your partner agrees to show you his or her embarrassing pictures from middle school, you know your relationship is going somewhere.

Autonomy refers to a state of independence and self-determination. In a way, it might seem that autonomy and intimacy are opposites, but that should not be the case. Intimacy and autonomy are actually both necessary in any healthy relationship. What is the perfect balance between autonomy and intimacy? Different relationships and different individuals at different points of their lives need to realize their needs. For example, an adolescent usually feels the need for more autonomy from family, but it is important that parents maintain intimacy with him or her to provide much-needed

> **HOMOPHOBIA** is the irrational fear of homosexuals.
> **INTIMACY** is a feeling of closeness in meaningful relationships characterized by sharing of personal experiences, thoughts, and emotions.
> **AUTONOMY** is a state of independence and self-determination.
> **DIALECTIC APPROACH** is the relationship model according to which relationships are characterized by an ongoing tension between intimacy and autonomy.
> **ATTACHMENT THEORY** is the theory that states that people's patterns of attachment are shaped by the intimate bonding they shared with their caregivers during infancy.
> **SOCIAL EXCHANGE THEORY** is the sociological perspective arguing that satisfaction in a relationship is enhanced when the rewards are greater than the costs.

guidance and affection. The level of intimacy can also be related to cultural factors. For example, in a 2008 study of the relationships of European Canadians and those of Chinese Canadians, it emerged that Chinese Canadians' more traditional gender roles caused lower levels of intimacy in their romantic relationships.[36]

THEORIES OF INTIMACY

Family theorists have developed different interpretations of the way intimacy works in marriage and family. According to the **dialectic approach**, relationships are characterized by an ongoing tension between intimacy and autonomy. The ideal family promotes closeness while at the same time allowing its members to cultivate their individuality. However, that perfect balance seldom exists, especially because of the differing personal needs of family members. For example, one family member might crave more time alone, while another family member may experience loneliness when not around others.[37]

Attachment theory focuses on the relationship between caregivers and care-seekers. Its basic assumption is that children are born with a need for intimate bonds that are met in different ways by the parents. The child develops patterns of attachment based on parental attention that will affect his or her way of interacting with other people. A child who receives immediate and effective responses to his or her needs will most likely feel self-confident and less likely to experience separation anxiety and grief.[38]

The **social exchange theory** argues that satisfaction in a relationship is enhanced when the rewards are greater than the costs. This means that if we invest more in a relationship than we receive from it, we are unhappy. The main assumption of the social exchange theory is that

<<< **The term** "bromance" has been coined to refer to nonsexual friendships between heterosexual men, characterized by intimacy and overt display of affection. **In the past few years, this kind of relationship has been the subject of many successful movies such as** *I Love You, Man*. **Do you think that overt affection between heterosexual men is more accepted today? Why or why not?**

INTIMACY AND GENDER

Gender is a very important variable in any aspect of a relationship, including intimacy. In our culture, for example, intimacy seems to have been ascribed mostly to women. Research seems to confirm that women tend to disclose more about themselves than men do.[42] Sociolinguist Deborah Tannen famously argued that women talk to create intimacy, whereas men talk to exchange information and assert their status.[43] Even recent studies among teens confirm these gender patterns. From a 2000 questionnaire given to 188 young people between the ages of 10 and 12, it emerged that, whereas girls tend to socialize more and develop more intimate friendships, boys focused more on physical activities (such as sports) in which intimacy skills were not required. In this sense, cross-sex friendships were deemed as fundamental to develop intimacy skills.[44]

every human interaction is actually an exchange of resources. Intimacy can therefore be seen as a resource that can be invested or received.[39]

The **circumplex model** suggests that balanced family systems are more functional than unbalanced ones. Researchers identify three characteristics of a balanced family system: family cohesion, flexibility, and communication. According to this model, balanced families share an emotional bond that brings them together (family cohesion), tolerate moderate changes in leadership and role relationships (flexibility), and are capable of communicating clearly and respectfully with one another (communication).[40]

Do's and Don'ts of Intimacy

Love

In literature and music, love has been described in countless metaphors

DON'T!

- Make emotional demands.
- Think your partner can read your mind.
- Resent lack of affection.
- Lose control when you are angry.
- Give up on your personal life.
- Run away from problems.
- Ask, "Do you love me?"
- Expect intimacy to come easily.

DO!

- Provide emotional support.
- Express your needs and expectations.
- Provide verbal and physical affection.
- Speak clearly about your feelings.
- Spend time together and alone.
- Learn to listen without judgment.
- Say, "I love you!"
- Accept that intimacy is built with time and effort.

Sources: Health Matters, "Intimacy and relationships."
http://www.taftcollege.edu/newTC/StudentServices/health/intimacy.htm

There are many ways to develop intimacy, as well as to prevent it. **How do you think negotiating intimacy can vary for family members, friends, and love partners?**

Culture and PDA

Public display of affection, or **PDA**, is viewed differently across different countries and regions of the world. For example, in some Mediterranean countries like Italy and Greece, and in Latin America, couples feel free to exchange kisses and hugs in the street, a practice that is less common in the United States. At the other end of the PDA spectrum is Jordan, where kissing in public is prohibited by Islamic law.

Without making generalizations, the truth is that the courtship script is more or less openly codified everywhere. In Mexico, for example, the practice of serenading is still common and taken seriously. On the other hand, Peruvians sometimes find the way young Americans dance in clubs a little too risqué.[41] As with other practices, even love and courtship around the world are going through a process of globalization, and in this sense, the United States still functions as a powerful exporter of behavior and style. Even so, knowing how affection is expressed in other cultures can be very useful in avoiding embarrassment while traveling.

comparing it to anything from a burning fire to a calm ocean. Love is something that is everywhere, yet hard to find. Love is full of sorrow, yet also full of joy. Love nourishes a relationship but can also lead to anxiety, emotional instability, and, in extreme cases, insanity. How is love viewed in marriage and in families? Professor Patricia Noller explained that love is usually characterized as emotional, cognitive, or behavioral.[45] The emotional component is exemplified by the enjoyment, caring, admiration, and respect we feel for someone we love, or by our passionate and sexual attraction toward that person. The cognitive component is exemplified by the expectations that we have for our relationships and by the decisions we make to actively commit to a love relationship. The behavioral component is exemplified by the behaviors we adopt to express our love, which can include verbal and physical affection, moral support, and even gifts and letters.[46]

THE INFLUENCE OF CULTURE AND GENDER

Many factors affect love, including culture and gender. A distinction has been made between individualistic and collectivistic countries. In individualistic countries such as the United States, love is mostly defined in terms of passion. In collectivistic countries like China, however, passion is looked down upon as disruptive of family and social order. For this reason, couples in individualistic countries tend to marry because they are in love, whereas couples in collectivistic countries often adopt practices such as arranged marriages.

The way people define and experience love is also affected by gender. Research shows an interesting difference between men and women, indicating that men love "passionately" and women love "compassionately."[48] This implies that women tend to look for more stable relationships, whereas men are mostly attracted by passionate love. In fact, it has been demonstrated that women fall out of love more easily than men.[49] According to researchers, the explanation might lie in the evolutionary process. As men were mostly preoccupied with finding a mate for procreation, women had to be more realistic and worry more about child care than passion.[50]

SEXUAL ORIENTATION, RACIAL DIFFERENCES, AND LOVE

Love is also influenced by **societal forces** such as shared values and beliefs, religious views, and, of course, prejudice. In this sense, same-sex couples and couples from racial minorities still suffer from discrimination in the United States.

According to estimates from 1994 and 2002, between 40 percent and 60 percent of gay men and between 45 percent and 80 percent of lesbians in the United States are in love relationships.[51] One difference between same-sex and heterosexual couples lies in social support, which is provided less to gay and lesbian couples (especially from family members). When compared with heterosexual couples with children, long-term relationships between same-sex couples seem also to end more frequently. Still, the percentage of long-term relationship among gay and lesbian couples is very high: About half of gay male couples and 40 percent of lesbian couples have been together for more than 10 years.[52]

Census data from 2000 show that African Americans tend to marry less and divorce more than Caucasian Americans.[53] A recent study suggests that there might be fundamental differences in the social, cultural, and

<<< **Passionate love has not always been a prerequisite of marriage. In fact, the ancient** Greeks considered passionate love a sort of insanity that should never affect marriage and family. **Medieval courtly love, with its image of love as a noble quest, was the first to establish the idealistic nature of passionate love.**[47] Why do you think passionate love has become so important to today's romantic relationships?

COMMITMENT is, according to Sternberg's triangular theory of love, the decision to love someone and maintain the love over time.

NONLOVE is a type of relationship where intimacy, passion, and commitment are absent.

LIKING is a type of relationship that is high in intimacy, but low in passion and commitment.

INFATUATION is a type of relationship that is high in passion and low in intimacy and commitment.

EMPTY LOVE is a type of relationship that is high in commitment, but low in intimacy and passion.

ROMANTIC LOVE is a type of relationship that is high in passion and intimacy, but low in commitment.

COMPANIONATE LOVE is a type of relationship that is high in intimacy and commitment, but low in passion; is defined by Sternberg as the love style focused more on feelings of trust and friendship than on sexual satisfaction.

FATUOUS LOVE is high in passion and commitment and low in intimacy.

CONSUMMATE LOVE is a type of relationship that is high in intimacy, passion, and commitment.

EROS is, according to John A. Lee, the love style characterized by overwhelming passion and deep emotional attachment.

LUDUS is, according to John A. Lee, the love style focused on love as play and on superficial or purely sexual relationships.

STORGE is, according to John A. Lee, the love style based on friendship and compatibility of values and beliefs.

PRAGMA is, according to John A. Lee, the love style combining ludus and storge and viewing love as realistic and pragmatic.

MANIA is, according to John A. Lee, the love style combining eros and ludus and characterized by possessiveness and jealousy.

AGAPE is, according to John A. Lee, the love style combining eros and storge and characterized by a mutual and altruistic interest in the partner's well-being.

historical contexts for the way African Americans view marriage and family. In fact, African American couples in the study reported more ineffective arguing, less satisfaction with the marriage (especially for women), and less social support than Caucasian couples. On the other hand, African-American couples appeared more assertive and less neurotic than their Caucasian counterparts, a resiliency that has been associated with successful unions.[54]

General Theories of Love

How do family scientists and sociologists interpret love? Here are a few perspectives:

THE TRIANGULAR THEORY OF LOVE

Psychologist Robert Sternberg postulated that love could be viewed as a triangle whose three sides are intimacy, passion, and **commitment**, and he called it Sternberg's triangular theory of love. Intimacy is emotional and includes feelings of affection, support, and closeness. Passion is motivational and includes sexual and romantic attraction and desire. Commitment is cognitive and refers to the conscious decision of loving someone and maintaining that love over time. Sternberg also identified eight fundamental types of love.[55] Think about which category Harry and Sally fit under when they first meet and at each of their subsequent meetings, especially when they first kiss.

Nonlove occurs when intimacy, passion, and commitment are absent, such as in a traditional hookup in which partners barely know each other and are not interested in continuing the relationship.

Liking is high in intimacy, but low in passion and commitment. This relationship usually describes friendships. If a friend is extremely missed or arouses passion, the relationship has become something more than just liking.

Infatuation is high in passion and low in intimacy and commitment. This can characterize secret crushes, like Charlie Brown's famous adoration for the Little Red-Haired Girl. Often, this type of love dwells on the surface and/or exists at a distance and involves idealization.

Empty love is high in commitment, but low in intimacy and passion. Empty love can characterize parents who are not in love anymore, but stay together for the sake of their children. In arranged marriages, empty love can be the first stage of the relationship.

Romantic love is high in passion and intimacy, but low in commitment. This often characterizes summer flings in which partners sincerely like each other, but know their relationship will end as soon as they return home. *Romeo and Juliet* may be seen as an example of romantic love because their feuding families prevent true commitment.

Companionate love is high in intimacy and commitment, but low in passion. This usually describes couples that have been together for a long time and appreciate communication and trust more than romantic and sexual attraction. The relationship between a parent and his or her child also may be described as companionate love.

Fatuous love is high in passion and commitment and low in intimacy. Relationships full of drama, breakups, and reconciliation are an example of this kind of love. One example is the French movie *Betty Blue* (1986), which shows an obsessive and self-destructive relationship between a writer and a wild, unpredictable woman.

Consummate love is high in intimacy, passion, and commitment. This is the goal for all romantic couples, but it is also difficult to maintain over time.

THE COLOR (STYLES) OF LOVE

Psychologist John Alan Lee outlined three different major love styles, and compared them to the primary colors. These styles are defined as **eros**, **ludus**, and **storge**.

Eros occurs when love is experienced like an overwhelming passion that can spark suddenly. It is intense and is exemplified by long conversations and physical affection. Ludus occurs when love is experienced as a game and is not taken seriously. Ludic lovers can have multiple partners at once, on the basis that people should simply have a good time. Storge refers to a love that is based on friendship; partners trust each other and share the same values, and sexual satisfaction comes in second.[56]

As in the color wheel, the three main types of love can overlap to create secondary types of love. **Pragma**, the combination of ludus and storge, describes love as realistic and pragmatic. Individuals look for the best possible partner for a rewarding life and are not too concerned about excitement. **Mania,** the combination of eros and ludus, sees love as a roller coaster. Individuals are possessive, jealous, and needy, and they expect things to go wrong. **Agape** is the sum of eros and storge. For agape, love is altruistic. Individuals are mostly concerned with the other's well-being and focus on the spiritual nature of their union.

THE PROTOTYPE APPROACH

Researchers have tried to create theories of love by gathering the opinions, beliefs, and feelings of people toward love. Called the "prototype approach," this method attempts to understand the prototypes that people use to identify love. Researchers asked a group of people to come up with as many types of love they could think of, and they then had another group rate the types of love for their closeness to their prototypical images of love. Maternal love was rated as the best example of prototypical love, followed by parental love, friendship, sisterly love, romantic love, and brotherly love. The lowest ratings were assigned to infatuation, sexual love, and puppy love.[57] A similar approach helped determine what people view as the main qualities of love, which emerged as trust, caring, honesty, friendship, respect, consideration for the other, loyalty, and commitment.[58]

Passionate Love vs. Companionate Love

Poet Elizabeth Barrett Browning wrote, "How do I love thee? Let me count the ways," and then gave a beautiful description of the type of love most coveted in literature: passionate love. **Passionate love** is overwhelming and encompassing, a true emotional storm that makes us feel alive like never before.

How does research view passionate love? Love theorists agree that passionate love usually starts suddenly and is characterized by **idealization**, or an unrealistic view of the loved one.[59] The emotions stirred by passionate love are intense, and lovers feel a strong physical attraction and a desire for exclusivity. When two people share passionate love, the result is a strong feeling of happiness and fulfillment for both. On the other hand, when love is unrequited, it causes feelings of anxiety, despair, and emptiness.[60] Overall, passionate love is usually associated with positive feelings by those who experience it. However, since passionate love makes one person the main focus of another person's life, negative emotions such as jealousy and obsession may also arise.[61] Research also confirms the fear that passionate love does not last long. If a couple is lucky, though, they might find that the decrease in passion does not correspond to the end of their love, but to the birth of a new type of relationship based on intimacy and commitment called companionate love.

Companionate love is based on feelings of trust and friendship and involves the enjoyment of each other's company in common activities and interests. Couples are more tolerant of each other's shortcomings and are willing to solve conflicts effectively. Couples at the beginning of a passionate relationship may shudder to hear this description, but in a survey of hundreds of couples married for more than 15 years, those couples explained that the secret to their long-lasting and happy unions was that they considered their partner their "best friend."[62] Indeed, research shows that, unlike passionate love, companionate love is always considered a positive experience.[63]

How to Increase Love in Your Relationships

In this chapter, we learned that there are different types of love depending mostly on the levels of passion, intimacy, and commitment. Ideally, a couple will want to progress smoothly from passionate love to companionate love. However, it is important to note that love is a mutable feeling that ebbs and flows, which means that relationships cannot be defined by one type of love only, and that during a relationship, couples embrace different kinds of love. The ideal of a mature and respectful love that always involves a sincere enjoyment of the other is often threatened by our quirks and immature behavior, or by external factors outside our control.

>>> **Joseph Lee postulated that there are** three types of love, just as there are three primary colors. These styles are called *eros*, *ludus*, and *storge*. The other types of love combine the different love styles. **Read the profiles for the six love styles and determine which one is yours. Then research an online questionnaire about the colors of love and complete it to find your love style.**

Whatever the problem might be, there are relationship rules that can help us make the right choices in terms of mate selection, learn something new about ourselves, and increase love in our relationships.

So, what are the rules of a loving relationship? A good relationship starts even before you meet "the right one." The truth is, people fall in love for many reasons, and not all of them are valid motives for committing to a long-term relationship. People think they are in love with someone because they feel a strong sexual attraction, or because they feel the other person would be a great mother, father, breadwinner, and so on. So, evaluate partners for their true personality, their generosity of spirit, and their compatibility with your ideals and core beliefs. Once you start a relationship, you should not lose your reason in the throes of romantic passion. Start an open conversation about your ideas of relationships. If you abhor marriage, crave a large family, or like spending weekends playing videogames on your own, then you should definitely inform your partner about these preferences before you decide to move in together.

In whatever relationship you might have, remember that you have to get to know your own needs and express them clearly. Then listen attentively to what your partner has to say and accept and even treasure your differences. Act as a team, so that similarities and differences become strengths. When you are confused, disappointed, or angry, speak up and be ready to negotiate. If you realize you're wrong, don't be afraid to apologize. Enjoy time spent together and maintain closeness. In all this, maintain your individuality, your self-respect, and your self-esteem. Finally, view your relationship as a living thing with its ups and downs and its necessity for change. If you allow your relationship to change and evolve, you will evolve, too.

Love Styles

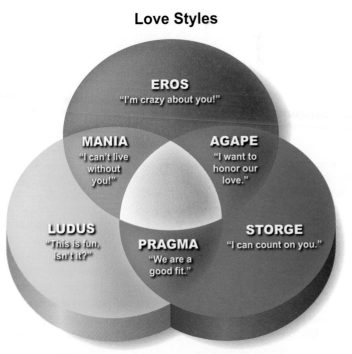

EROS
"I'm crazy about you!"

MANIA
"I can't live without you!"

AGAPE
"I want to honor our love."

LUDUS
"This is fun, isn't it?"

PRAGMA
"We are a good fit."

STORGE
"I can count on you."

10 Most Romantic Movie Lines EVER

1 "We'll always have Paris."
Casablanca (1942)

2 "I came here tonight because when you realize you want to spend the rest of your life with somebody, you want the rest of your life to start as soon as possible."
When Harry Met Sally (1989)

3 "Thank you for coming back to me."
Brief Encounter (1945)

4 "If there's any kind of magic in this world it must be in the attempt of understanding someone sharing something. I know, it's almost impossible to succeed but who cares really? The answer must be in the attempt."
Before Sunrise (1995)

5 "That's why they call them crushes. If they were easy, they'd call them something else."
Sixteen Candles (1984)

6 "You want the moon? Just say the word, and I'll throw a lasso around it and pull it down."
It's a Wonderful Life (1946)

7 "You are what you love, not what loves you. That's what I decided a long time ago."
Adaptation (2002)

8 "Sex alleviates tension and love causes it."
A Midsummer Night's Sex Comedy (1982)

9 "I was born when she kissed me. I died when she left me. I lived a few weeks while she loved me."
In a Lonely Place (1950)

10 "Look, in my opinion, the best thing you can do is find a person who loves you for exactly what you are. Good mood, bad mood, ugly, pretty, handsome, what have you, the right person is still going to think the sun shines out your ass. That's the kind of person that's worth sticking with."
Juno (2007)

Sources:
Casablanca: http://www.imdb.com/title/tt0034583/quotes; *When Harry Met Sally:* http://www.imdb.com/title/tt0098635/quotes;
Brief Encounter: http://www.imdb.com/title/tt0037558/quotes; *Before Sunrise:* http://www.imdb.com/title/tt0112471/quotes;
Sixteen Candles: http://www.imdb.com/title/tt0088128/quotes; *It's a Wonderful Life:* http://www.imdb.com/title/tt0038650/quotes;
Adaptation: http://www.imdb.com/title/tt0268126/quotes; *A Midsummer Night's Sex Comedy:* http://www.imdb.com/title/tt0084329/quotes;
In a Lonely Place: http://www.imdb.com/title/tt0268126/quotes; *Juno:* http://www.imdb.com/title/tt0467406/quotes

Movies have always been in love with. . . love. **Here is a list of the 10 most romantic move lines ever. What types of love do you think they describe?**

MAKE CONNECTIONS

Building Blocks of Successful Relationships

In this chapter, we analyzed how friendship, affection, intimacy, and love can be viewed as the building blocks of successful interpersonal relationships. In Chapter 14, we will discuss how these factors may also weaken and dissolve a relationship.

As you learned earlier in this chapter, researchers have identified many types of love. Each type has a different motivation and leads to a different outcome in the relationship. Researchers have also concluded that it is important in relationships to demonstrate both physical and verbal affection. This brings us to the content we discussed in Chapter 2, where physical and verbal affection were examined as factors that can strengthen families and marriages.

>>> ACTIVITIES

1. Conduct a survey among your friends to learn how many of them have experienced someone saying "I love you" just to have a sexual relationship.

2. How would you describe the environment you grew up in regarding verbal and physical affection? How did your experience growing up compare to that of your friends?

think marriages and families: WHAT ARE THE THEORIES BEHIND LOVE IN MARRIAGES AND FAMILIES?

Functionalism

Getting through a rejection, a breakup, or even a divorce is rightly considered a painful and difficult experience. As people struggle to rebuild their lives without their loved ones, they might wonder, "Why do we need love after all?" According to the functional theory, all patterns of human behavior have a specific function that aims at the preservation of the social order. From a functionalist point of view, the nuclear family constituted by parents and their children has the main function of preserving society by transmitting norms and **values** to future generations. Norms and values are basic concepts of functional theory. According to functionalists, norms guide and regulate human behavior in a society, whereas values motivate individuals to adhere to the norms. How does this apply to love? One norm in our society is that an individual cannot be married to more than one person at a time. From a functionalist point of view, monogamy contributes to the social order by providing a stable home in which parents are focused on the economical and emotional well-being of their children. Monogamy, though, has also become a value for most relationships, so much so that extramarital affairs are almost universally considered causes of distress and a valid reason for obtaining a legal separation.

In time, a society's norms and values can change. The idea that marriage should be a fulfilling experience for both spouses is a fairly recent one. Ana Carolina Fowler, at Tufts University, explains that in the first half of the 20th century the main function of marriage was to provide economic stability to the woman and to provide the man with someone to take care of the house and the children.[64] Gender roles today have changed significantly, and so have the norms and values affecting marriage. For instance, spouses today often share the economic responsibility and chores equally. Women who assume the role of breadwinner are no longer uncommon. There are also more partners who get married even if they do not want to have children, countering the traditional view that the main function of marriage is procreation.

Marriage today has become more a matter of personal fulfillment than of preservation of societal order. As emotional fulfillment and personal development have become values in our society, the norms concerning marriage will need to change accordingly. The debate about same-sex marriage is a great example of changing norms and values. Opponents of same-sex marriage argue that marriage's goal is procreation, so same-sex couples should not be entitled to it. On the other hand, supporters believe that two people in love—no matter their sexual orientation or their attitude toward procreation—should be able to marry and make joint decisions about their inheritance, health, and benefits.

Conflict Theory

Conflict theory is based on the assumption that change is always taking place, and that change is based on the struggle or conflict between different and competing interests. Conflict theory originated as a means to explain the struggle between classes at the beginning of the 19th century, but it has since been used to explain patterns of power imbalance within the family.

> **VALUES** are, according to functionalists, the cultural beliefs that motivate individuals to adhere to norms.
>
> **RITUALS** are prescribed sets of actions often connoted by symbolic value and usually adopted by religions and social groups through history.

Conflict theorists argue that love within the couple or within the family is influenced by an individual or group of individuals having more power than the other or others. A frequent instance of conflict is the one between parents and their teenaged children. Society allows more power and resources to parents (for example, money, freedom, physical power), but that is challenged by teens in their desire for more independence. Sometimes, conflicts arise from the fact that love is viewed as a limited resource. A husband might complain that the wife works too much and never spends time with him, finally accusing her of loving the job more than she loves him. This is a classic example of marital conflict, and research shows that the person with less personal investment in a relationship is the one who has more power.[65]

Conflict in marriages and families is not necessarily negative. When met by a willingness to listen and negotiate, conflict can help a relationship grow and deepen the love individuals feel for each other.

Symbolic Interactionism

"Do you want to see the rock?" a young woman asks her co-workers. Her boyfriend proposed the night before and gave her an engagement ring. Although the couple has been talking about marriage for a long time, the diamond ring seems to make it real. How is it possible for a cold little stone to carry so much meaning?

The basic assumption of symbolic interaction theory is that people assign meanings to elements of their environment. Interpretations of symbols are mostly transmitted across generations through family and society. In general, though, every time people come in contact with different things and experiences, they assign a symbolic meaning to them. In turn, people's interpretations of symbols influence their thoughts, behaviors, and expectations.

How does this relate to couples and family when discussing love? Couples and family use symbols to represent their idea of love. The engagement ring is a common symbol of committed love in society. For a man, though, giving his fiancée an engagement ring that belonged to his family can have additional meaning. Parents transmit their interpretation of the idea of love to their children by talking to them about love and by giving them physical and verbal affection. Love is also taught through **rituals**, which are very important objects of study for social interactionists. Consider a traditional birthday party for a young boy. Parents might be expected to provide a cake, a gift, and a card, and possibly to organize a birthday party. If one of the elements were missing, a child might feel hurt and think his parents do not care about him.

WRAP YOUR MIND AROUND THE THEORY

Functionalists believe that society survives through norms and values. **How do you think the norms and values concerning marriage will change in the upcoming decades?**

FUNCTIONALISM

Functional theory posits that all patterns of human behavior are functional to society's preservation and well-being. According to functionalists, the nuclear family is the most important social institution, because it transmits norms and values to future generations. Norms dictate how people should behave. In terms of love, for example, parents who mistreat and abuse their children can be prosecuted by law and even have their children taken away from them. The corresponding value is the agreed-upon need for a child to receive verbal and physical affection from the parents. In time, norms and values that characterize a society might change. In fact, the modern idea of love and marriage is very different from what it was even 60 years ago. Today, spouses are entitled to the same level of personal fulfillment, whereas in the past women had to adhere to a more restrictive gender role that often sacrificed their emotional satisfaction. On a larger level, society is struggling today to come to terms with changing values. The debate about same-sex marriage is an example.

CONFLICT THEORY

Conflict theorists believe that society is composed of groups that are in competition over resources. This theory is also applied to marriages and families, in which individuals may compete for resources such as money, time, affection, power, and so on. In the past, conflict within a couple could be exacerbated by more traditional gender roles that kept the woman in a subordinate position and allowed her less decision-making power within the family. Conflict theory can also be applied to love. It has been proven that the partner who feels less involved in a relationship holds more power. In this sense, love has become a resource. Conflict theory presupposes that conflict is normal. In fact, conflict can even be positive if it leads to more equality. Within marriage and family, conflict can be addressed through compromise and negotiation and can cause relationships to deepen and strengthen.

HOW DOES LOVE AFFECT MARRIAGE, FAMILY, AND SOCIETY?

SYMBOLIC INTERACTIONISM

Symbolic interactionists study the meanings that people assign to elements in their environment and to their interactions with others. Children learn to define love from their interactions with their parents. As they grow up, their interpretation of love changes according to the general interpretation given by society and by their interactions with other people. In this sense, the meaning of love is socially constructed. Rituals are especially rich in symbolic meaning. Engagements, weddings, baby showers, birthday parties, and such may communicate love in different ways. Another important element for social interactionists is the role that people assume in their interactions. Men, for example, are often required to "make the first move" to show their interest in a woman. Although the attitude toward courtship has changed significantly in recent times, a woman might find it easier and more socially acceptable to adopt a more passive role at the start of a relationship.

Conflict theorists argue that **family members can compete over resources. Consider a couple of siblings.** How can differing levels of intimacy and self-disclosure create conflict?

According to the symbolic interaction theory, **people attribute meaning to social interactions.** How do you think this relates to differing attitudes toward public displays of affection around the world?

discover marriages and families in action:
HOW CAN COUPLES ADDRESS INTIMACY PROBLEMS?

During the first period of a relationship, partners are sincerely curious about each other both emotionally and physically, and they do all they can to please and impress each other. As the couple settles into a long-term relationship, the initial energy fades and the two are left wondering how to maintain passion and intimacy.

Psychologists and sociologists agree that intimacy is the most important element in a successful relationship. However, many factors might hinder intimacy. People have a hard time expressing their emotions and may think giving up is easier than trying to communicate more effectively. Some people have developed issues of trust after failed relationships. Most couples, though, just let stress replace the moments of intimacy they initially shared.

The good news is that couples can learn to get around these hurdles. Through counseling, couples can learn how to communicate and correctly interpret the partner's desires and expectations. Partners should let go of romantic myths and misconceptions that only lead to disappointment.

Partners should try to rediscover physical affection in the form of kisses, hugs, and sexual intimacy. Couples can break routines, insert more humor in the relationship, and set aside time free from work or children. Couples are also encouraged to avoid making comparisons[66] and to accept the idea that their partner will make mistakes. Couples must realize that intimacy requires constant tending and attention. The magic of new love may be gone, but that does not mean that the future cannot be as intense and emotionally rewarding.

ACTIVITIES

1. Research some organizations and groups that offer intimacy retreats for couples. What suggestions do they have for couples who want to increase intimacy in their relationships? Can an individual learn intimacy skills without involving the partner or spouse?
2. Interview a couple that has been happily married for several years. Ask them to talk about what factors have contributed to their marital success. Be sure to question them on factors such as friendship, affection, love, and intimacy.

From Classroom to Community | Counseling for Young Spouses

Shelley is working on a bachelor's degree in mental health, and for the past year she has been volunteering at her city's youth and family counseling service. She mostly counsels young couples with children, teaching them intimacy and affection skills.

"When I first started working at the Youth & Family Center, I worked with a more experienced counselor and observed her during her sessions. Given my age, my superiors wanted to train me to work with younger couples.

"I feel I can relate to younger couples because I know the pressures they face. Many of them are doing their best to make their relationship work and be good parents, but they also resent the fact that their "fun life" has ended so abruptly. It is my job to help them redefine their priorities, but also to help them see the amazing rewards a family can offer.

"Most young couples have not been through long-term relationships before the marriage, and they never learned how to argue effectively. I teach them communication skills to help them understand what they really want and to express it clearly and without resentment. I also teach them how to listen. That is fundamental.

"I also teach parents techniques to help them be more assertive, but also more affectionate, toward their children. Younger parents may feel more overwhelmed at first, but they actually have a natural energy and capacity for connecting with the children.

"I have seen many positive results from my counseling, and I am very proud of my job. Most people think that love and intimacy should come naturally, but it takes some effort and sometimes the help of someone outside the relationship."

ACTIVITIES

1. Develop a short questionnaire which measures how often students have been "in love" with someone else. Pass it out to the class and then report your findings to the class.
2. Get together with a group of friends and acquaintances. Discuss the similarities and differences between love relationships and friendship relationships.

CHAPTER

05

HOW DO FRIENDSHIP, AFFECTION, LOVE, AND INTIMACY AFFECT MARRIAGES AND FAMILIES? 81

Friendship and love are affected by different patterns of intimacy, autonomy, and affection that vary across individuals, genders, life stages, and cultures. With regard to marriages and families, theorists have identified different types of love based on the interplay of intimacy, passion, and commitment.

WHAT ARE THE THEORIES BEHIND LOVE IN MARRIAGES AND FAMILIES? 91

Social exchange theorists analyze the way marriage and family help establish norms and values in a healthy society. Conflict theorists examine the imbalances of power in marriage and families due to competition over resources. Symbolic interactionists analyze the symbols associated with love, intimacy, and affection and how people interpret and react to them.

HOW CAN COUPLES ADDRESS INTIMACY PROBLEMS? 93

In a marriage, communication barriers and issues of trust can diminish the intimacy between spouses. Intimacy can be rebuilt by abandoning unrealistic expectations and creating time to be together without distractions or resentment.

Theory

FUNCTIONALISM 91
- the nuclear family transmits norms and values to future generations
- norms and values can change with time

CONFLICT THEORY 91
- spouses and family members compete over resources such as love, affection, and intimacy
- conflict is inescapable and can actually represent a chance of growth when resolved effectively

SYMBOLIC INTERACTIONISM 91
- people give meaning to their own behavior and the behavior of others
- the meaning of "love" is a social construction

Key Terms

dyadic relationship is a relationship between two people, that involves some kind of closeness and mutual affection 81

responsiveness is the affectionate and supportive understanding of another's needs, values, and desires 81

capitalization is being sincerely happy about a friend's well-being and success 81

social comparison refers to the habit of evaluating one's skills and qualities by comparing them to others 81

social support is the emotional, verbal, and material help received by others 81

dyadic withdrawal is the diminished involvement in outside social networks by a couple in a romantic relationship 82

hooking up is casual sexual activity with no strings attached between heterosexual people who are strangers or brief acquaintances 83

neuroticism is a personality trait characterized by negative emotions such as depression, anxiety,

anger, embarrassment, vulnerability, and impulsiveness 83

sexual double standard is the unwritten code of behavior that allows greater sexual freedom to men than to women 84

physical affection is the act of displaying affection through kisses, hugs, and physical contact 84

verbal affection is the act of displaying affection through compliments, assertions of love, laughter, etc. 84

affection exchange theory is the theory postulating that affectionate communication is an adaptive behavior that is instrumental to human survival and procreation 84

homophobia is the irrational fear of homosexuals 85

intimacy is a feeling of closeness in meaningful relationships characterized by sharing of personal experiences, thoughts, and emotions 85

autonomy is a state of independence and self-determination 85

dialectic approach is the relationship model according to which relationships are characterized by an ongoing tension between intimacy and autonomy 85

attachment theory is the theory that states that people's patterns of attachment are shaped by the intimate bonding they shared with their caregivers during infancy 85

social exchange theory is the sociological perspective arguing that satisfaction in a relationship is enhanced when the rewards are greater than the costs 85

circumplex model is a graphic model identifying three characteristics of a balanced family system: family cohesion, flexibility, and communication 86

public display of affection (PDA) is the physical show of affection in the view of other people 87

(continued)

societal forces are influences coming from or relating to society *87*

commitment is, according to Sternberg's triangular theory of love, the decision to love someone and maintain the love over time *88*

nonlove is a type of relationship where intimacy, passion, and commitment are absent *88*

liking is a type of relationship that is high in intimacy, but low in passion and commitment *88*

infatuation is a type of relationship that is high in passion and low in intimacy and commitment *88*

empty love is a type of relationship that is high in commitment, but low in intimacy and passion *88*

romantic love is a type of relationship that is high in passion and intimacy, but low in commitment *88*

companionate love is a type of relationship that is high in intimacy and commitment, but low

in passion; is defined by Sternberg as the love style focused more on feelings of trust and friendship than on sexual satisfaction *88*

fatuous love is high in passion and commitment and low in intimacy *88*

consummate love is a type of relationship that is high in intimacy, passion, and commitment *88*

eros is, according to John A. Lee, the love style characterized by overwhelming passion and deep emotional attachment *88*

ludus is, according to John A. Lee, the love style focused on love as play and on superficial or purely sexual relationships *88*

storge is, according to John A. Lee, the love style based on friendship and compatibility of values and beliefs *88*

pragma is, according to John A. Lee, the love style combining ludus and storge and viewing love as realistic and pragmatic *88*

mania is, according to John A. Lee, the love style combining eros and ludus and characterized by possessiveness and jealousy *88*

agape is, according to John A. Lee, the love style combining eros and storge and characterized by a mutual and altruistic interest in the partner's well-being *88*

passionate love is the love style characterized by overwhelming passion and emotional attachment that often characterizes the first stage of a romantic relationship *89*

idealization is an unrealistic view of the loved one *89*

values are, according to functionalists, the cultural beliefs that motivate individuals to adhere to norms *91*

rituals are prescribed sets of actions often connoted by symbolic value and usually adopted by religions and social groups through history *91*

Sample Test Questions

MULTIPLE CHOICE

These multiple-choice questions are similar to those found in the test bank that accompanies this textbook.

1. Why is social comparison more problematic for male friendships than female friendships?
   a. Male friendships tend to be less responsive.
   b. Male friendships tend to be less affectionate.
   c. Male friendships tend to be more superficial.
   d. Male friendships tend to be more competitive.

2. How does dyadic withdrawal affect young adults in relation to friendship?
   a. Young adults often change their social networks.
   b. Young adults focus more on exclusive friendships.
   c. Young adults focus more on meaningful friendships.
   d. Young adults look for friends with differing views and beliefs.

3. Which of the following is a recognized benefit of cross-sex friendships?
   a. Decreased casual sexual activity
   b. More equality between gender roles
   c. Less disclosure of personal information
   d. Increased satisfaction in same-sex relationships

4. Which of the following love styles MOST describes a traditional hookup?
   a. Nonlove
   b. Liking
   c. Infatuation
   d. Empty love

5. According to researchers, what is the MOST LIKELY reason women are more pragmatic than men in love?
   a. Women have overcome traditional gender roles.
   b. Women are more able to disclose their true feelings.
   c. Women are more interested in developing intimacy.
   d. Women learned to focus on childrearing and practical matters.

ESSAY

1. Discuss how intimacy in friendship is handled throughout the life cycle.

2. Discuss how autonomy and intimacy are balanced in the love styles defined by Sternberg.

3. How does the attachment theory relate to the display of verbal and physical affection in adulthood?

4. What are the reasons behind the lack of social support by families to same-sex couples?

5. Discuss the psychological effects of hookups on men and women.

WHERE TO START YOUR RESEARCH PAPER

For information about childhood and adolescent development, go to http://extension.oregonstate.edu/catalog/html/ec/ec1527/

For more information about psychological stages from adolescence to adulthood, go to http://www.psypress.com/pip/resources/chapters/PIP_adolescence.pdf

For more information about Sternberg's triangular theory of love, go to http://www.hofstra.edu/Community/slzctr/stdcsl/stdcsl_triangular.html

For an article about intimacy in relationships, go to http://www.psychologytoday.com/articles/199309/intimacy-the-art-relationships

For an overview of the attachment theory, go to http://www.personalityresearch.org/attachment.html

For an overview of the attachment theory in relation to personality development, go to http://www.personalityresearch.org/papers/cardillo.html

To find out more about same-sex families and relationships, go to http://www.apa.org/ppo/issues/lgbfamilybrf604.html

For more information about family response to homosexuality, go to http://community.pflag.org/Page.aspx?pid=194&srcid=-2

For more information about hookup culture, go to http://www.iwf.org/campus/show/20789.html

For a study on demographic and psychological correlates of hooking up, go to http://www.chs.fsu.edu/;ffincham/papers/ASB%20Owen%20et%20al.pdf

Answers: 1. d; 2. c; 3. b; 4. a; 5. d

Remember to check www.thethinkspot.com **for additional information, downloadable flashcards, and other helpful resources.**

In the

2008 movie *Never Forever*, Sophie, a beautiful and elegant Caucasian housewife, is married to Andrew, a very successful man of Korean descent. The two live in a beautiful house in New York. Despite the glamorous appearance of their lives and their love for each other, Andrew and Sophie are far from happy. They have been trying unsuccessfully to have a baby, but Andrew is infertile. This has caused Andrew to fall into a deep depression that culminates with a failed attempt to take his own life.

Sophie decides to address the situation and goes to a fertility clinic. She asks to be impregnated by a Korean donor, but the doctor tells her they need to have her husband's consent. Sophie is distraught: She knows that Andrew would never accept raising a child who is not his own. As Sophie is about to leave the clinic, she sees Jihah, a young Korean immigrant who is being turned down for sperm donation because he is undocumented. Jihah looks a lot like Andrew, and Sophie begins to wonder if she might have found a way to save her marriage. She follows Jihah to his apartment and proposes an arrangement in which she will pay him to sleep with her until she gets pregnant. Jihah is both surprised and conflicted by the offer, but eventually accepts.

During their first meetings, Sophie and Jihah do not speak a word to each other, and the sexual act is cold and mechanical. As the two get to know more about each other's lives and troubles, romance sparks between them, resulting in sexual encounters that are more intimate and passionate. When Sophie finally becomes pregnant, she announces it to her ecstatic husband and in-laws, who celebrate the news as a miracle. Sophie and Jihah agree not to see each other anymore, but, as weeks pass, they realize their bond cannot be so easily broken. Sophie and Jihah start meeting again, this time as lovers.

Andrew, in the meantime, has found new energy thanks to Sophie's pregnancy, and he becomes more and more affectionate toward her. He is crushed when the affair is eventually revealed. Andrew confronts Sophie as she returns from her latest tryst with Jihah. He states that he is willing to forgive her and start rebuilding their relationship, but he insists that Sophie must get an abortion. Sophie refuses, and the confrontation turns physical when Andrew tries, unsuccessfully, to throw Sophie down the stairs to cause a miscarriage. Their relationship is clearly over.

In the last scene of the movie, Sophie is seen playing on the beach with her son, now a toddler. She is happy—and pregnant again. Is Sophie with Jihah, expecting their second baby? The movie doesn't tell, but Sophie has clearly found her own independence and happiness.

SEX AND FERTILITY

CHAPTER 06

What lessons can we learn **from *Never Forever*?** **The movie engages many aspects of marriage:** the pressures of the longing to have a child, **the frustration over lack of communication,** and the tension created by an extramarital affair.

In the movie, Sophie has to bear the disapproval of her husband's Catholic family, who believe she could easily get pregnant if only she prayed enough. What roles do religion, race, and social conflict play on sexual norms and extramarital sex?

A few days ago I was talking with an old friend of mine. He is a divorced man in his mid-40s, and he raised his two children practically by himself. He asked me how I was coming along with the book you are reading, and when he found out about the content of this chapter, he offered to share his own experience with me. He told me that when he was getting a divorce he was required to explain his reasons to his attorney. He remembered saying, "When one spouse is having sex more often than the other, then it's time to get a divorce." He told me he can laugh about his comment now, but the entire situation was really painful for him.

Extramarital affairs affect many marriages and families. Over the years, the national press has been busy covering the infidelity of politicians, from the Clinton scandal to Governor Mark Sanford. The press and the public have been almost unanimous in their condemnation of extramarital affairs, but is judgment really that simple? In this chapter, we will analyze sexual norms and behaviors in our society, the theories behind sex and reproduction, and the issue of sex trafficking.

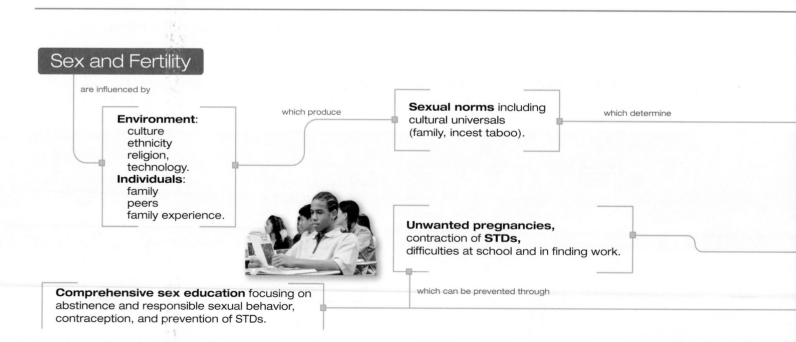

Sex and Fertility

are influenced by

Environment:
  culture
  ethnicity
  religion,
  technology.
Individuals:
  family
  peers
  family experience.

which produce

Sexual norms including cultural universals (family, incest taboo).

which determine

Unwanted pregnancies, contraction of **STDs,** difficulties at school and in finding work.

which can be prevented through

Comprehensive sex education focusing on abstinence and responsible sexual behavior, contraception, and prevention of STDs.

get the topic: HOW DO SEXUAL BEHAVIOR AND FERTILITY AFFECT MARRIAGES AND FAMILIES?

Sexual Norms

What are your thoughts on premarital sex? Extramarital affairs? Casual sex? Sex education in schools? Opinions on sexual behavior can vary from person to person and are also influenced by the society an individual lives in. The rules and expectations by which society channels and regulates the sexual behavior of its members are called **sexual norms**. Specifically, **proscriptive norms** tell what people should not do, such as avoiding unprotected, casual sex; whereas **prescriptive norms** establish what people should do, such as instituting sex education programs for teens.

Sexual behavior is also affected by **cultural universals**, or traits that are common in every known culture. Anthropologist George Murdock compared several hundred cultures to identify common patterns. One of the most common cultural universals is the family, whose function is to control sexual reproduction and protect and nurture children.[1] An important cultural universal concerning sexual behavior is the **incest taboo**, or the cultural restriction against sexual activity between close relatives.

SEXUAL NORMS are the rules and expectations by which society channels and regulates the sexual behavior of its members.

PROSCRIPTIVE NORMS are the rules that proscribe or prohibit certain behaviors.

PRESCRIPTIVE NORMS are the rules that recommend or require certain behaviors.

CULTURAL UNIVERSALS are the patterns or traits that are common to all human cultures.

INCEST TABOO is the cultural restriction against sexual activity between close relatives.

<<< **The hit series** *Sex and the City* **presented** women in their mid-30s **who were** sexually assertive and talked about sexuality very explicitly. **One cultural universal is that of gender roles.** How do you think the media portray gender roles when representing sex and sexuality?

Sexual behaviors and attitudes:
level of permissiveness
sexual double standard
etc.

exemplified by

Extramarital sex
Practiced by about half of people in relationships, but almost universally condemned.

and by

Teenage sex
Increasing number of sexually active teens; pregnancy rates among the highest in the Western world.

which can lead to

Effective family communication
that is open and respectful.

Sexual Norms and Cultural Universals

Sexual norms exist in every culture and can change over time. Looking back to Chapter 1, you can see how sexual norms have changed over time in the United States by focusing on current trends in families.

As you will learn in this chapter, issues associated with sex and fertility affect marriage and families greatly. Looking ahead to Chapter 9, you will see how variations within the family have also been affected by changing fertility rates and sexual norms.

>>> ACTIVITY Make a list of sexual norms that you think exist for college students. Then compare this list of sexual norms with sexual norms for college students in the 1950s, as described at this URL: http://www.theatlantic.com/doc/print/195711/sex-college

---

GENITAL INFIBULATION is the ritual cutting of the inner labia and surgical closure of the outer labia.

CONTRACEPTION is the use of devices or procedures to prevent pregnancy.

SEXUAL NORMS IN AMERICA

Sex and the City, Gossip Girl, Californication, Swingtown, Secret Diary of a Call Girl, Beverly Hills 90210, Desperate Housewives . . . What do they have in common? They are all successful TV shows about people leading extremely adventurous sex lives. Of course, no one can mistake those TV lives with the realities of everyday people, but how do these shows reflect the attitudes of Americans toward sex? Do we really want our lives to be as wild as in those seen on TV?

In 1997, the Gallup Poll published the result of a survey on Americans' attitudes toward sexual norms, and they were much tamer than television would lead us to expect.[2] In fact, it emerged that 39 percent of Americans over 18 considered premarital sex "wrong," although that percentage falls by almost half for Americans between 18 and 29. Almost half of participants stated that having a baby out of wedlock is wrong. This result, too, varies with age—only 39 percent of younger people share this opinion. Extramarital affairs are condemned by 79 percent of Americans—with no real difference of opinion between younger and older generations.

INFLUENCES ON SEXUALITY

What factors affect an individual's sexuality? Not surprisingly, family is very important, especially in terms of the level of self-esteem attained during the developmental years. People with higher self-esteem are most likely to be satisfied with their sexuality. Karraker and Grochowski explain that an individual's self-esteem is shaped by the love and acceptance he or she receives within the family, and that family communication should include age-appropriate talks about sex.[3]

Culture, in the form of tradition, ritual, and religion, also affects sexual norms. For example, cultures can differ in degrees of permissiveness. A study showed that Russians and Japanese are less tolerant than Americans of sexual activity between individuals who are not yet seriously committed to each other.[4] The fairly widespread practice of male circumcision for newborns is an example of how religious beliefs can regulate behavior in sexual health. For example, the Jewish faith includes male circumcision as evidence of a covenant with God. Although the practice has roots in religion, we now know of many positive reasons for circumcision, including a decreased risk of STDs.[5] For

females, female genital mutilation and **genital infibulation** (the ritual cutting of the inner labia and surgical closure of the outer labia, strongly opposed as a human rights' violation) are carried out in 28 African countries.[6] In the United States, differences in sexual norms have also been observed in different ethnicities. Studies report that Mexican American men are less likely to use **contraception**, mostly because of the Catholic Church's condemnation of birth control.[7]

SEXUAL ATTITUDES AND PREFERENCES

When a man and a woman have had many sexual partners, do people judge them in the same way? The answer is no, and research seems to confirm it. The sexual double standard that views men as "bros" and women as "hoes" when they have had multiple sexual partners is much weaker than it was decades ago, but still exists to some degree today.[8] Moreover, studies affirm that a woman who has contracted a sexually transmitted disease is more likely to be judged more negatively than a man in the same situation.

What about same-sex relationships? Same-sex marriage in the United States is still a divisive issue, and research shows that people's attitudes about it depend mostly on the origin that people attribute to homosexuality. When people consider homosexuality a choice rather than an inborn orientation, they are more likely to condemn it as "not acceptable."[9] However, it is very likely that Americans' attitudes are going to become more tolerant with time. In the 1997 Gallup polls, 59 percent of interviewees considered homosexuality morally unacceptable,[10] but this figure has decreased by about 10 percent in more recent years.[11]

Research has also investigated people's preferences about sex. A study of heterosexual couples showed that more than 90 percent of respondents prefer vaginal intercourse to other sexual activities. Watching the partner undress came in second with 50% of the preferences, followed by receiving and giving oral sex. Less data are available on homosexual couples, although national surveys reveal that both homosexual men and women consider hugging and caressing among their favorite bedroom activities.[12]

Sexual Behavior and Satisfaction

As much as we want to imagine our parents and grandparents as asexual beings who are solely and completely dedicated to our education and happiness, surveys show that older generations' lives are far from sexless. In 2004, AARP conducted a survey of almost 1,700 adults aged 45 and older, revealing that 66 percent of the men and 48 percent of the women consider a satisfying sexual relationship necessary for good quality of life.[13] About half of respondents with partners reported having sex at least once a week, although the number dropped to 34 percent for individuals over 70.[14]

Overall, studies associate marital sexuality with marital satisfaction. During the marriage and family cycle, sexual activity is shown to decrease with the arrival of children and then increase again when the children become adults and leave the house.[15] However, research shows that 49 percent of men and 54 percent of women in married couples are pleased with their sex lives, even if they have sex less than once a week.[16] Karraker even notes that married couples are more likely to have an orgasm during sex.[17] As for homosexual couples, researchers found that male gay couples tend to be more sexually active than lesbian couples in the first years of the relationships. As sexual activity diminishes with time, gay couples become more tolerant of sexual activity outside the relationship.[18]

SEXUAL SATISFACTION IN MARRIAGE AND LONG-TERM RELATIONSHIPS

"Did you like it?" Movies often make fun of this question, which many heterosexual men ask their partners at the end of their sexual encounters. Although in the movies these encounters are often between unmarried partners, the question of sexual satisfaction continues after a couple marries. A 2000 study of over 600 married women analyzed the predictors of women's **sexual satisfaction**.[19] It emerged that sexual satisfaction is directly related to women's overall satisfaction with the union and with nonsexual aspects of the relationship, such as emotional closeness and mutual respect. It could be that Sophie, in *Never Forever*, was not satisfied sexually because Andrew was distant and depressed after he learned of his infertility. She could not connect with her husband on an emotional level. Sexual satisfaction is also affected by the consistency and frequency of orgasms for both the spouses, and by noncoital sexual activities such as oral sex, anal sex, and masturbation. The study revealed that one's perception of God's view on sexuality (for example, sex for procreation or for enjoyment) is also associated with sexual satisfaction.[20] Other studies have also pointed out that sexual inactivity—often associated with age, the presence of children, or health problems—is a predictor of marital dissatisfaction.[21]

WHAT INCREASES SEXUAL SATISFACTION?

Just by looking at the number of self-help books and magazines promising to reveal the secrets to an explosive sex life, one could think that Americans are either inescapably sex-crazed or tragically incompetent

> **SEXUAL SATISFACTION** is an individual's positive feelings toward sexuality.
> **BODY IMAGE** is an individual's perception of his or her own physical appearance.
> **ADONIS COMPLEX** is a man's obsessive preoccupation that he is not muscular enough.

in bed. Despite the information overload, researchers agree that, for the most part, sexual enjoyment is a very personal sentiment related to an individual's experience and expectations,[22] his or her social and cultural background, and even biological factors.[23] Still, a 1997 study identified some general contributors to sexual satisfaction.[24] The study showed that sexual satisfaction is associated with young age, a nonreligious childhood (possibly because of many religions' condemnation of sexuality for enjoyment and not for procreation), and sexual confidence. Frequent sexual activity and frequent orgasms also help determine a person's satisfaction with his or her sex life.

The same study identified gender differences and pointed out that women are less likely to be satisfied with their sex lives. This is attributed to the fact that women generally start having sex later than men, hold more conservative attitudes toward sex, and usually have less sexual confidence. However, the ongoing emancipation of women even in the most private spheres of their lives makes one think that women will soon report the same level of sexual satisfaction and assertiveness as men.[25]

MIRROR, MIRROR

Let's look again at one of those women's magazines. The cover will almost certainly show a beautiful model or actress with impossibly glowing hair, a sparkling white smile, radiant and tanned skin, and a perfectly toned and curvy body. Men's magazines are no different, especially when they dedicate their covers to toned and tanned young men willing to share their secrets for perfect six-pack abs.

It is hard not to wonder: How does the myth of the perfect body affect our **body image**, or the ways we perceive our own physical attributes and, consequently, our sexual life? Not surprisingly, research has linked a positive body image with increased sexual activity and sexual satisfaction.[26] The better your opinion of your body, the more likely you are to find pleasure in sexual activities. The opposite is also true: A negative body image is associated with reduced sexual enjoyment. Scholars are talking about an ever-growing "**Adonis complex**" that makes many young men obsessed with becoming muscular. Still, studies show that women today are significantly more affected by body image concerns than men.[27] As mass media perpetuates the ideal of thinness

Attitudes Towards Homosexuality

% "Yes, it's acceptable"
% "No, it's not acceptable"

78 19 | 30 68

Inborn Choice

Source: Miller, Rowland S., *Intimate Relationships*. (New York, NY: McGraw-Hill, 2009), 275–279.

∧ ∧ ∧ **Studies show that** heterosexuals' views on the origins of homosexuality (inborn or chosen) **shape their attitudes toward it. How do you think these different attitudes affect the debate over** legal benefits for same-sex partners?

LIBIDO is sexual desire.

CYBERSEX refers to the virtual sexual activities practiced on the Internet.

as a basis of beauty, many women feel more and more uncomfortable with their own image. Researchers agree that eating disorders have spread dramatically in the past 30 years, and that a social climate in which thinness is synonymous with beauty is partly to blame.[28]

HEALTH AND SEXUAL SATISFACTION

It has now been established that people who consider themselves physically fit are also more likely to report an increased satisfaction with their sexual lives.[29] According to Pamela G. Rockwell, assistant professor of family medicine at University of Michigan Medical School, there are other health issues that are related to sexual satisfaction[30]:

Prescription Medications People should be aware of the possible side effects of medications they are taking. Diuretics can cause erectile dysfunction, and antidepressants can decrease one's interest in sex.

Cardiac Health Sex is not as likely to cause a heart attack as people might think. However, it is better to refrain from all kinds of physical activity, including sex, immediately after a heart attack or heart surgery.

Depression Untreated depression has been associated with sexual dysfunction, such as a lack of interest in sex and concerns about one's ability to perform any sexual activity.

Alcohol Although it is true that alcohol can increase one's desire to have sex by lowering inhibition, at the end its numbing effect diminishes pleasure considerably.

STDs Most sexually transmitted diseases can be prevented by the use of condoms, which doctors recommend using 100 percent of the time. People who have already contracted STDs can still enjoy sex, but protection is fundamental.

Stress When people are frantically trying to balance the many aspects of their work and family lives, the stress may cause them to lose some of their **libido**, or sexual desire.

Pregnancy Libido during pregnancy can vary from individual to individual, and sex during pregnancy usually poses no problem. As the pregnancy progresses, couples might need to become more creative with positions.

Menopause Women may experience changes in their sexual desire after menopause, but that does not impair their ability to have a healthy and enjoyable sex life in any way. Hormonal changes can begin during perimenopause, the years before menopause itself begins. Hormonal fluctuations such as the reduction of estrogen and progesterone can continue during menopause and postmenopause.[31]

Andropause Men may experience energy loss, depression, loss of libido, and sexual dysfunction during this time known as male menopause.[32]

Extramarital Affairs

The years 2008 and 2009 were tough on American politicians' wives. In March 2008, New York Governor Eliot Spitzer announced during a press conference that he was involved with prostitutes. In August 2008, Democratic presidential candidate John Edwards admitted he had an affair with a campaign aide. In June 2009, Republican senator John Ensign confessed that he had an affair with a member of his campaign staff, an embarrassing admission that soon turned into a veritable saga involving the other woman's family. Later in the same month, South Carolina Governor Mark Sanford went AWOL for a few days. After first

claiming that he had been on a hiking trip, the governor eventually admitted that he had been in Argentina with a mistress. Almost in tears, the governor gave a press conference in which he declared that, although his mistress was his "soul mate," he was willing to salvage his marriage and try to learn to love his wife again. The careers of Eliot Spitzer and John Edwards have been badly damaged by the scandals. As of today, Ensign and Sanford's scandals are still playing out, and many people are calling for their resignations.

Research showed that 90 percent of Americans consider extramarital affairs always wrong,[33] but that position may also be slightly hypocritical. Data from 1984 indicate that about 65 to 70 percent of men and 45 to 65 percent of women have had at least one extramarital affair.[34] It seems then that we can agree with the joke saying, "If it's not you, it's your wife."

Why do people have affairs? Researchers explain that often people have impossibly high expectations for the level of love and passion in their marriage. People in relationships often expect love to deepen and monogamy to be easy, whereas divorce rates and the number of extramarital affairs seem to show the opposite to be true. Within a relationship, some people tend to invest their partners with the main responsibility for their own emotional and sexual satisfaction, which can lead to disappointment and frustration. There is also the belief that extramarital sex will inevitably destroy the marriage. Although affairs can often lead to divorce, it is a fact that many couples use affairs to improve their relationship with their partner. Affairs can force partners to deal with their own expectations and face problems in the relationships. In *Never Forever*, Andrew is willing to forgive Sophie's affair and work on their marriage. It is her decision not to abort her child that he cannot forgive. On the other side of the spectrum, affairs can even be used to insert variety and excitement in a sexual relationship that has become predictable.[35]

Once again, researchers found differences in the way men and women approach extramarital affairs. A 1994 study suggested that men tend to have affairs because they feel sexually rejected by their wives or for the need for variety, whereas women have affairs mostly for emotional fulfillment rather than for sexual excitement.[36]

TECHNOLOGY AND MARITAL RELATIONSHIPS

If the likelihood of infidelity is increased by opportunity, can e-mails, text messaging, and Internet chat rooms actually encourage extramarital affairs? A study shows that technology is indeed making extramarital affairs easier, with almost a third of respondents admitting they used e-mail, text messaging, or chat rooms to flirt with others and to cultivate an affair.[37] The reason for this trend is that **cybersex** and online flirting are often conducted in anonymity, which makes online affairs seem easy and harmless. However, even online affairs can be extremely damaging, and many family practitioners believe that technology is directly responsible for the increased number of divorces obtained on the grounds of infidelity.[38]

What should people do if they find themselves caught up in an online affair? Experts suggest that cheating partners own up to their activities, end the affair, and possibly seek counseling to work with the partner to improve the relationship. Installing blocking software can help, too.

Adolescent Premarital Sex

In the past months, it was hard to ignore the headlines denouncing "sexting" (the exchange of racy messages and photos over the phone) as a spreading social plague among teenagers. But what is the truth about teenagers and sexuality?

In the last decades, the number of **sexually experienced** teenagers has increased. A study published by the U.S. Department of Health and Human Services (HHS) shows that the number of teenagers who have their first intercourse at the age of 15 has tripled from 1958 to 1994 (from 3 percent to 11 percent).[39] The same study shows that more than half of sexually active teenagers use condoms, mostly to avoid pregnancy. The percentage has increased by 10 percent between 1991 and 1999.[40] The study also shows that the number of sexual partners over a lifetime increases considerably with a lower age of first intercourse: Among young adults who were 20 in 1992, 74 percent of those who had their first intercourse at age 14 had six or more partners during their lifetime, compared to 10 percent of those who had their first intercourse at age 17 or older.[41]

VIRGINITY PLEDGES

In the last decade, the U.S. government has funded religious groups like the Silver Ring Thing to promote **sexual abstinence** among teenagers. On what grounds did the government make this decision? In the mid-nineties, the National Longitudinal Study of Adolescent

SEXUALLY EXPERIENCED means having had sexual intercourse.
SEXUAL ABSTINENCE is the practice of refraining from any sexual behavior or only from vaginal–penile intercourse.
VIRGINITY PLEDGE is the commitment to abstain from sexual intercourse until marriage.

Health (also known as Add Health) conducted a survey on the sexual activity of teenagers who took a **virginity pledge**, or vowed openly to remain sexually inactive until marriage. The study followed the participants from high school to early adulthood. Participants were categorized according to their response to the question, "Have you ever signed a pledge to abstain from sex until marriage?" and divided into strong pledgers (pledges were repeatedly confirmed), pledgers (pledges were confirmed in at least in one survey), weak pledgers (pledges were confirmed at least in one survey, but responses were inconsistent), and non-pledgers (never made a virginity pledge). The study concluded that adolescents who take a virginity pledge are less sexually active in high school and, as young adults, are less likely to

Sexual Activity: Virginity Pledges

	Non-Pledgers	All Pledgers	Strong Pledgers	Weak Pledgers
Ever Had Intercourse	89.92%	74.91%	65.01%	81.22%
Never Had Intercourse	10.08%	25.09%	34.99%	18.78%
Median Age of First Intercourse	16 years, 11 months	18 years, 8 months	19 years, 9 months	18 years, 3 months
Percent Having Intercourse Before Age 18	63.22%	39.25%	30.76%	44.67%
Average Number of Lifetime Sexual Partners	6.1	3.4	2.8	3.8

Source: The Heritage Foundation, "Sexual Activity by Wave III," http://www.heritage.org/Research/Family/upload/69372_1.gif, Accessed September 3, 2009.

∧
∧ **According to Add Health,** the average number of sexual partners over a lifetime for
∧ non-pledgers is more than double that for strong pledgers'. **How does this relate to the study on sexually active teenagers conducted for the HHS?**

FERTILITY is the occurrence of childbearing in a country's population.
DEMOGRAPHY is the science that studies human population.
CRUDE BIRTH RATE is the annual number of childbirths for every 1,000 people in a given population.
REPLACEMENT-LEVEL FERTILITY is the number of children necessary for women to replace themselves and their partners in the population, usually maintained at 2.1.

have unprotected sex and to give birth outside of wedlock. Other studies evaluated these results, and stated that virginity pledges are more effective for younger teenagers and work best when the pledger feels he or she is part of a community.[42] This also means that the pledges become weaker in situations in which there is no community support for premarital abstinence.[43]

SEX, CONTRACEPTION, AND PREGNANCY

What about pregnancy and contraception? Although the number of U.S. teen pregnancies has declined in the past decade, it is still among the highest in the Western world. Interestingly, about half of unintended teen pregnancies are caused by the ineffective use of contraceptives.[44] What factors are associated with prevention of unwanted pregnancies? Usually, unwanted pregnancies are less frequent when teenagers wait a long time before having sexual intercourse with their partners, when they talk about contraception before having sex, and when they take virginity pledges.[45] Research shows that teen pregnancies are more frequent in teenagers who run away from home or see themselves as risk takers. Depression and low self-esteem are also more frequent in girls who practice unprotected sexual activity than in boys.[46]

Family and schools also play a role in the prevention of teen pregnancies. For example, low levels of affection and support at home seem to lead to teenage depression and an increase in sexual behavior, especially in girls.[47] For boys, it emerged that good support can positively affect the sexual activity of boys, as they become more likely to adopt effective contraceptive methods and have fewer sexual partners (age of first intercourse and likelihood of sexual activity were not affected).[48] Family structure does not seem to have an influence on teenagers' sexual behavior, so there is no significant difference in families with married, single, divorced, or gay parents.[49] Parents who set limits for watching TV or discuss issues seen on TV with their children are proven to positively influence their children's sexual behavior, especially for sexual education and contraception.[50]

As far as school is concerned, teenagers who are actively engaged in their schools experience fewer unwanted pregnancies than high-school dropouts.[51] Low educational attainment,

∧∧∧ **The 2007 film** *Juno* **is about a** pregnant high-school girl **who decides to** give her baby up for adoption. **What school policies do you think could be implemented to reduce the number of teen pregnancies?**

frequent changes of school, attendance in schools with high levels of crime, and low test scores are also associated with increased unwanted pregnancies for teenagers.[52]

Fertility

From a demographic perspective, **fertility** is the occurrence of childbearing in a country's population. **Demography**, the science that studies human population, describes fertility through the **crude birth rate**, or the annual number of childbirths for every 1,000 people in a given population. What are the characteristics of fertility in the United States? According to the U.S. Census Bureau, childlessness has increased steadily since 1976 for women 40 to 44 years old. In 2008, approximately 18% of women in that age group were childless. This may be partially explained by the media's influence. When women see celebrities such as Nicole Kidman (baby at 41) or Marcia Cross and Jane Seymour (both had twins at 44), having babies so late, they may feel like they can also wait to have children, but then, at 40, they may have trouble conceiving. The U.S. Census Bureau also notes that women stop having children after an average of 2.1 children each, which is approximately **replacement-level fertility**. The highest level of fertility was recorded among women with graduate or professional degrees, and the peak age of fertility was between 24 and 30 years old. Today many women do not want children to prevent them from getting an education or from having a career, so many wait to have children until they are established in a profession.[53] In Chapter 8 we will discuss the decision to have children further, as well as infertility and new fertility technologies.

Teen Pregnancy

A study of birth rates and abortion among teenage girls between the ages of 15 and 17 shows that in 1972 the rate of pregnancy ending with birth was 76 percent. More recently, the number of pregnancies ending in birth has remained fairly steady around 50 percent. Although this number is less than it was in the 1970s, the number of teen births has increased from the 1980s, possibly because of a growing trend toward fewer abortions.[54] Compared with other countries, the number of teen pregnancies in the United States is alarming. In 1996, the United States had around 55 live births per 1,000 women aged 15 to 19. England and Canada (in 1995) each had only about 25 births, whereas Germany had closer to 10.[55] Teen pregnancies have a mostly negative effect on the teen mother and the child. Teen mothers often end up leaving school. Limited education leads to limited job options, which in turn affects the educational opportunities of the children and the overall economic stability of the home.[56]

Sexually Transmitted Diseases

Whatever dreams of a free love utopia may have bloomed during the sexual revolution of the 1960s and '70s came to a screeching halt when AIDS made its appearance in the early '80s. Suddenly, sexual expression could no longer be a carefree and spontaneous affair, but instead required strict safety measures. However, AIDS is only the most conspicuous example of a sexually transmitted disease, or **STD**. STDs are today also known today as **STIs** (sexually transmitted infections) and include all the illnesses, diseases, and infections that can be contracted through sexual and nonsexual contact of body parts and fluids.[57] Here are some of the most common STIs:[58]

CHLAMYDIA

This common pelvic inflammation is easily transmitted because of its relative lack of apparent symptoms. In the past years, the incidence of chlamydia in the United States has increased sharply. Interestingly, in 2007 there

STDs are sexually transmitted diseases.
STIs are sexually transmitted infections.

were three times as many cases of chlamydia among women than men, possibly because women undergo more screening than men.[59]

GONORRHEA

This infectious disease can be spread through sexual contact, but also from a mother to her child through lactation. Between 1975 and 1997, the incidence of the disease has decreased by 74 percent. According to the Centers for Disease Control and Prevention (CDC), in 2007 there were about 120 cases per 100,000 people in the United States.[60]

Women Who Had a Birth in the Last 12 Months Per 1,000 Women 15 to 50 Years Old by Selected Characteristics: 2006

| Characteristic | Number of Women | | Women Who Had a Birth in the Last 12 Months | | | | | |
| | | | Total | | Percent Distribution | | Births per 1,000 Women | |
	Estimate	Margin of Error[1]	Estimate	Margin of Error[1]	Estimate	Margin of Error[1]	Estimate	Margin of Error[1]
Total	76,172,507	26,845	4,182,942	36,517	100.0	—	54.9	0.5
Age								
15 to 19 years	10,551,372	20,447	278,446	9,200	6.7	0.2	26.4	0.9
20 to 24 years	10,134,195	22,267	935,039	16,091	22.4	0.4	92.3	1.6
25 to 29 years	9,976,440	17,922	1,173,652	20,143	28.1	0.4	117.6	1.9
30 to 34 years	9,679,647	14,300	987,324	15,739	23.6	0.3	102.0	1.6
35 to 39 years	10,559,537	37,669	583,591	10,656	14.0	0.2	55.3	1.0
40 to 44 years	11,354,220	36,790	170,791	6,111	4.1	0.1	15.0	0.5
45 to 50 years	13,887,096	24,830	54,100	4,219	1.3	0.1	3.9	0.3
Marital Status								
Married	36,225,985	90,172	2,698,790	28,954	64.5	0.4	76.6	0.8
Widowed	719,572	15,590	13,541	2,268	0.3	0.1	18.8	3.1
Divorced	7,378,966	40,798	167,767	7,159	4.0	0.2	22.7	0.9
Separated	2,317,577	27,685	113,275	6,442	2.7	0.2	48.9	2.8
Never Married	30,530,407	69,274	1,189,569	20,817	28.4	0.4	39.0	0.7
Educational Attainment								
Not a high school graduate	14,581,563	51,404	746,907	15,588	17.9	0.3	51.2	1.0
High school, 4 years	19,704,046	86,304	1,133,009	19,470	27.1	0.4	57.5	1.0
College, 1 or more years	41,886,898	97,318	2,303,026	26,629	55.1	0.5	55.0	0.6
Some college or associate's degree	23,475,815	71,672	1,171,936	18,786	28.0	0.4	49.9	0.8
Bachelor's degree	12,908,885	58,021	763,260	13,019	18.2	0.3	59.1	1.0
Graduate or professional degree	5,502,198	38,930	367,830	7,597	8.8	0.2	68.9	1.3

Source: *U.S. Census Bureau, "Fertility of Women: 2006," Issued August 2008.*

∧
∧ **Based on this** data from the U.S. Census Bureau, **what conclusions can you draw**
∧ **about the** relationship between fertility and age, marital status, and education **in the United States?**

HIV is the human immunodeficiency virus that causes AIDS.

AIDS is acquired immune deficiency syndrome.

HIV PREVALENCE ESTIMATE is the number of HIV-positive people at the end of a given year.

HIV INCIDENCE ESTIMATE is the number of new HIV infections contracted in a given year.

STIGMA is any kind of demeaning and discrediting characteristic attributed to a group or an individual.

EPIDEMIC is the outbreak of an infectious disease that affects a large number of people at the same time.

SYPHILIS

This disease is highly contagious and can be transmitted through sexual intercourse and also by close body contact with an infected individual. Syphilis had almost disappeared from the United States in the last part of the 20th century, but since 2001 it has made a comeback with an increase of more than 80 percent. The majority of cases are registered among African American men and women.[61]

CHANCROID

This disease is highly contagious and, when untreated, can facilitate the transmission of HIV. Cases of chancroid among the American population have been gradually declining since 2001, with only 23 cases reported nationwide in 2007.[62]

HUMAN PAPILLOMAVIRUS

The human papillomavirus (HPV) is actually not a single virus but a collection of viruses—more than 70—that in some cases can lead to cervical cancer. In recent years, a vaccine has been developed against some types of HPV. In a recent study, it was calculated that more than 25 percent of American women between 14 and 59 have contracted some kind of HPV. In 3.8 percent of participants, researchers detected the types of HPV that can lead to cervical cancer.[63]

PELVIC INFLAMMATORY DISEASE

Pelvic inflammatory disease (PID) is a serious inflammation of the female genital organs that can have life-threatening complications. It is estimated that about 100,000 women every year become infertile due to PID. Incidence of the disease has been declining since 2001, but has increased again between 2005 and 2006.[64]

HERPES SIMPLEX VIRUS

Commonly known as oral or genital herpes, herpes simplex virus (HSV) is the most common sexually transmitted infection, and can be passed through vaginal, oral, and anal intercourse. A mother can also transmit the virus to her newborn during birth. Precise data on the disease are not available, but HSV is estimated to affect more than 45 million American adults and teenagers.[65,66]

TRICHOMONIASIS

This disease affects more women than men and increases the risk of contracting HIV. It is considered the most easily curable STI, especially in young women. It is estimated that about 7.4 million cases are diagnosed each year in men and women.[67]

HUMAN IMMUNODEFICIENCY VIRUS AND ACQUIRED IMMUNE DEFICIENCY SYNDROME

Human immunodeficiency virus (HIV) is the virus that causes acquired immune deficiency syndrome (AIDS). When people with HIV develop certain indicators such as infections, cancers, or a low count of CD4 (a type of glycoprotein) in their blood, their HIV status develops into AIDS. No cure is yet available for the virus or the disease. HIV is transmitted when infected body fluids enter another person's bloodstream. The virus is therefore transmitted through unprotected sexual intercourse and use of unsanitary needles (in drug consumption but also in blood transfusions). It can also be passed from a mother to her child during pregnancy and lactation.[68]

How many people have HIV and AIDS in the United States? According to the CDC, the HIV prevalence estimate, or the number of HIV-positive people at the end of a given year, was 1,106,400 for 2006, with about 21 percent of people possibly not aware of having contracted the virus.[69] The estimated number of new HIV infections contracted in a year, expressed as HIV incidence estimate, was 56,300 in 2008, with half of that number representing gay or bisexual men. A reported 13,627 HIV cases were caused by heterosexual contact. It is estimated that 37,041 were diagnosed with AIDS in 2007. Over 70 percent of them were men, and about 64 percent were African Americans. The majority of people diagnosed with AIDS in 2007 were between the ages of 40 and 44, but there were also 500 cases among teenagers and 38 cases in the "under-13" category.[70]

Living with Herpes

Jeff is 28 and has had many sexual partners in his lifetime. A year ago, he found out he had genital herpes. This forced him to learn about the disease and take extra precautions.

"I always thought that using a condom during sex was enough to avoid STDs and unwanted pregnancies. Still, I have to admit I didn't use condoms every time I had sex. Sometimes my partners were taking the pill, and I trusted they didn't have any STDs. Then, one day I went to the doctor for some ulcers in my groin area, and I discovered I had genital herpes. The doctor told me there is no treatment for herpes; it is a lifelong condition. She told me I needed to take extra precautions during sex. I also needed to call my exes to tell them to get tested for HSV.

"I was devastated at first. I felt stupid, and guilty for putting my partners at risk. I became depressed and it took me a long time to enter a new relationship. Now I've learned to deal with the fact that you can live with herpes and that many other people are in my situation. I've had a girlfriend for the past two months, and I told her I have genital herpes before we became intimate. It was not easy, but we talked about it and decided to go on with our relationship.

"Today, I am much more careful about using protection during sex, and I avoid sexual contact during outbreaks. There are bad times and then periods when I am symptom-free. I have also been reading more about other STDs, and realized how little I knew about them. Living with herpes is not easy, but I have learned to deal with it."

Estimate of Diagnosed AIDS Cases from Start of Epidemic through 2007

Transmission Category	Adult and Adolescent Male	Adult and Adolescent Female	Total
Male-to-male sexual contact	487,695	–	487,695
Injection drug use	175,704	80,155	255,859
Male-to-male sexual contact and injection drug use	71,242	–	71,242
High-risk heterosexual contact	63,927	112,230	176,157
Other	12,108	6,158	18,266

Source: Centers for Disease Control and Prevention, "HIV/AIDS: Basic Statistics," http://www.cdc.gov/hiv/topics/surveillance/basic.htm#aidsrace, Accessed September 3, 2009.

∧
∧ **According to the Centers for Disease Control and Prevention,** the majority of men
∧ with AIDS contracted the disease through male-to-male sexual contact. **How do you think this influences or should influence prevention campaigns?**

It is estimated that more than 450,000 people in the United States live with AIDS today. So far, more than 580,000 people have died from AIDS in the United States.[71]

PREVENTION OF SEXUALLY TRANSMITTED DISEASES AND SEXUALLY TRANSMITTED INFECTIONS

HIV and STDs represent a growing threat not only to public health, but also to the economic well-being of many nations. STDs spread easily because of their rather asymptomatic nature, especially in their first stages. In the United States, STDs affect a disproportionate number of sex workers, immigrants, adolescents from poorer areas, detainees, and people with limited access to health care. Illicit drug usage has also been associated with an increase of STDs because it leads to risky sexual behavior (anonymous partners, unprotected sex, etc.), frequent exchange of sex for drugs, and sharing of needles. In addition, the **stigma** associated with STDs has become a significant factor in the **epidemic**. A study from 1995 showed that about one in five Americans in a sexual relationship had no knowledge of their partner's sexual

▶▶▶ GO GL⊕BAL

Religious Affiliation and Extramarital Sex among Men in Brazil

The **epidemic** of HIV in Africa has become a global emergency, but the truth is that the virus is spreading rapidly in South America, too. Brazil has the highest incidence of the virus, which has increased dramatically among heterosexuals in the past decades. A 1996 study of the sexual behavior of almost 4,000 Brazilian men from all regions of the country brought to light interesting considerations about religious affiliation and modality of extramarital affairs. According to the study, 12 percent of married or cohabiting men admitted having an affair during the previous year, with an average of 2.4 extramarital partners. Despite the fact that 99 percent of men were somewhat knowledgeable about HIV and AIDS, only 40 percent of those who had extramarital affairs reported using condoms during sex. Two-thirds of the affairs were conducted with acquaintances, 15 percent with strangers, and 4 percent with prostitutes. It is also interesting to note that there were no major differences in eco-nomic and educational backgrounds, so researchers encouraged policy makers to focus on the entire male population rather than on alleged *high-risk* groups.[72]

The study also highlights a connection between religious affiliation and sexual behavior in Brazilian men. Apparently, men belonging to the evangelical faith (increasingly popular in Brazil) were much less likely to have extramarital affairs compared to Catholic men. The reason might be that Catholicism is a religion by birth rather than conversion, so that new evangelical converts may be more determined than Catholics to adhere to religious values.[73]

SEX EDUCATION is a program of education about various aspects of human sexual behaviors including reproductive anatomy, sexual reproduction, sexual intercourse, contraception, and reproductive rights and responsibilities.

FAMILY PLANNING is the system of limiting the number of children in a family by birth control.

history, which explains how undiagnosed STDs can be transmitted even in monogamous relationships.

The National Prevention Information Network lists sexual abstinence and monogamous sexual activity between non-infected partners as the most effective preventive measures. Latex condoms, when used correctly, are very effective in preventing the transmission of HIV, chlamydia, gonorrhea, and trichomoniasis and are highly recommended in any penetrative intercourse. Sexually active individuals should also get regular checkups and screenings for STDs and ask their partners whether they have STDs (and urge them to get screened themselves).[74]

Families can also play an important role in prevention, especially if they maintain frequent and open communication with their children. It has been demonstrated that children in cohesive families start having sexual activity later and are more likely to use contraception that can prevent STDs.[75]

Sex Education

When children ask, "How are babies born?" they receive very disparate answers. Some parents go the zoological route by invoking the birds and the bees. Others believe they should never lie and enter into complicated anatomical descriptions that leave their children puzzled. Others run to the nearest bookstore to buy educational materials that will help them answer these questions with the least amount of trauma. Others simply ignore the question, hoping to postpone it until their children's wedding day. With this introduction to **sex education**, it's no surprise that many children—particularly teens—remain very confused about sex.

What is the best type of sex education? Recent evidence states that the most effective sex education is comprehensive in nature. This means it should encourage abstinence and responsible decision making, provide information about contraception and STIs, and dissipate prejudice about different sexual orientations.[76]

Government sex education programs have lately come under major criticism. Over the past decade, the U.S. government has invested $1.5 billion dollars in abstinence-only programs, which offer

very little information about the prevention of diseases, infections, and pregnancy.[77] Supporters of abstinence-only programs believe that abstinence is the only effective preventive technique and that comprehensive sex education only encourages reckless sexual activity.[78] However, research shows that not only does comprehensive sex education *not* have these effects, but also that abstinence-only programs actually have very little effect in preventing and delaying sexual activity in adolescence.[79] President Obama has publicly declared his support for abortion rights, prevention of STIs, and national and international **family planning**, or the system of limiting the number of children in a family through birth control.[80]

Criticism of abstinence-only programs also comes from some religious groups. In 2002, the Religious Institute on Sexual Justice, Morality, and Healing published the *Open Letter to Religious Leaders about Sex Education* to express its support for a more comprehensive sex education that promotes knowledge, respect for different sexual orientations, and a sense of responsibility and ethics toward sex. The document was signed by over 900 representatives of Christian and Jewish faiths. The letter by the Religious Institute wanted to show how human sexuality does not violate the tenets of religious faith.[81]

Still, the debate over sex education is not likely to end soon. A 2006 report on the effects of abstinence-only programs and comprehensive sex education adopted in schools has revealed that both approaches have little or no effect on the sexual activity of teenagers.[82] This is partly attributed to the sources of information outside school. This might mean that sex education needs to be rethought, or that we need an even more comprehensive approach that includes family and the media. Sex education and contraceptives will be covered more in Chapter 8.

FAMILY AND SEX EDUCATION

It is a common assumption that there is nothing more uncomfortable or cringe-worthy than talking about sex with one's parents. However, research shows that children and teenagers actually want their parents to talk to them about sex.[83] Families have been shown to play a significant role in the effectiveness of sex education. Programs have even been instituted in countries to prepare parents to have effective sex discussions. It is important that families maintain open and honest communication that takes into account the current cultural climate that children are exposed to and focuses on the children's specific needs.[84] Family scientists also stress the importance of sex education within the home for effective family planning.[85]

<<< **In 1997,** the school board of Franklin County, North Carolina, ordered that three chapters on AIDS, STDs, and contraception be removed from a ninth-grade textbook. **The board explained that the chapters did not comply with the abstinence-only program for children from kindergarten through ninth grade.** What role do you think schools should play in sex education of children and teenagers?

Katia is a college student who has been volunteering at a Planned Parenthood center for two years. Her job is to teach sex education classes for the parents of children and teenagers.

"The parents coming to my classes want to learn how to communicate better with their children about sex. They are often embarrassed, or they feel like they need to give long, technical lectures. So, I teach them what information is appropriate to share at each developmental stage. For example, I only learned about menstruation the day I got my first period at the age of 12. I was so scared and wished my parents had told me about menstruation before that day! I teach parents how to prepare children for the big changes coming in their lives.

"I also explain to parents that they should not talk about sex without mentioning intimacy, dating, and peer pressure. Children need to understand the emotional aspects related to their sexuality. Parents who provide clear and helpful information without sounding judgmental are going to win their children's trust.

"One of the most challenging parts is talking about sexual orientation. There are still too many instances of bullying and discrimination for gay teens or teens that are perceived as such. Most children learn about different sexual orientation from the media, and they are confused about it. Parents should talk to them about homosexuality before children are exposed to stereotypes.

"I would say that sex education should emphasize health, responsibility, and respect for oneself and others. These are important lessons to learn and to teach."

think marriages and families: WHAT ARE THE THEORIES BEHIND SEX AND SEXUAL REPRODUCTION?

SEX AND SEXUAL REPRODUCTION: THEORETICAL PERSPECTIVES

How do researchers interpret the role and modality of sex and sexual reproduction in society?

FUNCTIONALISM

Functional theory, which analyzes patterns of human behavior with their functions in society, argues that the survival of society is dependent on sexual reproduction. Since Sophie and Andrew, in *Never Forever*, cannot reproduce together, they are not adequately ensuring that society continues. To ensure their survival, societies have devised norms to control and regulate sexual reproduction and preserve social order. One norm that is common to almost every culture is that of the incest taboo, precluding sexual relationships between close relatives. The reason for this is biological: Offspring of close blood relatives are more likely to have physical or mental problems.[86]

Even though sex on its most basic level is intended for the continuation of the species, it can hardly be said that sex is mostly practiced for altruistic purposes. In this sense, functionalists argue that advancements in birth control have brought a distinction between the idea of sex for reproduction and sex for personal fulfillment.

CONFLICT THEORY

The basic assumption of the conflict theory is that people are in competition with each other over the control of resources. The theory has Marxist origins and primarily defines the conflict between social classes, but it has since been applied to microcosms such as the family and interpersonal relationships. It is easy to see how sex and sexual reproduction have created conflict in society. For example, the stereotype according to which women need to sacrifice their own personal aspirations to take care of their children is still widespread in modern society. Patriarchies historically put women, who were often seen as property, in conflict with their husbands, who felt they had all the power in the relationship. Despite the fact that sexual behaviors have changed over time, women still suffer from sexual bias. The same pattern exists when gays and lesbians are affected by the heterosexual bias in society, expressed in the forms of rejection by friends and family, harassment, and discrimination.[87]

SYMBOLIC INTERACTIONISM

The symbolic interaction theory analyzes the meanings that people associate with elements of their environment, and how these meanings are shared, interpreted, and transmitted. According to this perspective, sex and sexual reproduction are social constructions, highly dependent on symbolic associations of meanings that have developed through time. In this sense, children learn about their sexual roles from the input they receive from their families and from the outside world. Different groups in society view sex and sexual reproduction differently. For example, up until 1981, the Italian legislation admitted mitigating circumstances for the so-called "crimes of honor," in which individuals killed their spouses after discovering infidelity.[88] Because people socially construct their notions of sex and sexual reproduction, the meanings that are assigned and associated with these concepts can and do change over time. An interesting and fairly recent example is when President Bill Clinton famously denied having had any sexual relation with staffer Monica Lewinsky because he claimed there was a difference between "sexual relations" and "sexual intercourse."[89] Do you think Sophie viewed sex with Jihah differently at first, because her only intent was to reproduce?

WRAP YOUR MIND AROUND THE THEORY

Functionalists believe that sexual reproduction is at the base of a healthy society. **How do you think this view can reinforce bias against homosexual couples?**

FUNCTIONALISM

Why do people have sex? How does sexual reproduction help society? Functional theory believes that sexual reproduction is important for an orderly society because it is fundamental to the propagation of the species. Moreover, societies have devised sexual norms to make sexual reproduction more efficient. Cultural universals such as the incest taboo work to prevent health problems with offspring. The standard of monogamy makes sure children are taken care of by both parents and are educated about sexuality. Because functional theory is focused on a greater good that benefits all members of society, it has been criticized for ignoring diversity.

CONFLICT THEORY

Conflict theorists believe that society is comprised of groups that are in competition with each other over resources. The same assumption is translated to sex and sexual reproduction, which become cause for gender inequality in society. Society regulates the sexual behavior of women by investing them with the main responsibility for birth control. For example, news of the advent of the male contraceptive pill has been announced periodically, but women are still considered mostly responsible for the use (and purchase) of the birth control pill. Despite great advancements in the movement for gender equality, the sexual double standard still exists enough to condemn sexually active women as promiscuous and yet praise similarly active men as adventurous. Moreover, the prejudice against homosexuality and other sexual orientations is still strong.

WHAT ARE THE EFFECTS OF SEX AND SEXUAL REPRODUCTION ON SOCIETY?

SYMBOLIC INTERACTIONISM

Symbolic interactionists examine the meanings that people associate with elements of their environment and how these meanings are shared, interpreted, and transmitted. Theorists also believe that sex and sexual reproduction are socially constructed and vary greatly across different cultures, social classes, eras, and personal beliefs. For example, certain cultures do not view monogamy as a value. Views on masturbation are another great example of how symbolic association has changed over time. In Woody Allen's movie *Annie Hall,* the protagonist famously said, "Hey, don't knock masturbation. It's sex with someone I love." A joke like that would have not seemed very funny at the beginning of the 20th century, when masturbation was seen as a despicable act that could lead to mental and physical problems. What happened is not only that science demystified the physiology of masturbation, but also that the cultural prejudice against it has dissipated. However, some religions still speak out against masturbation.

As conflict theorists would see it, the fight against gender inequality and anti-homosexual bias is a continuing one. **To what extent to you think such attitudes reflect competition for resources as opposed to differences in personal viewpoints?**

According to symbolic interaction theory, culture and religion can affect the way people interpret and experience sex and sex reproduction. **How do you think religion affects how we view virginity? Do you think nonreligious people view virginity differently than religious people?**

discover marriages and families in action:

Sex Slavery and Sex Trafficking

Sex trafficking is a serious legal and human rights violation that occurs when someone is forced into commercial sex acts. Victims are usually minors and often transported illegally from one country to another. In 2007, the news reported the case of two young girls from Ukraine who came to the United States thinking they were going to work in an exchange-student program. They were met by two compatriots, who were kind at first, but instead of taking them to the student work program, the men got hold of their documents and forced them to work as strippers at a club. The captors forced the girls to work by threatening them with guns, but also by saying they would harm the girls' families back home if they did not cooperate. The girls suffered weeks of mental and physical abuse and threats before they were able to escape and turn in their captors to the FBI.[90]

It is estimated that each year in the United States about 17,000 girls are coerced into working in the sex industry.[91] According to a document published by the U.S. Department of Health and Human Services, girls are often kidnapped after being lured in by promises of career advancement or marriage into another country. Girls are often kidnapped, as the Ukrainian girls were in 2007, but some girls are sold by their parents or husbands. The people in charge of the trafficking often fail to see these women as human beings, but focus instead

SEX TRAFFICKING is the illegal practice of coercing people into commercial sex acts.
DEBT-BONDAGE is the illegal practice of controlling someone's life by claiming the person needs to pay a debt.
TRAUMATIC BONDING is the emotional attachment that victims end up feeling for their abusers.

on the large profits, potentially millions of dollars, that can be made. The girls are often held in **debt-bondage**, the illegal practice of controlling one's liberty by claiming the person needs to pay his or, more commonly, her debts. The victims of sex trafficking become, in effect, slaves. They encounter many risks, including physical and emotional injury and contracting of STDs, and are forced to use drugs and alcohol to the point of addiction. Among the psychological effects suffered by sex slaves are dissociated ego states, self-hatred, suicidal thoughts and suicide, and even **traumatic bonding**, the emotional attachment that victims sometimes began to feel for their abusers once their perceptions of reality become distorted.[92]

In 2000, the United States established The Trafficking Victims Protection Act to prosecute abusers and captors and help victims of trafficking (a "T-visa" can be provided for victims when they are undocumented).[93]

ACTIVITIES

1. Research practices of human trafficking and sex trafficking on the Internet. Compare the situation in the United States with other countries in the world.
2. Does your university have a policy on prostitution or sex trafficking? If so, do you agree with it? If there is no policy, write one that your university could use to prevent prostitution and sex trafficking.

>>> Organizations like The Coalition Against Trafficking in Women (CATW) are trying to raise awareness about sex trafficking **and promote legislation to prevent and prosecute this practice. CATW states in its Web site that** "sexual exploitation eroticizes women's inequality." **What does this statement mean?**

06

The sexual behavior of individuals is affected by sexual norms that are dictated by society and the family. Open and respectful communication within the family is associated with a responsible attitude toward sex, self-esteem, and sexual satisfaction. Teenage pregnancies and STDs can be prevented or limited by the joint efforts of family and education.

Functional theory sees sex and sexual reproduction as necessary for the propagation of the species. Symbol interactionists analyze the meanings that individuals and society associate with sex and sexual reproduction and believe sex is socially constructed. Conflict theorists believe sex and sexual reproduction are tied into sexual inequality, as women, gays, lesbians, and the transgendered are still victims of bias.

Sex trafficking is the illegal practice of coercing people (mostly women and minors) into commercial sex acts. Victims are threatened and constantly abused both mentally and physically.

Theory

FUNCTIONALISM 109
- the survival of society is dependent on sexual reproduction
- sexual norms like the incest taboo help control sexual reproduction to preserve the social order

SYMBOLIC INTERACTIONISM 109
- sex and sexual reproduction are socially constructed
- the meaning associated with sex and sexual reproduction change across different cultures, social groups, and time periods

CONFLICT THEORY 109
- sex and sexual reproduction are tied to social inequality
- bias still exist about sexual behavior of women, gays, and lesbians

Key Terms

sexual norms are the rules and expectations by which society channels and regulates the sexual behavior of its members 99

proscriptive norms are the rules that proscribe or prohibit certain behaviors 99

prescriptive norms are the rules that recommend or require certain behaviors 99

cultural universals are the patterns or traits that are common to all human cultures 99

incest taboo is the cultural restriction against sexual activity between close relatives 99

genital infibulation is the ritual cutting of the inner labia and surgical closure of the outer labia 100

contraception is the use of devices or procedures to prevent pregnancy 100

sexual satisfaction is an individual's positive feelings toward sexuality 101

body image is an individual's perception of his or her own physical appearance 101

Adonis complex is a man's obsessive preoccupation that he is not muscular enough 101

libido is sexual desire 102

cybersex refers to the virtual sexual activities practiced on the Internet 102

sexually experienced means having had sexual intercourse 103

sexual abstinence is the practice of refraining from any sexual behavior or only from vaginal-penile intercourse 103

virginity pledge is the commitment to abstain from sexual intercourse until marriage 103

fertility is the occurrence of childbearing in a country's population 104

demography is the science that studies human population 104

crude birth rate is the annual number of childbirths for every 1,000 people in a given population 104

replacement-level fertility is the number of children necessary for women to replace themselves and their partners in the population, usually maintained at 2.1 104

STDs are sexually transmitted diseases 105

STIs are sexually transmitted infections 105

HIV is the human immunodeficiency virus that causes AIDS 106

AIDS is acquired immune deficiency syndrome   *106*

HIV prevalence estimate is the number of HIV-positive people at the end of a given year   *106*

HIV incidence estimate is the number of new HIV infections contracted in a given year   *106*

stigma is any kind of demeaning and discrediting characteristic attributed to a group or an individual   *107*

epidemic is the outbreak of an infectious disease that affects a large number of people at the same time   *107*

sex education is a program of education about various aspects of human sexual behaviors including reproductive anatomy, sexual reproduction, sexual intercourse, contraception, and reproductive rights and responsibilities   *108*

family planning is the system of limiting the number of children in a family by birth control   *108*

sex trafficking is the illegal practice of coercing people into commercial sex acts   *111*

debt-bondage is the illegal practice of controlling someone's life by claiming the person needs to pay a debt   *111*

traumatic bonding is the emotional attachment that victims end up feeling for their abusers   *111*

Sample Test Questions

MULTIPLE CHOICE

These multiple-choice questions are similar to those found in the test bank that accompanies this textbook.

1. How is the sexual double standard related to STIs?
   a. Women are more likely than men to contract STIs.
   b. Women and men with STIs are stigmatized by society.
   c. Women with STIs are judged more negatively than men with STIs.
   d. Women have the sole responsibility to protect themselves from STIs.
2. Which of these factors positively affects sexual satisfaction for a couple?
   a. religious childhood
   b. presence of children
   c. importance of sexuality in one's life
   d. lack of nonsexual aspects of the relationship
3. According to research, what is one factor leading to more frequent teen pregnancies?
   a. changing schools frequently
   b. attending an abstinence-only program
   c. delaying first intercourse with the partner for a long time
   d. talking with the partner about contraception before first intercourse
4. Which is the most likely reason for the sharp increase in cases of chlamydia in the United States over the past years?
   a. The disease is almost without symptoms.
   b. More people get screened for the disease.
   c. Schools lack comprehensive sex education.
   d. People do not report the illness for fear of being stigmatized.
5. According to research, which of the following factors is associated with a greater number of sexual partners over a lifetime?
   a. lack of self-esteem
   b. lower age of first intercourse
   c. lack of comprehensive sex education
   d. availability of contraception methods

ESSAY

1. Discuss how the sexual double standard affects today's sexual norms.
2. What are the effects of the myth of the perfect body on people's body image and self-esteem?
3. How is communication technology redefining sexual norms?
4. Discuss the heterosexual bias affecting gays and lesbians today.
5. Discuss the rates of teen pregnancy and abortion today and the effect of both on a teenager's psychological well-being.

WHERE TO START YOUR RESEARCH PAPER

To learn more about American sexuality, go to http://nsrc.sfsu.edu/american_sexuality

For more information about genders and sexuality, go to http://emedicine.medscape.com/article/917990-overview

For an in-depth analysis of gender bias and the sexual double standard, go to http://people.mills.edu/spertus/Gender/pap/node7.html

For more information about body image and health, go to http://www.bodyimagehealth.org/

For more information about the causes of and prevention of eating disorders, go to http://www.nationaleatingdisorders.org/index.php

To find out more about online dating and cybersex, go to http://www.mekabay.com/cyberwatch/02dating_cybersex.htm

For an introduction to the effects of cybersex on relationships, go to http://www.calstatela.edu/univ/ppa/newsrel/cybersexsurvey.htm

To learn more about heterosexual bias in language, go to http://www.apa.org/pi/lgbc/publications/language.html

For a list of resources on sexual orientations, go to http://www.glbtss.colostate.edu/mission-statement.aspx

To find out more about bias against gays and lesbians, go to http://nsrc.sfsu.edu/category/tags/homophobia

To find out more about teen pregnancies and related services, go to http://news.stanford.edu/pr/93/931020Arc3093.html

For statistics on pregnancy and abortion in the United States, go to http://www.lib.umich.edu/govdocs/sthealth.html#abortion

For more information about the psychological effects of teen pregnancy and abortion, go to http://www.umich.edu/;msfc/index2.html

Answers: 1. c; 2. c; 3. a; 4. b; 5. b

Remember to check www.thethinkspot.com for additional information, downloadable flashcards, and other helpful resources.

WHAT ARE THE HISTORICAL AND CURRENT TRENDS IN DATING AND MATE SELECTION?
HOW DO THEORISTS VIEW DATING AND MATE SELECTION?
HOW ARE COUPLES AND FAMILIES FINDING CREATIVE WAYS TO DATE?

Toula

Portokalos is a frumpy, 30-year-old hostess in her family's Greek restaurant, whose unmarried status is a constant source of worry for her traditional Greek parents, Gus and Maria. Worried that life is passing her by, she convinces Gus (with Maria's help) to allow her to take computer classes at the local community college on the basis that it will benefit the family business. After encountering an attractive stranger at the restaurant, Toula is also motivated to improve her appearance. She exchanges her glasses for contact lenses and begins wearing makeup and more flattering clothes. She also starts working at her aunt's travel agency, which enables her to escape the family restaurant—but only after Toula's patriarchal father is convinced that the new career was all his idea.

While at the travel agency, Toula runs into the handsome stranger from the restaurant, a literature professor named Ian. They make plans for dinner, beginning a whirlwind courtship. Knowing that her family would vehemently object to her dating a non-Greek, Toula dates Ian in secret. However, the couple is caught when a neighbor sees Toula kissing Ian and tells her family. Horrified that their daughter is dating a non-Greek, her parents tell her to end the relationship. Toula, however, is determined to continue seeing Ian.

When Ian proposes, Toula's family is forced to accept him, and he gradually begins to win them over by attempting to learn Greek expressions and getting baptized in the Greek Orthodox Church. His efforts to learn the language are constantly thwarted by Toula's male relatives, who, to the amusement of the rest of the family, teach him highly inappropriate phrases and tell him that they are expressions of courtesy or religious blessings.

The wedding preparations are anything but smooth, with frequent cultural misunderstandings between Toula's eccentric family and Ian's reserved, upper middle-class parents. However, the wedding ceremony itself goes as planned, and the two families begin to socialize more easily during the reception (assisted by a few glasses of ouzo). During his speech, Gus heartwarmingly explains that Ian's last name originates from the Greek word for *apple*, while his family's last name means *orange* in Greek. Thus, even though the two families have many differences, they are, in the end, all fruit.

At the end of the film, a flash-forward shows Toula and Ian walking their reluctant young daughter to school. Demonstrating that she will continue some of her family's Greek traditions by sending her daughter to Greek school, Toula also rejects her father's patriarchal tendencies by promising her daughter that when she grows up, she can marry anyone she wants.

CHOOSING A PARTNER

CHAPTER 07

Although few families are as flamboyant and eccentric as Toula's Greek relatives in *My Big Fat Greek Wedding,* the film portrays some common modern dating scenarios **and raises interesting issues about family and culture.**

How important is it to obtain the approval of your family when you first start seeing someone new? Does it matter if a potential partner belongs to a different religion or is of a different race or ethnicity to your own? Since a landmark ruling in Virginia in 1967 that overturned a ban on whites marrying non-whites, interracial marriage has flourished in the United States. However, mixed-race or mixed-ethnicity couples may face challenges that other couples do not.

In the film, Ian is willing to convert to Toula's religion to please her family, but this may be a point of contention between two individuals with very different religious ideas. In extreme instances individuals in traditional or fundamentalist cultures may resort to "**honor killing**." Honor killings happen when a family member perceives that a female relative will bring or has brought shame on the family, usually through a suspected breech of cultural traditions or religious morals.

With the rising average age of women at the time of their first marriage, Toula is hardly an "old maid" at 30, but her feelings of discontent and a desire to settle down are common among American women who watch many of their friends get married in their 20s. When Toula meets Ian, she is initially worried about the reaction her family will have to a non-Greek vegetarian. However, she soon discovers that the benefits of dating the kind and generous teacher outweigh any difficulties she might encounter with her family—a concept we will examine later in the chapter when we look at the exchange theory of mate selection.

During a high school sociology course, I had to write a term paper about how the industrial revolution changed society. I remember reading an article about how the invention of the automobile changed the entire courtship process for young dating couples. Having a car meant that couples had a new degree of privacy, away from the prying eyes of gossiping neighbors. Today, technological advances continue to affect the dating scene. With the explosion of online dating services, we can narrow down potential suitors to an exact height, eye color, and preference for particular types of music or books.

In this chapter, we will examine the history of dating in the United States, look at today's dating trends, and learn about the theories of mate selection and the factors that affect them. We will also take a look at some of the creative ways in which dating couples are getting to know each other.

Choosing a Partner

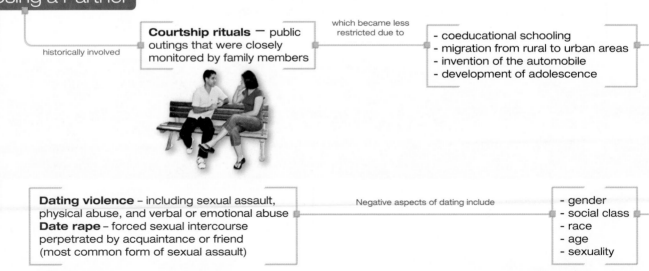

historically involved

Courtship rituals — public outings that were closely monitored by family members

which became less restricted due to

- coeducational schooling
- migration from rural to urban areas
- invention of the automobile
- development of adolescence

Dating violence – including sexual assault, physical abuse, and verbal or emotional abuse
Date rape – forced sexual intercourse perpetrated by acquaintance or friend (most common form of sexual assault)

Negative aspects of dating include

- gender
- social class
- race
- age
- sexuality

get the topic: WHAT ARE THE HISTORICAL AND CURRENT TRENDS IN DATING AND MATE SELECTION?

Dating

"Courtship [is] to marriage, as a very witty prologue to a very dull play."—
The Old Bachelor, William Congreve, playwright (1670–1729)

HISTORY OF DATING IN THE UNITED STATES

In colonial New England, parents strictly controlled the activities of their children, especially their daughters. Meeting a young man unsupervised was a cultural no-no; instead, potential suitors had to go through an elaborate public **courtship** ritual. Initial meetings typically took place at events such as sleigh rides, picnics, and church socials. Closely monitored by members of the family and local community, such meetings left little opportunity for couples to spend time alone together.

Although parents did not have the legal right to prevent an undesirable marriage, they exerted considerable influence over whom their children married. Colonial law stipulated that a man had to secure the permission of a woman's father before he could court her. Couples were often chaperoned on their dates by an older adult. A man was invited to "call" on his love interest, either by the lady's mother or by the lady herself. The couple would be granted some private time alone only if the relationship progressed toward an engagement.[1]

Despite its many restrictions, the courtship process in colonial America was far more liberal than the strict system of arranged marriages in aristocratic Europe. Courting couples exercised some autonomy over their choice of partner and married primarily for love. However, the colonists' interpretation of love was far more practical than today's head-over-heels version. Passion was viewed as wild and uncontrollable and therefore a dangerous basis for a long-term commitment. Instead, love was thought of in terms of sympathy and understanding. Practicality also played a large role. Men were advised to choose women with a strong work ethic over those with a pretty face, and women looked closely at a suitor's economic situation.

> **HONOR KILLINGS** happen when a family member perceives that a female relative will bring or has brought shame on the family, usually through a suspected breech of cultural traditions or religious morals.
>
> **COURTSHIP** is a publicly visible dating process with specific rules and restrictions.
>
> **DATING** is when two people meet at an agreed upon time and place to partake in a social activity.

From Courtship to Dating

The industrial revolution in the 1800s made it impossible for parents to maintain a tight leash on their children. The rise of coeducational schooling, mass migration to cities, and an increasing number of working women placed young women in numerous situations in which they might meet young men and created potential opportunities for unsupervised meetings. As noted earlier, the invention of the automobile increased mobility and provided time alone for young couples. New middle-class families no longer needed their children to work, which (coupled with new child labor laws) effectively extended the period of youth. By the 1920s, the term **dating** was used to refer to two people of the opposite sex meeting at an agreed upon time and place. Men were expected to pay all expenses, in return for companionship and possible physical intimacy. This new system shifted the balance of power from women, who were previously "called upon" in their own home, to men, who now had the advantage of being in control of the evening's entertainment.[2,3]

Modern Dating

During the 1960s, the women's movement empowered women to initiate dates rather than wait to be asked out. Couples increasingly split the cost of dates, and sexual intimacy became common. In the 1970s cohabitation before marriage became more widespread.[4] Today, dating is not necessarily oriented toward marriage. Men and women often remain single throughout their 20s, engaging in casual relationships or

which led to

Dating – meeting at an agreed time and place; shifted balance of power from women to men, who controlled dates pre-1960s

the modern forms of which include

- **hooking up**
(casual sexual encounters)
- **going steady**
(dating exclusively)
- **pack dating**
(dating in groups)
- **serious dating**
(considering long-term commitment)
- **engagement**
(public commitment to marry)

and are influenced by

- meeting at work or school
- meeting through a friend
- meeting at a social event
- meeting online
- meeting at church

typically result from

MARRIAGE MARKET is a system in which prospective partners evaluate the assets and liabilities of potential spouses and choose the best available mate.

GOING STEADY is dating one person exclusively.

PACK DATING is dating in small groups without committing to one person.

ENGAGEMENT is the public commitment to marry.

PRENUPTIAL AGREEMENT is a legal document stipulating financial arrangements in the event of a divorce.

DISENGAGEMENT is the breakdown of an engagement.

ONLINE DATING is when people use specialized dating Web sites such as Match.com or eHarmony to meet a potential spouse.

SPEED DATING is an accelerated form of dating in which men and women choose whether to see each other again based on a very short interaction.

hooking up—becoming sexually involved without emotional intimacy. This trend has led some researchers to dub today's dating scene a culture of "sex without strings and relationships without rings."[5]

REASONS FOR DATING

Dating has changed, but many aspects of it remain the same. Visit the home of a single man or woman on a typical Saturday night and you will likely witness a familiar routine: the primping and preening in front of the mirror, the nervous glancing at the watch, the hopeful conversations with friends and family members about tonight's date. But apart from the excitement of a night out, what do people get out of dating?

Dating fulfills a number of important functions in people's lives. It is a form of recreation that enables couples to socialize together and have fun. It provides companionship and intimacy. Dating also helps individuals learn social skills, gain self-confidence, and develop one-on-one communication skills. Through their relationships with other people, adolescents in particular develop a sense of their own identity, increasing their feelings of self-worth. Finally, dating is a possible opportunity to meet a future marital partner through the process of mate selection.

Researchers describe the dating process as a **marriage market**. Just as employers in a labor market attempt to hire the best possible employees for the lowest possible wage, potential spouses in the marriage market look for a partner with the highest number of desired characteristics and the fewest flaws. The three components to the marriage market include the *supply* of men and women who are looking for partners, the *preferences* of these men and women for particular physical characteristics and personal attributes in their

∧∧∧ **Going steady begins as early as middle school and marks a transition between childhood and adolescence, but these relationships rarely last more than a few weeks.**

What characteristics of going steady lead to such short courtships?

partners, and the *resources* that the men and women can offer potential partners themselves (attributes that other people are likely to find attractive). Unlike the labor market, which tends to value the same characteristics in all potential employees—for example, punctuality, reliability, and efficiency—the marriage market is extremely varied. Although most people value qualities such as honesty and integrity in a partner, few would agree on any one description of the perfect woman or perfect man.

TYPES OF DATING

Going Steady

A term that became common in the 1930s, **going steady** meant that two people were dating exclusively. Going steady sometimes led to engagement, although it was often a short-lived experience, lasting anywhere from a few days to a few years. In the 1950s, going steady became the dominant form of dating, and a 1958 study found that 68 percent of college coeds had gone steady at least once.[6] The practice of going steady was less about true love and more about status and peer pressure, representing the teenage desire for security and conformity.

Pack Dating

Popular among undergraduates, **pack dating** is a less pressurized form of dating, in which small groups of students go to dinner, watch movies, or go out dancing together. The packs (usually consisting of about five or six individuals) provide students with a sense of identity and self-assurance, but enable them to avoid long-term committed relationships. This may appeal to people who do not plan on settling down until their 30s or who have little free time to commit to a relationship between work and study responsibilities.[7]

Serious Dating

When a couple begins to date seriously, they see each other exclusively and usually spend most of their leisure time together. They may discuss marriage or the possibility of living together and begin to talk about the future as a couple, rather than as two individuals with independent life goals. Many couples are sexually intimate by this point, although the practice of premarital sex often depends on whether one or both partners have strong religious beliefs opposing premarital sex. Studies have found that religious commitment is inversely related to the age at first sexual intercourse and the number of lifetime sexual partners.[8,9]

Engagement

Engagement is a public commitment made by a couple when they announce their intention to marry. During the engagement period, couples plan their wedding

Relationship Escalation Model

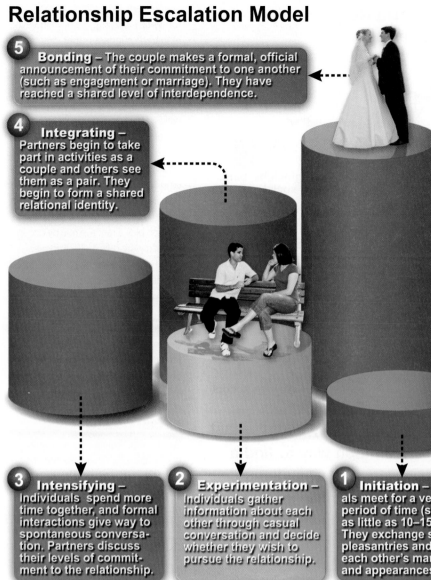

5 **Bonding** – The couple makes a formal, official announcement of their commitment to one another (such as engagement or marriage). They have reached a shared level of interdependence.

4 **Integrating** – Partners begin to take part in activities as a couple and others see them as a pair. They begin to form a shared relational identity.

3 **Intensifying** – Individuals spend more time together, and formal interactions give way to spontaneous conversation. Partners discuss their levels of commitment to the relationship.

2 **Experimentation** – Individuals gather information about each other through casual conversation and decide whether they wish to pursue the relationship.

1 **Initiation** – Individuals meet for a very short period of time (sometimes as little as 10–15 seconds). They exchange social pleasantries and observe each other's mannerisms and appearances.

Source: Knapp, Mark, *Interpersonal Communication and Human Relationships.* (Boston: Allyn & Bacon, 1984).

and discuss issues such as where they will live, whether they will have children, and what they hope to accomplish together in the future.

An engagement is also a chance for couples to test their compatibility and may be a time of high stress and conflict. Even without the cultural differences and parental disapproval that Toula and Ian had to deal with in *My Big Fat Greek Wedding*, couples must make important decisions. If one partner is considerably wealthier than the other, he or she may wish to draw up a **prenuptial agreement**, which stipulates what should happen financially in the event of a divorce. Researchers have discovered that prenuptial agreements are almost always sought by the economically stronger party in a relationship, usually masking underlying issues of power, trust, and sharing. When prenuptial agreements are used to legally reinforce unequal power in a relationship, they may negatively affect the couple's chance of a healthy marriage.[10]

The trend toward longer periods of engagement provides couples with more than enough time to question whether the relationship is truly right. This, coupled with high levels of stress, has led to an increasing number of **disengagements**—calling off the engagement to avoid a later divorce. Authors Rachel Safier and Wendy Roberts estimate that about

15 percent of all engagements are called off each year.[11] Some couples realize that they are incompatible before the big day, others are unable to work through the stresses that accompany marriage preparation, and many fear that the issues raised during the stressful planning period may soon escalate into divorce if they proceed with the wedding.[12]

MEETING POTENTIAL PARTNERS

"How did you two meet?" is a common question asked of new couples. Although traditional responses such as "through a friend" or "at work" are still the most popular answers, matchmaking is becoming an increasingly creative business. In addition, people can now meet potential partners on a singles cruise, during singles nights at their local supermarket, or even by placing a flirtatious bumper sticker on their car to let other drivers know that they are available. Other avenues include online dating and speed dating.

Online Dating

Once dismissed as the last resort, **online dating**—the use of specialist dating Web sites—has become an acceptable way to meet a potential partner. In a 2006 Pew survey of Internet users, 31 percent of American adults said that they knew someone who had used a dating Web site, and 15 percent said that they knew someone who was in a long-term relationship with a person that he or she had met online.[13]

Although online dating has proven to be highly successful, members of dating Web sites need to be wary of certain risk factors. Internet users do not necessarily portray themselves accurately—in one study, 81 percent of daters lied at least once on their online profile, most frequently about their weight, height, or age.[14] Others lie about their marital status or even their gender. Researchers also point to the use of the Internet as a forum for casual sexual encounters, increasing the potential risk of sexually transmitted diseases.[15]

Speed Dating

No time to socialize? Surely you can spare six minutes. That's how long potential couples usually spend getting acquainted while **speed dating**—an accelerated form of dating in which men and women choose whether to see each other again based on a very short interaction. Originally created for young Jewish singles in 1999, speed dating now provides homosexuals, heterosexuals, and a number of religious and ethnic groups with an opportunity to participate in quick, one-on-one dates with like-minded singles. Individuals spend six minutes talking to each date. If both individuals are interested, they are provided with each other's e-mail addresses.[16]

Although a fun dating strategy, speed dating is superficial by nature. Researchers have noted that speed-daters usually focus on physical attractiveness and rarely ask pertinent questions about char-

How People in Married or Long-term Relationships Met Their Current Partner

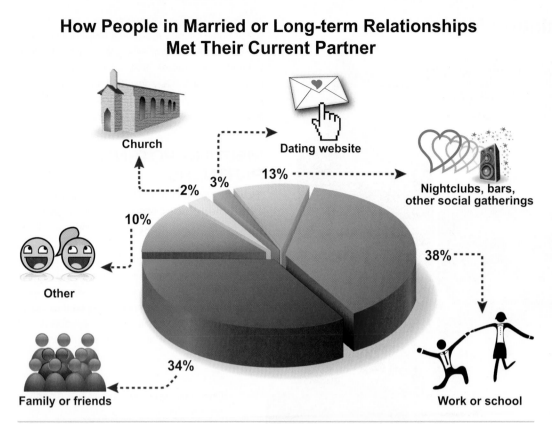

Church — 2%

Dating website — 3%

13%

Nightclubs, bars, other social gatherings

Other — 10%

38% — Work or school

Family or friends — 34%

> ∧
> ∧
> ∧ **Internet dating has rapidly increased in popularity over the last few years and is now the fourth most common way to find a partner.** Why do you think Internet or online dating is no longer considered a "last resort"?

acteristics such as education and religion.[17] When it comes to speed dating, social scientists Michèle Belot and Marco Francesconi note that women prefer men who are young and tall, and men prefer women who are young and thin. Both sexes prefer partners of a similar age, height, and education, and select partners according to physical attributes that might predict socioeconomic status (such as age, height, and weight).[18]

DIFFERENCES IN DATING PRACTICE

In *My Big Fat Greek Wedding*, Toula is expected to conform to her family's traditional gendered expectations of marrying a nice Greek boy, having Greek babies, and feeding everyone. When she meets Ian, she rejects her family's patriarchal ideals by dating a man who does not fit into the traditional mold. So, how do factors such as gender, class, race, age, and sexuality affect dating patterns?

Gender

Traditionally, men are expected to ask women out and pay for the evening's entertainment entirely. Recently,

women are increasingly leveling the romantic playing field. However, research suggests that traditional gender roles still influence the dating script. Women typically spend time preparing for the date, are picked up by the man, and create small talk, while men plan the activities, pay the bill, and walk the women to the door at the end of the evening.[19] Thus, men usually play a proactive role by organizing the date, providing transportation, and initiating sexual contact (such as a goodnight kiss), while women play a reactive role by accepting or rejecting sexual advances.

Researchers have also noted gender differences in the way men and women signal interest in each other. Women frequently use subtle and indirect tactics, such as "accidentally" being near males that interest them, while men typically choose to engage in direct verbal communication.[20]

Social Class

Since individuals from particular social classes share similar backgrounds and interests, most people in the United States tend to date and marry within their social class, even when partners belong to different racial or ethnic groups.[21] Researchers have discovered that dating behaviors vary within social classes.

Children from upper-class families are often encouraged to focus on education and career progression rather than romance, so they tend to start dating and marry later. Supervised parties and dances at exclusive schools and country clubs ensure that youngsters mingle among their social equals.

Middle-class parents are more likely to encourage their children to attend church groups or supervised school events such as

> <<< **Although it is now acceptable for women to ask men out, studies show that dates frequently follow a traditional gender-oriented script.** Do you think these patterns will change, and if so, how?

proms or homecoming parties.[22] However, teenagers are usually able to go on dates unsupervised, typically attending sports events or going out to dinner or a movie.

Lower-class youths are less likely to go on structured dates, instead choosing to hang out in groups at skating rinks, bowling alleys, or local bars.[23] Dating is often informal and unsupervised. When couples become serious, they often progress directly to marriage without an engagement period.

Race

Since non-whites are overrepresented within poorer communities, dating trends among minority groups are most likely to resemble those found in the lower classes. White adolescents are more likely than all other racial and ethnic groups to experience serious committed relationships, with the starkest difference between white girls and black girls.[24]

One racial imbalance is apparent—there are relatively few well-educated, eligible black men to partner the growing number of successful black women. Since 1976, nearly twice as many black women as black men have earned bachelor's, doctoral, and professional degrees, and approximately 12 percent of African American males in their 20s and early 30s are incarcerated.[25] This imbalance has contributed to a growing trend in **interdating**—dating members of other racial or ethnic groups. More than half of those surveyed (55 percent) had interdated at some point in their dating history.[26]

Age

Few people believed that the union between 26-year-old model Anna Nicole Smith and 89-year-old oil billionaire J. Howard Marshall was a love match. Why are we so cynical about such extreme age differences? In the United States, spouses tend to be just two to three years apart in age, with men typically older than women.[27] These differences are smallest in couples who marry at younger ages and greater between those who marry at older ages. One study of adolescents noted that males were willing to date females who were, on average, 1.57 years younger or six years older. Females, on the other hand, said they would date males 0.63 years younger to 5.9 years older.[28] Attitudes toward large age differences tend to be fairly negative, with a recent survey noting that 56 percent of men believe an age difference of five years or less is optimal in a relationship. Only 16 percent claim that age differences are not important.[29]

Sexuality

Most studies concur that the primary difference between homosexual and heterosexual relationships is the additional challenges homosexual couples face from being part of a **marginalized group**.[30,31] To be marginalized means to be relegated to a status outside the mainstream.

Researchers have found that steady relationships are equally important to gay and lesbian couples, and studies show that homosexual couples report the same levels of relationship satisfaction as heterosexual couples.[32]

However, researchers have noted some differences in dating. Gay male couples are more likely to report that sexual activity is the most important aspect of their relationship, whereas lesbian couples list emotional attachment as the number one criterion.[33] A study of Internet personal advertisements revealed that gay men are more likely to mention race preference in their ads than straight men.[34]

DATING VIOLENCE

When R&B singer Chris Brown was arrested for assaulting his girlfriend, pop star Rihanna, an ugly trend was brought to light. **Dating violence**—the perpetration or threat of an act of violence against a person in the context of a relationship, including sexual assault, physical abuse, and verbal or emotional abuse—is far more widespread than most people like to admit. Estimated rates of nonsexual dating violence range from 9 to 65 percent, depending on whether emotional and verbal aggression are included in the definition of violence. Consider these statistics:

- In a survey of college students, 88 percent reported at least one incidence of dating violence.[35]

- Among high school students, 96 percent reported experiencing psychological abuse. Of these, 59 percent were victims of physical violence.[36]

- In a study of 130 women who had experienced dating violence, the most frequent forms of physical abuse reported were pushing (67%), grabbing (52%), restraint (41%), and hitting (40%).[37]

- Females are more than twice as likely to experience sexual violence by a dating partner than males.[38]

Dating violence often stems from a desire to control a relationship and occurs more often when abusers have experienced physical aggression by a parent or guardian. Studies have found that violence toward children, even in

∧∧∧ **Once considered R&B's golden couple** Chris Brown and Rihanna's seemingly loving relationship turned sour when Brown was arrested for beating his girlfriend in February 2009. **The incident brought to light an alarmingly high incidence of teen dating violence.**

DATE RAPE is the act of forcing sexual intercourse on a non-consenting date or partner.

PARENT IMAGE THEORY is the psychoanalytic theory that men are more likely to select women who resemble their mothers, whereas women are more likely to select men who look like their fathers.

IDEAL MATE THEORY is the psychoanalytic theory that people develop a model image of their mate based on their early childhood experiences.

COMPLEMENTARY NEEDS THEORY suggests people select mates whose needs are opposite but complementary to their own.

EXCHANGE THEORY uses the concepts of rewards and costs to explain interpersonal attraction.

the context of discipline, increases the risk of children becoming victims or perpetrators of violence two- to threefold.[39,40] Unfortunately, dating violence is rarely a one-time event, since only about half of couples end the relationship after the first incidence of violence. Some studies suggest that frequent exposure to abusive behavior increases victims' investments in their violent relationships, making them less likely to leave.[41]

Date Rape

The more common type of sexual assault is **date rape**—the act of forcing sexual intercourse on a non-consenting partner. More than 85 percent of sexual assaults involve acquaintances or friends. Date rapes often go unreported and are notoriously difficult to prove, especially when alcohol or drugs may have impaired the victim's memory. Studies have found that the public regards stranger rape with harsher condemnation than date rape. The reason for this is that people are less willing to define non-consensual sex between acquaintances as "rape" and more likely to place blame on the victim.[42]

Theories of Mate Selection

How do we end up with the person we marry? Much as we would like to believe in the workings of fate or destiny, the reality is that our choice of partner is influenced by factors such as family background, socioeconomic class, race, and religion, and by practical constraints such as the geographic location in which we live and date.

PSYCHODYNAMIC THEORIES

Based on the ideas of Freud and Jung, psychodynamic theories postulate that our choice of mate is influenced by childhood experiences and family background.

Parent Image Theory

According to the **parent image theory**, men are more likely to select women who resemble their mothers, whereas women are more likely to select men who look like their fathers. Researcher Davor Jedlicka tested this idea among brides and grooms of mixed race parentage and found that 61 percent of brides married men of the same ethnicity as their father, whereas 59 percent of grooms married women of the same ethnicity of their mother.[43]

Ideal Mate Theory

The **ideal mate theory** states that people develop a model image of their mate based on their early childhood experiences. Researchers asked participants to describe their parents, significant others, and ideal significant others in terms of several personality characteristics. They found that for four out of eight personality variables, subjects' opposite-sex parents scored similarly to their partners. However, participants perceived their significant others as similar to their parents across all variables, supporting the idea that people tend to choose romantic partners they *perceive* to be similar to their opposite-sex parents, even if this is not necessarily the case.[44]

NEEDS THEORIES

According to Robert Winch's **complementary needs theory**, we select a mate whose needs are opposite but complementary to our own. For example, a person who enjoys nurturing others is likely to choose a partner who needs to be nurtured. A strong, dominant personality may be attracted to someone who is more submissive.[45] However, several other studies have suggested that we tend to be attracted to people who share similar personality characteristics to our own.

EXCHANGE THEORIES

Would you date an extremely wealthy person if he or she frequently embarrassed you in public? What about a person who was very attractive but unbearably boring? **Exchange theories** work on the premise of

From Classroom to Community} Safe Dating

Every week, Kim volunteers at her local community center, which runs a program to help prevent teen dating abuse.

"One of my friends was abused by her boyfriend, but I thought it was a pretty rare situation. When I read the statistics about teen dating violence, I was shocked and wanted to do something about it.

"I help out with the RESPECT program once a week, working with teens aged 13 to 19. Some of them are victims of dating abuse, and others are perpetrators of dating violence.

"We try to change the kids' attitudes about violence and gender stereotyping, and improve conflict management

ACTIVITY

Attend two different events for "singles" that are organized for singles to meet other singles. Examine the events using the scientific method discussed in Chapter 2 and from a "scientific" perspective. What processes or patterns do you see taking place?

skills so that they can stop a potentially violent situation before it escalates.

"I also work with individuals to create a Dating Bill of Rights and Responsibilities, which helps them to understand that they don't have to please others all the time and reinforces that it's OK to say "no" to anything they're not comfortable about in a relationship.

"We've had a lot of positive feedback about the program. I hope that the message we're sending out is reflected in lower teen violence statistics in the future."

cost–benefit analysis. We gain rewards from participating in a relationship, which might include physical attraction, social acceptance and approval, sexual fulfillment, and financial support. However, the relationship is also likely to come with costs, such as a partner's frugality, lack of humor, or the amount of time and effort required to maintain the relationship. When the rewards of being in the relationship outweigh the costs, the relationship is likely to continue.

Changing gender roles have resulted in a shift in the value of particular rewards and costs. Traditionally, men brought resources such as financial stability, education, and social status into a relationship, whereas women's assets included physical attractiveness and the ability to provide and care for children. As an increasing number of women earn college degrees and financial independence, they are able to be more selective in their choice of partners, dating men who are willing to share housework and child care responsibilities. Similarly, men now look not only at a potential partner's physical attractiveness, but also at her ability to contribute to the family's financial stability.

DEVELOPMENTAL PROCESS THEORIES

Developmental process theories describe mate selection as a process of narrowing down the vast number of potential partners using a filtering system. Each filter reduces the **field of eligibles**—the people whom society defines as acceptable marriage partners—until just one person is selected.

Propinquity Filter

Propinquity refers to geographic closeness, and it is one of the first factors to limit the number of people we meet and interact with frequently enough to date. A 1932 study by James Brossard in Philadelphia found that more than half the couples who applied for marriage licenses lived within 20 blocks of each other. Although mass transportation and online dating have expanded our romantic horizons, most people marry someone from the same geographic region as themselves. Institutional propinquity is equally important because most couples meet at work

or school or through social or religious institutions. In *My Big Fat Greek Wedding*, Ian obviously lives near Toula as they randomly run into one another twice, first when she is working at her family's restaurant, and later when she is working at her aunt's travel agency.

Physical Attractiveness Filter

Everyone has a different idea of what he or she finds physically attractive in a mate. Some studies suggest that we choose partners whose physical attractiveness is similar to our own.[46,47] For Americans, physical appearance is one of the primary factors in choosing a partner, with youth and slimness the two common attributes in people who are deemed attractive. Other cultures prize different physical attributes—among Mauritania's white Moor Arab population, for example, obesity is prized as a sign of wealth.[48]

Social Filter

Statistically, you are most likely to marry someone of the same class, race, age, education level, and socioeconomic background as yourself, a phenomenon that sociologists refer to as **homogamy** (sometimes used interchangeably with the term *endogamy*). Conversely, **heterogamy** (or *exogamy*) refers to the practice of marrying someone outside your own race, religion, or age group. Studies have found that couples are more likely to stay together because they have more in common and share similar values and beliefs.[49]

All eligible partners

Propinquity

Physical attraction

Homogamy and heterogamy

The Filter Theory of Mate Selection

<<< **The Filter Theory of Mate Selection.** According to filter theory, we narrow our choice of prospective partners by choosing someone we see regularly who is similar to us in terms of age, physical appearance, socioeconomic class, and religion. **To what extent do you think this theory accounts for a person's selection of a partner?**

Arranged Marriage in India

Although the concept of marrying without love seems alien to most Americans, it is a common and highly successful practice in India. Almost 95 percent of unions are arranged marriages. When parents or family elders seek out potential mates for their children, they consider occupational and cultural compatibility, class compatibility, and the family's moral history. Compatibility with future in-laws is particularly important because most couples live with the husband's parents after the wedding, even if they are financially independent.

Traditionally, the bride's family was expected to provide a **dowry**—material goods paid to the groom's family to increase their status by the marriage. The dowry system was prohibited in 1961, although the law is frequently flouted.[50]

Despite protests that they are outdated and subject women to various abuses, arranged marriages have a high success rate in India, with 94 percent of urban professionals rating their arranged marriages as "very successful."[51] Many young singles are opting for an arranged marriage even when it is not compulsory, trusting their parents to act in their best interests. Modern Indian parents often take their children's preferences into account and allow them to opt out of a proposed union if they do not like their chosen partner.

∧
∧ **Around 95 percent of**
∧ **marriages** in India are arranged by parents or family elders.

My Parents Picked My Spouse

A year ago, a 22-year-old Indian woman named Meeta Patel married her husband through an arranged wedding coordinated by her parents.

"I always knew that my parents would be the ones to find my husband. They also had an arranged marriage and are still happy together 25 years later.

"I trusted them to find me a husband that I would be equally happy with. The myth is that you cannot reject suitors that don't appeal to you. That is not the case. I turned down more than a dozen suitors before I met my husband.

"Another myth is that parents don't consult the wishes of their children. That is also not the case.

"My parents and I had many conversations about what I was looking for in a husband, and they used that information when considering matches.

"In the West, people marry for love—we see that in Western movies and shows.

"But in India, we marry to have a lasting union. That is what everyone does—it's our culture. The idea of marrying for "love" is very new.

"My husband has the same cultural background as me, which only adds to our ability to get along very well.

"It's true we didn't know everything about each other when we got married, but with each passing day our relationship grows stronger."

think marriages and families: HOW DO THEORISTS VIEW DATING AND MATE SELECTION?

FUNCTIONALISM

As we have learned in earlier chapters, structural-functionalism considers how society is made up of separate but interrelated parts (schools, families, churches, government, and economy) and how these parts contribute to the social system as a whole. Functionalists argue that marriage has a stabilizing effect on society. The traditional family system regulates sexual behavior, promotes orderly procreation, socializes and educates children, and provides protection and economic security for all its members.[52]

As the accepted forerunner to marriage in Westernized cultures, dating is part of this stabilizing process. Going on dates enables people to become acquainted and assess their compatibility before making a lifelong commitment of marriage. The mate selection process improves the chances of finding an ideal companion, increasing the likelihood that a long-term union will be successful. Dating also enables teens and young adults to develop their social skills, practicing roles that will later be required within marriage. Furthermore, dating contributes to a healthy economy. Think about the last date you went on. Did you go out to dinner? Watch a movie? Buy or receive flowers? Maybe you bought a new outfit to wear. However you spent your money, local businesses—and wider society by extension—benefited from your date.[53]

But is dating the most efficient means of contributing to a stable social system? If dating is such an effective method of mate selection, why is the U.S. divorce rate so high? Does dating really socialize young people to become good marriage partners? If so, why do we have domestic violence and spousal abuse? As with most social structures, dating has some negative consequences known as **dysfunctions**. Dysfunctions exist at a societal level (for example, divorce and domestic violence) and on a personal level (for example, betrayal and the fear of rejection). One reason that dating may not contribute to marital stability is a difference in structure and function. A date occurs within a limited time period, during which we are attempting to impress our date and not necessarily presenting our true selves. Hiding unsavory personality characteristics becomes trickier in a marriage when two people live together, making disagreements more likely.[54]

Functionalists believe that all aspects of a social system are interrelated, and dating is no exception. Dating habits are influenced by social values, gender roles, and demographics. For example, sex before marriage has far more serious implications in societies that value virginity. As we saw earlier in the chapter, gender roles affect expectations about how men and women behave on dates. And demographics determine opportunities and constraints in dating and mate selection. The **sex ratio** indicates the relationship between the number of men and the number of women of a given age in a society. Currently, there are roughly the same number of men and women in all age groups except those 65 and older. The comparatively small number of men compared to women in this age group provides men with more bargaining power when it comes to choosing a partner.[55]

CONFLICT THEORY

Conflict theorists examine an individual or group's ability to control the resources within society. Because resources are scarce, not every group is able to achieve its goal, resulting in conflict. Thus, conflict theorists view inequality as an inevitable aspect of most social relationships. For example, during the mid-1800s, Jim Crow laws passed by legislators in the southern states prevented interracial marriage in an attempt to segregate blacks and maintain a racial caste system. Today, similar prejudice exists against gay marriage, which is banned in all but six states. Opponents of gay marriage strive to keep the social status quo, arguing that legalizing same-sex unions will destroy the institution of marriage,

DOWRY is the material goods paid by the bride's family to the groom's family to increase their status by the marriage.

DYSFUNCTION is the negative consequence of a social structure.

SEX RATIO is the relationship between the number of men and the number of women of a given age in a society.

CONSENSUS is an agreement that is achieved in mate selection by choosing a partner with similar values and beliefs.

pave the way for polygamy and other non-traditional family arrangements, overburden the Social Security system, and force courts to place adoptive children in fatherless or motherless homes.[56] By maintaining the ban on gay marriage, opposition groups tilt the balance of power in favor of the dominant majority, marginalizing same-sex families.

Conflict exists not only between groups within society, but also between individuals. Family members frequently fight over issues ranging from possession of the remote control to the amount of time spent with in-laws during the holidays. Conflict theorists study how individuals can minimize the possibility of conflict by selecting mates who share their values and beliefs and by raising future children with these same values and beliefs. This process, known as agreement, or **consensus**, helps prevent the likelihood of insurmountable problems within a relationship.

Conflict theorists also study how differences of power and status influence social behavior, such as sexual attraction. Contrary to popular beliefs, research indicates that high status in males doesn't directly translate into sexiness. Rather, females find interpersonal power more attractive in males than high status. Interestingly, the same research study found that high status makes females more attractive to males.[57]

Sex Ratio in the United States (Number of Males per Female)

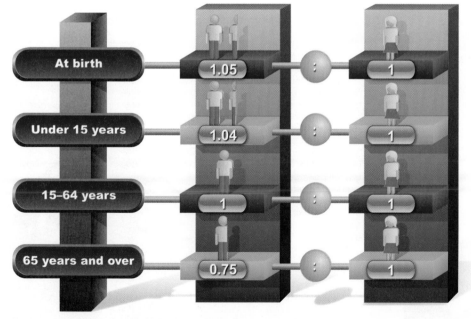

Source: www.cia.gov, CIA World Factbook, https://www.cia.gov/library/publications/the-world-factbook/geos/us.html, Accessed August 12, 2009.

∧
∧ The comparatively small number of men compared to
∧ women in the 65+ age bracket reduces women's options when it comes to finding a partner. **What social effects might this have for women in this age group?**

SYMBOLIC INTERACTIONISM

As we learned in previous chapters, symbolic interactionists consider how we socially construct a sense of self through our interactions with others. Daily interactions with friends, family members, and within society at large teach us cultural norms and values, influencing our behavior. We learn that it is polite to say "please" and "thank you" through persistent reminders from our parents, and we perceive that it is rude to cut in front of someone in line by the disapproving noises we hear among those behind us.

How might symbolic interactionists interpret our dating behavior? Consider the qualities and physical attributes you value in a partner. Where did you learn that kindness and honesty are desirable traits, whereas infidelity and deceitfulness are not? Images we see in the media, conversations we have with family and friends, and articles we read in newspapers shape our perceptions, and these perceptions are individually and culturally specific. As we have seen throughout the chapter, the concept of the ideal partner varies around the globe. Families in India place more importance on social status and compatibility between families as a whole

WRAP YOUR MIND AROUND THE THEORY

Researchers discovered **that children born and bred in the same kibbutz do not usually marry each other as adults.** How might this trend relate to the incest taboo in Western cultures in terms of social stability?

FUNCTIONALISM

Functionalists examine the role that dating and marriage play within society and how mating practices contribute to the stabilization or destabilization of social institutions. For example, a study of mate selection in kibbutzim in Israel revealed that children born and bred in the same kibbutz were extremely unlikely to marry each other as adults. Researchers suggested that this was the result of a self-imposed incest taboo—because the children grew up in close proximity to one another, they viewed peers as biological siblings. Examining the tendency to marry outside the kibbutz, researcher Yonina Talmon noted that the practice served to recruit new members, created strong ties between the kibbutz and the wider community, and prevented the emergence of powerful internal kinship groups.[59] However, the decision to marry outside the kibbutz was not an intentional effort to promote social stability, but rather an individual compromise between freedom and local continuity. Most second-generation members chose to stay in the kibbutz to continue their parents' lifelong work, but found the isolated community stifling and restrictive. Marrying outsiders counteracted this limitation by expanding their social horizons.[60]

CONFLICT THEORY

Conflict theorists study the struggles between individuals within families and between groups within societies to gain control over scarce resources. Conflict theorists believe that during the process of mate selection, potential partners seek to minimize the possibility of conflict by choosing a mate with similar values, attitudes, and beliefs to themselves. As we noted earlier in the chapter, most people tend to marry partners within the same age range, racial or ethnic group, educational background, and religion, increasing the likelihood of consensus. Some studies suggest that the most desirable mates are those who possess the highest status in society, indicating control of more of the resources.[63] In other words, people are naturally attracted to those with power.

WHAT FACTORS AFFECT MATE SELECTION?

SYMBOLIC INTERACTIONISM

Symbolic interactionists believe that we interpret meanings from our interactions with others. Single men and women commonly give flirtatious signals to indicate their interest in a member of the opposite sex. When psychologist Monica Moore recorded the flirtatious behaviors of 40 women at a local singles bar, university snack bar, university library, and university women's center, she noticed that the women were more likely to give flirtatious signals such as flipping their hair, smiling, or holding someone's gaze if they were in a location in which they were likely to meet single men. Regardless of the setting, the women who engaged in the most flirtatious behavior were approached by men most often.[61]

Although giving off flirtatious signals is a useful way to meet partners, researchers also consider the consequences of misinterpreting intended meanings. Many rapists claim to have interpreted signals from their victims as indicating a desire for sex.[62] They may mistake flirtatious behavior as an invitation to sex, although that is the farthest thing from the victim's mind. Regardless of how behavior is interpreted, most people agree that the victim is never at fault. The possibility of misinterpreting the intended meaning of a gesture or signal complicates the process of mate selection. Individuals must learn to decipher signals and accept that "no means no."

Conflict theorists believe **dating someone from the same educational background or religion indicates shared beliefs and values, minimizing the possibility of conflict.** Does this theory fit with your personal dating experiences?

According to symbolic interaction theory, **we interpret individual meanings from everyday situations.** How do we learn that gestures such as hair flipping and head tossing are signs of encouragement and not warnings to leave us alone?

than on physical attraction between potential spouses. Some countries in Africa view obesity as a sign of wealth and prosperity, whereas most Western cultures idealize slimness and youth.

Not only is it impossible to escape from societal influences on mate selection, researchers have found that parents also subtly affect their children's choice of partners. A study of campus sorority systems in the 1960s discovered that sororities tended to accept new members of a similar class, religion, and ethnic background, and that parents encouraged their daughters to join sororities that matched their backgrounds. Because sorority members primarily socialized with fraternity members of the same background, parents increased the likelihood that their daughters would date and marry someone from the same social group.[58]

discover marriages and families in action:
HOW ARE COUPLES AND FAMILIES FINDING CREATIVE WAYS TO DATE?

Keeping Dating Fresh

Since dating first started in the 1920s, it has evolved from a simple stroll in the park or trip in the car to a varied selection of activities, ranging from cooking classes to surfing lessons. Traditional dating patterns have also changed, and modern dates may commonly include gay or lesbian couples, single parents, or older widowers or divorcees. As such, couples and families are finding increasingly creative ways to fit dates into their changing lifestyles and to keep dating fresh and exciting.

FAMILY DATES

Many single parents find that child care arrangements limit their dating opportunities. Others go on dates with the intention of finding out whether their date would be a suitable role model for their children. One way of dealing with both situations is to bring the kids along. Family dates are an increasingly popular way for single parents to assess whether their families would integrate successfully or for nuclear families to spend some time together. Popular family activities include rafting or tubing on a local river, baking homemade cookies, flying kites, or playing board games. Although Toula and Ian from *My Big Fat Greek Wedding* do not have children while they are dating, her family is highly involved in their lives, so after their engagement, some of their dates include large family gatherings.

EDUCATIONAL DATES

Educational dates offer couples opportunities to learn new skills and enhance their knowledge while getting to know each other better. Couples may choose to visit a local museum, zoo, or art gallery, or to take a class together. Many community centers offer one-day classes in activities such as painting, photography, sailing, or dancing. If the date is a success, couples can then choose to enroll in a longer series of classes, potentially developing a shared hobby. Other educational options include taking a tour of a local factory, watching a documentary, visiting nearby historical sites, or visiting an arboretum.

CHARITABLE DATES

Charitable dates offer couples the chance to do something positive for their community while they get to know each other. Suggesting and accepting a charitable date may also offer some insight into a potential partner's personal values and beliefs, which, as we learned earlier in the chapter, is a key factor in successful mate selection. Couples with similar values are more likely to stay together than couples with widely divergent beliefs. Possible charitable dates might include taking part in a charity walk, run, or bike ride, volunteering at a fund-raising event, or reading stories to children in a local hospital.

ACTIVITY

Research different dating services in your community. Do they serve all populations, including heterosexuals as well as gays and lesbians? Do they provide services to set up dates?

MAKE CONNECTIONS

Dating and Mate Selection

As you have learned in this chapter, dating lays the groundwork for finding the individual you are going to spend the rest of your life with. It is vastly different from the casual practice of "hooking up" that we learned about in Chapter 5, which involves sexual activity without feelings or commitment.

In this chapter, we discussed many factors that can affect mate selection, including personal, societal, and family influences. Looking back to Chapter 3, you can see how poor communication may result in problems within a relationship. Conversely, positive communication results in stronger, more committed relationships. In Chapter 1, we learned that a person's family of origin has a lifelong impact on that person's life. In this chapter, we confirmed that this impact extends to the decisions a person makes about dating partners.

Sadly, violence is common within relationships. In this chapter, we learned what factors influence dating violence. Looking ahead to Chapter 13, we will examine stress, violence, and abuse within marriage and families in more detail.

>>> ACTIVITIES

1. Make a list of factors which are leading or propelling you toward marriage. Make a list of factors which are leading you away from marriage. How do your lists compare to empirical evidence that was presented in the chapter?

2. Ask five of your friends (include both males and females) what is the first feature or aspect that attracts them to someone. Compare and contrast the lists made by males and females. What are the similarities and differences?

WHAT ARE THE HISTORICAL AND CURRENT TRENDS IN DATING AND MATE SELECTION?   117

Dating in the United States has evolved from elaborate public courtship rituals to modern dating practices that include going steady, pack dating, serious dating, and engagement. Partners typically meet through friends or at work, but singles also use online dating and speed dating to meet their mates. Dating practices are influenced age, social class, education, gender, race, and sexuality. Dating violence is prevalent in many relationships, and date rape is the most common form of sexual assault.

HOW DO THEORISTS VIEW DATING AND MATE SELECTION?   124

Structural functionalists view dating as the socially accepted forerunner to marriage, and therefore believe it has a stabilizing effect on society. Conflict theorists believe that groups compete for scarce resources within society, with dominant groups struggling to keep power by maintaining the status quo. Hence, supporters of traditional marriage wish to prevent gay and lesbian couples from marrying. Symbolic interactionists believe that interactions between friends and family members and within society at large shape our cultural norms and values, influencing our perceptions of potential dating partners.

HOW ARE COUPLES AND FAMILIES FINDING CREATIVE WAYS TO DATE?   127

Couples and families are finding increasingly creative ways to fit dates into their changing lifestyles and to keep dating fresh and exciting. Modern creative dating includes family dates, educational dates, and charitable dates.

Theory

FUNCTIONALISM   124

- mating practices contribute to the stabilization or destabilization of social institutions
- social values, gender roles, and demographics influence dating habits

CONFLICT THEORY   125

- conflict exists between both groups and individuals within society
- individuals minimize the possibility of conflict by choosing a mate with similar values, attitudes, and beliefs as theirs

SYMBOLIC INTERACTIONISM   125

- individual perceptions are shaped through interactions with others
- people interpret meanings based on gestures and symbols

Key Terms

honor killings happen when a family member perceives that a female relative will bring or has brought shame on the family, usually through a suspected breech of cultural traditions or religious morals   116

courtship is a publicly visible dating process with specific rules and restrictions   117

dating is when two people meet at an agreed upon time and place to partake in a social activity   117

marriage market is a system in which prospective partners evaluate the assets and liabilities of potential spouses and choose the best available mate   118

going steady is dating one person exclusively   118

pack dating is dating in small groups without committing to one person   118

engagement is the public commitment to marry   118

prenuptial agreement is a legal document stipulating financial arrangements in the event of a divorce   119

disengagement is the breakdown of an engagement   119

online dating is when people use specialized dating Web sites such as Match.com or eHarmony to meet a potential spouse   119

speed dating is an accelerated form of dating in which men and women choose whether to see each other again based on a very short interaction   119

interdating is when people date members of other racial or ethnic groups   121

marginalized group is a group relegated to a social standing outside the mainstream   121

dating violence is the perpetration or threat of an act of violence against a person in the context of a relationship, including sexual assault, physical abuse, and verbal or emotional abuse   *121*

date rape is the act of forcing sexual intercourse on a non-consenting date or partner   *122*

parent image theory is the psychoanalytic theory that men are more likely to select women who resemble their mothers, whereas women are more likely to select men who look like their fathers   *122*

ideal mate theory is the psychoanalytic theory that people develop a model image of their mate based on their early childhood experiences   *122*

complementary needs theory is the theory that suggests people select mates whose needs are opposite but complementary to their own   *122*

exchange theory is the theory that uses the concepts of rewards and costs to explain interpersonal attraction   *122*

developmental process theory is the theory of mate selection in which individuals narrow down their choice of mate using a filtering system   *123*

field of eligibles is the group of people whom society defines as acceptable marriage partners   *123*

propinquity is geographic closeness   *123*

homogamy is the tendency to marry someone of the same race, class, age, and educational background; also called *endogamy*   *123*

heterogamy is the practice of marrying someone outside your own race, religion, or age group; also called *exogamy*   *123*

dowry is the material goods paid by the bride's family to the groom's family to increase their status by the marriage   *124*

dysfunction is the negative consequence of a social structure   *124*

sex ratio is the relationship between the number of men and the number of women of a given age in a society   *125*

consensus is an agreement that is achieved in mate selection by choosing a partner with similar values and beliefs   *125*

Sample Test Questions

MULTIPLE CHOICE

These multiple-choice questions are similar to those found in the test bank that accompanies this textbook.

1. What are the three components of the marriage market?
   a. supply, preferences, and resources
   b. supply, demand, and needs
   c. resources, exchange, and needs
   d. rewards, costs, and preferences

2. How do MOST people meet their long-term partners?
   a. at a religious institution
   b. at a nightclub or bar
   c. at work or school
   d. through family or friends

3. Which of these statements about dating practices is TRUE?
   a. Homosexual couples are typically happier than heterosexual couples.
   b. Traditional gender roles no longer exist during a typical date.
   c. Age differences are greatest in couples who marry at younger ages and smaller between those who marry at older ages.
   d. The higher the social class an individual is in, the more restricted he or she is likely to be regarding dating practices.

4. Dating violence:
   a. is usually a one-time event and does not recur.
   b. is common among young adults but not teenagers.
   c. occurs more often when abusers have experienced physical aggression by a parent.
   d. is often attributed to an unwillingness to take charge in a relationship.

5. According to the parent image theory, 26-year-old Danielle is most likely to:
   a. select a mate who resembles her father.
   b. select a mate who resembles her mother.
   c. select a mate with similar characteristics to her father.
   d. select a mate with similar characteristics to her mother.

ESSAY

1. Discuss the current dating trends in the United States.
2. Choose three common ways of meeting a partner and assess the advantages and disadvantages of each.
3. Analyze differences in gender in modern dating practices.
4. Choose one of the theories of mate selection and discuss its strengths and weaknesses.
5. How do changing family compositions affect modern dating practices?

WHERE TO START YOUR RESEARCH PAPER

For more information about the history of dating, go to
http://www.encyclopedia.com/doc/1O119-CourtshipandDating.html

For more data on dating violence statistics, go to
http://www.cdc.gov/ncipc/dvp/dating_violence.htm

For more information about teen dating violence, go to
http://www.focusas.com/Abuse-TeenDatingViolence.html

To find out more about online dating, go to
http://www.onlinedatingmagazine.com/

For more information about speed dating, go to
http://www.datingtrail.co.uk/history_speed_dating.php

For more information about modern arranged marriages, go to
http://www.startribune.com/lifestyle/family/15439136.html

To find out more about the theories of mate selection, go to
http://family.jrank.org/pages/1145/Mate-Selection-Factors-in-Relationship.html

Answers: 1. a; 2. c; 3. d; 4. c; 5. a

Remember to check www.thethinkspot.com for additional information, downloadable flashcards, and other helpful resources.

Tom

and Kate were both brought up in small families, so when they got married and started planning a family of their own, they agreed that they wanted to have a large brood. Twenty-three years of marriage and 12 children (7 boys and 5 girls) later, they seem to be handling their large family well. Both sacrificed their careers to make their family the priority; instead of working for a large university, Tom coaches football at a small local college, and Kate has given up a career as a newspaper journalist to be a full-time mom. Although their household might not be described as the most orderly, the Bakers seem to have a system that works. Their breakfast routine resembles an efficient assembly line, eldest daughter Nora helps out where she can, and, perhaps most importantly, Tom and Kate's marriage still has that spark. But when Tom and Kate are both offered promising professional opportunities, their well-oiled system starts to break down.

Tom's new job at a Division I school requires the family to move from Midland, their small suburban town, to big-city life in Chicago. Already against the relocation, the kids are dealt another blow when Kate gets a book deal from a major publisher that requires her to leave home for a promotional book tour. Tom is left to handle his new job and the household on his own. While Kate is away, Tom experiences some of her daily trials. Mark's pet frog seems to be perpetually missing, the two teenage girls of the family—Lorraine, the fashionista, and Sarah, the tomboy—are at each other's throats, and the clan wreaks havoc on a neighbor's birthday party. Nora's boyfriend offers additional negativity with his persistent dislike of her family, and the young, smug neighbors look down on the Bakers' lax discipline. The situation only grows worse when Kate calls Tom telling him her book tour has been extended for an additional two weeks and he'll have to survive on his own for a little while longer. The chaos reaches a dangerous peak, though, when Mark himself goes missing and is discovered on a train headed back to their old town. When Kate returns home after her book tour, their home is in disarray, and she is upset at Tom for not informing her that he couldn't deal with the responsibilities at home without her.

Once they finally realize how difficult these adjustments have been on the kids, Tom and Kate decide that their careers aren't worth their family's discontent. Tom gives up his career as the football coach at the large school to find a new job that allows him more time at home, and Kate's parenting book ends up on the best sellers' list, but she goes back to her job as stay-at-home mom.

PREPARING FOR CHILDREN AND PARENTING

CHAPTER 08

What lessons can we learn **from *Cheaper by the Dozen?* The 2003 movie, a remake of a 1950 movie,** which was based on a memoir, delivers some universal and enduring lessons about parenting and family life.

Tom and Kate's conflicted career decisions show one way that children can complicate family life. Parents must consider how every choice they make will affect not just themselves, but also their children. That's not to say that children are just a burden; in

Cheaper by the Dozen, they offer the perspective Tom and Kate need to help them make better career choices, not to mention the humor they bring to everyday life. Major life transitions, such as relocating, changing jobs, or even older children starting serious relationships of their own, can stretch families to their limits. But these challenges can also force families to work together and to compromise, which will ultimately bring them closer together. Siblings may not always get along, and discipline may not always work the way parents hope it will, but when all members of a family are working toward the same

goal—being a cohesive, functioning unit—they will have the bond they need to succeed.

When I was growing up, I remember having to work and do my chores before going outside to play. It never seemed fair that so many of my friends did not seem to have chores of their own. Although my siblings and I often thought our parents were unfair for making us do chores as we heard our friends play outside, we learned a strong work ethic from our parents. There are many lessons that children learn from parents. Some have positive consequences, and others have negative consequences. Parents need to seek out learning and teaching opportunities for their children. On the other hand, parents can also learn from their children. In this chapter, you will learn about how to prepare for children and parenting roles from empirical evidence and research findings.

Preparing for Children and Parenting

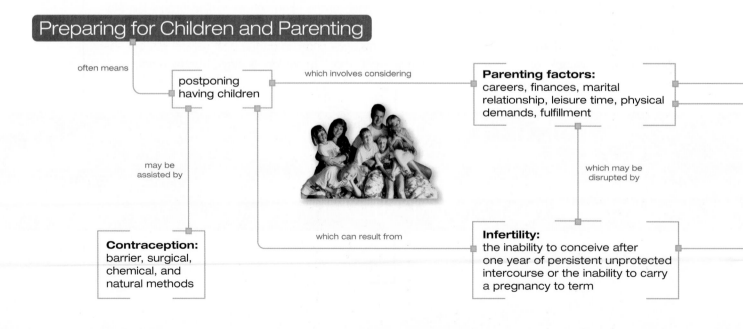

often means

postponing having children

which involves considering

Parenting factors: careers, finances, marital relationship, leisure time, physical demands, fulfillment

may be assisted by

which may be disrupted by

which can result from

Contraception: barrier, surgical, chemical, and natural methods

Infertility: the inability to conceive after one year of persistent unprotected intercourse or the inability to carry a pregnancy to term

get the topic: WHAT FACTORS SHOULD BE CONSIDERED WHEN MAKING PARENTING DECISIONS?

No woman can call herself free until she can choose consciously whether she will or will not be a mother.
—Margaret Sanger

Choosing to Parent

In 1909, the birth rate for the United States was 30 percent. Ninety-one years later, the birth rate had fallen to 14.4 percent.[1] In fact, in 2003, the United States' birth rate reached an all-time low.[2] In a country where health and life expectancy have improved and infant mortality rates have fallen, you would expect the birth rate to be skyrocketing. So, what caused this significant decrease rate of childbirths?

One of the reasons people are having fewer children is that they are living healthier, longer lives. Because of this, couples are waiting to have children. This may be because of money issues or because they want to establish careers and finish their education before settling down and starting a family.[3]

Social movements have also played a large role in this birth rate. Before the 1970s, only 10 percent of married women aged 40 to 44 were childless. However, after the women's liberation movement in the 1970s, this number increased dramatically; in 1976, the percentage of women without children in this age range rose to 19 percent.[4]

CHILDLESS AND CHILDFREE

Many women still follow the course of getting married and having children in their early 20s. Others may choose to be **childfree**, a term that describes women making the voluntary decision not to have children, as distinguished from **childless**, which describes people not having children for infertility reasons. In 2002, the birth rate fell to a record low of 13.9.[5] Does this mean that the number of women choosing to be childfree is at a record high? Maybe, but the statistics tell only part of the story. Because the birth rate is a ratio of the number of live births per 1,000 people in the population, the recent birth rate plunge can also be explained by a greater number of people in the population who are past childbearing age. However, in 2008, 18 percent of women at the end of their childbearing years were childless, doubling the 1980 percentage.[6]

Childlessness tends to occur with women who are highly educated and couples, called **DINKs** (double income, no kids), with high incomes, demanding careers, and a desire to work, travel, and

<<< **What factors must a woman consider when deciding whether or not to become a mother?** Are there any other decisions in life that have this magnitude of importance?

leads to decisions about

Parenting styles: permissive, authoritative, authoritarian, uninvolved

which can put additional strains on

which may be overcome with

Assisted reproductive technology (ART): AID, AIH, IVF, surrogates, donors, hormone therapy, ICSI, NSA

or

Adoption: legally taking a child parented by someone else as one's own

U.S. Birth Rates 1909–2000

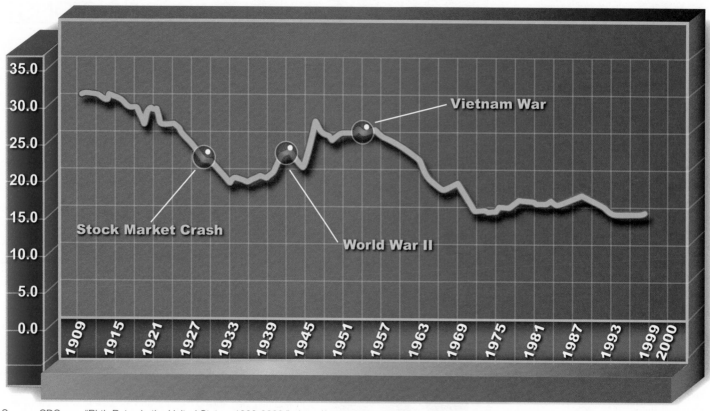

Source: CDC.gov, "Birth Rates in the United States, 1909-2000." <http://www.cdc.gov/nchs/data/statab/t001x01.pdf>, Accessed August 18, 2009.

The birth rate represents the number of live births per 1,000 in a population.

What factors might contribute to the rise and fall of birth rates in the United States?

focus on their marriage. In turn, these marriages tend to be happier throughout all stages of life with less work-family conflict, fewer bills, and fewer daily stressors.[7] But in what seems to be a contradiction, these couples are also more likely to divorce than couples with young children and to be viewed by their peers with pity, contempt, and suspicion.[8] The decline of mandated parenthood brought a decrease in the perception that children are an interference and an increase in the belief that fatherhood is fulfilling.[9] This suggests that increasing childlessness is a result of people giving more thought to whether parenting is best for them.

PARENTHOOD POSTPONED

Even more popular than a childfree lifestyle is the option to postpone having children. The National Survey of Families and Households (NSFH) found that the majority of 19- to 39-year-olds who didn't have children were planning to have them in the future.[10] Postponing parenting often follows naturally from wanting to first complete higher education, establish one's self professionally, and achieve financial stability, all of which may also cause both women and men to postpone marriage.

Women who postpone having children are, in effect, shortening the duration of their childbearing years. As a result, these women may have fewer children. Postponed marriages and a higher divorce rate may also cut childbearing years short. Couples may choose to have fewer children so that they still have time to focus on their careers and money to spend as they choose.

What are the social effects of smaller families and lower birth rates? There are arguments to be made in favor of larger families—children are often the ones who take care of their parents in old age, for instance. However, childfree couples tend to have more equitable gender roles than their parenting counterparts. Even those who put off having children get in the habit of sharing family responsibilities without succumbing to traditional roles.[11]

FINANCIAL CONSIDERATIONS

When considering whether to have a child, you should consider the cost. Raising a child from birth to age 18 amounts to a total cost that is three to four times the family's annual income.[12] Not every family can handle this financial pressure. One in five children in the United States lives in poverty,[13] which is many times caused by employment problems, teenage parents, and female-headed households earning less as a result of the gender gap.[14]

OTHER FACTORS TO CONSIDER

The decision to postpone having children may be the popular and even obvious choice for many heterosexual, college-educated, career-focused, married couples. But what other factors are considered when deciding whether to parent or not to parent?

Although perfectly natural, devoting your body to growing another human being for nine months isn't something a woman (or a couple) should enter into lightly. And although women may willingly, if not happily, abstain from certain activities, such as drinking alcohol, most would less likely welcome the postpartum depression that could beset them after giving birth. Although increasingly common—13 percent of women experience postpartum depression[15] and up to 85 percent of women experience some mood disturbances after giving birth[16]—these conditions still carry a stigma contrary to what is supposed to be the happiest time in a woman's life with a new "bundle of joy." In addition, a couple needs to consider whether their relationship is strong enough to handle the stress that a baby will bring, how they will share the responsibilities of caring for a child, and what kind of social support will be available to them.

Many of the factors that go into choosing whether or not to parent are the same no matter what a person's lifestyle. However, non-traditional parents have additional factors to consider as well.

Gay Couples

Conception is often the easiest part of parenting for a fertile, heterosexual couple, but even this stage involves significant planning and financial commitment for gay and lesbian couples. If they decide not to adopt,

lesbian couples have to decide who will carry the child and whose egg they'll use while gay male couples will have decide whose sperm to use and must find a surrogate. Gay couples may experience discrimination from their families and the community, which means less social support. Even medical professionals may discriminate against lesbian couples by refusing to recognize the pregnant woman's partner as a co-parent. The partner not carrying the child may not be able to take leave from work and may feel less bonded to the child. Additionally, lesbian couples' incomes tend to be 18 to 20 percent lower than their heterosexual equivalents.[17]

Single Parents

In 2006, nine percent of U.S. households were headed by single parents. So, it seems that as long as one parent is committed to parenting, the other can opt out of parenting whenever he or she wants. Of those 12.9 million single-parent families, 10.4 million were single mothers and only 2.5 million were single fathers.[18]

It probably comes as no surprise that single mothers outnumber single fathers, but 2.5 million single fathers represents almost 20 percent of single-parent households—a lot more than you might have assumed. Why might these fathers choose to parent even though society might give

Breakdown of Parenting Costs for Families Making $44,500–74,900 Annually

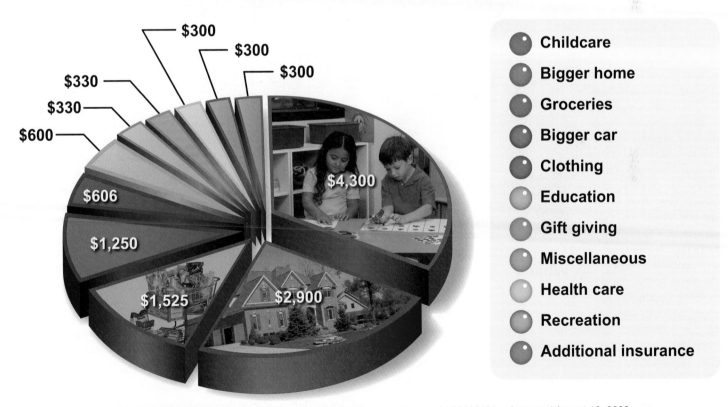

$300
$300
$300
$330
$330
$600
$606
$1,250
$1,525
$2,900
$4,300

- Childcare
- Bigger home
- Groceries
- Bigger car
- Clothing
- Education
- Gift giving
- Miscellaneous
- Health care
- Recreation
- Additional insurance

Source: MSNBC.com, "Cost of children? The numbers ain't kidding." <http://www.msnbc.com/id/20203458>, Accessed August 18, 2009.

∧
∧ **The cost of having a child for a family** who makes $44,500 to $74,900 annually is
∧ estimated at $197,700, according to the U.S. Department of Agriculture. **How might a childless couple spend $197,700?**

the impression that they are off the hook? One factor is the mother's fitness to parent. Fathers may step up if they feel that the mother has limitations that won't allow her to be a competent parent, such as mental illness or drug addiction. Other single fathers cite an inner sense of duty or describe being motivated not to repeat negative or nonexistent experiences with their own fathers.[19]

The societal conception of issues brought on by either the absence or presence of a father in a child's life is a hot-button topic. Issues of poverty and teenage pregnancy often take the blame for the absence of a father in a child's life.[20] The absence or presence of a father is also linked to the child's economic support, which,

∧
∧ **What** kinds of discrimination **might single fathers face?**

in turn, ultimately affects the child's nutrition, health, grades, emotional state, and behavior.[21] Children raised by single parents—mother or father—face outcomes both similar to and different from children brought up in two-parent families. The effects on children of single parents are covered in greater detail in Chapter 9.

Infertility

Even after a couple has considered all the factors and decided to have a child, they still have to get pregnant. For some people, that's not an easy task. In 1995 more than 9 million women and 2 million couples utilized infertility services.[22] **Infertility** is defined as the inability to conceive after one year of persistent unprotected intercourse or the inability to carry a

pregnancy to term.[23] Women and couples who have trouble conceiving have to devote considerable time and efforts to be defined as infertile. Then, an effort is made to find the cause of infertility.

CAUSES OF INFERTILITY

Along with the trend toward postponing having children comes the risk of postponing too long. Many cases of infertility are related to age: couples who wait too long after their peak age of fertility—27 in women and 35 in men—are likely to have greater difficulties conceiving.[24]

Male infertility may be a result of abnormality in their sperm: morphology (shape), impaired motility (movement), or low concentration of sperm. Possible causes for these difficulties include lifestyle factors: stress, nutrition, obesity, use or abuse of drugs, alcohol, and/or tobacco. Another possible complication is impaired delivery of viable sperm into a woman's vagina from erectile dysfunction or the absence of semen.

Causes of female infertility are similarly rooted in biological or lifestyle causes. Damaged or blocked fallopian tubes, endometriosis, ovulation or hormonal disorders, thyroid problems, early menopause, uterine fibroids, and pelvic adhesions can cause infertility in women. Certain medications, such as those used to treat cancer, as well as excessive caffeine intake may also be to blame.[25]

CONSEQUENCES OF INFERTILITY

Infertility affects people on personal, partner, and social levels. Couples who learn that they are infertile will likely go through a period of depression during which they are no longer motivated to participate in activities they may have once enjoyed. A couple's sex life may suffer as it can serve as a reminder of the problem at hand, or it may become stressful rather than enjoyable. Infertile individuals and couples may also feel isolated from friends who can't understand what they are going through and may feel the need to avoid child-centered activities like baby showers and birthday parties.[26]

Fertility Technologies

Identifying the cause of infertility isn't easy, and some couples may never pinpoint the reason that they can't conceive, even with the help of doctors and fertility specialists. With increasingly advanced technology, referred to as **assisted reproductive technology (ART)**, couples who can't conceive using the old-fashioned method don't have to give up trying.

ARTIFICIAL INSEMINATION

In 1884, Dr. William Pancoast was faced with an infertile couple. His solution was to anesthetize the wife and inseminate her with the sperm of a medical student. Although this incident was highly controversial at the time, it was also the first case of **artificial insemination by donor (AID)**.[27] Although the technique has benefited from ethics and technology since 1884, the general idea is the same: When infertility is caused by a male factor—or when a single woman desires to get pregnant—a donor male produces sperm through masturbation, which is then inserted into the woman's vagina when she is ovulating. From that point, pregnancy occurs naturally.

Cases in which the male partner has a low sperm count may be resolved using **artificial insemination by husband or male partner (AIH)**. The process is very much the same, except the male partner's sperm is put through a centrifuge to concentrate it and then inserted into the ovulating woman. AIH is generally preferable to AID. However, there remains a stigma attached to a man's wife being impregnated by another man, even if through artificial means. The Roman Catholic Church still considers it adulterous.

SURROGATES AND DONORS

In 1985, a young woman answered an ad in the Asbury Park Press and agreed to be artificially inseminated by a man, carry the pregnancy to term, and then give the child to the man and his wife in exchange for monetary compensation. However, when it came time to give the baby up, she decided she wanted to keep it. After being hashed out in the courts, custody of the child, dubbed Baby M, was awarded to the biological father. The surrogate mother was given visitation rights. This case exposes many of the legal, ethical, and social dilemmas inherent in cases of **gestational surrogacy**. Is it legal to exchange a baby for money? Does surrogacy exploit the women who carry the baby for another family out of financial necessity? Although some of these questions have begun to be sorted out legally, many of these dilemmas may never be resolved satisfactorily.

Some of these issues are alleviated with the use of egg or sperm donors, whose identities typically, though not always, remain anonymous. Yet, this commercialized reproduction is still a concern for many. Some worry about the practice of using a younger woman's egg to impregnate an older woman. Does this interfere with nature's biological safeguards that prevent an older woman from carrying a pregnancy due to the complications that might result? Often, sperm donors deposit multiple times, possibly fathering hundreds of children. This practice increases the risk of a serendipitous meeting of two half-siblings who may fall in love and try to conceive

together. Issues of parental rights and responsibilities are also raised with this technique.[28]

Another technique may alleviate some of these complex issues, though certainly not all of them. **Surrogate embryo transfer (SET)** involves using artificial insemination to impregnate a surrogate with either a donor or the male partner's sperm. When one of her eggs has been fertilized, it is flushed from the surrogate using a process called lavage. The fertilized egg is then implanted in the mother, who carries the pregnancy to term. However, lavage may be unsuccessful, leaving the surrogate to either have an abortion or carry an unwanted pregnancy to term.

IN VITRO FERTILIZATION

Although the success rate is low, **in vitro fertilization (IVF)** may help infertile couples have a child of their own. Drugs are taken to stimulate a woman's ovaries, releasing a glut of eggs. Eggs and semen are then medically collected and tested for viability. Those that pass the test are then united *in vitro* (literally, "in glass") and then transferred to the woman's uterus. To increase the chances of success, multiple embryos are implanted at once, which makes multiple births more likely.[29]

Though it seems an ideal solution for childless couples, IVF doesn't come cheap. The Advanced Fertility Center of Chicago advertises a single cycle of IVF at $9,500. Want to improve your odds? The multiple cycle option, which offers an 80-percent refund if you don't have a baby, costs $16,000 to $27,500. For multiple cycles and a 100-percent money-back guarantee, you have to shell out $24,500 to $32,000. These fees don't include qualification tests, pregnancy tests, medications, or consultations with physicians![30]

Intracytoplasmic Sperm Injection (ICSI)

A relatively newer form of IVF can be used in cases of male infertility without a donor. Microinsemination, or **intracytoplasmic sperm injection (ICSI)**, is similar to IVF. However, this method requires just a single spermatozoon, which is injected directly into an egg before the fertilized egg is implanted in the uterus. A similar method, **nonsurgical sperm aspiration (NSA)**, involves removal of sperm directly from the testes with a syringe.[31]

ADDITIONAL METHODS

Additional methods for having a child exist, and new ones are sure to arise. Women can try using **hormone therapy** to enhance the quality of their menstrual cycle to improve fertility by releasing more eggs. However, women who use fertility drugs are twice as likely to have multiple births. Women are having twins,

Multiples Birth Rate, 1990–2007

Source: U.S. National Center for Health Statistics, *National Vital Statistics Reports* (NVSR), 2006, 55: 1. 2011 Statistical Abstract of the United States, Table 81. U.S. Census Bureau. Accessed August 18, 2009.

∧∧ Families with multiple births have been in the spotlight in recent years. **What effect do multiple births have on parents and children?**

CRYOPRESERVATION is freezing eggs or sperm for later use.
PREIMPLANTATION GENETIC DIAGNOSIS (PGD) is the process to determine sex in embryos.
RHYTHM METHOD is avoiding intercourse during ovulation.
VOLUNTARY FETAL MORTALITY is induced abortion.
MEDICAL ABORTION is voluntary termination of a pregnancy by medication.

triplets, quadruplets, and even as many as eight children at a time. This increase in number of children has resulted in preterm babies with low birth weights. This puts the children at higher risk of dying or developing disabling diseases.[32]

Couples who can plan ahead might use **cryopreservation**. Both eggs and sperm can be frozen for later use by one's self or for donation. This method increases options for women or couples postponing having children or receiving chemotherapy or radiation therapy that might cause infertility.

The technology associated with fertility treatments has also led to advancements in genetic engineering technologies for sex selection. During IVF, embryos can be biopsied to determine sex in a process referred to as **preimplantation genetic diagnosis (PGD)**. Embryos with the desired sex can be implanted, and those of the other sex can be discarded or donated.[33] Proponents argue that this technique is a responsible method of family balancing[34] and avoiding the transmission of sex-specific genetic disorders. Opponents argue that it interferes with the natural reproductive process, destroys life, and contributes to male-favored biases.[35]

Contraception
BIRTH CONTROL METHODS

Just as much effort spent trying to get pregnant is spent trying not to get pregnant with the use of contraception. Sometimes, couples only want to prevent pregnancy temporarily, until they are ready to have a child. Some use the **rhythm method**—avoiding intercourse during ovulation—

but this requires self-control and lacks precision, since sperm can live for two days inside a woman. Other people want something more permanent. Surgical methods are most reliable: vasectomy for men and tubal ligation for women.

Barrier methods include the diaphragm (invented back in 1883), cervical cap, vaginal sponge, intrauterine device (IUD), male and female condoms (which, unlike other methods, are also useful in protecting against STIs), and vaginal spermicidal foams, jellies, suppositories, and films. Chemical methods deliver hormones via pill, injection, vaginal ring, and implant.[36]

CONTRACEPTIVES AND ADOLESCENTS

Most of the controversy surrounding contraceptive methods involves teen access to them. Many parents, educators, and legislators want to teach abstinence-only programs and limit teen access to information and contraceptives. Even among their peers, teens, especially females, who plan ahead to protect themselves during sex are burdened by an oversexed bad-girl stigma. They must often rely on the male to obtain contraception. However, these efforts fail to stop kids from having sex; instead, they stop them from doing so in a safe and informed manner. After a 1981 passage of a Minnesota law requiring parental notification for teen abortions, the birth rate for 15- to 17-year-olds went up 38.4 percent.[37]

Ending a Pregnancy before Birth

Even after conception, women still have the option of preventing a live birth through **voluntary fetal mortality**, which is induced abortion, legalized in the United States by the landmark 1973 Supreme Court case *Roe v. Wade*. Worldwide, an estimated one in four pregnancies will end in abortion.[38] Two methods of abortion are available to women when other birth control methods are unavailable or fail. **Medical abortion** uses two drugs, mifepristone followed by misoprostol, to terminate pregnancy after conception. This method can be used only up to 49 days after the beginning of the woman's last menstrual period.

Do Your Homework

"When my boyfriend and I started getting serious, I knew I should start finding out more information about how we could have sex safely. The first thing I did was talk to a lot of my friends. Even though most of them had a few sexual experiences, everyone told me something different. Some of them said you couldn't get pregnant if you had sex while you were having your period, but others said this wasn't true. One person told me that since we lived in an upper-class suburb, the chances of contracting sexually transmitted infections was so low that we didn't really need to worry about it. It became obvious to me

pretty quickly that I needed to find a more reliable source.

"My mom and I are close, so I felt comfortable asking her some questions. But there were still some nitty-gritty details that I needed more information about. I wasn't sure if you could get sexually transmitted infections from oral sex, but I couldn't say that to my mom!

"It took a lot of guts for me to walk into the local Planned Parenthood. I had to go to a part of town that I wasn't familiar with, and I felt like everyone would be looking at me wondering why I needed to be there. But I decided to be mature

about it and walked in the door. I was able to meet with someone one-on-one to discuss all of the questions I had.

"Turns out, you can get pregnant if you have sex during your period, you can get STIs no matter what part of town you live in, and you can get STIs from oral sex. The woman at Planned Parenthood gave me lots of additional information as well and several pamphlets that I was able to share with my confused friends. She also gave me a list of the services they provide, including general health care, abortion services, testing and vaccines, emergency contraception pill, and a lot more."

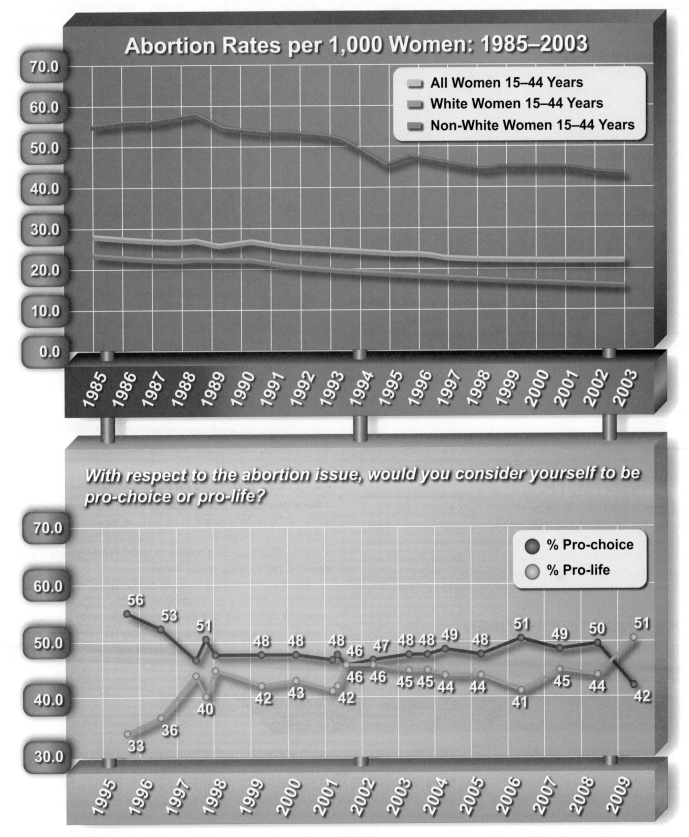

Abortion Rates per 1,000 Women: 1985–2003

- All Women 15–44 Years
- White Women 15–44 Years
- Non-White Women 15–44 Years

70.0
60.0
50.0
40.0
30.0
20.0
10.0
0.0

1985 1986 1987 1988 1989 1990 1991 1992 1993 1994 1995 1996 1997 1998 1999 2000 2001 2002 2003

With respect to the abortion issue, would you consider yourself to be pro-choice or pro-life?

- % Pro-choice
- % Pro-life

70.0
60.0
50.0
40.0
30.0

56 53 51 48 48 48 46 47 48 48 49 48 51 49 50 51
33 36 40 42 43 42 46 46 45 45 44 44 41 45 44 42

1995 1996 1997 1998 1999 2000 2001 2002 2003 2004 2005 2006 2007 2008 2009

Source: http://www.census2010.gov/compendia/statab/2008/tables/08s0096.pdf
Saad, Lydia, "More Americans 'Pro-Life' Than 'Pro-Choice' for First Time," Gallup. <http://www.gallup.com/poll/118399/more-americans-pro-life-than-pro-choice-first-time.aspx>, Accessed August 18, 2009.

∧ **Consider how abortion rates and attitudes about abortion have changed over time.**
∧ Are they consistent? What trends do you predict over the next 10–15 years?

Surgical abortion is completed by vacuum aspiration, which uses a narrow tube to remove the fetus from the uterus. Most surgical abortions take place during the first trimester; later-term abortions may be done in cases of complications that would endanger the life or health of the woman or fetus. A pregnancy may also terminate itself, usually if something has gone wrong during early development. **Involuntary fetal mortality** may be a **miscarriage** or **spontaneous abortion**, which occurs when a pregnancy ends itself mid-term, or **stillbirth**, a nonliving birth.[39] We will discuss abortion in more detail in Chapter 12.

Adoption

Tom and Kate from *Cheaper by the Dozen* are biological parents to all of their children; however, some families turn to adoption when they are childless or simply want another child. **Adoption** occurs when someone legally and voluntarily takes the child of other parents to raise as one's own. With legalized abortion and increased use of contraception, adoption is relatively uncommon. Less than four percent of households have adopted children.[40] The high cost of adoptions might also limit their number. Although subsidies, employer benefits, and tax credits help defer the expenses, adoptions can cost from $2,500 to more than $30,000.[41]

In a **closed adoption**, the child's biological parents are unknown, and there is limited information about them. In an **open adoption**, however, the adoptive parents and biological parents are in contact with one another, and the adopted child can grow up knowing both parents or may choose to meet his or her biological parents at a later point in life.[42]

U.S. agencies tend to discourage interracial adoptions due to concerns over children's identity problems, so most interracial adoptions are international. Adoption of older children often causes adopted children to be returned to the agency, because these children may have more trouble with attachment as a result of previous abuse or developmental impairments. Despite these challenges, adopted children tend to be well adjusted, and families tend to bond, probably as a result of deep commitment stemming from parents attempting to compensate for the lack of biological ties.[43]

ADOPTING STEPCHILDREN

When a parent with children remarries, he or she might decide to have the stepparent adopt the children. A survey of married adults conducted

<<< Once the lead plaintiff in a class-action lawsuit challenging Texas anti-abortion laws, which went to the Supreme Court as the famous *Roe v. Wade* case, Jane Roe (once Norma McCorvey) spent much of her life working in abortion clinics and advocating for abortion rights. **In 1995, she developed a relationship with the leader of Operation Rescue, an anti-abortion rights group.** She converted to Christianity under Rev. Phillip Behnam's guidance and started an anti-abortion rights group called Roe No More.

by the National Survey of Families and Households (NSFH) indicated that stepparents adopt about 1 in 10 stepchildren. Although many families choose not to go through a legal adoption, others see the process as a form of family unity. These proponents might also want the child to have the stepparent's name or gain legal rights.[48]

FOSTER PARENTING

In **foster parenting**, a couple will act as the parents for children who cannot live at home for a variety of reasons, or are waiting to be adopted. Many foster parents are already parents and take foster children into their homes to provide a loving home and family. Foster parents are given a stipend to pay for the children's needs.[49]

Foster parenting is not meant to be permanent. A child will stay in a foster home until the agency determines that the child's biological family is capable of taking care of them or an adoptive family has been found. However, when a foster child bonds with his or her foster family, many families will do what they can to adopt the child and make the child a legal part of the family.[50]

▶▶▶ GO GL◉BAL

The One-Child Policy in China

In 1949, China experienced a communist revolution and a rapidly growing population, with the average Chinese woman bearing 6.2 children. To control this population growth and depletion of natural resources, the Chinese government promoted "birth planning" and eventually a one-child policy that provided a government-funded subsidy to parents who agreed to the limitation. Much controversy surrounds China's one-child

policy, and China has received recommendations from scholars to revise the policy.[44] Critics of the one-child policy contend that fertility rates were already declining in China and that the policy didn't have as much of an effect as it may seem and that the policy forces Chinese women to have abortions and sterilizations.[45] The Chinese government declares that the one-child policy is to stay in place until 2010, at which time its critics are hoping it will be revised.[46]

One result of this policy was that because of gender biases that favor male

children, female babies were often abandoned so that parents' one-child wasn't "wasted" on a girl. In 1992, the Chinese government legalized foreign adoptions to find homes for these baby girls. Although international adoption agencies once encouraged assimilation, they now encourage bicultural competence, or positive identity within both cultures. This is successful when adoptive parents maintain a positive attitude about biculturalism and provide ethnic networks and access to ethnic communities for their children.[47]

Pregnancy and Childbirth

You've considered all the factors, thrown out the birth control, possibly seen a fertility doctor, and now you're finally pregnant. Although you're excited to have a baby, you're also complaining about weight gain, nausea, vomiting, mood swings, and stress.

During pregnancy women may experience at least a period of isolation, but they can also receive a great deal of emotional support.[51] Accompanying the criticism of the contemporary medical birth process involving hospitals and doctors has come the romanticizing of more primitive birthing practices. However, the safety and comfort of these pregnancies have been largely exaggerated. Women often have painful deliveries, and there is a high incidence of infant death.[52]

There are several less obvious effects of unwanted pregnancy on families. One study found a correlation between unwanted pregnancies and maternal behaviors, such as smoking or drinking alcohol, which had a negative effect on infant and child health.[53] Consistent with this finding, another study of young, low-income, first-time black mothers found that acceptance of one's pregnancy increases a child's attachment security and decreases the mother's feelings of parenting as burdensome.[54]

The Transition to Parenthood

The arrival of a child results in a remarkable alteration in the parents' everyday schedule. After childbirth, mothers may go through a time of incredible exhaustion and psychological strain. Race or cultural traditions, job possibilities, societal demands, and monetary factors influence the capability of males to operate well as fathers.[55] Parents frequently expect dissimilar roles for the genders of their children, depicting the male as more firm, attentive, and tough and the female as fragile, supple, and petite.[56] Parents must aid the child in their development, physically, emotionally, socially, and cognitively. Parents teach their child about love and acknowledgment, organization and order in life, aptitude, and self-assurance.[57]

Parents face many obstacles during parenthood including disturbed marriage responsibilities, lack of interaction, and the physical burdens

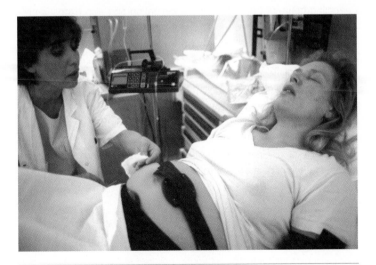

∧∧∧ Criticisms of contemporary birthing practices claim that the medicalization of pregnancy is harmful to women and babies. **What other arguments can you make for and against this point?**

SURGICAL ABORTION is voluntary termination of a pregnancy by vacuum aspiration.

INVOLUNTARY FETAL MORTALITY is self-terminating pregnancy.

SPONTANEOUS ABORTION or **MISCARRIAGE** is when a pregnancy ends itself mid-term.

STILLBIRTH is a nonliving birth.

ADOPTION is voluntarily taking the child of other parents as one's own.

CLOSED ADOPTION is the situation in which the child's biological parents are unknown, and there is limited information about them.

OPEN ADOPTION is the situation in which the adoptive parents and biological parents are in contact with one another.

FOSTER PARENTING is the situation in which a person or couple acts as temporary parents to a child or children who cannot live at home for a variety of reasons, or are waiting to be adopted.

PERMISSIVE PARENTING STYLE describes parents who exert little to no control and give few restrictions or guidelines, leaving children confused about what behaviors are acceptable.

AUTHORITARIAN PARENTING STYLE describes parents who attempt to shape children according to fixed standards by emphasizing obedience and punishment.

AUTHORITATIVE PARENTING STYLE describes parents who nurture children by providing warmth, support, and acceptance, and emphasizing positive reinforcement.

---

placed on the new caregivers.[58] Newborns need to be fed frequently and consoled when they cry. When the child grows into a toddler, turning the household into a safe and baby-friendly environment goes into effect, and the conflict between autonomy and reliance for the toddler arises.[59] These changes occur throughout every stage of a child's upbringing. When parents agree on how to raise the child, the adolescent receives clarity about the need for proper conduct.[60]

Parenting Styles

Interactions between parents and children can usually be typified according to parenting styles, each of which shows natural parenting values and behaviors. Researchers typically recognize four parenting styles: indulgent, authoritarian, authoritative, and uninvolved.[61] To meet the demands and responsibilities that come with parenting, there must be the appropriate level of nurturance, control, and support in the household.

INDULGENT STYLE

The indulgent style of parenting is also known as the permissive style. **Permissive** parents exert little to no control and impose few restrictions or guidelines, leaving children confused about what behaviors are acceptable. This style may also lead to children engaging in risky behaviors.[62]

AUTHORITARIAN STYLE

Authoritarian parents attempt to shape their children according to fixed standards by emphasizing obedience and punishment. One study suggests that when fathers exhibit this parenting style, children are more likely to engage in delinquent activities and use drugs.[63]

AUTHORITATIVE STYLE

Authoritative parenting is the most nurturing; it provides the most warmth, support, and acceptance, and it emphasizes positive reinforcement.[64] Children of authoritative parents display more instrumental and social competence and fewer problem behaviors.[65]

UNINVOLVED STYLE

Uninvolved parents rarely give their children rules and offer little attention. Children with uninvolved parents can become confused and anxious, and they often develop problems with self-control.[66]

FACTORS INFLUENCING CHILDREN'S WELL-BEING

Other factors also have an impact on the well-being of children. When parents exert high levels of psychological control, through intrusiveness, guilt trips, or withholding love, children's identity development problems cause them anxiety, depression, loneliness, and confusion. When combined with inadequate behavioral control, drug use, truancy, and other antisocial behaviors are likely.[67]

The expression of both active parenting and emotional bonding, especially by a child's father, is even more important to a child's well-being than economic support. In *Cheaper by the Dozen*, Tom learns that the financial gains of his new job are not as important as spending time with his children. **Active parenting** is exemplified by activities such as helping with homework, participating in projects, using non-coercive discipline, listening to problems, and offering advice. **Emotional bonding** is measured by strength of emotional ties, affection, mutual respect, and identification.[68]

GENDERED PARENTING STYLES

Often without realizing it, parents treat sons and daughters very differently. From the colors they paint the nursery to the toys they buy to the household chores they assign, parents treat their children according to traditional gender roles—socially constructed sets of behaviors based on gender. Girls are expected to be dependent, and boys are expected to be independent. When girls ask questions, they are likely to be led to the answer with much more hand-holding than boys, who are expected to figure things out independently.[69,70]

RACIAL AND ETHNIC DIFFERENCES IN PARENTING STYLES

Certain races and ethnicities present differences in parenting. African American parents often emphasize a child's self-esteem and encourage large community networks. Others in their family community, such as grandparents, often help parents in raising a child. In Hispanic American families, parents are often permissive in the early years but become more authoritarian as the child grows. Close mother-child relationships are highly encouraged in Hispanic homes. Although Asian American parents tend to be lenient in a child's early years, they become stricter, often focusing on the idea that a child's behavior reflects not only on them, but on the entire family. Asian American parents are also very devoted to education.[71]

SOCIAL CLASS AND PARENTAL BEHAVIOR

Differences in parenting can also occur because of social class. Blue-collar parents are more likely to parent based on the consequences of a child's actions. Parents use forms of punishment that are likely to produce immediate changes to behavior. On the other hand, middle-class parents focus their attention on the motivation behind the child's actions. Middle-class parents are more likely to see a child's action as reflective of their parenting.[72] Researcher Aryn Dotterer considered a parent's education (related to social class) in relation to the academic achievements of children. Students with less-educated parents had low math scores as a result of parent-child conflict. Dotterer speculated that parents of lower social classes were more likely to have harsh parenting tactics when children performed poorly, a method that did not increase child achievement.[73]

DISCIPLINE

Disciplinary methods are contentious, often because parents have trouble distancing their emotional reactions stemming from disappointment or frustration from the intended goals of the discipline. **Discipline** is training to correct an incorrect behavior. Logical and natural reinforcement, behavior modification, fairness, support, and consistency have been credited as integral practices within discipline. Power-assertive discipline including time-outs and physical discipline, such as spanking or slapping, is especially controversial.[74] One study found that when accompanied by an emotionally involved mother, power-assertive discipline was associated with well-adjusted children. When used in the context of a less emotionally involved mother, however, it tended to increase children's behavioral problems.[75] Discipline tends to be better received in adolescents not only when they feel that the disciplinary method is appropriate, but also when they perceive that the parents believe that it is appropriate.[76]

Spanking

The physical discipline method of spanking is especially controversial. Critics of spanking argue that the technique has a limited effectiveness in correcting behavior and promoting socialization and also exposes children to violence.[77] Although the practice of spanking as a means of discipline has declined, it is still widely practiced in the United States today.[78] A 2006 study revealed that 71.7 percent of Americans believed that spanking is "sometimes needed" to discipline children.[79] Also once assumed a practice of more violent families, research shows that spanking is a practice of both violent and nonviolent families.[80] The method of spanking as a form of discipline remains an issue for debate, as scholars continue to argue both its benefits, such as increasing effectiveness of other forms of discipline used with it, and its disadvantages, such as children being much more apt to externalize their emotions.[81]

Parent-Child Relationships
FAMILIES WITH YOUNG CHILDREN

Many couples with infants and young children feel that their home has been completely taken over by this new person. New mothers may become depressed due to the new stress and sleeplessness. Couples may also find that a young child dominates their relationship. When they may once have talked to each other about their own days, moms and dads now talk to each other about their child's day. This shift is one of the ways in which intimacy between couples can diminish, leading to an increase in marital dissatisfaction.[82] The overall marital satisfaction of a

"After Hurricane Katrina struck New Orleans, my mother, father, and I joined a group of volunteers to help build houses for those who had lost their homes.

When we arrived, all we had were materials.

Although the heat was nearly unbearable, we soldiered on, and by the time we left, we had actually created a house. Not only did this experience give me a great sense of purpose to see what I was able to do with my own two hands, I also learned a lot of new skills and enjoyed the amazing feeling of doing something really significant for someone else. This was also a major bonding experience for me and my family. We had never taken on such a large project that involved all of us.

"It was also interesting to see how many other different kinds of families came along with our group. By helping to change someone else's life, I also changed my own."

ACTIVITIES

1. Volunteer to babysit for a couple so they can take a night off and spend time together.
2. Observe for one hour at a local day care center. How do the children relate to the teacher and instructors? Even though the teacher and instructors are not the parents of the children, can you see some evidence of the patterns of parenting styles being used by the teacher and instructors of the children?

---

couple can increase or decrease based on the emotional connectedness of the marriage before they have a child. Couples who had a strong emotional connectedness before they had a child tend to have an increase in marital satisfaction. On the other hand, couples who had a weak emotional connectedness before they had a child tend to have a decrease in marital satisfaction.

Problems with familial intimacy may be even worse for low-income families, particularly for fathers. One study found that children from low-income families tend to have reduced involvement with their fathers than those from high-income families. These children also watch more television, which can negatively affect school performance, causing additional stress for the family unit.[83]

PARENTS WITH ADOLESCENTS

Adolescence spans the teen years to young adulthood. During this period, significant changes in their physical, sexual, and emotional selves makes life difficult not just for adolescents but for their parents as well. As a transition period, adolescence creates ambiguities about appropriate limits for adolescents. Many parents struggle with how much freedom to give their children during this time, and many adolescents demand the maximum. Teens are also learning how to behave more independently from their parents, so they need time alone with peers. Furthermore, because of all the hormonal changes going on in the bodies of adolescents, they may not have the capacity for reasoning or controlling their emotions in the same way that adults do.[84]

FAMILIES DURING THE POST-PARENT YEARS

After the stress of adolescence, parents and children may be glad to get some distance as the child begins his or her own adult life. Parent-child relationships during this time may flourish with mutual respect and appreciation for one another. However, if either party has trouble making the transition, this stage can be difficult. Parents may find it difficult to give up parental power and authority and may become inappropriately intrusive and overbearing in their children's adult lives. Children having trouble with this transition may not have been adequately prepared to take on all the responsibilities of adulthood and may hang on to parental protection—and maybe a room in the family basement—for way too long.[85]

think marriages and families: WHAT THEORIES DESCRIBE THE RELATIONSHIPS BETWEEN PARENTS AND CHILDREN?

Functionalism

As you recall from previous chapters, one of the functions of the family is to socialize its members so that they become functioning and productive members of our society. One way that children learn what is appropriate behavior is by watching their parents' examples of behaviors and actions.

Modeling occurs when children do what they see their parents do instead of what they tell them to do. This idea is supported by studies that have shown a correlation between criminal behavior, heavy drinking, and drug use in parents and children. Other behaviors are also subject to

> **MODELING** occurs when children do what they see their parents do instead of what their parents tell them to do.

modeling. Religious parents are more likely to have religious children.[86] Educational and occupational aspirations may also be handed down from parents to children via modeling.[87] Altruistic behaviors, such as volunteering, are also likely to be engaged in by children whose parents also volunteer.[88]

According to Albert Bandura's modeling-identification theory, children imitate adult behaviors because of vicarious reinforcement, and they

WRAP YOUR MIND AROUND THE THEORY

Families are important to maintaining the social order. **Besides the end of human civilization as we know it, what would be the effect on society if people stopped becoming parents?**

FUNCTIONALISM

Functionalism suggests that for society to function effectively, society's most important components, its families, must function effectively. Parents are responsible for teaching their children appropriate behavior by modeling it themselves. Parents need children to remind them of the importance of acting appropriately, even in situations when it may be easier or seem inconsequential to take a less appropriate course of action. Without parental figures in their lives to model appropriate behavior, children may never learn proper socialization. On some level, people continue to become parents to do their part to ensure that society continues to function and that people continue to act appropriately by modeling appropriate behaviors or by acting out the proper behaviors that were modeled to them.

CONFLICT THEORY

According to conflict theorists, life consists mainly of competing for resources. Money, food, and power are among those resources that are highly valued in contemporary society. Although these resources may not be particularly scarce at present, they are not unlimited. There are only so many jobs and only so many people who can hold power in society. By having children, families ensure the increase in numbers of those close to them with whom they can share these resources. In most cases, parents benefit from their children's money and power, particularly when parents reach the later stages of life that require their grown children to take care of them. Conflict theory suggests that people have children to have more people on their side when conflicts arise.

WHY DO PEOPLE HAVE CHILDREN?

SYMBOLIC INTERACTIONISM

Symbolic interactionists believe that each person's reality is based on his or her own interpretation of situations. This theory suggests that individuals have their own unique reasons for choosing to have children based on the advantages they expect that doing so will bring about. A man who grew up as an only child may choose to have several children because he interpreted the situation of being an only child as unfavorable and believes that having several of his own children could vicariously remedy his own past.

We are all familiar with family feuds. Conflict theory suggests that parents have children to protect themselves against conflict. **How might childless adults compensate for their lack of children during times of conflict?**

Our perceptions shape our realities. How might we handle situations that are clearly at odds with our expectations?

continue the behavior because of actual reinforcement. Vicarious reinforcement occurs when the model has power or when there is a close relationship between the model and the child. Both conditions hold true for children modeling parental behavior.[89]

Conflict Theory

For conflict theorists, it is conflict that affects the development of the people within a family. Some theorists state that people and families cannot grow without conflict, because without conflict there is no reason to change. So, the problems a family may face are simply an opportunity for the individuals and group as a whole to change and adapt to the situation.[90] Parent-child conflicts are anything but rare. They can occur as a result of or be exacerbated by generational conflicts, a child's desire for autonomy conflicting with a parent's need to exert control, and underlying hostility in the family environment. Theorists speculate that conflict with parents is a way that teenagers learn how to be autonomous and self-reliant. In other words, conflict helps them learn how to become adults.[91,92]

Symbolic Interactionism

Any situation can be viewed from the perspective that one is either completing an action or being acted upon. The combination of these two roles—how we see ourselves and how others see us—describes symbolic interaction theory. For these perceptions to serve us in society, we must be adequately socialized. Children become socialized by first playing at reality. This stage is obvious to anyone who has seen children playing imitative games of house, school, or grocery store. In order to apply what they learn during this play to the real world, children must also learn the social rules that exist in these situations in the real world. Socialization also occurs when children first recognize and fulfill the role of child in parent-child interactions.[93]

One study found that children who were physically punished as children grew up to use physical and verbal aggression during conflicts in their own marriages, to be controlling of their spouses, and to be less likely to look at a conflict from their spouse's perspective.[94] The ability to look at a situation from one's spouse's perspective is important to being able to act in a supportive manner, which in turn supports effective communication, which then makes role-taking easier.[95]

discover marriages and families in action:
HOW DO PEOPLE HANDLE INFERTILITY?

Despite the low success rates of fertility treatments, infertile couples are spending their time, money, and efforts at increasing rates for that small chance of getting pregnant and fulfilling their dream of having a child. Around 6.1 million women (and their partners) in the United States are infertile, and the number is rising. By 2025 it is expected that 7.7 million women will be infertile.[96] Most couples don't really consider the possibility that they might not be able to get pregnant until they are faced with the devastating fact, so they often have trouble just giving up without at least making some effort with the help of assisted reproductive technology (ART).

Fertility carries significant weight across cultures. In Nigeria, for example, most infertility is blamed on STIs, and infertile females may be shunned.[97] In Japan and Korea, an infertile woman is often seen as a woman made of stone. Infertility may be grounds for divorce, and attempts may be made to remedy it with rituals, prayer, or faith healers. In many cultures, adoption is uncommon and ART unavailable, so women may try fruitlessly to reverse infertility.[98]

Both male and female partners of infertile couples experience stress. However, women's stress may be more severe because treatment—even of male infertility—involves complicated and painful medical procedures on *her* body. Men may be more physically removed from the experience of infertility, although this distance may also lead to increased feelings of helplessness. Certainly, feelings of inadequate virility may be a problem, particularly in male social circles. Couples may also faces stresses because medical appointments interrupt their normal schedule, or lovemaking becomes routine and uninteresting.[99]

ACTIVITY

Visit a fertility clinic and ask what services it provides, its price range, and the confidentiality arrangements it has.

MAKE CONNECTIONS

Should I Become a Parent?

Becoming a parent is one of the most important roles and decisions an individual can have in our society. Looking back at this chapter, you can see what factors are important to consider before becoming a parent. There have been technological advancements that make it more convenient to plan to have children.

As you have learned in this chapter, there are many challenges to being a parent. A child is totally dependent on the parent for a good amount of time. A parent's job is 24/7. It never ends. As we discussed here, there are many parenting styles. Each one appears to have different outcomes for children. Looking ahead, in Chapter 10 we will discuss parenting in middle-aged and aging families.

>>> ACTIVITIES

1. Research information about birth control, abortion, pregnancy, and the morning-after pill on the Internet using at least three different Web sites. Compare and contrast the type and amount of information available at each site for each topic.

2. Take an informal poll of your friends concerning their attitudes and feelings about abortion. Why do you think some feel stronger about their attitudes and opinions on abortion when compared to the others?

Theory

FUNCTIONALISM   143

- Families are important social units in that parents teach children appropriate behavior through modeling.

CONFLICT THEORY   145

- Parent-child relationships endure conflicts over incompatible desires, which may be exacerbated by generational differences, struggles for autonomy and control, and underlying familial hostilities.

SYMBOLIC INTERACTIONISM   145

- Acting out roles during childhood helps prepare us for fulfilling them in real-life adulthood.

Key Terms

childfree describes the women who make the voluntary decision not to have children   *133*

childless describes people not having children for infertility reasons   *133*

DINKs are couples with high incomes, no kids, demanding careers, and a desire to work, travel, and focus on their marriage   *133*

infertility is the inability to conceive after one year of persistent unprotected intercourse or the inability to carry a pregnancy to term   *136*

assisted reproductive technology (ART) is any fertility treatment in which both egg and sperm are handled   *136*

artificial insemination by donor (AID) is inserting donor sperm directly into a woman's body   *137*

artificial insemination by husband or male partner (AIH) is inserting sperm directly into a woman's body   *137*

gestational surrogacy is using another woman's body to carry one's baby   *137*

surrogate embryo transfer (SET) is an artificial insemination method involving fertilization in a surrogate's body and implantation in the mother's   *137*

in vitro fertilization (IVF) is a fertility treatment involving fertilizing an egg outside the body   *137*

intracytoplasmic sperm injection (ICSI), is an in vitro fertilization method requiring just a single sperm   *137*

nonsurgical sperm aspiration (NSA), is an in vitro fertilization method involving direct removal of sperm from testes   *137*

hormone therapy is a fertility method taken by women to increase their monthly release of eggs   *137*

cryopreservation is freezing eggs or sperm for later use   *138*

preimplantation genetic diagnosis (PGD) is the process to determine sex in embryos   *138*

rhythm method is avoiding intercourse during ovulation   *138*

voluntary fetal mortality is induced abortion   *138*

medical abortion is voluntary termination of a pregnancy by medication   *138*

surgical abortion is voluntary termination of a pregnancy by vacuum aspiration   *140*

involuntary fetal mortality is self-terminating pregnancy   *140*

spontaneous abortion or **miscarriage**, is when a pregnancy ends itself mid-term *140*

stillbirth is a nonliving birth *140*

adoption is voluntarily taking the child of other parents as one's own *140*

closed adoption is the situation in which the child's biological parents are unknown, and there is limited information about them *140*

open adoption is the situation in which the adoptive parents and biological parents are in contact with one another *140*

foster parenting is the situation in which a person or couple acts as temporary parents to a child or children who cannot live at home for a variety of reasons, or are waiting to be adopted *140*

permissive parenting style describes parents who exert little to no control and give few restrictions or guidelines, leaving children confused about what behaviors are acceptable *141*

authoritarian parenting style describes parents who attempt to shape children according to fixed standards by emphasizing obedience and punishment *141*

authoritative parenting style describes parents who nurture children by providing warmth, support, and acceptance, and emphasizing positive reinforcement *141*

uninvolved parenting style describes parents who rarely give their children rules and offer little attention *142*

active parenting includes activities such as helping with homework, participating in projects, using non-coercive discipline, listening to problems, and offering advice *142*

emotional bonding is measured by the strength of emotional ties, affection, mutual respect, and identification *142*

discipline is training to correct an incorrect behavior *142*

adolescence is the period of life from the teen years to young adulthood *143*

modeling occurs when children do what they see their parents do instead of what their parents tell them to do *143*

Sample Test Questions

MULTIPLE CHOICE

These multiple-choice questions are similar to those found in the test bank that accompanies this textbook.

1. Birth rate is the measure of
   a. the number of women who give birth in a given year.
   b. the number of live births per 1,000 in a population in a given year.
   c. the percentage of women of childbearing age who give birth in a given year.
   d. the percentage of live births in all births in a given year.

2. Which of the following statements about infertility is true?
   a. Male fertility problems are often addressed within the woman's body.
   b. In the majority of cases, the cause of infertility is never identified.
   c. Due to ambiguities involved with surrogacy, several states have outlawed it.
   d. Infertility is most often caused by female factors.

3. Which of the following would most likely be associated with an authoritative parenting style?
   a. negative reinforcement
   b. leniency
   c. nurturance
   d. emotional bonding

4. Discipline is most effective when
   a. it occurs in an environment with high emotional involvement.
   b. it occurs in an environment with low emotional involvement.
   c. it occurs along with a permissive parenting style.
   d. it occurs along with an authoritarian parenting style.

5. Which of the following challenges are DINKs most likely to face?
   a. marital dissatisfaction
   b. financial strain of sending children to costly schools
   c. no one to take care of them in old age
   d. desire to change career paths

ESSAY QUESTIONS

1. How would different sociological theories interpret different parenting styles?

2. How do socioeconomic factors influence how couples handle infertility?

3. Discuss the ways in which gender can influence parent-child interactions.

4. Describe the factors a single woman must consider when deciding whether or not to have a child.

5. Discuss the possible outcomes of varying levels of teen access to contraception.

WHERE TO START YOUR RESEARCH PAPER

For more data on statistics, go to http://www.census.gov

For more on Planned Parenthood service and other information, go to http://www.plannedparenthood.org

For more on the rights of children born from donor sperm, go to http://donorsiblingregistry.com

For parenting tips, go to http://www.parenting.org

For more information about assisted reproductive technology, go to http://www.cdc.gov/ART

ANSWERS: 1. b; 2. a; 3. d; 4. a; 5. c

WHAT TYPES OF FAMILIES EXIST IN THE
21st CENTURY?
WHAT THEORIES ARE USED TO ANALYZE
DIFFERENT FAMILY TYPES?
WHAT FAMILY ISSUES ARE CURRENTLY
BEING DEBATED IN THE UNITED STATES?

Val

Goldman and Barbara Keeley are engaged to be married, but they couldn't come from two more different families. Barbara's father is a U.S. senator up for re-election and a founder of the right-wing, ultraconservative Coalition for Moral Order, which denounces, among other things, Jews and homosexuals. Val is the son of a gay man, Armand, conceived in the only heterosexual encounter of Armand's life. His father, who owns a South Beach gay nightclub, and his partner, Albert, who performs at the club as the star drag queen, raised him.

Worried about how her parents would react to a description of Val's real family, Barbara tells them that Armand is a diplomat and is married to a housewife. She changes their last name from Goldman to Coleman, too, so her parents won't suspect they are Jewish. However, her lies are in danger of being exposed when Senator Keeley needs to get out of town to avoid a political scandal and decides to pay his daughter's future in-laws a visit.

When Barbara finds out about her father's plans, she phones Val and explains her lies. They decide the best option is to try to fool her parents by acting as if the lies were true. Armand is angry, but Val persuades him to go along with the charade. Armand redecorates the house, changing the flamboyant colors and furnishings to grim, dark colors, so it won't look "gay." He also works on changing his speech, walk, and gestures so he can be seen as just one of the guys. Reluctantly, Armand agrees that the drag queen Albert has no chance of playing a convincing role as a straight male.

Although it hurts Albert deeply—he has served as Val's mother through his childhood—Val and Armand tell him that he can't attend the planned dinner. Instead, Armand enlists Val's biological mother, Katherine, to act the part of his wife when the couples meet for dinner.

The dinner is a comedy of errors. When Katherine is late, Armand emerges from his room dressed as a middle-aged mother and announces that she is Mrs. Coleman. During dinner, which consists of only a bizarre soup, she delivers a right-wing speech on the deterioration of American society and morals. The senator is impressed, but his wife is suspicious.

When Katherine arrives and announces that she is Mrs. Goldman, Val realizes he can't keep lying. He removes Armand's wig, explaining that Katherine is his biological mother but that Albert has filled the role of mother through his childhood. The senator is offended by both the fact that they are Jewish and gay, and prepares to leave in a huff. However, he and his wife have been followed by photographers, eager for a picture of the famous right-wing senator leaving a gay nightclub.

As everyone hides in a bedroom, wondering what to do, Val and Barbara explain why they felt they needed to lie to her parents. They are forgiven and in a moment of perfect irony, the senator's family escapes the photographers by dressing as drag queens and singing *We Are Family* from the nightclub's stage. Surprisingly, the senator isn't uncomfortable wearing a dress. At the end of the film, Barbara and Val are married in an interfaith ceremony attended happily by both families and their friends.

149

FAMILY VARIATION

CHAPTER 09

People often deal with sensitive subjects through satire or farce. As comical as some of the actions in *The Birdcage* may be, the movie—a 1996 remake of *La Cage aux Folles*—highlights the diversity of today's families, **the struggle to define** "acceptable" **families, and negative stereotypes faced** by gay and nontraditional families.

TRADITIONAL OR NUCLEAR FAMILY refers to a husband and wife who are legally married, have children, and live together.

Although Barbara's parents are initially narrow-minded and unaccepting of Val's family, their encounters show them that Armand, Albert, and Val have constructed a loving family regardless of society's opinions. In the end, the families come together through a feeling central to all types of families: love for their children.

When I was in college, one of my sociology professors tasked the class with examining sociology textbooks on the family published between the 1950s and 1980s. I still remember how amazed I was to see how the definition of a family had changed during that 30-plus-year period.

Before the industrial revolution began in the 18th century,

∧
∧   Today, there are many
∧   different types of families.
Traditional families—husband, wife, and children—only make up about a quarter of all U.S. families.[1]

the extended family—husband, wife, children, and grandparents all living together—was the dominant family format. After the revolution, the **traditional** or **nuclear family**—a legally married husband and wife who live together and have children—became dominant.

Many of the statistical trends in families changed drastically, too. There were increases in the divorce rate, the rate of people remaining single, the teenage birth rate, and the rate of unmarried people living together. People waited longer to get married, and the number of children per family decreased. Openly gay and lesbian couples became more common and adoption rates increased.

Today, there are cohabiting families, single-parent families, polygamous families, and a multitude of other types. In this chapter we will examine the variations in family groups.

Family Variation

has changed throughout history, from → **extended family** – three generations living together → which after the Industrial Revolution gave way to → **traditional** or **nuclear family** – husband, wife, and children

remarried, blended, or stepfamilies – families created when spouses are widowed or divorced and marry again
divorced families – characterized by legal termination of marriage

polygamous families – marriage between an individual and multiple spouses
grandparent families – grandparents have custody of grandchildren

get the topic: WHAT TYPES OF FAMILIES EXIST IN THE 21ST CENTURY?

Families in the United States

"Call it a clan, call it a network, call it a tribe, call it a family. Whatever you call it, whoever you are, you need one."

— Jane Howard (1935–1996)[2]

Historically, societies around the world have defined a family as husband, wife or wives, and biological children. But, as societies have changed, the definitions of family have changed to reflect social realities. Both cultural and legal definitions of families have expanded to include a variety of other types of families. For example, in certain cases Canada now recognizes the rights of **psychological parents**—adults serving as parents who are not biologically related to the child—as more important than the rights of a biological parent who has been absent from a child's life.[3] Some sociologists have suggested using the term **postmodern family** to include the many variations in current families.[4] However, as we can see from the attitudes of people such as Senator Keeley in *The Birdcage*, acceptance of some family variations is limited.

Although family patterns have changed greatly in recent years, 70 percent of all children still live in households with two parents. The following pie charts provide an overview of the living arrangements of children under the age of 18 in American households.[5]

TRADITIONAL OR NUCLEAR FAMILIES

Have you seen reruns of *The Adventures of Ozzie and Harriet* on TV? How about *Father Knows Best* or *Leave It to Beaver*? These shows, set in the 1950s and 1960s, presented what many thought were ideal, traditional families—husband, wife, and children living together. Back then, there were fewer nontraditional families and little social acceptance of families that didn't match the images presented on TV. Polls show that Americans still idealize the traditional family—in 2005, 71 percent of people polled agreed with the statement "God's plan for marriage is one man, one woman, for life." But, at the same time, only one-third defined a family as exclusively "husband, wife, and children."[6]

> **PSYCHOLOGICAL PARENT** is a person serving as a parent who is not biologically related to the child.
>
> **POSTMODERN FAMILY** is a term meant to include all family variations existing today.

Although the numbers of nontraditional families, like Val's in *The Birdcage*, have increased, about 6 out of 10 children in the United States live with both of their biological parents. But the percentage of children living with two parents varies widely by race and ethnicity: 87 percent of Asian children live with two biological parents, compared with 78 percent of non-Hispanic whites, 68 percent of Hispanics, and 38 percent of blacks.[7]

Studies show that there are clear benefits to a traditional marriage and family. Adults in traditional families enjoy a better financial situation because two people can live together as cheaply as about one and a half single people.[8] They can share the costs of furniture, a home, a car, food, and many other expenses. When one partner is sick, the other helps out, so health costs are lower as well. Married men earn more than single men because they have stable routines and a greater commitment or responsibility to work.[9]

Married people also live longer. Single men have mortality rates 250 percent greater than married men, and the mortality rate for single women is 50 percent higher.[10] Cancer rates for married people are lower, and married men and women enjoy greater life expectancies than singles. They also enjoy better mental health. Married men are much less likely to commit suicide and have much lower rates of alcohol problems. Married people have lower rates of depression and are much more likely to say they are happy with their lives, in part because the emotional support of a spouse helps individuals through tough times.[11]

And here's a surprise: Regardless of the images we see on TV and in the movies, married people enjoy better sex lives than singles. Married couples have sex more frequently than single people or couples living together, and more married men and women report that their sex life is emotionally and physically satisfying.[12]

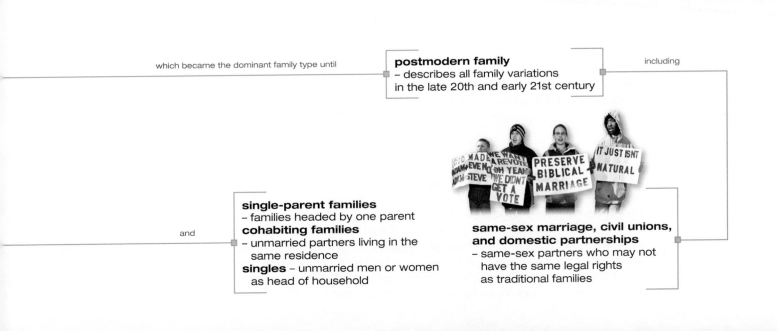

which became the dominant family type until

postmodern family
– describes all family variations in the late 20th and early 21st century

including

single-parent families
– families headed by one parent
cohabiting families
– unmarried partners living in the same residence
singles – unmarried men or women as head of household

and

same-sex marriage, civil unions, and domestic partnerships
– same-sex partners who may not have the same legal rights as traditional families

Children's Living Arrangements in the U.S. 2004

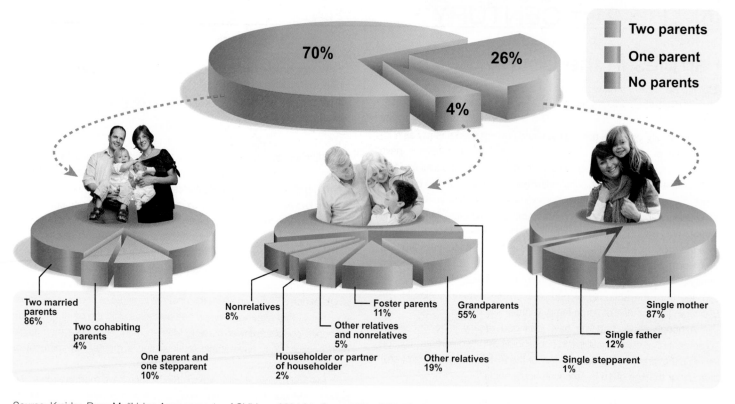

70%

26%

4%

- Two parents
- One parent
- No parents

Two married parents
86%

Two cohabiting parents
4%

One parent and one stepparent
10%

Nonrelatives
8%

Other relatives and nonrelatives
5%

Householder or partner of householder
2%

Foster parents
11%

Other relatives
19%

Grandparents
55%

Single mother
87%

Single father
12%

Single stepparent
1%

Source: Kreider, Rose M. "Living Arrangements of Children: 2004," in *Current Population Reports*, 5. Washington, DC: U.S. Census Bureau, 2007.

> ∧∧∧ Seventy percent of American children live with two parents, **while 26 percent live in single-parent households.** Are these figures higher or lower **than you would have predicted?**

SINGLE-PARENT FAMILIES

A **single-parent family** can be created when a spouse dies and doesn't remarry, a couple divorces or separates, a woman bears a child without marrying the father, or a single person adopts a child. The percentage of children adopted by a single person has soared—rising from approximately four percent of adopted children in 1970 to the current rate of approximately 33 percent.[13] The overall rate of single-parent families has slowly increased from 1994 to 2009, and now stands at about 11.2% of families.[14] As shown in the chart above, mothers head 87 percent of single-parent families.

Some social commentators have pointed to the growth of single-parent families since the mid-20th century as a source of many social problems. Studies have shown that single-parent families do expose children to certain risks as they grow up, but they may provide some unique, positive influences as well.

Possible Risks for Children in Single-Parent Families

Just as statistics show economic advantages for traditional families, they also show disadvantages for single-parent families. It is difficult for a single parent to provide the same income as two parents, and single parents don't enjoy the reduced costs of shared expenses. Examining recent changes in U.S. family structure, sociologist Paul Amato notes that single parents often can't provide the educational resources such as books, computers, and private tutoring that make it easier for their children to do well in school. In many cases, children in single-parent families live in neighborhoods with higher crime rates, inferior schools, and fewer community services, increasing the likelihood of behavioral problems.[15]

Because the demands on single parents are double those for a parent in a two-parent household, research suggests that beyond financial needs, single parents are rarely able to provide the same depth and breadth of parenting as their married counterparts. Compared to married parents, single parents typically provide their children with less emotional support, fewer rules, less supervision, and harsher but more inconsistent discipline.[16] Struggling with limited financial resources and often without the help of the other biological parent, most studies indicate that single parents find it difficult to fulfill their parental roles effectively.

Children in single-parent families are also exposed to higher levels of stress than those in traditional families, much of it caused by economic hardship. Single-parent families move much more frequently than traditional families, either because of financial difficulties or because single parents form new romantic attachments and move in with their partners. Custody and visitation issues after a divorce may also be a significant cause of stress for children of newly single parents.

Possible Benefits for Children in Single-Parent Families

Some people suggest that there are significant benefits for children in single-parent families that aren't possible in traditional families. Because only one parent is available, the bond between the parent and child may be stronger than in a family where attachments are split between two parents.[17]

In 1992, Hillary Clinton, then First Lady, published the book *It Takes a Village*. The title was taken from an African proverb, "It takes a village to raise a child."[18] For many single-parent families it does take a village, or at least an extensive network of friends and family, to raise a child. Because there are so many demands on a single parent's time, these parents often need to call on friends and family for help. This can establish a broad sense of community unknown in children raised in traditional families.

Even with a strong network of family and friends, children in single-parent families often need to help maintain the household. They might need to watch younger siblings, clean the house, cook dinner, or mow the lawn, simply because there is no one else to do it. These responsibilities can provide children with a variety of advanced skills and an appreciation of their own abilities as they move toward adulthood.

Finally, children in single-parent families often experience conflict and disappointment, such as not seeing both parents on holidays or having as much time to spend with friends, which may better prepare them for the future. By managing problems themselves or watching family members successfully navigate tough times, children may be better prepared to enter life as adults. Successful single-parent families let kids know that they are very important, but not the center of the universe. This may help children see themselves in a realistic position as they grow up.[19]

COHABITING FAMILIES

The federal government defines **cohabitation** as two unrelated adults of the opposite sex living in the same residence, although a broader

> **SINGLE-PARENT FAMILY** is a family in which one parent is responsible for the children in a household.
> **COHABITATION** refers to the condition of heterosexual couples living together without being married.
> **TRIAL MARRIAGE** is cohabiting to assess whether partners are sufficiently compatible for marriage.

definition would also include same-sex couples. In the not-so-distant past, cohabiting couples were said to be "living in sin," because some religions consider cohabitation without marriage a sin, but attitudes have changed dramatically over the past 30 years. In the United States, cohabitation increased 15-fold between 1970 and 2010 from 500,000 couples to 7.5 million couples, and more than half of all young adults now cohabit before marriage.[20] For many modern couples, relationships progress rapidly. One study of cohabiting couples found that over half of the couples surveyed moved in together after dating for just six months.[21]

Types of Cohabitation

Cohabitation is often seen as a **trial marriage**—a chance for couples to test their long-term compatibility before they tie the knot. However, recent studies suggest that many cohabiting couples have no intention of getting married. In a survey of 25 cohabiting couples, Sharon Sassler noted that trial marriage was rarely the principal reason for

Possible Risks and Benefits for Children in Single-Parent Families

Possible risks

- Economic hardship
- Less time and energy from single-parent
- Increased stress from issues such as divorce, frequently moving house, and additional family tension

Possible benefits

- Stronger bond with single parent
- Wider network of adult friends and community
- Extra responsibilities that build skills
- Learn to manage conflict and disappointment
- Realistic sense of place—not "center of the universe"

Sources: "Marriage and Child Well-Being. Why Do Single-Parent Families Put Children at Risk?" *The Future of Children*. (Princeton University and Brookings Institution. 2005). J. Wolf. "Positive Effects of Single Parenting." About.com http://singleparents.about.com/od/familyrelationships/tp/raised_single.htm#

⋀ **It's not easy for single parents to raise children,** but there can be some unique
⋀ advantages, too.

COHABITATION EFFECT is a phenomenon in which couples who cohabit before they marry are more likely to divorce.

SERIAL MONOGAMY is an involvement in a single exclusive relationship followed by another exclusive relationship.

cohabitation. Instead, couples pointed to financial reasons (the ability to share living expenses), the convenience of living together, and housing needs.[22] Similar results were found by Wendy Manning and Pamela Smock, who noted that couples often transition into cohabitation out of convenience, without making the conscious decision to move in together.[23]

Heuveline and Timberlake identify five categories of cohabitation[24]:

1. **Prelude to marriage:** Couples test their relationship with the expectation of transitioning into marriage. They usually marry or break up before having children.
2. **Stage in the marriage process:** Couples may postpone marriage to pursue other opportunities, often reversing the order of marriage and childbearing.
3. **Alternative to singlehood:** Couples prefer living together to living separately, but have no immediate plans to marry. They are often young and prone to breaking up.
4. **Alternative to marriage:** Couples are in stable relationships and may have children, but prefer not to marry.
5. **Indistinguishable from marriage:** Couples are indifferent to marriage rather than opposed to it and lack the incentive to formalize their relationships.

Disadvantages of Cohabitation

As we will discuss later in Chapter 14, couples who cohabit before they marry have a higher risk for divorce than non-cohabiting couples—a

phenomenon known as the **cohabitation effect**.[25] Recent research indicates that the cohabitation effect may not be as significant as was previously thought, especially if cohabiting couples live together once they are already engaged or planning to marry.[26] However, some studies suggest that cohabiting couples may experience other relationship problems, including more negative couple communication than married couples, higher levels of physical aggression, and more symptoms of anxiety and depression.[27] Researchers speculate that these factors may be the result of insecurity or instability in couples who are living together to test their relationship. When cohabiting couples plan to marry, the quality of their relationship does not differ from that of married couples.[28]

Although attitudes toward cohabitation have changed in recent years, not everyone is a fan. Many religious groups strongly oppose cohabitation because it conflicts with the religious emphasis on marriage. Others object on practical grounds, pointing to studies that highlight the lack of stability in cohabiting relationships and negative effects on health and happiness. Some point to possible negative effects on children raised in cohabiting families.[29]

But what are the negative effects for the five percent of children in the United States who live with cohabiting parents? Although few studies have been conducted on the well-being of children living in cohabiting families, early research indicates that children living with cohabiting couples have poorer school experiences and more emotional and social problems than children of married couples and possibly even more problems than teens living with a single mother alone.[30]

SINGLES

Some years ago, remaining single, especially for women, carried a clear social stigma. But these perceptions have changed as more and more people have chosen to stay single. The number of adults who have

∨
∨ Many well-known and accomplished people throughout history **have chosen to**
∨ **stay single.**

Famous Singles in History

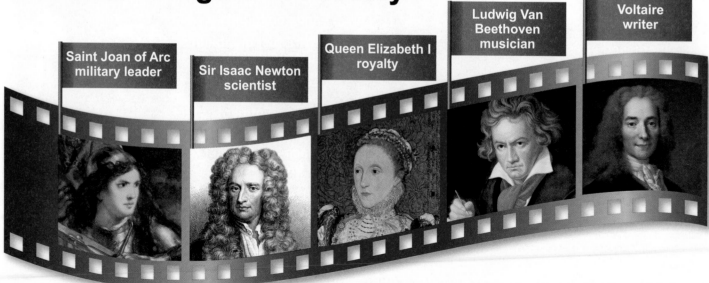

Saint Joan of Arc
military leader

Sir Isaac Newton
scientist

Queen Elizabeth I
royalty

Ludwig Van
Beethoven
musician

Voltaire
writer

Source: Trivia. TigerX.communications. http://tigerx.com/trivia/nomarry.htm]

A Cohabitation Trial

Jake is 23 and will graduate from college in one semester.

"Angela and I had been dating for about a year and a half and decided to move in together to save some money. We're probably going to get married in a few years.

"Her parents like me and thought it was fine that we were living together. But I didn't dare tell my parents. They live about 400 miles away and had never even met Angela.

"They're very religious and believe people should wait to have sex until they get married.

"I thought it would be a good idea to take Angela home to meet them at Christmas. I would have liked for us to be able to sleep together when we were there, but I couldn't get up the courage to talk about it with my parents, especially my mom.

"So, after we got there, I'm doing something else and Angela asks my mom which room is going to be ours. Well, my mom freaks out, and Angela asks, 'What's the big deal? We've been living together for six months.'

"That was the end of the visit, and we haven't spoken since. She kicked us out of the house and told us not to come back because we'd been living in sin."

---

never married has risen from 40 million in 1990 to over 74 million today—almost one in every three adults. If we categorize adults who have been widowed or divorced and haven't remarried as "singles," this number rises to about 114 million and 48 percent of all adults.[31] Unmarried men and women now head 45 percent of all the households in the United States.[32]

Today, people remain single for a variety of reasons. Some prefer to focus on educational goals or a career, intending to marry later on. However, the longer that people postpone marriage, the greater the likelihood of remaining single. In 2009, the median age at first marriage was 28 years for men and 26.2 years for women, compared to 23.1 years for men and 20.6 years for women in 1967.[33] Other singles say they haven't found a "soul mate" with whom they want to share the rest of their years. Greater career opportunities for women today make it much less likely that women marry for economic support.[34] Some successful women report that they don't have time to date and that men are often intimidated by their success.[35]

Today, many people are happily unmarried and show a wide range of interests, careers, cultures, and belief systems. Most singles also have strong friendships with both sexes, as well as strong family ties.[36] But singles do face some common problems. The physical safety of single women is always an issue. Some singles suffer from loneliness and strug-gle to satisfy their needs for intimacy, companionship, sex, emotional support, and for a stable romantic relationship.[37]

Commonly held beliefs about single men and women having a great time on the "singles scene" seem to be unrealistic. According to current research, most singles practice **serial monogamy**—involvement in a single exclusive relationship followed by another exclusive relationship. A few people have long-term dating relationships with other singles without thoughts of marriage.[38]

SAME-SEX MARRIAGE, CIVIL UNIONS, AND DOMESTIC PARTNERSHIPS

Should same-sex couples have the same legal rights as traditional couples? This question has created one of the most contentious social debates in recent years, involving the federal government and state legislatures, not to mention people such as radio talk-show host Rush Limbaugh and former Vice President Dick Cheney.

Before 2000, no gay or lesbian couple in the United States was entitled to the legal benefits awarded to traditionally married couples, regardless of how long they had been living together. Same-sex partners were ineligible for health insurance coverage, Social Security benefits, retirement savings, or hospital visitation rights, to name just a

Florence Nightingale nurse — James Buchanan president — Henry David Thoreau writer — Susan B. Anthony campaigner — J. Edgar Hoover FBI director

few. In fact, the federal government lists more than 1,100 legal rights and protections guaranteed to married couples that are not available to unmarried same-sex couples.[39]

Within the past decade, society has begun to address the rights and status of same-sex couples, resulting in several new legal terms. **Same-sex marriage** is a legal marriage between two people of the same sex. A **civil union** is a legally recognized union between same-sex couples that provides couples with legal rights. However, these rights are recognized only in the state in which the couple lives. A **domestic partnership** extends rights to unmarried heterosexual or same-sex couples, also at a state level.

Only same-sex marriage guarantees legal rights to couples at the state level. For example, in a state in which civil unions are recognized, one partner in a same-sex couple may obtain health insurance that covers his or her partner. However, unlike married couples, a same-sex couple must pay federal tax on the value of the health care premiums provided by the employer as if it were income.

In 1996, Congress passed the Defense of Marriage Act, which prohibited federal benefits to same-sex couples and allowed each state to choose whether it would recognize a same-sex union from another state. However, this statute conflicts with the U.S. Constitution's requirement that states recognize laws and contracts of other states and has not yet been tested in the courts.

Still, many states have plowed ahead in making their choices known. As of 2009, six states allow same-sex marriage; two others recognize these marriages as valid, whereas California got caught in-between. It allowed same-sex marriage in 2007 before Californian residents voted against it in 2008. The courts then ruled that the marriages performed during that year had to be recognized. In contrast, 30 states have language in their constitution that specifically defines marriage as a union between a man and a woman.[40]

Current Trends and Attitudes

The number of couples entering into civil unions may be slowing down. Gay rights groups say that many couples are waiting until they can gain the full legal protections of marriage rather than be subject to conflicting state and federal laws. Some couples say that entering a civil union has not provided the expected protections in employment, insurance, and health care.[41]

A recent national poll indicates that a majority of Americans—54 percent—oppose making same-sex marriage legal. However, there is a large difference of opinion among age groups. Although 58 percent of young adults aged 18 to 34 support same-sex marriage, the number drops steadily for older age groups—just over 40 percent of people aged 35 to 64 and only 24 percent of people aged 65 and over are in favor of legalizing same-sex marriage.[42]

Parent–Child Relationships

Because the legalities related to same-sex couples have only come into existence in the last decade and because there is such a wide variation in legal status and parenting circumstances in same-sex couples, little research has been completed on legal issues and parent–child relationships. Same-sex couples raising children have to negotiate a complex legal environment because these families do not have automatic legal recognition.[43]

Instead, most current research focuses on the emotional welfare of children raised in same-sex families. Studies indicate that children who are raised in same-sex households show little difference in their emotional and social development compared to children raised in traditional homes, and they are often more tolerant of diversity and more nurturing toward younger children.[44] Gay fathers, like Armand and Albert in *The Birdcage*, and lesbian mothers show a strong dedication to parenting roles, and most studies suggest that there is no significant difference in gender-identity confusion for children between heterosexual and homosexual homes.[45]

> ∧∧∧ Same-sex marriage **is the only form of same-sex union that guarantees couples the legal rights** and protections given to married heterosexual couples.

State Laws Governing Same-Sex Couples

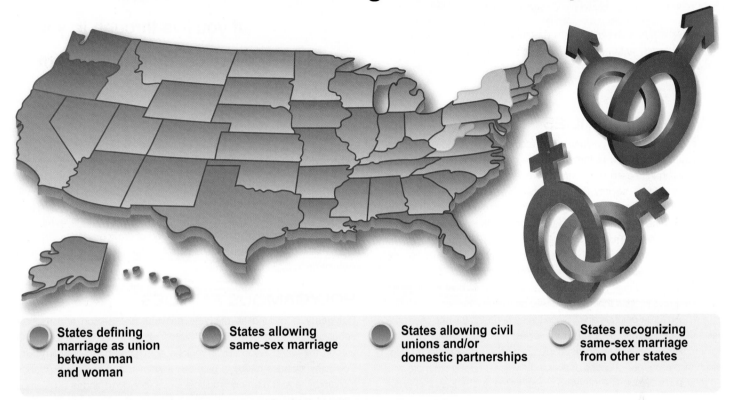

● States defining marriage as union between man and woman

● States allowing same-sex marriage

● States allowing civil unions and/or domestic partnerships

● States recognizing same-sex marriage from other states

Sources: National Conference of State Legislatures,
"Same Sex Marriage, Civil Unions and Domestic Partnerships," 2009. National Conference of State Legislatures

∧∧ The legal status and rights of same-sex couples **vary on a state-by-state basis.**

REMARRIED, BLENDED, OR STEPFAMILIES

When a spouse is widowed or divorced and then marries again, the new family is known by several, interchangeable names—a **remarried family**, **blended family**, or **stepfamily**. More than 12 million children in the United States were living in stepfamilies in 2004, about 17 percent of all children. Among children living with two parents, black children were most likely to be living in a blended family (28 percent), while Asian children were least likely to be in a remarried household (four percent).[46]

One issue facing stepparents and stepchildren is that the relationship is not legally recognized. For example, a man or woman may marry but not legally adopt the spouse's children. If the biological parent dies, the stepparent has no automatic legal right to maintain custody of the children even if he or she has been caring for them for many years. This problem may be solved through the process of adoption; however, once a stepparent adopts a child, the biological parent no longer has any legal rights or responsibilities.

Issues in Creating a Stepfamily

Beyond the legal issues faced by stepfamilies, parents and children must go through many emotional and social adjustments to create a functioning family unit. Psychologist Patricia Papernow identifies seven different stages of development in the life cycle of a stepfamily[47]:

Stage 1: Fantasy Family members fantasize about what life will be like as a stepfamily and have high expectations that later prove to be unrealistic. Families are often divided along biological lines, and children often still hope that their real parents will get back together.

Stage 2: Immersion Reality begins to set in, and family members find that their fantasies are at odds with reality. Stepparents may feel like outsiders, and children may feel split loyalties between their stepparent and their biological parent.

Stage 3: Awareness Family members begin to make sense of their situation, and stepparents begin to understand the biological parent–child connection and feel less uncertain about their own parenting abilities.

Stage 4: Mobilization Stepparents decide to take a firmer role in the new household. This often causes fights between family members, which can either draw attention to the need to work together to make changes or strain family relationships.

Stage 5: Action Couples work together to resolve their differences and to begin building a new family structure. The stepparent begins to taken on the disciplinary role in the family.

Stage 6: Contact Stepparents and stepchildren begin to get to know each other well and talk about their feelings, forging real relationships.

Stage 7: Resolution Family relationships are solid and reliable. The stepparent becomes an intimate outsider—someone who is close enough to know important details about their stepchildren's lives, but distant enough to play the role of a confidant.

Much research has been done on the effects of forming blended families on children at different ages and the best ways for stepfamilies to approach their new living situation. We will cover this in detail in Chapter 15.

DIVORCE is the legal termination of a marriage.

POLYGAMY is marriage between one person and more than one spouse, including marriage between a woman and multiple husbands (polyandry) and a man and multiple wives (polygyny); sometimes called plural marriage.

GRANDPARENT FAMILY is a type of family in which grandparents are responsible for raising their grandchildren.

DIVORCED FAMILIES

Divorce is the final legal termination of a marriage by law and allows both members of the couple to remarry. Some cultural commentators have pointed to an increased divorce rate in recent years as an indication of the collapse of U.S. society. Divorce statistics are often misreported and misinterpreted, which will be covered in Chapter 14.

The number of divorces per 1,000 people (which includes children and unmarried people) rose dramatically from about 1960 through the early 1980s. Researchers attribute this partly to the adoption of no-fault divorce in the United States, which made the legal process for divorce much easier. A couple could now mutually agree to a divorce without one spouse having to prove in court that the other was having an affair, was neglectful, or had been "cruel or inhumane." Since the early 1980s, the rate of divorce per 1,000 people has declined to the lowest rate since 1970.[49] Experts point to several different reasons: people are waiting longer to get married, which increases their chances of avoiding divorce, couples are more willing to attend marriage-strengthening programs to work through their prob-

Factors Affecting the Likelihood of Divorce	Result
Age	The younger males and females are when they marry, the greater the likelihood of divorce.[51]
Woman's economic independence	Women who can support themselves financially are not forced to stay in unhappy marriages and are more likely to divorce.[52]
Religious beliefs	Marriages in which both spouses attend religious services frequently are 2.4 times less likely to end in divorce than marriages in which neither spouse worships.[53]
Happiness and satisfaction in marriage	Women who are unhappy and dissatisfied with their marriage are more likely to initiate divorce proceedings than men.[54]
Children from divorced homes	Children from divorced homes are much more likely to divorce as adults—a concept known as the "intergenerational transmission of divorce."[55]
Identical twins	Identical twins are more likely to divorce than fraternal twins.[56] Researchers speculate that identical twins have more genetic material in common, and since factors such as drug abuse, alcoholism, and depression are affected by genes, the likelihood of divorce increases.[57]

"Being divorced is like being hit by a Mack truck. If you live through it, you start looking very carefully to the right and to the left."

—Jean Kerr (1922–2003)[48]

lems rather than divorcing, and more people are choosing to cohabit rather than marry so that separation doesn't lead to divorce.[50]

Refer to the table in the lower left corner for some of the factors that have been shown to influence the likelihood of divorce.

Chapter 14 provides more complete information on the effects of divorce on individuals and families.

POLYGAMOUS FAMILIES

Polygamy is defined as marriage between one person and multiple spouses. It is illegal in the United States, although it is widely practiced around the world, especially in regions dominated by the Muslim faith. Polygamy includes marriage between a woman and multiple husbands (polyandry) and a man and multiple wives (polygyny) and is sometimes called plural marriage.

Despite the threat of prosecution, some families still practice polygamy in the United States, particularly in Utah. Settlers who belonged to the Church of Jesus Christ of Latter-day Saints (commonly called Mormons) permitted polygamy before Utah became a state in 1890, and the practice still occurs among small, non-conformist sects. These sects are neither supported by nor are they members of the Church of Jesus Christ of Latter-day Saints. Today, Judaism and Christianity prohibit polygamy, whereas Islam permits the practice but encourages it only in certain conditions, such as when a couple cannot have children, a wife becomes chronically ill, or after a war when a large proportion of the men have been killed.[58]

Although only an estimated 20,000 to 40,000 people practice polygamy in the United States, which constitutes a tiny fraction of the population, two recent events have put polygamous families in the spotlight. In 2008, Texas Rangers raided the Yearning for Zion ranch where more than 400 children and teenagers and approximately 140 adult women lived and faced charges of forcing marriages of young girls to elderly leaders.[59] Polygamy also came to millions of Americans on the small screen in 2006 when HBO first aired the series Big Love, featuring a man with three wives.

Several studies indicate that polygamy has a variety of negative effects on families, including negative psychological and physical effects on wives and children and lower educational achievement for children.[60] Polygamous families are also reported to show increased rates of poverty, physical abuse, and illiteracy.[61] However, another study found no significant difference in the academic achievement of children raised in polygamous families. The researchers accounted for these differences by noting that studies by Western researchers may have different ways of measuring success and dysfunction than some of the cultures in Africa and Asia that had been studied.[62]

GRANDPARENT FAMILIES

The number of children being raised by their grandparents is on the rise. According to the U.S. Census, approximately 4.4 million grandchildren

Family Variations, Gender, and Partner Choices

In this chapter, you have learned about many of the family variations found in U.S. society today. Looking back to Chapter 4, you can see that an individual's gender and sexual orientation affect the type of family structure to which that person belongs. In Chapter 7, we reviewed factors associated with choosing a partner, which has a direct impact on both the family variation and how well the family functions. Looking ahead to Chapter 15, you will see in more detail some of the common issues for single-parent families, remarried families, and blended families, as well as some of the unique challenges that these types of families face.

>>> **ACTIVITIES** Write a short paper answering these questions:

1. How would you define the family that you grew up in?

2. What role in the family do you feel is the most important if any?

3. Of all the families that you have known, which family or families do you admire most? Why?

4. How has your cultural or ethnic identity impacted your experience and values about families?

5. What did you learn about families from this short activity?

---

under the age of 18 lived with their grandparents in 2000, representing six percent of children in all U.S. households.[63] Similar figures were noted in 2006.[64] Compare these statistics with the 2.2 million (3.2 percent) of children living with their grandparents in 1970, and you have some idea of just how dramatically the figure has increased over the past few decades.[65] The increase has been so great that there is now a housing development in New York solely for **grandparent families**, and there is a magazine devoted to grandparents raising children.[66] Researchers suggest that there are many reasons why grandparents take over parental responsibilities, including the death of one or more parents, divorce, unemployment, abandonment of children, child abuse, substance abuse problems, parental incarceration, teen pregnancies, and physical illness such as HIV/AIDS.[67]

Effects on Grandparents

Grandparents raising children take on a tough job. They face all the challenges of raising children felt by younger parents along with other issues related to their age and circumstances. Older caretakers may suffer from decreased stamina, fatigue, financial challenges, loss of personal time and time for friends, and tension between themselves and other family members who may resent their involvement. However, researchers have found many positive effects for grandparents raising children. Grandparents develop and maintain warm and close relationships with their grandchildren and have a positive view of their identities as grandparents.[68] This is true for grandmothers in particular, who typically find their relationships with their grandchildren more satisfying than grandfathers typically do.[69] Good relationships with the "middle generation"—the children's parents—help grandparents develop stronger bonds with their grandchildren.[70]

Effects on Grandchildren

Grandchildren raised by grandparents may have issues related to negative circumstances of their parents' leaving, such as divorce, substance or physical abuse, or incarceration.[71] In some cases, this can lead to ongoing behavioral problems, learning difficulties, or emotional or psychiatric disorders.[72] However, in general, children who are raised by their grandparents show no ill effects of being raised by grandparents when compared to children raised in other nontraditional households—they are just as healthy, perform at similar or higher academic levels, and have fewer behavioral problems.[73] In fact, research shows that grandparents often provide their grandchildren with more support and care than their own parents could provide for them.[74]

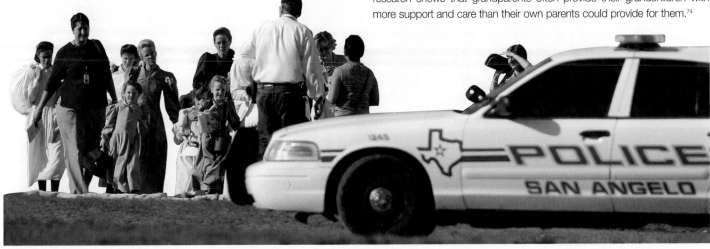

∧∧∧ **State authorities temporarily removed 416 children and teenagers** from the polygamous Yearning for Zion ranch in Texas following allegations of **child abuse and forced underage marriage.**

A Cultural Universal

A cultural universal is a social behavior or institution found in some form in every society on earth. Every society around the world has groups called families, although the composition of these groups varies greatly. In this chapter, we have listed nine family types found in the United States, but an international study would include many more variations.

The United Nations called 1994 the International Year of the Family. Its goal was to help governments, policy-makers, and people around the world appreciate the diversity of families and gain a greater understanding of family issues. So, what factors influence family diversity? As people moved from rural to urban settings during the industrial revolution, the dominant type of family changed from the extended family of three generations living together to the nuclear family of two generations. However, many societies in Africa are still built around extended families, including polygamous families and caretakers who are not biologically related to children within the household. The industrial revolution also foreshadowed the demise of the patriarchal family in Western societies—a household in which the father is the head of the family. As more women began to work outside the home, there was a move toward greater equality between the sexes.

Families around the world face many different challenges. In Asia and the Pacific, families are adapting to poor economic conditions, rapid rates of urbanization, and a new emphasis on greater equality between men and women. Families in Latin America and the Caribbean are dealing with increases in premarital sex and divorce, resulting in an increase in single-parent families. Meanwhile, families in the United States have one of the highest divorce rates in the world, along with high abortion rates and increasing numbers of single-parent families.[75] Commenting on these issues, then Secretary General Boutros Boutros-Ghali stated that families "are at the leading edge of change and are adapting to serious challenges" and are "essential to the fabric of society." In 2004, the U.N. celebrated the tenth anniversary of the Year of the Family.[76]

Every society has groups that it classifies as families, **but people's definitions of what constitutes a family vary greatly around the globe.**

think marriages and families: WHAT THEORIES ARE USED TO ANALYZE FAMILY ORGANIZATION AND RELATIONSHIPS?

FUNCTIONALISM

Sociologist Talcott Parsons, an early functional theorist, argued that families perform two basic, interrelated functions in society: socializing children and stabilizing adults into necessary social roles. When families perform these roles effectively, society is stable and functions efficiently.[77]

Parsons argued that these two functions were related to each other because children could only be properly socialized if society was organized into expected role structures. He maintained that the nuclear family was the ideal unit for a balanced society, with men taking on the "instrumental role" of family provider and protector, while women performed the "expressive role" of nurturer and caretaker.[78] This division of tasks between spouses, according to Parsons, was critical to making the family work. Because women focus on the household and childrearing tasks, men are free to leave the home and make a living for the family, and vice versa.[79] If Parsons' theory is true and a stable nuclear family contributes to a functioning family unit and a healthy society, how might today's varying family forms affect society?

Most functionalists would say that variations in the family lead to societal dysfunction. Sociologist David Popenoe believes that the institution of the family is in decline and that decline "should be cause for alarm."[80] According to Popenoe, family variations, specifically divorced and single-parent families, affect all other social institutions, including education, religion, government, and the economy. For example, the Kent State University Impact of Divorce Project studied more than 600 elementary school students from two-parent and single-parent households. This study showed that children from single-parent households consistently performed poorly on assessments of spelling, math, and reading skills and tests of mental and physical health as compared to their counterparts from two-parent households.[81] Research has also shown that poverty in single-parent homes is disproportionate to poverty in two-parent households. While some sociologists attribute this disproportion to other factors, such as the state of the economy, most put the blame on the declining family and divorce.[82]

CONFLICT THEORY

Conflict theory views the family as a microcosm of how social relations are structured in society as a whole. Conflict theorists believe that society is separated into two basic groups: the "haves" and the "have-nots." The "haves" control the majority of resources and have a vested interest in maintaining the status quo because it is advantageous to them. For example, in the United States today, Christians and heterosexual groups can be described as the "haves." Members of these groups often live in what we think of as "traditional families" and have automatic access to health insurance through an employer. These "haves" prevent the "have nots" from gaining access to these resources. For example, same-sex families and domestic partnerships are not permitted to have joint health insurance policies and must have

individual policies. The "haves" can use ideology to support and maintain their power by defining the type of family that is "normal" or "best" for society and denying resources and legal rights to other family variations. This ideology can operate as a justification for promoting inequality in the social structure, sometimes leading to homophobic or racist views by people who believe that their interpretation of the family is the only correct interpretation.[83]

Another group of conflict theorists—feminist theorists—have argued that the patriarchal structure of the family has contributed to male dominance. Feminist Charlotte Perkins Gilman noted that the "male function in the human race is to provide for the family," while the "female function [is] merely to serve the family."[84] Historically, male members of the family have had jobs outside the home and were the head of the household, while female members were expected to take on domestic tasks and be subservient to their husbands. Over time, as family variations began to emerge, women's role began to change. Women in both single-parent and two-parent households ventured out into the work field. Although women were given more economic and career opportunities, feminists argue that, even in two-parent homes, women are still expected to complete most of the domestic duties after spending a full day at work.[85]

SYMBOLIC INTERACTIONISM

Symbolic interactionists believe that people strive to create shared meanings. Individuals' identities are created and changed through interactions with others, and these interactions guide their behavior. In 2003, sociologists King-To Yeung and John Levi Martin tested the idea that people's definition of self is based largely on the interactions they have with others in a social environment.[86] This idea was not new, as sociologist Charles Cooley introduced the concept of the looking-glass self years before. However, Yeung and Martin expanded on Cooley's theory by determining that our close relationships most affect the way in which we view ourselves.[87] In other words, Yeung and Martin's research supported the idea that familial relationships are most important in developing our view of self. Through both verbal and nonverbal encounters with family members, our self is developed in both positive and negative ways. For example, if a mother praises a child's grades, that child might believe that his mother thinks he is intelligent and, in turn, view himself as intelligent. The reverse is also true. If a child is criticized, he or she might develop a negative view of self.

The socialization, or self development, process is reciprocal between parents and children—parents socialize children and children socialize parents—in an ongoing process. This reciprocal process is most apparent in families where identity negotiation is problematic. For example, researchers Hequembourg and Farrell examined how lesbian mothers negotiate an identity that combines the marginalized role of lesbian with the mainstream role of mother.[88] Other studies focus on immigrant families and the ways in which parents and children must negotiate new roles for themselves in unfamiliar cultural contexts.[89]

WRAP YOUR MIND AROUND THE THEORY

Functionalists believe that traditional families and gender roles promote well-adjusted children and parents and a stable society. Do you think traditional families promote a stable society more than other families?

Family Walk For Family Values
Organized by B.A.P.S.
Inspirer: H.D.H. Pramukh Swami Maharaj

FUNCTIONALISM

Functional theory holds that traditional families are an important force in maintaining a stable social order and that family life helps both children and adults. Children are taught societal expectations, and adults can settle into productive roles within the family and community. In the mid-1950s, Talcott Parsons saw "natural" parental roles for each gender. Men were breadwinners, made most of the major family decisions and managed much of the contact with the external world. Women used their "expressive" skills to manage internal family relationships. As gender roles and family relationships changed during the late 20th century, these theories applied to fewer and fewer people. In a 2000 study, functionalists Biblarz and Gottainer studied the outcomes of students with different family structures.[90] They found that children from divorced homes fared worse than children from two-parent homes on all levels.[91] However, children from widowed homes performed about the same as children from two-parent homes. This study showed that a family's structure is not the sole indicator of a child's future success.[92] In spite of these findings, many functionalists continue to campaign hard for a return to what they believe to be traditional families and gender roles.

IS ONE TYPE OF FAMILY PREFERABLE OVER ANOTHER?

CONFLICT THEORY

Conflict theorists believe that society is composed of groups that are in competition for scarce resources. Family resources include access to legal rights, insurance, health care, and child custody. Opposition to legal rights for same-sex marriages, domestic partnerships, civil unions, and cohabiting couples may prevent some types of families from gaining access to family resources. Conflict theorists view this as a way for the "haves" to use ideology to maintain their position at the top of the power structure. By defining the traditional family as the only acceptable family unit, the "haves" are able to maintain the social status quo.

SYMBOLIC INTERACTIONISM

Symbolic interactionists believe that each family defines its own roles and meanings through interactions among family members. For example, a family headed by a same-sex couple defines itself as a family even though it may not legally be recognized as one. Like Armand, Albert, and Val in *The Birdcage*, different types of families negotiate and define family roles, regardless of the views of society. In other words, these families do not internalize the views of others to define their family structure. For example, a single-parent family may rely on nonfamily members to meet some emotional or social needs. A cohabiting couple may make financial or custody agreements that are outside the legal system designed for married couples. Symbolic interactionists don't view family variations as right or wrong, but as unique constructs with meanings that are particular to each family and each individual family member.

Conflict theorists suggest **that opposition to rights and resources for same-sex couples is another way the "haves" can stay on top. What types of arguments** do opponents of same-sex rights use?

GOD MADE ADAM EVEN OH YEAH WE WANT A REVOTE WE DIDN'T GET A VOTE
PRESERVE BIBLICAL MARRIAGE

Symbolic interactionists believe that **each family is unique and negotiates important roles internally.**

discover marriages and families in action:
WHAT FAMILY ISSUES ARE CURRENTLY BEING DEBATED IN THE UNITED STATES

The Gay Blogger and Miss California

Beauty pageants are famous for controversy. In 1957, Miss USA was forced to resign when her in-laws revealed that she was only 18, not 21, as she had claimed, was already on her second marriage, and had two children. Since then, scandals relating to drug abuse, pregnancies, and risqué pictures have all caused a mild stir. However, few pageants have provoked as much debate as the 2009 Miss USA contest, when one of the judges asked Miss California for her opinions on gay marriage.

When pageant judge Perez Hilton, a gay man who writes a celebrity gossip blog, asked Carrie Prejean for her views on gay marriage, she answered honestly, "We live in a land that you can choose same-sex marriage or opposite marriage. And you know what, in my country, in my family I think that I believe that a marriage should be between a man and a woman. No offense to anybody there, but that's how I was raised and that's how I think it should be, between a man and a woman."

Hilton called it "the worst answer in pageant history" even though it sounded remarkably similar to the basic view expressed by President Obama. After she wasn't chosen as Miss USA, Prejean said, "I knew I wasn't going to win because of my answer . . . It's not about being politically correct; for me, it's about being biblically correct." Later, contest owner Donald Trump took away Prejean's Miss California crown, explaining that it wasn't because of her views, but because she had violated her contract by promoting outside organizations without permission.[93]

>>> Do you agree **or disagree with Miss California's views** on same-sex marriage?

From Classroom to Community } A Variety of Families

Two days a week, Jeff volunteers at the Boys and Girls Club near his college. He hangs out with the kids, shooting baskets and helping them with homework after school.

"I know the statistics about single-parent homes, but I was still surprised at how many of the kids at the club lived with just one parent. I was really amazed at how much responsibility some of them have, too.

"Hector is only 12 years old, but it's his job to watch his 8-year-old brother after school until his mom gets home. He has to make sure they get home O.K., fix his brother a snack, walk the family dog, and sometimes go shopping for supper. His mom works two part-time jobs just to get by, and she can't afford a sitter.

"Last summer, we threw a big party and told the kids that they could invite their families. Victoria seemed upset and said she wasn't coming. Later, she told me that she lived with her grandparents and she was ashamed of how old they were. She thought they would look out of place with the other parents.

"And then there's Walter. There are seven kids in Walter's family—two are his sister's children, and four are stepbrothers and sisters who moved into the family home when his father remarried. Walter is always reminding me that he likes his real mother better—I think he's secretly hoping his parents will eventually get back together."

09

WHAT TYPES OF FAMILIES EXIST IN THE 21ST CENTURY? 151

Prior to the 1970s, the dominant family type was a traditional family, consisting of husband, wife, and children. Since that time, there has been an increase in nontraditional family variations. Along with the traditional nuclear family, family variations in the United States today include single-parent families; cohabiting families; singles; same-sex marriages, civil unions, and domestic partnerships; remarried, blended, or stepfamilies; divorced families; polygamous families; and grandparent families. Each variation has its own challenges and benefits.

WHAT THEORIES ARE USED TO ANALYZE FAMILY ORGANIZATION AND RELATIONSHIPS? 161

Functionalists believe that traditional families provide stability for individuals and society. Conflict theorists view opposition to same-sex marriage, civil unions, and domestic partnerships as a means of "haves" maintaining control over "have-nots." Symbolic interactionists look at the family in small units and address ways that new roles are constructed within families through the process of socialization.

WHAT FAMILY ISSUES ARE CURRENTLY BEING DEBATED IN THE UNITED STATES? 163

Proposals for same-sex marriage, civil unions, and domestic partnerships have sparked debate across the country. As the number of nontraditional families continues to grow, support and opposition for their legal rights and for social recognition is becoming a key political issue.

Theory

FUNCTIONALISM 161

- the nuclear family socializes children to become members of adult society
- the nuclear family helps adults become stable, responsible members of society
- fixed gender roles within nuclear families keep society balanced

CONFLICT THEORY 161

- society is composed of groups that are in competition for scarce resources, and the dominant group wants to maintain the status quo
- opposition to legal rights for same-sex marriages, domestic partnerships, civil unions, and cohabiting couples may prevent some types of families from gaining access to family resources

SYMBOLIC INTERACTIONISM 161

- individuals construct their identities through interactions with family members
- each family is unique with family members continually renegotiating their individual roles

Key Terms

traditional or **nuclear family** refers to a husband and wife who are legally married, have children, and live together *150*

psychological parent is a person serving as a parent who is not biologically related to the child *151*

postmodern family is a term meant to include all family variations existing today *151*

single-parent family is a family in which one parent is responsible for the children in a household *152*

cohabitation refers to the condition of heterosexual couples living together without being married *153*

trial marriage is cohabiting to assess whether partners are sufficiently compatible for marriage *153*

cohabitation effect is a phenomenon in which couples who cohabit before they marry are more likely to divorce *154*

serial monogamy is an involvement in a single exclusive relationship followed by another exclusive relationship *155*

(continued)

same-sex marriage is marriage in which same-sex couples are united legally with all the legal rights guaranteed by the federal government to traditional married couples   *156*

civil union refers to same sex couples recognized in certain states without the legal rights guaranteed by the federal government to traditional married couples   *156*

domestic partnership refers to same-sex couples or cohabiting couples recognized in certain states but without the legal rights guaranteed by the federal government to traditional married couples   *156*

remarried family, blended family, or **stepfamily** describes the family of a person who remarries after divorce or death of the spouse, including all children   *157*

divorce is the legal termination of a marriage   *158*

polygamy is marriage between one person and more than one spouse, including marriage between a woman and multiple husbands (polyandry) and a man and multiple wives (polygyny); sometimes called plural marriage   *158*

grandparent family is a type of family in which grandparents are responsible for raising their grandchildren   *159*

Sample Test Questions

MULTIPLE CHOICE

These multiple-choice questions are similar to those found in the test bank that accompanies this textbook.

1. In which type of family do most children live?
   a. a family with one biological parent
   b. a family with two biological parents
   c. a blended family
   d. a grandparent family

2. Which of the following is NOT mentioned as a benefit of a traditionally married couple?
   a. a better sex life
   b. better health
   c. extensive family network
   d. economic advantages

3. Cohabiting couples:
   a. are less likely to divorce after they get married.
   b. experience more physical aggression than married couples.
   c. enjoy better health than singles.
   d. have the same legal rights as married couples.

4. The bond between a single parent and a child may be:
   a. weaker than in the parental bond in a traditional family.
   b. broken easily when there is too much stress.
   c. stronger than the parental bond in a traditional family.
   d. weakened when too many people are involved in parenting.

5. Civil unions and domestic partnerships:
   a. are only recognized in certain states.
   b. are legal terms developed in the 1970s.
   c. do not include cohabiting heterosexual couples.
   d. prevent same-sex couples from adopting children.

ESSAY

1. Discuss the positive effects of traditional families.
2. What are some of the benefits and challenges of choosing to stay single?
3. Discuss the reasons for the increase in grandparent families over the past few decades.
4. What are some positive and negative effects of single-parent families on children?
5. Discuss the legal and social issues caused by a recent increase in nontraditional families.

WHERE TO START YOUR RESEARCH PAPER

For more data on children's living arrangements, go to http://www.childtrendsdatabank.org/indicators/59FamilyStructure.cfm

For more data on U.S. families, go to http://www.census.gov/population/www/socdemo/hh-fam.html

To find out more about single-parent households, go to http://family.jrank.org/pages/1581/Single-Parent-Families.html

To learn more about cohabiting couples with children, go to http://www.urban.org/publications/310962.html

For more data on the unmarried and single population in the United States, go to http://www.census.gov/Press-Release/www/releases/archives/families_households/006840.html

To find out more about legal issues related to same-sex marriage, civil unions, and domestic partnerships, go to http://www.ncsl.org/?TabId=16430

For more information on stepfamilies, go to http://www.stepfamilies.info/

For more data on U.S. divorce statistics, go to http://www.cdc.gov/nchs/fastats/divorce.htm

For more information on polygamous families, go to http://www.polygamy.com/articles/templates/?a=171&z=3

For more data on grandparent families, go to http://www.census.gov/population/www/documentation/twps0026/twps0026.html

ANSWERS: 1. b; 2. c; 3.b; 4. c; 5. a

Remember to check www.thethinkspot.com for additional information, downloadable flashcards, and other helpful resources.

WHAT CHALLENGES DO MIDDLE-AGED AND
AGING FAMILIES FACE?
HOW DOES AGING AFFECT INDIVIDUALS,
FAMILIES, AND SOCIETY?
CAN ELDERLY PEOPLE AFFORD ESSENTIAL
PRESCRIPTION DRUGS?

In the

award-winning movie, *The Savages,* Wendy and Jon are a middle-aged brother and sister who don't like each other very much. Each has retreated into a rather solitary world: Jon teaches drama in Buffalo, New York, while Wendy strives to become a playwright in Manhattan. Neither is very happy with his or her relationships or prospects. Jon has a girlfriend from Poland who wants to marry him after four years of living together so she can stay in the country, but Jon refuses to make the commitment. Wendy has a purely sexual relationship with her married landlord and seems to like his dog better than she does him. She takes anti-anxiety drugs and works as an office temp where she steals stationery to keep her playwriting costs down. She imagines she will get a grant to complete her autobiographical play even though she is consistently turned down. Jon is struggling to complete a book for publication and can't quite get over the hump.

Always in the background are thoughts of their father, Leonard, who brought them up by himself after their mother abandoned them. He was alternately abusive and neglectful, and neither Jon nor Wendy has spoken to him in more than 20 years. He lives in a retirement community in Arizona with a girlfriend, but he is aging rapidly, showing increasing signs of memory loss and dementia.

The Savages are a truly fractured family, living many miles apart with little or no communication. There is no love lost between them until a crisis forces them to come together. Leonard slips more deeply into the shadowy world of memory loss and paranoia when he begins to write messages on the bathroom wall with his feces. Jon and Wendy travel to Arizona to figure out what to do, and after they arrive, Leonard's girlfriend dies suddenly. With no other relatives and no one else who will have him, Jon and Wendy bring Leonard back to Buffalo, where they place him in a nursing home.

As their father's death approaches, both Jon and Wendy battle contradictory emotions. They have to care for a father who deserves their anger but who is now so limited that he is beyond understanding his own behavior or their feelings. They also face making difficult decisions relating to his care. At one point, Jon and Wendy struggle to chose the right nursing home. Jon points out that the promises in the brochures are designed to play on the guilt of children. "Am I doing the right thing?" he asks out loud. "Is this nice enough? Would my older, wiser friends approve?" Wendy concludes one depressing visit to their father with an overly dramatic self-accusation: "We are horrible, horrible, horrible people."

Forced into living together and communicating with each other, the siblings travel a very bumpy road toward understanding themselves and each other a little better. After their father's death finally comes, it seems likely they will stay in touch and support each other a little more than in the past. In the end, Jon hopes to reconcile with his girlfriend in Poland. Wendy transforms her family's conflicts into a successful play that will be performed in a small, off-Broadway theater.

167

MIDDLE-AGED AND AGING FAMILIES

CHAPTER 10

The Savages aren't much of a family **at the beginning of the movie.** Mutual dislike and many miles separate them. **But blood proves thicker** than water in crisis.

Their father's illness and death force Jon and Wendy to face issues that many families must confront as parents age. In this chapter we will consider these issues. If parents are aging and less than capable of caring for themselves, who makes decisions concerning their care? What is it like to switch roles with a parent when a middle-aged child becomes the care-giver? Which health issues besides dementia might require extensive care? What priorities and limitations should be taken into account when deciding on care? Is it appropriate to address past family grievances when parents are no longer capable of fixing the wrongs they committed?

In *The Savages*, Leonard's neglect and abuse has a lifelong effect on Jon and Wendy, making it difficult for both of them to form committed relationships. But the movie also suggests that the trauma of her childhood and her reconnection with her family helped inspire Wendy as an artist. The ending of the movie suggests that the death of a family member can increase self-knowledge and also serve as a turning point that leads to other changes. The latter stages of life present unique challenges and opportunities to middle-aged and aging families.

My petite grandma had 13 children and never weighed more than 95 pounds. She was always active and never seemed to run out of energy, right up to the day she died. I'll never forget our massive family reunions every summer in Idaho. My grandma was always the life of the party, especially with the kids, since she was always playing with us and even going down the slide at the park like an eight-year-old. She was aging, but it didn't seem to faze her. She never acted like being older was a handicap or a hardship in any way. It was exciting to see her so active at her age. I remember thinking several times as I grew up that I wanted to be like my grandma when I was old. In this chapter we will look at how families cope when parents and grandparents, like my grandma, enter the final stages of life.

Middle-Aged and Aging Families

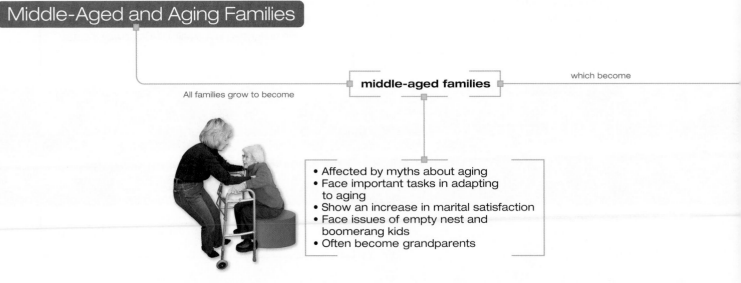

All families grow to become → **middle-aged families** → which become

- Affected by myths about aging
- Face important tasks in adapting to aging
- Show an increase in marital satisfaction
- Face issues of empty nest and boomerang kids
- Often become grandparents

get the topic: WHAT CHALLENGES DO MIDDLE-AGED AND AGING FAMILIES FACE?

"Middle age is when you choose your cereal for the fiber, not the toy."
— author unknown[1]

Middle-Aged Families

MIDDLE-AGE MYTHS

American culture emphasizes youth. Nearly every advertisement on TV, on the Internet, or in print exalts the looks and abilities of young people or encourages older people to try to recapture some of that glory. This theme shows up in all types of ads: The parties in beer ads are crowded with young, beautiful people; ads for foods and supplements promise older adults a return to the digestive regularity of their youth; skin creams and hair products entice women to take years off their appearance; and men are encouraged to use potency drugs that offer temporary periods of youthful virility. Our culture sells the idea that either you're young or you want to be young.

Some losses in physical abilities and social relationships are typical as people move through their middle years, a period usually considered to begin between the ages of 35 and 45. There is a general loss of physical strength and energy, as well as some reduction in hearing, sight, and other senses. Reflexes and metabolism usually change, making weight control more difficult. Diseases common in older people, such as cancer and diabetes, may reduce general health. And people actually shrink as they age through bone loss and the compression of spongy disks in the spine. People also lose elderly relatives and younger friends who die prematurely.[2]

But other common beliefs about the aging process are myths. Aging people are generally healthier than they were in previous generations. Sexual desire and enjoyment remain intact, and even increase for postmenopausal women. Intelligence remains stable, while verbal and social skills increase. It is also a myth that most people experience a midlife crisis related to their employment and social circumstances. People in their middle years are usually at the height of their earning power, job achievement, and satisfaction. Older workers may not be as suited for entry-level jobs relying on new technology, but they are more desirable for administrative or managerial positions because of their experience, discipline, and established social networks.[3]

Some middle-aged families belong to what is called the **sandwich generation** because they feel squeezed between two generations that require their attention. Because parents are having

---

<<< **The sandwich generation** may be squeezed between older and younger generations. **Does your family help care for** an elderly relative?

aging families ——— which eventually experience ——— **death, loss and grieving**

- Affected by social definitions of aging
- Ethnic groups show different patterns
- Some people are never married
- Face issues in work and retirement
- Experience reduced income
- Many women face old age alone
- Need to negotiate new roles with children
- Often face serious health issues

- Family responses are unique
- Four stages for families in adapting to a death
- Challenges in adapting to new role as widow or widower
- Society debates assisted suicide and euthanasia

EMPTY NEST is a home after the last child has left home.

SPACIOUS NEST is the transition to more physical room in the empty nest home and more psychological space for the marital relationship.

RENESTED FAMILY or **CLUTTERED NEST** is a home to which adult children have returned to live temporarily.

BOOMERANG KIDS are adult children who return to live with parents temporarily.

children later in life, they may have responsibilities for young children into their 40s and beyond. At the same time, their parents may be entering their 60s, 70s, or 80s. Certainly, young children require significant energy, attention, and investment. If parents need assistance at the same time because of physical or mental health issues, the generation in between is crushed by competing demands. Most of the people giving direct care to both generations are women, though this can vary in other cultures.[4,5]

The probability of families feeling squeezed by older and younger generations will likely increase in the coming years due to delayed parenting and declining birth rates.[6] However, the likelihood of caring for a younger and an older generation at the same time is low. More women than men are involved in caring for elders, but less than 10 percent of women in their 40s, and even smaller percentages of women in their 50s and 60s, combine full-time work with caregiving for both children and older adults. Only about 5 percent of older parents share a home with their children, though many more receive financial or other assistance.[7,8] Families who care for both children and aging parents don't show a great change in marital satisfaction during those years.[9] Those who do provide care for older generations are clearly affected by their previous relationships. One study notes that if a daughter had a close relationship with a parent, it is much easier to care for that parent later on.[10]

TASKS FOR MIDDLE-AGED FAMILIES

The middle years in a marriage are action-packed and affected by many different responsibilities and influences. Males and females need to address the needs of their spouse, children, other family members, and employers. In many cases, hard choices need to be made concerning how to best invest the precious commodities of time and money. At the same time, the richness of the environment can yield great rewards and satisfaction when a person advances at work, children gain skill and autonomy, older family members appreciate assistance, and spouses experience marital satisfaction.[11]

Negotiating changes in work roles and expectations is an important process for families during their middle years. For example, work expectations of men may change during this period. Many men are at the peak of their earning power, which provides greater opportunities for spouses and families to enjoy vacations, possessions, and other benefits. Men may also accept their current role at work, believing they have achieved their highest level of employment. However, women entering the work force after raising younger children to become more self-sufficient may feel less strain in balancing work with care for older children.[12]

Another challenge for families is changing their expectations and parenting strategies as children grow into adolescence and beyond. Children need less direct supervision, but still require significant attention and guidance from parents. Addressing these issues requires an understanding of children's development and attention to the individual needs of unique children. For example, is every child capable of staying home alone without trouble at the age of 12? At what age should kids have primary control over their own money? What about riding in a car with a

newly licensed friend? The parent-child relationship must continually change to adapt to the changing needs and abilities of children and the strengths and involvement of parents.[13]

MARITAL SATISFACTION AND CHILDREN

Studies show that satisfaction with a marriage follows a relatively predictable pattern. In early stages of the family life cycle, before children or during childbearing years, satisfaction is generally high. During middle stages of the family life cycle, between the time children turn three and the time they leave home, satisfaction drops to a lower level, reaching its lowest point when children are teenagers. Once children have been "launched" from the home and are predominantly responsible for themselves, parents typically experience greater satisfaction with their marriage.[14]

For years, people have used the image of a bird's nest to symbolize the care given to children by parents before their children are ready to fly on their own. This image inspired at least three terms that identify living arrangements and attitudes in middle-years families. The **empty nest** occurs when the last child leaves home. In many cases, empty nest syndrome is used to imply a state of loneliness and lack of purpose for parents, especially mothers. This may be true for parents whose children served to give them a sense of purpose and meaning or whose children helped stabilize a poor relationship between spouses. However, research shows that in most cases the end of daily care for a child in the home is a positive transition in parents' lives. Mothers experience a sense of freedom and look forward to new challenges and a renewed emphasis on marriage. Fathers interpret the transition as positive as well, as long as they have been significantly involved in parenting and don't feel they are losing a chance to establish a strong bond. Some people use the term **spacious nest** to describe the transition because there is more physical room in the home and more psychological space for the marital relationship to flourish.[15]

The home as a nest provides a further metaphor for the recent trend in which adult children return home to live temporarily. Adult children may move home while they establish or change a career or as a result of job loss or divorce. This arrangement is sometimes called a **renested family** or referred to as a **cluttered nest**. The children may be called **boomerang kids** because they have returned to their original spot. Researchers believe the rate of children returning to their parents' home temporarily has doubled in the last 50 years. Research shows that 30 percent of all parents with children in their 20s share their home with one or more of their children. This rate is likely to increase in coming decades and may indicate a clear change in the expected family life cycle. However, a renested family often involves stress when a child is unemployed or financially dependent on the parents or when a child is recovering from a divorce, especially if the child brings along their own children as well.[16,17]

BECOMING GRANDPARENTS

Although our mental image of grandparents is often one of elderly people, current demographics make it common for people to become grandparents during their middle years. The role of grandparent is defined differently in different cultures. For example, in some agricultural societies, grandparents remain the heads of the household and are given utmost respect and deference. However, in modern American culture, grandparents usually occupy one of many different roles.

For grandparents who are separated geographically from their children and grandchildren, there are few choices. Their relationships might be termed remote, with face-to-face visits limited to special occasions

The Family as a Nest

Parents spend time and energy raising young children so they can become self-sufficient.

When children leave, the empty nest can be a positive or negative experience for parents.

When "boomerang kids" return to the nest temporarily, new roles and relationships need to be established.

Why do you think that a "renested" family **is more common today?**

and holiday. But for grandparents who live geographically closer to their grandchildren, there are more options. They can serve as a "reserve parent" and provide care to their grandchildren as needed without needing to make or enforce disciplinary rules. They do not interfere with the relationship between a child and parent, although they may mediate some family disputes or provide family background and history to give children and parents needed perspective.[18,19] Children who are close to a grandparent on either the maternal or paternal side usually see a close relationship between the parent and grandparent on the same side.[20]

In certain cases, grandparents may take on a major role in raising their grandchildren, usually because a single parent needs assistance. In this case, grandparents do enforce discipline on grandchildren and the relationship may take on all the complexities of a parent-child relationship. There also may be tension between the parent and grandparent because the grandparent may be seen as interfering or the parent may be seen as lacking in skills or motivation.[21] The rates of grandparents providing child care for grandchildren are much higher for African Americans and Hispanics than for whites. This may be due to cultural differences as well as the prevalence of unemployed adults among these groups available to provide child care.[22] Another possibility is that it might be due to the greater percentages of single African American and Hispanic parents.[23]

In some cases, grandparents must step in to raise grandchildren because parents are absent for a variety of reasons: substance abuse and drug addiction; infection with HIV/AIDS; debilitating disease such as cancer; criminal involvement resulting in jail terms; and child abandonment, abuse, or neglect. This is the case for 10 percent of all grandparents and

more than 1 million kids. The rates for different ethnic groups are striking: 12 percent of African American children are being raised by grandparents compared to about 6 percent for Hispanics and 4 percent for whites. These grandparents suffer from increased physical and mental health risks because of their age and the fact that they have often been thrust into an unwelcome or unexpected role. In some cases, caring for grandchildren puts these caregivers under greater economic and occupational strain at a time when they had hoped to enjoy greater leisure and retirement. In most cases, the children are considered to be at risk because they have experienced the loss of one or more parents, making a variety of physical, mental, and social problems more likely.[24]

Aging Families

"I will never be an old man. To me, old age is always fifteen years older than I am." —Francis Bacon, Sr. (1561–1626)[25]

HOW OLD IS "OLD"?

Even people in their teens and 20s have mornings when they get out of bed and feel "old"—maybe their back is sore, their joints ache, or they just don't have a lot of energy. But because the aging process is variable and unique, there is no single set of physical attributes that distinguish someone who is old. There are 90-year-old athletes who run marathons, while some 20-year-olds can barely get off the couch. Which group is old? In essence, the terms to characterize different ages—including "old"—are socially constructed.

∨ ∨ ∨ **How important is** chronological age **when it comes to** physical skills and activity?

Traditionally in the United States, old age is considered 65 and higher. This benchmark was established in 1935 when the Social Security Act designated 65 as the age at which individuals qualify to receive old age benefits. Sixty-five was chosen based on custom rather than scientific study, and because it was the age many retirement programs used.[26] There have been a few modifications since then in government guidelines and private insurance plans, but over all, 65 is still the popularly held dividing line. However, an individual's self-image, as seen by Francis Bacon's quote above, doesn't always match the arbitrary divisions used by society. In the United States today, many people don't consider themselves old until well past 65, partially because life expectancy now averages about 78 years: 80 for women and 75 for men.[27]

Regardless of a person's attitude, researchers agree on five physical characteristics that characterize the aging process: Physiological changes are steady but gradual through adulthood into old age; the more complex the bodily function, the more rapidly it declines; individuals age at different rates, and tissues and systems within one person may age at different rates; aging lowers the ability to respond to stress; age brings a lower resistance to disease. Compared to other animals, one of the unique aspects of humans is that we typically live for an extended period of time after we have outlived our reproductive "usefulness."[28]

Society's expectations also play a role in aging. In general, "old people" are expected to be more socially and politically conservative than younger people, less tolerant, and more likely to suffer from depression and impairment. These expectations affect older people's image of themselves and result in a lower status in modern Western societies than in previous years. This means reduced access to financial resources, less decision-making power in both social and political settings, and reduced contact with other generations.[29]

Regardless of societal attitudes, research shows that the proportion of people in the world who are 65 or older has grown rapidly over the last 60 years. The percentage is projected to continue to grow into the middle of the 21st century. For example, in 1950, just over 5 percent of the world's population was 65 or older. However, by 2000, the percentage had risen to about 7 percent, and it is projected to rise to nearly 16 percent by 2050. In North America, the percentages were about 8 percent in 1950 and 12 percent in 2000, with a projected growth to over 20 percent by 2050. The primary reasons for this growth is a worldwide increase in life expectancy coupled with a reduction in the birth rate. As a result, today there are fewer younger people in comparison to older people.[30]

ETHNIC DIFFERENCES

The percentage of elderly individuals (65 and older) in different racial and ethnic groups greatly varies. For example, about 13 percent of all whites were elderly in 1990, compared to about 8 percent of blacks, 6 percent of Asians and Native Americans, and only 5 percent of Hispanics. These percentages have and will continue to change over time. They are expected to increase by 2050 to about 23 percent for whites, with rates for blacks and Native Americans roughly doubling, while the percentage for Hispanics will nearly triple to 14 percent.[31] The differences in these overall rates can be partially attributed to life expectancy. For example, the life expectancy for white males in 2010 is 76 years, while it is just 70 for black males. But the great increase in the percentage of the Hispanic elderly population illustrates what some have called "the Hispanic paradox." Hispanics as a group have lower education and income rates than the population as a whole. Normally, this would translate into a lower life expectancy. However, Hispanics in fact have a higher life expectancy—over 78 years in 2010—than the population as a whole. Although there is no official reason to explain this, one theory suggests that lifestyle choices in the Hispanic community may contribute to good health more than practices among other Americans.[32,33]

In general, the economic conditions of elderly people match the economic conditions of younger members of their ethnic group. For example, about 8 percent of elderly whites

were living in poverty in 1999 compared to 26 percent of blacks and 21 percent of Hispanics. Elderly blacks and Hispanics are also more likely to be living in substandard housing than whites.[34]

ELDERS WHO HAVE NEVER MARRIED, ELDER GAY MEN AND LESBIANS

About 8 percent of the elderly population has never married. In contrast to the popular idea that anyone who has never married has "missed the boat" and is necessarily unhappy and lonely, research shows that these elderly people are better adjusted than those who have experienced divorce or widowhood and enjoy as much general life satisfaction as married individuals. Although they tend to have fewer family contacts than married individuals, they have developed friends who provide close relationships and support similar to family members. Older single women are often better off financially than formerly married women, partially because of a strong work history and access to pensions.[35]

Aging gay men and lesbians exhibit many of the same patterns as heterosexuals who have never married. Instead of being lonely and dissatisfied, as the stereotypes suggest, gay males and lesbians have adapted well to their role in society and feel general satisfaction comparable to heterosexuals. Many have constructed a "family of choice" consisting of relatives, close friends, and current or former lovers. This "family" occupies a similar role in their lives as the traditional family formed by a heterosexual marriage. There may be significant changes in the lives of older gay males and lesbians in the future because many younger people in these groups do not hide their sexual orientation. Many elderly gays today lived "in the closet" to avoid negative reactions from family, friends, and society.[36] Some research indicates that the hardships of living in a society harshly biased against lesbians may have prompted them to develop strengths and adaptive strategies that serve them well as they grow older.[37]

FAMILY CHANGES IN LATER YEARS
Work and Retirement

As individuals change during the biological and social aging process, so do families. One of the greatest changes revolves around work. Those continuing to work in their later years must confront **ageism** or discrimination because of age. General, faulty stereotypes concerning older people have infiltrated the workplace. For example, myths about older workers suggest that they produce less and have less physical strength, endurance, drive, and imagination. Older workers are also seen as set in their ways, harder to train, and unable to get along well with younger workers. These perceptions affect older people who may be laid off or those who are looking for a new or different job. In some cases, companies have eliminated older workers who are paid more because of their

Percentage of Elderly, by Race and Hispanic Origin: 1990 and 2050

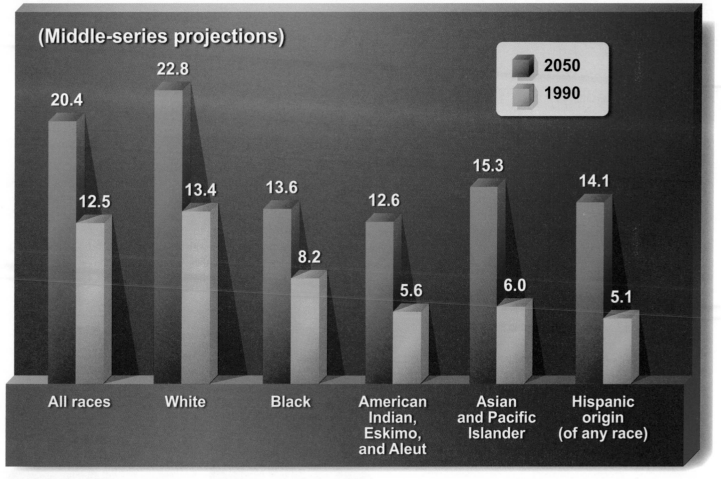

Source: U.S. Census Bureau

∧
∧
∧ **This graph illustrates the** "Hispanic paradox" **of increasing longevity in people of Hispanic origin.** One theory points to health-promoting lifestyle choices as a potential explanation.

Percentage of Older Population in the Labor Force, by Age and Sex: 1950, 1993 and 2010

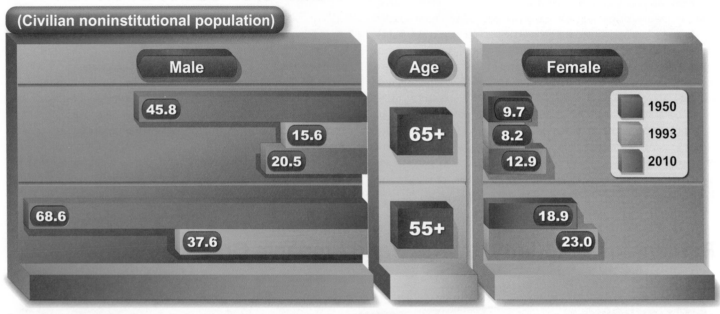

(Civilian noninstitutional population)

Male

Age

Female

	Male	Age	Female	
	45.8	65+	9.7	1950
	15.6		8.2	1993
	20.5		12.9	2010
68.6		55+	18.9	
37.6			23.0	

Source: United States Department of Labor, Bureau of Labor Statistics, Household Data Annual Averages (accessed through the U.S. Census Bureau web site)

∧
∧ **This graph shows** that rates for women working in their later years **have remained**
∧ **relatively stable** while the rates for men have dropped considerably. **Why do you think this is true?**

years of service to replace them with younger workers who earn lower wages. Since 1978, the federal government has prohibited age discrimination against workers up to the age of 70.[38]

There are changes for people who retire as well. Men are retiring earlier than in previous years. In 1950, 46 percent of the men aged 65 or older were still in the workforce, but that number had dropped to about 20.5 percent in 2010. The percentage for women during the same period rose slightly to about 13 percent. The rates for ethnic groups were remarkably similar: About 17 percent of older whites were still in the labor force compared to about 14 percent of blacks and Hispanics and about 20 percent of Asians.[39]

For decades in many families, one or both partners has been absent from home 40 or more hours each week because of work. When retirement occurs, usually at or around the age of 65, significant changes are necessary. A recently retired spouse, often the husband,

isn't accustomed to being at home during the day. A longtime housewife suddenly has an antsy partner puttering around the house, interrupting the routines that have worked for her for many years. Or a working wife may want to continue working and volunteering, spending little time at home with her retired husband. In general, couples have more time to do things together, which can be positive as long as the couple shares the same expectations for mutual time.[40]

>>> **Myths about old age may hamper older workers** when they attempt to change jobs **or apply for a new job.** What unique qualities do skilled older workers **bring to a job compared to younger workers?**

Couples may also struggle with maintaining or reigniting a romantic and sexual relationship after spending so many years preoccupied with work and children.[41]

Income and Lifestyle

What is a **fixed income**? Many couples who have retired rely on income that is fixed at a certain level, such as a pension or annuity. A fixed income promises an exact amount for a particular number of years or the duration of a person's life, regardless of inflation or rising costs. Some pensions or government programs allow only an increase related to the cost of living. Because the elderly are no longer working, they won't benefit from pay raises or job promotions. Their ability to purchase goods won't increase and may decline if they don't receive cost-of-living adjustments. The graph below indicates a clear decline in household income—starting at age 55 and dropping rapidly after age 65.

For example, a couple retired in 2000 with a fixed, combined retirement income of $30,000. They felt this amount would allow them to live comfortably in their later years. However, they found that because of inflation, their $30,000 income in 2009 had about the same buying power as $24,000 in 2000. Although their fixed income stayed the same, its value had decreased, with its buying power likely to drop even more in the future.[42] The expenses of retired couples may be lower because they have finished paying for their house and no longer support children. However, there is a probability of increased medical expenses and a rise in the costs for treatments and prescription drugs. Individuals or families who started their retirement near or below the poverty line may need to choose between paying for necessities such as food, drugs, and winter heat. A 1993 federal government report established that going hungry, being cold, or going without medication was an unpleasant choice for 12 percent of elderly people.[43] By 2006, 9 percent of elderly people were living in poverty—an obvious decrease from 1993. However, 9 percent amounts to 3 million elderly people below the poverty level.[44] Predictions also indicate that the financial status of baby boomers who start reaching 65 in 2010 is

Real Median Income by Age: 2007

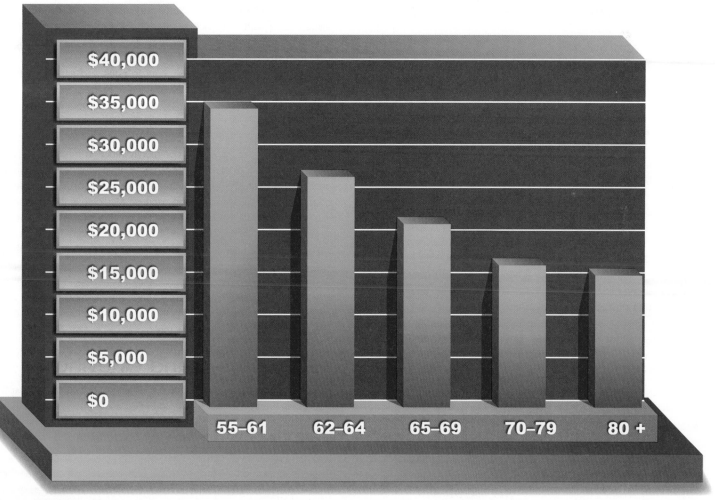

Source: U.S. Census Bureau

∧ **This graph illustrates** the steady decline in income **for Americans after age 55.**
∧ Do you think expenses for the elderly **decline at the same rate?**

very dependent on the performance of financial markets due to changes in work-related pensions and an increase in individual retirement accounts.[45]

Feminization of Old Age

During the last 80 years, women have lived longer than men in nearly every society. As a result, women make up a larger percentage of the elderly population. In the United States in 1930, there were approximately equal numbers of elderly men and women. Since then, the percentages have changed dramatically. In 2000, there were about 143 women aged 65 or over for every 100 men of the same ages. The ratio increases at advanced ages: There were 245 women aged 85 or over for every 100 men.[46,47] Experts predict a reduction in this ratio in coming years due to calls made by the U.S. Census and United Nations that males will gain longer life expectancy, though they expect women to continue to outnumber men in the elderly population throughout the foreseeable future.[48] A walk through any nursing home or care facility highlights the fact that more women than men will face issues such as chronic illness and dependence on medical care and shrinking economic resources. More women than men will have to confront a situation in which they have outlived their spouse.[49]

Children and Parents

The relationship between children and parents necessarily changes as both age. As discussed earlier, some children need to provide care for an aging parent or couple, either directly in their home or by planning for care in the parents' home or a care facility. Family conflicts from years before don't automatically disappear over time, as seen in *The Savages*. Some parents and children adapt by avoiding the issues that cause stress, which allows them to maintain the desired contact while reducing friction.[50]

In many cases, aging parents and adult children are able to change their relationships in ways that are satisfying for both. While adult children may assist parents in terms of care or management of a household, parents continue to assist their children in a variety of ways, from financial concerns to emotional support. However, when parents experience health issues and children take on the role of caregivers, their relationship may be severely tested. Sometimes, the relationship between caregiver and care receiver can bring about violence or abuse, which will be discussed in greater detail in Chapter 13. Several factors affect the challenges faced by children who are caregivers, including whether the health problems occurred gradually or suddenly; whether symptoms are progressive, constant, or recurring; the prognosis of the disease; and whether the parent suffers from incapacitation, incoherence, or other forms of impairment.[51]

Health Issues

Health issues also change a couple's relationship. Adapting to more minor health challenges associated with age, such as hearing loss or reduced physical strength, may prepare a couple to deal with more serious issues such as loss of mobility or life-threatening disease. In many cases, it is a spouse who initially assumes the major role of caregiving for the other spouse. One study suggests this care can be divided into two components: caring *for* a person involves meeting the person's physical needs; caring *about* a person involves the emotional side of the relationship. Both are critical in providing effective care, but neither is easy, especially when a person who is ill changes due to a reduction in physical and/or cognitive abilities.[52]

∧
∧ **Women are much more likely to face** the
∧ challenges of old age **than men** because their life expectancy is much higher. **Think of the elderly women in your life. Have you seen their challenges after the loss of a spouse?**

Access to health care assistance programs, such as Medicare, also makes a significant difference in managing the role of caregiver. Most recently, access to public and private health care has become an issue of debate in the elderly community. President Barack Obama's proposal for reforming health care includes cuts to rates and assessments on Medicare, steps to eliminate fraud and waste from the current system, as well as creation of the Medicare Payment Advisory Commission whose responsibility would be to recommend cost cuts that would be appropriated, unless voted down by Congress.[53] The proposal has frightened and drawn skepticism in the elderly community much in the same way as when Medicare originated in 1965 under then-President Lyndon B. Johnson. The fear and skepticism—whether founded or unfounded—can be somewhat understandable because Medicare is the sole health insurance most elderly people have. Although efforts have been made in the time between its origination and the proposed reform to ensure that all elderly persons have access to Medicare, some ethnic groups have less support. For example, studies show that elderly Hispanics less proficient in speaking English have significantly less access to Medicare and other health programs than others.[54] President Obama's proposal also seeks to bridge this gap, ensuring that all Americans receive the health care they need through affordable means.

Death, Loss, and Grieving

"In this world nothing can be said to be certain, except death and taxes."
—Benjamin Franklin (1706–1790)[55]

GRIEVING WITHIN FAMILIES

Benjamin Franklin was certain about governments collecting taxes and the fact that no one lives forever. Social scientists are just as certain that a death has wide-ranging effects on families. However, each family and individual reacts to a death in a unique way, and each death forces family members to make changes in their individual lives and in family roles and relationships.[56]

Social scientists have identified four basic tasks that families complete when they adapt to a death. These tasks encompass shared acknowledgement and acceptance, shared grief, reorganization of the family system, and re-investment in other relationships and pursuits.[57] These four tasks are considered sequential, but they often overlap. A family's mourning is not completed in a specific amount of time. Factors such as the timing of the death, nature of the death, and each individual's response to death play a part in the process.[58]

In the first step, the family must accept and acknowledge the death openly. This may be helped by family members communicating truthfully about the death, participating in the planning of a funeral and burial, and visiting a grave or other final resting place for the deceased. Trying to protect young family members or others considered fragile by not acknowledging the death is seen as counterproductive, usually leading to poor coping strategies such as denial.

The family also needs to share the experience of grief by accepting their own individual feelings and those of other family members. Individuals may feel a wide variety of emotions in response, including some that others might feel are inappropriate, such as ambivalence, relief, and anger. If these feelings aren't expressed or accepted, individuals may exhibit behavioral, physical, or psychological reactions or problems later on.

Death often leaves a vacuum in family roles and responsibilities. Families need to renegotiate and reassign these roles and tasks to learn to function in a healthy way again. For example, if the deceased was usually the peacemaker in a family dispute or was in charge of managing the family finances, a new family member or someone from outside the family needs to fill the role for the family to move ahead. Negative consequences usually arise in a family when no one fills a vacant role or when someone who is unprepared or unwilling takes it on.

Finally, families need to move beyond the death of a family member by becoming involved in new relationships and life pursuits. Holidays and other important dates often focus family members on their loss and, in some cases, moving ahead to new relationships or activities may be seen as disloyal to the family member who has died. At some point, successful families move on to new commitments without forgetting or ignoring their memories. They feel free to recall and discuss their memories without losing energy or interest in their current or future pursuits.[59]

Families that have experienced deaths in the past may rely on their history of strength and successful adaptation. Or they may feel overwhelmed by another loss if they have been unsuccessful in adapting in the past. Families that communicate more easily and accept the expression of strong emotions by their members are more likely to adapt to a death successfully than those who struggle to communicate or provide emotional support to members.

A family's religious and cultural background may also affect the family's grieving process. For example, Jewish families take a seven-day period after the death to "sit shivah." During this time, they refrain from normal activities and concentrate on remembering the deceased person and sharing their grief among themselves and with close friends. Similarly, African American families often openly express grief, and others in the community provide them with support during the grieving process. In contrast, white Anglo-Saxon Protestants sometimes discourage open mourning and favor quick funerals that require little of the extended family or community.[60]

DEATH OF A SAME-SEX PARTNER

The issues related to death and grieving become even more complicated when a death involves a member of a same-sex couple. Traditional families are expected to express their grief through communication with family and community members and participation in funerals or other ceremonies. However, a surviving same-sex partner is often denied these opportunities. For example, a person's family may have disapproved of the same-sex couple or tried to hide the relationship from family and friends. Because the couple is not legally recognized in most states, there are few social programs that offer support. Financial difficulties may also arise because the survivor is denied pension or medical benefits. Additionally, little acknowledgment may be forthcoming at work of the special needs of a grieving partner. These issues affect survivors of heterosexual couples who were not married as well.[62]

ADJUSTING TO LIFE AS A WIDOW OR WIDOWER

In *The Savages* Leonard and his girlfriend live together in the retirement community until her sudden death. What would have happened to Leonard if he did not have his children to care for him after losing his girlfriend? Because of the differences in life expectancy, women are much more likely to live as widows than men are to live as widowers. For ages 65 to 74, 77 percent of men and 53 percent of women are living with a spouse, but for ages 75 and older, the gap is much wider—67 percent of men live with a spouse but only 29 percent of women do. Both men and women need to adjust to a new role. Men often find that there are few role models and little social direction for widowers, while women are prone to consider deep questions about their past and future life. Paradoxically, the transition to becoming a strong, self-sufficient individual offers the greatest rewards for the men and women who were most dependent on their spouses during marriage. For these people, the ability to function independently is a greater challenge and, in the end, a significant achievement.[63] However, other research indicates that women who have a strong history in paid employment show social skills and strong self-esteem that help ease the transition into widowhood.[64]

When Death Is Unexpected

Juan's father died just a year ago, in the midst of his junior year in college.

"It was a great shock to all of us when my father died at 51. He was strong—he worked out in the sun every day as a carpenter—but I guess his heart wasn't as strong as we thought. I've got two younger sisters and a younger brother, ranging from eight to sixteen. My mom is even younger than my dad was.

"At first, I wanted to drop out of school and go home to stay, so I could help out, but everyone convinced me that wasn't the best idea. They said it wasn't what my dad would have wanted—he was always proud that I made it into college. He really wanted me to graduate. So, now I just go home most weekends instead of staying on campus. But things are different at home now. I get mad at my brothers and sisters now when they give my mom a hard time. I try to tell them to knock it off. But it doesn't usually work. They say, 'You're not our dad. We don't have to listen to you.' My uncle helps out a lot, but I'm the one that does a lot of the chores around the house. I'm learning how to take care of the car, but I sure wish my dad was around to teach me."

Some research indicates that losing a spouse at an expected time—during old age—makes for an easier adjustment than losing a spouse when young. However, older people usually have a smaller support network and battle poor health at the same time. Adult children, siblings, and friends are often central to helping a widow or widower adjust to a new life.[65] Living in a neighborhood near other widows and widowers seems to have a beneficial effect on overall health and mortality because there are more opportunities for interaction among peers and new social relationships are encouraged.[66]

THE DEBATE OVER ASSISTED SUICIDE AND EUTHANASIA

In 1998, the popular news show *60 Minutes* broadcast a videotape of the dying moments of Thomas Youk, who suffered from ALS, or Lou Gehrig's disease. The tape showed Jack Kevorkian, a former physician well known for his participation in many assisted suicides, speaking softly to Youk and then pressing a button that injected a lethal dose of drugs into his system. Kevorkian had previously been prosecuted four times for his role in **assisted suicides**, in which he provided a simple means for a person to end their own life, but he had never been convicted of a crime. However, after Kevorkian took the fatal action himself rather than allowing Youk to

do it, Kevorkian was convicted of second-degree murder and sentenced to 10 to 25 years in jail. He had committed **euthanasia**, or caused a person's death to relieve that person's suffering.[67]

Kevorkian was an outspoken proponent of what he called a "dignified death" for terminally ill, suffering patients. He felt a patient should be able to choose the time and place of death and be surrounded by chosen friends or family rather than gradually wasting away in a sterile environment with little or no consciousness and little quality of life. Opponents believe that some patients could be pressured to end their own life. They also believe that medical doctors are prevented from assisting in suicide by their Hippocratic oath, the modern version stating that "Above all, I must not play at God."[68,69]

There are currently two geographical areas where assisted suicide is legal under strict guidelines: Oregon and the Netherlands. In Oregon, many of the terminally ill patients do not choose assisted suicide to relieve pain, but to exercise some control over the circumstances of their death. In the Netherlands, doctors may perform euthanasia in certain conditions after a patient's request. However, one study found that doctors there performed euthanasia for some patients at a time when they were not competent to express their feelings, but had requested euthanasia previously.[70] There is no clear consensus on the outcomes of these laws, and the debate within the U.S. medical and patient communities continues. Some people use the term **passive euthanasia** to describe withholding treatment that will prolong the life of a terminally ill patient.[71] Somewhat associated with passive euthanasia is a Do Not Resuscitate (DNR) order.[72] Without a DNR, emergency personnel and medical staff are required by law to perform cardiopulmonary resuscitation (CPR).[73] A DNR order requests that in the event of a cardiac arrest, CPR will not be performed, nor other extraordinary measures.

▶▶▶ GO GLOBAL

Aging and Death around the World

The expectations and responses related to aging and death in America are unique to individuals and families. These expectations encompass a broad range of emotional, cultural, and practical actions and reactions. The same is true around the world. Different cultures view and respond to their aging members differently; consequently, rituals related to death cover a wide spectrum.

For example, there are few "old age homes" and no government care for the elderly in Nigeria. Families are left to care for sick and destitute elders. Most elders die at home. The death of an old man is treated as a time to celebrate, since he will be joining his ancestors in the land of the

dead, or, in Christian families, joining Jesus Christ. Most elderly people in Taiwan die at home as well, but in the urban atmosphere there, caring for the elderly may be viewed as an economic burden. Elders may be required to perform household maintenance as a form of payment for their care.

In contrast, most elderly people in Belgium and Austria die in old age homes or hospitals. In Austria, the cultural belief is that untrained family members know less about the aging process and death than trained professionals, so it is common for elderly parents to be left in institutions with little contact with the family. In Portugal, the rural custom is for elderly parents to live with a married child until death. The surviving spouse is then expected to tend the grave regularly, possibly daily, to keep it clean and supplied with flowers.[61]

∧
∧ **Different cultures have different**
∧ **expectations concerning care for the**
elderly. Do you think the expectations in U.S. culture are clear or confusing?

think marriages and families: HOW DOES AGING AFFECT INDIVIDUALS, FAMILIES, AND SOCIETY?

FUNCTIONALISM

The functionalist view of aging focuses on the functional roles played by adults that help create and maintain a stable society. Because stable societies require certain roles to be filled and certain jobs to be performed on a continuous basis, societies takes steps to ensure that these needs will be met. One way of ensuring this is by establishing an orderly transfer of power and responsibilities from an older generation to a younger one. This process is called "disengagement" by the older generation as they retire from the workplace and give up political and social leadership roles because of age. Society forces this disengagement in some cases, such as with a mandatory retirement age, whereas individuals may choose to become disengaged by giving up the roles of parent, worker, and social leader. Functionalists believe this disengagement is natural, inevitable, and necessary for individuals as they enter their later years.[74] Functionalists may study society using age stratification to identify similar groups, as well as looking at social and gender roles, ethnic influences, and age norms related to the aging process.[75]

CONFLICT THEORY

The work of Karl Marx promotes the idea that people in society constantly struggle over scarce resources. Marx saw these struggles as the result of a dominant class—the capitalists—exploiting workers to gain wealth for themselves and deny it to others. Within this context, aging workers were often discriminated against during the early years of the Industrial Revolution. They were fired or removed from physically demanding jobs and replaced by younger, stronger workers who could produce more. This often left the elderly without savings or government support. Regulations in the United States beginning in the early 20th century now make this type of ageism illegal. But conflict theorists note that older workers still face negative views of their work potential and are thus denied some economic resources available to others. They also point to the importance of large groups such as the American Association of Retired Persons (AARP) in lobbying Congress and policymakers to protect and promote the interests of the elderly.[76]

SYMBOLIC INTERACTIONISM

Symbolic interactionists focus on the ways that people interact using shared meanings and symbols. They reinforce the idea that the concept of being "old" is one that is socially constructed according to differing expectations and norms. For some elderly people and their families, age is not a primary factor in their relationships or interactions. For them, it may be true that "age is only a state of mind" in which self-expectations and the expectations of others are much more important than a chronological age. Although social norms are powerful influences, individuals and families create their own definitions and expectations related to age. Health problems can clearly affect these interactions, but in healthy individuals, age is determined within the context of the family by the actions and expectations of its members.[77,78]

discover marriages and families in action: CAN ELDERLY PEOPLE AFFORD ESSENTIAL PRESCRIPTION DRUGS?

It's statistically clear that as people grow older, they experience more health problems that require the use of prescription drugs. In many cases, there is only a single drug that addresses a particular health problem. However, prices in the United States for many prescription drugs stretch or break the budget for elderly individuals and families. Often, seniors do not buy or take essential prescription drugs for their health simply because they can't afford them while still paying for housing, food, and other costs.

A Congressional report in 2001 established that the uninsured elderly pay significantly more for drugs than those covered by insurance plans or Medicare. The reasons for this disparity in prices was that large insurance companies and government agencies such as the Veterans Administration and Medicare could use their bulk-purchasing power to purchase huge quantities of drugs to negotiate a lower unit price from drug companies. Anyone who wasn't a member of these large groups was forced to pay the highest prices—and sometimes skip their purchase and use because they couldn't afford it.[79]

Another Congressional report in 2003 found that seniors in the United States pay much more for prescription drugs than seniors in Canada, Europe, and Japan. At about the same time, Congress passed a bill that changed coverage for prescription drugs for seniors under Medicare but prevented Medicare from bargaining for lower prices for seniors. The results have been record profits for drug companies. President Barack Obama's proposed health care reform has requested that pharmaceutical companies cut costs by half for Medicare recipients.[80] In the meantime, seniors continue to shop for the best prices for drugs on the Internet, hoping to pay less than the prices required under Medicare or offered by retail pharmacies, but the prices are still much higher than in other comparable countries.[81]

ACTIVITIES

1. Talk to your local pharmacist. Ask them what type of issues they see relating to the cost of prescription drugs for the elderly. What types of options are available for the uninsured elderly?
2. Go to your local health department. Ask them what types of services are available for the elderly. Are there programs available to help the elderly pay for services? What types of common problems among the elderly do they see and serve the most frequently?

WRAP YOUR MIND AROUND THE THEORY

Functionalists **believe that older workers need to be "phased out"** so younger workers can learn to do their jobs effectively. **What do you think would happen** if people weren't forced to retire?

FUNCTIONALISM

Functional theory would suggest that a mandatory retirement age is one way that society can ensure stability. If old people were not "phased out" of jobs as they got older, they might continue to work until they died. At their death, there might be no one ready to perform their jobs, especially if the jobs required exceptional skills or training. By requiring that people retire at a certain age, such as 65, society transfers power and responsibility slowly and surely to the next generation. This form of disengagement from work goes hand in hand with other necessary and inevitable changes for elderly people as they give up responsibilities for child care and social leadership roles. These changes are important in building and maintaining a strong society and in allowing elders to make a natural progression that reflects the physical, mental, and social changes of aging.

CONFLICT THEORY

Conflict theorists might see a mandatory retirement age as another means for a dominant class to maintain its power over those below. If the retirement age did not apply to everyone equally, it could be used to deny older people a continued chance at gaining a greater share of economic resources. For example, if politicians and heads of companies were not forced to retire at a particular age—as is currently the case— they could continue to make policies that favor the upper class and continue to earn high salaries while those forced to retire would have little political voice and greatly reduced income. By forcing some of the most skilled workers to retire, whether they wanted to or not, the dominant class could reinforce their power over the newer, less skilled employees.

SHOULD THERE BE A MANDATORY RETIREMENT AGE?

SYMBOLIC INTERACTIONISM

Symbolic interactionists would argue that a mandatory retirement age does not take into account the fact that the effects of aging are unique to each individual and to smaller groups such as families or work-groups. Because the effects of aging depend on an individual's self-perception and the expectations of different groups they interact with, a mandatory retirement age forces some very capable workers to retire. An employer and society as a whole would benefit from using their skills, which may have been developed over decades. Skilled elderly workers may not want to retire, seeing their work as a foundation for their identity and expression of their achievements. Symbolic interactionists might also point to the fact that currently some of the most important positions in government—including President, Representative, Senator, and Supreme Court judge—have no age limitations. Supreme Court judges are appointed for life and often serve until they are quite elderly. These examples show that an arbitrary chronological age is not a good indicator of a person's abilities.

When older workers are forced to retire, **they often suffer economic disadvantages.** What will happen— or has already happened—**to your family's income when your parents retire?**

In some jobs, **people aren't required to retire.** Do you think their age **hampers their job performance?**

Intergenerational Relationships

No matter what our diet, exercise program, genetic makeup, or mental attitude, we all get older and eventually die, as Ben Franklin noted. In this chapter we established the fact that people are living longer now in comparison to the past and that medical and technological advancements can improve both our quantity and quality of life. However, in Chapter 4 we reviewed statistics that showed the lack of access to insurance and medical treatment in this country by millions of people that make it impossible for them to gain the benefits of both preventive and curative health care. In Chapter 11 we will examine the effects of work and the economy on marriage and family and how economic stress may cause problems within the family.

>>> ACTIVITIES

1. Interview the oldest member of your family or an older individual in your neighborhood. What types of experiences has that person had? What are some of the most difficult challenges and the greatest rewards that person has experienced during the aging process?

2. Visit a local grocery store and then a discount store. Look around for employees that are older. What types of work are they doing? What type of jobs do they have? Compare and contrast the grocery store with the discount store. What are the similarities and differences? How can you explain the differences and the similarities?

From Classroom to Community } Serving the Elderly

Esther volunteers a few hours each week at a local senior center. She enjoyed her relationships with her grandparents growing up and decided she would like to spend time with some seniors while she was in school.

"I picked Helen out almost immediately when I first started working there. A lot of the people can't remember my name or don't even know what day it is, but you can tell Helen is still very sharp, even though she is 83. She likes to play chess, and there wasn't anyone around she could play with. She said it was a favorite activity for her and her husband until he died about 10 years ago.

"She talked a lot about her life and I was amazed at all she had done. She enlisted as a nurse during World War II and again during the Korean War, which was how she met her husband. She'd been the head of nursing at large hospital and continued to volunteer there after she retired. They had kids late in their life, but she lost them both since her husband died.

"She really didn't have anyone left, but I was amazed at how positive she was every time I saw her. I guess that's what's helped her live so long. I'm going to do an oral history with her for a class project. I really hope I can be as positive living my life as she is in hers."

ACTIVITY

Research what types of organizations and associations are available for the aging population. How are they categorized and organized? Which one(s) do you see yourself joining when you are older? Why might you choose to join an organization when you are older? Why not?

Theory

FUNCTIONALISM   179

- society needs to "phase out" the elderly from important work and social roles through disengagement to allow a stable transfer of power to a younger generation
- this transfer of power is natural and necessary for both society and individuals, resulting in policies such as a mandatory or expected retirement age

SYMBOLIC INTERACTIONISM   179

- age is a socially constructed concept and is uniquely defined in families and relationships

- the self-images of individuals and the expectations within families concerning older people may not match the views of the broader society

CONFLICT THEORY   179

- discrimination against older people may be another way for a dominant class to retain power and economic control
- policies such as mandatory retirement are not applied equally across all positions in society and may favor those already in power

Key Terms

sandwich generation is the generation that may be responsible for care for aging parents and young children at the same time   *169*

empty nest is a home after the last child has left home   *170*

spacious nest is the transition to more physical room in the empty nest home and more psychological space for the marital relationship   *170*

renested family or **cluttered nest** is a home to which adult children have returned to live temporarily   *170*

boomerang kids are adult children who return to live with parents temporarily   *170*

ageism is discrimination in the workplace or other areas because of age   *173*

fixed income is income from a pension, annuity, or other source that is frozen at a certain level; fixed incomes may be increased with cost-of-living raises   *175*

assisted suicide refers to the situation in which one person supplies the means for another to commit suicide in order to prevent suffering   *178*

euthanasia is taking another person's life to prevent suffering   *178*

passive euthanasia is withholding treatment that would prolong life because the current quality of life is minimal   *178*

Sample Test Questions

MULTIPLE CHOICE

These multiple-choice questions are similar to those found in the test bank that accompanies this textbook.

1. Which of the following is a true statement about middle age?
   a. Most people experience a midlife crisis related to work or family.
   b. Sexual satisfaction is diminished, especially for women.
   c. Social contacts are reduced through the loss of family and friends.
   d. Middle-aged workers are less productive than younger workers.

2. "The sandwich generation" refers to:
   a. people whose parents are dead.
   b. people who take care of both their parents and their children.
   c. people born just after World War II.
   d. middle-aged families who have acquired greater economic opportunities.

3. Grandparents who fill in for parents because of the parents' absence:
   a. may be forced into an uncomfortable role.
   b. are offered significant economic assistance from government programs.
   c. do not need to establish or enforce discipline for children.
   d. are more common in white families than in African American or Hispanic families.

4. The percentage of elderly women compared to elderly men has:
   a. increased slightly in recent years.
   b. increased dramatically in the last 80 years.
   c. decreased since World War II.
   d. stayed level over the last 50 years.

5. The final step in families adapting to a death is:
   a. communicating honestly about the death.
   b. negotiating new roles within the family.
   c. establishing new relationships and life pursuits.
   d. accepting everyone's emotional reactions to the death.

ESSAY

1. Discuss the myths connected with aging. Which do you think are the most common? Which are the most harmful?

2. List some of the pressures on the sandwich generation. Which priorities do you think should be most important?

3. Describe the role of grandparents in your life. How would you change that if you could?

4. Describe the attitudes and actions of people in coping with the death of someone you knew. How do you think they were influenced by cultural expectations?

5. Take a position on assisted suicide and euthanasia. Explain your thinking.

WHERE TO START YOUR RESEARCH PAPER

For more information on myths about aging, go to
http://www.aging.pitt.edu/family-caregivers/myths/default.asp

For links to learn more about issues for the sandwich generation, go to
http://www.saferchild.org/sandwich.htm

For more information on the empty nest and women's reactions, go to
http://www.netdoctor.co.uk/womenshealth/features/ens.htm

For a selection of articles on boomerang kids, go to
http://www.aarp.org/community/search.bt?query=boomerang+kids

For a recent article on issues related to fixed incomes for seniors, go to
http://abcnews.go.com/Business/story?id=5292822&page=1

To information on the feminization of old age around the world, go to
http://www.un.org/documents/ecosoc/cn6/1998/ecn61998-4.htm

For basic information on the grieving process for families, go to
http://www.un.org/documents/ecosoc/cn6/1998/ecn61998-4.htm

For basic information on how different cultures react to death, go to
http://www.associatedcontent.com/article/407845/how_death_is_handled_in_various_cultures.html?cat=47

For a description of views on assisted suicide and euthanasia, go to
http://www.apa.org/pi/eol/arguments.html

ANSWERS: 1. c; 2. b; 3. a; 4. b; 5. c

Remember to check www.thethinkspot.com for additional information, downloadable flashcards, and other helpful resources.

WHAT ARE THE EFFECTS OF WORK AND UNEMPLOYMENT ON INDIVIDUALS AND FAMILIES?

HOW DOES SOCIAL CLASS AFFECT INDIVIDUALS AND FAMILIES?

WILL ENCOURAGING MARRIAGE REDUCE THE POVERTY RATE?

In the

2003 film *Daddy Day Care*, Charlie Hinton is a young parent working long hours as an advertising executive for a large food-products company. The challenge for his division is to create a children's breakfast cereal made from vegetables. He doesn't see a lot of his son, Ben, who is only three, or his wife, Kim, an attorney who is staying home to care for Ben. When it comes time for a focus group of young children, "Veggie-Os" is a complete flop. The children turn on the friendly company employees dressed as vegetables and pummel the carrot into submission.

Predictably, Charlie loses his job. After six weeks of looking for work, he has no leads. Because of their reduced income, Kim goes back to work and Ben is removed from Chapman Academy, the high-priced, very strict day care center that focuses on college-prep activities. Charlie is left to care for Ben, but continues to think of business schemes.

Suddenly, it hits him. There is no moderately priced day care program in the area, only Ben's previous school and a frightening, low-priced alternative called "A Touch of Eden." If he and his friend, Phil, who was laid off from the same company, can take care of their preschool children, how hard can it be to run their own day care program?

It turns out to be very hard. Charlie and Phil prove that they are totally out of touch with what kids want and need—they try to read a mission statement to their charges on the first day and use focus groups to learn what the kids like. After a few weeks, Phil observes, "Let's not kid ourselves. We don't know anything about day care. We're not even good parents." But after a few weeks of the children destroying Charlie's house, now called Daddy Day Care, and terrorizing Charlie and Phil, they learn to provide the kids with enough structure and enough latitude so that their center becomes popular enough to rival Chapman Academy.

The rest of the movie follows a predictable path. The severe head of Chapman Academy sees that Daddy Day Care is a threat to her business and does everything in her power to sabotage Charlie's enterprise. She reports them to a regulatory agency that pays regular visits to note code violations. Later, she wrecks a fund-raising event by cutting off power to a bouncy house and trapping the kids inside, releasing animals from a petting zoo, and putting cockroaches in the food. Still, Daddy Day Care survives and expands.

Charlie sells the franchise for a profit when he's offered a new advertising job. But he realizes that he loved working with his son and the other cute kids and quits the new job to go back and revive the business. In the end, Daddy Day Care thrives and the mean-spirited head of Chapman Academy is forced to take a job as school crossing guard.

THE EFFECTS OF WORK AND THE ECONOMY

Most critics were not kind to *Daddy Day Care,* viewing it as a too-predictable **comedy that simply wasn't very funny.**

But the basic premise is just as relevant today as when a similar movie, *Mr. Mom,* came out in 1983. How does a family react when the parents' work roles are reversed and their economic situation changes suddenly? Within the last couple of years, national and international economic changes have been as sudden and severe as any since the Great Depression 80 years ago. Workers at all levels—from the most highly compensated executives to workers paid minimum wage—have lost jobs that were crucial to their previous lifestyles. Families have been forced to adapt.

It's obvious that if one or two workers in a family lose a job, for whatever reason, it will have some impact on family spending for optional activities and purchases like vacations, eating out, new clothes, or children's camps or special lessons. The changes that families make in spending may be clear, but how those changes affect individual families isn't. What happens to family roles and relationships when someone is suddenly laid off or fired from a job? Is it okay for a father to stay at home and raise the children while a mother works? Are the issues for male and female caregivers the same or different? Societal and individual factors affect family's economic and social status as well. Charlie, in *Daddy Day Care,* chose to make changes because he couldn't find a new job right away. What societal and individual characteristics affect a person's ability to get a job?

In the 1970s, just before I became an adolescent, I wasn't always aware of my friends' family situations. But one family stood out. My friend Nancy had a father who was always home, taking care of the house and playing with her and her younger brother. It was especially noticeable during the summer, when her father would be the one to turn on the sprinkler so we could play in it or serve us Kool-Aid when we were hot. Her father was very friendly and seemed like he always knew a game to play. I realized I hardly knew her mother because she was always at work. This was at a time when it was rare for men to be in charge of watching the kids, even on weekends or evenings. But it worked out well for Nancy and the rest of her friends because, unlike Charlie and Phil early in *Daddy Day Care,* he didn't need a focus group to know what kids liked. Success at being a stay-at-home dad has been shown to occur when the father thinks of it as a job like any other, a job as a parent, unrelated to gender.[1]

The Effects of Work and the Economy

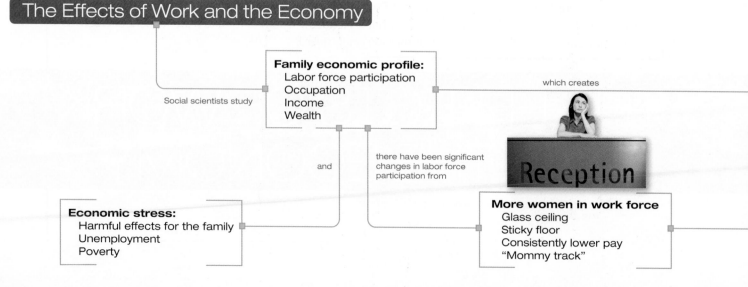

Social scientists study → **Family economic profile:**
Labor force participation
Occupation
Income
Wealth

which creates

and

there have been significant changes in labor force participation from

Reception

Economic stress:
Harmful effects for the family
Unemployment
Poverty

More women in work force
Glass ceiling
Sticky floor
Consistently lower pay
"Mommy track"

get the topic: WHAT ARE THE EFFECTS OF WORK AND UNEMPLOYMENT ON INDIVIDUALS AND FAMILIES?

Economic Stress

Research has documented a variety of negative effects on families related to economic hardship and stress. Children in these families receive less effective parenting and are subjected to more harsh parental reactions. They achieve less academically, have more conduct problems in school, suffer from higher rates of depression, and show lower self-esteem. Spouses in families feeling economic stress experience more marital tension and hostile behavior and show lower satisfaction in their marriages.[2]

A family's ability to deal with economic stress is affected by how family members rate the disruption. If, for example, they feel the economic changes are long-term, they may become demoralized. Certain groups cope with the stress better than others. For example, many African American families manage economic stress better than others because of their strong family bonds, shared values, and spiritual beliefs.[3]

A Family Economic Profile
LABOR FORCE PARTICIPATION

Social scientists use four basic characteristics to construct economic profiles for families: labor force participation, occupation, income, and wealth. **Labor force participation** refers to the number of people who either have a job or are looking for work. A number of factors make it more or less likely that a person is in the workforce. People with more formal education are more likely to be in the workforce. Women are still less likely than men to be

---

>>> **Women of the "baby boom" generation work at much higher rates than in previous years.** Did your mother work? How old was she when she started?

LABOR FORCE PARTICIPATION refers to the number of people who either have a job or are looking for work.

in the workforce, regardless of their education. Before the 1970s, the age of women affected their participation in the workforce because they usually didn't work once they married or became pregnant. But today, male and female rates fluctuate in similar ways for all ages. In recent years, the greatest gains in the labor force have been in the rates for women of the "baby boom" generation, especially married women. Before the 1970s, employment rates for married women were well below those for single women, but now their rates are nearly equal. In 2000, 78 percent of all married women aged 35 to 54 had a job.[4] Some of these baby boomers have retired since then.

OCCUPATION

In our society, and other industrialized societies, occupation may be the most important aspect of a person's social identity. Indeed, it is a primary factor in determining a person's social class status. For many adults, it indicates social information such as education, income, and residence. The

Social class:
Upper class
Middle class
Working class
Lower class

Upper class - increased its proportion of wealth in recent years
Middle class - includes most people and has important cultural power
Working class - is always at risk from job loss or layoff
Lower class - includes working poor who are not paid enough to live above poverty line

which often creates

Work-family conflict
Spillover model
Segmented model
Work-to-family and family-to-work model

U.S. Census Bureau and other organizations divide thousands of occupations into a few categories. Significant changes have occurred in the distribution of females in different occupations since 1970. For example, in 1970, about 53 percent of working women were either clerical workers or service workers, but that number dropped to about 40 percent in 2002.[5]

The International Labor Organization identified three continuing problems that contribute to the disparity in occupations and economic benefits for men and women worldwide. Two of these are identified with metaphors taken from buildings: "the glass ceiling" and "the sticky floor." The glass ceiling makes it appear that women can rise to the highest occupational levels, but a transparent barrier created by men in a patriarchal system doesn't allow it. On the other hand, the sticky floor keeps many women in jobs that offer low pay and no health or pension benefits. The third issue is the gender gap in pay. On average, women are paid about 80 percent of what men are for the same work.[6] A newer element is the so-called **glass escalator**, an invisible fast track for men entering previously female-dominated professions.

INCOME

Household income—earnings from work or investments—also helps measure a family's economic status. Real median household income provides a midpoint for all people in a group—half of them have incomes above and half below. Real median household income rose about 30 percent between 1967 and 2007, although it has always fallen during a recession.[7] Americans often judge a family's well-being by how they spend their money. People look at the houses people live in, their cars, their clothing, their vacations, and their expensive "toys," to assess economic status.[8] These judgments are not scientific, of course, just opinions about economic status.

There have always been large disparities between family income levels in America and incomes in other societies. But in recent years, these differences in the United States have become even more pronounced. For example, in 2002 the top 20 percent of families received about 50 percent of all the income in the United States, while the bottom 20 percent received only about 3 percent. This compares to the top 20 percent getting 43 percent of the income in the late 1960s and the bottom getting about 4 percent. Some people have termed this "the hourglass economy," in which large amounts of money go to a few people at the top, many families at the bottom receive a little, and the middle class is squeezed in between.[9]

There has been a marked difference in family income between white, non-Hispanic families and African American families ever since statistics have been gathered. A white family in 1947 had a median income of $20,870 (in 2001 dollars) compared to an African American family income of less than half that, at $9,644. Both groups enjoyed significant increases by 2001, with white families at more than $54,000 and African American families at about $33,500. How should these results be interpreted? The gap between white and African American families had been reduced;

∨
∨ **Real income has risen gradually over the last forty years.** What do you think the
∨ economic conditions were in the few years it declined?

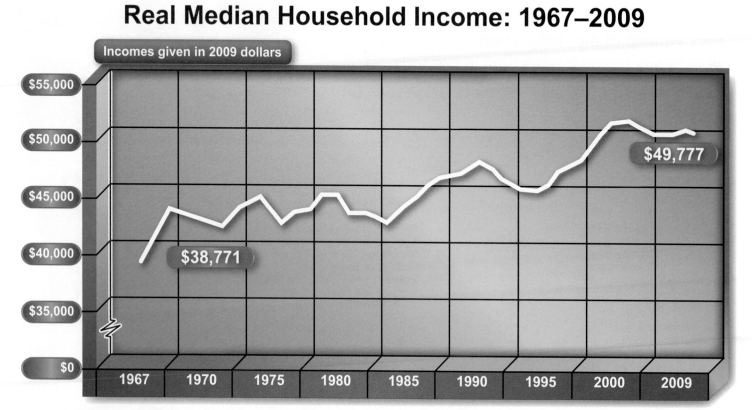

Real Median Household Income: 1967–2009

Incomes given in 2009 dollars

$38,771

$49,777

1967   1970   1975   1980   1985   1990   1995   2000   2009

Source: Carmen DeNavas-Walt, Bernadette D. Proctor, and Jessica C. Smith, Income, Poverty, and Health Insurance Coverage in the United States: 2009, *Current Population Reports*, U.S. Census Bureau.

African Americans earn 62 percent as much as whites in 2001 compared to only 47 percent in 1947. But the difference in actual dollars of income has increased, with whites receiving over $11,000 more in real income in 1947 and over $20,000 more in 2001. Researchers have determined that the major factor in accounting for these differences has been racial discrimination.[10]

Research also shows that women are paid less than men. This is true for the highest levels of CEOs in the United States, with women earning more than $500,000 but men earning an average of 30 percent more. Average female workers in the United States in 2008 earned 80 percent of what average males earned. These disparities are seen in nearly every culture in the modern world, with the exception of Sweden. Some of the differences can be ascribed to the fact that many women have been in the labor force for less time than men, and they are more likely to delay the completion of their education because of family responsibilities. But a stronger reason has been the history of discriminating against women in the labor market. The good news is that the gap between men's and women's pay in the United States is decreasing.[11]

WEALTH

Wealth, or net worth, is different from income and includes the total value of all assets such as a house, car, jewelry or other valuables, stocks and bonds, business ownerships, and savings minus any debts. Most people at the upper levels of wealth in the United States have inherited their wealth rather than created it during their lifetime. Surveys have shown that three factors are important predictors of a person's wealth: education, marital status, age, and race/ethnicity. People with a bachelor's degree or higher have a median net worth of twice or more of groups with less education, and older married people have the highest median net worth of any other age group. The differences for race and ethnicity are even greater. In 2000, the average white household had a net worth of $198,000 compared to $52,000 for Hispanic families and $35,000 for African American families.[12]

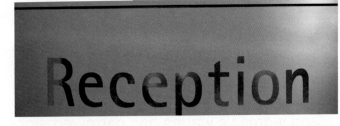

∧
∧ Women have often been stuck at
∧ the bottom of businesses by the "sticky floor" of clerical work, **which provides low pay, few benefits, and little satisfaction.**

The Effects of Work on Families

". . . We get our most important education not through books but through our work. We are developed by our daily task, or else demoralized by it, as by nothing else."
— Anna Garlin Spencer (1851–1931)[13]

In general, social scientists use three models to judge the relationship between work and family according to **work-family conflict** – incompatible role demands stemming from work or family that interfere with a person's functioning in either area. These conflicts can be based on competing demands for time or strains, such as a family illness or new job demand. For example, at the beginning of *Daddy Day Care*, Charlie knows very little about his son, or children in general, because he does

not balance his time between work and home. Another source of conflict can be behavioral expectations that do not mesh; aggressiveness at work may yield high performance, but result in negative effects at home. High levels of work-family conflict have been shown to have negative mental and physical health effects for men and women.[14]

THE SPILLOVER MODEL

The spillover model has gained a good deal of support and suggests that roles at work and at home may be very similar and that skills, stresses, and attitudes from work "spill over" into family life, and vice versa. For example, women may find that skills needed in managing a household are very similar to those needed in managing other workers. At the same time, the strain of managing her household may negatively affect a woman's ability to perform at work.[15] A study in Australia indicated that 89 percent of workers felt their family life was negatively affected by work-family conflict.[16] The success families experience in balancing these competing demands has been shown to have a significant effect on the emotional well-being and closeness of family members.[17] Women are much more likely to suffer the effects of negative spillover from home to work because they are more likely to turn down overtime or extra assignments to accommodate family needs, whereas men are more likely to take on additional work and responsibilities.[18]

THE SEGMENTED MODEL

The segmented model suggests that work and family are two different worlds, or segments, and that there is little or no overlap between them. This theory has lost support in recent years. Initially, some theorists used the functional theory of Talcott Parsons to describe the instrumental world of work as one dominated by men, while the expressive world at home was governed by women. However, neither the current world of work nor family life reflects these descriptions. Research has shown that there is considerable interchange between work and family segments. This model has been termed "the myth of separate worlds."[19]

THE WORK-TO-FAMILY AND FAMILY-TO-WORK MODEL

This model, which has gained wide acceptance in recent years, suggests a reciprocal relationship between work and family roles. For example, a woman might take advantage of a flexible schedule at work to help with family responsibilities. Changing roles at home then influence the woman's performance and relationships at work.[20] For both men and

Median Earnings of Full-Time Male and Female Workers: 1967–2009

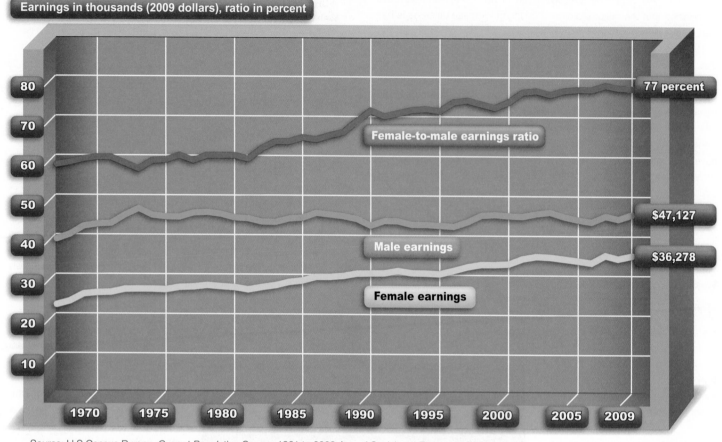

Earnings in thousands (2009 dollars), ratio in percent

80
70
60
50
40
30
20
10

77 percent

Female-to-male earnings ratio

$47,127

Male earnings

$36,278

Female earnings

1970 1975 1980 1985 1990 1995 2000 2005 2009

Source: U.S.Census Bureau, *Current Population Survey*, 1961 to 2009 Annual Social and Economic Supplements.

> ∧ ∧ ∧ **The gap between men's and women's wages has narrowed since 1960.** Do you think that trend will continue in the near future?

women, stability and satisfaction at home showed positive effects at work, with men affected more by satisfaction in the marital relationship and women by equitable arrangements for household work. Negative effects from family-to-work conflicts were most common for women with preschool-aged children.[21]

Working Women

One of the greatest changes in the intersection of work and families in the last 50 years has been the increase in the number of married women in the workforce. Less than 40 percent of married women worked before 1970, but more than 60 percent of married women are working today.[22] In 1950, there were 29 women working full-time year-round for every 100 men, but in 2000, the number rose to 70 women for every 100 men. However, women are consistently paid less than men. Although the differences in pay have narrowed in recent years, women in 2007 still earned just 78 cents for each $1 earned by men. The "sticky floor" of jobs in clerical work, which employs more than 40 percent of all women, accounts for much of this gap. The "glass ceiling" also results in only 14 percent of women working in executive, managerial, or administrative positions. In some cases, women choose

careers that pay less and offer fewer opportunities for advancement so there will be a reduced possibility of work-family conflict.[23]

"THE MOMMY TRACK"

There is ample evidence that career women are not paid as much and do not advance as quickly as men in professional areas such as colleges and universities, law firms, and other corporations and businesses.[24,25] The reasons for these results aren't clear. In *Daddy Day Care*, Charlie's wife returns to her job as an attorney after years of staying at home to care for Ben. This time off most likely affected her ranking among attorneys who had not taken time off. Felice Schwartz published a highly controversial article in the *Harvard Business Review* in 1989 that suggested two things: The cost of employing women was greater than employing men because of turnover related to maternity, and corporations should provide more flexible job arrangements for women who wanted to combine a career with raising a family. Critics quickly labeled her suggestion for flexible arrangements "**the mommy track**."[26] However, others have since suggested similar, flexible approaches for employers. Some of these attempts have shown success in allowing women to reduce work-family conflict while advancing in a professional career.[27,28]

LATCHKEY CHILDREN

One of the repercussions of the increase in dual-earner families is an increase in the number of **latchkey children**, or children who care for themselves for some portion of the day. Social scientists have struggled to create a consistent definition of latchkey children. For example, does a 12-year-old at home alone for an hour qualify? How about children who are supervised by older siblings or a neighbor? A 2003 survey found that about 25 percent of all school-aged children, about 14 million in total, spent some time unsupervised after school, with another 11 percent spending time supervised by a sibling.[29] Although there are some risks for unsupervised children, other research indicates positive results for some children, especially if there is contact with other adults or siblings. For example, children are able to develop their own self-care skills, self-responsibility, and other self-management skills.[30]

BOOMERANG KIDS

Another result of changes in the economy has been the recent increase in the number of boomerang kids, older offspring who leave home for a time but then return to live with their parents. Difficulties in finding a job or the cost of housing can force these children to delay their transition to adulthood. As a result, older parents may have to adjust their lives to continue parenting longer than expected, and the relationships between parents and children become more equal.[31]

Balancing Family and Work

The increase in women at work outside the home has created more dual-earner couples as well as more work-to-family and family-to-work

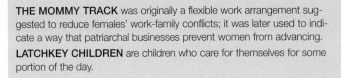

conflicts. Creating and maintaining a successful marriage and family when both spouses work is tricky. Social scientists believe that the issues can be addressed on two levels. One involves the interactions among family members. Successful families work hard at structuring their lives so that both work and family are valued and placed in the proper perspective.[32] One of the most important ways that a couple can manage the stress of two jobs is to make equitable arrangements for housework and other household needs. Although there has been some change, women still work at home for about twice as many hours as men. Marital conflict and unhappiness is much more common in dual-earner couples who do not share household responsibilities.[33]

The other avenue for balancing work and family relies on employers. Some employers have found that flexible scheduling, family leave, job sharing, and telecommuting allow employees to balance the demands of work and family more successfully. The results? Less employee turnover and greater productivity. In 1993, the federal government mandated that employers of 50 or more allow men or women up to 12 weeks of unpaid leave to care for a family member. But initially, few took advantage of it because they couldn't afford 12 weeks without pay. Regardless, research shows that both male and female workers report greater marital and job satisfaction and reduced work-to-family

Stay-at-Home Dads

Debbie grew up with a mother who worked long hours as a lawyer and a father who managed the household and did part-time work at home.

"I think I realized our family was different when I was three or four and it was my dad who took me to playgroups and hung out with a bunch of moms.

"Later on, my teachers were always surprised when my dad came to teacher conferences and school plays without my mother. My dad was good with other kids, so a lot of them thought it was cool for my dad to be there to play with us.

"My brother and I thought it was natural that my father went to the supermarket, bought our school supplies, and helped us pick out our Halloween costumes. We both went through a period of asking our parents why they had to be so differrent, but in the end we appreciated it.

"Our dad would have us help fix things around the house, like the door that wouldn't close and the chair with a broken leg, and then he'd have us help cook dinner, too. It was great to see that people are wrong when they think certain jobs are only for men or only for women."

>>> **More men are involved in managing a household than ever before.** How much was your father involved in things like shopping or child care?

Changing Roles for Working-Class Men in Japan

American men aren't the only ones struggling to adapt to new roles. In Japan, the accepted role for men in society for many years has been that of "salaryman"—dedicated almost exclusively to work with little involvement in household management or child care, and honored as the main breadwinner. But Japan has experienced many of the same changes as the United States after World War II. More women are working outside the home, and there is a greater demand for shared responsibilities at home. Laws in 1992 and 2005 allowed men and women to take leave from their jobs for child care responsibilities, but working-class men have a very hard time

taking advantage of this policy because they must find a substitute worker when they take leave.

Although their workdays may extend to 12 hours per day and include working a half-day on Saturday, many working-class men find time to spend with their children before bedtime and on weekends. However, the change from the head of the household and sole breadwinner to a more equal partner in household work causes a great deal of stress. Some men have formed support groups to discuss the challenges of their new roles, while others talk about these changes more informally at work. But the changes seem to have a positive effect for some young men, who take pride in their knowledge and experience in raising their children.[36]

>>> **Men in many countries around the world are** changing their traditional roles **as more women enter the workforce.**

conflict when offered flexible work options.[34,35] Federal and state governments have helped in other ways, such as giving parents the opportunity to take time from work for parent-teacher conferences or similar school functions.

Sexual Harassment

In 1991, a 35-year-old law professor, Anita Hill, was questioned about her former boss, a man she claimed had sexually harassed her for a two-year period 10 years earlier. She gave specific instances of his words and actions, including his many requests for dates, his repeated references to his enjoyment of pornographic movies, and other subtle and not-so-subtle sexual references.

She suffered physical symptoms related to the harassment, but did not file any charges against him at the time because she was afraid he might fire her or cause her to lose her job. She maintained cordial relations with him in recent years, she said, because cutting him off would have required explaining her reasons to her current boss, who was friendly with him. When someone accused her of making up the story, she stated flatly that she had nothing to gain by lying. "I am not given to fantasy," she said calmly,[37] and added that when she was asked about her boss' behavior, "I felt that I had to tell the truth."[38]

Why was Anita Hill's testimony so important? Because the man she was charging with sexual harassment was being considered for a lifetime appointment to the U.S. Supreme Court! Clarence Thomas, an African American, angrily denied all the charges and suggested that

they were racially motivated, even though Hill is African American as well. The committee never made a determination about who was telling the truth, but eventually Thomas was confirmed to his appointment in a close Senate vote, 52–48.

But the televised hearings and Hill's calm demeanor shed a new light on sexual harassment. A poll conducted soon after the hearings found that 70 percent of women in the military, 50 percent of women who worked in Congressional offices, and 40 percent who worked in federal agencies had suffered sexual harassment. Before Hill's story went public, such treatment was often viewed as a routine, if uncomfortable, part of employment for women rather than as illegal actions that significantly harmed the victim.[39]

The Equal Employment Opportunity Commission (EEOC) defines **sexual harassment** as "Unwelcome sexual advances, requests for sexual favors, and other verbal or physical conduct of a sexual nature" that affects a person's work. In 2008, almost 14,000 charges of sexual harassment were filed, about 16 percent by men. Payments of $47 million were made to those charging harassment. Employers are strongly encouraged to educate employees about sexual harassment, take steps to prevent it from occurring, and offer assistance if it does.[40]

Unemployment

We've considered the effects of work on individuals and families from a variety of perspectives. But what happens when people don't work? The national unemployment rate rose to nearly 10 percent in 2009, the highest in over 25 years, and it is predicted to keep climbing into 2010.[41] The rates in some areas are higher than at any time since before World War II.[42] What do social scientists predict, based on this information?

As you might guess, few of the predictions are good. Unemployment at these high levels affects all types of workers. In previous recessions, younger workers were affected the most because they lacked seniority, but currently the elimination of whole divisions, as well as cuts in administrative and managerial positions, affects older workers as well. Unemployment is connected to a variety of negative effects for individuals: greater rates of anxiety, substance abuse, sleep disorders, depression, and suicidal thoughts. The unemployed also suffer a reduction in self confidence and self-esteem. It isn't surprising that family instability, including divorce, is highest during periods of high unemployment.[43,44]

Social Class and Socioeconomic Status

"The distinctions separating the social classes are false; in the last analysis they rest on force." — Albert Einstein (1879–1955)[45]

For many years, in cultures around the world, a person's social class was determined at birth and could not be changed. For example, a child born as a Russian peasant would die a peasant, a baby born as an "untouchable" in India would remain in that group until death, and a member of the British nobility could do nothing to either advance in class or decline. Today **social class** refers to a group similar in educa-

SEXUAL HARASSMENT refers to unwelcome sexual advances, requests for sexual favors, and other verbal or physical conduct of a sexual nature that affects a person's work.

SOCIAL CLASS means a group whose members are similar in education, income, occupational status, housing, and lineage.

SOCIOECONOMIC STATUS (SES) quantifies education, income, and occupation on a continuum as an indicator of social class.

tion, income, occupational status, housing, and lineage. These broad categories assume some similar behaviors and attitudes among each group, but the members of a group will differ according to exactly what factors are used to define the class. **Socioeconomic status (SES)** uses formulas to quantify education, income, and occupation and places families on a continuum upon which class lines may be drawn. This approach highlights the fact that the differences between groups may be only slight.[46]

People can change classes quickly today—the stock market crash of 2008 caused free fall for people in the upper class, while a layoff or lost job can pull the rug out from under middle-class and working-class families. In *Daddy Day Care*, Charlie and his wife have to make certain changes after his job loss, such as taking their son out of his expensive prep school, to stay afloat. Luckily, Charlie's wife is able to find a job as a lawyer so they still have a good income. Social scientists differ on the number of classes in American society and their definitions. For simplicity, we will discuss four broad categories: the upper class, the middle class, the working class, and the lower class.[47]

THE UPPER CLASS

The upper class in the United States can be described as those in the upper 5 percent of wealth. For many years, it has been overwhelmingly white and Protestant, although that has changed slightly in recent years. Upper-class wealth has usually been inherited, and their percentage of the total wealth in the United States has grown recently. In 2005, the income of the top 3 million people in the United States, about 1 percent of the population, was equal to the income of the bottom 166 million people, or about 55 percent of the population. From 2003 to 2005, the income of the top 1 percent increased about 43 percent, while the middle fifth increased about 4 percent, and the bottom fifth improved just above 1 percent. The reasons for this growth aren't proven, but the increase in the value of the stock market and tax policies favoring the rich clearly contributed.[48,49] Yet, as with all social classes, the 2009 stock market plunge saw many of the upper class lose a large proportion of their investments or savings.

More than 100 years ago, it was suggested that society was governed by a "leisure class" of fabulously wealthy "old money" families who didn't work. In contrast, a recent qualitative study on members of the new working rich, including computer giant Bill Gates, airline owner Richard Branson, and investor Warren Buffet, show them working more hours than

∧
∧ **Unemployment rates in some areas are currently**
∧ **higher than any since the Great Depression.** Has unemployment affected your family? Do you think it will in the future?

Mean Annual Income of Each Fifth of Population: 1966–2007

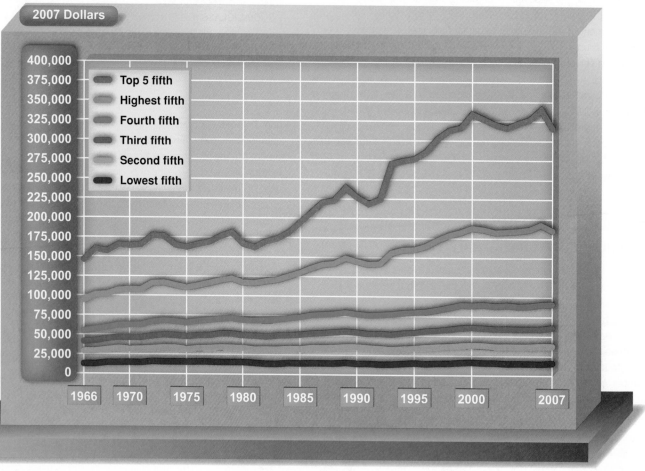

2007 Dollars

Legend:
- Top 5 fifth
- Highest fifth
- Fourth fifth
- Third fifth
- Second fifth
- Lowest fifth

Source: U.S. Census Bureau

∧
∧
∧ **The gap between upper-class and lower-class income has increased in recent years.**
How much do you think government policies have affected this change?

average Americans and living relatively modest lifestyles in comparison to their fortunes.[50]

The upper class typically live in exclusive neighborhoods in or near large cities and often own more than one home. They hold advanced degrees, serve as top executives, business owners, and senior government officials, and their children go to private schools and universities. They are also able to invest much more money on developing a child's interests and abilities, spending, on average, twice as much money to raise a child as a lower-class family.[51]

THE MIDDLE CLASS

Income for a middle class family usually ranges from the average national income to that just below the upper class, from about $40,000 to $170,000 per year. The middle class encompasses 40 to 45 percent of the U.S. population and wields enormous influence on American culture. Popular TV is often aimed at middle-class families and is sponsored by advertising appealing to the same group. Many national politicians have been successful using the phrase "How will it play in Peoria (Illinois)?" to guide their positions and statements so that they are attractive to middle-class voters.[52]

The middle class is often divided into upper and average middle class families, with the upper middle class graduating from college, serving as executives and professionals, owning a comfortable home, participating in local government and politics, and building wealth through investments. Members of the average middle class are more likely to be high school graduates, work in lower-level white-collar jobs such as clerks or counter staff in shops, or skilled blue-collar jobs such as electrician or plumber, and own their home in a modest neighborhood. Their modest wealth is involved in owning a home and building a retirement account.[53]

THE WORKING CLASS

About one third of American families are considered working class, earning less than the national average in blue-collar jobs such as factory work and less skilled construction jobs, which require discipline but offer less satisfaction and few health and pension benefits. Working-class families are at risk of financial troubles in the event of an illness or layoff. About half are able to own their own homes in neighborhoods that are less expensive and only about one-third of their children attend college.[54]

THE LOWER CLASS

The remainder of Americans, about 20 percent, can be classified as lower class. At the top of this group are the "working poor," estimated at more than 7 percent of the entire population, who work at jobs that don't provide enough income to provide for all of their family's basic needs.[55] For example, in 2009 if a single mother with two children worked full-time for 52 weeks at minimum wage, $7.25 per hour, she would earn a total of $15,080 in a year. Her income is below the federal government's poverty guidelines for a three-person family of $18,310—the level at which a family can meet only the most basic needs for food, clothing, and shelter.[56,57] Even with slight raises in pay or more part-time work by two adults, the working poor receive almost no benefits, such as health insurance, along with income that may not bring a family above the poverty level. This is one of the reasons the government is attempting to have government-sponsored health care.

Families without a working adult make up the remainder of the lower class. These families often qualify for government assistance in terms of food, shelter, clothing, or other needs. One study showed that lower-class families were more likely to have health coverage and the ability to pay their bills on time than the working poor.[58] Although the lower class is at significantly greater risk for poor health and involvement in crime and violence, they also show great resilience in meeting needs through family and community assistance.[59,60]

POVERTY

Defining Poverty

In 1964, President Lyndon Johnson declared "unconditional war on poverty in America." He sparked a variety of federal and state programs intended to improve what he called "a national problem."[61] This "war" showed initial success when the poverty rate dropped from above 20 percent of the population to just above 10 percent in 1970. However, since then, the poverty rate has remained between 10 and 15 percent of the population and fluctuates with the economy.[62]

All societies experience **relative poverty**, or the deprivation of some people in comparison to others. In contrast, **absolute poverty** involves deprivation that is life threatening. Worldwide, about 1 billion people, or one in every six, are in danger due to absolute poverty. Although the United States is one of the most affluent countries in the world, many of its people still suffer from poor health and malnutrition and live in dangerous and unhealthy conditions.

>>> **LBJ's** "War on Poverty" **was part of a group of programs called the Great Society.** Do you think his attempts to solve pervasive problems like poverty were commendable or misguided?

The U.S. government establishes poverty guidelines that determine eligibility for certain types of government assistance. The Health and Human Services guidelines depend on family size and are updated each year using changes in the Consumer Price Index.[63] For example, a family of two in 2009 is considered to be living in poverty if they earn less than $14,570 for the year, and a family of six is in poverty if they earn below $29,530.[64]

The People Who Live in Poverty

In 2009, almost 44 million people were living in poverty according to the Census Bureau's definition, equal to 14.3 percent of the population. Who are the people living in poverty? Race has a significant correlation. Although about two-thirds of all poor people are white, the rates for white non-Hispanics and those of Asian background are relatively low—about 9 percent and 12 percent, respectively. However, 26 percent of blacks and 25 percent of Hispanics live in poverty. Children under 18 are more likely to be poor compared to any other age group, because federal retirement programs, such as Social Security and Medicare, have reduced the risks for those 65 and over. Poverty occurs at higher rates within large cities and in rural areas away from cities. One of the most striking statistics is for single women who head a household: About 30 percent live in poverty compared to about 6 percent of married couples and 17 percent of male single parents.[65]

Theories on the Causes of Poverty

Social scientists and politicians have struggled for years to explain the causes of poverty for millions of people in an affluent society. Some point out that the poor in the United States are much better off than in other countries, but it is clear that poverty in the United States detracts from the health and happiness of more than one in ten people. There are two basic explanations suggested for the causes of poverty: blaming the victim or blaming society.

Some say that poor people have caused their own poverty by not working or not gaining the skills that allow them to work at a good job. Many Americans believe there are plenty of opportunities for any self-reliant person who wants to work their way out of poverty. Some research suggests that there is a "**culture of poverty**," which involves little planning for the future, little commitment to marriage, little or no work ethic, and dependence on government assistance. This culture may destroy people's ambition for improvement.[66,67]

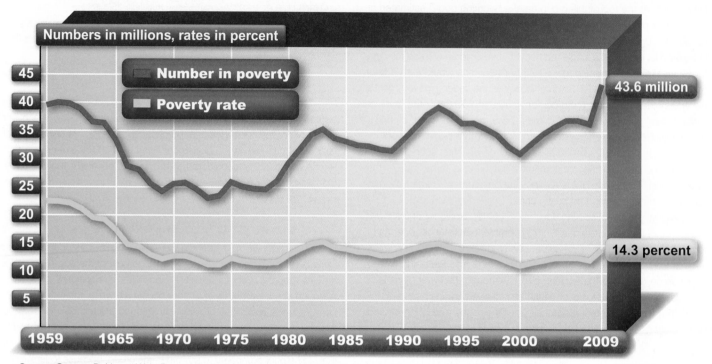

Number in Poverty and Poverty Rate: 1959–2009

Numbers in millions, rates in percent

Number in poverty
Poverty rate

43.6 million

14.3 percent

45 40 35 30 25 20 15 10 5

1959 1965 1970 1975 1980 1985 1990 1995 2000 2009

Source: Carmen DeNavas-Walt, Bernadette D. Proctor, and Jessica C. Smith, Income, Poverty, and Health Insurance Coverage in the United States: 2009, *Current Population Reports*, Issued September 2010, U.S. Census Bureau.

∧
∧ **The poverty rate has remained relatively stable for the last 25 years.** How successful
∧ was the War on Poverty, which began in the early 1960s?

A different explanation points to the failures of society in providing opportunities for people to escape poverty. One researcher, William Julius Wilson, studied an African American neighborhood in Chicago that had experienced dramatic changes from the early 1950s to the 1990s. It was once a solid, middle-class area where many African American families owned their homes and businesses thrived. It became a depressed and desolate slum where two-thirds of the people were unemployed. Wilson found that more than 800 businesses operated nearby in the 1950s, while only 100 did in the 1990s. Two major industrial employers closed in the 1960s when jobs were sent overseas. Wilson suggests that any lack of effort in getting a job is the result of limited opportunities rather than a cause of poverty.[68,69] Whatever the causes of poverty, its effect on families can be profound, insofar as it can hold people back for generations.

The Welfare System

The United States established a welfare system to assist poor people and dependent children in 1935, but during the latter part of the

century people pointed to continuing payments to some families over generations as a part of a culture of poverty. In 1996, the system implemented strict time limits on payments to individuals, and all recipients were expected to move from welfare payments to employment within a specified period. This change reduced the number of people receiving payments, although progress toward the greater goal of reducing poverty isn't clear. One study indicates that women who do move from welfare to work often remain in poverty.[70] Another shows that women with children who moved from welfare to employment were pleased with even a slight increase in income, but they suffered considerable work-to-family stress due to the job-related demands and the reduced time available to care for their children.[71]

Homelessness

It was estimated in 2000 that about 500,000 people are homeless each night in the United States, with about 3.5 million people experiencing homelessness at some point in the year. Homeless shelters have reported an increased

>>> **Millions of people experience homelessness each year in America.** Do you think the government should do more to address the problem?

demand for their help in recent years. People who say victims are responsible for their own situation point to statistics that indicate that one-third of all homeless people abuse alcohol or drugs and about one-fourth are mentally ill or unable to cope with society's demands. However, others point to societal changes that have increased the number of homeless people: A poor economy and widespread unemployment leave people without the money to rent or own a home; changes in the housing market have put owning or renting out of many people's reach; domestic violence drives women and children to leave a home for safety. Regardless of the cause, homeless men, women, and children are all at risk for physical and mental health problems, as well as involvement in violence and crime.[72,73,74]

From Classroom to Community } Working with Low-Income Families

Christine works a few hours each week as part of an aid program that provides subsidized housing for low-income families.

"One day I was working at the front desk, and Esperanza and her two kids came in. I went through the application process with her and watched as she managed two kids under five, listened to me, and filled out the paperwork at the same time.

"Later, my boss suggested that Esperanza's new apartment be my first home visit. The building where they lived was pretty depressing and scary. But when her door opened, it was another world. Everything was neat and clean, and the kids had a little space in the living room for books and toys.

ACTIVITIES

1. Research programs, services, and training opportunities in your community that help families and individuals move toward economic independence.
2. Attend a city council meeting. During the question period, ask what specific programs are provided to assist the economically disadvantaged in your area.

"Esperanza worked two part-time jobs while her mother watched the kids. Her income wasn't enough to move out of the building, but the kids always looked good and she loved to cook with beans, rice, and lots of spices. I realized that just by having an apartment, Esperanza was going to make a good life for her kids. Meeting her inspired me to look at a graduate degree in social work."

---

think marriages and families: HOW DOES SOCIAL CLASS AFFECT INDIVIDUALS AND FAMILIES?

FUNCTIONALISM

The functionalist view of work depends on theories published just after World War II. Researchers Kingsley Davis and Wilbert Moore suggest that the way society divides people into social and economic classes is a positive and necessary function. Certain jobs, such as household cleaning and answering a phone, can be performed by most people and are consequently paid at low rates. Other jobs, such as performing medical transplants and designing strong bridges and highways, can only be performed by certain people with specialized skills and training, and they merit much higher pay as a result. Kingsley and Moore suggested that this division of labor and compensation creates an efficient means of meeting society's needs. It encourages productivity and provides a necessary incentive for talented people to enter jobs that require training and involve important responsibilities by offering greater rewards.[75]

CONFLICT THEORY

Conflict theory uses the theories of Karl Marx and Max Weber, first published in the late 1800s, to advance the idea that capitalism promotes the interests of a few over the interest of the many. This approach suggests that there are only two economic classes: those that own the means of production, such as factory owners and administrative personnel, and those that sell their labor to others, such as factory workers. This theory was proposed at a time when a few industrialists, such as J. P. Morgan and John D. Rockefeller, amassed huge fortunes, earning an income that was sometimes 4,000 times the income of an average worker. Marx suggested that this structure would reproduce the same economic and social class structure in one generation after another, and that these inequities would eventually lead workers to revolt and overthrow the capitalist system. Today, conflict theorists can point to the increasing gap between the upper class and those below them as proof that the capitalist economic system continues to promote inequities and favor the "haves" over the "have-nots."[76]

SYMBOLIC INTERACTIONISM

Symbolic interactionists view economic distinctions from the viewpoint of their effect on the ways individuals and families interact. They point out

WRAP YOUR MIND AROUND THE THEORY

Functionalists believe that differing incomes for different occupations are a natural means of organizing society. Which occupations do **you** think should be paid the most?

FUNCTIONALISM

Functional theory would suggest social classes help organize society efficiently. The upper classes are people who have special skills or training that are needed and valued by society. For example, a physician invests thousands of dollars and years in training to be able to perform an essential function in society and is then compensated with a high salary and a respected social status. An electrician needs some special skills as well and also undergoes training, although not as long as a doctor, and is compensated at a lower level. Because our society believes nearly anyone can do the work of a janitor or a fast food worker, they are paid at the lowest levels. The economic rewards for each type of job are relative to the complexity of the job and its importance in our society. Functionalists believe that this type of system provides an efficient way to funnel people into appropriate jobs and social classes.

CONFLICT THEORY

Conflict theorists see social classes as a way to maintain the power and wealth of the upper class at the expense of the lower classes. They see the disparities in income and wealth between the upper and lower classes as unfair and inappropriate, reflecting the upper class's forceful hold on societal power rather than a fair distribution of resources. They view the "hourglass" shape of our economy as bloated at the top, with only a small percentage of people holding a large percentage of the wealth. Social classes help reinforce this system by allowing those at the top the greatest opportunities for continued leadership and power because of their economic resources. Those at the bottom are prevented from moving up in power or income by a lack of opportunities and too little time and money to gain access to better jobs and advance to a higher social class.

? HOW DOES SOCIAL CLASS AFFECT INDIVIDUALS AND FAMILIES?

SYMBOLIC INTERACTIONISM

For symbolic interactionists, social classes provide a way for people to interact with others who have similar economic resources and prospects. They also tend to reinforce the class structure by exposing children to the attitudes and expectations associated with their class. For example, Nancy and Jeremy come from a middle-class home and go to a public school with the other neighborhood children. They know the other families in the area and socialize with them. As they grow up, Nancy and Jeremy take on the middle-class values of their upbringing and are attracted to middle-class careers. On the other hand, Lilly and Richard come from an upper-class home and go to an exclusive, private school. Their parents socialize with other parents who have children at the school or with acquaintances from their business deals or clubs. Lilly and Richard take on the attitudes and expectations of many upper-class families, planning on careers in business or politics. Each family's interactions have helped shape its children and promote their entry into a social class similar to their parents'.

Conflict theorists believe that the upper class prevents the lower classes from gaining money and power. Has your social class presented any special opportunities or obstacles?

Children in private school mostly interact with other children in their own social class. What are the positives and negatives of this behavior?

that people of similar economic and social classes often live near one another and use the same businesses, schools, and parks. Consequently, people often interact with others of their own class. For example, people in a particular neighborhood probably have similar economic resources and jobs at essentially the same economic level. A middle-class family consisting of a male plumber and female teacher may live next door to a family consisting of a male who owns a small business and a female part-time receptionist. Although their particular jobs are different, their economic resources are similar. Their social interactions are important in supporting successful families through neighborhood and community assistance, and these interactions also reinforce social class through children's exposure to people with similar expectations and prospects.[77] On the other hand, the next-door neighbor might be someone living in poverty, perhaps through lost jobs or illness. Such circumstances can be a challenge for the interactions of neighbors with adequate economic resources.

discover marriages and families in action: WILL ENCOURAGING MARRIAGE REDUCE THE POVERTY RATE?

In 2003, President George W. Bush proposed a pilot program he believed would help reduce child poverty. The program would promote marriage between young, unmarried parents through a variety of government programs. The goal was to prevent children being raised in single-parent households, usually by women, which have a high poverty rate.

Backers of the program relied on several facts that they believed pointed to the importance of marriage in avoiding poverty. Each year, 1.3 million children are born to parents who aren't married, about one-third of all births. Although one-half of these parents are cohabiting at the date of birth, and nine out of ten mothers are romantically involved with the father and express interest in marrying him, less than one in ten actually marry within the next year. After a few years, most relationships deteriorate and the couples split. The percentage of unmarried mothers who live in poverty is about 55 percent, while the percentage for married mothers is only about 17 percent.[78]

> **ACTIVITY**
>
> Research the marriage rate and poverty rates for five different countries. Does the evidence from the countries you have selected support the hypothesis that increasing the marriage rate would reduce the poverty rate for children? Why or why not?

Critics claim that this idea neglects two significant facts. They say that there is actually a shortage of suitable fathers for the expectant mothers to marry because many exhibit drug, alcohol, or physical abuse problems. Also, they believe the earnings of the fathers are generally too low to lift the new family above the poverty line. Proponents of the program point to a survey called the Fragile Families Survey, which indicates that the fathers of these children are generally good marriage material, earning an average of $17,500 in the year before birth, enough to pull the new family above the poverty line.[79] Do you think the simple fact of increasing the marriage rate would reduce the poverty rate?

MAKE CONNECTIONS

Financial Stress and Hardship

In this chapter, we looked at how financial stress and hardship have a direct impact on family and marital relationships. Many factors can influence how the economy helps or hinders families. A few years ago, many families with investments in the stock market felt like they were getting richer all the time and were willing to spend money on vacations, cars, and kids' camps, lessons, and clothes. Then, suddenly, gas went up to $4 a gallon, and everyone's job was in jeopardy. The vacations, cars, and kids' activities weren't possible any more. There are very few people today who feel financially secure. In Chapter 13, we will review how stress, violence, and abuse affect marriages and families. You can assess how much financial, work, and economic stress impact these families and marriages.

>>> ACTIVITIES

1. Ask five of your friends if one or both of their parents worked outside the home for pay. Did any of them go to day care or receive some type of child care before or after school? Did any of them experience being a "latchkey" child?

2. Organize a group of friends or family members to serve a meal at the local homeless shelter.

WHAT ARE THE EFFECTS OF WORK AND UNEMPLOYMENT ON INDIVIDUALS AND FAMILIES? 187

Work significantly affects family life and may result in work-family conflicts from demands on a person's time, work and family strains, and roles that don't coincide. These conflicts can affect both work and family life. As more women have entered the workforce, they have especially felt the strains of work-family conflicts as they try to maintain a household while advancing in a career. Unemployment has universally negative effects on individuals and families.

HOW DOES SOCIAL CLASS AFFECT INDIVIDUALS AND FAMILIES? 197

Social classes are made up of people who have similar jobs, income, and other characteristics. The small upper class controls a disproportionate amount of the wealth in the United States and enjoys great advantages in job opportunities and children's education. The middle class consists of about 45 percent of the population and enjoys great cultural power and modest homes and wealth. The working class is generally at risk from the loss of a job or a lay-off. The lower class includes the working poor whose jobs don't pay enough to keep them out of poverty, people receiving government assistance, and the homeless.

WILL ENCOURAGING MARRIAGE REDUCE THE POVERTY RATE? 199

There is some evidence of a correlation between single-parent families and poverty in the United States, although there is dispute about ways to solve that problem. It does appear, however, that families with two parents are that much stronger and abler to lift themselves from poverty.

Theory

FUNCTIONALISM 198

- society uses an efficient economic system to order, value, and reward different jobs at different rates
- skilled people are encouraged to enter difficult and important jobs because they are rewarded with higher pay and social status

SYMBOLIC INTERACTIONISM 198

- people naturally interact with others of the same social class in neighborhoods and other associations
- children are exposed to the values and expectations of their own social class and often aspire to life at the same level

CONFLICT THEORY 198

- social classes are used as a way for the upper class to retain power and control through an uneven distribution of economic resources and opportunities
- lower classes are not given opportunities to rise in social class through training or access to economic resources

Key Terms

labor force participation refers to the number of people who either have a job or are looking for work *187*

glass escalator refers to an invisible fast-track for men entering previously female-dominated professions *188*

household income refers to earnings from work or investments *188*

wealth is net worth; it includes the total values of all assets such as a house, car, jewelry or other valuables, stocks and bonds, business ownerships, and savings minus any debts *189*

work-family conflict refers to the incompatible role demands stemming from work or family that interfere with a person's functioning in either area *189*

the mommy track was originally a flexible work arrangement suggested to reduce females' work-family conflicts; it was later used to indicate a way that patriarchal businesses prevent women from advancing *190*	verbal or physical conduct of a sexual nature that affects a person's work *192*	**relative poverty** refers to the deprivation of some people in comparison to others *195*
latchkey children are children who care for themselves for some portion of the day *191*	**social class** means a group whose members are similar in education, income, occupational status, housing, and lineage *193*	**absolute poverty** is deprivation that is life threatening *195*
sexual harassment refers to unwelcome sexual advances, requests for sexual favors, and other	**socioeconomic status (SES)** quantifies education, income, and occupation on a continuum as an indicator of social class *193*	**culture of poverty** refers to those cultural influences that involve little planning for the future, little commitment to marriage, little or no work ethic, and dependence on government assistance *195*

Sample Test Questions

MULTIPLE CHOICE

These multiple-choice questions are similar to those found in the test bank that accompanies this textbook.

1. Which of the following is NOT used as a way to assess a family's economic profile?
   a. income
   b. residence
   c. wealth
   d. occupation

2. "The myth of separate worlds" refers to:
   a. the segmented model of work-family conflict.
   b. the distance between the upper class and the lower classes.
   c. flexible work arrangements designed to allow women more freedom.
   d. the fact that the working class has little political power.

3. The greatest change in the U.S. workforce in recent decades has been the:
   a. reduction in the age of retirement.
   b. ability of women to break through the "glass ceiling."
   c. increase in women in the workforce, especially married women.
   d. the concentration of men in jobs on the "sticky floor."

4. In recent years, the upper class in the United States has:
   a. moved away from using private schools for its children.
   b. been less active in government and business leadership.
   c. expanded to include more citizens from other countries.
   d. increased its proportion of total wealth in the United States.

5. Which of the following groups is NOT overrepresented in poverty rates?
   a. African Americans
   b. single mothers
   c. children
   d. the elderly

ESSAY

1. Discuss the three models of evaluating work-family conflict and their strengths and weaknesses.

2. What do you think are the most significant barriers to women's advancement in the workplace?

3. Identify the unemployment rate for your local area or your home town and describe ways you think it is affecting individuals and the community.

4. Place your family in one of the four basic social classes. What effect did it have on your growth and current circumstances?

5. Which do you think is more important in creating poverty: individual actions or societal barriers?

WHERE TO START YOUR RESEARCH PAPER

For more information on family incomes, go to
http://www.census.gov/hhes/www/income/histinc/incfamdet.html

For more information on labor statistics worldwide, go to
http://laborsta.ilo.org/

For more information on U.S. income and poverty, go to
http://www.census.gov/prod/2008pubs/p60–235.pdf

For information on work and family conflicts, you can begin at
http://www.hrmguide.com/worklife/men_more_likely_to_leave.htm

To find out more about latchkey children, go to
http://findarticles.com/p/articles/mi_m1053/is_v13/ai_3243319/

To find out more about sexual harassment, go to
http://www.eeoc.gov/types/sexual_harassment.html

To find out more about social class in the United States, go to
http://www.nytimes.com/pages/national/class/

For basic information on welfare and its history in the United States, go to http://www.welfareinfo.org/history/

For more information on homelessness, go to
http://www.policyalmanac.org/social_welfare/homeless.shtml

ANSWERS: 1. b; 2. a; 3. c; 4. d; 5. d

Remember to check www.thethinkspot.com for additional information, downloadable flashcards, and other helpful resources.

HOW DO SOCIAL INSTITUTIONS SUCH AS EDUCATION, RELIGION, POLITICS, AND THE LEGAL SYSTEM IMPACT MARRIAGES AND FAMILIES?

HOW DO DIFFERENT THEORISTS VIEW MARRIAGES AND FAMILIES IN THE CONTEXT OF SOCIAL INSTITUTIONS?

HOW ARE FAMILY THERAPISTS RESPONDING TO DIVERSITY WITHIN MARRIAGES AND FAMILIES?

In the

movie *Stand and Deliver*, calculus teacher Jaime Escalante is starting a new job in Los Angeles at James A. Garfield High School, a tough school in which teachers are forced to focus on discipline rather than academics. Faced with a class of sub-literate, unmotivated, and disenfranchised Hispanic youths, Escalante vows to change the system and teach his students the value of a good education.

At first, Escalante is taunted and threatened by his unruly students. He responds to the class thug, "Tough guys don't do math. Tough guys fry chicken for a living." He loses the thug, but wins over the rest of the class, who realize that unless they improve themselves intellectually, they are destined to work in the fast food joints and auto repair shops of their poverty-stricken barrio.

Gradually, Escalante's innovative teaching techniques begin to have an impact on his class. He comes to class with a chef's hat, a meat cleaver, and some apples to teach fractions. He uses humor to explain other abstract math concepts and show their relevance to everyday life. Bonding with his students through a shared cultural heritage, Escalante tells them about famous Latin Americans whose accomplishments were made possible because of their ability to learn. "There are some people in this world who assume you know less than you do because of your name and your complexion," he tells them, "but math is a great equalizer." Eventually, even Angel, the most resistant student in the class, begins to pay attention.

Escalante initially teaches his class Math 1A, but soon realizes that their enthusiasm and potential will take them further than the school board's meager expectations. To the disbelief of fellow teachers, he develops a program that will enable his students to take the AP Calculus exam. Many of the students live in poverty and in single-parent households, and they have to deal with the contrast between what society expects of them and the higher expectations they have set for themselves.

When the students eventually take the AP Calculus test in the spring and receive their scores, they are overwhelmed to discover that they have all passed—a feat practically unheard of in the state of California. The Educational Testing Service is suspicious about the outstanding results and accuses Escalante's class of cheating. Outraged, Escalante believes that the students' racial and socioeconomic backgrounds have prejudiced the board's assessment of the results. He encourages the class to retake the test and prove everyone wrong. Despite only having a day to prepare for the second exam, all the students retake the test. When they pass the exam a second time, the students prove to the rest of the world that they truly did overcome the odds and deserve every bit of their success.

FAMILY AND SOCIAL INSTITUTIONS
Education, Religion, Politics, and the Legal System

CHAPTER 12

Stand and Deliver, based on a true story, **is a useful starting point in our evaluation of families and social institutions—** components in the social structure that address a basic social need, such as education.

Raised in working-class Hispanic families, Mr. Escalante's students received little support or encouragement from their parents. They drifted through high school with few reasons to pay attention in class. The other teachers focused on discipline rather than self-esteem or life skills.

Mr. Escalante became an important role model for his class, raising their expectations of themselves and driving them to improve their academic performance.

The film also addresses the wider social issues of prejudices and stereotypes. Would the Educational Testing Service have questioned the exam results if the students had been from a prestigious private school attended by upper-class white students? Mr. Escalante tells his class that education is a great equalizer, but does everyone receive the same quality of education? Some would argue that many students from disadvantaged or minority families are held to lower expectations than other students.

In my early 20s, I lived in Uruguay for 18 months. Several years before I arrived, a military coup had taken place, and the military ruled the country with brutal force. In 1981, General Gregorio Alvarez became the president. During his tenure, there were several protests against the military and the government. In 1984, the armed forces agreed to return civilian rule to the country. Watching the impact this experience had on the educational, legal, political, and religious aspects of family life forever changed my perspective.

Throughout this chapter, we will examine the impact that social institutions such as education, religion, politics, and the legal system have on family life. We will also consider how family therapists deal with diversity in modern family life.

>>> **Families and social institutions such as education form a complex bond.** Are children's educational achievements influenced by their family backgrounds?

Family and Social Institutions: Education, Religion, Politics, and the Legal System

Social institutions – components in social structure that address a basic social need

include

Education – provides members of society with knowledge including basic facts, job skills and cultural norms and values

which may be influenced by

– covenant marriage
– gay marriage
– gay adoption
– child care
– abortion

which considers issues such as

Legal system – legal and financial aid provided to families in government's **Family policy** – includes services such as family planning, food stamps, and child care

and

get the topic: HOW DO SOCIAL INSTITUTIONS SUCH AS EDUCATION, RELIGION, POLITICS, AND THE LEGAL SYSTEM IMPACT MARRIAGES AND FAMILIES?

Education

"Education is the ability to listen to almost anything without losing your temper or your self-confidence." — Robert Frost (1874–1963)[1]

Sociologists define **education** as the social institution through which society provides its members with knowledge that includes basic facts, job skills, and cultural norms and values. Most people in the United States today expect to spend a large percentage of their first 18 years in school, a concept that was unheard of several generations ago when education was a privilege enjoyed only by the wealthy. In 1940, less than one in four Americans aged 25 and older had graduated from high school, and only about 5 percent were college graduates.[2] In 2009, just a few decades later, almost 87 percent of adults in the United States aged 25 and older had at least completed high school, and almost 30 percent had at least a bachelor's degree.[3]

Changing educational patterns have resulted in a shift in family dynamics. With an increasing number of people attending college, we have also seen trends toward delayed marriage, a delay in the timing of childbirth and a reduced amount of childbearing, and a higher per-person income among young adult householders as discussed in earlier chapters of this book (See Chapters 1, 6, 7, and 8).

FAMILIES AND EDUCATIONAL OUTCOMES

At the beginning of the film *Stand and Deliver*, the students' educational attainment was negatively impacted by the low expectations held by their families. How strongly do families affect children's performance in school? Studies generally agree that compared to children in single-parent families, children with two parents fare better at school, have a lower risk of dropping out, achieve higher grades, and are more likely to attend college.[4]

However, researchers McLanahan and Sandefur found that regardless of family structure, children tend to do well when their parents provide

significant supervision of homework and leisure time.[5] Children are also more likely to succeed if their parents have strong roots within the community that provide them with additional support and supervision and create networks for personal and professional advancement.[6]

Developing networks within the community may be particularly important for children in low-income families. For example, churches that offer social and academic opportunities provide children with broader social networks, while fund-raising for a sports team or local youth group may help develop children's roles and responsibilities within the community.[7]

In addition to class and family structure, race may also play a role in educational attainment. Researchers have noted that even when factors such as family background, parental involvement, socioeconomic background, and academic preparation have been taken into account, an achievement gap between black students and white students still persists at all levels of schooling.[8] A study of underachieving but bright Puerto Rican high school students pinpointed five school-related factors that influenced their poor academic results: a lack of exposure to challenging and appropriate curricular experiences in elementary school; an absence of opportunities to develop or improve schoolwork discipline; negative interactions with teachers; an unrewarding curriculum; and poor experiences with guidance counselors.[9] In contrast, Puerto Rican students who did well in school primarily attributed their success to non–school-related factors, such as participating in church activities, the importance of their ethnic identities, and the influence of their mothers.[10] From these results, researchers concluded that school–community partnerships are a key factor in promoting the academic success of Puerto Rican and other Latino students.[11]

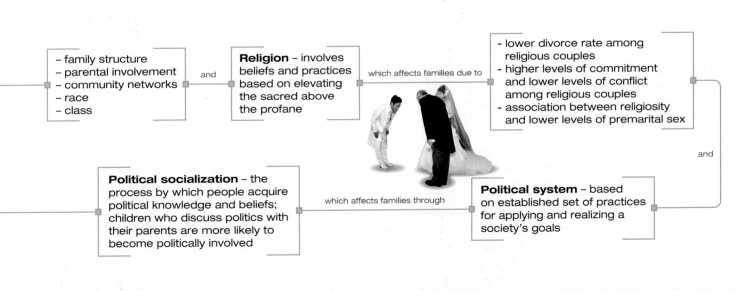

- family structure
- parental involvement
- community networks
- race
- class

and

Religion – involves beliefs and practices based on elevating the sacred above the profane

which affects families due to

- lower divorce rate among religious couples
- higher levels of commitment and lower levels of conflict among religious couples
- association between religiosity and lower levels of premarital sex

and

Political socialization – the process by which people acquire political knowledge and beliefs; children who discuss politics with their parents are more likely to become politically involved

which affects families through

Political system – based on established set of practices for applying and realizing a society's goals

Educational Attainment of U.S. Population, 1940–2007

Legend:
- High school diploma or more
- Bachelor's degree or more

Year	High school diploma or more	Bachelor's degree or more
1940	24.5	4.6
1950	34.3	6.2
1960	41.1	7.7
1970	52.3	10.7
1980	66.5	16.2
1990	75.2	20.3
2000	80.4	24.4

∧
∧ Today, more students graduate from college than in the past. **How does your family
∧ fit into the education status in the United States?**

PARENT INVOLVEMENT IN EDUCATION

Most recent research indicates that parent involvement in a child's schooling promotes higher student attendance rates, lower expulsion rates, student pride in his or her schoolwork, and higher academic achievement in reading and math.[12] Despite widespread knowledge of these facts, schools have traditionally been reluctant to enable parents to contribute to the educational process, which researcher Diana Hiatt Michael explains by looking at four forces: families' cultural beliefs, social structures of families, economic influences, and political pressures. **Cultural beliefs** affect issues such as which ethnic groups predominantly attend a school,

which language should be the dominant language spoken in school, and the level of parental expectations on academic achievement. **Social structures** include changes in family compositions, differing roles of family members, and the rate of population growth. **Economic influences** encompass employment opportunities, economic growth, and the gross national product allotted to education, while **political pressures** might stem from conflicts between local, state, and national government, or from changes of power.[13] Schools and families face a divide on several of these forces, thus causing a greater distance between the collaboration of parents and educators in a child's educational development.[14] A line can be drawn between parents and schools on any such issue that would fall under cultural, social, economical, and political forces.[15] For example, the modern technology adopted or the teaching of evolution theory and approach to world religions are some issues schools and families may disagree on. Sex education and its place in schools have been a topic of great debate and controversy, given that state and local governments often make the mandates on how the subject matter is taught.

During the period of industrialization and urbanization in the late 1800s and 1900s, the education system in the United States developed from the family-arranged system of home schooling and trade apprenticeships to a public, bureaucratic system. The attitude that teachers and educational professionals were solely qualified to make decisions about children's education relegated parents to the role of bystanders. Today, parents have become more involved in the educational process as a result of more families being better educated than in the past.[16] However, the need for parents to become even more involved in the educational process through collaboration with educators is evident. This partnership may face several challenges, including increased immigration from urban to rural areas resulting in more families for whom English is a second language, smaller families, longer working hours, and political and economic imperatives for a skilled, educated workforce.[17]

RECENT ISSUES IN EDUCATION

In addition to becoming more involved in their children's education, parents are facing a number of issues regarding schooling, including where to send their children, whether to opt for home schooling, and whether to continue their own education.

School Choice

Choosing where to send a child to school is no small consideration. Many parents specifically move to an area because of the perceived quality of public schooling. In 2003, 27 percent of parents in the United States indicated that their primary reason for selecting a neighborhood was the quality of education for their children.[18] Of the parents who actively choose the school their children will attend, most state that academic programs and high academic performance motivate their choices.[19] Parents with higher socioeconomic status are more likely to exercise choice when given the opportunity, and these parents will usually choose schools with fewer children from low-income families and racial minority families.[20] Put into law in 2001, under former President George W. Bush, the No Child Left Behind Act (NCLB) was implemented to ensure that all children have access to a high-quality education, regardless of socioeconomic status. NCLB served to reform the Elementary and Secondary Education Act of 1965, and one key revision was to focus on the educational opportunity of children who are less advantaged.[21] Under NCLB, after certain provisions have been met, any parent whose child attends a low-performing school has the option of transferring the child to a higher-performing school.[22]

Homeschooling

With the increase in comprehensive online learning providers, a growing number of parents are choosing to educate their children at home. The number of home-schooled students rose from an estimated 300,000 in 1990 to more than a million just a decade later.[23] Common reasons for homeschooling include avoiding the

---

CULTURAL BELIEFS are personal beliefs particular to a culture that may influence the power relationship between parents and school.
SOCIAL STRUCTURES are changes in family structures that may influence the power relationship between parents and school.
ECONOMIC INFLUENCES are economic factors that may influence the power relationship between parents and school.
POLITICAL PRESSURES are governmental pressures that may influence the power relationship between parents and school.
RELIGION is a social institution involving beliefs and practices based on recognizing and elevating the sacred above the profane.
SACRED refers to objects or concepts that inspire awe and respect.
PROFANE refers to everyday elements of ordinary life.

---

negative influences of public schools, concern with the quality of public school education, and a desire to include religious teachings in the curriculum.[24] Although most studies agree that there is little difference in student achievement between homeschooled and public-schooled students, three factors appear to influence academic achievement: Students who are homeschooled by more educated parents do better than those who are taught by less educated parents; students who are homeschooled by more conservative parents do better on standardized tests than those taught by more liberal parents; and children of parents who homeschool due to family needs have lower levels of achievement than those who are homeschooled for other reasons.[25] However, the primary factor directly linked to student achievement can best be attributed to the approach and teaching style of the parent.[26] For example, in the case of students who are taught by more conservative parents and do better on standardized tests than those taught by more liberal parents, this is most likely attributed to the conservative teaching style of teaching specific knowledge, whereas the more liberal parent might teach in an experimental or less formal approach, which would not be rewarded or recognized by standardized testing.[27]

Adult Education

As discussed in Chapter 8, people often marry later in life and therefore have children later in life. Many people also choose a nonstandard career path. As a result, many adults are choosing to return to school, possibly after they have had children. Students aged 25 or older currently comprise approximately 38 percent of the college student population.[28] Some studies suggest that a parent's return to education can impact a child's own educational aspirations. Researchers found that in families in which mothers successfully completed their undergraduate degrees following a return to school, most or all of the children also completed college by early adulthood.[29]

Religion

"Religion consists in a set of things which the average man thinks he believes and wishes he was certain."—Mark Twain (1835–1910)[30]

Most people are born into families who identify with some type of **religion**—a social institution involving beliefs and practices based on recognizing and elevating the **sacred** (objects or concepts that inspire awe and respect) above the **profane** (elements of everyday life). For example, Jewish people separate Shabbat, the holy day, from the rest

---

∧
∧ Approximately 38 percent of college students are 25 or older.

What factors might influence a person's decision to return to school?

RELIGIOUS PLURALISM is the existence of religious diversity within a community.

SHINTO is the native Japanese religion that emphasizes a love of nature.

POLITICAL SYSTEM is a social institution based on an established set of practices for applying and realizing a society's goals.

LIBERALS are individuals on the left of the political spectrum; generally associated in modern times with the Democratic party.

CONSERVATIVES are individuals on the right of the political spectrum; generally associated in modern times with the Republican party.

POLITICAL SOCIALIZATION is the process by which people acquire political knowledge, beliefs, and values.

of the days of the week by performing a candle-lighting ritual at the beginning and end of the day of celebration.

Although individuals may become more or less religious within their particular group, they rarely change their religious affiliation. The United States has a history of **religious pluralism**, in which people of many different religions coexist peacefully. As a nation of immigrants, this religious diversity is vast, encompassing Protestants, Catholics, Jews, Muslims, Buddhists, Hindus, and Sikhs, among many other religious denominations. Although 65 percent of all Americans state that religion is important in their daily lives, in 2009 the majority of Americans believe that the influence of religion in American life is waning, a view perhaps attributed to the shift from Republican to Democratic power in the 2008 presidential election.[31] Some view the Democratic party as the more secular of the two major political parties, in part, due to the Democratic party's emphasis on individual rights versus traditional institutions, such as organized religion.

RELIGION AND THE FAMILY

As we have seen throughout this book, religion plays a large role in determining social norms within marriages and families. Although interfaith dating and marriage is increasing, most people choose a partner within their own religious group, a factor that significantly lowers the risk of divorce.[32] Interfaith marriages face challenges. In Judaism, for example, the religion of the wife becomes the religion of the household over that of the husband. As a result, non-Jewish husbands can sometimes feel less satisfied in their influence over the household.[33] Generalizations and stereotypes can serve as challenges to the interfaith marriage as well.[34] In particular, the generalizations and stereotypes made by other family members can pose a great challenge for an interfaith married couple. Religiosity within a marriage is also associated with greater marital happiness. Studies show that couples who are religious enjoy higher levels of adjustment and commitment and lower levels of conflict.[35] A study of the relationship between marital stability and church attendance found that once all other variables had been taken into consideration, couples who attended church regularly had a divorce rate of 44 percent, compared with 60 percent for nonattenders.[36] Researchers have also discovered that:

- Religious couples are more likely to employ effective communication and conflict resolution skills than other couples, possibly due to a religious emphasis on prayer and forgiveness.[37]

- Religiosity is associated with lower levels of premarital sexual activity.[38]

- Evangelical wives spend approximately four to five more hours per week performing housework than their non-evangelical counterparts, especially on routine tasks traditionally defined as "women's work" such as cooking, cleaning, and laundry.[39]

- Frequent parent–child discussions about religion often contribute positively to a child's development, whereas frequent arguments about religion may foster division and conflict, delaying a child's development."[40]

Politics

"Politics is not the art of the possible. It consists in choosing between the disastrous and the unpalatable."—John Kenneth Galbraith (1908–2006)[44]

Politics, along with sex and religion, is one of the controversial topics that people are advised to steer clear of in polite company, because of its tendency to result in heated debates. The **political system**—a social institution based on an established set of practices for applying and realizing a society's goals—is an arena in which people hold widely diverging viewpoints. At one end of the political spectrum, **liberals** (associated in

Religious Composition of U.S. Population

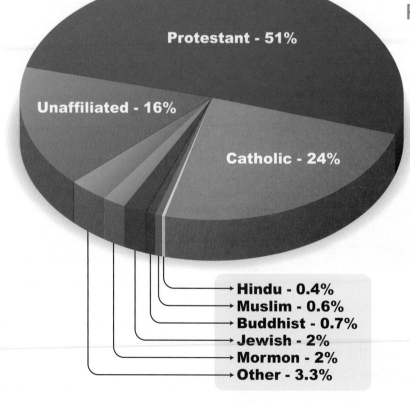

- Protestant - 51%
- Unaffiliated - 16%
- Catholic - 24%
- Hindu - 0.4%
- Muslim - 0.6%
- Buddhist - 0.7%
- Jewish - 2%
- Mormon - 2%
- Other - 3.3%

<<< The Religious Composition of U.S. Population shows **a high percentage of Protestants and Catholics and a low percentage of Muslims, Hindus,** and people unaffiliated with religion. **How does a person's religion affect their family life?**

Religion and Japanese Culture

Japan's traditions are cultural rather than religious, and few Japanese people consider themselves religious believers. Except for the small percentage of people who are practicing Christians (less than 2 percent), most families and individuals in Japan practice forms of folk religions, known as New Religions, that combine elements of Shinto, Buddhism, and Christianity.[41] These New Religions offer their members support through small group meetings and encourage solving problems through ritual and proper behavior.

The native Japanese religion is **Shinto**, which literally means "the way of the gods." Shinto followers worship nature in the form of *kami*—gods or spirits that personify aspects of nature such as the sky, trees, and mountains.[42] This love of nature is often expressed in Japanese poetry, landscape painting, and traditional landscaping and architecture. Although Shinto is associated with shrines and festivals, it has no fixed dogma or sacred scriptures, a fact that enables Japanese families to incorporate it into their lives along with aspects of other religions. For example, a Japanese funeral may assume the Buddhist customs of carrying prayer beads and bestowing a new Buddhist name on the deceased, while a Japanese wedding often incorporates Christian or Western elements such as cutting a cake, exchanging rings, and jetting off on a honeymoon after the ceremony.[43]

>>> Japanese weddings combine elements of Shinto and Christian rituals. **How might these religious elements affect the marriage?**

modern times generally with the Democratic party) support government regulation of the economy and programs to reduce income inequality. For example, President Obama's 2009 proposal for health care reform included funding that would come in part from increasing the taxes of the wealthiest members of society.[45] Socially, in general, liberals support equal rights and opportunities for gay and lesbian families, view abortion as a personal choice, and oppose the death penalty. At the other end of the political spectrum, **conservatives** (associated in modern times generally with the Republican Party) tend to believe that the government should play a limited role in the economy because a free market economy successfully regulates itself. They believe the economy is more productive without government intervention. Socially, conservatives, in general, support traditional family values and traditional gender roles—opposing gay marriage, abortion, and affirmative action programs.

So, where do most Americans fall on the political spectrum? In a 2009 Gallup poll, 40 percent of those interviewed identified themselves as "conservative," 21 percent viewed themselves as "liberal," and 35 percent told interviewers they were "moderate."[46] Despite the election of a Democratic president in 2008, most Americans say that their political views in recent years have become more conservative. For example, between 2004 and 2008 an increasing number of Americans opposed the banning of handguns and were more likely to say that the economy should be given priority over the environment when the two issues conflict. Conservative values regarding gay marriage, abortion, embryonic stem cell research, and church attendance remained stable, and of the seven values measured in 2004 and 2008, only one suggested a shift to the left—the decline in the belief that the government is responsible for promoting traditional values.[47] Conservatives are likely to look to faith-based organizations for moral and social guidance on values.

POLITICAL PARTICIPATION

Did you vote in the 2008 presidential election? The possibility of electing the first black president stirred many people into making the trip to the polling stations, particularly young and minority first-time voters. Exit polls show that 68 percent of voters in the 18–24 age group and 69 percent of voters in the 25–29 age bracket favored Barack Obama, along with 96 percent of black voters, 67 percent of Hispanic voters, and 63 percent of Asian voters.[48] Although many reports focused on the historic election of the nation's first black president, surveys indicated that age was a bigger factor in voter decision. Had he been elected, 73-year-old John McCain would have been the oldest president ever to be elected to the White House. At the time of the election, Barack Obama was 47.

Historically, voting turnouts for presidential elections have been low, with voting turnouts for state and local elections being even lower. Voting and playing an active role in the election process can be linked to the overall level of involvement of a family in political elections. One study found that among young adults eligible to vote under the age of 25, those who had frequent political discussions with their parents were far more likely to vote than those who did not discuss politics with their parents (38 percent compared with 20 percent).[49] By discussing routine knowledge such as where the polls are, who runs for election, how they voted, and what adult responsibilities and issues come with citizenship, parents provide the motive and the capacity to their children to become politically engaged.[50]

POLITICAL SOCIALIZATION

What impact do families have on their children's political beliefs? **Political socialization**—the process by which people acquire political knowledge, beliefs, and values—begins in childhood and continues throughout life. Because children spend a good amount of time with their parents, parental influence is considerable.

Children who speak to their parents about politics are more likely to be involved in political activities, and those who become involved in voluntary organizations are likely to acquire skills that facilitate inclusion into the adult world of politics. For example, young adults may run meetings, listen to others' ideas, argue viewpoints, and speak in public—all

National Voter Turnout in Federal Elections, 1960–2008

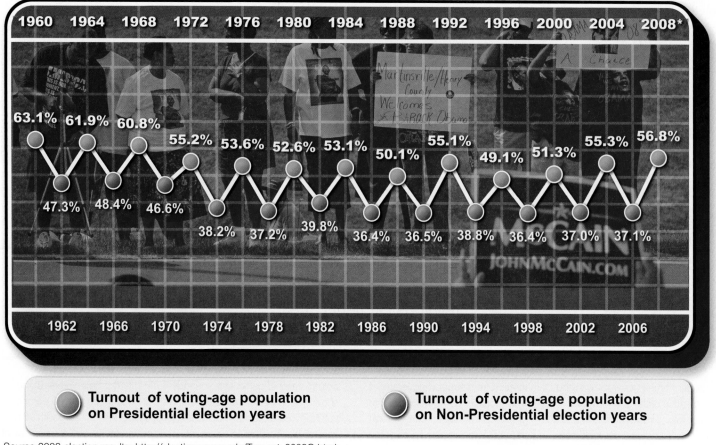

1960	1964	1968	1972	1976	1980	1984	1988	1992	1996	2000	2004	2008*

63.1% 61.9% 60.8%

55.2% 53.6% 52.6% 53.1%

50.1%

55.1%

49.1%

51.3%

55.3% 56.8%

47.3% 48.4% 46.6%

38.2% 37.2% 39.8% 36.4% 36.5% 38.8% 36.4% 37.0% 37.1%

| 1962 | 1966 | 1970 | 1974 | 1978 | 1982 | 1986 | 1990 | 1994 | 1998 | 2002 | 2006 |

● **Turnout of voting-age population on Presidential election years**

● **Turnout of voting-age population on Non-Presidential election years**

Source 2008 election results: http://elections.gmu.edu/Turnout_2008G.html.
n.a. = not available.

∧
∧ Voter turnout has varied from year to year. **What factors might have influenced**
∧ **more people** to vote during certain elections?

activities that teach the leadership skills and self-esteem required to take on active political roles in later life.[51]

Parents may pique their children's interest in politics, but do they influence their political attitudes and beliefs? Statistics suggest that parents are increasingly less likely to influence their child's choice of political party (known as **partisanship**). In 1958, 79 percent of children with Democratic parents and 72 percent of children with Republican parents adopted parental partisanship. By 1976, these figures had dropped to 62 percent and 56 percent, respectively, and in 1992 they had declined further, to 57 percent and 56 percent.[52]

When parental transmission does play a role in determining an individual's choice of political party, researchers Robert Erikson and Kent Tedin attribute it to one of three factors: simple communication between family members, the process of rational adaptation by which children learn that their parents' views are in their own best interests, and a genetic makeup in which similar genes display a tendency to respond openly or cautiously to contemporary political issues.[53]

Marriage and Political Socialization

Husbands and wives often spend just as much time together as parents and children, so do they also influence each other politically? The Michigan Socialization Study consisted of a series of surveys conducted

between 1965 and 1997 in which participants were interviewed about their political attitudes and beliefs. Researchers then compared the interviews to analyze how individuals' attitudes developed over time. They discovered that since people generally choose marriage partners from the same race, class, and religion, there was initially a positive relationship between the political opinions of husbands and wives taking part in the study. Over time, this relationship either remained the same or grew stronger. In general, wives became more politically similar to their husbands, rather than the reverse, and most of the shift in attitudes occurred early in the marriage.[54]

The Marriage Gap

The results from the Michigan Socialization Study may partly explain the **marriage gap** in politics—political disparities between those who are married and those who are single. Researchers have noticed that single people (including young people, those who marry late in life, gay men and lesbians, single parents, and cohabiting heterosexuals), are more likely to vote Democratic than married people. This gap has increased over the past three presidential elections. In 2008, McCain won the married vote by 5 points and Obama won the unmarried vote by 32 points—a difference of 37 points (compared with a 33-point difference in 2004 and a 28-point difference in 2000).[55]

Researchers have offered a number of explanations for the marriage gap, including several demographic theories. Because blacks are more likely to vote Democratic and less likely to be married, the discrepancy may be due to race rather than marital status. Married couples also tend to have higher incomes than single individuals, a factor positively associated with Republican voting. Furthermore, married people are more likely to own property and produce or expect children, creating a vested interest in protecting their wealth and maintaining social order—both conservative ideals promoted by the Republican party.[56]

The Legal System

"Laws are like cobwebs, which may collect small flies, but let wasps and hornets break through."—Jonathan Swift (1667–1745)[57]

How much influence should the government have over family life? Individual answers to this question depend on political leanings. Conservatives tend to believe that individuals are responsible for their own actions and financial stability, whereas liberals often believe that government intervention is required to help needy members of society. The extent of legal and financial aid provided to families is defined in the government's **family policy**—the range of services funded and sponsored by the government that affect families directly or indirectly. These services may include family planning, food stamps, foster care, child care, adoption, child development programs, and family counseling and therapy.

COVENANT MARRIAGE

Rising divorce rates and increases in nonmarital fertility, cohabitation rates, and "alternative" family arrangements have led to a perceived decline in traditional family values. In reaction to this, supporters of traditional marriage in some states, such as Arizona, Arkansas, and Louisiana, have helped legalize covenant marriages. A movement primarily spearheaded by

PARTISANSHIP is the support of a particular political party.

MARRIAGE GAP is the political disparities between those who are married and those who are single.

FAMILY POLICY is the range of services funded and sponsored by the government that affect families directly or indirectly.

COVENANT MARRIAGE is a heterosexual union that imposes strict regulations on entering and exiting the marriage in an effort to reduce divorce rates.

GAY MARRIAGE is a union of a same-sex couple with all the legal rights guaranteed by the federal government to heterosexual married couples.

Christian organizations, **covenant marriage** imposes strict regulations for entering into a union and even stricter regulations for dissolving it. Researchers debate the effectiveness of this legislation. John Crouch argues that covenant marriage will ensure that couples evaluate their decision to marry before entering into a union. Crouch adds that the premarital counseling required for a covenant marriage teaches vital communication and conflict resolution skills and enable couples to ensure their compatibility before tying the knot.[58]

However, others question the effect that covenant marriage may have on the children of parents who choose to stay together at any cost. Ashton Applewhite argues that a tense home environment may cause additional stress to children. A covenant marriage may also encourage women to remain in violent, abusive relationships.[59] So, in theory, it could mean the same for men who are victims of violent, abusive relationships. Covenant marriage is discussed in greater detail in Chapter 14 of this book.

GAY MARRIAGE

Gay marriage—the legal union of a same-sex couple—is now legal in six states. Marriage enables homosexual couples to publicly demonstrate their

From Classroom to Community } Encouraging the Youth Vote

Alyssa is a third-year college student who volunteers for a nonpartisan organization that encourages young people to participate in the democratic process.

"My parents are both passionate about exercising their right to vote, and I got involved with political campaigning from an early age. When I was at a fundraising event a couple of years ago, I met some of the *Engage* volunteers and thought that it sounded like a worthwhile cause. We don't promote any one party—our main aim is to get young people involved in the political process and become active citizens. We talk to students on college campuses all

over the country about how they can influence future political decisions by getting involved in the democratic process and speaking out about the issues that are important to them. I hear a lot of people make excuses about why they haven't voted in the past: they don't have time, they aren't registered, or they think their vote won't make a difference. It's encouraging that these excuses are beginning to dry up now that people are taking

ACTIVITY

Visit your local city or county voter registration office. Ask them to give you a tour and what issues may arise when individuals register to vote for the first time.

more of an active interest in the political process.

"During the 2008 presidential election, we set up voter registration tables on college campuses so that people could register to vote. Some of the volunteers even staged some guerilla theater performances to get people to the polls, which turned out to be pretty successful. I knew that the youth turnout had increased during the 2004 election, but I was still shocked at the response—young people who had never thought twice about voting were genuinely excited about the 2008 election. When the results came out, we found that for the first time in 20 years, the young voter share of the electorate surpassed that of voters over 65. That was a pretty good feeling. Hopefully, we'll get even more young votes in the 2012 election."

lifelong commitment to one another. It promises to remain a hot-button issue in the United States. Supporters urge lawmakers to push through new legislation for several reasons. Marriage entitles couples to legal benefits including tax deductions, inheritance rights, and Social Security benefits, as well as other benefits such as sick and bereavement leave. The Family Medical Leave Act (FMLA) is another benefit of married couples in which homosexual couples do not benefit. Under FMLA, an employee may be entitled to up to 12 weeks of unpaid leave to care for a spouse.[60] Currently the FMLA does not cover domestic partnership. Researchers have found that current attitudes toward gay marriage tend to be most accepting among nonparents with cohabiting experience, and least accepting among parents with no cohabiting experience. Women, whites, and young people are generally more approving than men, blacks, and older Americans.[61]

GAY ADOPTION

Gay adoption is another legal issue affecting some families. Currently, 65,000 adopted children are being raised by same-sex parents in the United States, while 14,100 foster children are living with gay or lesbian foster parents.[62] Although some states prohibit discrimination based on sexual orientation, many do not, leaving prospective adoptive parents at the mercy of judges and adoption agencies. As a result, some same-sex couples hide their sexual orientation during the adoption process. During an international adoption, one partner often adopts as the official single parent, leaving the other legally unrecognized, a fact that may cause strain within the couple's relationship.[63]

CHILD CARE

The vulnerability of children in the United States is a key concern for many families and organizations. The Children's Defense Fund reports that as of 2008, 11.3 percent of children do not have health insurance, one-third of all two-year-olds are not fully immunized, and 18 percent of children are living in poverty.[64] Many proponents of government reform argue that current policies regarding children are ineffective or insufficient. One particular area of concern is child care. Few families can afford the luxury of a parent staying home full-time to care for children. According to a 2005 U.S. Census Bureau report about working mothers, more than a third of children under the age of five spend time in an organized care facility while their mothers work. A further 30 percent are cared for by their grandparents, 25 percent receive care from their fathers, 3 percent by their siblings, and 8 percent by other relatives.[65] For families without the support of relatives, the financial cost of child care is a huge burden. Families in poverty who pay for child care spend 29 percent of their monthly income on child care arrangements (compared with 6 percent for families above the poverty line).[66]

Attitudes Toward Same-Sex Marriage

No legal recognition 32%

Undecided 5%

Civil union 30%

Legal marriage 33%

^^^ National opinion about the legality and morality of same-sex marriage is still divided. **However, some states have passed legislation that approves homosexual unions.** What opinions on same-sex marriage are most common in the area you live?

There are several policies currently in place to help struggling families. The government offers subsidies to states for child care and a tax credit to parents who spend money on child care. It also supports employers who provide on-site child care for parents. Is this sufficient? Some advocates believe that it is the government's responsibility to promote high-quality, affordable child care, while opponents protest that such expansion would overwhelm the federal budget.

ABORTION

Although abortion—the spontaneous or induced termination of a pregnancy—has been legal nationwide for more than 35 years, it continues to raise legal and ethical questions. On the grounds of a woman's right to privacy, the Supreme Court ruled in 1973 that the state's interest in preserving the life of a fetus occurs only when it is viable (capable of living unaided outside of the mother's womb), which occurs between 24 and 28 weeks of pregnancy. Recently, the major controversy has been over partial-birth abortions, which occur after week 26 and involve inducing a breech delivery with forceps. In 2003, President George Bush signed a law banning partial-birth abortions.

Researchers have discovered that people's attitude toward abortion varies according to circumstance. Approval ratings of abortion for medical reasons (such as serious birth defect, endangerment of the mother, or pregnancy as a result of rape) are consistently higher than for social reasons (such as not being able to afford a child or not wanting any more children).[67]

UNITED STATES FAMILY POLICY

Does the government do enough to help families? As a country, the United States spends considerably less on programs directed at families than other post-industrial Western countries. Between 1980 and 1998, the United States spent between 0.8 and 1.3 percent of its gross national product on family benefits. In contrast, Sweden doled out between 3.3 and 5.1 percent on family benefits during the same period.[68]

Whether or not the funding policy changes, researchers believe there are several key trends that will shape the future of families. These include an increase in the number of nontraditional families, high rates of marriage dissolution and serial marriages, a shift in family roles as the rate of women's employment continues to increase, and a redefinition of family due to increased life expectancy, with older people playing a key role in political participation and saving patterns as well as a dominant part in the workforce. Technology is likely to play an increasingly important role in family life, as trends such as e-learning and e-commerce enable people to work and study from the comfort of their own homes.[69]

think marriages and families: HOW DO DIFFERENT THEORISTS VIEW MARRIAGES AND FAMILIES IN THE CONTEXT OF SOCIAL INSTITUTIONS?

FUNCTIONALISM

Functionalists examine the way social institutions such as education and religion support the operation and stabilization of society. For example, schools supplement the role of the family by serving as a socializing agent that teaches children vital skills they will require in their adult lives to perform basic job functions. Schooling also teaches children cultural norms and values. Through civics classes, students learn about the political system, acquire patriotic sensibilities through daily repetition of the pledge of allegiance, and begin to understand concepts such as competitiveness, fair play, and compromise through sporting activities and educational games.

As Mr. Escalante's students learned in *Stand and Deliver*, schools also foster the notion that education results in upward social mobility. By rewarding talent and achievement regardless of social background, Mr. Escalante (and teachers nationwide) promote meritocracy—a system that encompasses the fundamental American values of freedom and opportunity. By passing the calculus exam, the students earned themselves the ability to pursue numerous different career directions.

A third function of education is the social integration of many different types of students. Children from all cultural, financial, and family backgrounds learn shared norms and values under one roof, creating a miniature "cultural melting pot" that facilitates students' integration into wider society.

Finally, education serves a number of secondary, unintentional functions. It provides child care for the increasing number of single-parent and dual-income families. It delays the age of marriage, reduces the likelihood of divorce for those who postpone tying the knot until after they graduate from college, and gives individuals a place to meet and develop relationships.[70] Further education also reduces the number of people in their teens and early 20s who would otherwise be competing for limited job opportunities in a shaky economy.

Other social institutions have similar stabilizing effects. Religion provides people with a sense of community that binds people together. Structural functional theorist Émile Durkheim argues that religion has three major functions: to unite people through shared symbolism, values, and norms (for example, through rituals such as baptism in the Christian church); to encourage people to obey cultural norms (through fear of disobeying "God's will"); and to provide a sense of greater meaning or purpose, making people less likely to despair in the face of change or tragedy.

CONFLICT THEORY

Conflict theorists challenge the idea that social institutions such as education develop talents and abilities equally. Conflict theorists instead believe that schooling helps perpetuate social inequalities. For example, the use of standardized testing to assign students to different types of educational programs is considered by some to be an unfair system.

Although efforts are made to eliminate any cultural bias from these tests, critics argue that elements of class, race, or ethnicity bias frequently place minority students at a disadvantage.[71] Because students from privileged backgrounds tend to do well on standardized tests, they are often placed in higher academic groups in school, and thereby receive a higher quality of education than those from disadvantaged families who tend to do less well on standardized tests.

Children from wealthier families are often educated in private rather than public schools, giving them the advantage of smaller class sizes, more intense coursework, and higher levels of discipline. These factors contribute to academic performance, which is generally stronger in private schools than in public schools.[72] Even within the public school system, inequalities exist due to differences in state funding and income levels within individual school districts. At the college level, the educational gap widens as a result of financial inequality; with annual tuition costing at least $3,000 a year even at a state-supported institution and most private university tuition fees exceeding $40,000, few low-income families can afford higher education.

Conflict theorists also believe that religion supports social inequality by legitimizing the status quo. For example, in British society, the head of the church is also the head of the state—the monarch. Thus, to challenge the political system is to challenge the church, effectively questioning the will of God. According to conflict theorists, religion also serves as a diversion, distracting people from the inequalities and injustices of their present situation in the hope of improved conditions in the afterlife. Karl Marx famously described religion as the "opiate of the masses"—a social institution that persuades families to accept the cards they are dealt rather than fight to improve their lot.[73]

> ∧
> ∧ Schools act as a socializing
> ∧ agent, **teaching children shared cultural norms and values such as the importance of learning to take turns and listen to the opinions of other students.** In what ways will this benefit the child's family life?

SYMBOLIC INTERACTIONISM

Symbolic interactionists consider how individuals create the reality of their daily lives through their interactions with others. For example, in the context of education, students' self-perception may influence how they perform in class. At the beginning of *Stand and Deliver*, Mr. Escalante's students believed themselves poor students (and subsequently performed poorly in class) because daily interactions with most teachers reinforced the stereotypes that they were illiterate, dangerous, and lazy.

An experiment performed by a teacher shortly after the assassination of Martin Luther King, Jr., in 1968 supported this idea of a self-fulfilling prophecy. When elementary school teacher Jane Elliott discovered that her all-white third grade class[74] held racist views about black people, she conducted an experiment on stereotypes. Noticing that all her children had either brown or blue eyes, she told them that children

WRAP YOUR MIND AROUND THE THEORY

Functionalists believe that education promotes meritocracy, **in which everyone is able to progress academically, regardless of their background.** Do you believe that schools promote upward mobility, **or do they help reproduce the class structure within society?**

FUNCTIONALISM

Functionalists believe that schools assist families by acting as additional socializing agents, fostering the notion of upward mobility and helping children to integrate into a culturally diverse society. By teaching children cultural norms and values, educators act as substitute parents, instilling ideas that will enable students to become productive members of society. Religion contributes to the operation of society by acting as a form of social cohesion and control and by providing children and families with a greater purpose.

Critics of functional theory argue that this account overlooks the problems within education and religion, such as the tendency for schools to reproduce the class system that exists within society, favoring privileged students over disadvantaged minorities. Strongly held religious beliefs often result in conflict rather than social cohesion, with many wars and acts of terror conducted in the name of religion.

CONFLICT THEORY

Conflict theorists believe that social institutions perpetuate social inequalities. Low-income and minority students may be denied access to many of the resources enjoyed by students from privileged backgrounds. A classic report by sociologist James Coleman confirmed that schools with large populations of color have larger class sizes, insufficient libraries, and fewer science labs.[76] However, the report also highlighted the importance of social capital—even with unlimited financial resources, a student will not succeed without the support of parents who value education.

Does education really promote social inequality? Critics point to the considerable resources dedicated to helping low-income families achieve academic success, such as flexible tracking assignments that enable students to progress from lower academic groups, the equal distribution of tax money in some states, the expansion of state-funded community colleges, and the plethora of scholarship programs geared toward students from low-income and minority families.

HOW DO SOCIAL INSTITUTIONS SUPPORT FAMILIES?

SYMBOLIC INTERACTIONISM

From a symbolic interactionist perspective, we develop a sense of self through our interactions with others. Our interpretations of these interactions often create self-fulfilling prophecies. Symbolic interactionists believe that students' academic performances are related to their self-perception. Families and teachers play a vital role in influencing these perceptions, and strong role models like Mr. Escalante in *Stand and Deliver* can change negative attitudes by instilling in students a sense of self-worth and self-esteem. Similarly, religious symbols acquire whatever meaning we give them, strengthening marriage bonds for couples who believe their union has been consecrated by God.

Critics of symbolic interaction theory argue that beliefs about superiority and inferiority are not created through individual interactions, but are ingrained in society. For example, the teachers at Mr. Escalante's school did not point out individual students but rather discounted the entire Hispanic class as "illiterate."

Conflict theorists view education as a means of promoting social inequality. Do you agree that children from **privileged families have an unfair advantage** when it comes to academic success?

Symbolic interactionists believe that we develop a sense of self through our interactions with others. Can one significant role model change a person's entire self-concept?

with brown eyes were smarter and worked harder than children with blue eyes. Within a short period of time, the children had fallen into their assigned roles, with the brown-eyed children performing better, speaking up more in class, and behaving in an advanced manner, while the blue-eyed children lost self-confidence and began underperforming. Elliott later used the lesson to teach her class about the negative impact of racial stereotypes.[75] Such stereotypes are learned not only within school but also within families. Daily interactions with family members influence our views both of ourselves (for example, if parents repeatedly tell younger children they are smart, brave, or scatterbrained, they tend to believe them) and of other people (for example, consistent disparaging remarks about groups of people).

Similarly, with regard to religion, symbolic interactionists believe that we create our own reality. Nothing inherent in a cross indicates that it is anything more than a shape. However, for Christians, the cross is a symbol of special significance because it represents the sacrifice made by Jesus Christ. Various rituals—such as Passover, Eid al-Fitr, and Christmas—help reinforce distinctions between the sacred and the profane. Marriage may have different implications for people who ascribe religious meaning to the union. When people believe that they have been joined together by God, the union acquires a significance that does not exist in a simple legal contract, making it harder to break the agreement. This may partly explain why divorce levels are lower among people with strong religious beliefs—for many, "'til death do us part" is a promise made to a higher power.

discover marriages and families in action:
HOW ARE FAMILY THERAPISTS RESPONDING TO DIVERSITY WITHIN MARRIAGES AND FAMILIES?

Family Diversity and Family Therapy

In earlier chapters, we discussed what comprises a family and how family structures have changed in recent years. Increases in the number of gay and lesbian households, cohabiting couples, and single-parent households have altered the typical composition of an American "family." Changes to the family coupled with an increased recognition and appreciation of minority groups and an end to some discriminatory laws and practices have altered the way that marriage and family therapists respond to diversity within families.

The trend toward acknowledging and studying diversity is highlighted in the number of research articles published in family therapy journals. Of the 1,850 articles published in *Journal of Marital and Family Therapy* and *Family Process* between 1970 and 2000, 208 articles (11.2 percent) were devoted to family diversity.[77] Of these, the primary issues considered were gender, followed by race, ethnicity, and culture, then divorce, and finally sexual orientation.

GENDER AND FAMILY THERAPY

Many of the articles regarding gender concern the issue of abuse. Over the past few decades, family therapists have moved away from viewing interdependence as the main problem within abusive relationships. No longer do they work with a couple to resolve their problems at the risk of further endangering an abused woman. Instead, family therapists recognize the vulnerability of the abused partner, hold the abuser accountable for his or her actions, and focus on altering the underlying values and beliefs that sustain abuse.[78] This trend has mirrored legal and political changes within society that have placed domestic violence at the forefront of national attention. For example, the passing of the 1994 Violence Against Women Act increased funding to domestic violence groups and increased the punishments for crimes based on gender.

Therapists have also increasingly explored the effects of gender on men in families. With an increasing number of single-parent families, interest has grown regarding the influence of absent fathers and how therapists can work with absent fathers in therapy.[79] For example, in 2008, President Obama raised the issue of absent fathers at a black church in Chicago, highlighting the disproportionate number of absentee fathers in the African American community.[80]

ACTIVITIES

1. Think of an example of how family diversity could affect religion, education, politics, and the legal system.
2. Visit the personnel or human resource office at your college or university. Ask staff members about their hiring policies concerning the religious or educational backgrounds of prospective employees.
3. Think of a problem faced by families within society. Design a social policy regarding that issue.

MAKE CONNECTIONS

Social Institutions and the Family

As you have learned in this chapter, all social institutions affect the family in some shape or form. Issues regarding particular social institutions may be more relevant to some families than others. For example, participating in the political process may be extremely important to some families and insignificant to others.

The legal issues surrounding abortion may be more important to members of a religious pro-life family than to members of a nonreligious family. In Chapter 8, we learned how some couples are unable to have children for one reason or another. To these couples, abortion may seem like a selfish or senseless action.

Earlier in this chapter, we learned that education is an important socializing agent that teaches children skills they need later in life and instills cultural norms and values. In Chapter 4, we learned how poor socialization results in serious problems within families.

>>> ACTIVITY Research political groups and organizations on the Internet. Find out which political groups or organizations support a specific agenda with which you agree. Create an advertisement for a specific group or organization.

12 **HOW** DO SOCIAL INSTITUTIONS SUCH AS EDUCATION, RELIGION, POLITICS, AND THE LEGAL SYSTEM IMPACT MARRIAGES AND FAMILIES?   205

Children tend to do well at school, regardless of social background, when their parents are involved in the educational process. Historically, teachers have discouraged parent involvement. However, this trend is shifting as a result of social forces, such as immigration. Religion shapes cultural norms in families, and religious couples typically have lower divorce rates and lower levels of conflict. Regular family discussions about politics encourage children's involvement in political activities. Current legal issues regarding the family include covenant marriage, gay marriage, gay adoption, child care, and abortion.

HOW DO DIFFERENT THEORISTS VIEW MARRIAGES AND FAMILIES IN THE CONTEXT OF SOCIAL INSTITUTIONS?   213

Structural functionalists believe that social institutions such as religion and education act as socializing agents that help maintain stability within society. Conflict theorists believe that social institutions perpetuate social inequalities. For example, they believe that underprivileged children receive a lower-quality education than children from wealthier families. Symbolic interactionists believe that individuals create their own experiences within social institutions; therefore they believe that strong educational or religious role models can influence children's self-perceptions.

HOW ARE FAMILY THERAPISTS RESPONDING TO DIVERSITY WITHIN MARRIAGES AND FAMILIES?   215

Family therapists are acknowledging and studying diversity within families and adapting their strategies. Issues such as domestic violence are treated differently today than they were 30 years ago as a result of changing social, legal, and political perspectives.

Theory

FUNCTIONALISM   213
- social institutions such as schools assist families by acting as additional socializing agents
- religion contributes to the operation of society by acting as a form of social cohesion and control and by providing children and families with a greater purpose

CONFLICT THEORY   213
- social institutions perpetuate inequalities within society
- the education system ensures that children from privileged backgrounds obtain better resources than children from low-income families, whereas religion supports social inequality by legitimizing the status quo

SYMBOLIC INTERACTIONISM   213
- individuals are shaped through their interactions with others, and their interpretations of these interactions often result in self-fulfilling prophecies
- teachers and religious leaders can act as role models and help develop a child's self-concept

Key Terms

social institution is the component in the social structure that addresses a basic social need   204

education is a social institution by which society provides its members with knowledge that

includes basic facts, job skills, and cultural norms and values   205

cultural beliefs are personal beliefs particular to a culture that may influence the power relationship between parents and school   206

social structures are changes in family structures that may influence the power relationship between parents and school   206

economic influences are economic factors that may influence the power relationship between parents and school   206

political pressures are governmental pressures that may influence the power relationship between parents and school   *206*

religion is a social institution involving beliefs and practices based on recognizing and elevating the sacred above the profane   *207*

sacred refers to objects or concepts that inspire awe and respect   *207*

profane refers to everyday elements of ordinary life   *207*

religious pluralism is the existence of religious diversity within a community   *208*

political system is a social institution based on an established set of practices for applying and realizing a society's goals   *208*

liberals are individuals on the left of the political spectrum; generally associated in modern times with the Democratic party   *208*

Shinto is the native Japanese religion that emphasizes a love of nature   *209*

conservatives are individuals on the right of the political spectrum; generally associated in modern times with the Republican party   *209*

political socialization is the process by which people acquire political knowledge, beliefs, and values   *209*

partisanship is the support of a particular political party   *210*

marriage gap is the political disparities between those who are married and those who are single   *210*

family policy is the range of services funded and sponsored by the government that affect families directly or indirectly   *211*

covenant marriage is a heterosexual union that imposes strict regulations on entering and exiting the marriage in an effort to reduce divorce rates   *211*

gay marriage is a union of a same-sex couple with all the legal rights guaranteed by the federal government to traditional married couples   *211*

Sample Test Questions

MULTIPLE CHOICE

These multiple-choice questions are similar to those found in the test bank that accompanies this textbook.

1. Which of these factors increases the likelihood that a child will receive a good education?
   a. homeschooling
   b. strong community support
   c. limited parental involvement
   d. living in a single-parent family

2. Which of these statements is TRUE about religion and the family?
   a. Religious couples are just as likely to get divorced as nonreligious couples.
   b. Religious couples are more likely to submit to traditional gender roles when it comes to housework.
   c. Most Americans believe that the influence of religion on family life is increasing.
   d. Discussing religion positively benefits child development, regardless of the tone of the discussion.

3. An individual with politically conservative views MOST LIKELY believes that:
   a. the government does not do enough to help low-income families.
   b. gay marriage should be legalized in all 50 states.
   c. the law banning partial-birth abortions should be overturned.
   d. individuals and families are responsible for their own well-being.

4. Why do some researchers and family workers oppose covenant marriages?
   a. They believe covenant marriages will lead to higher divorce rates.
   b. They believe covenant marriages are not legally binding.
   c. They believe couples will enter into marriage without due consideration.
   d. They believe strict regulations will cause women to remain in abusive relationships.

5. With which of these statements would a conflict theorist MOST LIKELY agree?
   a. Education contributes to a stable society by teaching children vital skills.
   b. Students' academic performances are related to their self-perception.

c. Standardized tests are inherently biased against children from minority families.
d. The education system promotes upward social mobility regardless of social background.

ESSAY

1. Choose one social institution (education, religion, politics, the legal system) and discuss the impact it has on families in the United States.

2. Discuss the arguments for and against government intervention in family life.

3. How can families influence their children's educational outcomes?

4. Choose a political viewpoint and develop an argument for a change in legal policy regarding gay marriage or gay adoption.

5. Discuss how changing family structures have altered the way family therapists view and treat families.

WHERE TO START YOUR RESEARCH PAPER

For more data on educational attainment in the United States, go to http://www.census.gov/population/www/socdemo/educ-attn.html

For more information about homeschooling in the United States, go to http://nces.ed.gov/pubs2006/homeschool/

For more information about the history of parental involvement in education, go to http://www.ed.gov/pubs/EdReformStudies/SysReforms/shields1.html

For more data on religion in the United States, go to http://www.census.gov/compendia/statab/cats/population/religion.html

To learn more about how liberals and conservatives view current political issues, go to http://www.studentnewsdaily.com/other/conservative-vs-liberal-beliefs/

For more information about family policy in the United States, go to http://www.familyandparenting.org/familyPolicyDigest

To find out more about the legal status of same-sex marriage, go to http://www.ncsl.org/default.aspx?tabid=16430

For global statistics on social institutions, including education and religion, go to http://www.nationmaster.com/index.php

ANSWERS: 1. b; 2. b; 3. d; 4. d; 5. c

Remember to check www.thethinkspot.com for additional information, downloadable flashcards, and other helpful resources.

Q WHAT ARE DIFFERENT STRESSORS THAT CAN
LEAD TO VIOLENCE AND ABUSE?
WHAT ARE SOME THEORIES THAT CAN EXPLAIN
VIOLENCE AND ABUSE?
HOW CAN SUBJECTIVITY ENHANCE DATA
COLLECTION ON DOMESTIC VIOLENCE?

In the

movie *Falling Down*, William "D-Fens" Foster is an average middle-aged man who has recently lost his job as a defense contractor. He is divorced from his wife, Beth, and doesn't have much of a relationship with his young daughter, Adele, because Beth has filed a restraining order against him. Although Foster has never hit her or her daughter, Beth feels he has a "propensity for violence."

One day Foster finds himself stuck in a Los Angeles traffic jam during a hot day. He waits patiently at first and takes in his surroundings: a bus of screaming children, men arguing on their cell phones, and a pesky fly buzzing around his head. Horns start to blare as Foster discovers that his car's air-conditioning has died. In the heat, with a long line of stopped cars stretching into the distance before him, Fosters grows impatient. The cacophony of horns, voices, and noises begin to irritate him. His frustration builds until, at last, he grabs his briefcase and abandons his car in the middle of the traffic jam.

Thus begins Foster's journey on foot through Los Angeles to his daughter's birthday party. Along the way he encounters various situations that he feels are unjust. In the past Foster would have tolerated these situations without resorting to violence, but in his current frame of mind Foster loses control. An argument with a convenience store clerk over excessively high prices quickly turns violent. Foster grabs the clerk's bat and smashes the store's shelves. Next a confrontation with two gang members leads Foster to attack the gang members with the baseball bat and take their switchblade. Later the gang members retaliate by trying to shoot Foster. When they crash their car, Foster takes their gun and shoots one of them in the leg.

After a string of these violent encounters, Foster begins looking for more. He launches a missile and blows up a construction site. He frightens a golfer with his weapons so much that the man has a heart attack. Despite the man's pleas, Foster leaves him to suffer.

During his journey, Foster makes several calls to his ex-wife. Each call becomes more and more threatening. Fearing for her safety, Beth calls the police.

When Foster finally approaches Beth's home, Beth takes Adele and flees. Inside Beth's house, Foster watches old home videos from Adele's previous birthdays and sees how happy they used to be as a family. But the video also reveals strain between Foster and Beth when he tried to force a frightened Adele to ride a toy horse.

Two police detectives, Prendergast and Torres, arrive at Beth's house. Foster shoots Torres and flees to Beth's favorite place, a nearby pier. There he finds his ex-wife and daughter and pulls out a gun. Prendergast follows him to the pier. During his conversation with Foster, Beth and Adele manage to escape. Prendergast aims his gun at Foster, who is shocked to learn that he has become "the bad guy." He moves to pull out a weapon. The detective shoots him just as he realizes that Foster had pulled out a water pistol.

STRESS, VIOLENCE, AND ABUSE IN MARRIAGES AND FAMILIES

CHAPTER 13

What lessons can we learn from *Falling Down*? **The movie** depicts ordinary people **with** everyday problems **that** manifest **themselves in** different ways.

Relatively common family problems such as marital separation, job loss, forced retirement, and the loss of a child can cause feelings of fear, inadequacy, frustration, and blame. These factors often create a deep divide between husbands and wives, as in the case of Foster and Beth, as well as between parents and children. Law enforcement also plays a role in situations of stress and violence. Although it is often effective, in some instances law enforcement doesn't protect victims.

Falling Down emphasizes how ordinary and even seemingly trivial situations can cause people suffering from stress to deviate from their behavior and act inappropriately. Foster is unable to deal with what he perceives to be an accumulation of injustices. The clerk at a convenience store won't give him change unless he buys something. He feels cheated at a fast food restaurant when what they serve him doesn't look like the advertised meal. These incidents, which many would consider mere irritations, spark Foster's violent outbursts.

The central message of *Falling Down* is that stress can drive a seemingly normal person to abnormal behavior. Foster's wife demonstrates one way that people deal with stress: They react with fear and withdrawal from life. Foster, on the other hand, demonstrates a more volatile reaction. It is significant that the name of Foster's character is unknown through most of the film. He is presented as an average, middle-aged man who has firm ideas about what is right and wrong. Yet his stress, anger, frustration, and sense of injustice cause him to go on a rampage. At the end of his journey, an incredulous Foster asks, "I'm the bad guy? How did that happen?" How, indeed, did circumstances lead this everyman not to notice the harm he was causing?

The other day at the grocery store I saw my friend Flo (not her real name). We hadn't seen each other for several months, so we hugged and spent some time catching up. She said that her parents were going downhill quickly, particularly her 86-year-old mother. Flo got teary-eyed as she discussed the stress and frustration of trying to care for her mom while working full-time and caring for her children. She also had a son serving in Iraq and another son about to deploy to Kuwait. Although her husband helps, Flo is very frustrated because her mom's condition has deteriorated so much that she says things that don't make sense and behaves erratically. Flo is overloaded. Like many people in our society, she is stressed-out.

In this chapter we will learn about stress and how to cope with it. We will also examine violence and abuse in families.

Stress, Violence, and Abuse

usually begins with

Stressors - events or transitions that cause change

can lead to

Crisis - an unstable conditions in which there aren't sufficient resources to manage the situation

Recovery depending on:
• **resiliency** - the ability to function within one's own pattern or create new patterns in the face of adversity or crisis
• perception of the stressor
• resources

when this is added to

Family violence - intentional abusive behavior against a family member
Domestic violence - intentional abusive behavior against an intimate partner
Intimate partner violence - intentional physical, emotional, or sexual abuse between partners or spouses

there is a higher risk of

• a need to control
• past experience of abuse
• poor social skills
• low self-esteem

get the topic: WHAT ARE DIFFERENT STRESSORS THAT CAN LEAD TO VIOLENCE AND ABUSE?

The stress level of Americans is on the rise. According to recent studies, financial concerns are the chief culprit for our growing anxiety. The current economic climate is certainly troubling Americans.[1] The rising cost of basic goods and services is also a major source of stress.[2] Other stressors include health concerns, sleeping troubles, pressure from work, and a general sense of feeling overwhelmed.

> **FAMILY STRESS** is a real or imagined imbalance between the demands on the family and the family's ability to meet those demands.
>
> **CRISIS** is an unstable condition in which there is a lack of sufficient resources to manage the situation.
>
> **COPE** is to manage and confront stress.

Stress

In *Falling Down*, Foster and his family are trying to come to terms with a newly defined situation. Foster has been laid off from his job. His wife doesn't want him around her or their daughter. This situation creates stress that affects the entire family.

Family stress is defined as "a real or imagined imbalance between the demands on the family and the family's ability to meet those demands."[3] These demands—also called stressors—are often events or transitions that cause change in a family.[4] Often, the way that family members perceive these stressors, combined with their ability to resolve conflicts and communicate with one another, determines whether or not the stressors cause a family **crisis**.[5] It is not uncommon for U.S. families to face big changes. Changes in marital status, employment, residence, finances, and school can cause stress that the family has to **cope** with, or manage.

Researchers have classified stress into two main categories: circumstances that cause stress and reactions to stress. The ability to cope with stress determines whether a reaction is positive or negative. Often, unwanted and unanticipated changes have a more negative outcome.[6] Researchers have found that if more stressful circumstances exist prior to a stressful event, the reaction may not be so negative.[7,8] For example, in the case of Foster, if the mother-father relationship prior to divorce was tumultuous, their daughter may feel better about the divorce and suffer less stress. On the other hand, if she didn't notice much friction prior to the divorce, her reaction to the change may be more severe.

TYPES OF STRESSORS

In 1967, Thomas Holmes and Richard Rahe created the Social Readjustment Rating Scale. Although the Social Readjustment Rating Scale is over 40 years old, it is still widely used today. The scale rates the effect of different stressors revolving around the family. On their scale, the higher the score, the more stressful the event. For example, the death of a spouse has a mean value of 100 while minor violations of the law have a mean value of 11.

Stressors from Outside the Family

Stressors are not only limited to those listed by Holmes and Rahe. Stressors may also originate outside the family, such as difficult economic times, disasters, school bullying, or violence in the community.[9] Children who constantly observe violence are likely to suffer long-term negative effects such as substance abuse, anxiety, depression, and post-traumatic stress.[10] The fear of natural and national disasters, as well as a community's slow recovery from a disaster, can also have long-term effects.[11] Bullying at school may cause preadolescent and adolescent children stress.[12]

MANAGING STRESS

Every family experiences some form of stress. As previously discussed, there are several factors that contribute to stress. Different families and marriages cope with stress in a multitude of ways. Why do some families successfully cope with a traumatic situation as others seem to fall apart?

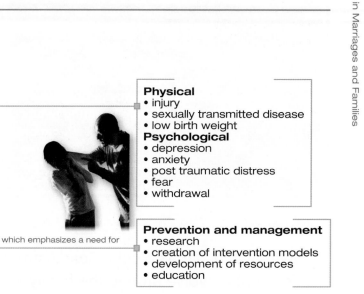

whose effects may be

Physical
• injury
• sexually transmitted disease
• low birth weight
Psychological
• depression
• anxiety
• post traumatic distress
• fear
• withdrawal

and can lead to

Ending the cycle of violence
• seeking help
• victim leaving abuser
• crisis intervention

A continual cycle of violence
• abuser repeats abusive behavior
• victim becomes the abuser

which emphasizes a need for

Prevention and management
• research
• creation of intervention models
• development of resources
• education

Holmes and Rahe's Social Readjustment Scale

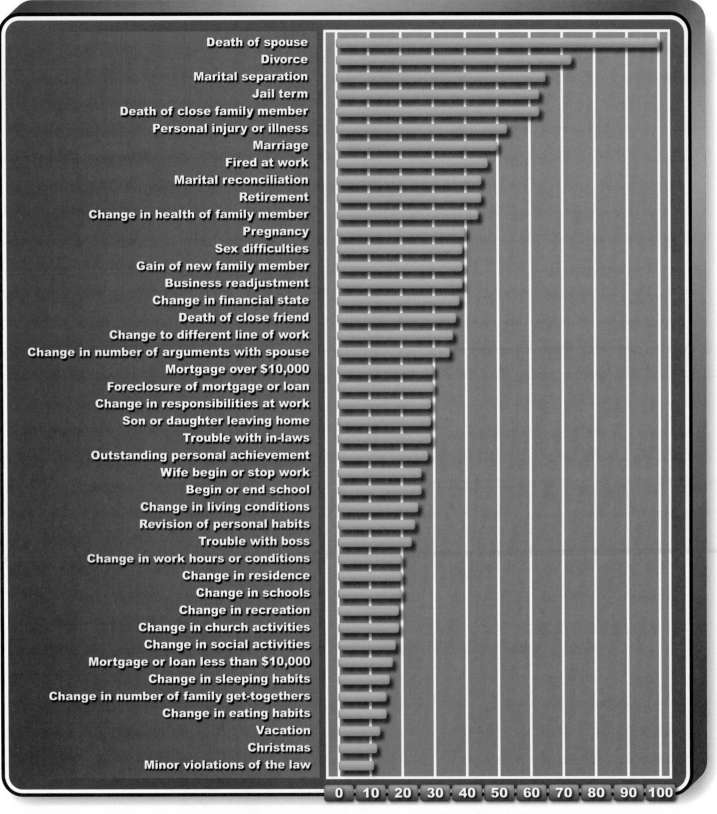

Source: Holmes, T., and R. Rahe, "The Social Readjustment Rating Scale," *Journal of Psychometric Research,* 1967. 11:213-218.

∧ Holmes and Rahe's Social Readjustment Rating Scale shows that the **most stressful**
∧ **life events revolve around the family.** For example, parents argue over a lost job or a new baby enters the household. **How would you rate these stressors?**

Resiliency

According to Hamilton McCubbin, **resiliency** is a family's ability to continue to function along established patterns of behavior despite stressful changes. However, resiliency also involves the ability to make changes to family patterns, if necessary, to function. Families with **elasticity** have the ability to "bounce back" from trauma or crisis. Part of resiliency is a family's **buoyancy**, or ability to keep afloat despite adversity.[13]

McCubbin points to several critical **recovery factors**, or qualities, that help a family overcome stress and/or crises. Various studies show that the ability of the family to recover from a crisis is due to family stability. Sources of stability include optimism, extended family support, recreation, routine, hope, spirituality, good communication, fairness, and a sense of order in the family system. Also significant is a family's ability to make adaptations that contribute to the functioning of the family's routine. A shared sense of values, beliefs, and rules is also an important factor in family recovery.[14] Family "hardiness," or the willingness to rally together, also helps a family confront crises.[15]

Researchers have also examined the characteristics of resilient individuals. These studies have focused on children who have overcome various crises, such as abuse, or found success despite conditions such as low socioeconomic status. The results show that resilient individuals possess good communication and problem-solving skills. They are socially competent, even-tempered individuals with a sense of autonomy, and yet they have the ability to ask for help from others. Additionally, resilient individuals have a tendency to believe in their value and purpose in life.[16]

Be Proactive

Research suggests that coping with stressful situations is often easier when individuals, partners, married couples, and families take a proactive approach. Stress can occur in many different kinds of situations. Although stress is often associated with negative situations, a stressor may be a positive situation or circumstance, such as marriage.[17] Personality and individual perceptions of a situation not only determine the level of stress, but also dictate how one copes with stress.[18,19]

Celia Ray Hayhoe suggests "the 5 Rs" as strategies for coping with stress: rethink, reorganize, reduce, release, and relax. Rethinking goals

in light of a new set of circumstances and reorganizing priorities accordingly can assist in coping. Reducing involves stepping back from activities. In other words, learning to stop biting off more than you can chew. By reducing the number of activities, the feelings of overwhelming anxiety should subside. This does not mean that everything should just be tossed to the side the moment overwhelming feelings start to surface. It means that realistic priorities should be placed on each task—what has to be accomplished, what would be nice to accomplish, and what does not need to be accomplished.[20] Releasing stress through physical activity and relaxing with the help of meditation or another restful activity can also have a positive effect on one's ability to cope with stress.[21] Relaxing allows the stress to take a backseat. Through methods such as meditation or deep breathing, one's focus can be placed on the moment as it is right now, rather than on worrying about all the what-ifs that the future holds.

Stressors come in many forms and can build up to cause an individual to act in violent ways. **How do you manage the different stressors in your life?**

Theories of Stress and Coping

Theories of coping with stress suggest that stress and its effects depend in part on how an individual or family perceives the source of stress.[22] In other words, one's perception of a change affects the degree of stress one experiences.[23] For example, in *Falling Down*, Beth perceives divorce as a positive change and suffers minimal stress from the decision. Foster perceives the divorce as a negative change and thereby suffers more stress.

Studies show that stressful experiences can be learning experiences, as long as the degree of stress is not too high.[24] Reuben Hill's ABC-X model of family stress shows how the degree of stress is related to the cause, the perception of the change, and the resources, or coping mechanisms, of a family.[25] Thus, according to this model, it stands to reason that a family with more coping resources or a more positive view of change will experience a lesser degree of stress. Carter and McGoldrick's model of family stress looks at stressors in the

∨ Hill's ABC-X model of family stress
∨
∨ shows the relationship between the degree of stress **and a family's perception and** resources to cope with the stressor.

family unit as well as stressors experienced by the family over time due to predictable and unpredictable life changes. The model suggests that stress levels depend on the age and experience of each family member.[26]

What Are Violence and Abuse?

In *Falling Down*, Foster's frustrations and stress due to his divorce and job loss lead him to go on a violent spree. Most people will likely concur that financial difficulties can cause stress. The vast majority of people do not react as Foster did when he lost his job, but could **family violence** be tied to a failing economy? A recent article reports that the nation's economic downturn may have caused increasing rates of domestic violence.[27]

Although anecdotal evidence may suggest a correlation between a bad economy and family violence, finances alone do not predict domestic abuse. It is a common misconception that family violence, also known as **domestic violence**, only affects certain groups, such as women who are poor or of color.[28] According to the National Coalition Against Domestic Violence (NCADV), domestic violence is "the willful intimidation, physical assault, battery, sexual assault, and/or other abusive behavior perpetrated by an intimate partner against another."[29] Statistics from NCADV show that 85 percent of victims of family violence are women, and women between the ages of 20 and 24 years old are at the greatest risk of non-fatal incidents of violence by a partner. However, victims of domestic violence and abuse are found in all demographics, regardless of gender, age, race, economic status, level of education, or religion.[30]

Family violence has both short-term and long-term effects, not only for the victim of violence but also for those that witnessed the violence.

ABC–X Model of Family Stress

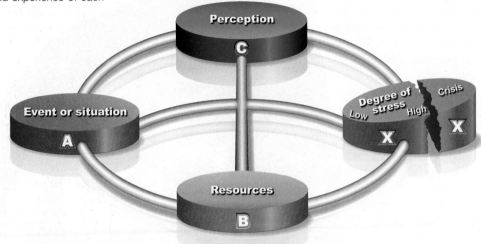

Source: Graphic is based on an image in Boss, Pauline, *Family Stress Management*. (Newbury Park, CA: Sage 1988) in Turner, Lynn H., and Richard West, *Perspectives on Family Communication*. (New York: McGraw-Hill, 2006).

There are the obvious short-term physical effects on the victim; however, long-term physical effects may include untreatable sexually transmitted diseases, ulcers, and even low birth weight in babies born to victims. There are also psychological effects for victims and witnesses. These may include post-traumatic stress disorder, low self-esteem, depression, suicidal thoughts, and high-risk sexual behavior.[31]

Just who are these abusers? As with victims of abuse, it is difficult to provide a demographic profile of an abuser. In many cases, an abuser may give a very different impression to the outside community and may appear to be a well-adjusted and caring individual. Think of how often friends and acquaintances of an abuser say, "I never would have suspected it" upon learning of abuse. Abusers may have been victims or witnesses of abuse themselves as children. Studies show

Balancing Work and Relaxation

Arno is a college sophomore who makes it a point to give himself time to work out and relax every day.

"This isn't about me being narcissistic or lazy; it's a lifeline. I grew up in a toxic family situation. My mom and dad fought constantly, and it often got physical. We kids weren't spared at all either. Stress and fear were basically the air we breathed every day.

"For a long time, I thought I never wanted to have kids. I was just too scared that I would end up being an awful parent. I grew up fearing and hating my own parents, but still wanting them to love me. Now, I mostly feel sorry for them. I think maybe I have a better perspective of how they were incapable of dealing with the difficulties of life.

"I'm learning to deal with stress in a healthy way. It isn't always easy since I didn't have many good role models. What works for me is to have an outlet. That's why I have to give myself part of the day to work out and relax just to release the tension. My girlfriend helps a lot, too, just by listening. I never had that before. A lot of people think that this is an obvious way to cope with stress, but when you grow up like I did, you don't know how to deal with all the messy feelings and tensions."

that there is a greater likelihood for victims or witnesses to become abusers themselves. Abusive behavior seems to stem from the need to control someone else, and many abusers exhibit poor communication and problem-solving skills, low self-esteem, or depression.[32]

A widely reported, extreme case of family violence and abuse was that of Austrian Josef Fritzl. Fritzl held his daughter captive in the basement and fathered her seven children in an incestuous relationship over a period of 24 years.[33] In this victim's case, she stayed with her abuser because she was locked in the basement; however, there are many cases in which victims are not physically prevented from leaving their abusers.

Why do they stay? Studies show that domestic violence is a continual cycle of violence, rather than a specific, isolated instance. These results might help answer the question. The cycle of violence is often categorized into three stages. The first stage is the onset of tension.[34] Sometimes, in this stage, verbal violence first shows its face. The second is the battering that takes place. The battering can take place during any period or amount of time—days, months, or even years.[35] The third and final stage of the cycle explains why women stay with their male abusers—the men show that they feel guilty and are extremely apologetic and remorseful for their violent actions, and the wives lovingly forgive them.[36]

There are many factors that further explain why victims stay with their abusers. One of the primary reasons is that the victim loves her abuser.[37] Additionally, victims often experience feelings of fear, compounded by threats that may be real or perceived. We have already discussed how a lack of resources can impact the degree of stress that an individual feels. In the case of victims of abuse, they often lack resources to overcome their fear and helplessness.[38] Feelings of helplessness are often deemed "learned helplessness," or the feeling that the victim cannot control her relationship with men and thus cannot control her relationship with other aspects of her life.[39] They also see in the final stage of the cycle their forgiving male abuser as the kind, loving spouse they always wanted, and out of love, they forgive again.[40]

Types of Violence and Abuse
INTIMATE PARTNER VIOLENCE

Intimate partner violence occurs in close relationships and is characterized by intentional physical, emotional, or sexual abuse, or intimidation via threats of physical or sexual abuse.[41] Intimate partner violence is not just limited to a partner or spouse. It can also occur as domestic violence between intimate family relations such as parent-child, sibling-sibling, and younger-elder intimates. According to the Centers for Disease Control and Prevention, this type of violence ranges from an isolated abusive event to recurrent abusive behaviors.[42] The effects of this violence can have a severe impact on the individual as well as the family as a whole, and the method by which the individual and the family unit react and handle the maltreatment has repercussions as well.

Female Victims

Statistically, most victims of intimate partner violence are females in heterosexual relationships. Although males experience victimization due to intimate partner violence, the number of cases of physical violence or rape of females is more than three times that of males.[43] Females are also more likely to be victims of nonfatal intimate partner violence, simple assault, aggravated assault, rape and sexual assault, and robberies.[44]

INTIMATE PARTNER VIOLENCE is intentional physical, emotional, or sexual abuse, or intimidation via threats of physical or sexual abuse, typically between partners or spouses, but including other intimate family relations.

WIFE RAPE is forced sex on a female spouse by a male spouse.

Researchers of domestic abuse and intimate partner violence on females have examined different aspects of the victims' experience, as well as their coping mechanisms. Researchers have found that women who were victims of sexual abuse by a family member are at risk for intimate partner violence in their relationships. Furthermore, women who witnessed intimate partner violence as children are more at risk for violence in their partnerships than if they had been victims of violence as children.[45]

Research on **wife rape**, or forced sex on a spouse, is not as common as research on date rape, or physical abuse of a romantic acquaintance. Studies show that people believe forced sex by a husband constitutes rape. However, studies also show mixed opinions, depending on the scenario. For example, studies indicate that people believe the wife is involved in the rape when she "leads on" her husband in a sexual encounter, says "no," and then her husband forces her to have sex.[46]

Researcher Sue Ellen Thomas has studied the perceptions of female victims of psychological abuse and domestic violence. Her research suggests that the main factor driving abusive patterns is control.[47] Demaris and Swinford examine fear and how it relates to partner violence. They found that women who were victims of forced sex or violence by their partners as well as those women who had sought help from counselors, lawyers, and shelters experience higher feelings of fear.[48]

How women cope with intimate partner violence and abuse has been the subject of many studies. In one study, victims of domestic or partner violence gave overall positive helpfulness ratings to the police who responded to their call for help. Overall, the victims found the police to be helpful but did not give such positive ratings for helping the victim find counseling.[49] In *Falling Down*, Beth calls the police on two occasions because she feels threatened by Foster. The fact that she calls the police reflects her positive perception of police intervention, which corresponds to research.

Male Victims

Much attention has been paid to female victims of intimate partner violence. However, researchers are turning their attention to the male victim and the origins of intimate partner abuse of a man by a woman in heterosexual relationships. One important finding is that males are more likely to be victims of dating violence, and women are more likely to be the perpetrators of violence toward men, especially in situations when both partners have been violent.[50]

Furthermore, researchers have isolated the issue of control and dominance in a relationship as a defining predictor of risk for violence, regardless of the gender of the dominant individual. In other words, relationships in which one partner is dominant have a higher probability for violence.[51] These findings undermine traditional assumptions that intimate partner violence is carried out exclusively by men against women.[52]

In *Falling Down*, Detective Prendergast's wife exhibits controlling behaviors. She becomes upset very easily, and he alters his behavior to accommodate her. His former partner, Detective Torres, notices and remarks on this. It is not until the final scene of the movie that we learn that Detective Prendergast and his wife lost their two-year-old daughter to sudden infant death syndrome. Did this single traumatic event trigger a dynamic in which Mrs. Prendergast must control and abuse her husband psychologically? It is clear from their interactions that an imbalance of power exists between them. This imbalance puts the Prendergasts' relationship at risk for abuse, which in this case is psychological.

One critical difference between the male and female abuser is that some women perpetrators of partner violence feed into the common expectation that the woman is the victim.[53] One study examines the dissatisfaction of males when they called the police for help after having been abused by their female partner. Combined with the fact that community resources are typically designed to assist the female victim, this situation has left male victims feeling trivialized and disparaged.[54] Furthermore, people often are less sympathetic to male victims of female abusers because there is a perception that males encourage the female perpetrator.[55]

It is not surprising that differences in perception regarding intimate partner violence exist across gender lines. Even the very language used to describe domestic violence reveals differential treatment of males and females: The passive voice tends to be used more to describe male-to-female violence, whereas the active voice is used more to describe female-to-male violence.[56] This notion seems to be consistent with the way that the media portray male violence to females and female violence to males.[57] A content analysis of the *Boston Globe* showed a passive voice ratio of 2 to 1 in reports covering sexual violence on females in which men were the perpetrators.[58] This difference emphasizes the female's active role and responsibility in a violent act, and according to researchers, such as Alexandra K. Frazer and Michelle D. Miller, the passive voice in media relations puts the victim in a position indicating them as the agent or cause of an action.[59] Regardless of the gender of the perpetrator and victim, researchers have concluded that nonconstructive conflict resolution processes in any relationship, heterosexual or homosexual, may lead to domestic violence.[60]

ABUSE IN SAME-SEX COUPLES

Abuse and violence in homosexual partner relationships have only recently received more media and cultural attention. Research shows that the rate of violence in same sex partnerships is similar to that of heterosexual partnerships.[61,62] What differs is that same-sex partners experiencing violence suffer not only violence in their intimate relationship, but also the added challenges incurred by negative societal perceptions of homosexuality.

Researchers agree that victims of same-sex couple violence experience similar types of violence that heterosexual victims of partner violence experience, but they also note that some victims of same-sex couple aggression tend to be more fearful of serious injury than their heterosexual counterparts.[63]

What are the similarities and differences between same-sex couple violence and heterosexual couple violence? One underlying feature in both scenarios is that the abuser tries to control and dominate the other partner. As a result, the victim may feel fearful and marginalized and may often blame himself or herself for the abuse.[64]

Although the rates and cyclical patterns of abuse are similar across heterosexual and gay couples, there are some distinguishing characteristics unique to gay couple abuse. The abuser in a gay couple may inflict emotional and verbal abuse by threatening the partner with "outing" him or her to others. Additionally, there are many false perceptions that homosexual abuse is mutual and that the partners abuse each other. Many battered gays and lesbians feel isolated and marginalized by a lack of community support, resources, and privacy. This isolation, in combination with challenges such as homophobia, sexism, and other forms of bigotry, present obstacles to victims who want to escape an abusive relationship.[65]

<<< Overall, victims of abuse find police intervention to be helpful.
Why might a victim not welcome police intervention?

Lesbian-to-Lesbian Abuse and Violence

Lesbian abusers tend to have similar personality traits to heterosexual male abusers, with a prevalence of substance abuse, low-self esteem, jealousy, and fear of abandonment. Some lesbian abusers exhibit antisocial disorders or a chronic mental health disorder linked to a dysfunctional perception and relation to others.[66] Some researchers suggest that lesbian violence is characterized more by aggression, rather than violence, with control as a main factor.[67] In other words, the abuser is more likely to try to dominate and control the relationship through violence, threats of outing, and aggression.[68,69] Researchers have also identified **fusion**, or "the intense emotional closeness and high level of interdependence of intimate partners," as a predictor of physically abusive lesbian relationships.[70,71] Researchers also found that the reason that some same-sex partners do not seek help is because they are ashamed or fearful of outsiders' homophobia, or prejudice against homosexuality.

Gay-to-Gay Abuse and Violence

In the case of male same-sex partnerships, the same predictors of violence in heterosexual relationships emerge: Intimate partner violence between males also tends to be cyclical, and abusers and victims have some history in their family of abuse.[72,73] Again, the power dynamic and control have been found to be the deciding factors. Dependency, jealousy, and substance abuse are also predictors of severity of the abuse.[74]

SIBLING-TO-SIBLING ABUSE

Violence and abuse among siblings is a frequent type of abuse.[75] Different from sibling rivalry, sibling-to-sibling abuse can be physical and emotional, with different levels of severity. Researchers have found that the decisive factors are parent instability, favoritism, and inequality in household fairness.[76,77]

Some studies link sibling violence to the socioeconomic status of a family.[78] Sibling violence is often attributed to families who face economic struggles. Researchers also suggest factors such as unemployment and divorce are linked to sibling violence.[79] However, the children's personality characteristics tend to be a greater factor than anything else.[80] In particular, younger children and younger children who are males show more signs of becoming violent toward siblings. Although sibling-to-sibling violence is most often mutual,[81] males are more likely to perpetrate abuse in a sibling relationship, so the percentage of male children in a family is another significant predictor of both severe and non-severe forms of sibling violence.[82]

Parental disciplinary processes and loss of temper also predict the severity of sibling violence.[83,84] Parents who are violent are often less responsive when siblings are violent toward each other. As a result, the child learns that the behavior is accepted and will continue to behave with violent responses.[85] If an individual is exposed to abusive behavior between parents or caretakers or negative parent-child interactions, the sibling relationship is more likely to be abusive or violent.[86] Unlike adults, children are unable to separate themselves from the

abusive situation, so the actions of the parents can sometimes become learned behavior for their children.[87] Similar to spousal abuse, sibling abuse is often brought on by a desire for control and power over another.[88] A sibling's need for control and power can be acted upon by violent means as a result of seeing the struggle between violent parents.[89]

Sibling-to-Sibling Sexual Abuse

Siblings perform the most common form of sexual abuse in families.[90] The United States Department of Health and Human Services, in 2002, reported that 2.3 percent of children had been sexually abused by a sibling.[91] As with other sibling-to-sibling abuse and violence, the family environment plays a critical role in sibling-to-sibling sexual abuse. Studies show that families who have heightened or suppressive attitudes toward sex show an increase in sibling-to-sibling sexual abuse.[92] In addition, the way a family approaches sexual abuse that has occurred is pivotal in the recovery process for the victim as well as for the entire family unit.

PARENT-TO-CHILD ABUSE AND VIOLENCE

Children as a group experience more long-term effects of abuse and violence. Childhood abuse can cause adverse psychological effects (e.g., low self-esteem, depression, and anxiety) and lead to self-destructive behaviors (e.g., suicide, self-mutilation, substance abuse, sexual promiscuity, and eating disorders).[93]

Graham-Bermann and Hughes review several different theoretical models designed to account for the adverse effects that family violence have on children. **Social learning theory** explains that violent and abusive behavior is learned. Simply put, abusive children learn abusive behaviors from the abuser. **Social cognition theory** explains that a child's interpretation of a certain situation may not be as hostile or aggressive as he or

∧
∧ In sibling-to-sibling abusive
∧ relationships, the male sibling is often the perpetrator. **What steps can a parent take to prevent violence among siblings?**

FAMILY SYSTEMS THEORY explains that different traits and coping mechanisms are passed from generation to generation within a family.

TRAUMA THEORY suggests that how a traumatic event is handled determines the extent of trauma that a victim experiences.

SOMATIZATION is the manifestation of physical symptoms from psychological problems.

PERSONAL RESILIENCE is an individual's ability to cope with and manage stress or a crisis.

she may perceive; changing the children's impressions may help children overcome the abusive situation. **Family systems theory** explains that different traits and coping mechanisms are passed from generation to generation within a family. This could be positive for a victim trying to survive sexual abuse. This can also perpetuate a violent cycle should the abusive and violent behavior pass from one generation to the next. Finally, **trauma theory** suggests that how a traumatic event is handled determines the extent of trauma that a victim experiences. If a victim cannot process the information and talk about the experience, he or she will be at risk for maladjustment.[94]

In a study of cases of fatal parent-to-child violence, perhaps the most striking findings were that most infant homicides were committed by the infant's mother and fathers committed more than two-thirds of adolescent homicides.[95]

Parent-to-Child Sexual Abuse and Violence

Sexual abuse on children and adolescents from adults is a prevalent issue in the United States. The effects of adults' sexual abuse on children can be severe, and even more severe when another family member caused the sexual abuse.[96] Female perpetrators tend to be the victim's primary caregiver, while male perpetrators are more likely to not be the primary caregiver. According to research, more girls than boys are abused by male sexual abusers, and female sexual abusers equally abuse both boys and girls.[97] In 2000, the adult perpetrator of sexual violence to children was a male 96 percent of the time. Females comprised 85 percent of the sexual violence victims.[98]

In addition to long-term psychological consequences of child sexual abuse, such as hostility, psychosis, anxiety, phobias, and depression, researchers have examined medical consequences of childhood sexual abuse, such as gastrointestinal problems, chronic pelvic pain, and **somatization**, which are physical symptoms brought about by psychological problems.[99,100,101] Research shows that the stressful events surrounding disclosure of sexual abuse can also cause long-term harm to young victims.[102] Given the much-cited cyclical nature of violence—when the victim becomes the abuser—**personal resilience** helps determine how well the survivor functions later in life.[103]

>>> Care providers at institutions and residential homes are often perpetrators of violence against elders.

As an administrator at a nursing home, how would you ensure that your employees were non-violent?

CHILD-TO-PARENT VIOLENCE AND ABUSE

Despite the common belief that domestic abuse between child and parent usually originates from the parent, a small percentage of incidents involve child-to-parent abuse. Pagani and colleagues have found in two separate studies that childhood violence patterns put adolescents at risk to commit acts of aggression toward their fathers and mothers.[104,105] Furthermore, children who witness parents hitting each other or other children are more likely to commit acts of child-to-parent aggression.[106] Also, the higher the "parent demandingness" toward a child, the more likely the child is to commit an act of domestic violence toward the parent.[107] In general, parental aggression toward a child increases the probability of that child's aggression toward the parent.[108] Brezina has suggested that violence toward the parent is often a survival response that helps the adolescent cope with negative treatment.[109]

ELDER ABUSE

Elder abuse can be physical, emotional, or sexual. Neglect or denying basic care and freedom are also considered forms of elder abuse.[110,111] Elder abuse often takes place at the hands of a caregiver or service provider in an institutional setting.[112] The majority of perpetrators of elderly abuse are somehow related to the victim—usually a child or spouse of the victim.[113] The victim usually relies on the perpetrator for financial support, and the victims of elder abuse tend to be female.[114] Researchers have found that victims of elder abuse are unable to defend themselves and often find it difficult to remove themselves from an abusive situation. This may be due to more traditional concepts of marriage, a lack of resources, and/or dependence on caregivers or service providers for personal and health care.[115] Several theories about what leads to elder abuse, including one theory that elder abuse from children serves as a means to "get even" for the abuse the child endured from the parent while growing up, exist.[116] However, given that elder abuse has only recently begun to be studied, no conclusive research yet exists.[117]

TEEN DATING VIOLENCE AND ABUSE

Dating violence is sexual, physical, or emotional violence that occurs between individuals who are dating. The Centers for Disease Control and Prevention (CDC) report that 25 percent of teens who date have experienced some form of dating violence, whether it is physical, emotional, or sexual. About 10 percent of these adolescents have reported being a victim of some form of physical dating violence.[118,119]

According to the CDC, the perpetrator of dating abuse most likely suffers from low self-esteem and depression. He or she resolves conflicts through violence, lacks anger management and communication skills, and experiences problems in school. Often, the abuser lacks parental supervision and is either the witness, victim, or perpetrator of abuse at home.[120]

Managing and Preventing Violence and Abuse

We have seen that family violence is largely influenced by early exposure to and experiences with violence. However, this is not the only explanation as to why family violence occurs. Violent and aggressive behaviors are learned. Families as well as individual family members can be proactive in protecting themselves and breaking the cycles that perpetuate abuse among intimates. As we learn more about the causes of family violence and understand the profiles of victim, offender, and victim-turned-offender, we as a society can begin to shape an intervention model that takes into account the diversity of victims' experiences as well as the commonalities that underlie and characterize the experiences of both the abuser and the abused. Through developing the

resources and interventions that can educate families as well as individual family members and help prevent violence regardless of severity, society as a whole can further the creation of a nurturing and supportive culture for victims, regardless of their age, sexual orientation, race, religion, or gender.

PROTECTING YOURSELF

There are several things you can do to protect yourself or escape abuse. All victims of abuse—man, woman, or child—may be able to use these same techniques, although each situation is different.

- Create a personal safety plan that identifies safe places and people whom you can trust during a crisis, as well as plans of action.[121]

- Should an abuser attempt to victimize you at work, notify the appropriate people in your workplace and request confidentiality to protect yourself.[122]

- Seek support, whether it is crisis intervention, legal assistance, or medical service.[123]

- If you are planning to leave your partner and fear violence, make sure you have a safety plan before you leave. Set some money aside in a safe place, and choose a place that will ensure your physical safety.

- If possible, urge your abusive partner to seek help through various community resources and advocates.

- Seek help from the appropriate law enforcement authorities, doctors, therapists, legal representation, or advocacy groups.[124]

From Classroom to Community } It Could Be Me

A year ago, Jenna started volunteering at a local shelter for abused women and children as part of a community service requirement.

"When I first started volunteering, I didn't think that I would be able to relate to any of these women or children. My life has always been relatively easy and free from hardship. I didn't even know anyone who had been a victim of abuse or violence.

"As I worked with these people and listened to their stories, I realized that practically the only difference between my story becoming one of their stories was the hand that I had been dealt. I think something resonated with me when I was talking to a woman on my third day here. Serena's background was very similar to mine. She had a loving family, a good job, a stable environment for her daughter. However, the long and drawn-out illness resulting in the death of a family member changed her family dynamic completely.

"During this time, her husband lost his job, and the financial strain added to the stress. She told me that she had always thought her family capable of dealing with stress, but when one thing piled on top of another, they just couldn't cope. It made her fearful, dependent, and withdrawn, and, unfortunately, it made her husband lash out. She said, 'I felt like I had nowhere to turn. I have no idea how my life even got to this point.' When I heard her story I realized that I, or basically anyone, could be in this woman's shoes without the right tools to get through a crisis."

ACTIVITIES

1. Suppose that you are a member of a community awareness organization. A recent report released by the local police department indicates that the number of reported victims of domestic violence has increase 350 percent in your community in the last 10 years. What type of propositions would you recommend to reduce the number of domestic violence victims in your city?
2. Visit your local Child Protective Service offices. Ask them what services they provide to children and families. What type of trends have they witnessed over time? What requirements do they have for a child or family to be taken off the "active case" list?

Violence on a Global Scale

Just as domestic violence transcends age, race, economic status, religion, and educational level, it also transcends borders. Studies suggest that the motivations for committing partner abuse differ. Culture may play a role in both an abuser's rationale for physical abuse as well as in acceptance or approval of domestic abuse. Traditional societies may be more likely to justify or approve the use of violence through measures such as spanking, sexual violence, or honor killings by a male against his spouse or another female family member, particularly where men and women are expected to fulfill traditional roles. In many of these traditional societies, even the women often accept and justify the man's right to discipline his wife by force. However, in developed nations and developing nations, there is a common thread of what sparks the violence. Studies show that the most consistent motivations include disobedience, talking back, parenting styles, finances, suspected infidelity, and—one of the most cited reasons—refusal to have sex.[125]

Physical Assault on Women by an Intimate Male Partner, Selected Population-based Studies, 1982–1999

Country/Area	Year of study	Sample			Proportion of women physically assaulted by a partner (%)	
		Size	Study Population*	Age (years)	During the previous 12 months	Ever
Africa						
South Africa	1998	10190	III	14–49	6	13
Zimbabwe	1996	966	I	≥15		17
Latin America and the Caribbean						
Colombia	1995	6097	II	15–49		
Puerto Rico	1995–1996	4755	III	15–49		13
North America						
Canada	1993	12300	I	≥18	3	29
United States	1995–1996	8000	I	≥18	1.3	22
Asia and Western Pacific						
Cambodia	1996	1374	III	—		16
India	1998–1999	89199	III	15–49	11	19
Europe						
Switzerland	1994–1996	1500	II	20–60	6	21
United Kingdom	1993	430	I	≥16	12	30
Eastern Mediterranean						
Egypt	1995–1996	7121	III	15–49	16	34

*Study population: I = all women; II = currently married/partnered women; III = ever-maried/partnered women

∧ The World Health Organization studied global rates of domestic violence.
∧ What cultural differences might explain the variance of violence in these countries?

think marriages and families: WHAT ARE SOME THEORIES THAT CAN EXPLAIN VIOLENCE AND ABUSE?

Functionalism

A functional theory of violence operates under the premise that violence serves a social function to help individuals attain social status, to set off much needed change in a community, and to warn a community or individual of danger.[126] Under this theoretical framework, researchers have found that family interaction was the key to inhibiting violent family encounters by focusing on the positive interrelationship between members of the family.[127] Additionally, intervention focusing on structural family systems has been found to be more effective than the typical intervention on an individual level for victims and perpetrators of family violence and abuse.[128] The family structure is examined in functional theory, and therapy that in a sense rebuilds the family structure has been shown to strengthen the family system as well as help end the cycle of violence within the family.[129] In other words, by changing the beliefs, norms, and attitudes of violence set deep within the family structure, violence within the family can be lessened.

Conflict Theory

A conflict theory of violence operates under the basic assumption that conflict among humans is unavoidable, and individuals and groups use violence to advance their own agendas. Conflict theory has been applied to family violence as seen through the lens of power and control.[130] Researchers found support for the notion that power and control are two important concepts that differentiate harmful behaviors and abuse that researchers call "intimate terrorism."[131] These researchers found that the defining features of abusive relationships were power and control. Other research has found that there is a "pro-arrest" preference for perpetrators of domestic abuse.[132]

Symbolic Interactionism

Symbolic interaction theory focuses on the meaning of violence and how violence is constructed. Social meanings among parties involved in violent episodes are explored in an effort to understand the dynamics, the encounters between participants of a violent situation, and the cycles of violent episodes.[133] The presentation of violence in American culture compared to other cultures can be examined through a symbolic interaction theory approach. For example, the presentation of violence through the media, video games, and even gun laws can shape the norms within American

Theoretical Explanations of Family Violence

Functionalism

Operates under the premise that violence serves a social function to

- help individuals attain social status
- set off much needed change
- warn a community or individual of danger

Conflict Theory

Operates under the basic premises that

- conflict among humans is unavoidable
- individuals and groups use violence to advance their own agendas
- conflict management is the way to bring about change

Symbolic Interactionism

- Focuses on the meaning of violence
- Explores how violence is constructed: dynamics, encounters between participants of a violent situation, cycles of violent incidents
- Examines social meanings among parties

∧
∧ Functionalism, conflict theory, and symbolic interactionism **are a few of the**
∧ **conceptual frameworks that researchers have** used to try to understand and explain the nature of violence and its effects on the individual and society. **Which theory presents ideas that you would agree with?**

WRAP YOUR MIND AROUND THE THEORY

Functionalists believe that positive family interaction can assist in preventing violent or abusive episodes. **What types of positive family interaction do you think can aid in providing a stable family structure?**

FUNCTIONALISM

When seen through the lens of functionalism, family violence is viewed as a vehicle for perpetrators of violence to attain social status when other means of advancing are not accessible. These acts of violence then act as agents of change in a community as well as warn the community of danger. Service providers and researchers focus on the positive interactions and relationships among family members in the intervention and prevention of violence. Violence may occur when negative emotions are purged through an aggressive act. Families that have more positive interactions, such as communication around the dinner table or a fun day playing at the park, are more likely to have a decreased level of negative emotions and therefore a reduced risk of violence.

CONFLICT THEORY

Conflict theory assumes that violence is a normal feature of the human experience, and conflict among humans is unavoidable. Perpetrators inflict violence on others so that they may advance their own interests or status. This violence is often used because other channels to seek change are blocked, unavailable, or exhausted. This perspective on violence operates under the model that conflict causes a confrontation, often violent, and in turn brings about change. The issue of power and control and its relationship to violence has been widely studied under the conflict theory. Power and control dynamics are part of the everyday human experience, which often lead to confrontation due to parties vying for dominance. These confrontations, that may come in the form of violent acts, then set off a change either in the power dynamic, the individual, or the community.

WHY DO PEOPLE COMMIT FAMILY VIOLENCE?

SYMBOLIC INTERACTIONISM

The meaning of violence and how individuals interpret social contexts is the focus of symbolic interaction theory. The individual's self-concept and understanding of social context and events figure into understanding how violence is constructed. Symbolic interaction theory explores social dynamics, interactions, and encounters, as well as how one may interpret those social dynamics, interactions, and encounters to gain insight into the cycle of violence. Social meaning plays an important role in our understanding of the behavior of both victim and perpetrator alike.

Conflict theory suggests that violence is a means for individuals to resolve conflict and assert their own control. **In what ways might this manifest itself in cases of domestic abuse?**

According to symbolic interaction theory, the meaning ascribed to an episode can account for the individual's behavior. **Can you think of a situation where the perceptions of each party in a violent episode may differ?**

culture. When violence and aggression are norms in greater society, they become norms within the family structure.[134] Symbolic interaction also examines the emerging self in the context and meaning of a situation. In this model, the meaning of the context of a situation or episode to the individual should be examined to try to account for an individual's behavior.[135] For example, one study on family violence research found that females who display more masculine traits are more likely to be perpetrators of violence.[136] Another example would be the feeling of "learned helplessness," which was discussed earlier in the chapter.

discover marriages and families in action:
HOW CAN SUBJECTIVITY ENHANCE DATA COLLECTION ON DOMESTIC VIOLENCE?

Researcher Niveditha Menon studied both domestic violence in cultural and familial contexts in India and the coping mechanisms of the women subject to abuse. Menon suggests that because a researcher has power and control over how the study participants' narrative will be interpreted and told to the greater audience, there should be some element of subjectivity to contextualize the participants' experiences.

When interviewing women for her study, Menon found that information that might otherwise have been lost could be gleaned through subjectivity. Over the course of five months of semi-structured interviews with Indian women, she found that two important factors in their coping strategies were their financial resources, which may have been economic independence or some type of financial support, and their familial resources, in terms of emotional support. Menon found that women's access to at least one of these resources was influential in their ability to be proactive in terminating the abusive relationship either by leaving or stopping the violent cycle.

Menon found that being attuned to certain non-objective aspects of research was helpful in gathering valuable information about the participants. Participants' silences, refusal to answer questions, and avoidance of certain topics gave her insight to the women's "overall life narratives." For example, in several cases the women preferred to talk about their poverty and financial lack of control instead of talking about their experiences with domestic violence. This helped Menon assess the importance women gave the violence.

She found that women without independent financial resources tended to perceive the violence as having little importance in the face of poverty.

Menon suggests that this kind of subjective information can help contextualize the participants' experience, not only in a broader social framework, but also in its emotional context. Approaching research as both quantitative and qualitative can help enhance the power of the knowledge gained in order to effect social change that will have a real impact on the women.[137] Menon's approach to research allowed her to examine further violence in India in ways that it had not before been examined. She was able to examine the two primary forms of domestic violence in India—situational couple violence and intimate terrorism—as well as the coping mechanisms used by Indian women in dealing with these two particular forms of domestic violence.[138]

ACTIVITY

Research the issues and dilemmas of collecting data on domestic violence and abuse. Are there specific issues that need to be taken into consideration when dealing with various populations such as minors and same-sex relationships?

MAKE CONNECTIONS

Reconnecting with the Family

All families experience stress. Stress can weaken the family, but frequently it creates many new family opportunities to grow and be strengthened. Throughout this chapter, you learned how individuals, couples, and families cope with stress and become stronger and more resilient.

As you have learned in this chapter, violence and abuse exist everywhere. No individual, couple, or family is immune from the possibility of violence and abuse. However, there are certain things that families can do to protect themselves from the likelihood of violence and abuse.

In Chapter 2, we discussed family stressors and family strengths as a way to study marriage and the family. Remember reading earlier that this is part of the natural development of relationships? Looking ahead, in Chapter 16 we will discuss how commitment and a positive attitude goes a long way in creating a successful and effective family.

>>> ACTIVITY

Plan and organize a fun family activity that requires the family to talk to each other free of distractions. No technical toys allowed (including cell phones).

WHAT ARE DIFFERENT STRESSORS THAT CAN LEAD TO VIOLENCE AND ABUSE? 221

Stress is the real or perceived inability to meet demands as a result of events or situations that cause change. The degree of stress depends on the stressor itself, an individual's or family's perception of the stressor, and the resources available to cope with the change. Stressors can range from predictable and unpredictable life events both within the family structure and outside the family structure. Most stressors stem from events that revolve around the family such as death of a family member, divorce, and money problems. Although some stressors may be positive, such as marriage, negative stressors and an individual's or family's inability to manage and cope with stress may lead to violence and abuse.

WHAT ARE SOME THEORIES THAT CAN EXPLAIN VIOLENCE AND ABUSE? 231

Functional theory suggests that violence serves a social function, helping bring about needed change. Conflict theory is based on the idea that conflict is unavoidable and that violence is used by people to advance their own agendas. The theory of symbolic interaction focuses on examining the meaning of violence as well as the social meaning that different parties attach to it.

HOW CAN SUBJECTIVITY ENHANCE DATA COLLECTION ON DOMESTIC VIOLENCE? 233

Subjectivity can enhance data collection on domestic violence by contextualizing the study participants' experiences. Including more subjective aspects of information can actually increase knowledge and provide clues and insights that might otherwise be missed. Being cognizant of the power and control relationships between the researcher, the participants, and the audience can provide a broader context for the subject, which can give the end result a greater impact in effecting social change.

Theory

FUNCTIONALISM 231
- violence serves a social function in helping individuals attain social status
- violence aids in sparking needed change in a community
- violence serves as a warning of danger to a community

CONFLICT THEORY 231
- conflict is unavoidable
- individuals and groups use violence to advance their agendas
- change can be brought about via conflict and confrontation

SYMBOLIC INTERACTIONISM 231
- social meaning of violent episodes can be examined to understand the dynamics of a violent situation or cycle
- the meaning that an individual or a group attributes to the context of a violent episode can give insight into the individual's or group's behavior.

Key Terms

family stress is a real or imagined imbalance between the demands on the family and the family's ability to meet those demands 221

crisis is an unstable condition in which there is a lack of sufficient resources to manage the situation 221

cope is to manage and confront stress 221

resiliency is the ability of an individual or family to function within familiar patterns or to create new patterns in the face of adversity or crisis 223

elasticity is the ability to recover from trauma or crisis 223

buoyancy is the ability of a family to keep afloat during adversity 223

recovery factors are qualities or characteristics of a family that assist recuperation from stress or a crisis 223

family violence is intentional abusive behavior against a family member that includes intimidation and physical and sexual assault *224*

domestic violence is intentional abusive behavior against an intimate partner that includes intimidation and physical and sexual assault *224*

intimate partner violence is intentional physical, emotional, or sexual abuse, or intimidation via threats of physical or sexual abuse, typically between partners or spouses, but including other intimate family relations *225*

wife rape is forced sex on a female spouse by a male spouse *225*

fusion is an extreme emotional connection and interdependence between intimate partners *227*

social learning theory explains that violent and abusive behavior is learned *227*

social cognition theory explains that a child's interpretation of a certain situation may not be as hostile or aggressive as he or she may perceive; changing children's impressions may help them overcome abusive situations *227*

family systems theory explains that different traits and coping mechanisms are passed from generation to generation within a family *228*

trauma theory suggests that how a traumatic event is handled determines the extent of trauma that a victim experiences *228*

somatization is the manifestation of physical symptoms from psychological problems *228*

personal resilience is an individual's ability to cope with and manage stress or a crisis *228*

Sample Test Questions

MULTIPLE CHOICE

These multiple-choice questions are similar to those found in the test bank that accompanies this textbook.

1. Based on theory, a family or individual is more likely to experience a high degree of stress if
   a. the event or situation leading to change is anticipated.
   b. the stressor is perceived negatively.
   c. there are ample resources available.
   d. the stressor originates in local or national events.

2. According to the research on family stress, which of the following is a factor that is most likely to aid in a family's recovery from stress or crisis?
   a. a shared sense of values
   b. a long history
   c. financial security
   d. independence of family members

3. According to the research on intimate partner violence, what is the main factor in predicting high risk to perpetrate intimate partner violence?
   a. The person has rage issues.
   b. The person comes from a family of divorce.
   c. The person has a desire to control.
   d. The person has no prior exposure to family violence.

4. Based on the literature on intimate partner violence, what adjective best describes the phenomenon of the victim becoming a perpetrator of violence or abuse?
   a. infinite
   b. cyclical
   c. terminal
   d. isolated

5. Which of the following is NOT a characteristic of a resilient individual?
   a. optimism
   b. dependence
   c. good communication skills
   d. low self-esteem

ESSAY

1. Discuss why building relationship skills is a successful form of family violence intervention.

2. Discuss how and why violence is perpetuated through different generations and how the cycle can be broken.

3. Discuss why family patterns are important in stress management.

4. Discuss the ways in which research on violence and abuse can aid in violence prevention.

5. Use Hill's ABC-X model of family stress to discuss a stressful situation that you or your family experienced.

WHERE TO START YOUR RESEARCH PAPER

For more information about building relationship skills to prevent family violence, go to http://endabuse.org http://www.familystresscenter.org/

To find out more about the cycle of violence, go to http://www.sciencedaily.com/releases/2008/09/080924153505.htm

To learn more about breaking the cycle of violence, go to http://www.breakthecycle.org/

To find out more about stress management, go to http://www.stressmanagementtips.com/family.htm

For more information about domestic violence prevention, go to http://www.ncadv.org/

To find out more about violence research, go to http://www.cdc.gov/ViolencePrevention/index.html

To learn more about the ABC-X model of family stress, go to http://cecp.air.org/vc/presentations/2selective/3lmcdon/HILL%27S_FAMILY_STRESS_THEORY_AND_FAST.htm

ANSWERS: 1. b, 2. a, 3. c, 4. b, 5. d

Remember to check www.thethinkspot.com for additional information, downloadable flashcards, and other helpful resources.

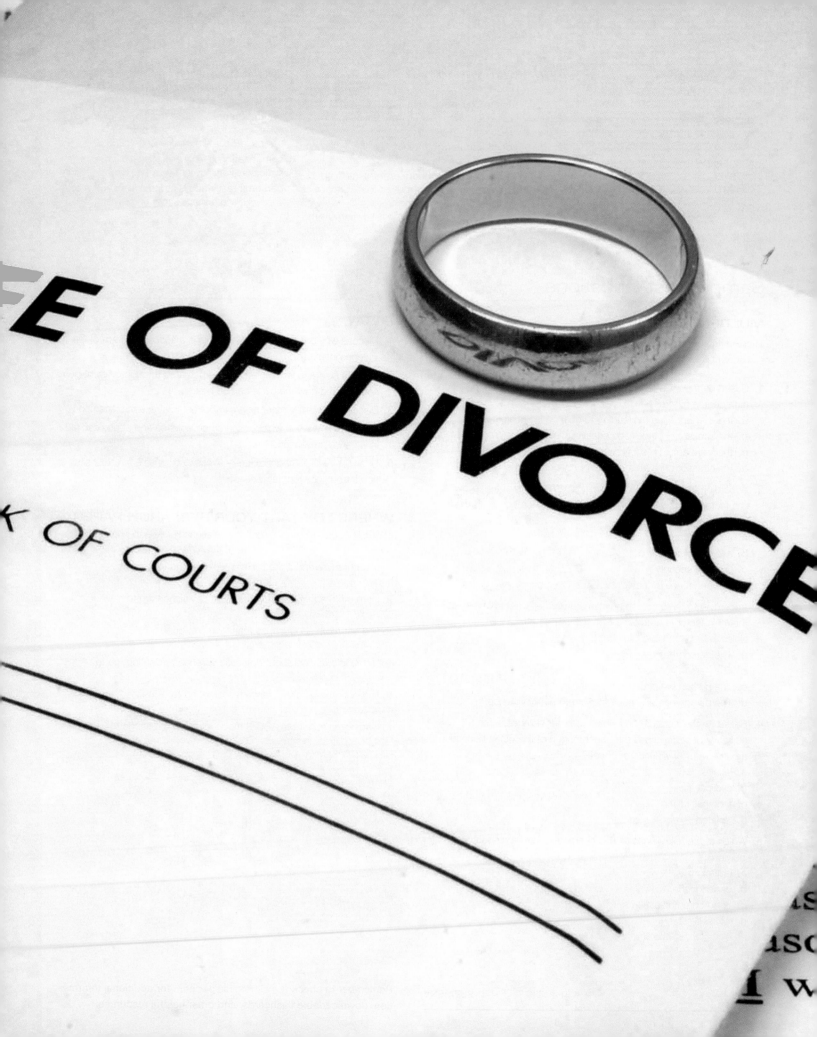

Eccentric

actor Daniel Hilliard specializes in dubbing voices for cartoon characters. He and his wife Miranda have three children: daughters Natalie and Lydia and son Chris. Daniel is a kind and loving father to his children, but Miranda increasingly begins to view him as a negative role model. She considers him to be a poor disciplinarian and thinks that he needs to grow up. When Daniel throws an elaborate surprise birthday party for Chris that goes horribly wrong, it is the final straw. Miranda, who objected to the idea of a birthday party to begin with because of Chris's failing grades, sees the mess and loses all patience with Daniel. She files for divorce and is awarded custody of the children.

Granted visitation rights to see his kids just once a week, Daniel is heartbroken. He discovers that Miranda is looking for a housekeeper to help her with the household duties and hatches an elaborate plan to spend more time with his children. With the help of his makeup artist brother, he transforms himself into Mrs. Doubtfire, a 60-something-year-old widow from Scotland. Having changed the phone number on Miranda's advertisement so that applicants can't reach her, he is the only person who applies for the job and soon finds himself immersed in cooking and cleaning chores. The position enables him to spend some time with his kids, and he finally has the opportunity to be the firm parental figure he failed to portray before the divorce.

For a while, the household runs smoothly. Miranda is delighted that Mrs. Doubtfire is doing such a great job with the children, and Daniel is thrilled that he can be an active participant in their lives. Eventually the ruse is discovered, first by Chris and then by the rest of the family during an eventful dinner. Miranda is furious with Daniel, and when they return to family court she seeks full custody. Although Daniel pleads that his actions were those of a desperate man who could not bear to be separated from his children, the judge finds his behavior disturbing and awards Miranda full custody.

At the end of the film, Miranda sees Daniel on a new children's television show in which he stars as Mrs. Doubtfire. She realizes that having him in their children's lives may be the solution to her problem of finding suitable day care and a way to keep Daniel involved on a daily basis, something he craves. She renegotiates the custody terms with her ex-husband, and they manage to come to an amicable agreement for the sake of the children. The film concludes with Miranda watching Daniel as Mrs. Doubtfire giving advice to the children of divorced parents on his television show.

237

SEPARATION AND DIVORCE

CHAPTER 14

What lessons can we learn **from *Mrs. Doubtfire*? Despite its eccentricities,** the film provides a realistic portrayal **of the painful process of divorce.**

The bitter custody negotiations between Miranda and Daniel illustrate how contentious separation and divorce can be, especially when children are involved. After a custody hearing, one parent is often dissatisfied with the outcome and feels pushed out of his or her children's lives. Although few fathers would disguise themselves as a Scottish nanny in an attempt to spend time with their kids, Daniel's desperate effort emphasizes the lengths that some parents will go to in order to be more involved with their children. Finally, the film shows that divorce is sometimes the only sensible option. Although Miranda and Daniel both love their children, it is clear that they are much happier as individuals than as a couple, and once they work everything out, the family is much happier overall.

∧
∧ Marriage does not always have a
∧ happy ending. **Over the past 30 years,** divorce has become a socially acceptable, **everyday occurrence.**

When I graduated from high school in 1981, I rarely heard anything about divorce. Despite its growing frequency, a negative social stigma was attached to separation and divorce that made divorcés superconscious of any signs of disapproval from friends and relatives. Fast-forward nearly 30 years, and look where we are now. People commonly throw divorce parties, post divorce announcements in newspapers, and set up divorce registries. Some newly reinstated singles even buy divorce cakes and wedding ring coffins! Far from the highly stigmatized process it once was, divorce is now a socially accepted, everyday occurrence. So, what happened? In this chapter, we will examine the history of divorce, the risk factors that make divorce more likely, and the consequences of divorce for both adults and children. We will also take a look at the theories behind divorce and examine how demographers calculate divorce rates.

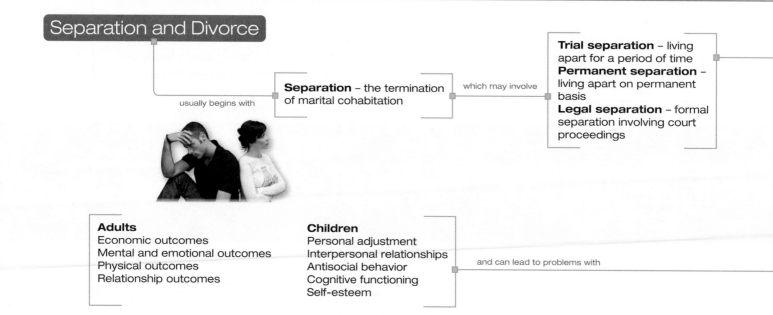

Separation and Divorce

usually begins with

Separation – the termination of marital cohabitation

which may involve

Trial separation – living apart for a period of time
Permanent separation – living apart on permanent basis
Legal separation – formal separation involving court proceedings

Adults
Economic outcomes
Mental and emotional outcomes
Physical outcomes
Relationship outcomes

Children
Personal adjustment
Interpersonal relationships
Antisocial behavior
Cognitive functioning
Self-esteem

and can lead to problems with

Separation

"The difference between a divorce and a legal separation is that a legal separation gives a husband time to hide his money" — Johnny Carson (1925–2005)

Except in some Muslim countries, where a husband can simply divorce his wife by uttering the words "I divorce thee" three times, divorce is not an immediate process. When a couple is first considering splitting up, they will usually separate for a period of time before making a final decision. **Separation** is the termination of marital cohabitation. Although it is not monitored as closely as divorce, research shows that separation has become a stage in the divorce process.[1] Separation may range from a short-term trial separation period to a permanent legal separation.

SEPARATION is the termination of marital cohabitation.

TRIAL SEPARATION is a type of separation in which a couple lives apart for a period of time in order to decide whether or not to separate permanently.

LIVING APART is a type of separation in which couples do not intend to get back together.

PERMANENT SEPARATION is a type of separation in which a couple begins living apart.

LEGAL SEPARATION is a formal separation involving court proceedings regarding property, alimony, child support, custody, and visitation rights.

SEPARATION AGREEMENT is a binding agreement between husband and wife regarding debts, assets, custody, child care, and support payments.

TYPES OF SEPARATION

There are four main types of separation. A couple may go through a **trial separation**, in which they live apart for a period of time to decide whether to separate permanently. If the couple does not reunite, they are said to be **living apart.** After a trial separation, or when a couple begins living apart on a permanent basis, they may undergo a **permanent separation**. In most states, property or debts accumulated after permanent separation are the responsibility of the person who acquired them. The most formal type of separation is a **legal separation**, which involves court proceedings. Both husband and wife sign a legally binding **separation agreement** that covers issues such as the distribution of debts and assets, custody, child care, and support payments. If the couple later divorces, decisions made in the separation agreement become part of the divorce judgment. During a legal separation, a court has the power to resolve all issues that would usually be resolved in a divorce, with the only difference being that when the order is entered by the court, the couple remains married.

Legal Separation or Divorce?

If a court rules on the same issues in a legal separation as in a divorce, why not just get a divorce? A couple might want to avoid the "D" word for several reasons. Some religions do not permit divorce, and a legal separation enables a couple to legally separate their financial rights and obligations without officially ending the marriage. Other couples might stay married to qualify for certain Social Security or pension benefits, or they may delay for financial reasons.

Some states require spouses to live apart for a period of time before granting a divorce. In other cases, couples may hope to eventually reconcile, but realize that they need some time apart in the mean time. In this instance, they may require a formal arrangement regarding child and spousal support and custody issues. Although data on marital reconciliation are few and far between, one study suggests that approximately 10 percent of married U.S. couples experience a separation and reconciliation.[2] Actor Sean Penn and his wife Robin Wright Penn famously began divorce proceedings in 2007 and reconciled four

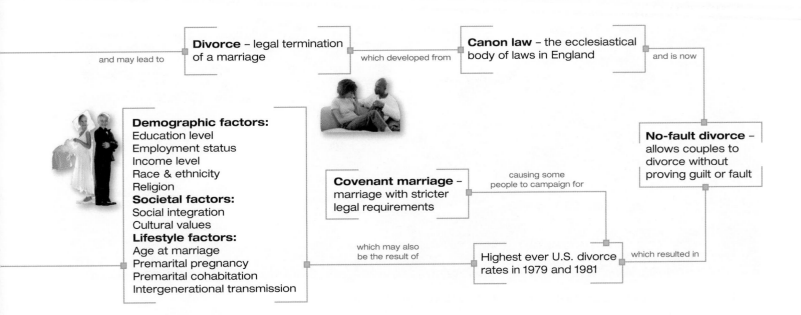

Divorce – legal termination of a marriage

and may lead to

which developed from

Canon law – the ecclesiastical body of laws in England

and is now

Demographic factors:
Education level
Employment status
Income level
Race & ethnicity
Religion
Societal factors:
Social integration
Cultural values
Lifestyle factors:
Age at marriage
Premarital pregnancy
Premarital cohabitation
Intergenerational transmission

Covenant marriage – marriage with stricter legal requirements

causing some people to campaign for

No-fault divorce – allows couples to divorce without proving guilt or fault

which may also be the result of

Highest ever U.S. divorce rates in 1979 and 1981

which resulted in

months later, only to file for a legal separation in April 2009 and then reconcile again in May 2009. Although celebrities are notorious for breaking up and making up, even in the real world, approximately one-third of divorced women attempted at least one marital reconciliation before signing the final divorce paperwork.[3]

Divorce

"American husbands are the best in the world; no other husbands are so generous to their wives, or can be so easily divorced."—Elinor Glyn (1864–1943)

After spending some time apart, a couple may decide to divorce. Divorce is the legal termination of a marriage, and it permits one or both spouses to remarry.

STATISTICAL TRENDS

Considering all the negative press about failing marriages, should newly-weds be pessimistic about their future or continue to look through rose-tinted glasses? Take a look at some recent statistics:

- The divorce rate in the United States has decreased over the past 30 years. In 1990, the divorce rate was 4.7 (per 1,000 people). In 2000, the rate was 4.2, and in 2005, it dropped to 3.6—the lowest divorce rate since 1970.[4] The divorce rate remained steady at 3.6 in both 2006 and 2007.[5]

- In 2004, Nevada had the highest divorce rate (6.4 per 1,000 people), closely followed by Arkansas (6.3), and then Wyoming (5.3). Washington, D.C., had the lowest divorce rate (1.7 per 1,000 people), followed by Massachusetts (2.2), and Pennsylvania (2.5).[6]

- Approximately 43.7% of custodial mothers and 56.2% of custodial fathers were separated or divorced in 2003.[7]

Patterns of Divorce

Why might divorce rates increase during times of social upheaval? Looking at the *Marriage and Divorce Rates* chart, we can see definite peaks and valleys over the last 85 years. Divorce rates increased gradually after World War I, then decreased in the 1930s during the Depression era. They rose significantly in the period following World War II, decreased in the 1950s, rose sharply again in the late 1960s and early 1970s, and reached an all-time high in 1981. As we have already observed, the divorce rate began to decrease in the 1980s and has been falling ever since.

So, what conclusions can we draw from these patterns? We can see that the divorce rate rises during major events, such as war, and decreases during times of economic hardship, such as the 1950s recession. Some sociologists attribute the peak at the end of World War II to divorces among people who married impulsively before the soldiers left for war and then found that they had little in common when they were eventually reunited.[8] Others point to the strains of families dealing with the aftermath of war, which caused many veterans to turn to alcohol or drugs.[9] Similar factors likely influenced the increase in divorce rates during the upheaval of the Vietnam War in the 1960s and 1970s. During this time, other social factors also came into play, such as the introduction of no-fault divorce laws (which we will discuss later in the chapter), changing gender roles, and the impact of feminism. During periods of relative social stability, divorce rates tend to decrease. In effect, divorce rates are lower today than they were between 1975 and 1990.[10] How might economic factors such as the bankruptcies of car manufacturing giants Chrysler and GM affect divorce rates over the next few years?

∨ **Both the** marriage rate and the divorce rate in the United States **have undergone a gradual**
∨ decline in recent years. **What socioeconomic factors may be responsible for these trends?**

Marriage and Divorce Rates, 1920–2007

Source: U.S. National Center for Health Statistics, and *Historical Statistics of the United States.*

Divorce Rates Around the World

How does the U.S. divorce rate compare with that of other countries? If you look at the graph below, you'll see that there is considerable variation in divorce rates around the world.

Three nations that are noticeably absent from any divorce surveys and statistics are Vatican City, Malta, and the Philippines. These are the only places that do not allow or recognize legal divorce, although a marriage can be easily annulled in the Philippines on psychological grounds. Elsewhere, however, cultural changes around the world are influencing divorce rates in almost every country. Let's take a look at several countries in depth to examine how each society views divorce.

Sweden

Why is the divorce rate so high in Sweden? The divorce laws are not that different from those in other European countries—once a spouse has filed for divorce, there is a six-month reconsideration period, after which a decree of divorce may be granted if one of the partners requests it. The high divorce rate is also surprising because many of the factors traditionally associated with divorce in the United States, such as brief courtship and teen pregnancy, are not as common in Sweden.

Ironically, one reason for the high percentage of failed marriages may be that Swedish couples often cohabit before marriage to test their long-term suitability. One might logically conclude that this would boost a couple's chances of a long and happy life together, but it seems to have the opposite effect. Swedish sociologist Jan Trost notes that the

marriage rate in Sweden is dropping as a result of cohabitation, yet divorce rates remain high.[11]

India

In a country that expected widows to throw themselves onto their husbands'

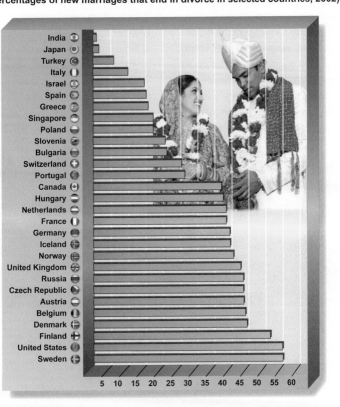

Divorce Rates Around the World
(Percentages of new marriages that end in divorce in selected countries, 2002)

India, Japan, Turkey, Italy, Israel, Spain, Greece, Singapore, Poland, Slovenia, Bulgaria, Switzerland, Portugal, Canada, Hungary, Netherlands, France, Germany, Iceland, Norway, United Kingdom, Russia, Czech Republic, Austria, Belgium, Denmark, Finland, United States, Sweden

5 10 15 20 25 30 35 40 45 50 55 60

∧
∧ Sweden has the highest percentage of
∧ marriages that end in divorce (54.9%),
and India has the lowest (1.1%). **Why do some countries have a higher divorce rate than others?**

funeral pyres not so long ago, it isn't surprising that the divorce rate in India is far lower than it is in most of the Western world. Before the Hindu Marriage Act was passed in 1956, Hindu women were banned from filing for divorce. Today, women in unhappy marriages are allowed

to seek a divorce, although the practice is far from socially acceptable. In both Hinduism and Islam, marriage is a sacred institution and divorced women are often ostracized by the community.[12] Although the divorce rate is increasing in urban areas, divorce is still extremely rare in rural parts of India.

Muslim Societies

Even though divorce rates in Muslim societies are low compared to the Western world, recent changes in divorce laws have resulted in a marked increase in the number of divorces. In Kuwait, where divorce was once a rarity, almost one-third of all marriages now end in divorce.[13] Legislation varies from country to country, though it is usually easier for a man to seek divorce than a woman. For example, in Turkey a husband can initiate divorce without needing to cite any reasons, whereas a wife is obligated to prove fault on her husband's part. Changes to divorce laws in Muslim society do not necessarily reflect a change in traditional values. In Morocco, a law was passed in 2004 stating that women were no longer legally required to obey their husbands. Divorce, however, is still a cause of great shame in Moroccan society.

What do these examples tell us about divorce around the world? Globally, divorce rates are rising. Increasingly liberal divorce laws are making the dissolution of marriage easier and less time-consuming. In Cuba, where couples pay a notary public $1.05 and are divorced within 20 minutes, almost 70 divorces occur for every 100 marriages.[14] Although religion and social status contribute to low divorce rates in many countries, global divorce rates are likely to continue to rise as the developing world becomes more westernized.

LEGAL TRENDS

Who was the first American to get divorced? You might be surprised to find out that the first divorce decree in the United States was actually granted to Mrs. James Luxford in 1639 by a Puritan court in Massachusetts. Early U.S. divorce laws were heavily influenced by **canon law**, the ecclesiastical body of laws used in England that governed the Catholic and Anglican churches. Not renowned for its liberal divorce policies, canon law saw marriage as a sacred union that could only be ended by the death of a spouse. Annulment was granted only in very limited circumstances, such as by proving that the marriage was not valid in the first place. This evolved into the **fault-based divorce** system, in which one partner was obligated to prove that the other had somehow violated the marriage contract. Until 1970, the fault-based system was used throughout the United States, though the grounds for divorce differed from one state to another. Typical grounds for divorce included adultery, neglect, desertion, and "cruel and inhumane treatment," such as mental or physical cruelty. Once a spouse successfully proved in court that his or her partner had violated the marriage

∧
∧ **The** fault-based divorce system **forced couples to**
∧ **play the blame game in court,** leading to acrimonious divorce trials.

contract, he or she would be granted an **absolute divorce**—the official end of a marriage, severing all legal bonds between a couple.

No-Fault Divorce

By the 1970s, divorce rates in the United States were skyrocketing, and public concern focused on the effects of divorce on both spouses and their children. The fault-based system created a highly adversarial atmosphere in court, in which spouses blamed each other for the failure of the marriage. Proposals were put forward for a no-fault divorce bill, which became a reality with the passing of California's Family Law Act in 1970. The new **no-fault divorce** allowed couples to divorce without proving guilt or fault on the part of the other. Instead, marital breakdowns were attributed to "irreconcilable differences," which allowed a judge to grant a divorce if he or she found that the marriage was irretrievably broken.

The liberalization of divorce laws quickly spread to other states—by 1979 all but three states had passed some type of no-fault divorce legislation, and by 1985 all 50 states had a no-fault clause allowance in their

marriage and divorce laws. So were these new laws responsible for the all-time highest divorce rates in history in 1979 and 1981? Many researchers believe they were an important contributing factor.[15] However, it is likely that other socioeconomic factors also played a role. In the 1960s and 1970s, the feminist movement encouraged women to enter the workplace, earn their own salaries, and celebrate their economic independence. Contraception and legal access to abortion also became more freely available in the 1970s, providing married women with the option of not having children. Women who were able to support themselves financially and did not have children dependent on them were more likely to dissolve unhappy marriages.[16]

COVENANT MARRIAGE

How should society deal with increased divorce rates and negative attitudes toward no-fault divorce laws? Some states have recently introduced a two-tiered system of marriage that allows couples to choose whether they want a traditional marriage or a marriage with a different set of legal requirements—a covenant marriage.

Covenant marriage was first introduced in Louisiana in 1997 and requires a couple to commit to a more strenuous set of legal requirements in an effort to strengthen their relationship. Supporters of the movement hope that the alternative to traditional marriage will create a stronger model of marriage for future generations and reduce the likelihood of divorce.

To partake in a covenant marriage, a couple generally has to undergo some form of premarital counseling. They must reveal any information that may affect the decision to marry, as well as pledge a lifelong commitment to each another. The couple must also agree to take part in counseling if they experience problems that threaten their marriage and agree to divorce only under very specific circumstances, such as abuse, adultery, or felony imprisonment.

Following its establishment in Louisiana, several other states, including Arkansas and Arizona, enacted their own covenant marriage legislation. To study attitudes toward this new type of marriage, researcher Alan Hawkins and his colleagues polled people in Louisiana and Arizona, because these states allow covenant marriage, and Minnesota, because it does not allow covenant marriage. The study revealed mixed feelings, but enabled Hawkins to draw four main conclusions[17]:

1. States in which the majority of people hold traditional, conservative values and are active in their religious community are more likely to pass covenant marriage legislation.
2. People who believe in traditional gender roles and participate in their religious community are more likely to participate in covenant marriages.
3. Some aspects of covenant marriage are more appealing than others. Although the majority of people in the study believed that pre-

marital counseling and marital education were important, they were less enthusiastic about the long waiting periods for divorce and had a lukewarm reaction to the policy as a package.

4. Sociodemographic factors such as age, education, income, and marital experience do not make a big difference to people's attitudes toward covenant marriage. Although people who were less religious and more liberal were not as enthusiastic about the legislation, there was an overall positive reaction to covenant marriage and its components.

Divorce Risk Factors

Is it possible to predict whether or not a couple will live happily ever after before they even marry? Demographic, societal, and lifestyle factors help explain why some people are more likely to divorce than others.

DEMOGRAPHIC FACTORS

Education Level

Overall, people who graduate from college have more stable marriages than those with only a high school education.[18] This is usually linked to other factors that affect marital success. For example, those who complete higher education are more likely to delay marriage and have higher incomes, and they are also better equipped to work out marital problems when they occur. However, research indicates that differences in educational levels within couples may have an impact on marital success. Divorce rates are lower if the husband is of a higher educational status than his wife than if they both have the same educational background, and highest if the wife is of a higher educational status than the husband.[19]

Income Level

Debt can be a major stressor for couples. Although high earners are not necessarily happier than people with low incomes, they are able to avoid some of the stress that results from large amounts of debt or mismanagement of family finances. Couples with sufficient financial resources are less likely to divorce than similar couples with inadequate income.[20]

Employment Status

Who's more likely to divorce—the factory worker or the lawyer? Among Caucasians, the answer is the factory worker. Generally, low-status occupations have a higher divorce rate than high-status occupations.[21] Unemployment also contributes to high divorce rates due to increased levels of marital stress. However, getting a high-powered job may not solve your marital woes—employment can create opportunities for spouses to meet new partners in the workplace. Changing and blended gender roles have also led to an increase in divorce levels, because working women are not as dependent on their husbands' income for stability and survival.[22]

Religion

Since all major religions discourage divorce, it is not surprising that religious couples are less likely to divorce than non-religious couples. Religious similarity and shared participation in religious activities may help sustain marital stability because they affirm the couple's compatibility in terms of traditions and values.[23] Couples who attend religious ceremonies regularly also have a source of support to help them work through problems that might otherwise lead to divorce. However, some studies indicate that if there is a difference between spouses in frequency of attendance, the risk of divorce increases. Researchers found that when wives attend weekly religious services but husbands do not, the risk of divorce is greater than it is for marriages in which neither spouse attends religious services.[24]

Race and Ethnicity

Divorce rates vary by race and ethnicity, with blacks facing the highest risk of divorce of any racial or ethnic group. One study found that after 10 years of marriage, 20 percent of first marriages for Asian Americans had dissolved, compared to 32 percent of first marriages for white women, 34 percent for Latina women, and 47 percent for black women.[25] Why might this be? Researchers point to the disproportionate level of poverty among blacks, leading to financial strain and unemployment. Some also suggest that divorce is more acceptable among African Americans than among other racial groups, with better community support for those going through the process.[26] Conversely, Hispanic cultures place the needs of the family and culture over the needs of the individual, making divorce less acceptable. Some researchers suggest that the high value Hispanics place on family may explain why divorce rates are lower in Hispanic communities, even though they are generally more educationally and economically disadvantaged than African Americans.[27] Additionally, Roman Catholicism plays a large role in the lives of many Hispanic families, further minimizing the risk of divorce.[28]

∧∧∧ **Why do** African Americans **have a** higher divorce rate **than any other racial group?**

SOCIETAL FACTORS

Social Integration

How well do you know your neighbors? The degree of interaction between individuals and their communities affects the likelihood of divorce. Couples who are tightly bonded to the community at large through social groups such as the Girl Scouts or Rotary Club or religious organizations such as the community church, mosque, or synagogue are more likely to remain married compared to couples with a loose bond. Social scientists believe that the diversity of sub-cultures, languages, and religious practices in the United States, as well as the tendency for people to move away from their family roots, has loosened social bonds in recent years, resulting in higher divorce rates.

Cultural Values

Are we becoming more selfish? Some researchers argue that the increasing emphasis on individual happiness and the pursuit of self-fulfillment over family commitments is the root cause of many divorces.[29] Materialism, changing priorities, and the portrayal of divorce as an everyday occur-rence in the media (for example, on TV shows such as *Divorce Court*) all reflect a cultural shift in values.

LIFESTYLE FACTORS

Age at Marriage

Many starry-eyed teens stubbornly ignore their parents' pleas to wait a few more years before making a lifelong commitment, proclaiming that they are "in love" and "ready now." However, statistics tell a different story. After 10 years of marriage, 48 percent of first marriages of

women under the age of 18 have dissolved, com-pared with 24 percent of first marriages of women who were 25 or older when they tied the knot.[30] Younger partners are less likely to be in a posi-tion to support their families financially, less likely to have the emotional maturity needed for a committed relationship, and less likely to possess the coping skills required to sus-tain a marriage.

Premarital Pregnancy

Premarital pregnancy or birth has a desta-bilizing effect on a marriage and significantly increases the likelihood of divorce. This is especially likely among adolescent parents, who usually do not have the education or income needed to maintain a stable family life.[31] Just look at 18-year-old Bristol Palin, daughter of former vice-presidential nominee, Sarah Palin. After it was announced that she was pregnant with her boyfriend's baby, the young couple quickly got engaged. However, soon after the baby was born, the couple went their separate ways.

Premarital Cohabitation

Many couples assume that living together before marriage helps iron out any poten-tial problems. However, according to statistics, cohabitation may increase the likelihood of divorce. In the United States, over 50 percent of cohabiting relation-

> ∧
> ∧ Marrying young **dramatically**
> ∧ increases **the** risk of divorce.

Top Ten Most Scandalous Divorces in American History

① 1735
Thrall v. Thrall
When William Thrall accused his wife Hannah of adultery, it split the tightly knit community of Windsor, Connecticut in two. Following years of lurid testimony that caused rifts between friends and neighbors, the court refused the divorce on the grounds that William's behavior had driven his wife away. William died in 1739, leaving Hannah a very wealthy 36-year-old widow.

② 1760
Lufkin v. Lufkin
Stephen Lufkin was granted a divorce from his wife Tabitha after William Haskell testified that he had indeed had sexual relations with her. The court took note of Haskell's testimony that Tabitha had said if he refused her she would find "Some other Man For She Did not Love her Husband Lufkin."

③ 1849
Butler v. Kemble
America's first celebrity divorce involved British stage star Fanny Kemble, and her American slaveholder husband Pierce Butler. After countering her husband's list of grievances with a narrative citing details of his infidelities, the scandal hit the newspapers. Fanny later withdrew her defense and accepted Butler's terms.

④ 1849
Forrest v. Forrest
Having been driven out of her house by actor husband Edwin Forrest, Catherine Forrest sued for divorce. The accusations began to fly on both sides, with both parties fighting allegations of infidelity. Catherine eventually won the case and was awarded the tidy sum of $3,000 a year.

⑤ 1869
McFarland v. McFarland
As recently divorced Abby Sage McFarland prepared to wed reporter Albert D. Richardson, her ex-husband, Daniel McFarland, burst into the New York *Tribune* offices and shot Richardson in the stomach. Clergyman Henry Ward Beecher married the dying man and his bride. McFarland was later acquitted of the murder.

ships dissolve within five years.[32] Researchers speculate that since cohabitation involves less commitment than marriage, cohabitating couples that marry maintain the attitude that relationships are temporary.[33] However, not all researchers agree with these findings. When Skinner et al. compared couples who had cohabited and married with couples who married but did not cohabit, they found no distinguishing characteristics.[34] Recent research indicates that the relationship between cohabitation and marital stability is a complex issue dependent on factors such as sexual history, cohabitation history, and race and ethnicity. For example, women who cohabited with only one partner prior to marriage had marriage dissolution rates similar to women who never cohabited.[35]

Intergenerational Transmission

Couples with divorced parents are at a surprisingly high risk of divorcing themselves. Why might this be? Children of divorced parents have a higher tendency to marry younger, cohabit before marriage, and have lower incomes—all of which can lead to divorce. They may also view divorce as a solution to marital difficulties and have a general suspicion that living "happily ever after" rarely happens in real life.[36] However, this relationship is not necessarily causal. Many sons and daughters of divorced parents are aware of the higher risk factor and take protective measures, such as undergoing counseling, to reduce the likelihood of divorce.

BOHANNON'S SIX STATIONS OF DIVORCE

Divorce is not something that just happens; it's a slow, generally painful process. Anthropologist Paul Bohannon suggests that there are six stations that every couple goes through during a divorce.

1 **Emotional Divorce** An emotional divorce generally happens well before legal divorce takes place. One spouse may start to slowly withdraw from the relationship or both parties may start to lose their sense of mutual trust and respect, potentially turning alienating behavior into conflict. Many couples delay divorce for as long as possible, often remaining married for the sake of the children. In a national study of people aged 40 and over, 17 percent claimed they had postponed getting a divorce for at least five years, citing their children's welfare as the primary reason.[37] By the time a couple has reached the end stages of an emotional divorce, apathy has often set in, and arguments are less common. For this reason, it may appear to an outsider that the couple's marriage is stable and content.

2 **Legal Divorce** Once a couple decides to get a divorce, they set off a complicated chain of events involving three parties: the husband, the wife, and the state. Although divorce laws vary from state to state, a typical legal divorce includes one spouse filing a petition, the other spouse responding to the petition, a waiting period that enables either party to change his or her mind, and finally a court settlement. During this stage, couples (often with the help of a lawyer) negotiate issues such as child custody and division of property. Legal divorce is an expensive process; if lawyers are involved, the average cost of a divorce in the United States is $20,000.[38]

3 **Economic Divorce** Long after the legal issues have been settled, a couple may continue to argue over financial matters such as ongoing child care expenses, debts, or property taxes. The economic divorce may therefore last for years, as former spouses return to court to try to renegotiate financial agreements. This stage is often not as significant for working-class couples, who often have fewer tangible assets to divide than wealthier couples do.

4 **Coparental Divorce** During the coparental divorce, spouses make decisions about child custody, financial support, and visitation rights. This is often a highly contentious stage with frequent disputes about which parent should receive sole custody, how often the noncus-

6
1911
Sinclair v. Sinclair
When author Upton Sinclair sued his unfaithful wife Meta for divorce, she told reporters that she wanted others to learn from her experience. Soon, the writer was facing intense public scrutiny, despite his insistence that he wanted no self-publicity.

7
1922
Stillman v. Stillman
When James Stillman, president of National City Bank, filed for divorce from his wife Anne, there were whispers that the couple's blond-haired, blue-eyed son looked a lot like Fowler McCormick—the teenage grandson of John D. Rockefeller. After a 5-year negotiation process costing almost a million dollars, the couple reconciled and lived happily ever after—until 15 years later, when 50-year-old Anne divorced James to marry 29-year-old Fowler McCormick.

8
1925
Rhinelander v. Rhinelander
When New York socialite Kip Rhinelander married domestic servant Alice Jones, the tabloids discovered she was of mixed race and had a field day. Kip's father sued for an annulment on the basis that Alice had duped her husband by passing herself off as white. After making her disrobe during the trial, jurors concluded that Kip must have known the truth and rejected the annulment.

9
1949
Bergman v. Lindstrom
When *Casablanca* actress Ingrid Bergman left her physician husband and small daughter to live with Italian director Roberto Rossellini, five and a half million American clubwomen voted to boycott her films and she was denounced on the floor of the U.S. Senate. An apology was eventually entered into the *Congressional Record* in 1972.

10
1982
Pulitzer v. Pulitzer
The divorce trial of publishing heir Herbert Pulitzer and his wife Roxanne received more news coverage than any divorce trial in recent history because of its graphic testimony—lesbian affairs, séances, cocaine use… Citing Roxanne's "gross immoral conduct," the judge ruled in favor of Herbert, granting him custody of the couple's two young boys.

todial parent should be allowed to visit, and which parent should make decisions about their children's education, religious upbringing, and daily lives. During the 20th century, courts adopted the view that women were better nurturers than men, and custody was typically awarded to the mother. In recent years this trend has started to shift, with one in six fathers being awarded sole custody in 2005.[39]

5 **Community Divorce** During the community divorce, a couple experiences changing social relationships. Friends may disappear out of loyalty for one spouse or from fear of being seen to take sides. Relationships with in-laws may also be severed. This can be a lonely and isolating time, especially if strong family traditions have been established with in-laws during special seasons such as Thanksgiving, Christmas, the high holidays, Easter, or Passover.

6 **Psychic Divorce** The psychic divorce occurs when one spouse gains a full sense of independence and is able to emotionally let go of the ex-spouse. Have you ever heard that your ex-boyfriend/girlfriend has started dating someone new and you realized that you genuinely didn't care? If so, you have gone through a psychic divorce. For people who are unable to let go of the pain, anger, and resentment of their marriage and its subsequent breakup, this final stage may never happen.

^^^ **What are the psychological effects of divorce on children? Studies show that** parental conflict **may have** more damaging long-term effects than the actual divorce.

CONSEQUENCES OF DIVORCE FOR ADULTS

After reviewing a decade of research literature from the 1990s, Paul Amato found that compared to married people, divorcés experienced lower levels of psychological well-being and happiness, more health problems and social isolation, and less satisfying sex lives. They also reported more economic problems and had a lower standard of living.[40] According to Kari Henley and Kay Pasley, divorce affects a couple in four major ways: economically, mentally, emotionally, and physically.[41]

Economic Outcomes

Since divorce reverses all the benefits of maintaining one household and saving and investing money as a couple, both spouses usually undergo an immediate decline in their standard of living. However, this effect changes over time. Generally, in the United States, women experience a decline in their economic status, whereas men experience a lesser decline, or even a slight increase in status. Studies indicate that there are three main reasons for this disparity: unequal wages for men and women; the gender division of labor within marriage that reduces women's career development during childbearing and child-raising years; and the high proportion of mothers with physical custody of children after divorce combined with low levels of child support payments.[42]

Mental and Emotional Outcomes

Divorced individuals show higher levels of depression and anxiety compared to married individuals, and they frequently have poorer self-concepts. Studies suggest that stress from divorce is cumulative, since people who have experienced two or more divorces suffer from higher levels of depression than people with only one divorce or those who have never divorced.[43]

Physical Outcomes

People who are divorced suffer from more health problems and higher early mortality compared to people who are married or single. They are also more likely to take part in risky behaviors, such as drug or alcohol use. Increased stress levels can lead to poor immune system functioning and increase the likelihood of illness.

Relationship Outcomes

People who are divorced experience more social isolation than married individuals. After a divorce, a person may find that he or she doesn't have much in common with married friends, or that friendships are lost because mutual friends are forced to choose sides.

CONSEQUENCES OF DIVORCE FOR CHILDREN

Just over half of all divorces involve children, and a major question that divorcing parents face is the potential impact separation may have on their offspring. David Demo and Alan Acock identify five factors to take into consideration: personal adjustment, interpersonal relationships, antisocial behavior, cognitive functioning, and self-esteem.[44]

Personal Adjustment

Research conducted over the past 60 years indicates that children from divorced homes tend to have more social and psychological problems compared to children from non-divorced homes, although some of the negative effects decrease over time. As we will see later in the chapter, some adults whose parents divorced when they were teenagers reflected that they had matured faster as a result of their parents' separation. The effects of divorce are greater on boys than on girls, and these effects may intensify if there is financial stress at home or if the parents are young. Parental conflict also plays a big role—high levels of conflict can have a greater impact on children than the actual divorce. Finally, the role of the noncustodial parent—that is, the parent who does not have primary custody—may affect how well children adjust to their new family dynamic. Children who see their noncustodial parent regularly adapt to the change in situation better than children who receive irregular visits from a noncustodial parent.[45]

Interpersonal Relationships

Divorce seems to have an impact on the way that children relate to others. Children of divorced homes are more likely to date early and engage in premarital sex than children from non-divorced homes. They are also more likely to choose high-risk partners, cohabit before marriage, and, as we noted earlier, get divorced themselves.[46]

Antisocial Behavior

Single mothers are often unfairly vilified in the press, though research shows that adolescents in mother-only households are more inclined to engage in deviant behavior such as drug-taking or truancy than teenagers in two-parent families. This is probably due to a lack of adequate supervision rather than the trauma of divorce—antisocial behavior is less likely to occur when there are two adults in the house, whether they are biological parents or not.[47]

Cognitive Functioning

Children from divorced homes tend to have lower academic records than children from intact households, as well as higher dropout rates from school.[48]

Self-Esteem

Research suggests that divorce in itself does not necessarily lower children's self-esteem; however, other factors may play a role. Children in households with high levels of parental conflict and children who receive little family support have lower self-esteem than other children, whether their parents are divorced or not.[49]

ADJUSTING TO DIVORCE

"A divorce is like an amputation; you survive it but there's less of you."—Margaret Atwood (b. 1939)

Why do some adults celebrate their new-found freedom by throwing elaborate and seemingly carefree divorce parties while others sink into a major depression? Divorce is a lengthy process, and it takes a long time for most individuals to adjust to their new status. This process is affected by **personal factors**—individual characteristics such as age, education level, and employment status, and **contextual factors**—outside factors such as the level of social support an individual receives during his or her time of need.

For example, some studies have found that older people have more difficulty adjusting to life after divorce because their employment options and chances of remarrying are more limited.[50] Other researchers found that older divorcés coped better because they did not have to worry about co-parenting issues once their children had grown up. Generally, adults with a high education level, high socioeconomic status, and high level of self-esteem cope better after a divorce than those who are financially insecure and less emotionally balanced. Having a job may also prove beneficial because it provides people with a social network as well as financial support.[51]

Whom do you call when you are in a crisis? After a divorce, most people lean heavily on their friends and family for support. A person with plenty of friends to call will generally find it easier to cope than someone who is socially isolated. Although jumping headfirst into a new relationship is probably not recommended, dating and remarriage are also key contextual factors associated with better post-divorce adjustment.

Finally, children are good sources of social support for divorcing parents. However, if there are co-parenting issues to deal with, children may also provide an additional source of stress for divorcing parents.[52]

POSITIVE OUTCOMES OF DIVORCE

Can divorce have positive outcomes? By the end of *Mrs. Doubtfire* it is clear that Daniel and Miranda are happier living apart than they ever were as a couple and that their children are beginning to adjust to the new situation. Although most research focuses on the negative aspects of divorce, some studies indicate that teenagers of divorced parents are more mature than teenagers in non-divorced homes, have higher self-esteem, and are better at empathizing with others.[53] A 20-year longitudinal study by Constance Ahrons concluded that most of the 173 grown-up children of divorce she interviewed had rebounded and functioned well after their parents' divorce, with some stating that the separation had made them stronger and wiser.[54]

Divorce may also provide ex-spouses with the chance to start a new and better life. Some studies indicate that people who are divorced experience increased levels of autonomy and personal growth.[55] Women in particular often report improved career opportunities, better social lives, and feeling happier and more fulfilled after a divorce.[56] Being back on the dating scene after a long period of time may also lead to an increase in self-confidence. For men, divorce may result in additional time and money to spend on themselves and their hobbies, an improved financial situation, and the ability to date new partners.[57] Some also report that their communication skills, often a key source of marital frustration, improved after a divorce.[58]

Although divorce is often the most viable option, not every troubled marriage is doomed to fail. Many couples who are considering divorce are able to rescue their marriage by undergoing therapy to help them work on issues such as communication, conflict resolution, and marital friendship. An analysis of data collected by the National Survey of Families and Households reported that 86% of unhappily married couples who stayed together were happy five years later.[59]

∧ **Sometimes,** divorce provides **a much-**
∧ **needed** escape for **people trapped in**
∧ unhappy marriages.

think marriages and families: WHAT ARE THE THEORIES BEHIND DIVORCE?

REWARD is a benefit.

COST is a detriment.

PROFIT is the ratio of reward to cost.

RATIONALITY is an alternative view of what constitutes a reward or a cost.

EXCHANGES AND EQUITY is a system of judging the reward and cost of a situation or relationship.

GENERALIZED SET OF REWARDS is an examination that tries to figure out why most people in general behave in a particular way.

Adjusting to Divorce: Theoretical Perspectives

How do sociologists view the process of divorce and the subsequent adjustment period? Here are two perspectives:

SOCIAL EXCHANGE THEORY

Everyone knows the risks of jumping out of a plane at 10,000 feet, yet skydiving is a hugely popular sport. Why? It's exhilarating, it's challenging, and it earns plenty of kudos from friends and family. Social exchange theorists view all human activity in a similar way—as a series of rewards and costs. Using the skydiving analogy, the **reward**, or benefit, is the exhilaration you feel as you fly through the air, while the **cost**, or detriment, is the long list of things that could go wrong the minute you pull the ripcord. When you

made the decision to step out of the plane, you considered the **profit**—the ratio of reward to cost—and decided that it was more beneficial to jump than to stay in the plane. Meanwhile, one of your fellow passengers may have opted to stay inside the plane because he or she had a different **rationality**—an alternative view of what constitutes a reward or a cost.

Social exchange theorists also consider two comparison levels. On the first level you might compare yourself to someone in the same position, such as the person in the plane next to you. On the second level you might also compare yourself to someone in an alternative position, such as a friend who enjoys a different extreme sport. You conduct your relationships through a system of **exchanges and equity**, in which you will maintain the relationship as long as it is fair and balanced. You continue to pay your skydiving club membership fee with the expectation that you will receive certain benefits. If the cost of each jump triples or you are suddenly expected to provide your own equipment, you will probably be less inclined to renew your subscription. Finally, exchange theorists consider the **generalized set of rewards**, which examines why most people in general behave in a particular way.[60]

So, how does this relate to the process of divorce? Take Mr. and Mrs. Carlton, who have been married for 15 years. At the beginning of the marriage, Mrs. Carlton felt that the marriage was fair and balanced: she and her husband split the household chores equally and she received plenty of love and attention from her other half. However, over time, the burden of chores has shifted, and she now feels as though she is doing the majority of the work without getting anything in return. She compares herself to Mrs. Smith next door, whose husband seems to be far more caring and affectionate and who helps out with the housework.

From Classroom to Community} When Divorce is the Only Option

Two days a week, Sara volunteers at her local Boys and Girls Club. She really enjoys her time there because she can relate to many of the children who participate.

When Sara was 12 years old her parents separated, and when she was 13 they divorced. Though the experience was traumatic at the time, she came to realize that it was the best option for her family.

"When I was growing up, my parents fought all the time. I used to hide under the covers at night in an attempt to muffle the sounds of dishes breaking.

"My mom and dad would slam doors and yell at each other. I thought it was my fault, so I tried really hard to be a better daughter and make them stop. I kept my room really clean and did all my chores, but it didn't help.

"When I was in elementary school, I was diagnosed with bipolar disorder.

"I was bullied all the time and didn't have many friends. A few years later, I started to cut myself when no one was watching. I couldn't handle the pressure from all the fighting at home.

"My parents divorced when I was 13.

"I had to go to court, which was terrifying. The judge asked me who I wanted to live with,

who I loved the most. How can you answer that? In the end, my parents got joint custody. I was given counseling to help me with my low self-esteem, and things started to get better. I realized that there was nothing I could have done to stop the fighting and that it wasn't my fault.

"Eventually, I also realized that divorce was the best option for my parents. They both got remarried and everyone is much happier with the way things are now.

"Counseling helped me to overcome my problems, and my self-esteem improved dramatically. Now, I like to help other children going through the same thing.

"I let them know that it's not their fault and even though divorce is painful, sometimes it's for the best."

ACTIVITY

Find a family counselor in your area and request an interview. Ask them what services are available for families going through a divorce. What are some common problems that children face when their parents decide to divorce? How does family therapy help them overcome these obstacles?

Mrs. Carlton considers the possibility of not being married and weighs up the profits and rewards of separation. On one hand, she would be free to seek a new beginning. On the other hand, the costs may include negative social stigma and a probable decrease in income. When Mrs. Carlton eventually decides that she wants a divorce, she has already had time to get used to the idea of separation and the adjustment process has begun.

DIVORCE-STRESS ADJUSTMENT THEORY

The **divorce-stress adjustment theory** views divorce as a stressful life transition to which the entire family must adjust. According to theorists, the process of divorce causes tension and anxiety in

DIVORCE-STRESS ADJUSTMENT THEORY is a theory that views divorce as a stressful life transition to which the entire family must adjust.

people's lives resulting from a number of different stressors. For adults, these stressors may include conflict with their former spouse, financial difficulties, and the pressures of sole parenting or loss of parental custody. For children, stressors may include reduced interaction with one of their parents, parental conflict, and a decline in family income. The adjustment process for both adults and children is mitigated by the amount of social support received, the family's economic situation, and demographic factors such as age and employment status.[61]

The Divorce-Stress Adjustment Perspective

Stressors

Adjustment

Adults
– sole parenting responsibility
– loss of custody of children
– conflict with ex-spouse
– economic decline
– other stressful
– divorce-related events

– family members successfully function in new family, work, or school roles
– identity is no longer tied to former marriage
– family members overcome psychological, behavioral or health problems caused by stress of divorce

Divorce Process

Mitigating Factors

Children
– decline in parental support
– loss of contact with one parent
– conflict between parents
– economic decline
– other stressful divorce-related events

- social support
- resources available to family
- demographic factors (age, income, employment status)

WRAP YOUR MIND AROUND THE THEORY

Functionalists **believe that the nuclear family is the most highly evolved social form. How might this prejudice people's views about** non-traditional families?

FUNCTIONALISM

Functional theory posits that society is made up of many intertwined parts that must all work together in order to function effectively. According to functionalists, the family is the most important social institution, with the traditional nuclear family being the ideal type. In the 1950s, anthropologist Talcott Parsons speculated that the nuclear family following World War II, made up of husband, wife, and children, was the culmination of many years of evolution.[62] Functionalists believe that strict gender roles, with husband as provider and wife as nurturer, help stabilize and maintain society. Once a family breaks apart through separation or divorce, it no longer performs its intended function and the fabric of society begins to fray. The functionalist position began to disintegrate in the 1970s, as people made more diverse choices about issues including marriage, divorce, sexuality, and abortion. However, traditional views still persist in social, political, and religious conservative ideology.

CONFLICT THEORY

Conflict theorists believe that society is composed of groups that are in competition for scarce resources—in short, that life is one big power struggle. In a marriage, these resources might include economic, social, or sexual factors. For example, if one partner controls the family finances and abuses his or her power, the relationship may suffer. Some conflict theorists argue that the traditional imbalance of power between men and women has shifted in recent years, as women are now able to meet their basic survival needs outside marriage. As a result, women today are far less likely to accept infidelity or domestic violence—burdens that may have been considered inevitable a hundred years ago.

WHY DO PEOPLE GET DIVORCED?

SYMBOLIC INTERACTIONISM

Symbolic interactionists look at the family on a micro level, by studying the meanings that people give to their behavior and to the behavior of others. According to the *Thomas Theorem*,[63] we create our own reality based on our interpretation of a situation. For example, if a husband perceives that his wife is flirting with another man at a party, he may become jealous and angry, picking an argument with his wife. The consequences of his interpretation are real, regardless whether his wife was actually flirting. Symbolic interaction theory examines the roles that people construct for themselves, which may evolve over time. How might this lead to divorce? Spouses assign meanings to their daily interactions and create a role for themselves as a parent, as a spouse, and as a man or a woman. People's evaluations of themselves and their partners change over time, which can affect a relationship either positively or negatively. If a wife does not live up to the image that her husband has created for her (or vice versa), the relationship may deteriorate.

Conflict theorists argue **that the balance of power between the two sexes** is shifting in favor of women. How **might this lead to higher divorce rates?**

According to symbolic interaction theory, **self-fulfilling prophesies may initiate the breakdown of a relationship. Do you agree that perception can influence reality?**

discover marriages and families in action:
HOW DO DEMOGRAPHERS MEASURE DIVORCE?

Measures of Divorce

You've probably heard that half of all marriages end in divorce at some point. But what does this actually mean? Does it indicate that half of all couples who get married today will eventually divorce? That half of all couples who are currently married will one day split up? That half of all people who are ever married will divorce at some point in their lives? Demographers use several different measures of divorce[64]:

Marriage to Divorce Ratio

The **marriage to divorce ratio** compares the number of divorces in a given year to the number of marriages. Let's say there are 500 divorces and 1,000 marriages in a given year. This means the ratio would be one divorce for every two marriages. This is not an accurate way of measuring the divorce rate, because the people who are divorcing in any given year are not the same as those who are marrying. In other words, the statistic compares two unlike populations.

Crude Divorce Rate

The **crude divorce rate** is the number of divorces per 1,000 people. This is a good general indicator; however, the rate represents the total population. This includes people who are not at risk to divorce, such as young children and older single people.

Refined Divorce Rate

The **refined divorce rate** is the number of divorces per 1,000 married women. This is a more accurate method of measurement than the crude divorce rate, but it does not take age into account. Since younger married people are far more likely to divorce than older married people, the statistics

MARRIAGE TO DIVORCE RATIO compares the number of divorces in a given year to the number of marriages.

CRUDE DIVORCE RATE is the number of divorces per 1,000 people.

REFINED DIVORCE RATE is the number of divorces per 1,000 married women.

AGE-SPECIFIC DIVORCE RATE is the number of divorces per 1,000 married women in each age category.

STANDARDIZED DIVORCE RATE is the statistic based on the age-specific divorce rate in each age category that is calculated by adding the total number of divorces across all age categories, dividing the sum by the standard population size, and multiplying this number by 1,000.

may be misleading if demographers compare two population areas with an uneven age distribution.

Age-Specific Divorce Rate

The **age-specific divorce rate** is the number of divorces per 1,000 married women in each age category. This takes any discrepancies in age distribution into account.

Standardized Divorce Rate

The **standardized divorce rate** is a single statistic based on the age-specific divorce rate in each age category. It is calculated by adding the total number of divorces across all age categories, dividing the sum by the standard population size, and multiplying this number by 1,000. A standardized divorce rate is useful for demographers because it provides a single statistic for comparison purposes, although it loses a lot of information in the condensing process.

ACTIVITIES

1. Ask your friends and family members what it means when they hear that half of all marriages end in divorce. Compare and contrast their answers.
2. Locate research articles on divorce or articles in magazines that discuss how many people get divorced. What type of statistics and measures of divorce do they use?

MAKE CONNECTIONS

Divorce and Family Relationships

Divorce breaks down the nuclear family, but frequently creates many new family variations. Looking back at Chapter 9, you can see how remarriage creates step-families, often blending several families together in the same household. Other divorced parents remain single and live alone, whereas still others return to their parental home so that the grandparents can take care of the children.

As you have learned in this chapter, divorce is more of a process than a single event. Various stressors can create the conditions that lead to divorce, including constant conflict between spouses. Looking back to Chapter 3, you can see how poor communication results in conflicts within families and understand the consequences of not managing conflict constructively. Sometimes, there is an imbalance of power in a relationship, which may shift following a divorce. Remember reading earlier in the chapter how people often report feelings of greater autonomy after a divorce? If one spouse makes all the decisions in a relationship, separation can instill a sense of power and freedom in his or her partner.

>>> ACTIVITIES

1. Look at the magazines located in the check out line of your favorite grocery store. How many of the cover stories appear to discuss the topic of relationships or provide relationship advice? Do any of the topics appear to relate to separation and divorce? What does this tell you about our society?

2. Interview a few of your close friends who have experienced a parental divorce or separation. What are some of the things they have experienced during the transitional process of the parental divorce or separation? Are there common themes among their responses? How do their comments compare to the researched presented in this chapter?

14

WHAT ARE THE STATISTICAL, LEGAL, AND HISTORICAL TRENDS IN DIVORCE? 239

The divorce rate peaked in the United States in 1981 and has been falling ever since. Divorce rates are affected by social upheaval. The introduction of no-fault divorce laws in the 1970s simplified the legal process, and in most westernized societies there is no longer a social stigma attached to divorce.

WHAT ARE THE THEORIES BEHIND DIVORCE? 248

Social exchange theorists view marriage as a series of rewards and costs. As long as the rewards of being married outweigh the costs, a couple is likely to remain together. According to the divorce-stress adjustment theory, divorce is a painful transitional process that is influenced by various stressors.

HOW DO DEMOGRAPHERS MEASURE DIVORCE? 251

They measure divorce through several different measures, including the marriage to divorce ratio, crude divorce rate, refined divorce rate, age specific divorce rate, and standardized divorce rate.

Theory

FUNCTIONALISM 250

- the nuclear family is the ideal social institution
- once a family breaks apart, it no longer performs its intended function

SYMBOLIC INTERACTIONISM 250

- people give meanings to their own behavior and the behavior of others
- perception influences people's actions, which may have negative consequences

CONFLICT THEORY 250

- marriage is made up of resources, including financial, sexual, and social resources
- partners compete for resources, and an imbalance of power may lead to conflict

Key Terms

separation is the termination of marital cohabitation *239*

trial separation is a type of separation in which a couple lives apart for a period of time in order to decide whether or not to separate permanently *239*

living apart is a type of separation in which couples do not intend to get back together *239*

permanent separation is a type of separation in which a couple begins living apart *239*

legal separation is a formal separation involving court proceedings regarding property, alimony, child support, custody, and visitation rights *239*

separation agreement is a binding agreement between husband and wife regarding debts, assets, custody, child care, and support payments *239*

canon law is the ecclesiastical body of laws used in England that governed the Catholic and Anglican churches *242*

fault-based divorce is a type of divorce in which one partner is obligated to prove that the other had somehow violated the marriage contract *242*

absolute divorce is the official end of a marriage in which all legal bonds between a couple are severed *242*

no-fault divorce is a type of divorce that allowed couples to divorce without proving guilt or fault on the part of the other *242*

personal factors are individual characteristics such as age, education level, and employment status *247*

contextual factors are outside factors such as the level of social support an individual receives during their time of need *247*

reward is a benefit *248*

cost is a detriment *248*

profit is the ratio of reward to cost *248*

rationality is an alternative view of what constitutes a reward or a cost *248*

exchanges and equity is a system of judging the reward and cost of a situation or relationship *248*

generalized set of rewards is an examination that tries to figure out why most people in general behave in a particular way *248*

divorce-stress adjustment theory is a theory that views divorce as a stressful life transition to which the entire family must adjust *249*

marriage to divorce ratio compares the number of divorces in a given year to the number of marriages *251*

crude divorce rate is the number of divorces per 1,000 people *251*

refined divorce rate is the number of divorces per 1,000 married women *251*

age-specific divorce rate is the number of divorces per 1,000 married women in each age category *251*

standardized divorce rate is the statistic based on the age-specific divorce rate in each

age category that is calculated by adding the total number of divorces across all age categories, dividing the sum by the standard population size, and multiplying this number by 1,000 *251*

Sample Test Questions

MULTIPLE CHOICE

These multiple-choice questions are similar to those found in the test bank that accompanies this textbook.

1. Which of the following statements about legal separation is TRUE?
   a. Couples that are legally separated are no longer married.
   b. Legal separation does not establish alimony or child support.
   c. A couple may file for a legal separation while waiting for a divorce.
   d. Unlike divorce proceedings, a court ruling in a legal separation is not binding.

2. Which of these was NOT a legitimate reason for divorce under the fault-based divorce system?
   a. Neglect
   b. Infidelity
   c. Cruel and inhumane treatment
   d. Irreconcilable differences

3. According to divorce statistics, which of the following people is MOST LIKELY to divorce?
   a. A 30-year-old newlywed man with a college education
   b. A 45-year-old wife who regularly attends church with her husband
   c. A 27-year-old woman who lived with her husband for five years before marriage
   d. A 50-year-old millionaire who organizes annual charity events in her community

4. A teenager whose parents have recently divorced is most likely to:
   a. have low self-esteem.
   b. avoid marriage later on.
   c. start dating later than other teens.
   d. get lower grades in school than other teens.

5. The most accurate measure of divorce is the:
   a. marriage to divorce ratio.
   b. crude divorce rate.
   c. refined divorce rate.
   d. age-specific divorce rate.

ESSAY

1. Discuss the positive and negative effects of no-fault divorce laws.
2. What factors should you keep in mind when reading and interpreting divorce statistics?
3. What are the major differences between legal separation and divorce, and why might a couple choose one over the other?
4. How do sociologists from the three sociological paradigms view divorce?
5. What socioeconomic factors influence patterns of divorce in the United States?

WHERE TO START YOUR RESEARCH PAPER

For more data on U.S. divorce statistics, go to http://www.cdc.gov/nchs/fastats/divorce.htm

For more data on global divorce statistics, go to http://www.nationmaster.com/graph/peo_div_rat-people-divorce-rate

For more information about correlations of divorce, go to http://www.divorcereform.org/cor.html

To find out more about divorce law, including state specific divorce laws, go to http://www.divorcelawinfo.com/

To learn more about the effects of divorce on children, go to http://www.medscape.com/viewarticle/405852_4

For more information about the history of divorce in the United States, go to http://www.americanheritage.com/articles/magazine/ah/2000/7/2000_7_38.shtml

To find out more about covenant marriage, go to http://www.covenantmarriage.com/

For an overview of the arguments for and against no-fault divorce, go to http://www.divorce360.com/divorce-articles/news/trends/divorce-too-easy-in-us.aspx?artid578

For more information about the process of dissolution, go to http://www.lectlaw.com/files/fam23.htm

For general information about divorce, including divorce risk factors and the effects of divorce on adults and children, go to http://www.divorcehelpguide.info/index.html

ANSWERS: 1. c; 2. d; 3. c; 4. d; 5. d

Remember to check www.thethinkspot.com **for additional information, downloadable flashcards, and other helpful resources.**

WHAT ARE THE CHARACTERISTICS OF
SINGLE-PARENT FAMILIES, REMARRIED
FAMILIES, AND STEPFAMILIES, AND WHAT
CHALLENGES DO THEY FACE?
HOW DO DIFFERENT THEORISTS VIEW
SINGLE-PARENT FAMILIES, REMARRIED
FAMILIES, AND STEPFAMILIES?
WHAT ORGANIZATIONS CAN ASSIST
STEPFAMILIES AND BLENDED FAMILIES?

Working

as an executive assistant at a top Manhattan modeling agency, Helen Harris is a popular, ambitious 20-something without a care in the world. She spends her days hobnobbing with the superficial stars of New York's fashion industry and her nights partying at the hottest clubs in town. But Helen's carefree days come crashing to a halt when she learns that her sister Lindsay and Lindsay's husband have been killed in a car accident. To the surprise of the rest of the family (especially uptight older sister Jenny), Helen is given custody of Lindsay's three children—15-year-old Audrey, 10-year-old Henry, and 5-year-old Sarah. Although Jenny—a conservative suburban mom who raised Helen and Lindsay after their parents died—would seem the natural choice for the children's guardian, Helen accepts the challenge. Helen brings the kids home to live with her in her Manhattan apartment.

Quickly learning that parenthood does not fit well with her hectic 24/7 schedule, Helen begins to struggle at work. Unable to juggle schedules, clients, and the requirements of a job that requires frequent travel, she is forced to sacrifice both her career and her lifestyle. Moving the kids to a more affordable, but comparatively run-down apartment in Queens, Helen enrolls them in a nearby Lutheran school and finds a job as a receptionist at a local car dealership. Finding support from her sister Jenny, her neighbor Nilma, and the friendly school principal, Pastor Dan (with whom she begins a romantic relationship), Helen slowly begins to navigate her way through the pitfalls of parenthood, gradually transforming from a cool, hip aunt into a responsible mom. She faces many battles, not only as a new mom but also as a comforter of three children who have just lost their parents. Foremost among Helen's concerns is 15-year-old Audrey, who has to be kept from smoking, using a fake ID, and dating a highly undesirable high school senior on the verge of being expelled from school. When Audrey's prom date takes her to a motel using Helen's credit card with the intention of taking Audrey's virginity, Helen is unable to handle the situation and calls on Jenny to deal with it instead. Feeling like a failure, Helen passes the children on to Jenny, breaks off her relationship with Pastor Dan, and returns to her safe, carefree life in Manhattan.

At the end of the film, Helen discovers that Lindsay chose her to take care of the kids because Helen reminded Lindsay so much of herself. Knowing that her sister had faith in her ability to learn how to become a parent, Helen regains custody of the children and renews her blossoming relationship with Pastor Dan.

SINGLE-PARENT FAMILIES, REMARRIAGE, AND STEPFAMILIES

CHAPTER 15

Raising Helen **brings up some interesting issues** regarding single parenthood. **Although the simultaneous deaths of two parents are rare,** becoming an instant parent is an everyday occurrence.

People often marry into blended families. This creates a host of challenges, with new stepparents struggling to parent their partners' children, and stepchildren struggling to get used to a completely different set of household rules and expectations.

Divorce, death, or separation may also cause people to become instant single parents, creating a different set of issues. As Helen finds out, balancing a family with a career as a single parent is no easy feat. Is it possible for single parents to have it all without compromising the welfare of their children?

Sociologists study the impact of single parenthood on children by measuring factors such as educational achievement, rates of drug and alcohol abuse, and rates of depression compared to children in two-parent families.

Like many people, in June 2009 I was bombarded with salacious details about the separation of Jon and Kate Gosselin, stars of the reality TV show *Jon & Kate Plus 8* and parents of a set of twins and sextuplets.

Following their legal separation, Jon and Kate instantly became single parents, and within weeks reports of new partners hit the media. Should either of them remarry, it will create complex new blended families. In this chapter, we will study the characteristics of single-parent families, remarried families, and stepfamilies and consider the issues that each type of family faces. We will also examine the theories behind these types of families and consider the support systems currently available for them.

>>> With eight children to consider, the divorce of reality TV stars Jon and Kate Gosselin may create complicated family dynamics in the future. **What effects might this kind of mass television exposure have on a family?**

Single-Parent Families, Remarriage, and Stepfamilies

Single-parent families - created through divorce, widowhood, or births to unmarried women

face challenges such as

but are successful when they

– allow losses to be mourned
– have realistic expectations
– nurture couple relationships
– establish family traditions
– gradually develop step-relationships
– cooperate with the absent parent

– financial strain
– difficulty adapting to new roles as stepparents
– differences in parenting styles
– lack of couple bonding time
– issues with children and ex-spouses

get the topic: WHAT ARE THE CHARACTERISTICS OF SINGLE-PARENT FAMILIES, REMARRIED FAMILIES, AND STEPFAMILIES, AND WHAT CHALLENGES DO THEY FACE?

Modern Families

As we have seen throughout this book, today's families are distinctly different from those of the traditional family system, which was based on lifetime marriage and an intact nuclear family. The modern pluralistic system includes families created by divorce, remarriage, births to single women, or, as seen in the film *Raising Helen*, adoption. America's high divorce rate does not seem to discourage people from tying the knot again—in fact, a third of Americans are expected to marry, divorce, and remarry at some point during their lives.[1] On the other hand, many people choose not to remarry after a divorce or the death of a spouse, and others choose not to marry in the first place. In 2010, approximately 26% of all American households with children were single-parent households.[2]

Historically, the distribution of children's living arrangements in American households did not change much between 1880 and 1970, with the number of children living in mother-only households increasing just three percent, from 8 percent in 1880 to 11 percent in 1970. During this time, the vast majority of children (around 84 percent) lived in two-parent households. Between 1970 and 1990, however, these trends shifted dramatically, with the number of children in mother-only households doubling from 11 percent to 22 percent (partially as a result of the no-fault divorce laws that were introduced in the early 1970s). Over the past 20 years, the figures have stabilized as efforts to lower divorce rates and strengthen marriages (such as the Bush administration's Healthy Marriage Initiative) have been introduced (see graph below).[3]

Historical Living Arrangements of Children 1880 to 2010

Percent distribution: 100, 90, 80, 70, 60, 50, 40, 30, 20, 10, 0

1880, 1890, 1900, 1910, 1920, 1930, 1940, 1950, 1960, 1970, 1980, 1990, 2010

- No parents
- Father only
- Mother only
- Two parents

Source: 1880-1960: Integrated Public Use Microdata Series: Version 2.0 made available by the Historical Census Projects; 1968-1995: U.S. Census Bureau, Current Population Survey; 1996-2004: U.S. Census Bureau, Survey of Income and Program Participation, Wave 2. For 1880-1940, children in group quarters are included (1 percent or less of all children); U.S. Census Bureau, Current Population Survey, 2010 Annual Social and Economic Supplement.

∧
∧ **What other factors do you think caused the** drop in
∧ two-parent households?

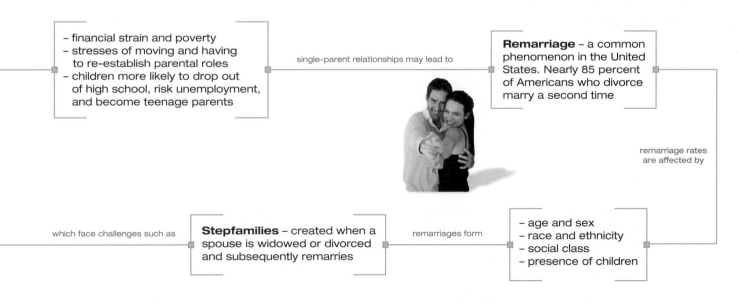

- financial strain and poverty
- stresses of moving and having to re-establish parental roles
- children more likely to drop out of high school, risk unemployment, and become teenage parents

single-parent relationships may lead to

Remarriage – a common phenomenon in the United States. Nearly 85 percent of Americans who divorce marry a second time

remarriage rates are affected by

which face challenges such as

Stepfamilies – created when a spouse is widowed or divorced and subsequently remarries

remarriages form

- age and sex
- race and ethnicity
- social class
- presence of children

Types of Single-Parent Families

As we noted in Chapter 9, a single-parent family may be created through marital separation or divorce, widowhood, or births to unmarried women. Most modern single-parent families are headed by women, although the percentage of father-only households in the United States is on the rise, increasing from 10 percent of the total in 1970 to 13 percent of the total in 2010.[4]

According to statistics, the number of single-parent households created by births to unmarried women is increasing at a faster rate than the number of single-parent families created through divorce.[5] In 2006, 39 percent of all births were to unmarried mothers.[6] Although shows such as MTV's *16 and Pregnant* often give the impression that unmarried mothers are primarily promiscuous or naïve teens, most births to single mothers are to women over 20. An increasing number of women in their 30s and 40s are choosing unmarried parenting because they have not found a suitable partner and are worried about declining fertility.

Although negative attitudes toward single parents have declined over the past 20 years, there has been a recent conservative backlash against unwed mothers and their "illegitimate children." In 2008, conservative columnist Ann Coulter published a book called *Guilty*, in which she linked single motherhood with crime, poverty, and moral decline in society. Prejudiced opinion or point of fact? A look at the research findings for single-parent families may help answer some pressing sociological questions.

FAMILIES HEADED BY MOTHERS

Recent studies of families headed by single mothers have found that children raised in single-mother families created by the death of a father fare better than children raised in divorced single-mother families. Researchers discovered that children raised in widowed single-mother families have higher levels of educational attainment, occupational status, and happiness in adulthood than children from divorced single-mother families. Although there were no noticeable differences in family values, gender roles, or child-rearing practices, sociologists Timothy Biblarz and Greg Gottainer speculated that the discrepancies might be the result of the relative social statuses of the two family types. Divorced single mothers tended to be more financially stressed, held lower occupational positions, and worked longer hours than their widowed counterparts.[7]

Single-mother families are more likely to live in hazardous environments than are other types of families. Researchers found that single-mother families were overrepresented in hazardous environments in 14 U.S. metropolitan areas compared with other family types. Some studies link pollution with negative effects on individuals' physical and mental health and development, especially in children.[8]

Supportive mothering within single-mother families helps reduce the likelihood of teenage delinquency, whereas the impact of father involvement in single-mother families varies by ethnic group. Researchers found that for black adolescents, nonresidential father involvement helped buffer the effects of delinquency and drug use, whereas Asian American and Hispanic father involvement in single-mother families increased the likelihood of problem behavior. One explanation for this contrast is that the Asian American and Hispanic families have less experience with single-mother homes. Although black families have learned to accept that father figures are not always present, in other ethnic groups, the father's presence might only cause more problems since families have not yet learned to live peaceably in this particular situation.[9]

Single-mother families are more likely to be living in poverty than are two-parent families. In 2000, 25 percent of single-mother families lived in poverty, compared with 12 percent of single-father families and five percent of married-couple families.[10]

FAMILIES HEADED BY FATHERS

Recent studies of single-parent families headed by fathers have found that, compared to married parents, single fathers spend 18 percent more on food consumed away from the home and 28 percent more on alcohol and tobacco products than do married parents.[11]

Single fathers earn less than married fathers, have lower household incomes, are less educated, and are more likely to be reliant on public transfer programs. On average, married fathers earn at least $14,000 a year more than single fathers and have total household incomes of at least $20,000 more a year. The socioeconomic gap between married and single fathers is increasing. Between 1984 and 1996, the percentage of married fathers who completed 12 or more years of education increased from 46 percent to 56 percent, whereas rates for single fathers were stagnant.[12]

Gender often plays a role in father custody. Most studies of single custodial fathers indicate that fathers are more likely to take custody of boys than girls.[13]

∧
∧ **Single-father families** are more likely to eat out
∧ than are married-parent families. **Why might this be the case?**

CHALLENGES FOR SINGLE-PARENT FAMILIES

Although the majority of children from single-parent homes do well, there are risks associated with single parenthood. Children from single-parent homes are twice as likely to drop out of high school, run a greater risk of unemployment, and are twice as likely to become teenage parents as are children from two-parent families.[14] These factors are often linked to the stresses families have to deal with following a divorce. Single parents (especially single mothers) experience a dramatic decrease in household income after a divorce, which child support, spousal support, and public assistance typically do not offset. One issue with child support is that fathers often aren't paying the full amount owed. In 2001, 51 percent of divorced and separated mothers were given the full amount of child support owed, while 27 percent received partial payment and 22 percent received nothing.[15] Children of divorced parents also frequently undergo drastic lifestyle changes, such as moving to different accommodations (often for economic reasons), re-establishing individual parental roles, and adapting to the emotional stresses caused by the divorce. Studies indicate that one of the most important factors in children's well-being after a divorce is co-parenting. The risks of single parenthood are greatly reduced if parents are able to develop a cooperative co-parental relationship rather than one that is conflicted and hostile.[16]

BINUCLEAR FAMILIES

After a divorce, families are divided into a **binuclear family** system, in which the original nuclear family is split in two. A binuclear family consists of two nuclear families—one headed by the mother (the ex-wife), and the other headed by the father (the ex-husband). Single-parent families and stepfamilies are both forms of binuclear families, and the former often turn into the latter when divorcees begin to date, cohabit, and eventually remarry.

DATING AND COHABITING AFTER DIVORCE

When couples divorce, former partners often become involved in the process of courtship—seeking and selecting a mate. However, the courtship norms of second and subsequent marriages are not as clear-cut as they were the first time around, with divorced people less willing to waste time on potentially unsuitable dates. Strained finances, the necessity of making childcare arrangements, and changed sexual ethics also alter courtship rituals for divorced parents.[17] Children may find a parent's decision to date difficult to accept, often hoping that their biological parents will reunite. Ex-spouses frequently complicate matters, too, whether because they are jealous that their former partner is dating someone new or fearful that they will be shut out of their children's lives. Despite these complications, remarriage courtships tend to be short, and many people resume dating prior to the divorce decree.[18] Almost one-third of divorced individuals marry within a year of their divorces.

Dating

Although some parents find the experience of being single after a divorce liberating, many do not enjoy being alone and quickly re-enter the dating scene. Researchers have found that:

- A year after a parent's divorce, children have typically met two new dating partners.[19]

- The strongest contributor to a divorced adult's well-being is the formation of a satisfying romantic relationship.[20]

- Rates of mothers finding a new partner are generally lower and slower than that of fathers.[21]

- Younger adults (aged 20–35) are more optimistic about finding another long-term partner than older adults (aged 40–65), who generally experience a more limited pool of potential partners.[22]

Cohabitation

Some divorced people may be reluctant to marry a second time, instead choosing long-term cohabitation. Others consider cohabitation a way of testing a relationship before remarriage, especially if children are present. Half of all remarriages begin with cohabitation, and living together is actually more common after a divorce than before a first marriage.[23] Researchers have also discovered that:

From Classroom to Community } Poverty and the Single Parent

Through her father's company, Jessica became involved with the Business Community Anti-Poverty Initiative in her town. She helps organize job preparation fairs for people living below the poverty line.

"Almost a third of the people living below the poverty line in my town are from single-parent families. Most of them are women who are finding it hard to support their families.

"I've met a lot of single parents through the volunteer group, and some of their stories are heartbreaking. One lady was living in a fairly nice area, but couldn't afford to stay there after she got divorced.

"She had to move her kids to a new house and a new school, and the stress of it all was really getting to them. The kids' grades had started dropping, they were beginning to disrespect her authority, and they'd begun hanging out with a rough crowd at school. I referred her to the youth group we have here.

"Volunteering has definitely opened my eyes to some of the issues surrounding impoverished families. It's extremely rewarding when someone we've coached calls back to tell us they've got a job. It feels like we're really making a difference."

ACTIVITY

Think about the family you grew up in. How was money handled? Do you think the type of family someone grew up in affects how money is handled?

Marital History of Men and Women, 40–49 Years Old

	Men	Women
Never married	14%	12%
Married once	67%	65%
Married twice	16%	19%
Married three or more times	3%	4%

Source: Adapted from Table 3, U.S. Census Bureau, "Detailed Tables—Number, Timing, and Duration of Marriages and Divorces. 2004."
http://www.census.gov/population/www/socdemo/marr-div/2004detailed_tables.html

What reasons might explain the difference between how many men and women remarry?

- Cohabitation after a divorce is more likely than remarriage: Twenty years after the dissolution of a marriage, 56 percent of women and 62 percent of men reported forming a cohabiting relationship, whereas only 16 percent of women and 20 percent of men had remarried.[24]

- Instability in remarried relationships is around 65 percent greater for cohabiters than for non-cohabiters.[25]

- White women are more likely than black women to enter into a cohabiting relationship after the breakdown of a first marriage. Women who have no religious affiliation, few or no children, and who live in communities with low rates of male unemployment, poverty, and receipt of welfare are also more likely to enter into post-divorce cohabiting relationships.[26]

Remarriage

"I don't think I'll get married again. I'll just find a woman I don't like and give her a house."—Lewis Grizzard, American humorist (1946–1994)

Despite the pain and trauma caused by divorce, remarriage is a common phenomenon in the United States, creating a booming industry in support services, books, and magazines such as *reMarriage* and *Bride Again*. Nearly 85 percent of Americans who divorce end up remarried, half of them within three years. About 13 percent of men and women have been married twice, and three percent have married three or more times.[27] Although the remarriage rate in the United States is the highest in the world, it has declined slightly in recent years. This decline may be partly due to the increasing preference for cohabitation over marriage, a factor that is also affecting first marriages in the United States. A number of factors affect if and when people remarry, including age, sex, race and ethnicity, and social class.

AGE AND SEX

The probability of remarrying is higher for men than for women, with recent statistics indicating that 52 percent of divorced men and 44 percent of divorced women over the age of 25 are remarried.[28] Women who are older than 25 when they divorce are less likely to remarry than women under 25, possibly because men tend to marry women younger than themselves. Older women face more competition in the dating pool, and although the number of eligible potential spouses increases for men over time,

>>> The male preference for younger women **reduces the prospects of remarriage for women who divorce after the age of 25.** What kinds of problems might arise in relationships in which **older men marry younger women?**

it decreases for women. Older women are also more likely to have custody of children—a fact that may restrict their ability to socialize or reduce their appeal as potential spouses. According to researchers, women are most likely to walk down the aisle a second time if they married at a young age the first time around, have few marketable skills, and want children.[29]

RACE AND ETHNICITY

Of all racial and ethnic groups, white women are the most likely to remarry. Within five years of divorcing, researchers found that nearly 60 percent of white women, 44 percent of Hispanic women, and approximately 33 percent of black women had remarried.[30]

Sociologists believe that the disproportionately high rates of unemployment, incarceration, and mortality among black males reduce marriage prospects for college-educated African American women. In addition, many college-educated black men marry younger, less educated women or marry across racial-ethnic boundaries, further reducing the dating pool.

Asian Americans have the lowest rates of remarriage in the United States, attributed to their tendency to marry later the first time around and the social stigma still attached to divorce in the Asian American community.

SOCIAL CLASS

As many "sugar daddies" can testify, wealth drastically improves a man's chances of remarriage. Conversely, some studies have found that women with lower incomes are more likely to remarry because they require the financial support. The addition of another wage earner may reduce the negative economic impact of a divorce.[31] Similarly, although men with high levels of education are likely to remarry, well educated women have less to gain from remarriage because they are more likely to be financially independent.[32] However, other researchers contend that remarriage has little to do with socioeconomic status and that working women are actually more likely to repartner because they have opportunities to meet potential future spouses in the workplace.[33]

CHILDREN

In *Raising Helen*, the title character finds it extremely difficult to juggle her sister's children, a career, and a romantic life. Generally, the presence of children reduces the probability of remarriage for both men and women, but especially for women.[34] Although some people relish the idea of having a ready-made family, the concept does not appeal to everyone. Divorced mothers are often busy trying to support their families or are restricted to dating men who are financially able to provide for a larger family. For women, having children from a previous relationship also increases the chances of a subsequent marriage ending in divorce.[35]

REMARRIAGES VERSUS FIRST-TIME MARRIAGES

Remarriage differs from first marriage in several ways. New partners must get to know each other during a time of significant life changes, adding a level of stress that does not exist in first marriages. Previous marital experience often adds an element of caution to new relationships, and although partners hope they will avoid past mistakes, there is also the fear that hurts from previous marriages may recur.[36]

Whereas partners in a first marriage are able to develop an intimate bond before the arrival of children, a second marriage may introduce an entire network of half siblings, stepsiblings, and stepgrandparents. Any rules that existed between the nuclear family in the first marriage have to be renegotiated, and new boundaries and expectations have to be established between stepparents and stepchildren.

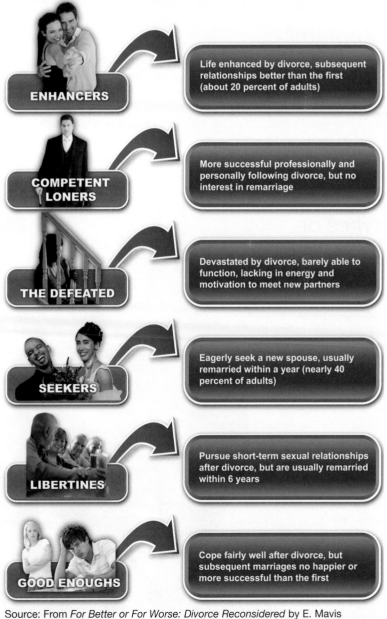

Patterns of Response to Divorce

ENHANCERS — Life enhanced by divorce, subsequent relationships better than the first (about 20 percent of adults)

COMPETENT LONERS — More successful professionally and personally following divorce, but no interest in remarriage

THE DEFEATED — Devastated by divorce, barely able to function, lacking in energy and motivation to meet new partners

SEEKERS — Eagerly seek a new spouse, usually remarried within a year (nearly 40 percent of adults)

LIBERTINES — Pursue short-term sexual relationships after divorce, but are usually remarried within 6 years

GOOD ENOUGHS — Cope fairly well after divorce, but subsequent marriages no happier or more successful than the first

>>> **Sociologist E. Mavis Hetherington** identified six patterns of response to divorce.

Source: From *For Better or For Worse: Divorce Reconsidered* by E. Mavis Hetherington & John Kelly. Copyright 2002 by E. Mavis Hetherington and John Kelly. Used by permission of W. W. Norton & Company, Inc.

People who remarry may find themselves at different stages in their life cycles with conflicting goals. An older man looking forward to a relaxing retirement may marry a younger woman with ideas of starting a family. Alternatively, a woman who already has children may enter a second marriage with strong career goals and no interest in expanding her family.

Stepfamilies

As we noted in Chapter 9, when a spouse is widowed or divorced and subsequently remarries, the new family is known by several, interchangeable names—a remarried family, stepfamily, or blended family. We will use the term **stepfamily** for the remainder of this chapter. The Stepfamily Association of America (SAA, 2009) disagrees with the usage of *blended family* because remarriage does not "blend" two families into something entirely new or sever prior family connections. Children do not lose their individuality or their attachment to the non-residential parent when they become part of a stepfamily.[37]

TYPES OF STEPFAMILIES

The number of stepfamilies in the United States is increasing, with nearly one-third of all children experiencing a married or cohabiting stepfamily before they are 18 years old.[38] There are several types of stepfamilies, defined by the parent-child relationship. In a **mother-stepfather family**, the household comprises the mother's biological children, who are the father's stepchildren. In a **father-stepmother family**, the household comprises the father's biological children, who are the mother's stepchildren. In a **joint stepfamily**, the household comprises at least one biological child of both parents as well as at least one biological child of only one parent (with the other parent

as stepparent). In a **complex stepfamily**, both partners have children from previous relationships.

STRUCTURAL DIFFERENCES

Researchers have identified six key structural distinctions between stepfamilies and first-marriage families[39]:

1 **All members of a stepfamily have experienced important losses.** Whether because of the loss of a spouse or parent through death or divorce, family members may feel anger and hostility, which negatively affects relationships within a stepfamily.

2 **Family members all have histories.** Whereas partners in a first marriage establish rules and expectations before having children, stepfamilies must immediately renegotiate all former parenting strategies, rules, and traditions with children already in the picture.

3 **Parent-child bonds predate the relationship between new partners.** Children often form close bonds with a parent in a single-family structure and may view a new stepparent as an unwelcome outsider.

4 **A biological parent lives outside the family.** Children may be caught in a power struggle between the absent parent and the custodial parent, causing tension within the family. There may be jealousy between the absent parent and the stepparent.

5 **Children in stepfamilies are often members of two households.** Children must often learn to function in two households with two different sets of rules and expectations.

6 **The role of a stepparent is ill defined.** Stepfamilies may encounter disciplinary problems if a stepparent is unwilling to assume a parenting role, or if they create resentment by trying to fill the role too quickly.

CHALLENGES OF BUILDING A STEPFAMILY

A recent report published by the Department of Health and Human Services concluded that children in stepfamilies face similar risks as children in single-parent families. Compared to children living with two biological parents, they are less likely to do well in school and more likely to suffer from depression, experience behavioral problems such as drug and alcohol abuse, indulge in premarital sex, and get arrested.[40] Why might this be the case?

<<< When a parent remarries, the sudden change in family dynamics may cause **feelings of anger, fear, and resentment.** How can such feelings be minimized?

As we noted in Chapter 9, stepfamilies go through several stages of development, ranging from early hopes of an instant nuclear family to a gradual understanding of new boundaries, rules, and expectations. During this time, adults may be under financial strain as a result of child support and spousal support owed to their "former" families. They may also be having difficulties determining where to draw disciplinary boundaries or how to respond to stepchildren. Research shows that relations between stepparents and stepchildren are often characterized by less warmth and support than in biological relationships, and stepparents are often less involved in monitoring and controlling their stepchildren's activities.[41] Differences in parenting styles may also cause tension between spouses, and a lack of bonding time without children makes it difficult for new couples to cement their relationship and form a solid parenting team.

Meanwhile, children in stepfamilies often feel a loss of power and control when their biological family dissolves, causing feelings of helplessness.[42] They may feel angry about having to change home or schools, or about having to share their biological parent with a new family, resulting in disruptive behavior.[43] Loyalties divided between divorced parents can be a further source of stress and conflict, especially if children are caught in the middle of an acrimonious split. Children may feel they are betraying their biological parent by developing a close relationship with a stepparent, which may cause them to put up emotional barriers.[44]

Unlike a nuclear family, a stepfamily does not have an established social model to deal with these complex challenges. There are no guidelines to determine how a stepparent and

stepchild should interact.[45] The time and energy required to deal with these challenges increases the likelihood that stepparents will be less attentive, less available, and more likely to experience conflict with each other, as well as with ex-spouses, biological children, and stepchildren.[46]

CHARACTERISTICS OF SUCCESSFUL STEPFAMILIES

Overcoming the challenges associated with stepfamily life is not an easy task, and many families fall apart under the pressure. Approximately 60 percent of remarriages end in divorce.[47]

Despite the risks, many stepfamilies do function successfully. Marriage and family therapists Emily Visher and John Visher identify several key characteristics in successful stepfamily relationships[48]:

1 **They allow losses to be mourned.** Adults grieve for the loss of a previous relationship and allow children to share feelings of anger, fear, and guilt about their parents' divorce.

2 **They have realistic expectations.** Adults and children come to realize that their stepfamily will be different from their first family and that expectations of instant love and adjustment are not realistic. They understand that relationships develop over time.

3 **Adult couples have a strong relationship.** Remarried adults find time away from the children to nurture their relationship.

4 **They establish family traditions.** Successful remarried families develop their own rituals and traditions to help them bond as a family.

5 **They develop step-relationships.** Stepparents gradually take on a disciplinary role, allowing the biological parent to perform primary parenting duties until a solid relationship with the stepparent is formed.

6 **They cooperate with the absent parent.** Stepfamilies are able to collaborate over child care arrangements, enabling children to transfer between households without being caught in the crossfire between parents and stepparents.

Median Duration of Second Marriages in the United States, 2004

	Total (in years)	White	Black	Hispanic
Men	8.6	8.4	10.2	10.3
Women	7.2	6.8	8.3	8.2

Source: Adopted from U.S. Census Bureau, "Number, Timing, and Duration of Marriages and Divorces: 2004," Table 6. http://www.census.gov/population/www/socdemo/marr-div/2004detailed_tables.html

∧
∧ **Median duration of second marriages in the United States, by** race and ethnicity, as of 2004.
∧

Divorce, Separation, and Remarriage in Austrian Families

The divorce and remarriage trends in the United States are often replicated in other developed countries around the world. In Austria, the divorce rate is 46 percent (relative to the number of marriages per year), and the majority of people who get divorced marry again—around 60 percent of people who divorce before they hit 30.[51] As in the United States, gender differences become significant after the age of 30, with 55 percent of divorced men but only 46 percent of divorced women remarrying within 10 years of their divorce.[52]

However, unlike typical marital life cycles in the United States, second marriages in Austria tend to be lifelong, and very few people divorce a second time. Sociologists have also noticed a new form of partnership emerging in Austrian families that is uncommon in the United States, in which couples choose to live in different households regardless of whether they are married. Dubbed LATs (living apart together relationships), partners in these types of relationships are typically older, have individual careers, and choose to live separately for personal or professional reasons.[53]

REDIVORCE IN STEPFAMILIES

Sociologists attribute the high levels of divorce among second marriages to three main causes: intrapersonal factors that predispose individuals to leave relationships quickly, cultural factors such as inadequate social support for stepfamilies, and interpersonal factors such as the stress caused by family conflicts.[49]

The two primary sources of conflict in remarriages are finances and children.[50] In the film *Raising Helen*, Helen discovers that the resources involved in providing for three children are considerable. In a stepfamily, couples have to work out how to provide for their offspring, as well as how financial resources will be allocated. Additionally, many remarried couples are dependent upon former partners for spousal support, creating tension and stress when payments are late or unpaid. Meanwhile, diverging views about the proper behavior of children frequently create conflicts between couples. Without the positive characteristics identified above, constant stress and conflict can wear down second marriages, leading to another divorce.

think marriages and families: HOW DO DIFFERENT THEORISTS VIEW SINGLE-PARENT FAMILIES, REMARRIED FAMILIES, AND STEPFAMILIES?

TRIANGULATION is a situation in which two family members unite against a third family member, causing loyalty conflicts.

FUNCTIONALISM

Functionalists view the family as a social institution that helps continue, preserve, and sustain society. Functional theorists examine family structures in terms of how they promote social stability. In the eyes of early theorists such as Talcott Parsons, the ideal family form is the nuclear family, in which men and women take on specific roles within a family. Men are expected to take on the instrumental role of family provider and protector, while women are expected to take on the expressive role of nurturer and caregiver, maintaining positive internal relationships within the family.

If we try to apply this model to remarried families and stepfamilies, we immediately run into a problem. Functional theory states that every individual within a family has a specific purpose, but stepfamilies often have two male and two female heads of households—the biological parents and the stepparents. So, who should fill the instrumental and expressive roles? Researchers frequently identify the blurring of parental and stepparental responsibilities as one of the primary causes of conflict within stepfamilies. Biological parents may resent a stepparent disciplining their child, while stepchildren may respond to attempts at authority with cries of "You can't tell me what to do; you're not my real mother/father." Original family members will often unite against an "outsider" in the family (a situation known as **triangulation**), causing loyalty conflicts that hinder stepfamily functioning.

Research suggests that it takes four to seven years for stepfamilies to negotiate these blurred role boundaries in order to progress through the developmental stages required to become a successful functioning stepfamily, and not every family is able to do so.[54] An inability to agree on clear relationship boundaries and to determine parental roles and expectations is a key cause of stress that often leads to the dissolution of second marriages.

CONFLICT THEORY

Conflict theorists believe that conflict is natural and necessary for the survival of social systems. Conflict enables groups who are repressed to challenge the status quo, ensuring the continual progression and development of society. For example, the success in some states of the current campaign to legitimize gay marriage has resulted in a transfer of power, enabling gay couples access to legal rights and social resources that they were previously denied.

Individuals within families compete for resources such as time, attention, money, and space, whereas individuals within society compete for jobs, educational achievements, social status, political equality, and financial success. Are individuals at a disadvantage when they have to compete for scarcer resources? Children from single-parent families often have to compete for the attention of a lone parent, whose time may be restricted because longer work hours are necessary to provide for the family. Children from stepfamilies may have to share their biological parent both with a stepparent and with any other children. Financial resources within the household may also be stretched because of support (alimony, child support) paid to other families. Sociologists frequently question whether accessibility to resources places some families at an advantage over others.

Most researchers agree that, on average, intact two-parent families have higher household income and that higher socioeconomic status is associated with lower levels of adolescent psychological distress.[55] Adolescents from intact families also report the highest-quality relationships with their parents (similarly associated with lower levels of psychological distress).[56] However, rather than being inherent in family structure, this trend may be primarily caused by the amount of resources parents are willing to invest in their children. Parents who invest more social capital in their children (such as time and energy) are more likely to have non-delinquent, well-adjusted youth. Since stepparents typically invest their time and energy in their new spouses and biological children, adolescent stepchildren are often deprived of parental resources compared to children from intact families.[57] Conversely, in successful stepfamilies, children may benefit from additional resources, including multiple role models and an extended kin network.

roles, attitudes, beliefs, and behaviors that we develop through our interactions with others. For example, how do children learn what is considered socially appropriate behavior? If a child in the United States burps after a meal, he will probably be admonished by a parent and learn that burping in public is considered rude. In China, the behavior would likely be encouraged because it is interpreted as a compliment to the person who prepared the meal. Thousands of similar interactions between parents and children, husbands and wives, and other family members help us socially construct appropriate and inappropriate behavior.

Just as we socially construct actions and behaviors, so too do we attribute meanings to terms and expressions based on our experiences. What images spring to mind when you read the words *single mother*? Maybe you grew up in a single-parent family and envision your own childhood experiences. Perhaps you have little personal experience with single-parent families and base most of your assumptions on newspaper articles or television shows. As feminist researchers Sally Lloyd, April Few, and Katherine Allen point out, the term *single mother* is used to cover differing family situations, from a woman with children who lives with her parents (and is financially supported by them), to a mother struggling to pay the bills because she does not receive regular child support from her children's father. In *Raising Helen,* Helen is a young professional who has to uproot herself and three children to support their new life together as a family. Although the women in these three situations have little else in common, they would all be classified as "single mothers" in most studies.

Now consider the term *single father*. Does a single father perform exactly the same role as a single mother? How does the role of a single father differ from that of a married father? Feminist sociologist Barbara Risman found that men who were divorced or widowed and took on full parenting responsibilities adopted parenting behaviors similar to those of women who were mothers rather than the behaviors of married fathers. From this, Risman concluded that gender is socially constructed through everyday interaction, rather than something that is inherent within us.[58]

∧
∧ **Symbolic interactionists believe** that we learn
∧ traditional gender roles through our everyday
interactions with others. **To what extent do you agree?**

SYMBOLIC INTERACTIONISM

Symbolic interactionists study the family on a micro level by examining how family members interact with each other based on their individual interpretations of actions and behaviors. Meaning is not inherent in objects or situations—we assign meanings to people's actions and react to them accordingly. This system of interpretation provides a basis for the

WRAP YOUR MIND AROUND THE THEORY

Negative stereotypes about gay and lesbian parents continue to persist, **even though research suggests that children fare equally well in gay households as in traditional households.** Why do you think this is the case?

FUNCTIONALISM

According to functionalists, individuals have the greatest chance of success if they grow up in a nuclear family, in which the male head of household performs an "instrumental" role and the female head of household performs an "expressive role." When individuals grow up in nontraditional households, these roles may become confused. This blurring of role boundaries frequently results in conflicts, and the stress these conflicts cause may lead to marital dissolution. Researchers frequently discover that children in stepfamilies, compared to children in two-parent families, are more likely to experience behavioral problems and are less likely to perform well in school.[59] The challenges faced by gay and lesbian stepfamilies differ from those that confront heterosexual families, because of negative attitudes about homosexuality, enduring myths about stepfamilies, and a lack of support for parenting within the gay community.[60] However, studies indicate that children raised in same-sex households show little difference in their emotional and social development from children raised in traditional homes, and they are often more tolerant of diversity and more nurturing toward younger children.[61]

CONFLICT THEORY

Conflict theorists believe that family members compete for resources such as time, money, space, and attention. Because these resources are often stretched very thinly in single-parent families with only one adult or in stepfamilies with several sets of children, individuals growing up in nontraditional families are often placed at a disadvantage. However, successful stepfamilies may provide individuals with a wealth of resources that compensate for the negative consequences of divorce and living with a single parent. These benefits might include gaining multiple role models, acquiring new values, ideas, or interests, gaining additional siblings, and potentially improving their economic situation.

HOW DOES GROWING UP IN A NONTRADITIONAL FAMILY AFFECT INDIVIDUALS?

SYMBOLIC INTERACTIONISM

Symbolic interactionists believe that meaning is not inherent in objects or behaviors, but is attributed to them through everyday interactions. We learn how to behave appropriately through the reactions we receive from other people. Some sociologists believe that the most important way to learn how to be a parent is to actively participate in raising a child from a young age.[62] Since most stepparents are unable to do this, they must socially construct what it means to be a stepparent using other sources. Parenting magazines such as *Parenting World*, *Today's Parent*, and *Stepfamily Magazine* offer stepparents their interpretations of how to discipline, communicate, and bond with other stepfamily members, but some things must be learned through interaction. For example, Heather Gallardo points out that her identity as a stepmother could only be formed by interacting with her new stepchildren. She addresses the rules she set for her stepson. He resented these rules, feeling they were too strict and different from those his biological mother demanded. In this case, Gallardo did not like her new role as the evil stepmother. Gallardo later explains how her stepdaughter called her at work one evening, asking for help on an assignment. From their previous interactions, both had learned that this was part of her mothering role.[63]

According to symbolic interaction theory, we socially construct roles based on our everyday experiences. **How much can one learn about how to be a stepparent from reading parenting magazines?** What kinds of things can only be figured out through experience?

discover marriages and families in action:
WHAT ORGANIZATIONS CAN ASSIST STEPFAMILIES AND BLENDED FAMILIES?

As stepfamilies begin to outnumber traditional nuclear families in America, the number of support systems and resources available to assist these types of families is increasing. Here are just a few of the many available stepfamily organizations.

THE STEPFAMILY FOUNDATION

Founded in 1975, the Stepfamily Foundation offers professional counseling for stepfamily members via telephone and in person. The foundation's counseling model is based on the premises of business management. Counselors help families create an action plan defining the roles, rules, responsibilities, and contributions of each in-house family member and any visiting children. Building on couple strength and communication skills, they then work through common stepfamily issues such as discipline, co-parenting, and visitation. Couples typically attend six to eight sessions (and complete additional homework), and the foundation claims to have an 84 percent success rate.

www.stepfamily.org

THE NATIONAL STEPFAMILY RESOURCE CENTER (NSRC)

The NSRC serves as a clearinghouse of information for stepfamilies, including facts and statistics, frequently asked questions, legal policies relating to stepfamilies, research summaries, and useful articles about stepfamilies

ACTIVITIES

1. Research organizations and sources in your community and county that help stepfamilies.
2. Speak to a marriage counselor about the recurring issues that affect remarried families and stepfamilies.

from various magazines. The organization provides a list of stepfamily support groups and professional counselors by state, and it also offers educational resources to enable stepfamilies to learn how to work through problems themselves.

www.stepfamilies.info

THE SECOND WIVES CLUB

As its name suggests, the Second Wives Club specifically targets stepmoms and second wives. It offers a number of resources, including articles by lawyers, councilors, therapists, and other stepmoms, and enables members to blog about their experiences. Members can also join discussion groups to ask advice from other stepmoms or to vent about the challenges they face at home.

www.secondwivesclub.com

SHAREKIDS.COM

ShareKids.com is an online co-parenting system that enables divorced families and stepfamilies to manage child sharing between homes. When parents set up an account, they are able to access tools such as a color-coded calendar that shows which parent the children are with at any given time. The Web site also offers systems that track events and activities, children's medical records, school and homework assignments, and shared parental expenses. Parents can also set up a list of rules organizing court orders and custody arrangements to avoid any potential conflict or misunderstandings.

www.sharekids.com

MAKE CONNECTIONS

Nontraditional Families

As you have learned in this chapter, the number of nontraditional families in society is growing rapidly, shifting perceptions about what it means to be part of a "normal" family. In this chapter, we covered single-parent families, remarried families, and stepfamilies in detail. In Chapter 9 we learned about a wider variety of family types, including cohabiting families and same-sex families.

Today, the United States is represented by many family variations, each adding to the complexity and diversity of American society. Although some types of families face more challenges than others, it is possible for every type of family to experience the happiness and satisfaction of a successful family relationship. In Chapter 16 we will examine some of the common patterns and characteristics of effective families.

>>> ACTIVITY

Ask several of your friends if they are part of stepfamily. If yes, who was in the family? Did everyone get along? What type of issues existed? What did they do for the holidays?

WHAT ARE THE CHARACTERISTICS OF SINGLE-PARENT FAMILIES, REMARRIED FAMILIES, AND STEPFAMILIES, AND WHAT CHALLENGES DO THEY FACE? 257

Single-parent families may be created through marital separation or divorce, widowhood, or births to unmarried women. Most modern single-parent families are headed by women. Following a divorce, families are divided into a binuclear family system, consisting of two nuclear families—one headed by the mother (the ex-wife), and the other headed by the father (the ex-husband). Stepfamiles are created when a spouse is widowed or divorced and subsequently remarries. They are structurally different from first-marriage families and face issues of financial strain, the blurring of role boundaries, and disagreements about parenting.

HOW DO DIFFERENT THEORISTS VIEW SINGLE-PARENT FAMILIES, REMARRIED FAMILIES, AND STEPFAMILIES? 264

Functionalists believe that every individual in the family has a specific role. In stepfamilies, this results in a blurring of role boundaries because there are two mothers or two fathers within the family. Conflict theorists believe that individual family members compete for resources such as time, money, and attention. These resources are often scarce in single-parent families and stepfamilies. Symbolic interactionists believe that we construct meaning through our interactions with others. These interactions teach us appropriate and inappropriate behavior.

WHAT ORGANIZATIONS CAN ASSIST STEPFAMILIES AND BLENDED FAMILIES? 267

Organizations such as the Stepfamily Foundation, the National Stepfamily Resource Center, the Second Wives Club, and ShareKids.com provide stepfamily members with information, counseling, and support from peers to help them deal with the challenges of living in a stepfamily.

Theory

FUNCTIONALISM 264
- in a nuclear family, the male head of household performs an "instrumental" role, while the female head of household performs an "expressive role."
- when individuals grow up in nontraditional families, these roles may become confused

CONFLICT THEORY 264
- family members compete for resources such as time, money, space, and attention
- individuals in nontraditional families may be at a disadvantage if these resources are stretched too thinly

SYMBOLIC INTERACTIONISM 265
- meaning is attributed to objects and behaviors through everyday interactions
- stepparents socially construct their role as stepmother or stepfather using resources such as the mass media

Key Terms

binuclear family is a post-divorce family structure comprised of two nuclear families, one headed by the ex-wife and the other by the ex-husband *259*

stepfamily is a family with a married couple who care for at least one child who is not the biological offspring of both adults *262*

mother-stepfather family is a household that comprises the mother's biological children and father's stepchildren *262*

father-stepmother family is a household that comprises the father's biological children and mother's stepchildren *262*

joint stepfamily is a household that comprises at least one biological child of both parents as well as

at least one biological child of only one parent (with the other parent as stepparent) *262*

complex stepfamily is one in which both partners have children from previous relationships *262*

triangulation is a situation in which two family members unite against a third family member, causing loyalty conflicts *264*

Sample Test Questions

MULTIPLE CHOICE

These multiple-choice questions are similar to those found in the test bank that accompanies this textbook.

1. Which of these statements is true about single-parent families?
   a. The number of single-father families is decreasing.
   b. Most single mothers give birth before age 20.
   c. The socioeconomic gap between married fathers and single fathers is increasing.
   d. Single-father families are more likely to be living in poverty than single-mother families.

2. Which factor does NOT usually affect post-divorce courtship?
   a. strained finances
   b. child care arrangements
   c. changed sexual ethics
   d. reluctance to date

3. What are the two primary sources of conflict in a remarriage?
   a. finances and children
   b. children and ex-spouses
   c. ex-spouses and career
   d. career and finances

4. According to sociological research, which of these people is MOST LIKELY to remarry?
   a. a recently divorced 40-year-old woman with two children
   b. a college-educated, middle-aged black woman
   c. a wealthy, college-educated man with no children
   d. a 30-year-old Asian American man

5. Which of these statements would MOST LIKELY be voiced by a symbolic interactionist?
   a. We learn how to behave within a family unit through our dealings with other family members.
   b. The primary purpose of a family is to continue, preserve, and sustain society.
   c. Social systems survive through competition for scarce social resources.
   d. The nuclear family is the only form in which individuals thrive.

ESSAY

1. The divorce rates for second marriages are higher than the divorce rates for first marriages. Discuss the factors that lead to the lower rates of marital stability.

2. What challenges do single parents face, and how can they minimize the risks associated with single parenthood?

3. How do stepfamilies differ from first-marriage families?

4. Discuss the limitations of functionalist theory in light of the increasing number of nontraditional families in the United States.

5. Examine the resources currently available to stepfamilies within your local area and evaluate whether they are sufficient.

WHERE TO START YOUR RESEARCH PAPER

For more data on single-parent households over the past 20 years, go to http://www.census.gov/compendia/statab/tables/09s1293.pdf

For more information about the effects of single parenthood on children, go to www.census.gov/prod/3/97pubs/cb-9701.pdf

For more information about resources for single parents, go to http://singleparentsnetwork.com/

To find out more about remarriage, including facts and statistics, go to http://www.remarriage.com/Remarriage-Facts/

To learn more about the characteristics of a successful stepfamily, go to http://helpguide.org/mental/blended_families_stepfamilies.htm

For more information about current trends in marital status, go to http://www.census.gov/population/www/documentation/twps0483/twps0483.pdf

For more information about dating after divorce, go to http://www.divorceinfo.com/dating.htm

For global statistics on marriage and family, including divorce rates and single-parent statistics, go to http://www.nationmaster.com/index.php

ANSWERS: 1. c; 2. d; 3. a; 4. c; 5. a

Remember to check www.thethinkspot.com for additional information, downloadable flashcards, and other helpful resources.

WHAT ARE THE CHARACTERISTICS OF AN
EFFECTIVE MARRIAGE AND A SUCCESSFUL
FAMILY?
WHAT ARE THE THEORIES THAT ANALYZE
FAMILY RELATIONSHIPS AND THE ROLE OF
THE FAMILY IN SOCIETY?
HOW DOES RESEARCH DEFINE A SUCCESSFUL
FAMILY?

Meet Me

in St. Louis is a classic musical film set in St. Louis, Missouri, in 1903, just before the famous 1904 World's Fair. The story focuses on the character of 17-year-old Esther, the middle child in the Smith family. Esther is close to Rose, her eldest sister, and follows her romantic dates and marriage prospects while also taking care of her little sisters, Agnes and Tootie.

The story is narrated in four vignettes representing the four seasons. The first vignette illustrates a typical summer day in the Smith household: Mr. Smith is at work at a law firm, and Rose is waiting for a long-distance call from a boyfriend who might finally propose to her. Esther tries unsuccessfully to exchange flirtatious glances with the boy next door, John Truett. Mrs. Smith supervises the preparation of a pot of ketchup, and Tootie comes back home with the man who sells ice around the neighborhood.

The autumn vignette takes place on Halloween night. Tootie's Halloween pranks end up bringing Esther and John Truett together romantically, and the family is shocked when Mr. Smith announces that he has been put in charge of the New York office of his law firm. The family will have to leave St. Louis right after Christmas and before the much-anticipated World's Fair. The girls are especially upset by the idea of leaving their beloved St. Louis and their love interests, schoolmates, and beautiful house. After the first protests, however, the family accepts the father's decision, and the children gather around the piano to watch their parents sing together.

During the winter vignette, Esther receives a marriage proposal from John Truett, which she accepts tearfully, thinking about the upcoming move. Little Tootie has not accepted the decision to move yet, and in an act of rebellion she destroys all the snowpeople she had built with her sisters in the yard. When Mr. Smith sees the wreckage, he gathers the family and announces his intention to renounce the promotion and stay in St. Louis. As the whole family celebrates the good news, Rose's boyfriend storms into the house and proposes to her.

The last vignette takes place in springtime, when the family sets out in their best clothes to attend the opening of the World's Fair. As they stroll happily around the fairgrounds, they marvel at the beauty that is "right here where we live. Right here in St. Louis."

ENDURING MARRIAGES AND FAMILIES:
Successful Patterns of Commitment

CHAPTER 16

In *Meet Me in St. Louis*, the Smiths face an important decision that will affect all their lives. Mr. Smith's promotion and move to New York mean not only an opportunity to advance his career, but also a jump in prosperity for the whole family.

As the day of the move approaches, however, Mr. Smith realizes he needs to take into account the emotional well-being of his children, and he decides to sacrifice his professional ambitions in the name of stability.

The movie, released in 1944 and set at the beginning of the 20th century, certainly represents a model of family that is very different from today's. If a movie version of *Meet Me in St.*

Louis were released today, it would certainly show a very different family dynamic. For instance, the contemporary Mrs. Smith would most likely hold a full-time job and earn a salary comparable to (or higher than) her husband's. Furthermore, she wouldn't be likely to let her husband announce his big plans to relocate the family without consulting her first.

Despite its somewhat old-fashioned content, *Meet Me in St. Louis* raises questions about family commitment that are relevant today. When confronted with important decisions, every family must evaluate what their interpretation of commitment is. This involves not only the commitment between husband and wife, but also that between all family members. In this chapter, we will examine the factors that enhance understanding

between spouses and family members, the characteristics of enduring marriages and families, and how social context shapes the idea of family and commitment. We will also take a look at the theories behind the role of the family in society and behind the relationships and dynamics within families.

V
V
V Some military families are relocated six or seven times during a family member's military career. **What kinds of challenges do you think repeated relocations could have on a family?** What do you think the government or society could do **to help families in this situation?**

Enduring Marriages and Effective Families

are characterized by → **commitment** towards the other members of the family and towards the family as a whole → which is maintained through → quality time together, communication, encouragement and affection, agreed values, rules, trust, ability to cope with stress, creation of rituals

resistance to globalization by maintaining traditions, gender roles. — but also — **Westernized characteristics**—decreased birthrates, widespread contraception, increased cohabitation, increased divorce rate, fewer arranged marriages — which is causing around the world

get the topic: WHAT ARE THE CHARACTERISTICS OF AN EFFECTIVE MARRIAGE AND A SUCCESSFUL FAMILY?

Different people have different ideas about the importance of family in their lives. When I first began to teach at the university in 1993, I had eight weeks of summer vacation. It seemed only natural to me to spend my entire vacation in my hometown, visiting my parents, my younger sister, and other family members. Many of my friends and colleagues were shocked by my vacation plans. They could not understand how anybody would want to spend more than a few days with their families each year. "Don't we have national holidays for that?" a good friend would say. Another friend informed me, "A long weekend with my mother is really all I can take without losing my mind." My friends may have more distant relationships with their family members than I do, but since I moved away from my relatives, I really love spending time with them. It might sound like an overly sentimental cliché, but I consider my family my best friends. In this chapter we will look at factors that research reports suggest are important for the success and effectiveness of a family.

AMERICANS AND THE FAMILY

In December 2005, Gallup, an organization providing statistical data, conducted a poll asking American people about their favorite way to spend an evening. According to the poll, 32 percent of Americans prefer spending an evening at home with their families. Watching TV

>>> **As an evening pastime,** watching TV is experiencing a slow decline in the preferences of Americans, **whereas spending time with the family seems to have become more popular.**

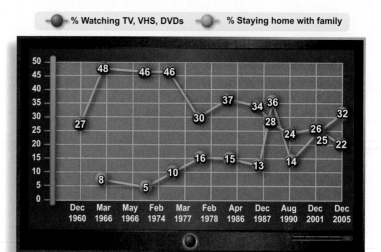

Favorite Way to Spend an Evening: Trend 1960–2005

% Watching TV, VHS, DVDs — % Staying home with family

	Dec 1960	Mar 1966	May 1966	Feb 1974	Mar 1977	Feb 1978	Apr 1986	Dec 1987	Aug 1990	Dec 2001	Dec 2005
% Watching TV	27	48	46	46	30	37	34	36	24	26	32
							28			25	22
% Staying home	8		5	10	16	15	13		14		

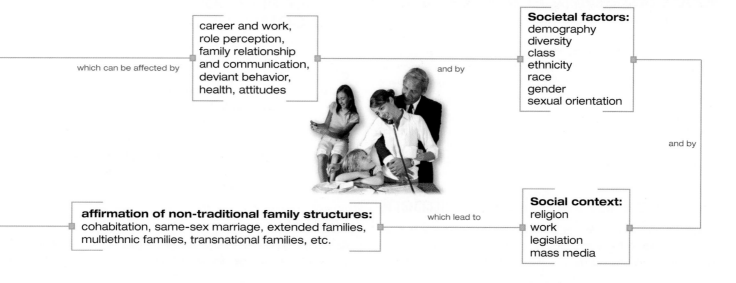

which can be affected by → **career and work, role perception, family relationship and communication, deviant behavior, health, attitudes**

and by → **Societal factors:** demography, diversity, class, ethnicity, race, gender, sexual orientation

and by →

which lead to → **Social context:** religion, work, legislation, mass media

affirmation of non-traditional family structures: cohabitation, same-sex marriage, extended families, multiethnic families, transnational families, etc.

comes in second, with 22 percent.[1] Given the result of this poll, I guess my decision to spend eight weeks of vacation with my family looks less remarkable.

Spending time with the family has not always been Americans' preferred way to spend the evening. In fact, for the past 60 years, family time has mostly come in second to watching TV, which topped the list of favorite evening pastimes from 1960 to 1986 and again in 1990.

The article that accompanied the release of the poll's results pointed out that, according to the people interviewed, "spending time with the family" does not exclude watching TV together as a family. However, in their responses, people stressed that what they valued was spending time with their families, regardless of the other activities taking place during family time.

What Is Commitment?

As discussed in Chapter 5, Yale psychology professor Robert J. Sternberg formulated his "triangular theory of love," which states that love is made up of three components: passion, intimacy, and commitment.[2] The basic assumption is that commitment is twofold: It originates in the decision to love someone (**short-term commitment**) and is reinstated in the effort to maintain that love over time (**long-term commitment**). Through commitment, spouses declare their willingness not just to love each other, but also to honor each other's values and personal happiness.

Karpinus and Johnson, however, detail three types of commitment: personal, moral, and structural. Personal commitment is one's desire to maintain the relationship. This commitment is determined by attraction both to the relationship and to the partner, as well as a relationship identity. A moral commitment comes from a sense of duty to finish what you start, one's values, and your personal obligation to another person. Structural commitment stems from valuing the time and energy you have put into a relationship.[3]

Commitment does not only affect the happiness of married couples. National studies have shown that couples that commit to their marriage and their family will mostly likely encounter fewer behavioral problems and conflicts with their children, whereas children whose parents divorce are likely to enter romantic relationships with more insecurities and less trust than their peers have.[4,5] The essential aspects of commitment, such as love, trust, and respect, are important not only for romantically involved couples, but also for entire families.

Factors that Affect Commitment

Toward the end of *Meet Me in St. Louis,* Mr. Smith decides that he is not going to uproot his family and upset his children by moving the family to New York. By making this decision, Mr. Smith demonstrates that he is more committed to his family's happiness than to his own professional growth. Mr. Smith is not alone in his strong commitment to family, but not everyone would make the choice that he made. In fact, research shows that many factors can affect an individual's level of family commitment.

CAREER AND WORK

There has been an increase in the number of **dual-earner families** (families in which both parents work) in the second half of the 20th century.[6] As a result, couples today often juggle the complex relationship between their roles in the family and their roles at work: They try to be successful workers, successful parents, and successful spouses all at the same time. Although research shows that a strong commitment to work and family can produce increased satisfaction in both spheres, when this commitment does not have positive results in either category, it can result in high levels of stress and dissatisfaction that can in turn lead to marital problems.[7] **Work-family conflict**, or the imbalance between family and work roles, can also be exacerbated by gender differences that are still very much a part of the modern American workplace. Despite the accomplishments of the feminist movement in the second half of the 20th century, women today receive fewer promotions and less consideration when they get married and start a family than do their male counterparts.[8] (See Chapter 14 for more information about how work can interfere with family life.)

ROLE PERCEPTION IN MARRIAGE

Sociology explains that people perceive that their role in the family has a job description. To a certain degree, tradition influences **role perception**, including the stereotypical image of the husband as the family's breadwinner and the wife as the children's caregiver. However, younger generations have set aside traditional gender roles in favor of defining their own lifestyles based on their values of self-fulfillment, equality, and fairness. In other words, younger generations are creating their roles as they go along, regardless of established norms.[9]

WILLINGNESS TO SACRIFICE

An essential result of commitment is the willingness to make sacrifices. Scott Stanley claims that people are more likely to make sacrifices if they have a close bond with the other person. In other words, higher levels of commitment lead to a greater willingness to make sacrifices for others. However, sacrifices should not be detrimental to either person involved.[10]

FAMILY RELATIONSHIPS AND COMMUNICATION

Spouses and family members view positive feelings such as trust, intimacy, love, and support within the family as necessary results of a committed relationship. Family communication is essential to carrying out any kind of commitment. The open and frequent exchange of ideas is an indicator of a cohesive family in which parents and children spend time together and respect each other's ideas and feelings.[11] Moreover, parents who are actively committed to talking with their children and being close to them are more likely to help their children improve their school achievements[12] and encounter fewer problems with **deviant behavior** such as drug abuse and criminality.[13]

HEALTH

As you might remember from Chapter 13, Hill's ABC-X model of family stress proposes that the total amount of stress that a family must endure is the sum of the stressor itself, the resources that the family has to deal with the stressor, and the family's perception of the stressor. A family member's health problems can serve as a stressor in families that are not emotionally equipped to deal with the situation. Pediatricians explain that when families need to provide extensive and long-term care to a child at home, those families can have trouble adjusting to their new responsibilities. For instance, parents who commit themselves to being full-time nurses instead of parents and spouses can negatively affect their children's development and their own relationship.[14] Families might also struggle with a relative's drug addiction or alcohol abuse, chronic pain, or terminal illness, among other health-related challenges. One recent case study examined how an elderly mother's prescription drug addiction changed—and damaged—her relationship with the middle-aged daughter who cared for her.[15]

On the positive side of the health equation, strong family relationships can actually improve an individual's health: People who have love and support from family members tend to get sick less often than do people who lack familial support.

ATTITUDES AND OVERALL HAPPINESS

A good predictor of a happy and enduring marriage is the attitude that spouses have toward each other. People who accentuate the positive have more fun together and show their affection more. One recent study found that generally happy individuals who have positive personal attitudes are more likely to have marriages that remain happy over time.[16] It may sound simplistic, but fun and mutual enjoyment should not be taken for granted in a long-term relationship. Not every interaction in a relationship needs to be positive, but researchers Janice Driver and John Gottman have found that couples who use humor and affection in small ways in their everyday lives are more likely to resolve conflicts positively and amicably.[17]

Creating and maintaining a positive attitude in a relationship might require a change in each individual's personal goals. There is evidence that people who maintain active commitments to family and to other non-competitive aspects of life, such as friendship and social involvement, are generally more satisfied with their lives than are people who don't share those commitments. Further evidence suggests that a person who is committed to competitive goals (such as career advancement and material gain) is likely to be less happy than his or her non-competitive peers.[18]

Characteristics of Effective Marriages

Every marriage is different, and each couple needs to find its own recipe for success. A few key ingredients to an effective marriage do exist, however. First of all, each spouse needs to promote his or her own individual well-being as well as the partner's well-being and the well-being of the relationship itself. In a successful marriage, each spouse has the right to be respected, nurtured, and encouraged to grow. Of course, there will be discord, but arguments are another key ingredient in a marriage: Although disagreements can be painful, if they take place in a healthy relationship, they often lead to better understanding and communication between partners. Finally, every couple should be aware that the only constant in marriage is, ironically, change. Marriages have ups and downs, and it's the spouses' responsibility to face each situation as an occasion to grow together and offer each other safety, protection, and love.

∧∧∧ Parents who monitor their children's studies **and encourage success without being overbearing are shown to help their children improve their achievement in school.** How do you think communication increases a child's sense of responsibility?

TWELVE CHARACTERISTICS OF SUCCESSFUL MARRIAGES

As we discussed earlier, there is no single recipe for a good marriage. However, an analysis of the literature on effective marriages seems to point to 12 basic characteristics of effective marriages:

1. **Listen, talk, and be nice!** Spouses communicate freely, openly, and politely.
2. **Help, then help some more.** Spouses are willing and ready to help each other and do not put themselves first as individuals.
3. **Become a cheerleader.** Spouses give each other unconditional support and encouragement. They genuinely respect and admire each other, and they show it.
4. **Bring your souls together.** Spouses share basic moral values and demonstrate respect and tolerance for each other's spiritual beliefs.
5. **Remember the trinity of happiness.** Spouses engage in a three-fold commitment: to their own individual happiness, to the happiness of the marriage, and to the happiness of the family.
6. **Show that you mean it.** Spouses find their own ways to express affection both physically and verbally on a regular basis.
7. **Marriage is fun!** Spouses spend an adequate amount of time together and are able to laugh and have fun together.
8. **Be together in the trenches.** Spouses find creative ways to cope with crises and times of stress and frustration.
9. **Trust and be trustworthy.** Spouses know they can depend on each other's promises and can count on each other's commitment.
10. **Divide and conquer.** Spouses are responsible to each other and the rest of the family. They agree on shared responsibilities that match their role expectations.
11. **Put yourself in your partner's shoes.** Spouses are able to empathize with their partner, identifying with their thoughts and feelings.
12. **Celebrate change.** Spouses accept each other's differences and adapt to changes in their lives and personalities as their marriage evolves.

In addition to these 12 characteristics, marriage researcher John Gottman and his colleagues have compiled a set of skills that help couples communicate effectively and maintain a positive attitude. For example, Gottman suggests that couples avoid personal critical attacks,

EGALITARIAN ROLES in a family, are when the roles of the parents are regarded as equal.

contemptuous behaviors (such as eye-rolling), and defensive responses to a partner's complaints. Instead, says Gottman, couples should address contentious issues by taking time to calm down, using specific and non-accusatory language to identify problems, and making every effort to understand and validate each other's emotions by listening attentively and empathetically.[19]

Even cursory online research into the secrets of a happy marriage will bring up literally hundreds of thousands of Web sites ready to "solve" any relationship problem. Although several of these prescribed solutions are supported by research, many of these Web sites are far from trustworthy, and avid Googlers should keep in mind that even scientifically valid studies may not hold the key to their unique relationship challenges.

For example, in September 2006, a British magazine published the result of a study suggesting that flirting with strangers may be the secret to a successful marriage. About 25 percent of people interviewed admitted that flirting with strangers increased their sex drive and made them feel more attractive, thus increasing their desire for their partner.[20] Additional studies have shown that people often do flirt just for fun, not to attract a mate. People in completely platonic relationships have been known to flirt with one another, indicating that sometimes the pleasure of flirting is in the act itself.[21] However, critics have countered that while flirting may work for 25 percent of people, it's not for everyone, and it's certainly not the secret to a long-lasting and happy marriage. These findings clearly show that marital happiness is more complex and more subject to individual needs and expectations than we might initially assume.

In one noteworthy study, researchers relied on the ENRICH inventory, an assessment tool that analyzes certain variables in a marriage, to study 5,039 married couples. The researchers' objective was to determine whether the ENRICH inventory could reveal any difference between happily married couples and unhappily married couples. First, researchers differentiated between the two types of couples by asking participants whether they were satisfied with their marriage and whether they had ever considered separation or divorce. Then, each couple and individual were scored on the following variables: personality issues, communication, conflict resolution, financial management, leisure activities, sexual relationship, children and parenting, family and friends, **egalitarian roles**, and religious orientation. The results of the study indicate that, when using either individual or couples' scoring, happily married couples can be distinguished from unhappily married couples with accuracy as high as 85 to 90 percent. It is also interesting to note that the mean scores of men and women who participated in the study were mostly consistent in every one of the aforementioned variables, especially among happily married individuals.[22]

∨
∨   **According to the study,** 57 percent of happily married couples scored high on
∨   conflict resolution, as opposed to 17 percent of unhappily married couples. **What do this and the other striking discrepancies in the graph tell you about the characteristics of an effective marriage?**

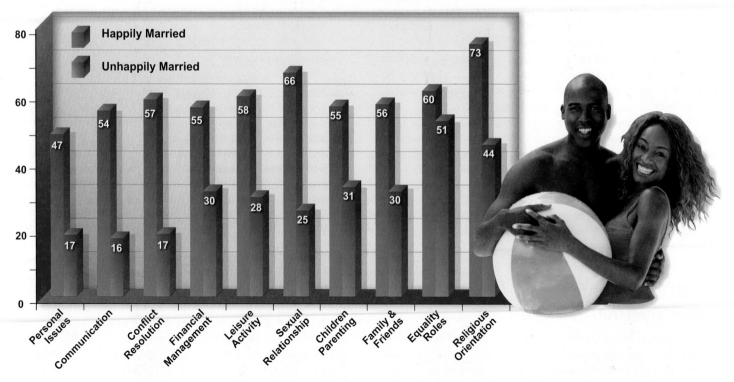

Happily Married Couples vs. Unhappily Married Couples: The ENRICH Inventory, 1989

Legend: Happily Married / Unhappily Married

Variable	Happily Married	Unhappily Married
Personal Issues	47	17
Communication	54	16
Conflict Resolution	57	17
Financial Management	55	30
Leisure Activity	58	28
Sexual Relationship	66	25
Children Parenting	55	31
Family & Friends	56	30
Equality Roles	60	51
Religious Orientation	73	44

Characteristics of Effective Families

"Happy families are all alike; every unhappy family is unhappy in its own way." — Leo Tolstoy, Russian mystic and novelist (1828–1910), from *Anna Karenina*

The other night, I watched part of an episode of *The Andy Griffith Show* on the TV Land channel. The show is a sitcom from the 1960s about a widower sheriff in North Carolina. The easygoing and down-to-earth sheriff lives with his aunt Bee and his young son Opie, played by Ron Howard—who later played Richie Cunningham in another famous TV family series, *Happy Days*. Have the wholesome, endearing families in those old TV series ever given us an accurate portrayal of family life? Sitcoms from the 1960s generally present only one facet of the family: a "typical" white, middle-class family with two heterosexual parents. Of course, not all families fit this description then, and even fewer families fall into these categories today. However, as limited as their perspective may be, these old sitcoms do illustrate several of the principles that characterize happy and effective families of all ethnicities and compositions.

You might wonder what sociologists mean when they talk about "effective families." A 1990 study stated that **effective families** are those that are able to successfully transmit values that allow the children to start successful families themselves. Because this is a difficult criterion to observe—few researchers have the time and resources to observe a family develop over three generations—researchers focused also on parents' satisfaction with both their family and personal lives and their ability to raise well-adjusted and autonomous children.[23]

In an earlier study, researchers observed 200 families across the nation that were judged to be "effective" and "successful" by their local churches. The result of the study identified behaviors that parents should adopt to create effective families.[24] First of all, an effective family begins with an effective marriage, so parents need to nurture their union and commitment to each other. Second, it is important that parents support and respect their children and spend time with them. In an effective family, children are not only given both verbal and physical affection; they are also rewarded for good behavior in order to learn the value of good work and responsibility. Finally, effective families can cope with adversity by maintaining open lines of dialogue and creatively redefining roles and responsibilities in ways that enrich the family experience.

More recent opinions encourage some of the same practices for effective families. In 1997, best-selling author Dr. Stephen R. Covey published *The 7 Habits of Highly Effective Families*. In his book, Covey suggests that when families encounter a major or minor problem, family members should refrain from getting actively upset and blaming each other. Instead, they should pause for a moment to cool down and consider possible solutions to the problem. Covey also says that strong families work together to solve problems, and they respect and value each member's unique perspectives. Finally, Covey reminds families that they need to prioritize. Families should make a clear commitment, possibly reworking their weekly schedule, to create openings for family time. In this sense, family rituals are highly recommended, as they promote family unity and bring family members closer together.

Experts suggest that families focus on spending quality time together by telling each other stories, eating together, playing and joking, creating family rituals, and generally enjoying each other's company. On top of this, parents have responsibilities to their children, but they have responsibilities to themselves as partners in a married couple. According to experts, parents should try not to fight in front of the children, and they should keep their voices down when they need to set rules.[25]

∧
∧ **The representation of the family has changed on television, too.** In the 1970s, the
∧ wholesome *Happy Days* presented the perfect all-American Caucasian family with the father as breadwinner and the mother as caregiver. **In the 1980s, it was the turn of the successful, dual-earner African American family of *The Cosby Show*.** Today, *The New Adventures of Old Christine* tells the story of a divorced mother living with her brother and her son while coping with her ex-husband's new relationship. **How do you think the movie industry represents family and parental gender roles today?**

ETHNICITY refers to a group of people sharing the same language, geographical origin, culture, and traditions.
BIRTHRATE is the average number of births on a given year.

INTERNATIONAL FAMILY STRENGTHS MODEL

Researcher John Defrain and his colleagues developed the International Family Strengths Model. This model, based on a study of over 24,000 family members in the United States, reveals that even though families face unique joys and challenges, family strengths are similar across cultures.[26] Defrain lists six qualities that represent strong families: appreciation and affection, commitment, positive communication, enjoying time together, spiritual health, and the effective management of stress.[27]

Defrain believes that members of a strong, or effective, family will openly express love for one another. They are also committed to the family, meaning that activities outside the home do not interfere with time and energy put into the family. Defrain points out that a committed marriage is part of this characteristic. Communication is extremely important when facing conflict, but day-to-day communication should also be positive. Families should be able to perform their daily routines with productive communication but should also make time just to talk in order to connect.[28]

One of the key qualities of a strong family is time spent together. In his study, Defrain found that the majority of people cited their favorite memory as a time spent with their family. Rarely was this an extravagant trip to Disney World, for example, but more often the most positive memories were small camping trips or nice meals that the family shared.[29]

Although some may find the inclusion of spiritual well-being controversial, Defrain insists that a strong family must have it. This spirituality can be in the form of organized religion, but also include any type of faith, hope, or connection to the world. Spiritual health, Defrain says, helps people connect to one another on a level of love and compassion. Finally, Defrain's model focuses on the family's ability to deal with conflict. Even strong families face hardships, but they can often prevent troubles, or they work together to face them when they come.[30]

The Family Today and Tomorrow

WHAT IS A FAMILY?

In the U.S. legal system, the family has been traditionally defined as a unit consisting of a heterosexual married couple and their child or children, which corresponds to the term nuclear family. Some sociologists, including researcher David Popenoe, argue that the nuclear family is the healthiest environment in which to raise children. Popenoe theorizes that alternative family arrangements have led to the decline of the family and to a dangerous societal de-emphasis on children.[31,32]

Other sociologists argue that family is not declining; it is simply changing. Many scholars have a more flexible definition of "family," taking into account the extended family of grandparents, aunts and uncles, and cousins, and sometimes even people who are not related by blood at all. What about separated and divorced parents, same-sex couples with adopted children, cohabiting couples with children, and other combinations of adults with responsibilities for children? According to many (but not all) people's definitions, these are families, too.

A person's definition of family is likely to be affected in part by his or her racial or ethnic background. For example, African Americans are more likely than European Americans to hold a broad view of family, including extended family members as well as close friends in the familial mix.[33] More broadly, we can say that each individual's

>>> Americans' opinions about many aspects of marriage have changed over time. In the 1950s, very few people approved of marriages between African Americans and whites, but by 2007, nearly 80% of poll respondents approved of these marriages. What other opinions about marriage have changed over time?

Percentage of Americans Approving of Marriage Between African-Americans and Whites

Source: Gallup Poll (http://www.gallup.com/poll/117328/Marriage.aspx)

perspectives on the family will differ based on his or her background, values, and beliefs.

In modern U.S. society, the question of what makes a family is at the center of several significant cultural debates, and each person brings his or her own answers to the table to consider. Most people agree, however, that changing social values are currently affecting and possibly expanding the traditional definition of the family in the United States.

REDEFINING THE CONCEPT OF FAMILY

What factors are redefining the concept of family today? First of all, it is important to look at changes in the demography—or makeup—of the American society. According to the United States Census Bureau, the number of cohabiting couples, or unmarried couples of the opposite sex living together, was 12 times as large in 2006 as it was in 1960. In 2010, more than a third of those cohabiting couples had children under 18 years of age.[34] Marriage can no longer be considered the only basis of the American family.

Class, race, and **ethnicity** are other important factors to consider as we redefine what makes a family. The traditional, middle-class Caucasian family with lots of cheerful children depicted in many classic movies has always been a projection of the class that produced it rather than a reality. Not only is U.S. society a composite of many different economical statuses, but it is also made up of different races and an increasing variety of ethnicities[35] that are in turn mixing to create interracial and multi-ethnic families. Different cultures are bound to have different definitions of family, commitment, and even affection, since cultural context strongly influences the values shared by couples and families.

What about same-sex couples and their families? According to the Census Bureau, in 2000 there were 594,391 cohabiting same-sex couples in the United States.[36] In 2005, that figure had increased by 20 percent,[37] which represents the willingness of same-sex couples to affirm their partnerships on one hand, and that the stigma associated with same-sex families is being relieved on the other. As the battle for same-sex marriage continues on the national and international stage, it is matched by the struggle to guarantee adoption rights to same-sex couples or, where these rights are already granted, to have them made legally equal to the rights of heterosexual couples. Despite criticism by some U.S. voters, there is a growing consensus that children raised by same-sex couples do not suffer any

disadvantages when compared with children raised by heterosexual families.[38] Same-sex couples have now been granted the right to adopt in 22 states and the District of Columbia. In 2007, it was estimated that same-sex partners cared for about 65,000 adopted children and 14,000 foster children.[39]

FAMILY ACCORDING TO THE LAW

What do governments have to say about the ways in which the concept of family is changing? Although many states in the United States still only consider a family legal if it is a nuclear family, other family forms are being recognized across the country. Around the world, many countries are struggling with ever-increasing demands to legally redefine the family to include cohabiting couples, same-sex partners, and polygamous marriages. In Canada, the notion of marriage has been expanded to mean "conjugal relationship," allowing unmarried, heterosexual couples living together and same-sex couples in long-term relationships to claim rights previously held only by heterosexual married couples.[41] These rights commonly include access to tax benefits and family health plans, acknowledgement of each partner as decision-maker in case of serious health conditions of the other partner, and the right to inheritance and Canada's equivalent of Social Security payments after the death of a partner.[42]

The issue of family is often discussed in cases involving the custody of children and non-biological parents. For example, a case from 2003 involved 12-year-old Timmie, whose mother had just died. Both father and stepfather were given joint custody, and Timmie was allowed to choose his stepfather as his primary caregiver.[43] In a case from the 1990s an Israeli woman and her husband had her eggs fertilized with his sperm and then frozen. When the couple divorced, the woman wanted to implant the fertilized eggs in a surrogate, but the husband refused. After many appearances in court, the woman won the right to the eggs.[44] After Michael Jackson's death in June 2009, the biological mother of two of his children requested custody, even though she turned full custody over to Jackson in 1999.[45] So, does Jackson's family have a right to seek custody of the children, or should the children be with their biological mother?

∧
∧ **For five months in 2008, same-sex**
∧ **marriage was legal in California.**

Critics argue that same-sex marriage would weaken the institution of marriage. **Supporters counter that the bonds of marriage would actually be enriched and strengthened.** What do you think are the reasons for both positions?

FAMILIES AROUND THE WORLD

How are families changing around the world? Countries throughout the Western world have experienced changes in the family system similar to the changes taking place in the United States. For example, **birthrates** are decreasing due to the widespread availability of contraception;

the average age of individuals at their first marriages has increased; the boundaries between traditional gender roles are becoming increasingly blurred; and there are more domestic partnerships and higher **divorce rates** than there have been in the past.

Non-Western countries have undergone equally remarkable changes. Extended households are giving way to nuclear households, divorce is less stigmatized, and parents are exerting less control over their children's lives (for example, there has been a recent decline in the number of arranged marriages, those in which the marital partners were chosen by people other than the spouses[46]). Low-income women in developing countries still face considerable financial, legal, and social barriers to contraception and other family planning tools. As women around the world gain greater access to information and technology, however, their countries' birthrates may very well decrease, mirroring birthrate trends in more developed nations.[47]

Globalization and recent international events, such as the economic crisis that exploded in 2008, are also reshaping traditional family systems around the world. For example, adolescence—that stage of life so familiar to American teenagers, when rebelling against authority figures and challenging parents' viewpoints are popular pastimes—began as a 20th-century Western phenomenon. Now, however, young people around the world are embracing an American-style, consumption-focused adolescent experience, and their relationships with their parents and guardians are changing as a result of this Western influence.[48] As people find themselves reading the same books and newspapers, listening to the same music, and watching the same movies as their fellow human beings around the world, they begin to consider—and occasionally embrace—new values and new images of families.

FUTURE OF THE FAMILY

Given the changes that the American family has undergone in the past 60 years, one cannot help but wonder what will happen next. In *Families With Futures: A Survey of Family Studies for the Twenty-first Century*, sociologists Meg Wilkes Karraker and Janet R. Grochowski address several issues affecting families today and hypothesize what future families will look like.[49] For example, it is hard not to wonder how technology will change the relationship we have with our families. As more and more people become glued to their computer screens and mobile phones, families may have to go to extra efforts to find the time to sit together at the dinner table. And if our culture continues to place an emphasis on monetary success and working long hours, parents will have to develop new strategies for balancing work and family life.

Around the world, there has been a **paradigm** shift, or a change of assumptions, in the way that family is perceived. People's concepts of love, marriage, and family are already very diverse and are constantly changing. Will people embrace marriage or abandon it? Will more people have fewer children at a later age or start larger families at a younger age? Will **monogamy** become more or less popular with time? How important will gender and sexual orientation be for future families? We may not be able to predict what families will look like 50 or 100 years in the future, but we can act as critical thinkers and interested observers as the values and beliefs of our cultures shift and change.

Marriages and Families in the 21st Century: U.S. Families in Social Context

Let's take a step back now and look at the U.S. family as we know it. How does social context affect the U.S. family? After all, culture—shared beliefs, values, behaviors, and ideas passed from a generation to the next—bear a significant impact on marriages and families. Social institutions, too, can have a tremendous impact on families.

RELIGION

Religious beliefs can strongly affect the way couples view their relationship and commitment. Religions often support marriage and family theoretically by taking clear positions on matters such as gender roles, premarital sex, divorce, and abortion. Religions also support marriage and family by implementing services such as premarital and marital counseling, family centers, and programs for the education and entertainment of the children.

WORK

Industrialization and the redefinition of gender roles in a more egalitarian direction are still affecting how families function. In dual-earner families with small children, parents rely more and more on day care centers and babysitters to look after their kids while they are at work. In other families, the work-family conflict is avoided by having a parent, most commonly the mother, give up or suspend a professional life to care for the children at home. For lower-income families, the work-family conflict can be difficult to resolve, leading some parents to explore non-traditional work hours and part-time or telecommuting solutions. Because their hourly wage is low, many lower-income families find themselves working more than a traditional 40-hour week, which results in parents' being away from their children more often.[50] In any case, the demands of the parents' work lives influence the way they handle and share responsibilities at home and the time they can dedicate to their children and to each other.

LEGISLATION

There is a wide variety of family issues on which the government legislates, from tax benefits for married couples and parents with dependent children to alimony in case of legal separation or divorce. For example, in May 2009, the U.S. government introduced the Reuniting Families Act to bring together immigrant families that are currently living apart due to long immigration-processing times.[51] Recently, state legislation has focused on the issue of same-sex marriage, which, as of June 2009, is legal in the states of Connecticut, Maine, Iowa, Massachusetts, Vermont, and New Hampshire.[52] In 2008, the controversial Proposition 8 changed the California state constitution by banning same-sex marriages five months after they had been legalized by the state courts. Proposition 8 states that, for the state of California, marriage is only valid if it is between a man and a woman. Gay rights groups have challenged the decision by arguing that the ban required legislative approval and should not have been put to the voters. However, on May 26, 2009, California's Supreme Court upheld the ban, albeit guaranteeing the validity of same-sex marriages celebrated before the passing of Proposition 8.[53]

LEADERSHIP

What image of the family do our leaders promote? In May 2009, President Barack Obama was invited to deliver the commencement address at Notre Dame University, a Catholic university. The event was

Religious Couples and Marriage Satisfaction (1973–1994)

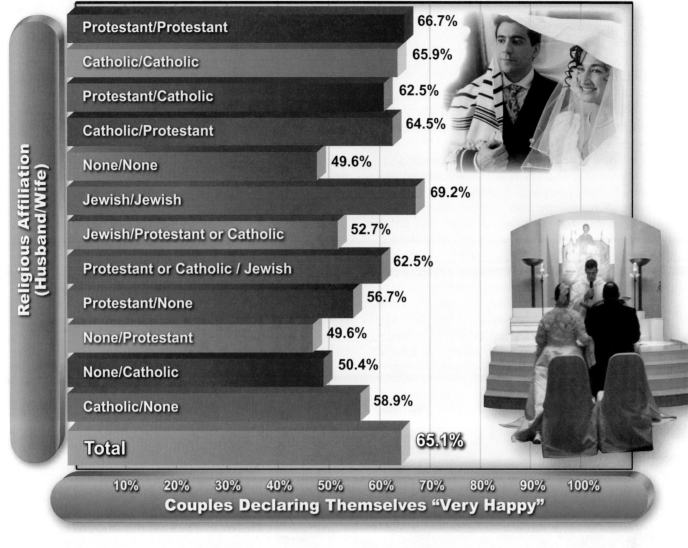

Religious Affiliation (Husband/Wife)

Protestant/Protestant	66.7%
Catholic/Catholic	65.9%
Protestant/Catholic	62.5%
Catholic/Protestant	64.5%
None/None	49.6%
Jewish/Jewish	69.2%
Jewish/Protestant or Catholic	52.7%
Protestant or Catholic / Jewish	62.5%
Protestant/None	56.7%
None/Protestant	49.6%
None/Catholic	50.4%
Catholic/None	58.9%
Total	65.1%

10% 20% 30% 40% 50% 60% 70% 80% 90% 100%

Couples Declaring Themselves "Very Happy"

Source: http://www.trinity.edu/~mkearl/fam-inst.html

Studies show that couples who share the same religious beliefs display **greater satisfaction with their marriages than couples who do not share the same beliefs.** Based on what you have learned on factors that determine successful marriages, **how would you explain these results?**

highly publicized because of the president's support for abortion rights and stem cell research, both of which the Catholic Church opposes. In his speech, President Obama acknowledged that the debate on abortion has no clear solution and that the opposing views on the matter are "irreconcilable."[54] Nonetheless he argued that both sides adopt a respectful and open exchange of ideas, so that neither side of the matter could be reduced "to caricature." President Obama then called for legislation that supports safe and effective family planning and women's empowerment in developing countries. President Obama's views on abortion are different from the staunch anti-abortion view professed by his predecessor President George W. Bush. At the beginning of his first

term, President Bush placed restrictions on international funding for family planning, banning any language in counseling that mentioned abortion as an option (rules that were repealed by President Obama in January 2009).[55] The guidance we get from our leaders depends in part on their own moral and political outlook.

Even First Lady Michelle Obama has spoken on matters that concern the family, stating that U.S. society is in need of more family-friendly policies. At a meeting of Corporate Voices for Working Family, a non-profit organization dedicated to improving work-family balance, Mrs. Obama declared that her mission as First Lady would be that of promoting a healthier balance between work and family. She spoke in favor of paid sick leave, more flexible work schedules for working parents, and paid leave in cases of birth, adoption, or serious illness of a child.[56]

MASS MEDIA

The **mass media** have played a significant role in family life over the past century, and chances are good that they will continue to do so. A 1999 study revealed that children in the United States spend an average of 42 hours every week using various media (watching TV, playing videogames, etc.).[57] That's as much time as many adults spend at a full-time job! But what is the effect of children's in-depth exposure to mass media? That seems to depend on the nature of the content. Research shows that inappropriate images in the media have been associated with aggressiveness, substance abuse, diminished self-esteem, poor school achievements, and obesity.[58] For these reasons, pediatricians recommend that parents gain control their children's media time and monitor the content of the media their children are exposed to.[59] However, educational programming may actually stimulate the child to learn and can even encourage positive social behavior. A 2005 study on the influence of anti-smoking campaigns showed that mass media, and television in particular, could actually become an effective tool to curb pre-teen and teenage smoking.[60]

Mass media can also be used to positively influence adult family members. In 1992, two multimedia campaigns were launched in Nigeria with the goal of promoting family planning and contraceptive techniques. Approximately 1,500 Nigerian men and women of childbearing age were interviewed at the end of the campaigns by researchers from the Johns Hopkins School of Public Health, and the interviews revealed that the campaign had been successful in reaching their target audience. People admitted having conversations at home about family planning, and there was an increase of 7 percent in the use of contraceptives.[61]

Mass Media and Parenting

In 1998, the U.S. Centers for Health Communication at the Harvard School of Public Health sponsored a study of the relationship between mass media and parenting education.[62] The study concluded that mass media affects parenting both positively and negatively. On one hand, mass media promotes interest in parenting education. The study points out that books on parenting currently constitute about 20 percent of the psychology literary market, and the presence of child-rearing advice is mushrooming on television and in the electronic media.[63] In recent years, television shows such as *Supernanny* and *Nanny 911* have been providing advice on basic techniques of discipline to frustrated parents around the country. On the Web, a Christian Web site helps parents monitor the content of movies watched by their children by posting detailed reviews of violence, sexual content, immorality, and generally anti-Christian views in released movies. Software developers are trying to help parents monitor their children's online activities through parental control software that blocks inappropriate Web content, instant messaging, and social networking Web sites. NEWPIN, a program aimed at child protection and parental education, notes that the media focuses on negatives by assigning labels such as "abusive mother" and relating horror stories. The organization has attempted to focus on the positive aspects of changing one's behavior by encouraging headlines such as "Giving our dads a helping hand" or "Struggling mums aided."[64]

On the other hand, the information presented by mass media is often scattered and contradictory, and parenting guidance is often undermined by unrealistic representations of family in the entertainment media. Many people have expressed concern about sitcoms and films that represent stereotypical gender roles and images of teenagers as inescapably rebellious and prone to crime and drug abuse. One example is presented by the successful teen drama *Gossip Girl,* which focuses on the lives of scheming privileged teenagers in New York's Upper East Side and their complicated amorous lives. Provocatively, a famous campaign presented the series as "every parent's nightmare."

Despite the contradicting attitudes of mass media toward parenting and the family, the researchers at the U.S. Centers for Health Communication concluded that the media's increased attention to family issues can serve as an opportunity for parents. If helpful information presented by the media is validated and consolidated by experts, it could become a valuable resource for parents, associations, health care providers, advocates, and policy makers.[65] NEWPIN agrees that positive information on aid programs and successful parenting stories should be presented by the media to encourage parents to seek the help they need to raise happy and healthy children.[66]

∧ In 2009, Michelle Obama launched the White
∧
∧ House Kitchen Garden **with the help of students from the Bancroft Elementary School in Washington, D.C.** Michelle Obama is promoting better eating habits at home and at school. **How can government encourage parents' responsibility to their children's health?**

Family Commitment and Adversity

Even effective families are bound to face adversity and stress from time to time. If difficult situations are handled with responsibility and mutual respect, however, they can become opportunities for growth as well as a chance to reinforce family commitment. Looking back to Chapter 1, you can see how families are affected by individual and societal factors. When couples and families are able to cope with adversity and stress, they develop the characteristics essential to effective marriages and families.

Do you remember reading earlier about factors that can affect the future of the family? When a family does not respond well to adversity or stress, it may develop an alternative family structure to deal with the situation. Economic crises can reshape a family's ability to spend an appropriate amount of time together. If parents are stressed about money after a job loss, for example, they may spend too much time budgeting or looking for additional employment. Then, the children may not get the time they need with their parents. The marriage itself may become broken if couples are fighting over the situation and not giving positive attention to one another. Other families find that they grow closer during adversity because they have to work together, which can promote communication and diminish selfishness, to overcome their difficult circumstances.

>>> ACTIVITY

Identify two religious leaders in your community. Ask them the following questions:

Define family commitment.
Which factors are the most important in contributing to family commitment?
Which factors are the least important?
What recommendations do you have for families who wish to increase their level of family commitment?

▶▶▶ GO GL🌐BAL

Future Families

Are we able to predict what families will look like around the world in the future? Making predictions implies considering the deep effects that socioeconomic changes have on our society, and realizing that the concept of the family as we know it can change dramatically.

Kenya

A recent survey conducted by Northern Illinois University asked several Kenyans between 20 and 50 years of age living in the United States to make their predictions about what families in Kenya will look like 10 years from now. Participants were encouraged to make their predictions based on existing socioeconomic conditions. They expressed their opinions on a variety of family-related issues such as courtship, mate selection, fertility, family structure, children's education, and so on.

Interestingly, respondents made the distinction between families in the cities and those in the rural areas of Kenya. Interviewees reflected on modern Kenyan cities where cohabitation is increasingly more common, as is the use of dating Web sites. What will most likely be the effect of these lifestyle changes? Respondents predicted that the number of egalitarian relationships (and, consequently, the number of divorces) will increase. In the rural areas, fixed gender roles are not expected to disappear as quickly, and some respondents predicted a strengthening of traditional values as a deliberate rejection of more egali-

tarian relationships. Respondents believed that the growing availability of contraception will lead to a larger number of couples without

∧ **International organizations such as the U.S. President's Emergency Plan for AIDS Relief (PEPFAR) are implementing programs to aid families with members affected by HIV and AIDS through counselling and medical assistance.** How do you think such program affect the dynamics of families affected by HIV and AIDS?

children, as well as to reduced influence of extended family members in decisions about family planning.

Respondents also made several interesting comments about the future of parenting in Kenya. In 2001, the Children's Act established detailed provisions about parental responsibility and the rights of children. According to the Act, Kenyan children have the right to be protected against physical and psychological abuse, exploitation, and abandonment.[67] Respondents who held more traditional values expressed concern that families would become too child-centered and that parents would lose their control and authority over their children. Finally, respondents predicted that the AIDS epidemic will create a growing number of families in which grandparents will take primary care of their orphaned grandchildren. This potential change will lead to new family dynamics and the need for different parenting skills.[68]

What does this study tell us about the future of the family worldwide? One conclusion we can draw is that globalization will continue to export Westernized ways of experiencing courtship, marriage, and parenting to non-Western countries. Marriage and the family structure will become more diversified, leading governments to issue new policies to protect and define families according to different criteria. In certain areas, globalization will also be rejected, and old traditions will probably be strengthened and adjusted to meet the needs of the modern world.

think marriages and families: WHAT ARE THE THEORIES THAT ANALYZE FAMILY RELATIONSHIPS AND THE ROLE OF THE FAMILY IN SOCIETY?

SEXUAL REGULATION is the practice of restricting sexual activity to the spouse only.

SOCIAL PLACEMENT is the transmission of role and social status from one generation to the next.

TRANSNATIONAL FAMILIES are families settled in one place but with relationships across countries.

MARRIAGES AND FAMILIES: THEORETICAL PERSPECTIVES

How do sociologists view the role of the family in society and the workings of family relationships? Here are three perspectives:

Functionalism

"Why are we doing this?" This must be the question that many newlyweds ask themselves after the honeymoon, when all the adrenaline of the wedding preparation, ceremony, gift opening, and traveling has worn off. Those couples will need some time to adjust to their routines, but their question is deeper than they might think.

The functional theory views social institutions such as marriage and family as the means to respond to collective needs. Anthropologist George Murdock, a functionalist, celebrated the role of the nuclear family, defined as an economic and reproductive entity sharing the same residence.[69] According to functionalists and their definition, the nuclear family fulfills many roles. First of all, the family has a role in socialization, because parents teach their children to become valuable members of society. Then, family helps **sexual regulation** in society by restricting sexual activity to spouses and encouraging marriage outside the family. One example of sexual regulation is the incest taboo that is common in every culture to prevent physical and mental damage to the children of close relatives. Families play a role in maintaining **social placement**, because they transmit their ethnicity, religion, and social status to their children. Finally, families ensure affection and emotional support for their children, making them emotionally equipped to deal with the challenges of the outer world.[70]

So, how can we answer the confused newlyweds' question from a functionalist point of view? First, those newlyweds should know that the propagation of the species is dependent on their sexual relationship as non-related male and female. Thanks to their union, their children will inherit their parents' cultural background and social status and find a place in an orderly society. In addition, the parents will provide all the love and affection that their children need to become well-adjusted adults. According to functionalists, those newlyweds have plenty to do.

Conflict Theory

Who makes the important decisions in a family? Is compromise always preferable to imposition? Is power equally shared by all members of the family? Conflict theory looks at the patterns of power struggle in the family structure. Starting from the assumption that, in society, whoever controls the most important resources has the most power, conflict theory looks at the way families organize around a hierarchical structure and how such a structure might generate conflict. What resources are valuable within a family? Resources can be age, money, physical strength, ability to reproduce, ethnicity (especially in multiethnic families), and the responsibility to make decisions. In a family with children over the age of 16, car keys immediately become a resource. As power is distributed in the family, competitive structures may arise between spouses, between parents and children, and even between siblings. A household in which the man works and expects the woman to stay home and take care of the meals and the laundry is one of male dominance. If the man is the only one bringing in money, he can exert power over his spouse by withholding money or making certain demands about the care of the household. Although these are extreme examples, men hold the power in many relationships. To deal with the conflict that arises from competition, families must learn the delicate balance between negotiation, compromise, persuasion, and the establishment of rules.

Conflict theory can be used to examine the dynamics in **transnational families**, or families in which some members are settled in one place but the family relationships spread across countries. Transnational families include families that separate for immigration purposes and families with children adopted from foreign countries. Immigrant families are growing in the United States. About 12.5% of the population in the United States is foreign born.[71] These people, although living in America, often still have ties to their home country. Transnational families benefit from having strong social and family support, which makes maintaining their cultural identify easier.[72] When a family adopts a child from another country, the family needs to define what kind of relationship the child will maintain with his or her home country and how much of that country's tradition and culture to integrate into the family. As communication technology becomes more refined, studies show that transnational families in the United States are less likely to identify with U.S. values and culture. Instead, they often define themselves as belonging to a multicultural environment.[73]

Symbolic Interactionism

What were your toys when you were a child? If you are a woman, it's likely that you had more dolls than toy cars. For the most part, you did not choose those toys; they were given to you by adults who thought that boys and girls have very different tastes. You could have been the toughest tomboy on the block, but you most likely received at least one smiling doll with a flowery dress to remind you that you are a girl, and girls like dolls and flowers. Of course, you know by now that not all girls like dolls and flowers, and not all boys hate them, either. So why do people make these types of gender-based associations?

The analysis of the meaning that people associate with elements of their environment is the scope of symbolic interaction theory. This theory assumes that people learn to associate meanings from their interactions with others. According to Ingoldsby, Smith, and Miller, newborns are "asocial," as they are not born with any preconceived idea about the world around them.[74] As the babies grow up, they become aware of themselves and learn to respond to situations based on what they have learned from the interaction with their family members, especially their parents.[75] In the early 20th century, sociologist Charles Cooley put forth the theory of the looking-glass self to explain this type of development: Cooley argued that we monitor ourselves by imagining how we appear to other people. Furthermore, we imagine what other people's judgments of our behaviors must be, and we react emotionally to those imagined judgments, going so far as to base our identity—our sense of self—on those judgments.[76] Cooley's concept of the looking-glass self is a classic example of symbolic interaction theory.

The concept of family itself can be seen through symbolic interaction theory. What are the symbols used to describe the family? The family tree is used to represent an extended family as a living organism that grows with time. Many families tell their stories in quilts that represent how all family members are patches of the same story. The dinner table is a symbol of togetherness, so the ritual of a dinner together becomes very important to many families. In art and photography, the image of a mother, father, and child is immediately associated with the concept of family, just like a house with a smoking chimney or a bird's nest indicates a family that lives together in harmony.

Certain symbols such as hugs or smiles usually indicate happiness and love. When these are present within a family, each member is likely to feel important and special. Negative symbols such as a parent absent from the dinner table or yelling in conversations have the opposite effect. Families in which such behaviors are present may feel more isolated from one another.

Louis Thomas invented "The Universal Family Flag" to create a symbolic image of what he believes to be the greatest institution of the world, the family. The flag represents a family of four—parents of both sexes, legally married—holding hands under a rainbow. Above them, a shining sun symbolizes the love of God. Below them, a tree, bearing many different fruits, symbolizes the cycle of life, but also stability and strength of character.[77]

The Universal Family Flag represents a rather traditional image of the family. What symbols should a flag display to include non-traditional families? As the family continues to evolve and transform, there will be many more symbols that represent the family in all of its forms and structures.

∧
∧
∧ Angelina Jolie, actress and Goodwill Ambassador **for the United Nations High Commissioner for Refugees,** has adopted three children from three different countries: **Maddox from Cambodia, Zahara from Ethiopia, and Pax from Vietnam.** According to the United Department of State, **U.S. families adopted 11,568 children in 2008, 4,632 of whom came from Asia.**

WRAP YOUR MIND AROUND THE THEORY

Functionalist Talcott Parsons **stated that parents had definite roles according to their sexes, with men being "instrumental" and women being "expressive."** How does this view relate to work-family conflict, as described in Section I?

FUNCTIONALISM

Functional theorists believe that marriage and family have specific functions in society, namely the preservation of the species and the transmission of values and knowledge that are essential to the individual and to a healthy society. In this sense, the nuclear family is viewed as a subsystem of society. A family is functional when parents adhere to their responsibilities toward the children by maintaining an exclusive sexual relationship (sexual regulation), by teaching their children to be valuable members of society (socialization), by transmitting their social status, ethnicities, religion, and moral values (social placement), and by providing unconditional affection and support (affection and emotional support). When families are functional, society functions, too. Because of its conservative view of the family—parents are married and of opposite sexes, and families live together—functional theory is not as popular today as it was in the 1950s, when it was championed by Harvard anthropologist Talcott Parsons.

CONFLICT THEORY

Conflict theorists believe that social classes are in competition for the ownership of resources. The same dynamics apply to the study of marriage and the family, so spouses and family members display hierarchical structures based on economic power, gender, age, ethnicities, and so on. For example, in certain families the breadwinner might feel entitled to make the final decision on how money is spent, but also on the education of the children and the time management of the spouse. This might lead to imbalance and conflict in the family. Although conflict is recognized as an avoidable element of marriage and family life, it requires intelligent negotiation, bargaining, and compromise not to damage family relationships.

? WHY DO PEOPLE GET DIVORCED?

SYMBOLIC INTERACTIONISM

Symbolic interaction theorists examine the meaning that people associate with elements of their environment. People learn to make these associations from the interaction they have first with their family and then with other members of society. In 2005, researcher Carolyn Tubbs studied the quality of family time in low-income families. She found that common daily activities such as communication and playing allowed mothers proper nurturing of their children. Twenty-five percent of mothers had "talk time," face-to-face conversation, with their children. Walks, meals, and bedtime are key times for these talks. Thirty-nine percent of mothers said that they played with their children regularly. Family play was focused on the child's enjoyment and oftentimes, their learning.[78]

Experts explain that, **as teenagers approach young adulthood, they often display rebellious behavior due to their need to find their individuality and become independent.** Based on the characteristics of effective families you read about earlier in this chapter, how can parents cope with this kind of conflict?

According to Tubbs, rituals such as playing outdoors help us understand our commitment to family. **What do the symbols in households you are familiar with tell you about family commitment?**

discover marriages and families in action:
HOW DOES RESEARCH DEFINE A SUCCESSFUL FAMILY?

Measures of Success

"If the family were a fruit, it would be an orange, a circle of sections, held together but separable—each segment distinct."

Letty Cottin Pogrebin, American author and editor, *Family and Politics* (1939–)

One of Douglas Coupland's most popular novels is titled *All Families Are Psychotic* (2002). In recent years, the success of movies like *The Royal Tenenbaums* (2001) and *Little Miss Sunshine* (2006) suggests that people identify with **dysfunctional families**. As the media, researchers, and policy makers focus their attention on dysfunctional families, it becomes more and more important to understand what makes a successful family, and if there really is such a thing.

What are the criteria that identify a successful family? This question has received many answers from psychiatrists, sociologists, anthropologists, and psychologists around the world. Studies have been set up to identify characteristics of strong families per se or in comparison with dysfunctional families. In *Identifying Successful Families: An Overview of Constructs and Selected Measures,* authors Krysan, Moore, and Zill explain that successful families can be identified by the characteristics of each family member, by the way family members interact with each other, and by the role that

DYSFUNCTIONAL FAMILIES are families that do not fulfill their role toward their members and society.

the family plays in society.[79] Some researchers believe that a successful family is one in which parents are able to raise well-adjusted children in an atmosphere of support and affection. Other researchers focus their attention on families' ability to deal with stress and maintain open and constructive communication, thus becoming more cohesive and satisfied units.[80]

Do successful romantic relationships lead to successful families? Ted L. Huston and Heidi Melz theorize that warm-hearted, even-tempered people who marry each other are likely to maintain friendly, loving marriages. Huston and Melz strongly suggest that these "warm" marriages are successful both because they are unlikely to end in divorce and because they are affectionate, nurturing, and healthy.[81] It's not such a stretch to imagine that a warm, successful marriage can serve as the foundation for a warm, successful family.

Whatever the criteria, understanding what makes a successful family can be an invaluable tool for sociologists, psychologists, counselors, advocates, and policy makers to develop effective programs to help families.

ACTIVITIES

1. How would you define a successful family? What criteria would you use to measure the characteristics of successful families? Make a list of characteristics that you think define a successful family.
2. Ask your friends and family members about what they think constitutes a successful family. Compare and contrast their responses with your own definition of a successful family.

From Classroom to Community } Random Acts of Kindness

Throughout her life, Naomi has fostered rescued dogs with her family. Her family has also been active with other volunteering activities. At the age of 19, Naomi realizes that volunteering as a family helped her family remain united even in times of crisis.

"My father loves animals and has always been active at the local shelter. I can't remember a time when we weren't taking care of a rescue dog. Taking care of rescue dogs is not as easy as it seems.

"Puppies need training and socialization. Older dogs might still be traumatized by abuse or abandonment. It takes a strong commitment to help them.

"My parents made sure that my brother and I took responsibility for the dogs' well-being. Sure, it was fun to play with the puppies, but I also knew I needed to walk them often, clean after them, and give them some basic training. As I grew up, my responsibilities increased. I would go with the rest of my family to the shelter to clean and walk the dogs, or we'd help out at adoption events. We also prepared fliers and organized a few fund-raising events.

"I have to admit, there were times I would have rather stayed at home and relaxed or just gone out with my friends.

"Looking back, though, I realize that our volunteering was important to me for so many reasons. Taking responsibility made me more self-confident and taught me the value of commitment. Then, spending time with my family and

doing something valuable for the community brought me closer to my parents and my brother. We learned to work together and to depend on each other's commitment. I'm also glad that I have so many fun memories from the time that my family spent together volunteering.

"When my father lost his job last year, it was hard on everybody. It took him a while to find another job, and in the meantime we all had to pull together to get through.

"But I realize now that we all stepped up to the plate immediately. I started tutoring kids in the neighborhood, and my brother began waiting tables at a restaurant. I think that we were used to working together, and responsibility didn't faze us. I'm very proud of my family."

16

WHAT ELEMENTS CHARACTERIZE AN EFFECTIVE MARRIAGE AND A SUCCESSFUL FAMILY? 273

Although the definitions of marriage and family are always changing in time and across different geographical areas, researchers agree that effective marriages and successful families are based on a long-term commitment to open and respectful communication, a constant display of affection and encouragement, lots of time together, and the willingness to cope with stress and adversity.

WHAT ARE THE THEORIES THAT ANALYZE FAMILY RELATION- SHIPS AND THE ROLE OF THE FAMILY IN SOCIETY? 284

Functional theorists believe that the nuclear family has the role of promoting and maintaining the social order. Conflict theorists analyze family relationships based on the conflict generated by hierarchy and the difference in goals. Symbolic interaction theorists analyze the meaning that people associate with symbols, behaviors, and roles in marriage and family.

HOW DOES RESEARCH DEFINE A SUCCESSFUL FAMILY? 287

A successful family is one in which family members take care of the well-being of each other as individuals and of the family as a whole.

Theory

FUNCTIONALISM 284

- the nuclear family plays a role in the preservation of society
- parents need to raise children that are valuable members of society

CONFLICT THEORY 284

- spouses and families experience conflict when there is an imbalance of power
- spouses and families cope with conflict through negotiation, bargaining, and compromise

SYMBOLIC INTERACTIONISM 284

- people adopt behaviors based on their interpretation of the environment
- people learn to associate meaning to reality from their interactions with other people

Key Terms

short-term commitment according to Steinberg, is the decision to love someone else *274*

long-term commitment according to Steinberg, is the decision to maintain the love for a person over time *274*

dual-earner family is a family in which both parents hold a job *274*

work-family conflict is the discord between roles adopted in the work place and in the family *274*

role perception is the view of the role one assumes within the family or in society *274*

deviant behavior is the set of actions that deviate from the common, accepted cultural rule, such as delinquency or drug abuse *274*

egalitarian roles in a family, are when the roles of the parents are regarded as equal *276*

effective families are families that promote the satisfaction of both the individual members and the family as whole *277*

ethnicity refers to a group of people sharing the same language, geographical origin, culture, and traditions *278*

birthrate is the average number of births on a given year *278*

divorce rate is the average number of divorces on a given year *280*

paradigm is a set of assumption shared by a community at a given time *280*

monogamy is the custom of sharing a permanent sexual relationship with only one partner *280*

mass media are all means of mass communi- cation including newspapers, books, music, radio television, Internet, etc. *282*

sexual regulation is the practice of restricting sexual activity to the spouse only *284*

social placement is the transmission of role and social status from a generation to the next *284*

transnational families are families settled in one place but with relationships across countries *284*

dysfunctional families are families that do not fulfill their role toward its members and society *287*

Sample Test Questions

MULTIPLE CHOICE

These multiple-choice questions are similar to those found in the test bank that accompanies this textbook.

1. According to researchers, the risk of a teenager's drug abuse is increased by:
   a. competitiveness with siblings.
   b. hierarchical structure in the family.
   c. enforcement of established rules from parents.
   d. exposure to inappropriate mass-media content.

2. According to functionalists, how do parents ensure social placement for their children?
   a. by socializing their children
   b. by supporting their children economically
   c. by transmitting their class, values, and culture to the children
   d. by providing a stable and non-judgmental environment for their children

3. Which of the following is a recognized challenge for transnational families?
   a. shifting family roles
   b. lack of communicated values
   c. non-egalitarian roles of parents
   d. increased incidence of deviant behavior in children

4. According to psychologists, what is an effect of diverging definitions of commitment in a couple?
   a. feelings of isolation
   b. work-family conflict
   c. lack of family rituals
   d. hierarchical gender roles

5. Which of the following is NOT a change that has recently affected the family in the Western world?
   a. decreased birthrates
   b. equalization of gender roles
   c. increased number of divorces
   d. decreased number of domestic partnerships

ESSAY

1. Discuss the relationship between gender roles and work-family conflict.
2. Why do you think rituals are so important in creating an effective marriage and a successful family?
3. What is the relationship between parents' commitment and deviant behavior in their children?
4. How do functional and conflict theorists view family commitment?
5. How is globalization affecting the concept of family around the world?

WHERE TO START YOUR RESEARCH PAPER

For more data on U.S. family statistics, go to
http://www.census.gov/population/www/socdemo/hh-fam.html

For more information on gender issues and their relationship to the workplace, go to http://www.gpac.org/

For more information about recent studies on gender roles and work, go to http://www.hope.edu/academic/psychology/335/webrep/genroles.html

For more information about parenting education and recommendations, go to http://www.pta.org/topics.asp

For more information about troubled teens and teen drug abuse, go to http://www.parentingteens.com/index/

For more data on U.S. children, go to
http://www.census.gov/population/www/socdemo/children.html

For more information about sociological concepts and functionalism, go to http://www.sociology.org.uk/rload.htm

For more information about a variety of family issues, go to http://www.psychwww.com/resource/selfhelp/family.html

For research about families around the world, go to http://www.fww.org/articles.html

For a study on rituals and family strength, go to http://www.directionjournal.org/article/?654

For statistical data about children and women around the world, go to http://www.unicef.org/statistics/index.html

Answers: 1. d; 2. c; 3. a; 4. a; 5. d

GLOSSARY

absolute divorce is the official end of a marriage in which all legal bonds between a couple are severed. (242)

absolute poverty is deprivation that is life threatening. (195)

active parenting includes activities such as helping with homework, participating in projects, using non-coercive discipline, listening to problems, and offering advice. (142)

adolescence is the period of life from the teen years to young adulthood. (143)

Adonis complex is a man's obsessive preoccupation that he is not muscular enough. (101)

adoption is voluntarily taking the child of other parents as one's own. (140)

affection exchange theory is the theory postulating that affectionate communication is an adaptive behavior that is instrumental to human survival and procreation. (84)

affectionate communication is the way affection in expressed. (49)

affective behavior is that in which people tend to rely a lot on nonverbal communication. (53)

affiliated kin are nonrelated individuals who are accepted as part of a family. (7)

agape is, according to John A. Lee, the love style combining eros and storge and characterized by a mutual and altruistic interest in the partner's well-being. (88)

ageism is discrimination in the workplace or other areas because of age. (173)

age-specific divorce rate is the number of divorces per 1,000 married women in each age category. (251)

AIDS is acquired immune deficiency syndrome. (106)

androgynous describes a person who has a balance of both male and female characteristics so that neither predominates. (63)

arranged marriage is a type of marriage in which the families of the bride and groom negotiate an arrangement before the two parties enter into a relationship. (5)

artificial insemination by donor (AID) is inserting donor sperm directly into a woman's body. (137)

artificial insemination by husband or male partner (AIH) is inserting sperm directly into a woman's body. (137)

asexual describes those who are attracted to neither sex. (70)

assisted reproductive technology (ART) is any fertility treatment in which both egg and sperm are handled. (136)

assisted suicide refers to the situation in which one person supplies the means for another to commit suicide in order to prevent suffering. (178)

attachment theory is the theory that states that people's patterns of attachment are shaped by the intimate bonding they shared with their caregivers during infancy. (85)

authoritarian parenting style describes parents who attempt to shape children according to fixed standards by emphasizing obedience and punishment. (141)

authoritative parenting style describes parents who nurture children by providing warmth, support, and acceptance, and emphasizing positive reinforcement. (141)

autonomy is a state of independence and self-determination. (85)

binuclear family is a post-divorce family structure comprised of two nuclear families, one headed by the ex-wife and the other by the ex-husband. (259)

birthrate is the average number of births on a given year. (279)

bisexual describes those who are attracted to members of both sexes. (70)

body image is an individual's perception of his or her own physical appearance. (101)

boomerang kids are adult children who return to live with parents temporarily. (170)

boundaries are emotional barriers that define a system and separate the system from its environment and other systems. (16)

buoyancy is the ability of a family to keep afloat during adversity. (223)

canon law is the ecclesiastical body of laws used in England that governed the Catholic and Anglican churches. (242)

capitalization is being sincerely happy about a friend's well-being and success. (81)

case study is an intensive study of a single case or a small number of cases that share common characteristics. (35)

childfree describes the women who make the voluntary decision not to have children. (133)

childless describes people not having children for infertility reasons. (133)

chronosystem is the research model that examines the impact of normative and nonnormative life transitions on family processes and child development over time. (16)

circumplex model is a graphic model identifying three characteristics of a balanced family system: family cohesion, flexibility, and communication. (86)

civil union refers to same sex couples recognized in certain states without the legal rights guaranteed by the federal government to traditional married couples. (156)

closed adoption is the situation in which the child's biological parents are unknown, and there is limited information about them. (140)

coercion is being forced to act against one's interests. (17)

coercive power is based on a family member using physical or psychological force to impose his or her will on others, often with a threat of fear or loss of privilege. (51)

cognition is the process of logical thought. (45)

cohabitation effect is a phenomenon in which couples who cohabit before they marry are more likely to divorce. (154)

cohabitation refers to the condition of heterosexual couples living together without being married. (153)

commitment is, according to Sternberg's triangular theory of love, the decision to love someone and maintain the love over time. (88)

communication channel is the method through which information is conveyed, such as speech, gestures, and writing. (46)

communication is the act of conveying verbal and nonverbal information to another person. (45)

communication patterns are the recurring characteristics of verbal and nonverbal exchange between two or more people. (48)

companionate love is a type of relationship that is high in intimacy and commitment, but low in passion; is defined by Sternberg as the love style focused more on feelings of trust and friendship than on sexual satisfaction. (88)

comparison level of alternatives is the evaluation by individuals of their relationships in the light of available alternatives. (16)

complementary needs theory is the theory that suggests people select mates whose needs are opposite but complementary to their own. (122)

complex stepfamily is one in which both partners have children from previous relationships. (262)

conflict management is the process of dealing with conflict. (54)

conflict resolution is the process of attenuating or eliminating a source of conflict. (54)

conflict theory is the theory that analyzes patterns of conflict resulting from competition over resources. (55)

consensus is an agreement that is achieved in mate selection by choosing a partner with similar values and beliefs. (125)

conservatives are individuals on the right of the political spectrum; generally associated in modern times with the Republican party. (209)

consummate love is a type of relationship that is high in intimacy, passion, and commitment. (88)

contextual factors are outside factors such as the level of social support an individual receives during their time of need. (247)

contraception is the use of devices or procedures to prevent pregnancy. (100)

control is the conflict-management style that is carried out through the use of blame, personal attacks, and mean jokes. (53)

control variables are factors that remain constant across experimental subjects and throughout experimental trials. (34)

controlling communication style is one in which the sender does not allow the receiver to express his or her ideas. (46)

conversation orientation is the degree to which families encourage open exchange of ideas on a variety of subjects. (49)

cope is to manage and confront stress. (221)

cost is a detriment. (248)

costs are the negative outcomes, energy invested, or rewards foregone as a result of choosing one behavior over another. (16)

courtship is the process of seeking and selecting a mate. (117)

covenant marriage is a type of marriage that requires a couple to commit to a more strenuous set of legal requirements in an effort to strengthen their relationship and reduce the possibility of divorce. (211)

crisis is an unstable condition in which there is a lack of sufficient resources to manage the situation. (221)

cross-cultural study is a research study in which subjects from two or more cultures are observed. (35)

crude birth rate is the annual number of childbirths for every 1,000 people in a given population. (104)

crude divorce rate is the number of divorces per 1,000 people. (251)

cryopreservation is freezing eggs or sperm for later use. (138)

cultural beliefs are personal beliefs particular to a culture that may influence the power relationship between parents and school. (206)

cultural universals are the patterns or traits that are common to all human cultures. (99)

culture of poverty refers to those cultural influences that involve little planning for the future, little commitment to marriage, little or no work ethic, and dependence on government assistance. (195)

cybersex refers to the virtual sexual activities practiced on the Internet. (102)

date rape is the act of forcing sexual intercourse on a non-consenting date or partner. (122)

dating is when two people meet at an agreed upon time and place to partake in a social activity. (117)

dating violence is the perpetration or threat of an act of violence against a person in the context of a relationship, including sexual assault, physical abuse, and verbal or emotional abuse. (121)

debt-bondage is the illegal practice of controlling someone's life by claiming the person needs to pay a debt. (111)

demography is the science that studies human population. (104)

dependent variable is the factor that is affected by the independent variable during an experiment. (34)

developmental process theory is the theory of mate selection in which individuals narrow down their choice of mate using a filtering system. (123)

deviant behavior is the set of actions that deviate from the common, accepted cultural rule, such as delinquency or drug abuse. (274)

dialectic approach is the relationship model according to which relationships are characterized by an ongoing tension between intimacy and autonomy. (85)

DINKs are couples with high incomes, no kids, demanding careers, and a desire to work, travel, and focus on their marriage. (133)

discipline is training to correct an incorrect behavior. (142)

disengagement is the breakdown of an engagement. (119)

divorce is the legal termination of a marriage. (154)

divorce rate is the average number of divorces on a given year. (280)

divorce-stress adjustment theory is a theory that views divorce as a stressful life transition to which the entire family must adjust. (249)

domestic partnership refers to same-sex couples or cohabiting couples recognized in certain states but without the legal rights guaranteed by the federal government to traditional married couples. (156)

domestic violence is intentional abusive behavior against an intimate partner that includes intimidation and physical and sexual assault. (224)

dowry is the material goods paid by the bride's family to the groom's family to increase their status by the marriage. (124)

dual-earner family is a family in which both parents hold a job. (274)

dyadic relationship is a relationship between two people, that involves some kind of closeness and mutual affection. (81)

dyadic withdrawal is the diminished involvement in outside social networks by a couple in a romantic relationship. (82)

dynamic communication style is one in which the sender uses motivational phrases to encourage the receiver. (46)

dysfunction is the negative consequence of a social structure. (124)

dysfunctional families are families that do not fulfill their role toward its members and society. (287)

economic influences are economic factors that may influence the power relationship between parents and school. (206)

education is a social institution by which society provides its members with knowledge that includes basic facts, job skills, and cultural norms and values. (205)

effective families are families that promote the satisfaction of both the individual members and the family as whole. (277)

egalitarian communication style is one in which the sender encourages feedback from the receiver. (46)

egalitarian relationships are unions in which power is shared equally between partners. (52)

egalitarian roles in a family, are when the roles of the parents are regarded as equal. (276)

elasticity is the ability to recover from trauma or crisis. (223)

emotional bonding is measured by the strength of emotional ties, affection, mutual respect, and identification. (142)

empty love is a type of relationship that is high in commitment, but low in intimacy and passion. (88)

empty nest is a home after the last child has left home. (170)

engagement is the public commitment to marry. (118)

epidemic is the outbreak of an infectious disease that affects a large number of people at the same time. (107)

eros is, according to John A. Lee, the love style characterized by overwhelming passion and deep emotional attachment. (88)

ethnic group is a group of people characterized by cultural factors, such as language, religion, and shared customs, that are passed from one generation to the next. (12)

ethnicity refers to a group of people sharing the same language, geographical origin, culture, and traditions. (279)

ethnography is a study that attempts to understand a group from the point of view of its members. (36)

euthanasia is taking another person's life to prevent suffering. (178)

exchange theory is the theory that uses the concepts of rewards and costs to explain interpersonal attraction. (122)

exchanges and equity is a system of judging the reward and cost of a situation or relationship. (248)

exosystem refers to the outside influences that a child may not interact with personally, but that have a large impact on the child. (16)

expert power is based on the specific expertise of a member of the family that leads him or her to make decisions in that area. (51)

extended family is a group constituted by a nuclear family and their relatives. (47)

family is a group of two people or more related by birth, marriage, or adoption and residing together. (6)

family career is the family experience of an individual over a lifetime. (27)

family development theory proposes that families proceed through common, identifiable stages. (25)

family diversity refers to the variation in family structures, experiences, and circumstances between families. (12)

family life course is a model that focuses on how families integrate changes over time and the meanings that individual family members give to those changes. (25)

family life cycle is a theory that identifies eight specific stages for families beginning after marriage. (25)

family narrative is made up of family stories that are told and retold that help define family history and character. (30)

family of origin describes the family in which an individual is raised. (11)

family planning is the system of limiting the number of children in a family by birth control. (108)

family policy is the range of services funded and sponsored by the government that affect families directly or indirectly. (211)

family stress is a real or imagined imbalance between the demands on the family and the family's ability to meet those demands. (221)

family systems theory explains that different traits and coping mechanisms are passed from generation to generation within a family. (228)

family violence is intentional abusive behavior against a family member that includes intimidation and physical and sexual assault. (224)

father-stepmother family is a household that comprises the father's biological children and mother's stepchildren. (262)

fatuous love is high in passion and commitment and low in intimacy. (88)

fault-based divorce is a type of divorce in which one partner is obligated to prove that the other had somehow violated the marriage contract. (242)

fertility is the occurrence of childbearing in a country's population. (104)

field of eligibles is the group of people whom society defines as acceptable marriage partners. (123)

fixed income is income from a pension, annuity, or other source that is frozen at a certain level; fixed incomes may be increased with cost-of-living raises. (175)

focus group is a small group brought together by a researcher to discuss a particular subject. (36)

foster parenting is the situation in which a person or couple acts as temporary parents to a child or children who cannot live at home for a variety of reasons, or are waiting to be adopted. (140)

functional theory asserts that the family performs an important function in the preservation of social order. (55)

fusion is an extreme emotional connection and interdependence between intimate partners. (227)

gay marriage is a union of a same-sex couple with all the legal rights guaranteed by the federal government to traditional married couples. (211)

gender is made up of the social practices that a culture defines as masculine and feminine. (63)

gender roles are sets of expected behaviors associated with males and females. (48)

generalized set of rewards is an examination that tries to figure out why most people in general behave in a particular way. (248)

genital infibulation is the ritual cutting of the inner labia and surgical closure of the outer labia. (100)

gestational surrogacy is using another woman's body to carry one's baby. (137)

glass escalator refers to an invisible fast-track for men entering previously female-dominated professions. (188)

going steady is dating one person exclusively. (118)

grandparent family is a type of family in which grandparents are responsible for raising their grandchildren. (158)

heterogamy is the practice of marrying someone outside your own race, religion, or age group; also called exogamy. (123)

heterosexual describes those who are attracted to the opposite sex. (70)

HIV incidence estimate is the number of new HIV infections contracted in a given year. (106)

HIV is the human immunodeficiency virus that causes AIDS. (106)

HIV prevalence estimate is the number of HIV-positive people at the end of a given year. (106)

homogamy is the tendency to marry someone of the same race, class, age, and educational background; also called endogamy. (123)

homophobia is the irrational fear of homosexuals. (85)

homosexual describes those who are attracted to members of the same sex. (70)

honor killings happen when a family member perceives that a female relative will bring or has brought shame on the family, usually through a suspected breech of cultural traditions or religious morals. (116)

hooking up is casual sexual activity with no strings attached between heterosexual people who are strangers or brief acquaintances. (83)

hormone therapy is a fertility method taken by women to increase their monthly release of eggs. (137)

household income refers to earnings from work or investments. (188)

household refers to all people who occupy a housing unit regardless of relationship. (6)

hypothesis is a proposed explanation of behavior that is not proven but can be tested. (32)

ideal mate theory is the psychoanalytic theory that people develop a model image of their mate based on their early childhood experiences. (122)

idealization is an unrealistic view of the loved one. (89)

in vitro fertilization (IVF) is a fertility treatment involving fertilizing an egg outside the body. (137)

incest taboo is the cultural restriction against sexual activity between close relatives. (99)

independent variable is the factor that is manipulated by the researcher during an experiment. (34)

infatuation is a type of relationship that is high in passion and low in intimacy and commitment. (88)

infertility is the inability to conceive after one year of persistent unprotected intercourse or the inability to carry a pregnancy to term. (136)

informational power is based on one family member having access to information that is denied to the other members of the family. (51)

interdating is when people date members of other racial or ethnic groups. (121)

interpersonal communication is the verbal and nonverbal messages exchanged by two people. (46)

intimacy is a feeling of closeness in meaningful relationships characterized by sharing of personal experiences, thoughts, and emotions. (85)

intimate partner violence is intentional physical, emotional, or sexual abuse, or intimidation via threats of physical or sexual abuse, typically between partners or spouses, but including other intimate family relations. (225)

intracytoplasmic sperm injection (ICSI), is an in vitro fertilization method requiring just a single sperm. (137)

involuntary fetal mortality is self-terminating pregnancy. (140)

joint stepfamily is a household that comprises at least one biological child of both parents as well as at least one biological child of only one parent (with the other parent as stepparent). (262)

labor force participation refers to the number of people who either have a job or are looking for work. (187)

latchkey children are children who care for themselves for some portion of the day. (191)

legal separation is a formal separation involving court proceedings regarding property, alimony, child support, custody, and visitation rights. (239)

legitimate power is based on the belief that power should be delegated to a specific member of the family. (51)

liberals are individuals on the left of the political spectrum; generally associated in modern times with the Democratic party. (208)

libido is sexual desire. (102)

liking is a type of relationship that is high in intimacy, but low in passion and commitment. (88)

living apart is a type of separation in which couples do not intend to get back together. (239)

longitudinal study is a research study in which subjects are observed over a long period of time. (35)

long-term commitment according to Steinberg, is the decision to maintain the love for a person over time. (274)

looking-glass self is a concept of self in which interpretations of other people's opinions become a dominant aspect of identity. (15)

ludus is, according to John A. Lee, the love style focused on love as play and on superficial or purely sexual relationships. (88)

macro-social perspective focuses on groups of families at the community or cultural level. (31)

macrosystem is the culture in which an individual lives. (16)

mania is, according to John A. Lee, the love style combining eros and ludus and characterized by possessiveness and jealousy. (88)

marginalized group is a group relegated to a social standing outside the mainstream. (121)

marriage gap is the political disparities between those who are married and those who are single. (210)

marriage is a legally recognized union between a man and a woman. (5)

marriage market is a system in which prospective partners evaluate the assets and liabilities of potential spouses and choose the best available mate. (118)

marriage to divorce ratio compares the number of divorces in a given year to the number of marriages. (251)

mass media are all means of mass communication including newspapers, books, music, radio television, Internet, etc. (282)

matriarchy is a social system in which women dominate men. (65)

medical abortion is voluntary termination of a pregnancy by medication. (138)

mesosystem is the description of how different parts of the child's microsystem interact. (16)

micro-social perspective focuses on individuals and single family groups. (31)

microsystem is a child's immediate environment, including any immediate relationships or organizations that the child interacts with. (16)

modeling occurs when children do what they see their parents do instead of what their parents tell them to do. (143)

mommy track, the was originally a flexible work arrangement suggested to reduce females' work-family conflicts; it was later used to indicate a way that patriarchal businesses prevent women from advancing. (190)

monogamous marriage is a type of marriage in which one person is married to another person of the opposite sex. (5)

monogamy is the custom of sharing a permanent sexual relationship with only one partner. (280)

mother-stepfather family is a household that comprises the mother's biological children and father's stepchildren. (262)

multigenerational patterns of communication are the transfer of communication patterns from one generation to the next. (49)

nepotism is favoritism shown to one's kin. (17)

neuroticism is a personality trait characterized by negative emotions such as depression, anxiety, anger, embarrassment, vulnerability, and impulsiveness. (83)

no-fault divorce is a type of divorce that allowed couples to divorce without proving guilt or fault on the part of the other. (242)

non-confrontation is the conflict-management style that involves withdrawal and avoidance. (53)

nonlove is a type of relationship where intimacy, passion, and commitment are absent. (88)

nonsurgical sperm aspiration (NSA), is an in vitro fertilization method involving direct removal of sperm from testes. (137)

nonverbal communication is the information conveyed through body language, gestures, and facial expressions. (45)

norms are societal expectations for appropriate behavior, including those for gender. (64)

nuclear family is a group constituted by the parents and their own or adopted children. (47)

online dating is when people use specialized dating Web sites such as Match.com or eHarmony to meet a potential spouse. (119)

open adoption is the situation in which the adoptive parents and biological parents are in contact with one another. (140)

pack dating is dating in small groups without committing to one person. (118)

pansexual describes those who display a broad range of sexual attractions, including attraction to those who do not fall into the simple gender categories of males and female. (70)

paradigm is a set of assumption shared by a community at a given time. (280)

parent image theory is the psychoanalytic theory that men are more likely to select women who resemble their mothers, whereas women are more likely to select men who look like their fathers. (122)

partisanship is the support of a particular political party. (210)

passionate love is the love style characterized by overwhelming passion and emotional attachment that often characterizes the first stage of a romantic relationship. (89)

passive euthanasia is withholding treatment that would prolong life because the current quality of life is minimal. (178)

patriarchal family is a family structure in which the eldest male has the most authority. (51)

patriarchy is a social system in which men dominate women. (64)

permanent separation is a type of separation in which a couple begins living apart. (239)

permissive parenting style describes parents who exert little to no control and give few restrictions or guidelines, leaving children confused about what behaviors are acceptable. (141)

personal factors are individual characteristics such as age, education level, and employment status. (247)

personal resilience is an individual's ability to cope with and manage stress or a crisis. (228)

phenotype refers to the anatomical and physical characteristics that distinguish one race from another. (12)

physical affection is the act of displaying affection through kisses, hugs, and physical contact. (84)

political pressures are governmental pressures that may influence the power relationship between parents and school. (206)

political socialization is the process by which people acquire political knowledge, beliefs, and values. (209)

political system is a social institution based on an established set of practices for applying and realizing a society's goals. (208)

polygamous marriage is a type of marriage in which one person is married to multiple husbands or wives. (5)

polygamy is marriage between one person and more than one spouse, including marriage between a woman and multiple husbands (polyandry) and a man and multiple wives (polygyny); sometimes called plural marriage. (158)

postmodern family is a term meant to include all family variations existing today. (151)

pragma is, according to John A. Lee, the love style combining ludus and storge and viewing love as realistic and pragmatic. (88)

preimplantation genetic diagnosis (PGD) is the process to determine sex in embryos. (138)

prenuptial agreement is a legal document stipulating financial arrangements in the event of a divorce. (119)

prescriptive norms are the rules that recommend or require certain behaviors. (99)

profane refers to everyday elements of ordinary life. (207)

profit is the ratio of reward to cost. (248)

propinquity is geographic closeness. (123)

proscriptive norms are the rules that proscribe or prohibit certain behaviors. (99)

psychological parent is a person serving as a parent who is not biologically related to the child. (151)

public display of affection (PDA) is the physical show of affection in the view of other people. (87)

qualitative research examines and interprets an issue to discover underlying meanings or patterns of relationships; uses words, pictures, or objects to describe the issues being studied. (33)

quantitative research uses the scientific method to test a specifically defined hypothesis; uses numbers to describe and explain the issues being studied. (33)

race is a group of people who are classified according to their phenotype. (12)

random sampling is a procedure through which participants in an experimental study are chosen at random. (34)

rationality is an alternative view of what constitutes a reward or a cost. (248)

receiver is the person to whom a verbal or nonverbal message is addressed. (46)

reciprocity is the exchange of favors. (17)

recovery factors are qualities or characteristics of a family that assist recuperation from stress or a crisis. (223)

referential power is based on affection and the creation of bonds between members of the family. Feelings like affection, friendship, and attraction can help create alliances within the family. (51)

refined divorce rate is the number of divorces per 1,000 married women. (251)

relative poverty refers to the deprivation of some people in comparison to others. (195)

religion is a social institution involving beliefs and practices based on recognizing and elevating the sacred above the profane. (207)

religious pluralism is the existence of religious diversity within a community. (208)

relinquishing communication style is one in which the receiver is invited to participate in the communication as much as the sender. (46)

remarried family, blended family, or **stepfamily** describes the family of a person who remarries after divorce or death of the spouse, including all children. (157)

renested family or **cluttered nest** is a home to which adult children have returned to live temporarily. (170)

replacement-level fertility is the number of children necessary for women to replace themselves and their partners in the population, usually maintained at 2.1. (104)

resiliency is the ability of an individual or family to function within familiar patterns or to create new patterns in the face of adversity or crisis. (223)

resource theory is the idea that power originates from the control of resources. (51)

responsiveness is the affectionate and supportive understanding of another's needs, values, and desires. (81)

reward is a benefit. (248)

reward power offers physical and psychological rewards to family members who comply with certain requests. (51)

rewards are the pleasures or satisfactions we enjoy from participating in a relationship. (16)

rhythm method is avoiding intercourse during ovulation. (138)

rituals are prescribed sets of actions often connoted by symbolic value and usually adopted by religions and social groups through history. (91)

role is the part we are expected to play in society, learned through interactions with others. (15)

role perception is the view of the role one assumes within the family or in society. (274)

romantic love is a type of relationship that is high in passion and intimacy, but low in commitment. (88)

rules of transformation are the means by which a system governs the way in which inputs from the environment are changed to outputs. (16)

sacred refers to objects or concepts that inspire awe and respect. (207)

same-sex marriage is marriage in which same-sex couples are united legally with all the legal rights guaranteed by the federal government to traditional married couples. (156)

sandwich generation is the generation that may be responsible for care for aging parents and young children at the same time. (169)

scientific method is a systematic approach to observing phenomena, drawing conclusions, and testing hypotheses. (32)

script is a sequence of automatic behaviors. (49)

secondary data analysis is quantitative research that uses studies that have already been completed and analyzes the data in ways not originally planned. (35)

self is the concept of identity that develops through interactions with others. (15)

sender is the person who conveys a verbal or nonverbal message. (46)

separation agreement is a binding agreement between husband and wife regarding debts, assets, custody, child care, and support payments. (239)

separation is the termination of marital cohabitation. (239)

serial monogamy is an involvement in a single exclusive relationship followed by another exclusive relationship. (155)

sex education is a program of education about various aspects of human sexual behaviors including reproductive anatomy, sexual reproduction, sexual intercourse, contraception, and reproductive rights and responsibilities. (108)

sex ratio is the relationship between the number of men and the number of women of a given age in a society. (125)

sex refers to the biological differences that differentiate men and women, including internal and external sexual organs, hormonal profiles, and chromosomes. (63)

sex roles are attitudes and behavioral expectations that go along with the biological aspects of being male or female. (63)

sex trafficking is the illegal practice of coercing people into commercial sex acts. (111)

sexism is the belief that one sex is superior to the other. (65)

sexual abstinence is the practice of refraining from any sexual behavior or only from vaginal-penile intercourse. (103)

sexual double standard is the unwritten code of behavior that allows greater sexual freedom to men than to women. (84)

sexual harassment refers to unwelcome sexual advances, requests for sexual favors, and other verbal or physical conduct of a sexual nature that affects a person's work. (192)

sexual norms are the rules and expectations by which society channels and regulates the sexual behavior of its members. (99)

sexual orientation is the sex a person is attracted to. (47)

sexual regulation is the practice of restricting sexual activity to the spouse only. (284)

sexual satisfaction is an individual's positive feelings toward sexuality. (101)

sexuality is made up of social practices related to erotic desire, pleasure, and reproduction. (63)

sexually experienced means having had sexual intercourse. (103)

Shinto is the native Japanese religion that emphasizes a love of nature. (209)

short-term commitment according to Steinberg, is the decision to love someone else. (274)

single-parent family is a family in which one parent is responsible for the children in a household. (152)

social class means a group whose members are similar in education, income, occupational status, housing, and lineage. (193)

social cognition theory explains that a child's interpretation of a certain situation may not be as hostile or aggressive as he or she may perceive; changing children's impressions may help them overcome abusive situations. (227)

social comparison refers to the habit of evaluating one's skills and qualities by comparing them to others. (81)

social exchange theory is the sociological perspective arguing that satisfaction in a relationship is enhanced when the rewards are greater than the costs. (85)

social institution is the component in the social structure that addresses a basic social need. (204)

social learning theory explains that violent and abusive behavior is learned. (227)

social placement is the transmission of role and social status from a generation to the next. (284)

social structures are changes in family structures that may influence the power relationship between parents and school. (206)

social support is the emotional, verbal, and material help received by others. (81)

socialization is the shaping of an individual's behavior to conform to social or cultural norms. (12)

societal forces are influences coming from or relating to society. (87)

society refers to the process of socialization in which we interpret meanings of symbols and learn about our roles. (15)

socioeconomic status (SES) quantifies education, income, and occupation on a continuum as an indicator of social class. (193)

solution orientation is the conflict-management style that involves logical reasoning, compromise, and a focus on mutual agreement. (53)

somatization is the manifestation of physical symptoms from psychological problems. (228)

spacious nest is the transition to more physical room in the empty nest home and more psychological space for the marital relationship. (170)

speed dating is an accelerated form of dating in which men and women choose whether to see each other again based on a very short interaction. (119)

spontaneous abortion or **miscarriage,** is when a pregnancy ends itself mid-term. (140)

standardized divorce rate is the statistic based on the age-specific divorce rate in each age category that is calculated by adding the total number of divorces across all age categories, dividing the sum by the standard population size, and multiplying this number by 1,000. (251)

STDs are sexually transmitted diseases. (105)

stepfamily is a family with a married couple who care for at least one child who is not the biological offspring of both adults. (262)

stigma is any kind of demeaning and discrediting characteristic attributed to a group or an individual. (107)

stillbirth is a nonliving birth. (140)

STIs are sexually transmitted infections. (105)

storge is, according to John A. Lee, the love style based on friendship and compatibility of values and beliefs. (88)

stratification is a division into similar layers or groups. (25)

stressor is a situation or event causing stress. (4)

subcareer is one of four distinct roles that a person may experience at any time and that affect the individual and the family. (27)

subsystem is part of a system that can be analyzed separately in relation to its exchanges with the system and with other subsystems. (16)

suicidal ideation refers to thoughts about committing suicide. (54)

surgical abortion is voluntary termination of a pregnancy by vacuum aspiration. (140)

surrogacy is the process through which a woman agrees to carry and deliver a baby for another couple. (47)

surrogate embryo transfer (SET) is an artificial insemination method involving fertilization in a surrogate's body and implantation in the mother's. (137)

symbolic interaction theory is the theory that people attach symbolic meaning to elements in the world around them. (55)

symbols are objects, events, or ideas that have acquired cultural significance beyond their literal meaning. (55)

tactics are the behaviors that people adopt to carry out their conflict-management styles. (54)

traditional or **nuclear family** refers to a husband and wife who are legally married, have children, and live together. (150)

transnational families are families settled in one place but with relationships across countries. (284)

trauma theory suggests that how a traumatic event is handled determines the extent of trauma that a victim experiences. (228)

traumatic bonding is the emotional attachment that victims end up feeling for their abusers. (111)

trial marriage is cohabiting to assess whether partners are sufficiently compatible for marriage. (153)

trial separation is a type of separation in which a couple lives apart for a period of time in order to decide whether or not to separate permanently. (239)

triangulation is a situation in which two family members unite against a third family member, causing loyalty conflicts. (264)

uninvolved parenting style describes parents who rarely give their children rules and offer little attention. (142)

values are, according to functionalists, the cultural beliefs that motivate individuals to adhere to norms. (91)

variety is the extent to which a system is able to adapt to changes in the environment. (16)

verbal affection is the act of displaying affection through compliments, assertions of love, laughter, etc. (84)

verbal communication is the information conveyed through spoken language. (45)

virginity pledge is the commitment to abstain from sexual intercourse until marriage. (103)

visual communication is the information conveyed through visual cues such as typographical signs, illustrations, and images. (45)

voluntary fetal mortality is induced abortion. (138)

wealth is net worth; it includes the total values of all assets such as a house, car, jewelry or other valuables, stocks and bonds, business ownerships, and savings minus any debts. (189)

wife rape is forced sex on a female spouse by a male spouse. (225)

withdrawal communication style is one in which either participant shows no interest in the exchange. (46)

work-family conflict is the discord between roles adopted in the work place and in the family. (274)

work-family conflict refers to the incompatible role demands stemming from work or family that interfere with a person's functioning in either area. (189)

ENDNOTES

CHAPTER 1

1. *Hyde v. Hyde and Woodmansee*, 1866, summarized at http://www.uniset.ca/other/ths/LR1PD130.html (accessed August 2, 2009).
2. "Divorce soars in India's middle classes," *The Daily Telegraph*. October 1, 2005, http://www.telegraph.co.uk/news/worldnews/asia/india/1499679/Divorce-soars-in-Indias-middle-class.html (accessed August 2, 2009).
3. Stephanie Coontz, *Marriage, A History: From Obedience to Intimacy, Or How Love Conquered Marriage* (New York: Viking, 2005).
4. U.S. Census Bureau, *Current Population Report*, 2008. http://www.census.gov (accessed June 20, 2009).
5. Tillman, K.H. and C.B. Nam, "Family structure outcomes of alternative family definitions," *Population Research and Policy Review* 27 (2008): 367–384.
6. P. Dilworth-Anderson, L. M. Burton, and W. L. Turner, "The importance of values in the study of culturally diverse families," *Family Relations* 42 (July 1993): 238–242.
7. Philip Greven, *Four Generations: Population, Land and Family in Colonial Andover, Mass* (Ithaca, NY: Cornell University Press, 1970).
8. Steven Mintz and Susan Kellog, *Domestic Revolution: A Social History of American Family Life* (New York: Free Press, 1988), 14.
9. Ibid.
10. Ernest W. Burgess and Harvey J. Locke, *The Family: From Institution to Companionship* (New York: American Book Publishers, 1945).
11. Steven Mintz and Susan Kellog, *Domestic Revolution: A Social History of American Family Life* (New York: Free Press, 1988), 171.
12. "Family and the Schools," *Newsweek*, May 17, 1948. Vol. 31, 92.
13. U.S. Census Bureau, 2004. http://www.census.gov/Press-Release/www/releases/archives/facts_for_features_special_editions/001780.html (accessed June 21, 2009).
14. David Popenhoe and Barbara Dafoe Whitehead, *The State of Our Unions* (Piscataway, NJ: Rutgers University, National Marriage Project, 2005).
15. U.S. Census Bureau, 2008. http://www.census.gov/Press-Release/www/releases/archives/families_households/013378.html (accessed June 21, 2009).
16. U.S. Census Bureau Newsroom, *Census Bureau Reports Nearly 1 in 3 Unmarried Women Who Give Birth Cohabit*, November 4, 2010.
17. U.S. Census Bureau News, Facts for Features, March 9, 2010 and April 20, 2010.
18. U.S. Census Bureau, Current Population Survey, 2010 Annual Social and Economic Supplement.
19. Michael Hout and Caroline Hanley, "The overworked American family: Trends and nontrends in working hours, 1968–2001," *Survey Research Center* (University of California, Berkeley, 2002), 11.
20. John R. Weeks, *Population: An Introduction to Concepts and Issues*, 9th edition (Belmont, CA: Wadsworth Thomson Learning, 2005).
21. Jason Fields and Lynne M. Casper, "America's Families and Living Arrangements: March 2000," *Current Population Reports*, P20-537, U.S. Census Bureau (2001), http://www.census.gov/prod/2001pubs/p20-537.pdf (accessed August 3, 2009).
22. John R. Weeks, *Population: An Introduction to Concepts and Issues*, 9th edition (Belmont, CA: Wadsworth Thomson Learning, 2005).
23. Ibid.
24. U.S. Census Bureau, 2006. http://www.census.gov/Press-Release/www/releases/archives/facts_for_features_special_editions/006560.html (accessed June 21, 2009).
25. Deborah Feyerick and Sheila Steffen, "Same-sex marriage in Massachusetts, 4 years later." CNN.com, June 16, 2009. http://www.cnn.com/2008/US/06/16/feyerick.samesex.marriage/index.html.
26. Gary J. Gates, et al., "Adoption and foster care by gay and lesbian parents in the United States," *The Williams Institute & The Urban Institute* http://www.law.ucla.edu/Williamsinstitute/publications/Policy-Adoption-index.html (accessed July 23, 2009).
27. Jessie Bernard, "Women, marriage, and the future," *Futurist* 4 (1970): 41–43.
28. Ibid.
29. Elizabeth Jelin and Ana Rita Díaz-Muñoz, *Major trends affecting families: South America in perspective*. United Nations Department of Economic and Social Affairs Division for Social Policy and Development Programme on the Family (2003), 2.
30. Ibid., 4.
31. Ibid., 4–7.
32. Ibid., 6
33. Ibid., 8.
34. Ibid., 11.
35. Ibid., 14.
36. The United States Conference of Mayors, *Hunger and homelessness survey: A Status Report on Hunger and Homelessness in America's Cities A 25-City Survey*, 2008. http://www.usmayors.org/pressreleases/documents/hungerhomelessness-report_121208.pdf.
37. Annette Lareau, *Unequal Childhoods* (Berkeley, CA: University of California Press, 2003), 29.
38. J. Ross Eshleman, *The Family: An Introduction*, 2nd edition. (Boston: Allyn and Bacon, 1978), 10.
39. C. Ross. C., J. Mirowsky, and K. Goldsteen, "The Impact of the Family on Health," in *Contemporary Families: Looking Forward, Looking Back*, Alan Booth, ed., (Minneapolis: National Council on Family Relations, 1991).
40. U.S. Census Bureau Newsroom, *Census Bureau Reports Nearly 1 in 3 Unmarried Women Who Give Birth Cohabit*, November 4, 2010.
41. Jesse D. Mckinnon and Claudette E. Bennett, "We the People: Blacks in the United States: Census 2000 Special Reports," U.S. Bureau of the Census (2005), 6, http://www.census.gov/prod/2005pubs/censr-25.pdf (accessed August 2, 2009).
42. William A. Vega, "Hispanic Families," in Alan Booth, ed., *Contemporary Families: Looking Forward, Looking Back* (Minneapolis: National Council on Family Relations, 1991).
43. Vonnie C. McLoyd, et al., "Marital processes and parental socialization in families of color: A decade review of research," *Journal of Marriage and the Family* 62(4) (2000): 1070–1093.
44. Karen R. Humes, Nicholas A. Jones, and Roberto R. Ramirez, Overview of Race and Hispanic Origin: 2010, *2010 Census Briefs*, U.S. Census Bureau.
45. Vonnie C. McLoyd, et al., "Marital processes and parental socialization in families of color: A decade review of research." *Journal of Marriage and the Family* 62(4) (2000): 1070–1093.
46. Masako Ishii-Kuntz, "Japanese American Families," in *Families in Cultural Context*, Mary Kay DeGenova, ed., (Mountain View, CA: Mayfield, 1997).
47. Kerrily Kitano and Harry H. L. Kitano, "The Japanese-American Family," in C. Mindel, R. Habenstein, and R. Wright, Jr., eds., *Ethnic Families in America: Patterns and Variations*, 4th edition (Upper Saddle River, NJ: Prentice Hall, 1998), 311–330.
48. Karen R. Humes, Nicholas A. Jones, and Roberto R. Ramirez, Overview of Race and Hispanic Origin: 2010, *2010 Census Briefs*, U.S. Census Bureau.
49. Michael Yellowbird and C. Matthew Snipp, "American Indian Families," in *Minority Families in the United States: A Multicultural Perspective*, Ronald L. Taylor, ed., (Englewood Cliffs, NJ: Prentice Hall, 1994).
50. Susan Miller Okin, "Families and feminist theory: Some past and present issues," in Hilda Lindeman Nelson (ed.), *Feminism and Families* (New York: Routledge, 1997), 13–24.
51. Bron B. Ingoldsby, Suzanne R. Smith, and J. Elizabeth Miller, *Exploring Family Theories* (Los Angeles: Roxbury Publishing Company, 2004), 189–192.
52. Charles Horton Cooley, *Human Nature and the Social Order* (New York: Scribner's, 1902), 184.
53. Urie Brofenbrenner, "Ecology of the family as a context for human development: Research perspectives," *Developmental Psychology*, 22 (6) (1986): 723–742.
54. Ibid.
55. Richard J. Gelles, "Abused Wives: Why Do They Stay?" *Journal of Marriage and the Family* 38 (1976): 659–668.
56. Fred Rothbaum, "Family Systems Theory, Attachment Theory, and Culture," *Family Process* 41 (2002): 328–350.
57. Roy H. Rodgers and Reuben Hill, "The developmental approach," in *Handbook of Marriage and the Family*, Harold T. Christensen, ed., (Chicago: Rand McNally, 1964).
58. Evelyn Millis Duvall and Reuben Hill, eds., *Dynamics in Family Interaction* (New York: Women's Foundation, 1948).
59. Joan Aldous, *Family Careers, Developmental Change in Families* (New York: John Wiley & Sons, 1978).
60. Leslie A. Baxter, Dawn O. Braithwaite, and John H. Nicholson, "Turning points in the development of blended families," *Journal of Social and Personal Relationships*, 16(3) (1999): 291–313; Richard C. Friedman, "On sexual orientation and family development," *The American Journal of Orthopsychiatry* 68 (4) (1998).
61. Pierre L. van den Berghe, "Race and Ethnicity: A Sociobiological Perspective," *Ethnic and Racial Studies* 1 (1978): 401–411.
62. Pierre L. van den Berghe, *Human Family Systems: An Evolutionary View* (New York: Elsevier, 1979).
63. Nancy Kingsbury and John Scanzoni, "Structural-functionalism," in., *Sourcebook of Family Theories and Methods: A Contextual Approach*, Pauline G. Boss, et al., eds. (New York: Plenum, 1993), 195–217.
64. Richard B. Felson, "Parents and reflected appraisal process: A longitudinal analysis," *Journal of Personality and Social Psychology* 56 (1989): 965–971.
65. Richard L. Miller, Philip Brickman, and Diana Bolen, "Attribution versus persuasion as a means for modifying behavior," *Journal of Personality and Social Psychology* 31(3) (1975): 430–441.
66. Janice E. Stockard, *Daughters of the Canton Delta: Marriage Patterns and Economic Strategies in South China, 1860–1930* (Stanford, CA: Stanford University Press, 1989).
67. Frank F. Furstenberg, Jr., and Graham Spanier, eds., *Recycling the Family—Remarriage after Divorce*, rev. ed. (Newbury Park, CA: Sage, 1987).

CHAPTER 2

1. "Family Development Theory: Basic Concepts and Propositions, Critiques, Research, Conclusion," *Marriage and Family Encyclopedia*, http://family.jrank.org/pages/519/Family-Development-Theory.html (accessed June 30, 2009).

2. "Family Development Theory: Critiques," *Marriage and Family Encyclopedia*, http://family.jrank.org/pages/516/Family-Development-Theory-Critiques.html (accessed June 30, 2009).

3. Evelyn Millis Duvall, *Family Development*, 4th edition (Philadelphia: J.P. Lippincott, 1971), 519-532.

4. Jenifer Kunz, *Marital Satisfaction over the Family Life Cycle*. Thesis for Brigham Young University, Sociology Department (1989).

5. John B. Lansing and Leslie Kish, "Family Life Cycle as an Independent Variable," *American Sociological Review* 22(5) (1957): 512-519, http://www.jstor.org/stable/2089474 (accessed June 30, 2009).

6. Carolyn A. Kapinus and Michael P. Johnson, "The Utility of Family Life Cycle as a Theoretical and Empirical Tool," *Journal of Family Issues* 24(2) (2003): 155-184.

7. Graham Spanier, William Sauer, and Robert Larzelere, "An Empirical Evaluation of the Family Life Cycle," *Journal of Marriage and Family* 41(1) (1979): 27-38, http://www.jstor.org/stable/351728 (accessed June 30, 2009).

8. Steven L. Nock, "The Family Life Cycle: Empirical or Conceptual Tool?" *Journal of Marriage and the Family* 41(1) (1979): 15-26. http://www.jstor.org/stable/351727 (accessed June 30, 2009).

9. D. Russell Crane and Tim B. Heaton, *Handbook of Families and Poverty* (Thousand Oaks, CA: Sage Publications, 2008).

10. Harold Feldman, "Development of the husband-wife relationship," *Report of research to NIMH* (Ithaca, NY: Dept. of Child Development and Family Relationships, New York State College of Home Economics, Cornell University, 1965).

11. Harold Feldman and Margaret Feldman, "The Family Life Cycle: Some Suggestions for Recycling," *Journal of Marriage and the Family* 37(2) (1975): 277-284.

12. John DeFrain and Sylvia M. Asay, "Family Strengths and Challenges in the USA," *Marriage & Family Review* 41(3) (2007): 281-307. http://dx.doi.org/10.1300/J002v41n03_04 (accessed June 30, 2009).

13. Donald J. Hernandez, "Child development and the social demography of childhood," *Child Development* 68(1) (1997): 149-169.

14. John DeFrain and Sylvia M. Asay, "Family Strengths and Challenges in the USA," *Marriage & Family Review* 41(3) (2007): 281-307. http://dx.doi.org/10.1300/J002v41n03_04 (accessed June 30, 2009).

15. Ibid.

16. Ibid.

17. Irene Hoiutman and Karen Jettinghoff, "Raising Awareness of Stress at Work in Developing Countries," *Protecting Worker's Health Services No. 6* (Geneva: World Health Organization, 2007).

18. Brandeis University Institute for Health Policy, "Substance abuse: The nation's number one health problem," 2001, cited by National Council on Alcoholism and Drug Dependence, http://www.ncadd.org (accessed June 30, 2009).

19. "Actual causes of death in the United States, 2000," National Center for Chronic Disease Prevention and Health Promotion (2004) http://www.cdc.gov/ (accessed June 30, 2009).

20. John DeFrain and Sylvia M. Asay, "Family Strengths and Challenges in the USA," *Marriage & Family Review* 41(3) (2004): 281-307. http://dx.doi.org/10.1300/J002v41n03_04 (accessed June 30, 2009).

21. Leanne O. Wolff, "Family Narrative: How Our Stories Shape Us," address given at the 1993 Annual Meeting of the Speech Communication Association, Miami, Florida.

22. Dennis K. Orthner, Hinckley Jones-Sanpei, and Sabrina Williamson, "The Resilience and Strengths of Low-Income Families," *Family Relations* 53(2) (2004): 159-167.

23. Patricia Kain Knaub, "Professional Women Perceive Family Strengths," *Journal of Home Economics* 77(2) (1985): 52-55.

24. Harriet K. Light and Ruth E. Martin, "American Indian Families," *Journal of American Indian Education* 26(1) (1986), http://jaie.esu.edu.erl.libb.byu/V26/v26S1ame.htm (accessed June 30, 2009).

25. William A. Katz, "*Strengths of Black Families* by Robert Hill: A Review," *Equal Opportunity Review* (1973).

26. John DeFrain and Sylvia M. Asay, "Family Strengths and Challenges in the USA," *Marriage & Family Review* 41(3) (2007): 28-307. http://dx.doi.org/10.1300/J002v41n03_04 (accessed June 30, 2009).

27. John DeFrain and Sylvia M. Asay, "Epilogue," *Marriage & Family Review* 41(3) (2007): 447-466. http://dx.doi.org/10.1300/J002v41n03_10 (accessed June 30, 2009).

28. Ibid.

29. Ibid.

30. Ibid.

31. Science Museum of Minnesota. St. Paul, Minnesota. http://www.smm.org/catal/introduction/glossary/ (accessed June 30, 2009).

32. Peter Lassman, ed., and Ronald Speirs, tr., *Weber: Political Writings* (Cambridge, England: Cambridge University Press, 1994), http://www.criticism.com/md/weber1.html.

33. Corrine Glesne and Alan Peshkin, *Becoming Qualitative Researchers: An Introduction* (White Plains, NY: Longman, 1992).

34. Greenstein, T., *Methods of Family Research* (Thousand Oaks, CA: Sage Publications, 2001), 74-77.

35. "Advantages and Disadvantages of Experimental Research," *Writing Guides: Conducting Experiments* (Colorado State University) http://writing.colostate.edu/guides/research/experiment/pop5d.cfm (accessed August 2, 2009).

36. Theodore N. Greenstein, *Methods of Family Research* (Thousand Oaks, CA: Sage Publications, 2001), 80-85.

37. "Advantages and Disadvantages of the Survey Method," *Writing Guides: Conducting Experiments* (Colorado State University) http://writing.colostate.edu/guides/research/survey/com2d1.cfm (accessed August 2, 2009).

38. Theodore N. Greenstein, *Methods of Family Research* (Thousand Oaks, CA: Sage Publications, 2001), 85-88.

39. Gerard Keegan, *Higher Psychology: Approaches and Methods* http://www.gerardkeegan.co.uk/resource/observationalmeth1.htm (accessed August 2, 2009).

40. Theodore N. Greenstein, *Methods of Family Research* (Thousand Oaks, CA: Sage Publications, 2001), 164-175.

41. Ibid. 100-102

42. Winston Tellis, "Introduction to Case Study," *The Qualitative Report* 3(2) (1993) http://www.nova.edu/ssss/QR/QR3-2/tellis1.html (accessed August 2, 2009).

43. Theodore N. Greenstein, *Methods of Family Research* (Thousand Oaks, CA: Sage Publications, 2001), 102-103.

44. "Ethnography," Project Tools http://www.tiresias.org/tools/ethnography.htm (accessed August 2, 2009).

45. Theodore N. Greenstein, *Methods of Family Research* (Thousand Oaks, CA: Sage Publications, 2001), 103-104.

46. James M. White and David M. Klein, *Family Theories,* 3rd edition (Thousand Oaks, CA: Sage Publications, 2008), 46-47.

47. Ibid. Ch. 7

48. Ibid. Ch. 4

49. Stephen F. Duncan and Kristi McLane, "Family Strengths: Identifying Family Strengths," *School of Family Life* Brigham Young University, 2002. http://www.foreverfamilies.net/xml/articles/family_strength.aspx (accessed August 2, 2009).

50. B.F. Grant, "Estimates of US children exposed to alcohol abuse and dependence in the family," *American Journal of Public Health* 90 (1) (2000): 112-115, http://www.alcoholfreechildren.org/en/research/briefs.cfm?doc_id=2334 (accessed August 2, 2009).

CHAPTER 3

1. Janet Yerby, Nancy Buerkel-Rothfuss, and Arthur P. Bochner, *Understanding Family Communication* (Scottsdale, AZ: Gorsuch Scarisbrick Publishers, 1995), 34-38.

2. Ibid.

3. Uttara Manohar, "Interpersonal Communication," http://www.buzzle.com/articles/interpersonal-communication.html (accessed August 5, 2009).

4. Ibid.

5. Kory Floyd and Mark T. Morman, eds., *Widening the Family Circle: New Research on Family Communication* (Thousand Oaks, CA: Sage Publications, 2006).

6. Lynne H. Turner and Richard West, *Perspectives on Family Communication* (New York: McGraw-Hill, 2006), 355-360.

7. Stephen A. Anderson and Ronald M. Sabatelli, *Family Interaction: A Multigenerational Developmental Perspective* (Boston: Pearson Education, Inc, 1995), 159-161.

8. Ibid.

9. Ibid.

10. Betty Yorburg, *Family Realities: A Global View* (Upper Saddle River, NJ: Prentice Hall, 2002), 147-158.

11. "Multigenerational Transmission of Communication Patterns," *Genograms*, http://www.genograms.org/patterns.html (accessed June 21, 2009).

12. André M. Ledbetter, "Family Communication Patterns and Relational Maintenance Behavior: Direct and Mediated Association with Friendship Closeness," *International Communication Association* 35 (2009): 130-147.

13. Ibid.

14. Sachiyo M. Shearman and Rebecca Dumlao, "A Cross-Cultural Comparison of Family Communication Patterns and Conflict Between Young Adults and Parents," *Journal of Family Communication* 8 (2008): 186-211.

15. Sherry L. Beaumont, "Adolescent Girls' Conversations with Mothers and Friends: A Matter of Style," *Discourse Processes* 20 (1995): 109-132.

16. Ibid.

17. Yong S. Park, Leyna P. Vo, and Tuying Tsong, "Family Affection as a Protective Factor Against the Negative Effects of Perceived Asian Values Gap on the Parent-Child Relationship for Asian American Male and Female College Student," *Cultural Diversity and Ethnic Minority Psychology* 15(1) (2009): 18-26.

18. Rick Peterson and Stephen Green, "Families First—Keys to Successful Family Functioning: Communication," *Virginia Cooperative Extension*, Virginia Tech, http://pubs.ext.vt.edu/350/350-092/350-092.html (accessed June 22, 2009).

19. "Communication Skills for You and Your Family," *Families Matter!* Cooperative Extension, University of Delaware, http://ag.udel.edu/extension/fam/fm/issue/communicationskills.htm (accessed June 22, 2009).

20. Brian Jory, "Power: Family Relationships," http://family.jrank.org/pages/1316/Power.html (accessed June 22, 2009).

21. Ronald O. Blood and Donald M. Wolfe, *Husbands & Wives: The Dynamics of Married Living* (New York: The Free Press, 1960), 11-47.

22. Brian Jory, "Power: Family Relationships," http://family.jrank.org/pages/1316/Power.html (accessed June 22, 2009).

23. Ibid.

24. Robert H. Lauer and Jeanette C. Lauer, *Marriage & Family: The Quest for Intimacy* (New York: McGraw-Hill, 2009), 218-219.

25. Brian Jory, "Power: Family Relationships," http://family.jrank.org/pages/1316/Power.html (accessed June 22, 2009).

26. Daniel Workman, "World's Most Emotional Countries," http://regional-business-profiles.suite101.com/article.cfm/worlds_most_emotional_countries, Accessed June 26, 2009.

27. Ibid.

28. Lynne H. Turner and Richard West, *Perspectives on Family Communication* (New York: McGraw-Hill, 2006), 171-174.

29. Kathleen M. Galvin, Carma L. Bylund, and Bernard J. Brommel, *Family Communication: Cohesion and Change.* (Boston: Pearson Education, Inc, 2004), 223-226.

30. Lynne H. Turner and Richard West, *Perspectives on Family Communication* (New York: McGraw-Hill, 2006), 174-178.

31. Ibid.

32. Ibid.

33. Ibid.

34. John M. Gottman and Lowell J. Krokoff, "Marital Interaction and Satisfaction: A Longitudinal View," *Journal of Consulting and Clinical Psychology* 57(1) (1989): 47-52.

35. Patricia Noller, et al., "A Longitudinal Study of Conflict in Early Marriage," *Journal of Social and Personal Relationships* 11 (1994): 233-252.

36. Annmarie Cano, K. Daniel O'Leary, and Wanda Heinz, "Short-term consequences of sever marital stressors," *Journal of Social and Personal Relationships* 21(4) (2004): 419-430.

37. Eric W. Lindsey and Malinda J. Colwell, "Family conflict in divorced and non-divorced families: Potential consequences for boys' friendship status and friendship quality," *Journal of Social and Personal Relationships* 23(1) (2006): 45-63.

38. Shobha C. Shagle and Brian K. Barber, "Effects of family, marital, and parent-child conflict on adolescent self-derogation and suicidal ideation," *Journal of Marriage and the Family* 55(4) (1993): 964-974.

39. Shelley Mallet, Doreen Rosenthal, and Deborah Keys, "Young people, drug use and family conflict: Pathways into homelessness," *Journal of Adolescence* 28 (2005): 185-199.

40. Joaquin Borrego, Jr., et al., "Parent-child interaction therapy with domestic violence populations," *Journal of Family Violence* 23 (2008): 495-505.

41. Stephen A. Anderson and Ronald M. Sabatelli, *Family Interaction: A Multigenerational Developmental Perspective* (Boston: Pearson Education, Inc, 1995), 177-189.

42. Ibid.

43. Ibid.

44. Eileen Hayes, "Saying 'no' to everything," *Parenting* (2008), BBC, http://www.bbc.co.uk/parenting/your_kids/toddlers_no.shtml (accessed June 19, 2009).

45. "The Family: An Example of a Primary Group," Peerpapers.com, http://www.peerpapers.com/essays/Family-Example-PrimaryGroup/134514.html?read_essay (accessed June 29, 2009).

46. "Frequently Asked Questions on Marriage and Family Therapists," American Association for Marriage and Family Therapy, http://www.aamft.org/faqs/index_nm.asp#why (accessed June 29, 2009).

47. Ibid.

48. "Family Therapy: Healing Family Conflicts," MayoClinic.com, http://www.mayoclinic.com/health/family-therapy/hq00662 (accessed June 29, 2009).

CHAPTER 4

1. Cliff Jahr, "Patti," *New York Times Magazine,* December 26, 1975, http://www.oceanstar.com/patti/intervus/751226nt.htm (accessed August 5, 2009).

2. "What is the difference between sex and gender? *Monash University Medicine, Nursing, and Health Sciences*, Victoria, Australia, 2009 http://www.med.monash.edu.au/gendermed/sexandgender.html (accessed August 5, 2009).

3. C. Lynn Carr, "Tomboyism or Lesbianism? Beyond Sex/Gender/Sexual Conflation," *Sex Roles* 53(1/2) (2005): 119-131.

4. Brian K. Williams, Stacey C. Sawyer, and Carl M. Wahlstrom, *Marriages, Families, Intimate Relationships* (Boston, MA: Pearson Education, 2009), 90-92.

5. JoNell Strough, et al., "From Adolescence to Later Adulthood: Femininity, Masculinity, and Androgyny in Six Age Groups," *Sex Roles* 57 (2007): 385-396.

6. Ward Goodenough, "Cultural anthropology and linguistics," *Language and linguistics* 9 (1957):168.

7. *American Heritage Dictionary of the English Language*, Houghton Mifflin, 2000. http://education.yahoo.com/reference/dictionary/entry/culture;_ylt=Auz x8rW46PeFKcSNyIQ1_8.sgMMF (accessed August 5, 2009).

8. Marie Richmond-Abbot, *Masculine and Feminine* (New York: McGraw Hill, 1992, 1983), 56-58.

9. Margaret Mead, quoted in *Masculine and Feminine*, Marie Richmond-Abbot (New York: McGraw Hill, 1992, 1983), 57.

10. John Tierney, "As Barriers Disappear, Some Gender Gaps Widen," *New York Times,* September 8, 2008, http://www.nytimes.com/2008/09/09/science/09tier.html?_r=2&scp=9&sq=sex%20differences%20in%20health&st=cse (accessed August 5, 2009).

11. Melissa J. Perry and George W. Albee, "The Deterministic Origins of Sexism," *Race, Gender & Class* 5(3) (1998): 122-128.

12. Floyd M. Martinson, "Youth, Socio-Sexual Norms and Systems II," *Family in Society* (New York: Dodd, Mead & Company Inc, 1970), 262-276.

13. David Sutton, "Another World Is *Still* Possible," *Identities: Global Studies in Culture and Power* 14 (2007): 631-647.

14. Lisa Sanchez Gonzalez, "Sexism in Latino Studies Programs," *Latino Studies* 4 (2006): 154-161.

15. Betty J. Collier and Louise N. Williams, "Towards a Bilateral Model of Sexism," *Human Relations* 34(2) (1981): 127-139.

16. U.S. Equal Employment Opportunity Commission, "Sex-Based Discrimination," 2008, http://www.eeoc.gov/types/sex.html (accessed August 5, 2009).

17. Nicole V. Benokraitis, *Marriage and Families* (Upper Saddle River, NJ: Pearson Education, 2008), 144-145.

18. U.S. Equal Employment Opportunity Commission, "Sexual Harassment," 2008, http://www.eeoc.gov/types/sexual_harassment.html (accessed August 5, 2009).

19. J.Z. Rubin, F. Provenzano, and Z. Luria, "The eye of the beholder: Parents' views on sex of newborns," *American Journal of Orthopsychiatry* 44 (1974): 512-519.

20. Barrie Thorne, *Gender Play: Girls and Boys in School* (New Brunswick, NJ: Rutgers University Press, 1993), 2.

21. J.S. Eccles, J. Jacobs, and R. Harold, "Gender role stereotypes, expectancy effects, and parents' socialization of gender differences," *Journal of Social Issues* 46 (1990): 186-201.

22. Susan A. Basow, *Gender Stereotypes and Roles,* 3rd edition (Pacific Grove, CA: Brooks/Cole Publishing Company, 1992).

23. Diane N. Ruble, "Sex role development," in Marc H. Barnstein and Michael E. Lamb, eds., *Developmental Psychology: An Advanced Textbook*, 2nd ed. (Hillsdale, NJ: Erlbaum, 1988).

24. Rob Kuznia, "Survey: Hispanic Teens Say Parents Biggest Influence on Decisions about Sex," HispanicBusiness.com, 2009, http://www.hispanicbusiness.com/news/2009/5/19/survey_hispanic_teens_say_parents_biggest.htm (accessed August 5, 2009).

25. J.S. Eccles, J. Jacobs, and R. Harold, "Gender Role Stereotypes, Expectancy Effects, and Parent's Socialization of Gender Differences," *Journal of Social Issues* 46(2) (1990): 183-201.

26. Jennifer L. Kornreich, "Sibling influence, gender roles, and the sexual socialization of urban early adolescent girls," *Journal of Sex Research*, http://findarticles.com/p/articles/mi_m2372/is_1_40/ai_101530214 (accessed August 5, 2009).

27. John Macionis, *Sociology* 11th edition (Upper Saddle River, NJ: Pearson Education, 2007), 127-133.

28. Ibid.

29. Sara Amon, Shmuel Shamai, and Zinaida Ilatov, "Socialization Agents and Activities of Young Adolescents," *Adolescence* 43(170) (2008): 374-394.

30. "Children and Watching TV," *Facts for Families*, American Academy of Child and Adolescent Psychiatry 54 (2001), http://www.aacap.org/cs/root/facts_for_families/children_and_watching_tv (accessed August 5, 2009).

31. Norman Herr, "Television and Health. The Sourcebook for Teaching Science" (2007), http://www.csun.edu/science/health/docs/tv&health.html#tv_stats (accessed August 5, 2009).

32. Judith Worell, *Encyclopedia of Men and Women: Vol 2* (San Diego, CA: Academic Press, 2001), 808.

33. Ibid., 677-678.

34. Ibid., 678.

35. Ibid., 679.

36. Trina Buss, "Second Shift for Employed Mothers," *Online Encyclopedia of Family Stress and Coping* (2007), http://familystressencyclopedia.blogspot.com/2007/08/second-shift-for-employed-mothers.html (accessed August 5, 2009).

37. "Sexuality," *Health and Well-Being* (2004), http://health.ninemsn.com.au/article.aspx?id=689611 (accessed August 5, 2009).

38. "Sexual Orientation and Homosexuality," *APA Help Center*, American Psychological Association (2009), http://www.apahelpcenter.org/articles/pdf.php?id=31 (accessed August 5, 2009).

39. Juniper Russo Tarascio, "Straight, Gay, Bi and . . . Pansexual?" Associated Content Society (2008), http://www.associatedcontent.com/article/1047717/straight_gay_bi_and_pansexual_html?cat=47 (accessed August 5, 2009).

40. "APA Reiterates Position on Reparative Therapies," American Psychiatric Association, *Psychiatric News* 36(2) (2001): 34.

41. Brian W. Litzenberger and Margaret C. Buttenheim, "Sexual Orientation and Family Development; Introduction," *American Journal of Orthopsychiatry* 68 (3) (1998): 344-351.

42. "Study Suggests Difference Between Female And Male Sexuality," *ScienceDaily* (2003), http://www.sciencedaily.com/releases/2003/06/030613075252.htm (accessed July 15, 2009).

43. "Exploring the Biological Contributions to Human Health: Does Sex Matter?" Institute of Medicine of the National Academy of Sciences (Washington DC: National Academy Press, 2001), http://www.nap.edu/openbook.php?record_id=10028&page=28 (accessed August 5, 2009).

44. Robert Pear, "Sex Differences Called Key in Medical Studies," *New York Times,* April 25, 2001, http://www.nytimes.com/2001/04/25/us/sex-differences-called-key-in-medical-studies.html?scp=1&sq=Sex%20Differences%20Called%20Key%20in%20Medical%20Studies.%E2%80%9D%20&st=cse (accessed August 9, 2005).

45. E. Barrett-Connor, "Coronary Heart Disease: Why Are Women So Superior?" *Circulation* 95 (1995): 252-264.

46. The University Hospital, "Stroke Statistics," University of Medicine and Dentistry of New Jersey, http://www.theuniversityhospital.com/stroke/stats.htm (accessed August 6, 2009).

47. P.A. Tataranni, D.E. Larson, and E. Ravussin, "Body fat distribution and energy metabolism in obese men and women," *Journal of the American College of Nutrition* 13(6) (1994): 569-574.

48. MayoClinic.com, "Depression in Women: Understanding the Gender Gap," Mayo Foundation for Medical Education and Research (MFMER), 2008, http://www.mayoclinic.com/health/depression/MH00035 (accessed August 5, 2009).

49. Sam Vaknin, "Is there any difference between male and female narcissists?" Buzzle.com, 2003, http://www.buzzle.com/editorials/6-5-2002-19796.asp (accessed August 5, 2009).

50. World Health Organization, *Eliminating Female Genital Mutilation*, (Geneva, Switzerland: WHO Press, 2008).

51. Ann Bradley and Diane Miller, "NIAAA Researchers Estimate Alcohol and Drug Use, Abuse, and Dependence Among Welfare Recipients," National Institutes of Health (1996), http://www.nih.gov/news/pr/oct96/niaaa-23.htm (accessed August 5, 2009).

52. U.S. National Center for Health Statistics, "National Vital Statistics Reports (NVSR)," *Deaths: Final Data for 2005*, 2008. 56(10). http://www.census.gov/compendia/statab/tables/09s0100.pdf (accessed August 5, 2009).

53. Ricky L. Langley, *Sex and Gender Differences in Health and Disease*, Carolina Academic Press (2003): ix–xi. http://www.cap-press.com/pdf/1284.pdf (accessed August 5, 2009).

54. Ibid.

55. "Culture of Belarus," *Countries and Their Cultures*, http://www.everyculture.com/A-Bo/Belarus.html (accessed August 5, 2009).

56. "SIGI Rankings 2009," *Social Institutions and Gender Index*, Organization for Economic Co-operation and Development (OECD) (2009), http://genderindex.org/ranking (accessed August 5, 2009).

57. Talcott Parsons, "Age and Sex in the Social Structure of the United States," *American Sociological Review* 7(5) (1942): 604–616.

58. Wesley R. Burr, et al., *Contemporary Theories about the Family* (New York: The Free Press, 1979), 242–243.

59. James M. White and David M. Klein, *Family Theories*, 3rd edition (Thousand Oaks, CA: Sage Publication, 2008), 196–198.

60. John Macionis, *Sociology*, 11th edition (Upper Saddle River, NJ: Pearson Prentice Hall, 2007), 352.

61. Sheldon Stryker, "From Mead to a Structural Symbolic Interactionism and Beyond," *Annual Review of Sociology* 34 (2008): 15–31.

62. Ibid., 101–103.

63. Cheryl A. Rickabaugh, *Sex and Gender* (Boston: McGraw Hill, 1998), 19–21.

CHAPTER 5

1. Rebecca G. Adams, Rosemary Blieszner, and Brian De Vries, "Definitions of friendship in the third age: Age, gender, and study location effects," *Journal of Aging Studies* 14(1) (2000): 117–134.

2. Rowland K. Miller and Daniel Perlman, *Intimate Relationships* (New York: McGraw-Hill, 2009), 216–221.

3. Ibid.

4. Aurora M. Sherman, Brian De Vries, and Jennifer E. Lansford, "Friendship in childhood and adulthood: Lessons across the life span," *International Journal of Aging and Human Development* 51(1) (2000): 31–51.

5. Ibid.

6. Maarten Selfhout, et al., "In the eye of the beholder: Perceived, actual, and peer-rated similarity in personality, communication, and friendship intensity during the acquaintanceship process," *Journal of Personality and Social Psychology* 96(6) (2007): 1152–1165.

7. Sarah Greenberg, et al., "Friendship Across the Life Cycle" *Journal of Gerontological Work* 32(4) (2000): 7–23.

8. Vanessa M. Buote, Eileen Wood, and Michael Pratt, "Exploring similarities and differences between online and offline friendships: The role of attachment style," *Computers in Human Behavior* 25 (2009): 560–567.

9. Darius K.-S. Chan and Grand H.-L. Cheng, "A comparison of offline and online friendship qualities at different stages of relationship development," *Journal of Social and Personal Relationships* 21(3) (2004): 305–320.

10. Vanessa M. Buote, Eileen Wood, and Michael Pratt, "Exploring similarities and differences between online and offline friendships: The role of attachment style," *Computers in Human Behavior* 25 (2009): 560–567.

11. Gustavo S. Mesch and Ilan Talmud, "Similarity and the quality of online and offline social relationships among adolescents in Israel," *Journal of Research on Adolescence* 17(2) (2007): 455–466.

12. Roger Baumgarte and Donna Webster Nelson, "Preference for same- versus cross-sex friendships," *Journal of Applied Social Psychology* 39(4) (2009): 901–917.

13. Rowland S. Miller and Daniel Perlman, *Intimate Relationships* (New York: McGraw-Hill, 2009), 229–233.

14. Ibid.

15. Ibid.

16. Kathleen A. Bogle, *Hooking Up: Sex, Dating, and Relationships on Campus* (New York: New York University Press, 2008), 783–784.

17. Kathleen A. Bogle, "The shift from dating to hooking up in college: What scholars have missed," *Sociology Compass* 1(2) (2007): 775–788.

18. Jesse J. Owen, et al., "'Hooking up' among college students: Demographic and psychosocial correlates," *Archives of Sexual Behavior* (2008).

19. Ibid.

20. Gary Gute and Elaine M. Eshbaugh, "Personality as a predictor of hooking up among college students," *Journal of Community Health Nursing* 25 (2008): 26–43.

21. Elaine M. Eshbaugh and Gary Gute, "Hookups and sexual regret among college students," *The Journal of Social Psychology* 148(1) (2008): 77–89.

22. "Hooked on 'hooking up,'" *The Huntington News*, http://www.huntington-news.com/2.6302/hooked-on-hooking-up-1.1644208 (accessed July 26, 2009).

23. William F. Flack, et al., "Risk factors and consequences of unwanted sex among university students: Hooking up, alcohol, and stress response," *Journal of Interpersonal Violence* 22(2) (2007): 139–157.

24. Kathleen A. Bogle, *Hooking Up: Sex, Dating, and Relationships on Campus* (New York: New York University Press, 2008), 158–186.

25. Ibid.

26. Kory Floyd, *Communicating Affection: Interpersonal Behavior and Social Context* (New York: Cambridge University Press, 2006), reviewed in *Journal of Communication* 57 (2007), 176–178.

27. M.P. González, et al., "What is Affection?" *Biopsychology.org 1998-2006*, http://www.biopsychology.org/biopsychology/papers/what_is_affection.html (accessed August 6, 2009).

28. "The Importance of Touch in Parent-Infant Bonding," Texas School for the Blind and the Visually Impaired (2002), http://www.tsbvi.edu/Outreach/seehear/fall00/infantbonding.htm (accessed July 27, 2009).

29. Ibid.

30. Andrew K. Gulledge, Michelle H. Gulledge, and Robert F. Stahmann, "Romantic physical affection types and relationship satisfaction," *The American Journal of Family Therapy* 31 (2003): 233–242.

31. Mary Kay DeGenova, *Intimate Relationships, Marriages and Families* (New York: McGraw-Hill, 2008), 47.

32. Elizabeth Vaquera and Grace Kao, "Private and public display of affection among interracial and intra-racial adolescent couples," *Social Science Quarterly* 86(2) (2005): 484–508.

33. Hilary N. Fouts, Michael E. Lamb, Jaipaul L. Roopnarine, "Social experience and daily routines of African American Infants in Different Socioeconomic Contexts," *Journal of Family Psychology* 21(4) (2007): 655–664.

34. Kory Floyd, Jack E. Sargent, and Mark Di Corcia, "Human affection exchange: VI. Further tests of reproductive probability as a predictor of men's affection with their adult sons," *The Journal of Social Psychology* 144(2) (2004): 191–206.

35. Ibid.

36. Tara C. Marshall, "Cultural differences in intimacy: The influence of gender-role ideology and individualism—collectivism," *Journal of Social and Personal Relationships* 25(1) (2008): 143–168.

37. Beth A. Le Poire, *Family Communication: Nurturing and Control in a Changing World* (Thousand Oaks, CA: SAGE, 2005).

38. Debra J. Mashek and Arthur Aron, *Handbook of Closeness and Intimacy* (Philadelphia: Lawrence Erlbaum Associates, 2004).

39. Geraldine K. Piorkowski, *Too Close for Comfort: Exploring the Risks of Intimacy* (New York: Perseus Publishing, 1994).

40. David H. Olson and Dean M. Gorell, "Circumplex Model of Marital & Family Systems," *Normal Family Processes* (New York: Guilford, 2003).

41. The Big Green, "Rules of Affection" (2004), http://thebiggreen.net/article.php?id=576 (accessed July 28, 2009).

42. "Intimacy: Intimacy and Gender," http://family.jrank.org/pages/947/Intimacy-Intimacy-Gender.html (accessed July 28, 2009).

43. Deborah Tannen, *You Just Don't Understand: Women and Men in Conversation* (New York: William Morrow and Company, 1990).

44. Lynne Zarbatany, Patricia McDougall, and Shelley Hymel, "Gender-differentiated experience in the peer culture: Links to intimacy in preadolescence," *Social Development* 9(1) (2000): 62–79.

45. Patricia Noller, "What is this thing called love? Defining the love that supports marriage and family," *Personal Relationships* 3 (1996): 97–115.

46. Ibid.

47. Rowland S. Miller and Daniel Perlman, *Intimate Relationships* (New York: McGraw-Hill, 2009).

48. Jungsik Kim and Elaine Hatfield, "Love types and subjective well-being: A cross-cultural study," *Social Behavior and Personality* 32(2) (2004): 173–182.

49. Jerold Heiss, "Gender and Romantic-Love Roles," *The Sociological Quarterly* 32(4) (1991): 575–591.

50. Ibid.

51. Lawrence A. Kurdek, "Are gay and lesbian cohabiting couples really different from heterosexual married couples?" *Journal of Marriage and Family* 66(4) (2004): 880–900.

52. Ibid.

53. Lawrence A. Kurdek, "Differences between partners from Black and White heterosexual dating couples in a path model of relationship commitment," *Journal of Social and Personal Relationships* 25(1) (2008): 51–70.

54. Ibid.

55. Rowland S. Miller and Daniel Perlman, *Intimate Relationships* (New York: McGraw-Hill, 2009).

56. Pamela C. Regan, *The Mating Game: A Primer on Love, Sex, and Marriage* (Thousand Oaks, CA: Sage Publications, 2008).

57. Ibid.

58. Ibid.

59. Ibid.

60. Robert J. Sternberg and Karin Weis, *The New Psychology of Love* (New Haven, CT: Yale University Press, 2006).

61. David A. Gershaw, "A Line on Life: Love Triangles" (2002), http://virgil. azwestern.edu/;dag/lol/LoveTriangles.html (accessed July 30, 2009).

62. Rowland S. Miller and Daniel Perlman, *Intimate Relationships* (New York: McGraw-Hill, 2009).

63. Pamela C. Regan, *The Mating Game: A Primer on Love, Sex, and Marriage* (Thousand Oaks, CA: Sage Publications, 2008).

64. Ana Carolina Fowler, "Love and marriage through the lens of sociological theories," *Journal of the Sociology of Self-Knowledge* 5(2) (2007): 61-72.

65. Bron B. Ingoldsby, Suzanne R. Smith, and J. Elizabeth Miller, *Exploring Family Theories* (Los Angeles: Roxbury Publishing Company, 2004).

66. UCSD University Communication, "Rekindle the Romance" (2005), http://ucsd-news.ucsd.edu/thisweek/2005/feb/02_22_relationships.asp (accessed August 2, 2009).

CHAPTER 6

1. John Macionis, *Sociology* (Upper Saddle River, NJ: Pearson Education, Inc, 1987), 72, 82, 197.

2. "Gallup Poll Review from the Poll Editors," The Gallup Organization (1997), http://www.hi-ho.ne.jp/taku77/refer/sexnorm.htm (accessed July 9, 2009).

3. Meg Wilkes Karraker and Janet R. Grochowski, *Families With Futures: A Survey of Family Studies for the 21st Century* (Marwah, NJ: Lawrence Erlbaum Associates, Inc, 2006), 168-172.

4. Pamela C. Regan, *The Mating Game: A Primer on Love, Sex, and Marriage* (Thousand Oaks, CA: Sage Publications, Inc, 2008), 207-209.

5. "Sexual Health: Circumcision," *Sexual Conditions Guide*, http://www.webmd.com/sexual-conditions/guide/circumcision (accessed August 12, 2009).

6. Ibid.

7. Lynne H. Turner and Richard West, *Perspectives on Family Communication* (New York: McGraw-Hill, 2006), 333-335.

8. Rowland S. Miller and Daniel Perlman, *Intimate Relationships* (New York: McGraw-Hill, 2009), 275-279.

9. Ibid.

10. "Gallup Poll Review from the Poll Editors," The Gallup Organization (1997), http://www.hi-ho.ne.jp/taku77/refer/sexnorm.htm (accessed July 9, 2009).

11. "Americans Evenly Divided on Morality of Homosexuality," The Gallup Organization (2008), http://www.gallup.com/poll/108115/americans-evenly-dividedmorality-homosexuality.aspx (accessed July 9, 2009).

12. Pamela C. Regan, *The Mating Game: A Primer on Love, Sex, and Marriage* (Thousands Oaks, CA: Sage Publications, 2008), 207-209.

13. "Attitudes about sexuality and aging," AARP.org (2008), http://www.aarp.org/health/conditions/articles/harvard__sexuality-in-midlife-and-beyond_2.html (accessed July 9, 2009).

14. Ibid.

15. Meg Wilkes Karraker and Janet R. Grochowski, *Families With Futures: A Survey of Family Studies for the 21st Century* (Marwah, NJ: Lawrence Erlbaum Associates, Inc., 2006), 185-186.

16. Ibid.

17. Ibid.

18. Marilyn Coleman and Lawrence H. Ganong, *Handbook of Contemporary Families: Considering the Past, Contemplating the Future* (Thousand Oaks, CA: Sage Publications, Inc, 2004), 108-109.

19. Michael Young, et al., "Sexual satisfaction among married women," *American Journal of Health Studies* 16(2) (2000): 73-84.

20. Ibid.

21. Hope College, "Sex and Marital Satisfaction" (2009), http://www.hope.edu/academic/psychology/335/webrep/marital/html (accessed May 21, 2009).

22. Elina Haavio-Mannila and Osmo Kontula, "Correlates of increased sexual satisfaction," *Archives of Sexual Behavior* 24(4) (1997): 399-419.

23. Tina M. Penhollow and Michael Young, "Predictors of sexual satisfaction: The role of body image and fitness," *Electronic Journal of Human Sexuality* (2008), http://www.ejhs.org/volume11/Penhollow.htm (accessed June 11, 2009).

24. Elina Haavio-Mannila and Osmo Kontula, "Correlates of increased sexual satisfaction," *Archives of Sexual Behavior* 24(4) (1997): 399-419.

25. Ibid.

26. Ibid.

27. Ibid.

28. Kristen Harrison, "Does interpersonal attraction to thin media personalities promote eating disorders?" *Journal of Broadcasting & Electronic Media* 41(4) (1997): 478-500.

29. Tina M. Penhollow and Michael Young, "Predictors of sexual satisfaction: The role of body image and fitness," *Electronic Journal of Human Sexuality* (2008), http://www.ejhs.org/volume11/Penhollow.htm (accessed June 11, 2009).

30. "9 Health Issues That Can Impact Sexual Satisfaction," *University of Michigan Health System Newsroom* (2007), http://www2.med.umich.edu/prmc/media/newsroom/details.cfm?ID=677 (accessed June 11, 2009).

31. "Stages of Menopause," http://www.menopausenatural.com/menopause_stages.html (accessed August 14, 2009).

32. Christopher J. Gearon, "Dealing with Male Menopause," *Men's Health Center*, http://health.discovery.com/centers/mens/articles/andropause.html (accessed August 14, 2009).

33. Judith Treas and Dierdre Giesen, "Sexual infidelity among married and cohabiting Americans," *Journal of Marriage and the Family* 62 (February 2000): 48-60.

34. Linda L. Lindsey, *Gender Roles: A Sociological Perspective* (Upper Saddle River, NJ: Prentice Hall, 1997), 189-192.

35. Ibid.

36. Ibid.

37. "Internet Infidelity: Technology's Dramatic Effect on Relationships," *Surviving Marital Infidelity* (2007) http://www.survivinginfidelity911.com/internet-infidelity-technologys-dramatic-effect-on-relationships (accessed July 12, 2009).

38. Ibid.

39. "Behavioral Health: Sexual Activity and Fertility," *Trends in the Well-Being of America's Children and Youth* (2000) http://aspe.hhs.gov/hsp/00trends/contents.htm#SD (accessed July 13, 2009).

40. Ibid.

41. Ibid.

42. Peter S. Bearman and Hannah Brückner, "Virginity Pledges and First Intercourse," *The American Journal of Sociology* 106(4) (2001): 856-912.

43. Ibid.

44. Jennifer Manlove, Suzanne Ryan, and Kerry Franzetta, "Perspective of contraceptive use within teenagers' first sexual relationships," *Perspectives on Sexual and Reproductive Health* 35(6) (2003): 246-255.

45. Ibid.

46. Lori Kowaleski-Jones and Frank L. Mott, "Sex, contraception and childbearing among high-risk youth: Do different factors influence males and females?" *Family Planning Perspective* 30(4) (1998): 163-169.

47. Kristin A. Moore, et al., "Nonmarital school-age motherhood: Family, individual, and school characteristics," *Journal of Adolescent Research* 13(4) (1998): 433-457.

48. Chien-Chung Huang and Wen-Jui Han, "Child support enforcement and sexual activity of male adolescents," *Journal of Marriage and Family* 69 (2007): 763-777.

49. Erin Calhoun Davis and Lisa V. Friel, "Adolescent sexuality: disentangling the effects of family structure and family context," *Journal of Marriage and Family* 63 (2001): 669-681.

50. Melina Bersamin, et al., "Parenting practices and adolescent sexual behavior: A longitudinal study," *Journal of Marriage and Family* 70 (2008): 97-112.

51. Jennifer Manlove, "Influence of High School Dropout and School Disengagement on the Risk of School-Age Pregnancy," *Journal of Research on Adolescence* 8 (2) (1998): 187-220.

52. Kristin A. Moore, et al., "Nonmarital school-age motherhood: Family, individual, and school characteristics," *Journal of Adolescent Research* 13(4) (1998): 433-457.

53. John R. Weeks, *Population: An Introduction to Concepts and Issues*, 9th ed. (Belmont, CA: Wadsworth Publishing, 2007).

54. "Behavioral Health: Sexual Activity and Fertility," *Trends in the Well-Being of America's Children and Youth* (2000), http://aspe.hhs.gov/hsp/00trends/contents.htm#SD (accessed July 23, 2009).

55. Statistics Canada, "International Comparisons," http://www.statcan.gc.ca/kits-trousses/preg-gross/edu04_0134g-eng.htm (accessed August 14, 2009).

56. "Behavioral Health: Sexual Activity and Fertility," *Trends in the Well-Being of America's Children and Youth* (2000), http://aspe.hhs.gov/hsp/00trends/contents.htm#SD (accessed July 23, 2009).

57. Nicole V. Benokraitis, *Marriages and Families: Changes, Choices, and Constraints* (Upper Saddle River, NJ: Pearson Education, Inc, 2008), 216.

58. "Sexually Transmitted Diseases Surveillance, 2007," Centers for Disease Control and Prevention, http://www.cdc.gov/std/stats07/toc.htm (accessed, July 15, 2009).

59. "Sexually Transmitted Diseases Surveillance, 2007: National Overview," Centers for Disease Control and Prevention, http://www.cdc.gov/std/stats07/natoverview.htm (accessed July 27, 2009).

60. Ibid.

61. Ibid.

62. "Sexually Transmitted Diseases Surveillance, 2007: Other Sexually Transmitted Diseases," Centers for Disease Control and Prevention, http://www.cdc.gov/std/stats07/other.htm (accessed July 27, 2009).

63. Ibid.

64. Ibid.

65. Ibid.

66. "Sexual Health: Genital Herpes," *Genital Herpes Guide* (2007), http://www.webmd.com/genital-herpes/guide/sexual-health-genital-herpes (accessed July 15, 2009).

67. "Trichomoniasis," *Sexual Conditions Health Center* (2007), http://www.webmd.com/sexual-conditions/trichomoniasis (accessed July 15, 2009).

68. "Sexual Health: HIV and AIDS," *HIV and AIDS Guide* (2009), http://www.webmd.com/hiv-aids/guide/sexual-health-aids (accessed July 27, 2009).

69. "Basic Statistics," Centers for Disease Control and Prevention (2007), http://www.cdc.gov/hiv/topics/surveillance/basic.htm#def (accessed, July 15, 2009).

70. Ibid.

71. Ibid.

72. Zelee E. Hill, John Cleland, and Mohamed M. Ali, "Religious Affiliation and Extramarital Sex among Men in Brazil," *International Family Planning Practices* 30 (2004): 20-26.

73. Ibid.

74. "STD Prevention Today," National Prevention Information Network, http://www.cdcnpin.org/scripts/std/prevent.asp (accessed July 16, 2009).

75. "What is the Role of the Family in HIV Prevention?" University of California, San Francisco (2003), http://www.caps.ucsf.edu/pubs/FS/family.php (accessed July 16, 2009).

76. "Strong Evidence Favors Comprehensive Approach to Sex Ed," Guttmacher Institute (2007), http://www.guttmacher.org/media/nr/2007/05/23/index.html (accessed July 16, 2009).

77. "The History of Federal Abstinence-Only Funding," Advocates for Youth (2007), http://www.advocatesforyouth.org/index.php?option=com_content&task=view&id=429&Itemid=177 (accessed July 16, 2009).

78. Milton Diamond and Hazel G. Beh, "Abstinence-only sex education: Potential developmental effects," *Human Ontogenetics* (2008) 2(3) (2008): 87–91.

79. "Strong Evidence Favors Comprehensive Approach to Sex Ed," Guttmacher Institute (2007), http://www.guttmacher.org/media/nr/2007/05/23/index.html (accessed July 16, 2009).

80. "A New Day: The Obama Administration and U.S. Sexual Policy and Reproductive Health Policy," Guttmacher Institute (2007), http://www.guttmacher.org/media/nr/2009/03/04/index.html (accessed July 16, 2009).

81. "Open Letter to Religious Leaders about Sex Education," Religious Institute (2002), http://religiousinstitute.org/publications.html (accessed July 16, 2009).

82. Joseph J. Sabia, "Does sex education affect adolescent sexual behaviors and health?" *Journal of Policy Analysis and Management* 25(4) (2006), 783–802.

83. Triece Turnbull, Anna van Hersch, and Paul van Schaik, "A review of parental involvement in sex education: The role for effective communication in British families," *Health Education Journal* 67(3) (2008): 182–195.

84. Ibid.

85. Y.D.M. Batwa, "The role of parents in family and sex education for development: With special reference to Tanzania," *Journal of the Faculty of Arts and Social Sciences* 8(1) (1986): 13–26.

86. John J. Macionis, *Sociology*, 11th edition (Upper Saddle River, NJ: Pearson, 2007), 197.

87. R.T. LeBeau and W. A. Jellison, "Why get involved? Exploring gay and bisexual men's experience of the gay community," *Journal of Homosexuality* 56(1) (2009): 56–76.

88. "Honor Killing in Italy Spurs Quest for Justice," Women's eNews (2009), http://www.womensenews.org/article.cfm/dyn/aid/3268 (accessed July 27, 2009).

89. "1998: Clinton's Grand Jury Testimony Released," *On This Day*, BBC News, http://news.bbc.co.uk/onthisday/hi/dates/stories/september/21/newsid_2525000/2525339.stm (accessed July 27, 2009).

90. "Sex Slaves, Human Trafficking . . . in America?" MSNBC.com (2007), http://www.msnbc.msn.com/id/22083762 (accessed July 20, 2009).

91. Ibid.

92. "Sex Trafficking Fact Sheet," U.S. Department of Health and Human Services (2009), http://www.acf.hhs.gov/trafficking/about/factsheets.html (accessed July 20, 2009).

93. "Prosecution," Humantrafficking.org (2006), http://www.humantrafficking.org/combat_trafficking/prosecution (accessed July 20, 2009).

CHAPTER 7

1. Beth L. Bailey, *From Front Porch to Back Seat: Courtship in Twentieth-Century America* (Baltimore, MD: John Hopkins University Press, 1988).

2. Ibid.

3. Betty Yorburg, *Family Realities A Global View* (Upper Saddle River, NJ: Prentice Hall, 2002), 111–117.

4. Andrew J. Cherlin, *Public and Private Families* (New York: McGraw-Hill, 1995), 221–243.

5. David Popenoe and Barbara Dafoe Whitehead, *Sex Without Strings: Relationships Without Rings* (Piscataway, NJ: The National Marriage Project, Rutgers, 2002).

6. Robert R. Bell and J. B. Chaskes, "Premarital sexual experience among coeds, 1958 and 1968," *Journal of Marriage and the Family* 32 (1970): 82–84.

7. Trip Gabriel, "Pack Dating: For a Good Time, Call a Crowd," *New York Times*, January 5, 1997, http://www.nytimes.com/1997/01/05/education/pack-dating-for-a-good-time-call-a-crowd.html (accessed August 1, 2009).

8. Rodney L. Bassett, et al., "Why do Christian college students abstain from premarital sexual intercourse?" *Journal of Psychology and Christianity* 21 (2002): 121–132.

9. F. Scott Christopher and Susan Sprecher, "Sexuality in marriage, dating, other relationships: A decade in review," in *Understanding Families into the New Millennium: A Decade in Review*, R. M. Milardo, ed. (Minneapolis, MN: National Council on Family Relations, 2001), 218–236.

10. Sam Margulies, "The psychology of prenuptial agreements," *Journal of Psychiatry and Law* 32(4) (2003): 415–432.

11. Rachel Safier and Wendy Roberts, *There Goes the Bride: Making Up Your Mind, Calling It Off and Moving On* (San Francisco, CA: Jossey-Bass, 2003).

12. Pamela Paul, "Calling it off," Time.com, http://www.time.com/time/magazine/article/0,9171,490683-1,00.html (accessed Aug 1, 2009).

13. Mary Madden and Amanda Lenhart, "Online Dating," Pew Internet and American Life Project (2006), http://www.pewinternet.org/Reports/2006/Online-Dating.aspx (accessed August 1, 2009).

14. Catalina L. Toma, Jeffrey T. Hancock, and Nicole B. Ellison, "Separating fact from fiction: An examination of deceptive self-presentation in online dating," *Personality and Social Psychology Bulletin* 34 (2008): 1023–1037.

15. Danielle Couch and Pranee Liamputtong, "Online dating and mating: Perceptions of risk and health among online users." *Health, Risk & Society* 9(3) (2007): 275–294.

16. Marian L. Houser, Sean M. Horan, and Lisa A. Furler, "Dating in the fast lane: How communication predicts speed dating success," *Journal of Social and Personal Relationships* 25 (2008): 749–769.

17. Robert Kurzban and Jason Weeden, "Do advertised preferences predict the behavior of speed daters?" *Personal Relationships* 14 (2007): 623–632.

18. Michèle Belot and Marco Francesconi, "Can anyone be 'the' one? Evidence on mate selection from speed dating." Discussion Paper 2377, *Institute for the Study of Labor (IZA)* (Bonn, Germany: 2006).

19. Marie Liege Laner and Nicole A. Ventrone, "Egalitarian daters/traditionalist dates," *Journal of Family Issues* (1998), http://jfi.sagepub.com/cgi/content/abstract/19/4/468 (accessed August 1, 2009).

20. Catherine L. Clark, Philip R. Shaver, and Matthew F. Abrahams, "Strategic behaviors in romantic relationship initiation," *Personality and Social Psychology Bulletin* (1999), http://psp.sagepub.com/cgi/content/abstract/25/6/709 (accessed August 5, 2009).

21. Mathijs Kalmijn, "Trends in black/white intermarriage," *Social Forces* (1993), http://www.questia.com/PM.qst?a=o&d=77517573 (accessed August 1, 2009).

22. Maxine Baca Zinn and D. Stanley Eitzen, *Diversity in Families* (New York: HarperCollins, 1996), 210–211.

23. Ibid.

24. Sarah R. Crissey, "Race/ethnic differences in the marital expectations of adolescents: The role of romantic relationships," *Journal of Marriage and Family* 67 (2005): 697–709.

25. Paige M. Harrison and Jennifer C. Karberg, "Prison and jail inmates at midyear 2002," Bureau of Justice Statistics Bulletin (2003), http://www.ojp.usdoj.gov/bjs/pub/pdf/pjim02.pdf (accessed August 3 2009).

26. Alison Stein Wellner, "U.S. attitudes toward interracial dating are liberalizing," Population Reference Bureau (2005), http://www.prb.org/en/Articles/2005/USAttitudesTowardInterracialDatingAreLiberalizing.aspx (accessed August 1, 2009).

27. Joan Delaney, "Do older men prefer younger women?" *The Epoch Times* (2008), http://www.theepochtimes.com/n2/life/older-men-younger-women-2276.html (accessed Aug 1, 2009).

28. Douglas T. Kenrick, et al., "Adolescents' Age Preferences for Dating Partners: Support for an Evolutionary Model of Life-History Strategies," *Child Development* 67 (1996): 1499–1511.

29. Joan Delaney, "Do older men prefer younger women?" *The Epoch Times* (2008), http://www.theepochtimes.com/n2/life/older-men-younger-women-2276.html (accessed Aug 1, 2009).

30. Gary W. Harper and Margaret Schneider, "Oppression and discrimination among lesbian, gay, bisexual, and transgendered people and communities: A challenge for community psychology," *American Journal of Community Psychology* 31 (2003): 243–252.

31. Jonathan J. Mohr and Ruth E. Fassinger, "Sexual orientation identity and romantic relationship quality in same-sex couples," *Personality and Social Psychology Bulletin* 32 (2006): 1085–1099.

32. Meg Wilkes Karraker, "Forming Relationships: Dating, Cohabitating, and Staying Single," *Families with Futures: A Survey of Family Studies for the 21st Century* (Mahwah, NJ: Lawrence Erlbaum Associates, 2006), 212.

33. Ibid.

34. Voon Chin Phua and Gayle Kaufman, "The crossroads of race and sexuality: date selection among men in Internet "personal" ads," *Journal of Family Issues* 24(8) (2003): 981–994.

35. Melody J. Slashinski, Ann L. Coker, and Keith E. Davis, "Physical Aggression, Forced Sex, and Stalking Victimization by a Dating Partner: An Analysis of the National Violence Against Women Survey," *Violence and Victims* 18(6) (2003): 610.

36. Ibid.

37. Ibid.

38. Ibid.

39. Ibid., 612.

40. Ibid., 613.

41. Deborah L. Rhatigan and Amy E. Street, "The impact of intimate partner violence on decisions to leave dating relationships: a test of the investment model." *Journal of Interpersonal Violence* 20 (2005): 1580–1597.

42. Candice M. Monson, Jennifer Langhinrichsen-Rohling, and Tisha Binderup, "Does "no" really mean "no" after you say "yes"?: Attributions about date and marital rape," *Journal of Interpersonal Violence* 15(11) (2000): 1156–1174.

43. Davor Jedlicka, "A test of the psychoanalytic theory of mate selection," *The Journal of Social Psychology* 112 (1980): 295–299.

44. Glenn Geher, "Perceived and actual characteristics of parents and partners: A test of a Freudian model of mate selection," *Current Psychology* 19(3) (2000): 194–212.

45. R.F. Winch, "Another look at the theory of complementary needs in mate selection," *Journal of Marriage and the Family* 29 (1967): 756–762.

46. Ellen Bersheid, et al., "Physical attractiveness and dating choice: A test of the matching hypothesis," *Journal of Experimental Social Psychology* 1 (1982): 173–89.

47. Alan Feingold, "Matching for attractiveness in romantic partners and same-sex friends: A meta-analysis and theoretical critique," *Psychological Bulletin* 104 (1998): 226–35.

48. Pascale Harter, "Mauritania's 'wife-fattening' farm," BBC News, January 26, 2004, http://news.bbc.co.uk/2/hi/africa/3429903.stm (accessed Aug 3, 2009).

49. Charles T. Hill, Zick Rubin, and Letitia A. Peplau, "Breakups before marriage: The end of 103 affairs," *Journal of Social Issues* 32(1) (1976): 147–168.

50. Leela Mullatti, "Families in India: Beliefs and realities," *Journal of Comparative Family Studies* 26(1) (1995): 11–25.

51. I.A.R. Lakshmann, "Marriage? Think logic, not love," *Baltimore Sun*, September 22, 1997.

52. Linda L. Lindsey, *Gender Roles: A Sociological Perspective* (Upper Saddle River, NJ: Prentice Hall, 1997), 172.

53. Linda P. Rouse, *Marital and Sexual Lifestyles in the United States: Attitudes, Behaviors, and Relationships in Social Context* (New York: Routledge, 2001).

54. Ibid.

55. Ibid.

56. "Gay Marriage: Why Would It Affect Me? Ten Arguments Against Same Sex Marriage," http://www.nogaymarriage.com/tenarguments.asp (accessed Aug 3, 2009).

57. John Levy Martin, "Is Power Sexy?" *American Journal of Sociology* 111(2) (2005): 408–46.

58. John Finley Scott, "The American college sorority: Its role in class and ethnic endogamy," *American Sociological Review* 20 (1965): 514–527.

59. Yonina Talmon, "Mate selection in collective settlements," *American Sociological Review* 29(4) (1964): 491–508.

60. Ibid.

61. Monica M. Moore, "Nonverbal courtship patterns in women: Context and consequences," *Ethology and Sociobiology* 64 (1985): 237–247.

62. Neal King, "Knowing women: Straight men and sexual certainty," *Gender and Society* 17(6) (2003): 861–877.

63. David M. Buss, et al., "A Half Century of Mate Preferences: The Cultural Evolution of Values," *Journal of Marriage and Family* 63 (2001), 502.

CHAPTER 8

1. "Birth Rates in the United States, 1909–2000," CDC.gov, http://www.cdc.gov/nchs/data/statab/t001x01.pdf (accessed August 18, 2009).

2. "U.S. Birth Rate Reaches Record Low," U.S. Department of Health and Human Services, http://www.hhs.gov/news/press/2003pres/20030625.html (accessed July 30, 2009).

3. Meg Wilkes Karraker, *Families with Futures: A Survey of Family Studies for the 21st Century* (Mahwah, NJ: Lawrence Erlbaum Associates, 2006), 277–282.

4. Ibid.

5. "U.S. Birth Rate Reaches Record Low," U.S. Department of Health and Human Services, http://www.hhs.gov/news/press/2003pres/20030625.html (accessed July 30, 2009).

6. Jane Lawler Dye, Fertility of American Women: 2008, *Population Characteristics*, issued November 2010, U.S. Census Bureau.

7. Marie Richmond-Abbott, *Masculine and Feminine: Gender Roles Over the Life Cycle* (New York: McGraw-Hill, 1992), 203–204

8. Betty Yorburg, *Family Realities: A Global View* (Upper Saddle River, NJ: Prentice Hall, 2002), 180–181.

9. Arland Thornton and Linda Young-DeMarco, "Four Decades of Trends and Attitudes Toward Family Issues in the United States: The 1960s Through the 1990s," *Journal of Marriage and the Family* 63(4) (2002): 1009–1037.

10. Tim B. Heaton, T.B., Cardell K. Jacobson, and Kimberlee Holland, "Persistence and Change in Childless Intentions," *Journal of Marriage and the Family* 61 (1999): 531–539, summarized in *Family Planning Perspective* 11 (1999): 254–255.

11. Marie Richmond-Abbott, *Masculine and Feminine: Gender Roles over the Life Cycle* (New York: McGraw-Hill, 1992), 203.

12. Stephen A. Anderson and Ronald M. Sabatelli, *Family Interaction: A Multigenerational Developmental Perspective* (Boston: Allyn & Bacon, 1999), 204.

13. Carmen DeNavas-Walt, Bernadette D. Proctor, and Jessica C. Smith, Income, Poverty, and Health Insurance Coverage in the United States: 2009, Current Population Reports, issued September 2010, U.S. Census Bureau.

14. Daniel T. Lichter, "Poverty and Inequality among Children," *Annual Review of Sociology* 23 (1997): 121–145.

15. Michael W. O'Hara and Annette M. Swain, "Rates and Risk of Postpartum Depression—A Meta-Analysis," *International Review of Psychiatry* 8(1) (1996): 37–54.

16. Laura F. Petrillo, et al., "Course of Psychiatric Illness During Pregnancy and the Postpartum," in *Review of Psychiatry 24. Mood and Anxiety Disorders during Pregnancy and Postpartum*, Lee S. Cohen and Ruta M. Nonacs, eds. (Arlington, VA: American Psychiatric Publishing, 2005).

17. Lori E. Ross, "Perinatal Mental Health in Lesbian Mothers: A Review of Potential Risk and Protective Factors," *Women & Health* 41(3) (2005): 13–128.

18. Mike Bergman, "Single-Parent Households Showed Little Variation Since 1994, Census Bureau Reports," U.S. Census Bureau. http://www.census.gov/Press-Release/www/releases/archives/families_households/009842.html (accessed July 30, 2009).

19. Roberta L. Coles, "Black Single Fathers: Choosing to Parent Full-Time," *Journal of Contemporary Ethnography* 31(4) (2002): 411–439.

20. William Marsiglio, et al., "Scholarship on Fatherhood in the 1990s and Beyond," *Journal of Marriage and Family* 62 (2000): 1173–1191.

21. Ibid.

22. K.A. Horvath, "Infertility Treatment: An Argument for Mandated Coverage," *Journal of Health Law* 32(3) (1999): 445–469.

23. Diane D. Aronson, "Defining Infertility," *Public Health Reports* 115(1) (2000): 6.

24. David Dunson, Donna Baird, and Bernardo Colombo, "Increased Infertility with Age in Men and Women," *Obstetrics and Gynecology* 103(1) (2004): 51–56.

25. "Infertility Causes," Mayo Foundation for Medical Education and Research (2009), http://www.mayoclinic.com/health/infertility/DS00310/DSECTION=causes (accessed June 27, 2009).

26. Diana C. Parry and Kimberley J. Shinew, "The Constraining Impact of Infertility on Women's Leisure Lifestyles," *Leisure Science* 26 (2004): 295–308.

27. Rona Achilles, "Desperately Seeking Babies: New Technologies of Hope and Despair," in *Family Patterns, Gender Relations*, Bonnie J. Fox, ed. (Toronto: Oxford University Press, 1993), 213–229.

28. Betty Yorburg, *Family Realities: A Global View* (Upper Saddle River, NJ: Prentice Hall, 2002), 178–182.

29. Meg Wilkes Karraker, *Families with Futures: A Survey of Family Studies for the 21st Century* (Mahwah, NJ: Lawrence Erlbaum Associates, 2006), 277–282.

30. "Cost of IVF at the Advanced Fertility Center of Chicago," Advanced Fertility Center of Chicago, http://www.advancedfertility.com/ivfprice.htm (accessed July 30, 2009).

31. Élise de La Rochebrochard, "Men Medically Assisted to Reproduce: AID, IVF, and ICSI, an Assessment of the Revolution the Medical Treatment of Male Factor Infertility," *Population-E* 58 (4–5) (2003): 487–522.

32. Betty Yorburg, *Family Realities: A Global View* (Upper Saddle River, NJ: Prentice Hall, 2002), 180.

33. Ibid.

34. G. Pennings, "Family Balancing As a Morally Acceptable Application of Sex Selection," *Human Reproduction* (1996): 2339–2343.

35. Rona Achilles, "Desperately Seeking Babies: New Technologies of Hope and Despair," in *Family Patterns, Gender Relations*, Bonnie J. Fox, ed. (Toronto: Oxford University Press, 1993), 213–229.

36. John R. Weeks, *Population: An Introduction to Concepts and Issues* (Belmont, CA: Wadsworth Publishing, 2005), 223–231.

37. Marie Richmond-Abbott, *Masculine and Feminine: Gender Roles Over the Life Cycle* (New York: McGraw-Hill, 1992), 168.

38. Stanely K. Henshaw, Susheela Singh, and Taylor Haas, "The Incidence of Abortion Worldwide," *International Family Planning Perspectives* 25 (1999): S30–S38.

39. John R. Weeks, *Population: An introduction to Concepts and Issues*, 9th edition (Belmont, CA: Wadsworth Publishing, 2007), 231.

40. Betty Yorburg, *Family Realities: A Global View* (Upper Saddle River, NJ: Prentice Hall, 2002), 181.

41. "Cost of Adopting," Adoption.com, *http://statistics.adoption.com/information/statistics-on-cost-of-adopting.html* (accessed August 18, 2009).

42. Betty Yorburg, *Family Realities: A Global View* (Upper Saddle River, NJ: Prentice Hall, 2002), 182.

43. Laura Hamilton, Simon Cheng, and Brian Powell, "Adoptive Parents, Adaptive Parents: Evaluating the Importance of Biological Ties for Parental Investment," *American Sociological Review* 72(1) (2007): 95–116.

44. Peter Ford, "Chinese county reins in birth-rate—without a one-child limit," http://www.csmonitor.com/2007/0227/p01s04-woap.htm (accessed September 8, 2009).

45. John R. Weeks, *Population: An Introduction to Concepts and Issues*, 9th edition (Belmont, CA: Wadsworth Publishing, 2007), 258–260.

46. Ibid.

47. Kristy A. Thomas and Richard C. Tessler, "Bicultural Socialization Among Adoptive Families: Where There Is a Will, There Is a Way," *Journal of Family Issues* 28(9) (2007): 1189–1219.

48. Susan D. Stewart, *Brave New Stepfamilies: Diverse Paths Toward Stepfamily Living* (Thousand Oaks, CA: Sage Publications, 2007), 85–88.

49. Meg Wilkes Karraker, *Families with Futures: A Survey of Family Studies for the 21st Century* (Mahwah, NJ: Lawrence Erlbaum Associates, 2006), 277–282.

50. Teresa Toguchi Swartz, "Mothering for the State: Foster Parenting and the Challenges of Government-Contracted Carework," *Gender & Society* 18(5) (2004): 567–587.

51. Shelly Romalis, "Childbirth as Culture, Experience and Politics," in *Family Patterns, Gender Relations*, Bonnie J. Fox, ed. (Toronto: Oxford University Press, 1993), 237–241.

52. Lawrence Z. Freedman, L.Z. and Vera Masius Ferguson, "The Question of 'Painless Childbirth' in Primitive Culture," *American Journal of Orthopsychiatry* 20(2) (1950): 363–372.

53. Theodore J. Joyce, Robert Kaestner, and Sanders Korenman, "The Effect of Pregnancy Intention on Child Development," *Demography* 37(1) (2000): 83–94.

54. Jean M. Ispa, et al., "Pregnancy Acceptance, Parenting Stress, and Toddler Attachment in Low-Income Black Families," *Journal of Marriage and* Family 69(1) (2007): 1–13.

55. Meg Wilkes Karraker, *Families with Futures: A Survey of Family Studies for the 21st Century* (Mahwah, NJ: Lawrence Erlbaum Associates, 2006), 287–289.

56. Marie Richmond-Abbott, *Masculine and Feminine: Gender Roles over the Life Cycle* (New York: McGraw-Hill, 1992), 67–68.

57. Judy C. Pearson, "The Development of the Family: From Cradle to Classroom," *Communication in the Family: Seeking Satisfaction in Changing Times* (New York: Harper & Row Publishers, 1989), 191–94.

58. Marie Richmond-Abbott, *Masculine and Feminine: Gender Roles Over the Life Cycle* (New York: McGraw-Hill, 1992), 205.

59. Betty Yorburg, *Family Realities: A Global View* (Upper Saddle River, NJ: Prentice Hall, 2002), 183–184.

60. Stephen A. Anderson, "Families with Young Children," *Family Interaction: A Multigenerational Developmental Perspective* (Boston, MA: Allyn and Bacon, 1999), 198.

61. Stephen Anderson and Ronald M. Sabatelli, *Family Interaction: A Multigenerational Developmental Perspective*, 4th edition (Boston: Pearson Education, 2007), 215–216.

62. Stephen A. Anderson and Ronald M. Sabatelli, *Family Interaction: A Multigenerational Developmental Perspective*, 2nd edition (Boston: Allyn and Bacon, 1999), 198.

63. Jacinta Bronte-Tinkew, J., Kristin A. Moore, and Jennifer Carrano, "The Father-Child Relationship, Parenting Styles, and Adolescent Risk Behaviors in Intact Families," *Journal of Family Issues* 27(6) (2006): 850–881.

64. Stephen Anderson and Ronald M. Sabatelli, *Family Interaction: A Multigenerational Developmental Perspective*, 4th edition (Boston: Pearson Education, 2007), 215–216.

65. Ibid.

66. Ibid.

67. Ibid.

68. Paul R. Amato and Joan G. Gilbreth, "Nonresident Fathers and Children's Well-Being: A Meta-Analysis," *Journal of Marriage and Family* 61(3) (1999): 557–573.

69. Lynne H. Turner and Richard West, *Perspectives on Family Communication* (New York: McGraw-Hill, 2006), 127–131.

70. Marie Richmond-Abbott, *Masculine and Feminine: Gender Roles over the Life Cycle* (New York: McGraw-Hill, 1992), 67–70.

71. Stephen Anderson, *Family Interaction: A Multigenerational Developmental Perspective* (Boston: Allyn and Bacon, 1999), 198.

72. Wesley Burr, *Contemporary Theories about the Family* (New York: The Free Press, 1979), 37–38.

73. Aryn Dotterer "A Longitudinal Examination of the Bidirectional Links Between Academic Achievement and Parent-Adolescent Conflict," *Journal of Family Issues* 29 (2007): 762–779.

74. Nissa R. Towe-Goodman and Douglas M. Teti, "Power Assertive Discipline, Maternal Emotional Involvement, and Child Adjustment," *Journal of Family Psychology* 22(3) (2008): 648–651.

75. Ibid.

76. Laura M. Padilla-Walker and Gustavo Carlo, "'It's not Fair!' Adolescents' Constructions of Appropriateness of Parental Reactions," *Journal of Youth and Adolescence* 33(5) (2004): 389–401.

77. Patrick Sandora, "Ten Reasons to Not Spank Your Child," http://www.micheleborba.ivillage.com/parenting/archives/2009/06/10-reasons-to-not-spank-your-c.html (accessed September 9, 2009).

78. Christopher G. Ellison and Matt Bradshaw, "Religious Beliefs, Sociopolitical Ideology, and Attitudes toward Corporal Punishment," *Journal of Family Issues* 30(3) (2009): 320–340.

79. Ibid.

80. B.B. Robbie Rossman and Jacqueline G. Rea, "The Relation of Parenting Styles and Inconsistencies to Adaptive Functioning for Children in Conflictual and Violent Families," *Journal of Family Violence* 20(5) (2005): 261–277.

81. Goran Jutengren and Kerstin Palmérus, "A Comparison of Swedish and US Fathers' Self-reported Use of Parental Discipline," Children & Society 16 (2002): 246–259.

82. Kathleen M. Galvin, Carma L. Bylund, and Bernard J. Brommel, *Family Communication: Cohesion and Change* (Boston: Pearson Education, 2004), 282–297.

83. W.J. Yeung and R. Glauber, "Children's Time Use and Parental Involvement in Low-Income Families," In *Handbook of Families and Poverty*, ed. D. Russell Crand and Tim B. Heaton (Thousand Oaks, CA: Sage, 2008): 288–310.

84. Kathleen M. Galvin, Carma L. Bylund, and Bernard J. Brommel, *Family Communication: Cohesion and Change* (Boston: Pearson Education, 2004), 282–297.

85. Stephen A. Anderson, *Family Interaction: A Multigenerational Developmental Perspective*, 4th edition (Boston: Pearson Education, 2007), 231–245.

86. Casey Copen and Merril Silverstein, "Transmission of Religious Beliefs across Generations: Do grandparents Matter?" *Journal of Comparative Family Studies* (2007): 497–499.

87. Andrew O. Behnke, Kathleen W. Piercy, and Marcelo Diversi, "Educational and Occupational Aspirations of Latino Youth and Their Parents," *Hispanic Journal of Behavioral Sciences* 26(1) (2004): 16–35.

88. René Bekkers, "Intergeneration Transmission of Volunteering," *Acta Sociologica* 50(2) (2007): 99–114.

89. Wesley Burr, *Contemporary Theories about the Family* (New York: The Free Press, 1979), 317–364.

90. James M. White and David M. Klein, *Family Theories* (Thousand Oaks, CA: Sage Publications, 2008), 185–190.

91. Ping-Yin Kuan, "Peace, Not War: Adolescents' Management of Intergenerational Conflicts in Taiwan," *Journal of Comparative Family Studies* (2008): 592–610.

92. Jean S. Phinney, "Autonomy and Relatedness in Adolescent-Parent Disagreements: Ethnic and Developmental Factors," *Journal of Adolescent Research* 20(1) (2005): 8–39.

93. James M. White and David M. Klein, *Family Theories* (Thousand Oaks, CA: Sage Publications, 2008), 93–119.

94. Alicia D. Cast, David Schweingruber and Nancy Berns, "Childhood Physical Punishment and Problem Solving in Marriage," *Journal of Interpersonal Violence* 2 (2006): 244–261.

95. Alicia D. Cast, "Role-Taking and Interaction," *Social Psychology Quarterly* 67(3) (2004): 296–309.

96. Lynne Clark Callister, "The Pain and Promise of Unfulfilled Dreams: Infertile Couples," *Handbook of Families and Health: Interdisciplinary Perspectives*, ed. D. Russell Crane and Elaine S. Marshall (Thousand Oaks, CA: Sage Publications, 2006), 97.

97. Ibid., 98.

98. Ibid.

99. Ibid., 99–100.

CHAPTER 9

1. "Poll: Americans Idealize Traditional Marriage," *Religion and Ethics Newsweekly*, PBS Online (2005), http://www.pbs.org/wnet/religionandethics/week908/survey.html (accessed October 26, 2009).

2. *Words of Women Quotations for Success*, Power Dynamics Publishing (1997), http://creativequotations.com/one/1157.htm (accessed October 26, 2009).

3. Nicholas Bala and Rebecca Jeremko Bromwich, "Context and Inclusivity in Canada's Evolving Definition of the Family," *International Journal of Law, Policy and the Family* 16 (2002): 145–180.

4. Marian F. Zeitlin, et al., "The Postmodern Family," *Strengthening the family—Implications for international development* (1995), http://www.unu.edu/unupress/unupbooks/uu13se/uu13se03.htm, (accessed October 26, 2009).

5. Rose M. Kreide, "Living Arrangements of Children: 2004," in *Current Population Reports*, U.S. Census Bureau (2007), 70–114, http://blueprod.ssd.census.gov/prod/2008pubs/p70-114.pdf (accessed October 26, 2009).

6. "Faith and Family in America," *Religion and Ethics Newsweekly*, PBS Online (2005) http://www.pbs.org/wnet/religionandethics/week908/ReligionAndFamily_Summary.pdf (accessed October 26, 2009).

7. Sam Roberts, "Most Children Still Live in Two-Parent Homes, Census Bureau Reports," *New York Times*, February 21, 2008, http://www.nytimes.com/2008/02/21/us/21census.html?_r=3&oref=slogin (accessed October 26, 2009).

8. Linda J. Waite and Maggie Gallagher, *The Case for Marriage* (New York: Broadway Books, 2000).

9. Linda J. Waite, "Does marriage matter?" *Demography* 32 (1995): 483–507.

10. Catherine E. Ross, John Mirowsky, and Karen Goldsteen, "The impact of the family on health: Decade in review," *Journal of Marriage and the Family* 52 (1990): 1059–1078.

11. Linda J. Waite and Maggie Gallagher, *The Case for Marriage* (New York: Broadway Books, 2000).

12. Ibid.

13. Social Explorer Tables: ACS 2005 to 2009 (5-Year Estimates) (SE), ACS 2005–2009 (5-Year Estimates), Social Explorer; U.S. Census Bureau.

14. Social Explorer Tables: ACS 2005 to 2009 (5-Year Estimates) (SE), ACS 2005–2009 (5-Year Estimates), Social Explorer; U.S. Census Bureau.

15. Paul R. Amato, "The impact of family formation change on the cognitive, social, and emotional well-being of the next generation," *Marriage and Child Wellbeing* 15(2) (2005): 75–96.

16. E. Mavis Hetherington, Edward R. Anderson, and W. Glenn Clingempeel, "Coping with marital transitions," *Monographs of the Society for Research in Child Development* 57 (1992): 2–3, University of Chicago Press; R. L. Simons and Associates, *Understanding Differences between Divorced and Intact Families* (Thousand Oaks, California: Sage, 1992); Nan Marie Astone and Sara S. McLanahan, "Family structure, parental practices, and high school completion," *American Sociological Review* 56 (1991): 309–20; Elizabeth Thomson, et al., "Family structure, gender, and parental socialization," *Journal of Marriage and the Family* 54 (1992): 368–78.

17. David M. Kleist, "Single-Parent Families: A Difference that Makes a Difference?" *The Family Journal* 7 (1999): 373–378.

18. Kerby Anderson, "It Takes a Village: An Analysis of Hillary Clinton's Book," Leadership University, Christian Leadership Ministries. http://www.leaderu.com/orgs/probe/docs/village.html (accessed October 26, 2009).

19. Jennifer Wolf, "Positive Effects of Single Parenting," http://singleparents.about.com/od/familyrelationships/tp/raised_single.htm# (accessed October 25, 2009).

20. Rose M. Kreider, Housing and Household Economic Statistics Division Working Paper, September 15, 2010, U.S. Bureau of the Census, Washington, D.C.

21. Sharon Sassler, "The process of entering into cohabiting unions," *Journal of Marriage and Family* 66 (2004): 491–505.

22. Ibid.

23. Wendy D. Manning and Pamela M. Smock, "Measuring and modeling cohabitation: New perspectives from qualitative data," *Journal of Marriage and Family* 67 (2005): 989–1002.

24. Patrick Heuveline and Jeffrey M. Timberlake, "The role of cohabitation in family formation: The United States in comparative perspective," *Journal of Marriage and Family* 66 (2004): 1214–1230.

25. Catherine L. Cohan and Stacey Kleinbaum, "Toward a Greater Understanding of the Cohabitation Effect: Premarital Cohabitation and Marital Communication," *Journal of Marriage and the Family* 64 (2002): 180–192; David Popenoe and Barbara Dafoe Whitehead, *Should We Live Together? What Young Adults Need to*

Know about Cohabitation before Marriage (New Brunswick, NJ: Rutgers University, National Marriage Project, 1999).

26. Galena H. Kline, et al., "Timing is everything: Pre-engagement cohabitation and increased risk for poor marital outcomes," *Journal of Family Psychology* 18(2) (2004): 311–318.

27. Galena K. Rhoades, Scott M. Stanley, and Howard J. Markman, "Couples' reasons for cohabitation: Associations with individual well-being and relationship quality," *Journal of Family Issues* 30(2) (2009): 233–258.

28. Susan L. Brown and Alan Booth, "Cohabitation versus marriage: A comparison of relationship quality," *Journal of Marriage and Family* 58 (1996): 668–678.

29. Marisa A. Head, "What are the Benefits and Challenges of Living with a Roommate?" *Associated Content Society* (2007) http://www.associatedcontent.com/article/348898/what_are_the_benefits_and_challenges.html (accessed October 25, 2009).

30. Sandi Nelson, Rebecca L. Clark, and Gregory Acs, "Beyond the Two-Parent Family: How Teenagers Fare in Cohabitating Couple and Blended Families," *Urban Institute* (2001) http://www.urban.org/publications/310339.html (accessed October 25, 2009).

31. Social Explorer Tables: ACS 2005 to 2009 (5-Year Estimates) (SE), ACS 2005–2009 (5-Year Estimates), Social Explorer; U.S. Census Bureau.

32. U.S. Census Brureau, "Unmarried and Single Americans Weeks," *Facts for Features*, July 19, 2010.

33. U.S. Census Bureau, "300 Million," *Facts for Features* (2006), http://www.census.gov/PressRelease/www/releases/archives/facts_for_features_special_editions/007276.html (accessed October 26, 2009).

34. Lindy Williams and Michael Philip Guest, "Attitudes toward Marriage among the Urban Middle-Class," *Journal of Comparative Family Studies* 36 (2005): 163–186.

35. Kris Frieswick, "Too Successful for a Mate?" MSN.com (2008), http://articles.moneycentral.msn.com/Investing/HomeMortgageSavings/TooSuccessfulForAMate.aspx?GT1=33009#pageTopAchor (accessed October 26, 2009).

36. "Famous People Who Never Married," http://tigerx.com/trivia/nomarry.htm (accessed October 26, 2009).

37. Yun Chen, "Relationship Choices and Lifestyles," Warren Township High School (2008), http://blue.wths.net/faculty/chen/ah/social/Relationship%20Choices%20and%20Lifestyles.ppt (accessed October 26, 2009).

38. Jeffrey Jensen Arnett, *Emerging Adulthood: The Winding Road from the Late Teens Through the* Twenties (New York: Oxford University Press, 2004) 97–98.

39. *Defense of Marriage Act*, GAO/OGC-97-16, U.S. General Accounting Office (1997), http://www.gao.gov/archive/1997/og97016.pdf (accessed October 26, 2009).

40. "Same Sex Marriage, Civil Unions and Domestic Partnerships," National Conference of State Legislatures (2009), http://www.ncsl.org/?TabId=16430 (accessed October 25, 2009).

41. Andrea Stone, "Some Say Civil Unions Dropping Off," *USA Today*, April 19, 2007, http://www.usatoday.com/news/nation/2007-04-19-civil-unions_N.htm (accessed October 26, 2009).

42. "CNN Poll: Generations Disagree on Same Sex Marriage," *Current Affairs* (2009) http://thecurrentaffairs.com/cnn-poll-generations-disagree-on-same-sex-marriage.html (accessed October 26, 2009).

43. Ramona Faith Oswald and Katherine A. Kuvalanka, "Same-Sex Couples: Legal Complexities," *Journal of Family Issues* 29 (2008): 1051–1066.

44. William Meezan and Jonathan Rauch, "Gay marriage, same-sex parenting, and America's children," *The Future of Children* 15(2) (2005): 98–107.

45. James G. Pawelski, et al., "The Effects of Marriage, Civil Union, and Domestic Partnership Laws on the Health and Well-being of Children," *Pediatrics* 118 (2006): 349–364.

46. Rose M. Kreide, "Living Arrangements of Children: 2004," in *Current Population Reports*, U.S. Census Bureau (2007): 70–114, http://blueprod.ssd.census.gov/prod/2008pubs/p70-114.pdf (accessed October 26, 2009).

47. Patricia L. Papernow, *Becoming a Stepfamily* (San Francisco: Jossey-Bass Publishers, 1993).

48. Robert Berkvist, "Jean Kerr, Playwright and Author, Dies," *The New York Times*, January 7, 2003, http://www.nytimes.com/2003/01/07/theater/jean-kerr-playwright-and-author-dies-at-80.html (accessed October 26, 2009).

49. "U.S. Divorce Rate Falls to Lowest Level Since 1970," msnbc.com, May 10, 2007, http://www.msnbc.msn.com/id/18600304/#storyContinued (accessed October 26, 2009).

50. Ibid.

51. "Divorce Rate," divorcerate.org (undated), http://www.divorcerate.org/ (accessed October 26, 2009).

52. Randall G. Kesslring and Dale Bremmer, "Female Income, the Ego Effect, and the Divorce Decision," *Amsterdam Institute for Advanced Labour Studies* (2004), http://www.rose-hulman.edu/~bremmer/professional/divorce_micro.pdf (accessed October 27, 2009).

53. Vaughn R.A. Call and Tim B. Heaton, "Religious Influence on Marital Stability," *Journal for the Scientific Study of Religion* 36(3) (1997): 382–392.

54. John B. Kelly, "Divorce: The Adult Perspective," in *Handbook of Developmental Psychology*, B. Wolman and G. Stricker, eds. (Englewood Cliffs, NJ: Prentice-Hall, 1982), 734–750.

55. Jenifer Kunz, "The Intergenerational Transmission of Divorce," *Journal of Divorce and Remarriage* 34(1/2) (2001): 169–175.

56. Alana Levy, "Are You Genetically Predisposed to Leave Your Mate?" *Psychology Today* (2001), http://www.psychologytoday.com/articles/pto-20011101-000020.html (accessed October 28, 2009).

57. Ibid.

58. Jamal Badawim, "Polygamy in Islamic Law," *Islam for Today* (1998), http://www.islamfortoday.com/polygamy5.htm (accessed October 26, 2009).

59. "Zion Raid: The Ranch Has Not Given Up All Its Secrets," *The Independent*, April 13, 2008, http://www.independent.co.uk/news/world/americas/zion-raid-the-ranch-has-not-yet-revealed-all-its-secrets-808370.html (accessed October 26, 2009); Law offices of Bill Baskette, "Texas High Court Rules Yearning for Zion Children Must Be Returned," *FindLaw.com* (2009), http://knowledgebase.findlaw.com/kb/2009/Apr/1267618_11.html, (accessed October 26, 2009).

60. Sultan Abdulla Al Shamsi and Leon C. Fulcher, "The impact of polygamy on United Arab Emirates first wives and children," *International Journal of Child and Family Welfare* 1 (2005): 46–55.

61. Cynthia T. Cook, "Polygyny: Did Africans get it right?" *Journal of Black Studies* 38(2) (2007): 232–250; Riley Bove and Claudia Valeggia, "Polygyny and women's health," *Social Science & Medicine* 68 (2009): 21–29; Alean Al-Krenawi and John R. Graham, "A Comparison of Family Functioning, Life And Marital Satisfaction, and Mental Health Of Women in Polygamous And Monogamous Marriages," *International Journal of Social Psychiatry* 52(1) (2006): 5–17.

62. Salman Elbedour, et al., "The Effect of Polygamous Marital Structure on Behavioral, Emotional, and Academic Adjustment in Children: A Comprehensive Review of the Literature," *Clinical Child and Family Psychology Review* 5(4) (2002): 255–271.

63. U.S. Census Bureau, "Children and the households they live in: 2000," *Census 2000 Special Reports* (2004), http://www.census.gov/prod/2004pubs/censr-14.pdf (accessed October 26, 2009).

64. U.S. Census Bureau, "Families and Living Arrangements: Living Arrangements of Children," Tables 1-4 (2006), http://www.census.gov/population/www/socdemo/hh-fam.html (accessed October 26, 2009).

65. U.S. Census Bureau, "Co-resident grandparents and their grandchildren: Grandparent maintained families" (1998), http://www.census.gov/population/www/documentation/twps0026/twps0026.html (accessed October 27, 2009).

66. Abby Ellin, "Grandparents Helping Grandparents Help the Kids," *New York Times*, October 17, 2004, http://query.nytimes.com/gst/fullpage.html?res=9C07E4DE143AF934A25753C1A9629C8B63&pagewanted=all; Timothy Williams, "A Place for Grandparents Who Are Parents Again," *New York Times*, May 21, 2005, http://query.nytimes.com/gst/fullpage.html?res=9B0CE7DE1539F932A15756C0A9639C8B63&sec=&spon=&pagewanted=all (accessed October 26, 2009).

67. Catherine C. Goodman and Merril Silverstein, "Grandmothers raising grandchildren: Family structure and well-being in culturally diverse families," *The Gerontologist* 42(5) (2002), 676–689; Margaret Platt Jendrek, "Grandparents who parent their grandchildren: Circumstances and decisions," *The Gerontologist* 34(2) (1994), 206–216.

68. Donald C. Reitzes and Elizabeth J. Mutran, "Grandparent identity, intergenerational family identity, and well-being," *The Journals of Gerontology Series B: Psychological Sciences and Social Sciences* 59 (2004): 213–219.

69. Ibid.

70. Valarie King and Glen H. Elder, Jr., "The legacy of grandparenting: childhood experiences with grandparents and current involvement with grandchildren," *Journal of Marriage and Family* 59 (1997): 848–859.

71. Catherine C. Goodman and Merril Silverstein, "Grandmothers who parent their grandchildren: An exploratory case of close relations across three generations," *Journal of Family Issues* 22(5) (2001), 557–578.

72. Nancy M. Pinson-Millburn, et al., "Grandparents raising grandchildren," *Journal of Counseling & Development* 74 (1996), 548–554.

73. Jennifer Crew Solomon and Jonathan Marx, "To grandmother's house we go: Health and school adjustment of children raised solely by grandparents," *The Gerontologist* 35(3) (1995), 386–394.

74. Nancy M. Pinson-Millburn, et al., "Grandparents raising grandchildren," *Journal of Counseling & Development* 74 (1996): 548–554.

75. United Nations, "Families around the world: universal in their diversity—UN emphasis on the importance of the family in social development and change—International Year of the Family, 1994—Cover Story," *U.N. Chronicle* (1994), http://findarticles.com/p/articles/mi_m1309/is_n1_v31/ai_15282799/ (accessed October 26, 2009).

76. United Nations, "Proclamation of the Tenth Anniversary of the International Year of the Family" (2004), http://www.un.org/esa/socdev/family/TenthAnv/Proclamation%20of%20Tenth%20Anniversary.PDF (accessed October 26, 2009).

77. James M. White and David M. Klein, *Family Theories*, 3rd edition (Thousand Oaks CA: Sage Publications, 2008), 38–39.

78. Ibid.

79. Ibid.

80. David Popenoe, "Family Decline, 1960–1990: A Review and Appraisal," *Journal of Marriage and the Family* 55(3) (1993): 527–542.

81. David Popenoe, *Life Without Father: Compelling New Evidence That Fatherhood and Marriage Are Indispensable for the Good of Children and Society* (New York: Free Press, 1996).

82. Stephanie Coontz, *The Way We Never Were: American Families and the Nostalgia Trap* (New York: Basic Books, 2000).

83. Meg Wilkes Karraker and Janet R. Grochowski, *Families with Futures: A Survey of Family Studies for the 21st Century* (Mahwah NJ: Lawrence Erlbaum Associates, 2006), 36–37.

84. Gail Bederman, *Manliness and Civilization: A Cultural History of Gender and Race in the United States, 1880-1917* (Chicago: University of Chicago Press, 1996).

85. Arlie Russell Hochschild, with Anne Machung, *The Second Shift: Working Parents and the Revolution at Home* (New York: Penguin Books, 2003).

86. King-To Yeung and John L. Martin, "The Looking Glass Self: An Empirical Test and Elaboration," *Social Force* 81(3) (2003): 843-879.

87. Ibid.

88. Amy L. Hequembourg and Michael P. Farrell, "Lesbian Motherhood: Negotiating Marginal-Mainstream Identities," *Gender and Society* 13(4) (1999): 540-577.

89. Ilene Hyman, Nhi Vu, and Morton Beiser, "Post-migration stresses among Southeast Asian refugee youth in Canada: A research note," *Journal of Comparative Family Studies* 31(2) (2000): 281-293.

90. James M. White and David M. Klein, *Family Theories*, 3rd edition (Thousand Oaks CA: Sage Publications, Inc., 2007), 36-40.

91. Ibid.

92. Ibid.

93. "Miss California Controversy," comment by David Waters in "On Faith" blog, *Washington Post*, April 22, 2009, http://newsweek.washingtonpost.com/onfaith/undergod/2009/04/miss_california_controversy.html (accessed October 26, 2009).

CHAPTER 10

1. The Quote Garden, "Quotations about Age," 2009 http://www.quotegarden.com/age.html (accessed September 15, 2009).

2. Betty Yorburg, *Family Realities: A Global View* (Upper Saddle River, NJ: Pearson Education, 2002), 207-208.

3. Ibid., 208-209.

4. Ibid., 209-211.

5. Hong-kin Kwok, "The Son Also Acts as Major Caregiver to Elderly Parents: A Study of the Sandwich Generation in Hong Kong," *Current Sociology* 54(2) (2005): 257-272.

6. Ingrid Arnet Connidis, *Family Ties and Aging*, 2nd edition (Los Angeles, CA: Pine Forge Press, 2010), 160-161.

7. Betty Yorburg, *Family Realities: A Global View* (Upper Saddle River, NJ: Pearson Education, 2002), 209-212.

8. Alex Johnson, "A Generation Caught Between 2 Others," msnbc.com, February 13, 2007 http://www.msnbc.msn.com/id/17134636/ (accessed September 15, 2009).

9. Russell A Ward and Glenna Spitze, "Sandwiched Marriages: The Implications of Child and Parent Relations for Marital Quality in Midlife," *Social Forces* 77(2) (1998):647-666.

10. Betty Yorburg, *Family Realities: A Global View* (Upper Saddle River, NJ: Pearson Education, 2002), 209-212.

11. Ibid., 232.

12. Ibid., 234-236.

13. Ibid., 236-237.

14. Jenifer Kunz and Claudia Stuart, *Sociology: The New Millennium*, 2nd edition (Dubuque, IA: Kendall/Hunt Publishing, 2005), 167-185.

15. Stephen A. Anderson and Ronald M. Sabatelli, *Family Interaction: A Multigenerational Developmental Perspective*, 4th edition (Upper Saddle River, NJ: Pearson Education, 2007), 232-234.

16. Ibid., 240-241.

17. David H. Olson, John Defrain, and Linda Skogrand, *Marriage and Families: Intimacy, Diversity, and Strengths*, 6th edition (Boston: McGraw Hill Higher Education, 2008), 372.

18. Stephen A. Anderson and Ronald M. Sabatelli, *Family Interaction: A Multigenerational Developmental Perspective*, 4th edition (Upper Saddle River, NJ: Pearson Education, 2007), 251-253.

19. Betty Yorburg, *Family Realities: A Global View* (Upper Saddle River, NJ: Pearson Education, 2002), 216-217.

20. Christopher G. Chan and Glen H Elder, "Matrilineal Advantage in Grandchild-Grandparent Relations," *The Gerontologist* 40(2) (2000): 179-190.

21. Betty Yorburg, *Family Realities: A Global View* (Upper Saddle River, NJ: Pearson Education, 2002), 216-217.

22. Ingrid Arnet Connidis, *Family Ties and Aging*, 2nd edition (Los Angeles: Pine Forge Press, 2010), 197.

23. Reynolds Farley and John Haaga, eds, *The American People Census 2000* (New York: Russell Sage Foundation, 2005), 183. http://books.google.com/books?id=nN-H76pipyAC&printsec=frontcover&source=gbs_navlinks_s#v=onepage&q=&f=false (accessed September 15, 2009).

24. Elizabeth McConnell Heywood, "Custodial Grandparents and their Grandchildren," *The Family Journal* 7 (1999): 367-372.

25. ThinkExist.com, "Francis Bacon, Sr. Quotes," http://thinkexist.com/quotes/francis_bacon,_sr./ (accessed September 15, 2009).

26. John R. Weeks, *Population: An Introduction to Concepts and Issues*, 9th edition (Belmont, CA: Wadsworth/Thomson Learning, 2005), 368-370.

27. David Brown, "Life Expectancy Hits Record High in United States," *Washington Post*, June 12, 2008. http://www.washingtonpost.com/wp-dyn/content/article/2008/06/11/AR2008061101570.html (accessed September 15, 2009).

28. John R. Weeks, *Population: An Introduction to Concepts and Issues*, 9th edition (Belmont, CA: Wadsworth/Thomson Learning, 2005), 376-377.

29. Ibid., 378.

30. Ibid., 369-376.

31. U.S. Census Bureau, "Current Population Reports, Special Studies, P23-190, 65+ in the United States," 1996 http://www.census.gov/prod/1/pop/p23-190/p23190-f.pdf (accessed September 15, 2009).

32. U.S. Census Bureau, "United States Population Projections by Age, Sex, Race, and Hispanic Origin," 2008 http://www.census.gov/population/www/projections/methodstatement.pdf (accessed September 15, 2009).

33. David Brown, "Life Expectancy Hits Record High in United States," *Washington Post*, June 12, 2008. http://www.washingtonpost.com/wp-dyn/content/article/2008/06/11/AR2008061101570.html (accessed September 15, 2009).

34. John R. Weeks, *Population: An Introduction to Concepts and Issues*, 9th edition (Belmont, CA: Wadsworth/Thomson Learning, 2005), 392-393.

35. Marilyn Coleman and Lawrence H. Ganong, eds., *Handbook of Contemporary Families* (Thousand Oaks, CA: Sage Publications, 2004), 145-146.

36. Ibid., 146-147.

37. Sarah G. Gabbay and James J. Wahler, "Lesbian Aging," *Journal of Gay & Lesbian Social Services* 14(3) (2002): 1-21.

38. Susan Hillier and Georgia M. Barrow, *Aging, the Individual, and Society*, 7th edition (Belmont, CA: Wadsworth Publishing Company, 1999), 168-173.

39. United States Department of Labor, Bureau of Labor Statistics, Household Data Annual Averages (accessed through the U.S. Census Bureau web site).

40. Stephen A. Anderson and Ronald M. Sabatelli, *Family Interaction: A Multigenerational Developmental Perspective*, 4th edition (Upper Saddle River, NJ: Pearson Education, 2007), 247-248.

41. Lynne H. Turner and Richard West, *Perspectives on Family Communication*, 3rd edition (Boston: McGraw Hill, 2006), 241-242.

42. Bureau of Labor Statistics, "Inflation Calculator," 2009 http://data.bls.gov/cgi-bin/cpicalc.pl (accessed September 15, 2009).

43. Felicia R. Lee, "Fear of Hunger Stalk Many Elderly," *New York Times*, November 16, 1993 http://www.nytimes.com/1993/11/16/nyregion/fear-of-hunger-stalks-many-elderly.html (accessed September 15, 2009).

44. Melissa F. Stoeltje, "Hard Times Hardest on Elderly Poor," *Express News*, November 23, 2008 http://www.mysanantonio.com/news/Hard_times_hardest_on_elderly_poor.html (accessed September 15, 2009).

45. Elizabeth A. Kutza, "The Intersection of Economics and Family Status in Late Life: Implications for the Future," *Marriage & Family Review* 37(1) (2005): 9-26.

46. John R. Weeks, *Population: An Introduction to Concepts and Issues*, 9th edition (Belmont, CA: Wadsworth/Thomson Learning, 2005), 385-386.

47. Leonid A. Gavrilov and Patrick Heuveline, "Aging of the Population," *The Encyclopedia of Population*, ed. Paul Demeny and Geoffrey McNicoll (New York: Macmillan Reference USA, 2003) http://longevity-science.org/Population_Aging.htm (accessed September 15, 2009).

48. John R. Weeks., *Population: An Introduction to Concepts and Issues*, 9th edition (Belmont, CA: Wadsworth/Thomson Learning, 2005), 385-386.

49. Joan Ditzion, "Our Later Years," *Our Bodies, Ourselves: A New Edition for a New Era* (Boston: Women's Health Book Collective, 2005) http://www.ourbodiesourselves.org/book/excerpt.asp?id=35 (accessed September 15, 2009).

50. Ibid., 243-244.

51. Stephen A. Anderson and Ronald M. Sabatelli, *Family Interaction: A Multigenerational Developmental Perspective*, 4th edition (Upper Saddle River, NJ: Pearson Education, 2007), 253-256.

52. Ingrid Arnet Connidis, *Family Ties and Aging*, 2nd edition (Los Angeles: Pine Forge Press, 2010), 84.

53. Health Reform.gov, "America's Seniors and Health Insurance Reform: Protecting Coverage and Strengthening Medicare" http://www.healthreform.gov/reports/seniors/index.html (accessed September 16, 2009).

54. Lena G. Caesar, "English Proficiency and Access to Health Insurance in Hispanics Who Are Elderly," *Hispanic Journal of Behavioral Sciences* 28(1) (2006): 143-152.

55. Benjamin Franklin, *The Works of Benjamin Franklin*, The Phrase Finder http://www.phrases.org.uk/meanings/death-and-taxes.html (accessed September 16, 2009).

56. Stephen A. Anderson and Ronald M. Sabatelli, *Family Interaction: A Multigenerational Developmental Perspective*, 4th edition (Upper Saddle River, NJ: Pearson Education, 2007), 266.

57. Ibid., 266-267.

58. Ibid., 266-268.

59. Ibid., 267-268.

60. Ibid., 268-273.

61. Bert N. Adams and Jan Trost, *Handbook of World Families* (Thousand Oaks, CA: Sage Publications, 2005).

62. Ingrid Arnet Connidis, *Family Ties and Aging*, 2nd edition (Los Angeles: Pine Forge Press, 2010), 116-118.

63. Meg Wilkes Karraker and Janet R. Grochowski, *Families with Futures: A Survey of Family Studies for the 21st Century* (Mahwah, NJ: Erlbaum Associates, 2006), 258-260.

64. Manacy Pai and Ann E. Barrett, "Long-Term Payoffs of Work? Women's Past Involvement in Paid Work and Mental Health in Widowhood," *Research on Aging* 29(5) (2007): 436-456.

65. Ingrid Arnet Connidis, *Family Ties and Aging*, 2nd edition (Los Angeles: Pine Forge Press, 2010), 108-115.

66. V. Subramanian, Felix Elwert, and Nicolas Christakis, "Widowhood and Mortality among the Elderly: The Modifying Role of Neighborhood Concentration of Widowed Individuals," *Social Science & Medicine* 66 (2008): 873-884.

67. R.F. Holznagel and Paul Hehn, "Jack Kevorkian," Who2 Biography http://www.answers.com/topic/jack-kevorkian (accessed September 16, 2009).

68. American Psychological Association, "End of Life Issues and Care: Assisted Suicide," 2009 http://www.apa.org/pi/eol/arguments.html (accessed September 16, 2009).

69. Lasagna, Louis, "The Hippocratic Oath: Modern Version," *Doctor's Diaries,* PBS Online, 2009 http://www.pbs.org/wgbh/nova/doctors/oath_modern.html (accessed September 16, 2009).

70. American Psychological Association, "End of Life Issues and Care: Assisted Suicide," 2009 http://www.apa.org/pi/eol/arguments.html (accessed September 16, 2009).

71. E. Garrard and S. Wilkinson, "Passive Euthanasia," *Journal of Medical Ethics* 31 (2005): 64-68.

72. ProCon.org. "What is a Do-Not-Resuscitate order (DNR)?" *Euthanasia* http://euthanasia.procon.org/viewanswers.asp?questionID=188 (accessed September 15, 2009).

73. Ibid.

74. William C. Cockerham, *This Aging Society,* 2nd edition (Upper Saddle River, NJ: Prentice Hall, 1997), 50-55.

75. Susan Hillier and Georgia M. Barrow, *Aging, the Individual, and Society,* 7th edition (Belmont, CA: Wadsworth Publishing Company, 1999), 74-76.

76. William C. Cockerham, *This Aging Society,* 2nd edition (Upper Saddle River, NJ: Prentice Hall, 1997), 68-71.

77. Susan Hillier and Georgia M. Barrow, *Aging, the Individual, and Society,* 7th edition (Belmont, CA: Wadsworth Publishing Company, 1999), 27-30, 83-85.

78. William C. Cockerham, *This Aging Society,* 2nd edition (Upper Saddle River, NJ: Prentice Hall, 1997), 65-68.

79. Congressional Research Service, "CRS Report for Congress: The Cost of Prescription Drugs for the Uninsured Elderly and Legislative Approaches," Library of Congress, 2001.

80. Health Reform.gov. "America's Seniors and Health Insurance Reform: Protecting Coverage and Strengthening Medicare" http://www.healthreform.gov/reports/seniors/index.html (accessed September 16, 2009).

81. Minority Staff, Committee on Government Reform, U.S. House of Representatives. "Drug Pricing Analysis: Prescription Drug Prices for Uninsured Seniors in the U.S. Are Higher than Prices in Canada, Europe, and Japan," 2003 http://oversight.house.gov/documents/20040628104816-38372.pdf (accessed September 16, 2009).

CHAPTER 11

1. Ann M. Duffett, "Dissertation Abstracts International, A: The Humanities and Social Sciences," 67(12) (2007): 4711.

2. Meg Wilkes Karraker and Janet R. Grochowski, *Families with Futures: A Survey of Family Studies for the 21st Century* (Mahwah, NJ: Erlbaum Associates, 2006), 372-373.

3. Ibid.

4. John R. Weeks, *Population: An Introduction to Concepts and Issues,* 9th edition (Belmont, CA: Wadsworth/Thomson Learning, 2005), 425-426.

5. Ibid., 428-430.

6. U.S. Bureau of Labor Statistics, "Highlights of Women's Earnings in 2008," Report 1017, July 2009, 1. http://www.bls.gov/cps/cpswom2008.pdf (accessed August 14, 2009).

7. Carmen DeNavas-Walt, Bernadette Proctor, and Jessica Smith, "Income, Poverty, and Health Insurance Coverage in the United States: 2007," U.S. Census Bureau (2008), http://www.census.gov/prod/2008pubs/p60-235.pdf (accessed August 14, 2009).

8. John R. Weeks, *Population: An Introduction to Concepts and Issues,* 9th edition (Belmont CA: Wadsworth/Thomson Learning, 2005), 429-431.

9. Ibid.

10. Ibid., 431-433.

11. U.S. Bureau of Labor Statistics, "Highlights of Women's Earnings in 2008," Report 1017, July 2009, 1. http://www.bls.gov/cps/cpswom2008.pdf (accessed August 14, 2009).

12. John R. Weeks, *Population: An Introduction to Concepts and Issues,* 9th edition (Belmont, CA: Wadsworth/Thomson Learning, 2005), 435-438.

13. Anna Spencer, *Woman's Share in Social Culture* (New York: Arno Press. 1972), 121, http://books.google.com/books?id=c5Qdx9Ed3PoC&pg=PP7&dq=spencer+we+are+developed+by+our+daily+task&source=gbs_selected_pages&cad=5 (accessed August 14, 2009).

14. Meg Wilkes Karraker and Janet R. Grochowski, *Families with Futures: A Survey of Family Studies for the 21st Century* (Mahwah, NJ: Erlbaum Associates, 2006), 349-350.

15. Sue Mennino, Beth Rubin, and April Brayfield, "Home-To-Job And Job-To-Home Spillover: The Impact of Company Policies and Workplace Culture," *The Sociological Quarterly* 46 (2005): 107-135.

16. Sandra A. Lawrence, "An integrative model of perceived available support, work-family conflict and support mobilization," *Journal of Management and Organization* 12(2) (2006): 160.

17. Daphne Pedersen Stevens, Gary Kiger, and Pamela J. Riley, "His, hers, or ours? Work-to-family spillover, crossover, and family cohesion," *The Social Science Journal* 43 (2006): 425-436.

18. Jennifer Reid Keene and John R. Reynolds, "The Job Costs of Family Demands: Gender Differences in Negative Family-to-Work Spillover," *Journal of Family Issues* 26(3) (2005): 275-299.

19. Shelley J. Correll and Chris Bourg, "Abstract: Trends in Gender Role Attitudes, 1976-1997: The Continued Myth of Separate Worlds," *American Sociological Association* (1999).

20. Ann C. Crouter, "Spillover from Family to Work: The Neglected Side of the Work-Family Interface," *Human Relations* 37 (1984): 425-442.

21. Daphne Pedersen Stevens, et al., "Examining the Neglected Side of the Work-Family Interface," *Journal of Family Issues* 28(2) (2007): 242-262.

22. Meg Wilkes Karraker and Janet R. Grochowski, *Families with Futures: A Survey of Family Studies for the 21st Century* (Mahwah, NJ: Erlbaum Associates, 2006), 375-377.

23. Ibid., 377-378.

24. Deborah L. Rhode, "The unfinished agenda: Women in the legal profession," Chicago: American Bar Association Commission on Women in the Profession. Cited in Noonan, M. and M. Corcoran, 2004. "The Mommy Track and Partnership," *Annals: AAPS* 596 (2001): 130-150.

25. Helene A. Cummins, "Mommy Tracking Single Women in Academia when They Are Not Mommies," *Women's Studies International Forum* 28 (2005): 222-231.

26. Douglas Hall, "Promoting Work/Family Balance: An Organizational Change Approach," *Organizational Dynamics* (Maryland Heights, MO: Elsevier Science Publishing Co., 1990), 5-18.

27. E. Jeffrey Hill, et al., "Beyond the Mommy Track: The Influence of New-Concept Part-Time Work for Professional Women on Work and Family," *Journal of Family and Economic Issues* 25(1) (2004): 121-136.

28. Julia Draznin, "The Mommy Tenure Track," *Academic Medicine* 79(4) (2004): 289-290.

29. After School Alliance, "America After 3 PM: A Household Survey on Afterschool in America," 2003. http://www.afterschoolalliance.org/documents/AA%203%20pm_Executive_Summary.pdf (accessed August 14, 2009).

30. Dave Riley and Jill Steinberg, "Four Popular Stereotypes about Children in Self-Care: Implications for Family Life Educators," *Family Relations* 53(2004): 95-101.

31. Barbara A. Mitchell, "Changing Courses: The Pendulum of Family Transitions in Comparative Perspective," *Journal of Comparative Family Studies* (June 22, 2006): 325, 336.

32. Shelley A. Haddock, et al., "Ten adaptive strategies for family and work balance: Advice from successful families," *Journal of Marital and Family Therapy* 27 (4) (2001): 445-458.

33. Meg Wilkes Karraker and Janet R. Grochowski, *Families with Futures: A Survey of Family Studies for the 21st Century*, (Mahwah, NJ: Erlbaum Associates, 2006), 384-385.

34. Ibid., 381-382.

35. Jeane M. Brett and Sara Yogev, "Restructuring Work for Family," *Journal of Social Behavior and Personality* 3(4) (1998): 159-174.

36. Masako Ishi-Kuntz, "Working Class Fatherhood and Masculinities in Contemporary Japan," *Handbook of Feminist Studies,* ed. Sally A. Lloyd, April L. Few, and Katherine R. Allen (Los Angeles: Sage Publications, 2009), 192-204.

37. Jill Smolowe, et al., "She Said, He Said," *Time,* October 21, 1991. http://www.time.com/time/magazine/article/0,9171,974096-1,00.html (accessed August 14, 2009).

38. Anita Hill, "Opening Statement: Sexual Harassment Hearings Concerning Judge Clarence Thomas," Testimony in the Thomas hearings, October 11, 1991, Gifts of Speech, http://gos.sbc.edu/h/hill.html (accessed August 14, 2009).

39. Linda Lindsey, *Gender Roles: A Sociological Perspective,* 3rd edition (Upper Saddle River, NJ: Prentice Hall, 1997), 341-343.

40. U.S. Equal Employment Opportunity Commission, "Sexual Harassment," 2008 http://www.eeoc.gov/types/sexual_harassment.html (accessed August 14, 2009).

41. Financial Forecast Center, "U.S. Civilian Unemployment Rate Forecast," 2009. http://forecasts.org/unemploy.htm accessed 7/24/09 (accessed August 14, 2009).

42. Tom Abate, "State unemployment rate highest since 1941," *San Francisco Chronicle,* March 18, 2009. http://www.sfgate.com/cgi-bin/article.cgi?f=/c/a/2009/04/17/MNPQ174BVL.DTL (accessed August 14, 2009).

43. Meg Wilkes Karraker and Janet R. Grochowski, *Families with Futures: A Survey of Family Studies for the 21st Century* (Mahwah, NJ: Erlbaum Associates, 2006), 373-375.

44. Kornelius Kraft, "Unemployment and Separation of Married Couples," *Kylos* 54(1) (2001): 67-88.

45. Haythum Khalid, *Book of Famous Quotes* (2009), http://www.famous-quotes.com/topic.php?tid=196 (accessed August 14, 2009).

46. Stephen A. Anderson and Ronald M. Sabatelli, *Family Interaction: A Multigenerational Developmental Perspective,* 2nd edition (Boston, MA: Allyn and Bacon, 1999), 86-88.

47. John Macionis, *Sociology,* 11th edition (Upper Saddle River, NJ: Pearson Education, 2007), 284-287.

48. David Cay Johnston, "Report Says Rich Getting Richer Faster, Much Faster," *New York Times,* December 15, 2007, http://www.nytimes.com/2007/12/15/business/15rich.html?_r=1 (accessed August 14, 2009).

49. U.S. Census Bureau News, "The Desert Is Desirable," U.S. Census Bureau, Department of Commerce, 2005 http://www.census.gov/Press-Release/www/releases/archives/population/006142.html (accessed August 14, 2009).

50. Chris Rojek, "Leisure and the Rich Today: Veblen's Thesis after a Century," *Leisure Studies* 19 (2000): 1-15.

51. John Macionis, *Sociology*, 11th edition (Upper Saddle River, NJ: Pearson Education, 2007), 289.

52. Ibid., 286-287.

53. Ibid.

54. Ibid., 287.

55. Ibid.

56. U.S. Dept. of Labor, "Compliance Assistance—Fair Labor Standards Act" (2009), http://www.dol.gov/esa/whd/flsa/ (accessed August 14, 2009).

57. U.S. Dept. of Health and Human Services, "The 2009 HHS Poverty Guidelines" (2009), http://aspe.hhs.gov/poverty/09poverty.shtml (accessed August 14, 2009).

58. Dennis K. Orthner, Hinckley Jones-Sanpei, and Sabrina Williamson, "The Resilience and Strengths of Low-Income Families," *Family Relations* 53(2004): 159-167.

59. John Macionis, *Sociology* 11th edition (Upper Saddle River, NJ: Pearson Education, 2007), 288.

60. Keniv M. Roy, Carolyn Y. Tubbs, and Linda M. Burton, "Don't Have No Time: Daily Rhythms and the Organization of Time for Low-Income Families," *Family Relations* 53 (2004): 168-178.

61. Lyndon B. Johnson, "Annual Message to the Congress on the State of the Union," January 8, 1964. http://www.lbjlib.utexas.edu/johnson/archives.hom/speeches.hom/640108.asp (accessed August 14, 2009).

62. Carmen DeNavas-Walt, Bernadette D. Proctor, and Jessica C. Smith, *Income, Poverty, and Health Insurance Coverage in the United States,* U.S. Government Printing Office, 2008.

63. U.S. Dept. of Health and Human Services, "Frequently Asked Questions Related to the Poverty Guidelines and Poverty" (2009), http://aspe.hhs.gov/poverty/faq.shtml#developed (accessed August 14, 2009).

64. U.S. Dept. of Health and Human Services, "The 2009 HHS Poverty Guidelines" (2009), http://aspe.hhs.gov/poverty/09poverty.shtml (accessed August 14, 2009).

65. Carmen DeNavas-Walt, Bernadette D. Proctor, and Jessica C. Smith, Income, Poverty, and Health Insurance Coverage in the United States: 2009, *Current Population Reports,* Issued September 2010, U.S. Census Bureau.

66. John Macionis, *Sociology*, 11th edition (Upper Saddle River, NJ: Pearson Education, 2007), 295-296.

67. Richard T. Schaefer, *Racial and Ethnic Groups,* 11th edition (Upper Saddle River, NJ: Pearson Education, 2008), 278-279.

68. William Julius Wilson, *When work disappears: The world of the new urban poor* (New York: Knopf, 1996).

69. John Macionis, *Sociology*, 11th edition (Upper Saddle River, NJ: Pearson Education, 2007), 296-297.

70. Lydia L. Blalock, Vicky R. Tiller, and Pamel A. Monroe, "They Get You Out of Courage: Persistent Deep Poverty Among Former Welfare-Reliant Women," *Family Relations* 53 (2004): 127-137.

71. Andrew S. London, et al., "Welfare Reform, Work-Family Tradeoffs, and Child Well-Being," *Family Relations* 53 (2004): 148-158.

72. John Macionis, *Sociology*, 11th edition (Upper Saddle River, NJ: Pearson Education, 2007), 298-300.

73. Kimberly A. Tyler, "A Qualitative Study of Early Family Histories and Transitions of Homeless Youth," *Journal of Interpersonal Violence* 21(10) (2006): 1385-1393.

74. Linda Anooshian, "Violence and Aggression in the Lives of Homeless Children," *Journal of Family Violence* 20(6) (2005): 373-387.

75. John Macionis, *Sociology*, 11th edition (Upper Saddle River, NJ: Pearson Education, 2007), 264-265.

76. Ibid., 265-269.

77. Ibid., 269-270.

78. Robert E. Rector, et al., "Increasing Marriage Would Dramatically Reduce Child Poverty," *Handbook of Families and Poverty*, ed. Crane, D. and T. Heaton (Los Angeles: Sage Publications, 2008), 457-470.

79. Ibid.

CHAPTER 12

1. Quote DB, "Education Quotes" http://www.quotedb.com/quotes/714 (accessed September 21, 2009).

2. U.S. Census Bureau, "Educational Attainment: 2000, 2003." http://www.census.gov/prod/2003pubs/c2kbr-24.pdf (accessed September 21, 2009).

3. U.S. Census Bureau, U.S. Census of Population, 1970 and 1980, Vol. 1; Current Population Reports, P20-550, and earlier reports; and "Educational Attainment," http://www.census.gov/population/www/socdemo/educ-attn.html.

4. Valarie King, Kathleen Mullan Harris, and Holly E. Heard, "Racial and ethnic diversity in nonresident father involvement," *Journal of Marriage and the Family* 66 (2004): 1-21; Coleman, James S., "Families and Schools," *Educational Researcher* 16 (1987): 32-38.

5. Sarah McLanahan and Gary Sandefur, *Growing Up with a Single Parent* (Cambridge: Harvard University Press. 1994).

6. Ibid.

7. Robin L. Jarrett, "Growing up poor: The family experiences of socially mobile youth in low-income African American Neighborhoods," *Journal of Adolescent Research* 10 (1995): 111-135.

8. Kenneth I. Spenner, Claudia Buchmann, and Lawrence R. Landerman, "The black-white achievement gap in the first college year: Evidence from a new longitudinal case study," *Social Stratification and Mobility* 22 (2004): 187-216.

9. Eva I. Diaz, "Perceived factors influencing the academic underachievement of talented students of Puerto Rican descent," *Gifted Child Quarterly* 42 (1998): 105-122.

10. Rene Antrop-González, William Vélez, and Tomas Garrett, "Examining familial-based academic success factors in urban high school students: The case of Puerto Rican female high achievers," *Marriage and Family Review* 43 (2008): 140-163.

11. Ibid.

12. Joyce L. Epstein, *School, Family, and Community Partnerships: Preparing Educators and Improving Schools* (Boulder: Westview Press. 2001); Hiatt-Michael, Diana B., *Promising Practices for Family Involvement in Schooling across the Continents* (Greenwich: Information Age Publishing. 2005).

13. Diana B. Hiatt-Michael, "Families, their children's education and the public school: An historical review," *Marriage and Family Review* 43 (2008): 39-66.

14. Ibid.

15. Ibid.

16. Ibid.

17. Ibid.

18. National Center for Educational Statistics, "Parental choice of schools," 2007 http://nces.ed.gov/programs/coe/2009/section4/indicator32.asp (accessed September 21, 2009).

19. D. Armor and B. Peiser, "Interdistrict Choice in Massachusetts," *Learning from School Choice,* ed. Paul E. Peterson and Bryan C. Hassel (Washington, DC: Brookings Institution, 1998), 157-186.

20. Paul Teste and Mark Schneider, "What research can tell policymakers about school choice," *Journal of Policy Analysis and Management* 20(4) (2001): 609-631.

21. US Department of Education, "Key Policy Letters Signed by the Education Secretary or Deputy Secretary," 2001 http://www.ed.gov/policy/elsec/guid/secletter/010813.html (accessed September 21, 2009).

22. US Department of Education, "Four Pillars of NCLB," July 01, 2004 http://www.ed.gov/nclb/overview/intro/4pillars.html (accessed September 21, 2009).

23. Patricia M. Lines, "When homeschoolers go to school: A partnership between families and schools," *Peabody Journal of Education* 75 (2000): 159-186; Hammons, Christopher W., "School @ Home," *Education Next* 1(4) (2001): 48-55.

24. Ed Collom, "The ins and outs of homeschooling: The determinants of parental motivations and student achievement," *Education and Urban Society* 37(3) (2005): 307-335.

25. Ibid.

26. Ibid.

27. Ibid.

28. National Center for Education Statistics, *Digest of Education Statistics,* Washington, DC: National Center for Education Statistics, 2003.

29. J. Jill Suitor et al., "Unforeseen consequences of mothers' return to school: Children's educational aspirations and outcomes," *Sociological Perspectives* 51(3) (2008): 495-513.

30. ThinkExist.com, "Mark Twain Quotes" http://thinkexist.com/quotation/religion_consists_of_a_set_of_things_which_the/158208.html (accessed September 21, 2009).

31. Lydia Saad, "Americans Believe Religion is Losing Clout: Percentage saying influence of religion is slipping at 14-year high," Gallup, 2008 http://www.gallup.com/poll/113533/Americans-Believe-Religion-Losing-Clout.aspx (accessed September 21, 2009).

32. Joshua G. Chinitz and Robert A. Brown, "Religious homogamy, marital conflict, and stability in same-faith and interfaith Jewish marriages," *Journal for the Scientific Study of Religion* 40(4) (2001): 723-733.

33. Ibid.

34. Mark Furlong and Abe W. Ata, "Observing Different Faiths, Learning About Ourselves: Practice with Inter-married Muslims and Christians," *Australian Social Work* 59(3) (2006): 250-264.

35. Howard M. Bahr and Bruce A. Chadwick, "Religion and Family in Middletown, USA," *Journal of Marriage and Family* 47 (1985): 407-414; Annette Mahoney et al., "Marriage and the spiritual realm: The Role of proximal and distal religious constructs in marital functioning," *Journal of Family Psychology* 13 (1999): 321-338.

36. Annette Mahoney et al., "Religion in the home in the 1980s and 90s: A meta-analytic review and conceptual analyses of links between religion, marriage and parenting," *Journal of Family Psychology* 15 (2001): 559-196.

37. Annette Mahoney et al., "Marriage and the spiritual realm: The Role of proximal and distal religious constructs in marital functioning," *Journal of Family Psychology* 13 (1999): 321-338.

38. C. Daniel Batson, Patricia Schoenrade, and W. Larry Ventis, *Religion and the Individual* (New York: Oxford University Press. 1993).

39. Christopher G. Ellison and John P. Bartkowski, "Conservative Protestantism and the division of household labor among married couples," *Journal of Family Issues* 23(8) (2002): 950-985.

40. John P. Bartkowski, Xiaohe Xu, and Martin L. Levin, "Religion and child development: Evidence from the early childhood longitudinal study," *Social Science Research* 37 (2008): 18-36.

41. Linda Schneider and Arnold Silverman, *Global Sociology: Introducing Five Contemporary Societies,* Fifth Edition (Boston: McGraw Hill, 2009).
42. Ibid.
43. Ibid.
44. QuoteWorld.org, "John Kenneth Galbraith," http://www.quoteworld.org/quotes/5169 (accessed September 21, 2009).
45. Office of Management and Budget, "Transforming and Modernizing America's Health Care System," http://www.whitehouse.gov/omb/fy2010_key_healthcare/ (accessed September 21, 2009).
46. Terence P. Jeffrey, "Conservatives now outnumber liberals in all 50 states, says Gallup poll," CNSNews.com, 2009 http://www.cnsnews.com/news/print/52602 (accessed September 21, 2009).
47. Lydia Saad, "Special report: Ideologically, where is the U.S. moving?" Gallup, 2009 http://www.gallup.com/poll/121403/special-report-ideologically-moving.aspx (accessed September 21, 2009).
48. CNN, "Exit polls: Obama wins big among young, minority voters," 2008 http://www.cnn.com/2008/POLITICS/11/04/exit.polls/ (accessed September 21, 2009).
49. Molly W. Andolina et al., "Habits from home, lessons from school: Influences on youth civic development," *PS: Political Science and Politics* 36(2) 2003: 275-80.
50. Nancy Burns, Kay Schlozman, and Sidney Verba, *The Private Roots of Public Action: Gender, Equality, and Political Participation* (Cambridge, MA: Harvard University Press. 2001).
51. Herbert W. Marsh, "Extracurricular activities: Beneficial extension of the traditional curriculum or subversion of academic goals?" *Journal of Educational Psychology* 84 (1992): 553-62.
52. Robert S. Erikson and Kent L. Tedin, *American Public Opinion: Its Origins, Content, and Impact* (New York: Pearson Longman, 2007).
53. Ibid.
54. M. Kent Jennings et al., *Youth-Parent Socialization Panel Study, 1965-1997, Four Waves Combined* (Ann Arbor, MI: University of Michigan, Center for Political Studies/Survey Research Center, 2004).
55. Selected exit poll comparisons, 2000-2004-2008, http://observationalism.com/2008/11/09/selected-exit-poll-comparisons-2000-2004-2008/ (accessed September 21, 2009).
56. Herbert F. Weisberg, "The demographics of a new voting gap: Marital differences in American voting," *Public Opinion Quarterly* 51 (1987): 335-43; Martin Plissner, "The marriage gap," *Public Opinion* (Feb-March 1983): 53.
57. AllGreatQuotes.com, "Law Quotes." http://www.allgreatquotes.com/law_quotes.shtml (accessed September 21, 2009).
58. Lynne H. Turner and Richard L. West, *Perspectives on Family Communication* (New York: McGraw-Hill, 2006).
59. Ibid.
60. United States Department of Labor, "Wage and Hour Division," http://www.dol.gov/esa/whd/fmla/ (accessed September 22, 2009).
61. Stacey M. Brumbaugh et al., "Attitudes toward gay marriage in states undergoing marital law transformation," *Journal of Marriage and Family* 70 (2008): 345-359.
62. Taylor Gandossy, "Gay adoption: A new take on the American family," CNN, 2007 http://www.cnn.com/2007/US/06/25/gay.adoption/index.html (accessed September 22, 2009).
63. Sally A. Lloyd, April L. Few, and Katherine R. Allen, eds, *Handbook of Feminist Family Studies* (Thousand Oaks, CA: Sage Publications, 2009).
64. Children's Defense Fund, "Children in the United States," Nov 2008. http://www.childrensdefense.org/child-research-data-publications/data/state-data-repository/cits/children-in-the-states-2008-all.pdf (accessed September 22, 2009).
65. U.S. Census Bureau, "Nearly half of preschoolers receive child care from relatives," 2008 http://www.census.gov/Press-Release/www/releases/archives/children/011574.html (accessed September 22, 2009).
66. Ibid.
67. Donald Granberg and Beth Wellman Granberg, "Abortion attitudes, 1965-1980: Trends and determinants," *Family Planning Perspectives* 12 (1980): 250-261; Elaine J. Hall and Myra Marx Ferree, "Race differences in abortion attitudes," *Public Opinion Quarterly* 50 (1986): 193-207.
68. Martha N. Ozawa, "Social welfare spending on family benefits in the United States and Sweden: A comparative study," *Family Relations* 53(3) (2004): 301-309.
69. Joseph F. Coates, "What's ahead for families: Five major forces for change," *The Futurist,* World Future Society (Sept-Oct 1996).
70. John Macionis, *Sociology,* Eleventh edition (Upper Saddle River, NJ: Pearson Education, 2007), 530.
71. James Crouse and Dale Trusheim, *The Case Against the SAT* (Chicago, IL: University of Chicago Press, 1988).
72. James S. Coleman and Thomas Hoffer, *Public and Private High Schools: The Impact of Communities* (New York: Basic Books, 1987).
73. Karl Marx, "Zur Judenfrage," *Deutsch-Französische Jahrbucher,* 1844.
74. Frontline, *A Class Divided* http://www.pbs.org/wgbh/pages/frontline/shows/divided/ (accessed September 21, 2009).
75. John Macionis, *Sociology,* Eleventh edition (Upper Saddle River, NJ: Pearson Education, 2007), 531.
76. James S. Coleman et al., *Equality of Educational Opportunity,* U.S. Department of Health, Education and Welfare, 1966.
77. Leigh A. Leslie and Goldie Morton, "Family therapy's response to family diversity: Looking back, looking forward," *Handbook of Contemporary Families: Considering the Past, Contemplating the Future,* ed. Marilyn Coleman and Lawrence H. Ganong (Thousand Oaks, CA: Sage Publications, 2004), 526.
78. Rhea Almeida and Michele Bograd, "Sponsorship: Holding men accountable for domestic violence," *Journal of Feminist Family Therapy* 2 (1991): 243-259; Judith Myers Avis, "Where are all the family therapists? Abuse and violence within families and family therapy's response," *Journal of Marital and Family Therapy* 18 (1992): 225-232.
79. Phoebe Kazdin Schnitzer, "Tales of the absent father: Applying the story metaphor in family therapy," *Family Process* 32 (1993): 441-458.
80. Julie Bosman, "Obama sharply assails absent black fathers," NYTimes.com, June 16, 2008 http://www.nytimes.com/2008/06/16/us/politics/15cnd-obama.html (accessed September 21, 2009).

CHAPTER 13

1. Rick Nauert, "America's Stress Level is Rising," Psych Central, http://psychcentral.com/news/2008/10/06/americas-stress-level-is-rising/3074.html (accessed August 13, 2009).
2. Harris Interactive, "Money, Trouble Sleeping and Over-scheduling Major Hassles for Americans," http://www.harrisinteractive.com/harris_poll/index.asp?PID=977 (accessed August 13, 2009).
3. Clemson University Extension, "From Family Stress to Family Strengths," http://www.clemson.edu/psapublishing/PAGES/FYD/HEL70.pdf (accessed August 13, 2009).
4. Ibid.
5. Ibid.
6. Family.jrank.org, "Stress—Exposure and Responses to Stressors, Effects of Economic Stressors on Marital Behaviors, Societal Differences, Demographic Factors, and Family Stressors" http://family.jrank.org/pages/1644/Stress.html (accessed August 14, 2009).
7. Blair Wheaton, "Life Transitions, Role Histories, and Mental Health," *American Sociological Review* 55 (1990): 209-223.
8. Susan M. Jekielek, "Parental Conflict, Marital Disruption, Children's Emotional Well-Being," *Social Forces* 76 (1998): 905-935.
9. Contemporary Families, "Economic Woes = Family Stress," July 23, 2008 http://www.contemporaryfamilies.org/subtemplate.php?t=briefingPapers&ext=EconomyandFamily (accessed August 26, 2009).
10. Eugene Asienberg and Todd Herrenkohl, "Community Violence in Context: Risk and Resilience in Children and Families," *Journal of Interpersonal Violence* 23 (3) (2008): 296-315.
11. David Brunsma and J. Steven Picou, "Disasters in the Twenty-First Century: Modern Destruction and Future Instruction," *Social Forces* 87(2) (2008): 983-991.
12. Susan W. Langdon and William Preble, "The Relationship between Levels of Perceived Respect and Bullying in 5th through 12th Graders," *Adolescence* 43 (2008): 485-503.
13. Hamilton I. McCubbin, et al., *Families Under Stress: What Makes Them Resilient,* Adapted from the 1997 American Association of Family and Consumer Sciences Commemorative Lecture (1997).
14. Ibid.
15. Ibid.
16. Meg Wilkes Karraker and Janet R. Grochowski, *Families with Futures: A Survey of Family Studies for the 21st Century* (Mahwah, NJ: Lawrence Erlbaum Associates, Inc., Publishers, 2006), 66-70.
17. Celia Ray Hayhoe, "Families Taking Charge: Dealing with the Stress," Virginia Polytechnic Institute and State University, http://pubs.ext.vt.edu/2811/2811-7016/2811-7016.html (accessed August 14, 2009).
18. Ibid.
19. Anita DeLongis and Susan Holtzman, "Coping in Context: The Role of Stress, Social Support, and Personality in Coping," *Journal of Personality* 73 (2005): 1633-1656.
20. Celia Ray Hayhoe, "Families Taking Charge: Dealing with the Stress," Virginia Polytechnic Institute and State University, http://pubs.ext.vt.edu/2811/2811-7016/2811-7016.html (accessed August 14, 2009).
21. Ibid.
22. Dawn O. Braithwaite and Leslie A. Baxter, eds., *Engaging Theories in Family Communication: Multiple Perspectives* (Thousand Oaks, CA: Sage Publications, 2006), 282-287.
23. Lynne H. Turner and Richard West, *Perspectives on Family Communication* (New York: McGraw-Hill, 2006), 228-232.
24. Meg Wilkes Karraker and Janet R. Grochowski, *Families with Futures: A Survey of Family Studies for the 21st Century* (Mahwah, NJ: Lawrence Erlbaum Associates, Inc., Publishers, 2006).
25. Lynne H. Turner and Richard West, *Perspectives on Family Communication* (New York: McGraw-Hill, 2006), 228-232.
26. Betty Carter and Monica McGoldrick, *The Expanded Family Life Cycle* (Boston: Allyn and Bacon, 1999).
27. Frank Eltman, "Economy May Contribute to Rise in Family Violence," ABC News, http://abcnews.go.com/US/wireStory?id=7308490 (accessed August 14, 2009).
28. Meg Wilkes Karraker and Janet R. Grochowski, *Families with Futures: A Survey of Family Studies for the 21st Century* (Mahwah, NJ: Lawrence Erlbaum Associates, Inc., Publishers, 2006), 351-368.
29. NCADV, "Domestic Violence Facts," http://www.ncadv.org/files/DomesticViolenceFactSheet(National).pdf (accessed August 14, 2009).

30. Ibid.

31. Meg Wilkes Karraker and Janet R. Grochowski, *Families with Futures: A Survey of Family Studies for the 21st Century* (Mahwah, NJ: Lawrence Erlbaum Associates, Inc., Publishers, 2006), 351–368.

32. Ibid.

33. Nicholas Kulish, "Life Sentence in Austria Incest Case," *The New York Times*, March 20, 2009, http://www.nytimes.com/2009/03/20/world/europe/20austria.html?_r=1&scp=2&sq=incest&st=cse (accessed August 14, 2009).

34. Lenore E. Walker, "Who Are the Battered Women?" *Frontiers: A Journal of Women Studies* 2(1) (1977): 52–57.

35. Ibid.

36. Ibid.

37. Ibid.

38. Meg Wilkes Karraker and Janet R. Grochowski, *Families with Futures: A Survey of Family Studies for the 21st Century* (Mahwah, NJ: Lawrence Erlbaum Associates, Inc., Publishers, 2006), 351–368.

39. Lenore E. Walker, "Who Are the Battered Women?" *Frontiers: A Journal of Women Studies* 2(1) (1977): 52–57.

40. Ibid.

41. Centers for Disease Control and Prevention, "Understanding Intimate Partner Violence Fact Sheet," 2006, http://www.cdc.gov/HomeandRecreationalSafety/index.html (accessed August 22, 2009).

42. Ibid.

43. Meg Wilkes Karraker and Janet R. Grochowski, *Families with Futures: A Survey of Family Studies for the 21st Century* (Mahwah, NJ: Lawrence Erlbaum Associates, Inc., Publishers, 2006), 351–368.

44. Bureau of Justice Statistics, "Intimate Partner Violence in the U.S., Victim Characteristics," http://www.ojp.usdoj.gov/bjs/intimate/circumstances.htm (accessed August 22, 2009).

45. Solveig Karin Bø Vatnar and Stål Bjørkly, "An Interactional Perspective of Intimate Partner Violence: An In-depth Semi-structured Interview of a Representative Sample of Help-seeking Women," *Journal of Family Violence* 23 (2008): 265–279.

46. Kathleen C. Basile, "Attitudes Toward Wife Rape: Effects of Social Background and Victim Status," *Violence and Victims* 17(3) (2007): 341–354.

47. Sue Ellen Thompson, "Components of Psychological Abuse of Female Victims in Domestic Violence," *Dissertation Abstracts International* 50(11) (1990): 4989.

48. Alfred Demaris and Steven Swinford, "Female Victims of Spousal Violence: Factors Influencing Their Level of Fearfulness," *Family Relations* 45(1) (1996): 98–106.

49. Robert Apsler, Michele R. Cummins, and Steven Carl, "Perceptions of the Police by Female Victims of Domestic Partner Violence," *Violence Against Women* 9 (11) (2003): 1318–1335.

50. Murray A. Straus, "Dominance and Symmetry in Partner Violence by Male and Female University Students in 32 Nations," paper presented at conference on Trends in Intimate Violence Intervention, New York University, May 23, 2006.

51. Denise A. Hines, Jan Brown, and Edward Dunning, "Characteristics of Callers to the Domestic Abuse Helpline for Men," *Journal of Family Violence* 22 (2007): 63–72.

52. Ibid.

53. Ibid.

54. Eve S. Buzawa and Thomas Austin, "Determining Police Response to Domestic Violence Victims The Role of Victim Preference, *American Behavioral Scientist* 36 (5) (1993): 610–623.

55. Roseann Hannon et al., "Judgments Regarding Sexual Aggression as a Function of Sex of Aggressor and Victim," *Sex Roles* 43(5/6) (2000): 311–322.

56. Alexandra K. Frazer and Michelle D. Miller, "Double Standards in Sentence Structure: Passive Voice in Narratives Describing Domestic Violence," *Journal of Language and Social Psychology* 28(1) (2009): 62–71.

57. Ibid.

58. Ibid.

59. Ibid.

60. Carl A. Ridley and Clyde M. Feldman, "Female Domestic Violence Toward Male Partners: Exploring Conflict Responses and Outcomes," *Journal of Family Violence* 18(3) (2003): 157–170.

61. Pam Elliot, "Shattering Illusions: Same-Sex Domestic Violence," *Journal of Lesbian Social Services* 4 (1996): 1–8.

62. Erika Lawrence, et al., "Mechanisms of Distress and Dissolution in Physically Aggressive Romantic Relationships," *Handbook of Divorce and Relationship Dissolution,* ed. Mark A. Fine and John H. Harvey (New York: Routledge and Taylor, 2006): 263–286.

63. Ibid.

64. Aardvark.org, "Domestic Violence in Gay and Lesbian Relationships," http://www.aardvarc.org/dv/gay.shtml (accessed August 24, 2009).

65. Ibid.

66. Vallerie E. Coleman, "Lesbian Battering: The Relationship Between Personality and the Perpetration of Violence," *Violence and Victims* 9(2) (1995): 139–152.

67. Diane Helene Miller, et al., "Domestic Violence in Lesbian Relationships," *Women & Therapy* 23(3) (2001): 107–127.

68. Paula B. Poorman and Sheila M. Seelau, "Lesbians Who Abuse Their Partners: Using the FIRO-B to Assess Interpersonal Characteristics," *Women & Therapy* 23(3) (2001): 87–105.

69. Bette Speziale and Cynthia Ring, "Intimate Violence among Lesbian Couples," *Journal of Feminist Family Therapy* 18 (2006): 85–96.

70. Ibid.

71. Diane Helene Miller, et al., "Domestic Violence in Lesbian Relationships," *Women & Therapy* 23(3) (2001): 107–127.

72. Shonda M. Craft and Julianne M. Serovich, "Family-of-Origin Factors and Partner Violence in the Intimate Relationships of Gay Men Who Are HIV Positive," *Journal of Interpersonal Violence* 20 (2005): 777–791.

73. Moisés Próspero, "Effects of Masculinity, Sex, and Control on Different Types of Intimate Partner Violence Perpetration," *Journal of Family Violence* 23 (2008): 639–645.

74. Joan C. McLennan, Anne B. Summers, and Charles Vaughan, "Gay Men's Domestic Violence," *Journal of Gay & Lesbian Social Services* 14(1) (2002): 23–49.

75. Meg Wilkes Karraker and Janet R. Grochowski, *Families with Futures: A Survey of Family Studies for the 21st Century* (Mahwah, NJ: Lawrence Erlbaum Associates, Inc., Publishers, 2006), 351–368.

76. Kristi L. Hoffman and John N. Edwards, "An Integrated Theoretical Model of Sibling Violence and Abuse," *Journal of Family Violence* 19(3) (2004): 185–200.

77. Ibid.

78. Shelley Eriksen and Vickie Jensen, "All in the Family? Family Environment Factors in Sibling Violence," *Journal of Family Violence* 21 (2006): 497–507.

79. Ibid.

80. Ibid.

81. Heather Hensman Kettrey and Beth C. Emery, "The Discourse of Sibling Violence," *Journal of Family Violence* 21 (2006): 407–416.

82. Shelley Eriksen and Vickie Jensen, "A Push or a Punch Distinguishing the Severity of Sibling Violence," *Journal of Interpersonal Violence* 24(1) (2009): 183–208.

83. Shelley Eriksen and Vickie Jensen, "All in the Family? Family Environment Factors in Sibling Violence," *Journal of Family Violence* 21 (2006): 497–507.

84. Ibid.

85. Kristi L. Hoffman, K. Jill Kiecolt, and John N. Edwards, "Physical Violence between Siblings: A Theoretical and Empirical Analysis," *Journal of Family Issues* 26(8) (2005): 1103–1130.

86. Ibid.

87. Ibid.

88. Ibid.

89. Ibid.

90. Mark S. Kiselica and Mandy Morrill-Richards, "Sibling Maltreatment: The Forgotten Abuse," *Journal of Counseling and Development* 85(2) (2007): 148.

91. Ibid.

92. Ibid.

93. Meg Wilkes Karraker and Janet R. Grochowski, *Families with Futures: A Survey of Family Studies for the 21st Century* (Mahwah, NJ: Lawrence Erlbaum Associates, Inc., Publishers, 2006), 351–368.

94. Sandra A. Graham-Bermann and Honore M. Hughes, "The Impact of Domestic Violence and Emotional Abuse on Children: The Intersection of Research, Theory, and Clinical Intervention," *Journal of Emotional Abuse* 1(2) (1999): 1–21.

95. Jenifer Kunz and Stephen J. Bahr, "A Profile of Parental Homicide Against Children," *Journal of Family Violence* 11(4) (1996): 337–352.

96. American Psychological Association, "Understanding Child Sexual Abuse, http://www.apa.org/releases/sexabuse/ (accessed September 28, 2009).

97. Kathy A. McCloskey and Desreen N. Raphael, "Adult Perpetrator Gender Asymmetries in Child Sexual Assault Victim Selection: Results from the 2000 National Incident-Based Report System," *Journal of Child Sexual Abuse* 14(4) (2005): 1–24.

98. Ibid.

99. Muhammad Haj-Yahia and Safa Tamish, "The Rates of Child Sexual Abuse and Its Psychological Consequences as Revealed by a Study Among Palestinian University Students," *Child Abuse & Neglect* 25 (2001): 1303–1327.

100. Carol D. Berkowitz, "Medical Consequences of Child Sexual Abuse," *Child Abuse & Neglect* 22(6) (1998): 541–550.

101. National Library of Medicine, "Somatization disorder," http://www.nlm.nih.gov/medlineplus/ency/article/000955.htm (accessed August 26, 2009).

102. Simona Ghetti, et al., "Legal Involvement in Child Sexual Abuse Cases Consequences and Interventions," *International Journal of Law and Psychiatry* 25 (2002): 235–251.

103. Daniel T. Wilcox, Fiona Richards, and Zerine C. O'Keeffe, "Resilience and Risk Factors Associated with Experiencing Childhood Sexual Abuse," *Child Abuse Review* 13 (2004): 338–352.

104. Linda S. Pagani, et al., "Risk Factor Models for Adolescent Verbal and Physical Aggression toward Fathers," *Journal of Family Violence* 24 (2009): 174–182.

105. Ibid., 528–537.

106. Arina Ulman and Murray A. Straus, "Violence by Children against Mothers in Relation to Violence between Parents and Corporal Punishment by Parents," *Journal of Comparative Family Studies* 34 (2003): 41–60.

107. Lynette Levy, "Child on Parent Assault: The Impact of Parental Nurturance and Demandingness," *Dissertation Abstracts International: Section B: The Sciences and Engineering* 61 (2-B) (2000): 1087.

108. Ibid.

109. Timothy Brezina, "Teenage Violence toward Parents as an Adaptation to Family Strain Evidence from a National Survey of Male Adolescents," *Youth & Society* 30(4) (1999): 416–444.

110. Meg Wilkes Karraker and Janet R. Grochowski, *Families with Futures: A Survey of Family Studies for the 21st Century* (Mahwah, NJ: Lawrence Erlbaum Associates, Inc., Publishers, 2006), 351–368.

111. Seniors Canada, "Facts on the Abuse of Seniors," http://www.seniors.gc.ca/c.4nt.2nt@.jsp?lang=eng&geo=106&cid=155 (accessed August 26, 2009).

112. Kari Brozowski and David R. Hall, "Growing Old in a Risk Society: Elder Abuse in Canada," *Journal of Elder Abuse & Neglect* 16(3) (2004): 65–81.

113. Ibid.

114. Ibid.

115. Silvia M. Straka and Lyse Montminy, "Responding to the Needs of Older Women Experiencing Domestic Violence," *Violence Against Women* 12(3) (2006): 251–267.

116. Jill E. Korbin, Georgia Anetzberger, and Craig Austin, "The Intergenerational Cycle of Violence in Elder and Child Abuse," *Journal of Elder Abuse & Neglect* 7(1) (1995): 1–15.

117. Kari Brozowski and David R. Hall, "Growing Old in a Risk Society: Elder Abuse in Canada," *Journal of Elder Abuse & Neglect* 16(3) (2004): 65–81.

118. CDC.gov, "Intimate Partner Violence. Dating Violence Fact Sheet," http://www.cdc.gov/ViolencePrevention/intimatepartnerviolence/datingviolence.html (accessed August 26, 2009).

119. Ibid.

120. CDC.gov, "Understanding Teen Violence Fact Sheet," http://www.cdc.gov/ViolencePrevention/pdf/DatingAbuseFactSheet-a.pdf (accessed August 26, 2009).

121. National Coalition on Domestic Violence, "My Personal Safety Plan," http://www.ncadv.org/protectyourself/MyPersonalSafetyPlan.php (accessed August 27, 2009).

122. National Coalition on Domestic Violence, "Workplace Guidelines," http://www.ncadv.org/protectyourself/WorkplaceGuidelines.php (accessed August 27, 2009).

123. National Coalition on Domestic Violence, "Getting Help," http://www.ncadv.org/protectyourself/GettingHelp.php (accessed August 27, 2009).

124. American Psychological Association, "Partner Violence; What Can YOU Do?," http://www.apa.org/pi/violenceathome.html (accessed August 27, 2009).

125. Who.int, "The World Report on Violence and Health," http://www.who.int/violence_injury_prevention/violence/global_campaign/en/chap4.pdf (accessed August 14, 2009).

126. Richard J. Gelles and Murray A Straus, "Determinants of Violence in the Family: Toward a Theoretical Integration," *Contemporary Theories about the Family* Vol. I, ed. W.R. Burr, et al., (New York: The Free Press, 1979): 549–581.

127. Robert Marion Brown, "An Examination of the Individual and Combined Effects of Selected Socio-Demographic and Socio-Psychological Factors in Explaining Family Violence," *Dissertation Abstracts International A: The Humanities and Social Sciences* 61(8) (2001): 3368.

128. Richard J. Gelles and Peter E. Maynard, "A Structural Family Systems Approach to Intervention in Cases of Family Violence," *Family Relations* 36(3) (1987): 270–275.

129. Ibid.

130. Silvia M. Straka and Lyse Montminy, "Family Violence: Through the Lens of Power and Control," *Journal of Emotional Abuse* 8(3) (2008): 255–279.

131. Ibid.

132. Amanda L. Robinson, "Conflicting Consensus," *Women & Criminal Justice* 10(3) (1999): 95–120.

133. Richard J. Gelles and Murray A Straus, "Determinants of Violence in the Family: Toward a Theoretical Integration," *Contemporary Theories about the Family* Vol. I, ed. W.R. Burr, et al., (New York: The Free Press, 1979): 549–581.

134. Tracy L. Dietz and Jana L. Jasinsik, "Female-Perpetrated Partner Violence and Aggression: Their Relationship to Gender Identity," *Women & Criminal Justice* 15(1) (2003): 81–99.

135. Carl A. Bersani and Huey-Tsyh Chen, "Sociological Perspectives in Family Violence," *Handbook of Family Violence*, ed. Vincent B. Van Hasselt, et al. (New York: Plenum, 1998): 57–84.

136. Tracy L. Dietz and Jana L. Jasinsik, "Female-Perpetrated Partner Violence and Aggression: Their Relationship to Gender Identity," *Women & Criminal Justice* 15(1) (2003): 81–99.

137. Niveditha Menon, "Feminist Methodology in Practice: Collecting Data on Domestic Violence in India," *Handbook of Feminist Family Studies*, ed. Sally A. Lloyd, April L. Few, and Katherine R. Allen (Thousand Oaks, CA: Sage Publications, 2009): 249–263.

138. Ibid.

CHAPTER 14

1. Wayne W. Mcvey, "Is separation still an important component of marital dissolution?" *Canadian Studies in Population* 35(1) (2008): 187–205.

2. Howard Wineberg and James McCarthy, "Separation and reconciliation in American marriages," *Journal of Divorce & Remarriage* 20(1–2) (1993): 21–42.

3. Howard Wineberg, "The timing of remarriage among women who have a failed marital reconciliation in the first marriage," *Journal of Divorce & Remarriage* 30(3/4) (1999): 57–69.

4. Jeffrey Cottrill, ed., "U.S. Divorce Statistics," *Divorce Magazine* http://www.divorcemag.com/statistics/statsUS.shtml (accessed May 1, 2009).

5. National Vital Statistics Report, *Births, Marriages, Divorces, and Deaths: Provisional Data for July 2007*, Vol 65 (14) (2008) http://www.cdc.gov/nchs/data/nvsr/nvsr56/nvsr56_14.pdf (accessed June 9, 2009).

6 Divorce Magazine, "U.S. Divorce Statistics," http://www.divorcemag.com/statistics/statsUS.shtml (accessed May 1, 2009).

7. Ibid.

8. Ernest R. Mowrer, "War and family solidarity and stability," *The American Family in World War II*, ed. R.A. Abrams (New York: Arno and New York Times, 1972), 100–106.

9. William M. Tuttle, Jr., *Daddy's Gone to War: The Second World War in the Lives of America's Children* (New York: Oxford University Press, 1993).

10. Robert Schoen and Vladimir Canudas-Romo, "Timing effects on divorce: 20th century experience in the United States," *Journal of Marriage and Family* 68 (August 2006): 749–758.

11. Jan Trost, *Unmarried Cohabitation* (VästerAs, Sweden: International Library, 1980).

12. Paul R. Amato, "The impact of divorce on men and women in India and the United States," *Journal of Comparative Family Studies* 25 (1994): 207–221.

13. Fahad Al Naser, "Kuwait's families," *Handbook of World Families*, eds. Bert N. Adams and Jan Trost (Thousand Oaks, CA: Sage, 2005), 507–535.

14. "Divorce is easy in Cuba, but a housing shortage makes breaking up hard to do," *New York Times*, Dec 31, 2007, http://www.nytimes.com/2007/12/31/world/americas/31cuba.html (accessed May 1, 2009).

15. Douglas W. Allen, Krishna Pendakur, and Wing Suen, "No-fault divorce and the compression of marriage ages," *Economic Inquiry* 44 (2006): 547–559.

16. Charles Lee Cole and Jessica Broussard, "The social context and history of divorce in the U.S.," *Family Therapy Magazine* (May/June 2006): 6–9.

17. Alan J. Hawkins, et al., "Attitudes about covenant marriage and divorce: Policy implications from a three state comparison," *Family Relations* 51 (2002): 166–175.

18. Rose M. Kreider, *Number, Timing, and Duration of Marriages and Divorces, 2001*. U.S. Census Bureau, Current Population Reports (2005): 70–97.

19. Larry Bumpass, Teresa Castro Martin, and James A. Sweet, "The impact of family background and early marital factors on marital disruption," *Journal of Family Issues* 12(1) (1991): 22–42.

20. Graham B. Spanier and Paul C. Glick, "Marital instability in the United States: Some correlates and recent changes," *Family Relations* 31 (July 1981): 329–338.

21. T.C. Martin and L.L. Bumpass, "Recent trends in marital disruption," *Demography* 26 (Feb 1989): 37–51.

22. Lynn K. White, "Determinants of divorce," *Contemporary Families: Looking Forward, Looking Back*, ed. A. Booth (Minneapolis, Minnesota: National Council on Family Relations, 1991).

23. Howard Wineberg, "Marital reconciliation in the United States: Which couples are successful?" *Journal of Marriage and the Family* 56 (Feb 1994): 80–88.

24. Vaughn A. Call and Tim B. Heaton, "Religious influence on marital stability," *Journal for the Scientific Study of Religion* 36(3) (September 1997): 382–392.

25. Rose M. Kreider and Jason M. Fields, *Number, timing, and duration of marriages and divorces: 1996*. U.S. Census Bureau, Current Population Reports (2002): 70–80.

26. Charles V. Willie and Richard J. Reddick, *A New Look at Black Families*, 5th edition (Walnut Creek, CA: AltaMira, 2003).

27. Adriana J. Umana-Taylor and Mark A. Fine, "Predicting commitment to wed among Hispanic and Anglo partners," *Journal of Marriage and Family* 65 (2003): 117–139.

28. Ibid.

29. Frank Pittman, *Grow up! How Taking Responsibility Can Make You a Happy Adult* (New York: Golden Books, 1999).

30. L.A. Kurdek, "Predicting marital dissolution: A 5-year prospective longitudinal study of newlywed couples," *Journal of Personality and Social Psychology* 64 (2) (1993): 221–42.

31. Jay D. Teachman, "Premarital sex, premarital cohabitation, and the risk of subsequent marital dissolution among women," *Journal of Marriage and Family* 65 (May 2003): 444–55.

32. Anne Milan, "One hundred years of families," *Canadian Social Trends* 56 (2000): 1–13.

33. Pamela J. Smock and Sanjiv Gupta., "Cohabitation in contemporary North America," *Just Living Together*, ed. A. Booth and A.C. Crouter (Mahwah, NJ: Lawrence Erlbaum, 2002), 53–84.

34. Kevin B. Skinner, et al., "Cohabitation, marriage, and remarriage," *Journal of Family Issues* 23 (2002): 74–90.

35. J. Teachman, "Premarital sex, premarital cohabitation and the risk of subsequent marital dissolution among women," *Journal of Marriage and Family* 65 (2003): 444–455.

36. Paul R. Amato, "Explaining the intergenerational transmission of divorce," *Journal of Marriage and the Family* 58 (Aug 1996): 628–640.

37. X.P. Montenegro, *Divorce Experience: A Study of Divorce at Midlife and Beyond* (Washington, DC: AARP, 2004).

38. Divorce Guide, "How much does it cost to hire a divorce lawyer in the USA?" 2009. http://www.divorceguide.com/usa/divorce-information/how-much-does-it-cost-to-hire-a-divorce-lawyer-in-the-usa.html (accessed May 6, 2009).

39. Timothy Grall, *Custodial Mothers and Fathers and Their Child Support: 2005*, U.S. Census Bureau, Current Population Reports (2007): 60–234.

40. Paul R. Amato, "The consequences of divorce for adults and children," *Journal of Marriage and the Family* 62(4) (Nov 2000): 1269–1287.

41. Kari Henley and Kay Pasley, "Divorce: Effects on couples," *International Encyclopedia of Marriage and Family* 2nd edition, ed. J. Ponzetti (New York: Macmillan, 2003) 480–486.

42. Pamela J. Smock, "The economic costs of marital disruption for young women over the past two decades," *Demography* 30(3) (1993): 353–71.

43. Lawrence A. Kurdek, "The relations between reported well-being and divorce history, availability of a proximate adult, and gender," *Journal of Marriage and the Family* 53 (1991): 71-78.

44. David H. Demo and Alan C. Acock, "The impact of divorce on children," *Journal of Marriage and the Family* 50(3) (Aug 1988): 619-648.

45. Jenifer Kunz, "The effects of divorce on children," *Family Research: A Sixty-Year Review 1930-1990*, volume 2, ed. S. Bahr (New York: Lexington Books, 1992), 325-376.

46. Ibid.

47. Ibid.

48. Ibid.

49. Ibid.

50. Gay C. Kitson and Leslie A. Morgan, "The Multiple Consequences of Divorce: A Decade Review," *Journal of Marriage and the Family* 52 (1990): 913-924.

51. Kari Henley and Kay Pasley, "Divorce: Effects on couples," *International Encyclopedia of Marriage and Family*, 2nd edition, ed. J. Ponzetti (New York: Macmillan, 2003), 480-486.

52. Ibid.

53. David Gately and Andrew Schwebel, "Favorable outcomes in children after parental divorce," *Journal of Divorce & Remarriage* 18 (1992): 57-77.

54. Constance Ahrons, *We're Still Family: What Grown Children Have to Say About Their Parents' Divorce* (New York: HarperCollins, 2005).

55. Gay C. Kitson, *Portrait of Divorce: Adjustment to Marital Breakdown* (New York: Guilford Press, 1992).

56. Alan C. Acock and David H. Demo, *Family Diversity and Well-Being* (Thousand Oaks, CA: Sage Publications, 1994).

57. X. P. Montenegro, *Divorce Experience: A Study of Divorce at Midlife and Beyond* Washington, D.C., AARP (2004).

58. Catherine K. Riessmann, *Divorce talk: Women and Men Make Sense of Personal Relationships* (New Brunswick, NJ: Rutgers University Press, 1990).

59. Linda J. Waite, et al., *Does Divorce Make People Happy? Findings from a Study of Unhappy Marriages*, Institute for American Values (2002).

60. David M. Klein and James M. White, *Family Theories: An Introduction* (Thousand Oaks, CA: Sage Publications, 1996), 59-85.

61. Paul R. Amato, "The consequences of divorce for adults and children," *Journal of Marriage and the Family* 62(4) (Nov 2000): 1269-1287.

62. Talcott Parsons, "The American Family: Its Relations to Personality and to the Social Structure," *Family, Socialization, and Interaction Process*, ed. T. Parsons and R. F. Bales (New York: Free Press, 1955).

63. William I. Thomas and Dorothy S. Thomas, *The Child in America: Behavior Problems and Programs* (New York: Alfred A. Knopf, 1928), 571-572.

64. J. Lynn England and Phillip R. Kunz, "The application of age-specific rates to divorce," *Journal of Marriage and the Family* 37(1) (1975): 40-46.

CHAPTER 15

1. Megan Sweeney, "Remarriage and the nature of divorce: Does it matter which spouse chose to leave?" *Journal of Family Issues* 23(3) (2002): 410-440.

2. U.S. Census Bureau, Current Population Survey, 2010 Annual Social and Economic Supplement.

3. Ibid.

4. Ibid.

5. Ailsa Burns and C. Scott, *Mother-Headed Families and Why They Have Increased* (Hillsdale, NJ: Erlbaum. 1994).

6. U.S. National Center for Health Statistics, National Vital Statistics Reports (NVSR), "Births: Preliminary Data for 2006," 56(7) (December 5, 2007).

7. Timothy J. Biblarz and Greg Gottainer, "Family structure and children's success: A comparison of widowed and divorced single-mother families," *Journal of Marriage and the Family* 62 (2000): 533-548.

8. Liam Downey, "Single mother families and industrial pollution in metropolitan America," *Sociological Spectrum* 25(6) (2005): 651-675.

9. En-ling Pan and Michael P. Farrell, "Ethnic differences in the effects of intergenerational relations on adolescent problem behavior in U.S. single-mother families," *Journal of Family Issues* 27(8) (2006): 1137-1158.

10. Min Zhan and Shanta Pandey, "Economic well-being of single mothers: Work first or postsecondary education?" *Journal of Sociology and Social Welfare* 31(3) (2004): 87-112.

11. Kathleen M. Ziol-Guest, "A single father's shopping bag: Purchasing decisions in single-father families," *Journal of Family Issues* 30(5) (2009): 605-622.

12. Brett V. Brown, "The single-father family," *Marriage & Family Review* 29(2) (2000): 203-220.

13. Geoffrey L. Greif, *The Daddy Track and the Single Father* (Lexington, MA: Lexington Books, 1990); Marilyn Ihinger-Tallman, K. Pasley, and C. Buchler, "Developing a middle-range theory of father involvement post divorce," *Fatherhood: Contemporary Theory, Research and Social Policy* ed. William Marsiglio (Thousand Oaks, CA: Sage, 1995), 55-77.

14. Sarah McLanahan and Gary Sandefur, *Growing Up with a Single Parent: What Hurts, What Helps* (Cambridge, MA: Harvard University Press, 1994).

15. Mark A. Fine and John H. Harvey, *Handbook of Divorce and Relationship Dissolution* (New York: Routledge, 2006).

16. Paul R. Amato, "The consequences of divorce for adults and children," *Journal of Marriage and the Family* 62 (2000): 1269-1288.

17. Graham B. Spanier and Linda Thompson, *Parting: The Aftermath of Separation and Divorce*, revised edition (Newbury Park, CA: Sage, 1987).

18. Edward R. Anderson, et al., "Ready to take a chance again: Transitions into dating among divorced parents," *Journal of Divorce and Remarriage* 40 (2004): 61-75.

19. Ibid.

20. Hongyu Wang and Paul R. Amato, "Predictors of divorce adjustment: Stressors, resources and definitions," *Journal of Marriage and the Family* 62 (2000): 655-668.

21. Sandra Petronio and Thomas Endres, "Dating and the single parent: Communicating in the social network," *Journal of Divorce* 9 (1985): 83-105.

22. Debora P. Schneller, et al., "After the breakup," *Journal of Divorce and Remarriage* 42(1) (2004): 1-37.

23. Xiaohe Xu, Clark D. Hudspeth, and John P. Barkowski, "The role of cohabitation in remarriage," *Journal of Marriage and Family* 68 (2006): 261-274.

24. Zheng Wu and Christoph M. Schimmele, "Repartnering after first union disruption," *Journal of Marriage and Family* 7 (2005): 27-36.

25. Lawrence Ganong and Marilyn Coleman, *Remarried Family Relationships* (Newbury Park, CA: Sage Publications, 1994).

26. M. D. Bramlett and W. D. Mosher, *Cohabitation, Marriage, Divorce, and Remarriage in the United States*. National Center for Health Statistics. Vital Health Stat 23 (2002), 22.

27. Rose M. Kreider, *Number, timing, and duration of marriages and divorces: 2001*. U.S. Census Bureau, Current Population Reports, 70-97, www.census.gov; Kreider, Rose M. and Jason M. Fields, *Number, timing, and duration of marriages and divorces*, 2002; 1996. U.S. Census Bureau, "Current Population Reports, 70-80." www.census.gov (accessed July 22, 2009).

28. U.S. Census Bureau. "Current Marital Status by Age and Sex for Those Ever Divorced: 2004," Table 4. www.census.gov (accessed July 22, 2009).

29. Zheng Wu, "Remarriage in Canada: A social exchange perspective," *Journal of Divorce and Remarriage* 21 (3/4) (1994): 191-224.

30. M. D. Bramlett and W. D. Mosher, *Cohabitation, Marriage, Divorce, and Remarriage in the United States*. National Center for Health Statistics. Vital Health Stat 23 (2002), 22.

31. Marianne E. Page and Ann H. Stevens, "The economic consequences of absent parents," *The Journal of Human Resources* 39(1) (Winter 2004): 80-107.

32. Zheng Wu, "Remarriage in Canada: A social exchange perspective," *Journal of Divorce and Remarriage* 21(3/4) (1994): 191-224.

33. Lawrence Ganong, Marilyn Coleman, and Jason Hans, "Divorce as prelude to stepfamily living and the consequences of redivorce," *Handbook of Divorce and Relationship Dissolution*, ed. Mark A. Fine and John H. Harvey (Mahwah, NJ: Lawrence Erlbaum, 2006), 409-434.

34. Lawrence Ganong, Marilyn Coleman, and Mark Fine, "Reinvestigating remarriage: Another decade of progress," *Journal of Marriage and the Family* 62(4) (Nov 2000): 1288-1307.

35. Jay Teachman, "Complex life course patterns and the risk of divorce in second marriages," *Journal of Marriage and Family* 70 (2008): 294-305.

36. Betty Carter, *The Changing Family Life Cycle*, 2nd edition, Monica McGoldrick, ed. (Boston, MA: Allyn and Bacon, 1989).

37. Stepfamily Association of America, "What is a stepfamily?" 2009. http://www.stepfamilies.info/faqs/faqs.php (accessed July 23, 2009).

38. Larry L. Bumpass, R. Kelly Raley, and James A. Sweet, "The changing character of stepfamilies: Implications of cohabitation and nonmarital childbearing," *Demography* 32 (1995): 425-436.

39. Emily B. Visher and John S. Visher, *Stepfamilies: A Guide to Working with Stepparents and Stepchildren* (New York, NY: Brunner/Mazel, 1979).

40. M. D. Bramlett and W. D. Mosher, *Cohabitation, Marriage, Divorce, and Remarriage in the United States*. National Center for Health Statistics. Vital Health Stat 23 (2002), 22.

41. Susan D. Stewart, "Boundary ambiguities in stepfamilies," *Journal of Family Issues* 26(7) (Oct 2005): 1002-1029.

42. N. Kalter, et al., "Locus of control in children of divorce," *Journal of Personality Assessment* 48(4) (1984): 410-414.

43. Lisa Stroschein, "Parental divorce and child mental health trajectories," *Journal of Marriage and Family* 67(5) (2005): 1286-1300.

44. Z. Kheshgi-Genovese and T. A. Genovese, "Developing the spousal relationship within stepfamilies," *Families in Society* 78(3) (1997): 255-264.

45. C. Parent and M. Beaudry, "Le couple dans la famille recomposée: Problèmes et Strategies" [The stepfamily couple: Problems and strategies], *Science et comportement* 25(1) (1996): 3-21.

46. Noel Schultz, S. L. Schultz, and D. H. Olson, "Couple strengths and stressors in Australian stepfamilies," *Journal of Marriage and the Family* 53 (1991): 555-569.

47. Andrew J. Cherlin, *Marriage, Divorce, Remarriage* (Cambridge, MA: Harvard University Press, 1992).

48. Emily B. Visher and John S. Visher, "Dynamics of successful stepfamilies," *Journal of Divorce and Remarriage* 14(1) (1990): 3-12.

49. Lawrence Ganong and Marilyn Coleman, *Stepfamily Relationships* (New York: Kluwer/Plenum, 2004).

50. Marilyn Coleman, Mark Fine, Lawrence Ganong, K. Downs, and N. Pauk, "When you're not the Brady Bunch: Identifying perceived conflicts and resolution strategies in stepfamilies," *Personal Relationships* 8 (2001): 55-73.

51. Bert Adams and Jan Trost, eds., *Handbook of World Families* (Thousand Oaks, CA: Sage Publications, 2005), 207-209.

52. Ibid.

53. Ibid.

54. Patricia Papernow, *Becoming a Stepfamily* (San Francisco, CA: Jossey-Bass, 1993).

55. Alan C. Acock and David H. Demo, *Family Diversity and Well-Being* (Thousand Oaks, CA: Sage, 1994); Goodman, E., "The role of socioeconomic status gradients in explaining differences in US adolescents' health," *American Journal of Public Health* 89 (1999): 1522–8; K. Call and J. Nonnemaker, "Socioeconomic disparities in adolescent health: Contributing factors," *Annals of the New York Academy of Science* 896 (2000): 352–355.

56. E. M. Hetherington, M. Cox, and R. Cox, "Effects of divorce on parents and children," *Nontraditional Families: Parenting and Child Development* ed. M. E. Lamb (Hillsdale, NJ: Lawrence Erlbaum, 1982), 233–285; T.M. Videon, "The effects of parent-adolescent relationships and parental separation on adolescent well-being," *Journal of Marriage and Family* 64 (2002): 489–503.

57. Marilyn Coleman, Lawrence Ganong, and Mark Fine, "Reinvestigating remarriage: Another decade of progress," *Journal of Marriage and the Family* 62 (2000): 1288–1307.

58. Barbara J. Risman, "Intimate relationships from a microstructural perspective: Mothering men," *Gender and Society* 1 (March 1987).

59. M. D. Bramlett and W. D. Mosher, *Cohabitation, Marriage, Divorce, and Remarriage in the United States.* National Center for Health Statistics. Vital Health Stat 23 (2002), 22.

60. Roni Berger, "Gay stepfamilies: A triple-stigmatized group," *Families in Society* 81 (5) (2000): 504–516.

61. William Meezan and Jonathan Rauch, "Gay marriage, same-sex parenting, and America's children," *The Future of Children* 15(2) (2005): 98–107.

62. R. Hill and J. Aldous, "Socialization for Marriage and Parenthood," *Handbook of Socialization Theory and Research* ed. D. A. Goslin (Chicago: Rand McNally, 1969), 885–950.

63. Heather Gallardo, "Stepmothering and Identity: A Co-constructed Narrative," *Journal of Divorce and Remarriage* 48(1) (2007): 125–139.

CHAPTER 16

1. Joseph Carroll, "Family Time Eclipses TV as Favorite Way to Spend an Evening," The Gallup Organization (2006), http://www.gallup.com/poll/21856/Family-Time-Eclipses-Favorite-Way-Spend-Evening.aspx (accessed June 2, 2009).

2. Robert Sternberg, *The Triangle of Love: Intimacy, Passion, Commitment* (New York: Basic Books, 1988).

3. Carolyn Kapinus and Michael Johnson, "The Utility of Family Life Cycle as a Theoretical and Empirical Tool," *Journal of Family Issues* 24(2) (2003): 155–184.

4. Stephen F. Duncan, "Family Strengths: Commitment," http://www.foreverfamilies.net/xml/articles/commitment.aspx (accessed June 2, 2009).

5. Kelly van Schaick and Arnold L. Stolberg, "The impact of paternal involvement and parental divorce on young adults' intimate relationships," *Journal of Divorce & Remarriage* 36(1/2) (2001): 99–121.

6. D.D. Bielby, "Commitment to Work and Family," *Annual Review of Sociology Contemporary Perspectives in Family Research* 18 (1992): 281–302.

7. Kristin M. Perrone, et al., "Work-family interface: Commitment, conflict, coping, and satisfaction," *Journal of Career Development* 2 (March 2006): 286–300.

8. Scott Coltrane, "Elite careers and family commitment: It's (still) about gender," *The Annals of the American Academy, AAPSS* 596 (November 2004): 214–220.

9. Daniel Eckstein, Fern Clemmer, and Armando Fierro, "The use of image exchange in examining relationship role perceptions," *The Family Journal: Counseling and Therapy for Couples and Families* 14, 1 (January 2006): 71–76.

10. Scott Stanley, "Sacrifice as a Predictor of Marital Outcomes," *Family Process* 45(3) (2006): 289–303.

11. Desirée Baolian Qin, "Doing well vs. feeling well: Understanding family dynamics and the psychological adjustment of Chinese immigrant adolescents," *Journal of Youth Adolescence* 37 (2008): 22–35.

12. D.B. Davalos, E.L. Chavez, and R.J. Guardiola, "Effects of perceived parental school support and family communication on delinquent behaviors in Latinos and White non-Latinos," *Cultural Diversity and Ethnic Minority Psychology* 11(1) (2005): 57–68.

13. Robert Crosnoe, Kristan G. Erickson, and Sanford M. Dornbusch, "Protective functions of family relationships and school factors in the deviant behavior of adolescent boys and girls: Reducing the impact of risky friendships," *Youth & Society* 33(4) (June 2002): 515–544.

14. Doreen A. Crawford, "Keep the focus on the family," *Journal of Child Health Care* 6(2) 2002: 133–146.

15. Martha Morgan and Whitney A. Brosi, "Prescription drug abuse among older adults: a family ecological case study," *Journal of Applied Gerontology* 26(5) (2007): 419–432.

16. Claire M. Kamp Dush, Miles G. Taylor, and Rhiannon A. Kroeger, "Marital happiness and psychological well-being across the life course," *Family Relations* 57(2) 2008: 211–226.

17. Janice L. Driver and John M. Gottman, "Daily marital interactions and positive affect during marital conflict among newlywed couples," *Family Process* 43(3) 2004: 301–314.

18. Bruce Headey, "Life goals matter to happiness: A revision of set-point theory," *Social Indicators Research* 86 (2008): 213–231.

19. Victor W. Harris (summarizing John Gottman), "9 Important Skills for Every Relationship," Utah Marriage. http://utahmarriage.org/htm/dating/important-skills (accessed July 28, 2009).

20. Valentina Ibeachum, "Is Flirting the Key to a Successful Marriage?" http://www.relationshipwrks.com/cgi-bin/np/viewnews.cgi?category=4&id=1161186428 (accessed June 4, 2009).

21. David Henningsen, "Flirting with Meaning: An Examination of Miscommunication in Flirting Interactions," *Sex Roles* 50 (2004): 481–489.

22. Blaine J. Fowers and David H. Olson, "ENRICH marital inventory: A discriminant validity and cross-validation assessment," *Journal of Marital and Family Therapy* 15(1) (1989): 65–79.

23. Maria Krysan, Kristin A. Moore, and Nicholas Zill, "Identifying Successful Families: An Overview of Constructs and Selected Measures," U.S. Department of Health and Human Services, 1990. http://aspe.hhs.gov/daltcp/reports/idsucfam.htm (accessed June 4, 2009).

24. W. G. Dyer and P. R. Kunz, *Effective Mormon Families: How Do They See Themselves* (Salt Lake City: Deseret Book, 1986).

25. Denise Mann, "15 Secrets of Happy Families," WebMD. http://www.webmd.com/parenting/features/15-secrets-to-have-a-happy-family (accessed June 4, 2009).

26. John Defrain and Sylvia M. Asay, "Family Strengths and Challenges in the USA," *Marriage and Family Review* 41(3) (2007): 281–307.

27. Ibid.

28. Ibid.

29. Ibid.

30. Ibid.

31. David Popenoe, "American family decline, 1960–1990: A review and appraisal," *Journal of Marriage and the Family* 55(3) (1993): 527–542.

32. David Popenoe, "Can the nuclear family be revived?" *Society* (July/August 1999): 28–30.

33. Pearl Stewart, "Who is kin?" *Journal of Human Behavior in the Social Environment* 15(2) (2007): 163–181.

34. U.S. Census Bureau. "Table UC-1: Unmarried Partners of the Opposite Sex, by Presence of Children: 1960 to Present," http://www.census.gov/population/www/socdemo/hh-fam.html#history (accessed June 6, 2009); Source: U.S. Census Bureau, Current Population Survey, 2010 Annual Social and Economic Supplement.

35. U.S. Census Bureau, "Table 1: United States–Race and Hispanic Origins: 1790 to 1990." http://www.census.gov/population/www/documentation/twps0056/twps0056.html (accessed June 4, 2009).

36. Tavia Simmons and Martin O'Connell, "Married-Couple and Unmarried-Partner Households: 2000," *Census 2000 Special Reports*, 2003.

37. Adam P. Romero, et al., *Census Snapshot: United States*, The Williams Institute, 2007.

38. Medscape Today, "Children of Same-Sex Couples Do as Well as Other Children," http://www.medscape.com/viewarticle/514477 (accessed June 6, 2009).

39. Gary Gates, "Adoption and Foster Care by Lesbian and Gay Parents in the United States," Urban Institute. http://www.urban.org/publications/411437.html (accessed June 6, 2009).

40. "Same-sex marriage around the world," CBCnews.ca, June 3, 2009. http://www.cbc.ca/world/story/2009/05/26/f-same-sex-timeline.html (accessed June 4, 2009).

41. Nicholas Bala and Rebecca J. Bromwich, "Context and Inclusivity in Canada's Evolving Definition of the Family," *International Journal of Law, Policy and the Family* 16 (2002): 145–180.

42. FactCheck.org. "What Is a Civil Union?" http://www.factcheck.org/what_is_a_civil_union.html (accessed June 6, 2009).

43. Melissa Holtzman, "Definitions of the Family as an Impetus for Legal Change in Custody Decision Making: Suggestions from an Empirical Case Study," *Law and Social Inquiry* 31 (2006) 1–37.

44. Daphna Birenbaum-Carmeli, "Contested Surrogacy and the Gender Order: An Israeli Case Study," *Journal of Middle East Women's Studies* 3 (2007): 21–44.

45. "Deal Near on Jackson Service, as Custody Battle Looms," *The New York Times*. July 2, 2009. http://www.nytimes.com/2009/07/03/us/03jackson.html (accessed July 27, 2009).

46. Arland Thornton, Georgina Binstock, and Dirgha Ghimire, "International Networks, Ideas, and Family Change," *PSC Research Report No. 04-566*. (October 2004).

47. Martha Campbell, et al., "Barriers to fertility regulation: A review of the literature," *Studies in Family Planning* 37(2) (2006): 87–98.

48. Paula S. Fass, "Children in global migrations," *Journal of Social History* 38(4) (2005): 937–953.

49. Meg Wilkes Karraker and Janet R. Grochowski, *Families with Futures: A Survey of Families Studies for the Twenty-first Century* (Philadelphia: Lawrence Erlbaum Associates, 2005).

50. Christina E. Gringeri, "The Poverty of Hard Work: Jobs and Low Wages in Family Economics of Rural Utah Households," *Journal of Sociology and Social Welfare* 28 (2001): 3–22.

51. Advocate.com, "Reuniting Families Act Introduced," http://www.advocate.com/news_detail_ektid88218.asp (accessed June 15, 2009).

52. "New Hampshire Passes Gay Marriage," *BBC News*, June 3, 2009, http://news.bbc.co.uk/2/hi/americas/8082250.stm (accessed June 6, 2009).

53. John Schwartz, "California high court upholds gay marriage ban," NewYorkTimes.com, May 26, 2009. http://www.nytimes.com/2009/05/27/us/27marriage.html (accessed June 6, 2009).

54. "Obama Confronts Abortion Debate, Urges Notre Dame Grads to Seek Common Ground," FoxNews.com, May 17, 2009. http://www.foxnews.com/politics/2009/05/17/obama-urges-notre-dame-graduates-seek-common-ground/ (accessed June 6, 2009).

55. "Obama Reverses Rules on U.S. Abortion Aid," *New York Times*, January 24, 2009. http://www.nytimes.com/2009/01/24/us/politics/24obama.html?_r=2&scp=9&sq=obama%20abortion&st=cse (accessed June 6, 2009).

56. "Michelle Obama Calls for More Family-Friendly Workplace Policies," FoxNews.com, May 8, 2009. http://www.foxnews.com/politics/2009/05/08/michelle-obama-calls-family-friendly-workplace-policies/ (accessed June 6, 2009).

57. American Academy of Pediatrics, "Children, Adolescents, and Television," *Pediatrics* 107(2) (2001): 423–426.

58. Ibid.

59. Ibid.

60. I. Cheng et al., "The influence of mass media and family communication on adolescent smoking," Paper presented at the annual meeting of the International Communication Association, Dresden International Congress Centre, Dresden, Germany. http://www.allacademic.com/meta/p93296_index.html (accessed June 8, 2009).

61. K. S. Kiragu et al., *Promoting Family Planning Through Mass Media in Nigeria: Campaigns Using a Public Service Announcement and a National Logo* (Baltimore, MD, Johns Hopkins Center for Communication Programs, July 1996).

62. A. Rae Simpson, "The Role of the Mass Media in Parenting Education," *Parenthood in America* 1998, http://parenthood.library.wisc.edu/Simpson/Simpson.html (accessed June 6, 2009).

63. Ibid.

64. Linda Mondy, "Engaging the Community in Child Protection Programmes: The Experience of NEWPIN in Australia," *Child Abuse Review* 13 (2004): 433–440.

65. A Rae Simpson, "The Role of the Mass Media in Parenting Education," *Parenthood in America* 1998, http://parenthood.library.wisc.edu/Simpson/Simpson.html (accessed June 6, 2009).

66. Linda Mondy, "Engaging the Community in Child Protection Programmes: The Experience of NEWPIN in Australia," *Child Abuse Review* 13 (2004): 433–440.

67. "Representing Children Worldwide: Kenya," http://www.law.yale.edu/RCW/rcw/jurisdictions/afe/kenya/frontpage.htm (accessed June 8, 2009).

68. Dorothy Rombo and Jane Rose Muthoni Njue, "Future Families: The Case of Kenya," http://www.ncfr.org/pdf/membersvc/Dec_2006_Focus.pdf (accessed June 8, 2009).

69. Trinity University, "Marriage and Family Processes," http://www.trinity.edu/~mkearl/family.html (accessed June 8, 2009).

70. "Family," Encyclopædia Britannica Kids, http://student.britannica.com/comptons/article-200537/family (accessed June 8, 2009).

71. Lee Ann DeReus, "A Note From the Guest Coordinators," *Family Relations* 57 (2008): 415–418.

72. Ibid.

73. Bahira Sherif Trask, Raeann R. Hamon, and Bethany Willis Hepp, "How Transnational Families and International Adoption Will Further Diversity Families of the Future," http://www.ncfr.org/pdf/membersvc/Dec_2006_Focus.pdf (accessed June 8, 2009).

74. Bron B. Ingoldsby, Suzanne R. Smith, and J. E. Miller, *Exploring Family Theories* (Los Angeles: Roxbury Publishing Company, 2004).

75. Ibid.

76. Thomas J. Scheff, "Looking-glass self: Goffman as symbolic interactionist," *Symbolic Interaction* 28(2) (2005): 147–166.

77. The Universal Family Flag, "What is the Universal Family Flag, and what does it mean?" http://www.the-universal-family-flag.com/index.html (accessed June 10, 2009).

78. Carolyn Tubbs, "Family Ties: Constructing Family Time in Low-Income Families," *Family Process* 44(1) (2005): 77–91.

79. Maria Krysan, Kristin A. Moore, and Nicholas Zill, "Identifying Successful Families: An Overview of Constructs and Selected Measures," http://aspe.hhs.gov/daltcp/reports/idsucfam.htm (accessed June 4, 2009).

80. Ibid.

81. Ted L. Huston and Heidi Melz, "The case for (promoting) marriage: The devil is in the details," *Journal of Marriage and Family* 66(4) (2004): 943–958.

PHOTO CREDITS